A JOYFULLY SERIOUS MAN

A Joyfully Serious Man

THE LIFE OF ROBERT BELLAH

MATTEO BORTOLINI

PRINCETON UNIVERSITY PRESS

PRINCETON & OXFORD

Published by Princeton University Press
41 William Street, Princeton, New Jersey 08540
6 Oxford Street, Woodstock, Oxfordshire OX20 1TR

press.princeton.edu

All Rights Reserved
ISBN 978-0-691-20440-6
ISBN (e-book) 978-0-691-20439-0

British Library Cataloging-in-Publication Data is available

Editorial: Fred Appel and James Collier
Production Editorial: Jenny Wolkowicki
Jacket and text design: Pamela L. Schnitter
Production: Erin Suydam
Publicity: Kate Hensley and Kathryn Stevens
Copyeditor: Maia Vaswani

Jacket image: courtesy of the Bellah family

This book has been composed in Arno Pro

Printed on acid-free paper. ∞

Printed in the United States of America

10 9 8 7 6 5 4 3 2 1

For my beautiful son, Riccardo
We can never love, respect, or praise our children enough

CONTENTS

ILLUSTRATIONS

Writing Bob Bellah

BOLOGNA, CAMBRIDGE, BERKELEY, ERFURT, 2006–2020

The classification of the constituents of a chaos, nothing less is here essayed

—HERMAN MELVILLE, *MOBY DICK*

THE LIGHT SPILLED THROUGH the bay windows on a cold November evening as Marc and Sheila Andrus welcomed their guests at the bishop's residence in San Francisco's Pacific Heights. Robert Neelly Bellah sat on a couch, his long legs crossed at sharp angles, chatting with a dear Jesuit friend. They were elegantly dressed, both wearing those flashily patterned ties that Americans tend to favor and that Europeans like me find a little too garish. Every now and then someone approached. They all said the same thing: "I am so happy to finally meet you. I just wanted to tell you how powerful your writings and your example have been." The room was filled with a diverse crowd of people smiling and waving, eating grapes and cheese, sipping chardonnay. Visibly thrilled to be under the spotlight, the old man nodded and shook hands, sharing an occasional anecdote about this and that.

It was November 20, 2011, a special day for Robert Bellah. That morning hundreds of scholars, students, and friends had packed the Yerba Buena salon of the Marriott Marquis Hotel—the flashy post-modern extravaganza where the annual meeting of the American Academy of Religion was taking place—to pay their homage to the retired Berkeley professor and hear what a panel of distinguished colleagues had to say about his long-awaited masterpiece, *Religion in Human Evolution*. The crowd burst into a warm applause as the master of ceremonies, Mark Juergensmeyer, introduced his guest with the simplest of questions: "So, Bob . . . how did this book begin?" A tall, slender man, Bellah looked fragile in his loose-fitting suit. He smiled, modestly: "I am not sure I am the best person to know that. . . . It's mysterious how one gets involved with things."[1]

Still, he tried to answer. After a quick ride through the ups and downs of a sixty-year intellectual career, Bellah's remarks took a rather surprising turn. "Every subatomic particle in our body comes from the Big Bang," he said, "We are part of the universe, literally—not metaphorically or poetically, but quite literally." As much as religion is a uniquely human phenomenon, he added, to understand it we have to take into account the entirety of our past, all the way back to the beginning of time, before man and before life itself. Eyebrows were raised. But Robert Bellah—or Bob, as he invited everyone to call him—knew how to make his public smile. "Recently somebody asked me: Why are you writing this book about religion when you should write your autobiography? I said: I *am* writing my autobiography, it's the autobiography of the human race!" The crowd cheered.

Under its apparent humility, Bellah's quip spoke of the desire of the Enlightenment to embrace all that exists through pure scientific reason, and yet it suggested that only myths and narratives might be able to capture the essence of the human condition through innumerable individual examples. As such it was an almost perfect representation of its author and his scholarly quest. Born in 1927, Robert Bellah became in the 1950s one of the most visible and esteemed students of Talcott Parsons, the Harvard sociologist who led the vanguard of the behavioral sciences after the end of World War Two. Bellah came of age professionally during a time imbued with a faith in scientific and technological advancement, and in the postwar academic elites who, from their perches in lavishly funded universities, research institutions, and professional associations, were seen as key assets in the confrontation between the Soviet Union and the "Free World." It was a time of hope and enthusiasm among established and up-and-coming social scientists as their disciplines seemed on the cusp of attaining the predictive maturity and prestige of the natural sciences.

As an early career participant in these novel national and international scholarly networks, Bellah first focused on Japanese history and religion. His destiny, however, was not to become a specialist. Soon after he brought his doctoral studies to a conclusion, Parsons picked him to enter an exclusive club of "theorists"—those engaged in the delicate task of creating abstract conceptual frameworks. As one of the elects, Bellah in the mid-1950s devised an awe-inspiring project, one that would have been inconceivable two or three decades earlier: to spend his entire life working on a general explanation of the evolution of human culture founded on a full-fledged scientific theory of religion.

From the time Bellah established himself as a leading social scientist, the world never stopped changing around him. From the assassination of John F. Kennedy to the rise and fall of the sixties counterculture, from the ambiguous achievements of the civil rights movement to national disaster in Vietnam, the bracing, optimistic postwar vision of unlimited upward progress soon fell apart. By the 1970s, the global leadership of the United States and its allegedly scientific justification, modernization theory, were trashed at home and abroad. Repeated economic crises, the rise of neoconservatism, and political and ideological polarization fatally wounded the authority that social scientists had achieved as the watchmen of both Roosevelt's New Deal and Johnson's Great Society. The economic and cultural milieu that had nurtured Bellah's ascent and his ambitious scholarly dreams was gone.[2]

By the mid-1970s, Bellah had practically abandoned the study of Japan and had set aside his project on religious evolution to enter the field of American studies as an expert and critic of the relationship between religion and politics. Perhaps more importantly, he had moved from the rarified realm of professional social science into the public sphere. He had acquired a new persona: that of the caustic but hopeful critic of the political myths upon which the United States had been built. His doubtful, ever-changing work on what he called the "American civil religion" embodied his most deep-rooted political and moral conviction—that nations and countries are good only insofar as they contribute to the realization of universal values in the world. By the time of the 1985 publication of *Habits of the Heart*, his most successful book and one coauthored with four colleagues, he was a well-known public intellectual. In a political milieu where the rift between neoliberalism and conservative evangelicalism, on the one side, and radical secularism, on the other, was becoming more and more irremediable, the combination of Bellah's progressive politics with a strong argument for a "public church" placed him in an interesting, and at times difficult, position. When he finally returned to his lifelong dream of working on a general theory and history of religious evolution, Bellah was well past seventy and the social sciences were on the defensive from both a scholarly and a political point of view.[3]

If biography is the art of illuminating patterns through personal lives, then Bellah's story might be seen as the perfect prism for looking at the history of contemporary social science in its connection to wider political, social, and cultural transformations. Using the words of his close friend and intellectual ally, the anthropologist Clifford Geertz, one might say that a detailed narrative of Bellah's life might help to shed light on at least two revolutions in "the way we think about the way we think": the rise of the postwar behavioral sciences and their defeat at the hand of the strangest among bedfellows—the post-modern blurring of genres and the radical reductionism of experimental natural science.[4]

But the story of Robert Neelly Bellah reveals not only a collective, national, or global history. It also illuminates the life of a man who wrestled with modernity and who responded to the historical and cultural shifts of his epoch in unique ways. He grew up in the dreamland of Western consumerism, Los Angeles, and became a self-directed, hyperachieving individual after the early loss of his father to suicide. As a young man in Cambridge, Massachusetts, he took on the identity of the highbrow, open-minded scholar, as incarnated by his mentor Talcott Parsons. Not content to follow in his teacher's footsteps, Bellah chose an even more difficult road than Parsons's, one that combined the role of the postwar professional social theorist with an older, classical idea of the universal scholar. Not only would he become an expert on cybernetics and systems theory, but he would master a dozen modern and ancient languages and bring out a definitive comparative work on the evolution of religion as a bridge for the unification of the humanities and the social sciences.

This latter, grandiose project was born not only from Bellah's inexhaustible intellectual curiosity, but also from the high expectations his peers and teachers placed upon him. In his twenties he was taught to revere a handful of classical thinkers and persuaded himself that he could become one of them—that he could be, without any irony, the next Max Weber. This unbridled ambition of the young Bellah and his seemingly irresistible career trajectory toward the professional heights would soon clash with all-too-human personal limitations. And yet for decades he produced work imbued with penetrating insights and always characterized by a readiness to change his mind whenever evidence and reflection pushed him to do so.

Crucial to Bellah's trajectory was the horrifying loss of two of his four daughters between 1973 and 1976, an upheaval that led at the end of that decade to a complex and painful period of personal clarification. This time of self-realization, when Bellah reached a deeper, more textured grasp of his own limits and potential, coincided with the period of his greatest successes: the collaborative effort of *Habits of the Heart*, which turned Bellah into a prominent public intellectual; the radical reshaping of his relationship with his wife, Melanie Hyman; his reembracing of religion as a vocal and committed member of the Episcopal Church; and the rethinking of some of his ideas on American politics and religion, which eventually brought him to see the Protestant Reformation as "a mistake, though a necessary one."[5] After President Bill Clinton awarded him the National Humanities Medal in 2000, Bellah returned to his most rigorous scholarly persona and accomplished the task he had given himself some forty years earlier—publishing a book comparable to Max Weber's *Essays in the Sociology of Religion*.

Bellah's favorite poet, Wallace Stevens, wrote in his diary as a nineteen-year-old that "the mind cannot always live in a 'divine ether.' The lark cannot always sing at heaven's gate. There must exist a place to spring from—a refuge from the heights, an anchorage of thought." This refuge, continued Stevens, is *study*: "Study ties you down; and it is the occasional wil[l]ful release from this voluntary bond that gives the soul its occasional over-powering sense of lyric freedom and effort. Study is the resting place—poetry, the adventure."[6] Bellah began his professional life anchored in study, and then, with a deliberate and impetuous move, swung toward poetry. At that point, however, study and poetry became one with him, and could never be separated again. What the young Stevens saw as two necessary but autonomous sides of a whole, Bellah reunited into one, single practice of creative tension, a practice where resting and moving became indistinguishable.

More universally, through his work and his many lives, Bellah bore witness to the fact that everyone is subject to fragmentation in their lives. He called "religion" those symbols, myths, and practices through which the pieces are collected and assembled into a whole. "Religion is a world where one tries to discover the plot of the whole thing," Bellah wrote in one of his diaries in 1971, "or perhaps better *to live that plot*, as an individual or a group, through a symbolic form which seems most adequately to express it." Religion brings together, if only for a moment, the scattered pieces of the human condition.[7]

Once he had defined religion, Bellah spent his entire life attempting to figure out how it works, and his final word on the matter, the one he left enshrined in *Religion in Human Evolution*, is that no religion by itself can fully mend what is broken. No individual religion can save human beings from fragmentation. Different ways of symbolizing and narrating wholeness, different ways of gesturing at and incorporating wholeness into everyday practices, are not mutually exclusive, but rather are elements of yet another, mysterious and incomplete, whole. "I would reject the notion that all religions are basically the same—different paths to the same end," Bellah told his sociologist friend Hans Joas in a conversation published in 2012, "They're not all the same. And yet, at some level, particularly at the most general theological and ethical level, they do share some profound commitments. It's their very difference that is so important to us, because what the Buddhists know and what the Hindus know are things that Christians often don't fully know. . . . So it's that sense," he concluded, "neither homogenizing nor denying a profound resonance among the great traditions." Unity and wholeness can be found only by moving incessantly from one perspective to the other.[8]

And yet for Bellah, all efforts at regaining wholeness are destined to be provisional and incomplete. He was drawn to an understanding of religion as "something that disrupts and calls all our expectations into question, [something] that keeps us from settling into a groove." This disruptive force, which Bellah sometimes called the sacred, compels us to exercise continuous self-judgment, to move beyond our limits toward a new consciousness of ourselves. The sacred, for Bellah, is a domain of change and infinite creativity: we can never be satisfied with who and what we are. We must continuously reflect on who we are and who we want to be—and then we must change our lives.[9]

As another of Bellah's favorite poets wrote in one of his last letters, "Man can embody truth but he cannot know it." At the heart of the human condition lies an impossible hope of wholeness and redemption.[10] When we look at Robert Neelly Bellah we see still another attempt to win back what is lost to the lived life—without, however, having to choose between reason and belief, resting and moving, safety and adventure, study and poetry.

In the course of researching this book, I interviewed Robert N. Bellah six times—on July 9, 11, 13, 19, 20, and 27, 2007—in Berkeley, CA. And I had informal encounters with him in Budapest and Erfurt, Germany, in 2008; Berkeley, CA, in 2009 and 2011; and Freiburg and Heidelberg in 2012. I also conducted in-person interviews with Andrew Barshay (July 17, 2007, Berkeley, CA), John A. Coleman, SJ, (December 13, 2013, San Francisco), Harvey Cox (May 6, 2009, Cambridge, MA; October 18, 2016, Trento, Italy), Shmuel N. Eisenstadt (June 28, 2008, Budapest), Steve Foster (April 25, 2019, Paris; August 24, 2019, New York City), Renée C. Fox (August 26, 2019, Philadelphia),

Carl Kaysen (May 1, 2008, Cambridge, MA), Victor Lidz (June 27, 2008, Trento, Italy, plus repeated informal encounters), Richard Madsen (August 3, 2007, Berkeley, CA), Paul Rabinow (July 31, 2007, Berkeley, CA), Eli Sagan (April 28, 2008, Englewood, NJ), Neil J. Smelser (August 3, 2007, Berkeley, CA), William M. Sullivan (July 27, 2007, Berkeley, CA; August 9, 2019, New York City plus repeated informal encounters), Ann Swidler (July 23, 2007, Berkeley, CA, plus repeated informal encounters), Steven M. Tipton (July 24, 2007, Berkeley, CA), and Edward A. Tiryakian (June 28, 2008, Budapest). And I corresponded by letter and e-mail with Randy Alfred, Jan Assmann, Jennifer Bellah Maguire, Hally Bellah-Guther, Norman Birnbaum, Richard Bulliet, Gordon M. Burghardt (who also provided e-mails, 2010–2013), John Chernoff, Albert M. Craig, Timothy Doran, Dexter Dunphy, Alessandro Ferrara, Estelle B. Freedman, Victoria Lanakila Generao, Daniel Hartwig, Hans Joas (who also provided e-mails, 2011–2013), Leonard W. Johnson, Don Jones, Bill Kelly, Clive Kessler, David Kirp, Martin E. Marty, Douglas Mitchell (who also provided e-mails, 1998–2011), Dunbar Moodie, Tony Namkung, Donald S. Nesti, Dan Orr, Tom Piazza, Samuel C. Porter (who also provided e-mails, 1999–2005), Arvind Rajagopal (who also provided e-mails, 2007–2013), Russell Richey, Heiner Roetz, Stephen G. Salkever, Andrew Schmookler, Harlan Stelmach, Jeffrey Stout, David W. Stowe, Anna Sun, Charles Taylor, Stephen Tobias, John Torpey (who also provided e-mails, 2010–2012), Bruce J. Vermazen, Ezra Vogel, Bill Wetherall, Björn Wittrock, James Wolfe, Anthony Wrigley, Robert Wuthnow, David Yamane, and Yang Xiao (who also provided e-mails, 2002–2013).

Over the years, I have published diffusely on Bellah: articles, book chapters, small pieces, book reviews, and even edited a "companion" to his work. Any differences or inconsistencies between this book and all my previous work should be understood as the result of further research and reflection on my part.[11]

ACKNOWLEDGMENTS

LONG PROJECTS CREATE MANY DEBTS. I want first to thank all the institutions and the people who gave me the chance to pursue my research: my own University of Padova; the Center for Cultural Sociology at Yale University, where I was a visiting fellow in the fall of 2006; the Department of Sociology at the University of California, Berkeley, where I was a visiting fellow in the summer of 2007, and where I taught a sociology of religion class (Bob's course!) during the 2016 summer session; the Department of Sociology at Harvard University, where I was a visiting fellow in the spring of 2009 and where I taught a classical social theory class during the 2013 summer session. Tim Driscoll, Ed Copenhagen, and Juliana Kuipers at the Harvard University Archives; Alessandro Monteverdi at the Giovanni Agnelli Foundation; Fran O'Donnell at the Andover-Harvard Theological Library Archives; Alex Suthern at the McGill University Archives; Lee R. Hiltzik at the Rockefeller Archive Center; the Rare Book and Manuscript Library at Columbia University; the Special Collections Research Center at the University of Chicago; Matthew Burke at Adams House, Harvard University; Chris Reed at Gnomon Copy in Cambridge, MA. The individuals who helped me from afar: Mary Curtis Horowitz at the Horowitz Foundation for Social Policy; Todd T. Ito at the University of Chicago Law School; Melinda Wallington at the University of Rochester Library; David Stiver at the Berkeley GTU Library; Matthew Beland at the Drew University Library; Kevin Proffitt at the American Jewish Archives; Lisa Sharik at the Texas Military Forces Museum; Carol Jasak and Brian Basore at the Oklahoma Historical Society; Hélène Favard and Caroline Louret at the IMEC, Saint-Germain-la-Blanche-Herbe; Carmencita E. Solidum at Los Angeles High School; Tim Noakes at Stanford University; James Collier, Jenny Wolkowicki, and Lisa Black at Princeton University Press. I gratefully acknowledge the kind permission of the Bellah family, specifically Hally Bellah-Guther and Jennifer Bellah Maguire, for access to the private papers of Robert Bellah. I would also like to thank the anonymous compilers and webmasters of the countless websites that I used for research, without whom a big part of this book would not have been written.

I would like to thank all my American sponsors and friends: Ron Eyerman, Philip Smith, and Nadine Amalfi at Yale; Michael Burawoy, Rebecca Chavez, Carmen Privat-Gilman, David Nasatir, and Beppe and Francine Di Palma at Berkeley; Michèle Lamont, Mary C. Brinton, and Suzanne Ogungbadero at Harvard. Thanks to the people who helped with my research: Randy Alfred, Jan Assmann, Andrew Barshay, Richard Bulliet, Gordon Burghardt, John Chernoff, John Coleman, SJ, Luca Corchia, Albert Craig, Timothy Doran, Dexter Dunphy, Claude Fischer, Estelle Freedman (and Daniel Hartwig), Victoria Lanakila Generao, Andreas Guther, Kathleen Hurty, Bill Kelly, Clive Kessler, David Kirp, Jakob Köllhofer, Christopher Jencks, Martin Marty, Christine Mitchell, Dunbar Moodie, Jerry Muller, Tony Namkung, Martha Nussbaum, Dan Orr, Tom Piazza, Arvind Rajagopal, Russell Richey, Heiner Roetz, Andrew Schmookler, Jeffrey Stout, Anna Sun, Charles Taylor, Ed Tiryakian, Andrew Tobias, Stephen Tobias, John Torpey, Bruce Vermazen, Bill Wetherall, Björn Wittrock, James Wolfe, Anthony Wrigley, Robert Wuthnow, David Yamane, and Yang Xiao.

Thanks to Andrew Abbott, Margaret Archer, Stefano Barbieri, Marina Bertoncin, Matteo Bianchin, Amy Borovoy, Alice Brombin, Chas Camic, Francesca Capelletti, René Capovin, Jaysi Chander, Dario Comuzzi, Bruno Cousin, Luisa Da Re, Paola Da Re, Christian Dayé, Leonardo De Bernardini, Mario Del Pero, Nina Eliasoph, Patrizio Ercolini, Elena Esposito, Gary Alan Fine, Marcel Fournier, Rossella Ghigi, Phil Gorski, Neil Gross, Jeff Guhin, Renzo Guolo, Scott Kraemer, Paul Lichterman, Stephen Maguire, Giorgio Manfré, Neil McLaughlin, Alessandro Mongili, Ken Nakayama, Michael Pettit, Simona Pinelli, Gianfranco Poggi, Doug Porpora, Riccardo Prandini, Claudio Riva, Roland Robertson, Armando Salvatore, Robert Sampson, Marco Santoro, Silvio Scanagatta, Cherry Schecker, Peppino Sciortino, Giorgia Sinatra, Mark Solovey, Charles Stang, David Stark, Helmut Staubmann, Andrew Strabone, Ajantha Subramanian, Javier Treviño, Bryan Turner, Stephen Turner, Gary Urton, Jonathan VanAntwerpen, Marcella Veglio, Martina Visentin, Giovanni Zampieri, and the late Donald Levine, Eli Sagan, Shmuel Eisenstadt, Norman Birnbaum, Don Jones, Carl Kaysen, Neil Smelser, Paul Rabinow, Ezra Vogel, and Douglas Mitchell.

I wrote most of the book in the congenial milieu of the Max-Weber-Kolleg für kultur- und sozialwissenschaftliche Studien of the Universität Erfurt. I want to thank Bettina Holstein and Kathleen Rottleb for their help along the

way. At the MWK I shared food, beer, and words with Emiliano Rubens Urci-
uoli, Chad Alan Goldberg, Cécile Stehrenberger, Matteo Santarelli, Tullio
Viola, Michael Sauder, Luca Pellarin, Stefania Maffeis, Carmen González
Gutiérrez, Elisa Iori, Barbara Thériault, Tiziana Faitini, Giulia Pedrucci, Ca-
milla Smith, Dylan Kennedy, Tanja Visic, and Fouad Gehad Marei.

Hans Joas offered me the Erfurt fellowship as an unexpected, wonderful
gift. Jeff Alexander boldly assumed the key role of helping me land a book
contract in the complex world of American academic publishing. Ann Swidler,
Steven Tipton, Richard Madsen, and Hally Bellah-Guther helped me in all too
many ways, occasional conflicts included. Fred Appel, my editor, has been a
constant source of wisdom, especially in some very dark moments. I have been
blessed to know them.

Jennifer Bellah Maguire helped in so many ways that any list would not suffice: she gave me continuous insight on the developments and vicissitudes of
her family from the very inside, contributed to a step-by-step editing of the
text, and made her amazing negotiating powers available when needed—and
invited me to a wonderful Christmas Eve party during my trip to California in
2013, when the idea of switching from an intellectual to a "full" biography first
surfaced. William M. Sullivan and I shared lunches, trips, and memories, and
he never failed to complete my theoretical or factual guesses as I wrote. They
both helped me in finding the right balance between the public and the private
sides of Bob Bellah's life with friendship and firmness when needed. For that
I am immensely grateful.

Elisa Scalabrin and our daughter Ester Emilia supplied me with chance and
community chest. Steve Foster and Harlan Stelmach helped me in two exceedingly difficult moments. Teresa Roversi arrived just at the right time and has
been here ever since. Paolo Costa, Andrea Cossu, Sam Porter, and Victor Lidz
have been a continuous presence. Bob Bellah and Massimo Rosati would have
been too, had they not decided to leave. I am sure they are together some-
where, weary of life but not satiated with life.

A JOYFULLY SERIOUS MAN

1

From Father to Son

OKLAHOMA TO CALIFORNIA, 1916–1944

IT WAS JUNE 23, 1916, when Luther Hutton Bellah Jr. hopped on the evening train to Oklahoma City. Excited as he was, he still did not know that his days at the southern border would be boring and inconsequential. He had just turned twenty, and adventure was all he was looking for—or maybe he was just trying to work his way out of the dusty little hole he called home. Drawn by economic opportunity, Hutton's parents had left Texas to resettle in Hollis when he was eight, and their gamble had paid off. After Oklahoma had been granted statehood in 1907, the small town had steadily grown in prominence as the seat of the newly created Harmon County and a station on the railway line connecting Altus and Wellington. In a handful of years its population had doubled, reaching the thousand mark by 1910, and the drugstore run by Luther H. Bellah and "Molly" Emaline Jones had soon become a staple of the town's thriving commercial scene.

Not that Hutton had the slightest intention of becoming a shopkeeper. A tall, handsome boy, he had done all he could to outshine his parents and peers, and keep himself busy in the meantime: studying, reading, writing, sports, theater—everything. In the summer of 1913, just after finishing high school with the highest honors, he had failed the admission test at the Annapolis Naval Academy, and had spent some time looking for jobs and a lucky break in Oklahoma and Missouri. When he came back to Hollis in December of that year, Hutton knew it would not be for long.[1]

It was the Mexican revolutionary General Francisco "Pancho" Villa, of all people, to give him a new excuse to leave. When President Woodrow Wilson issued a mobilization order calling up the National Guard of all states to

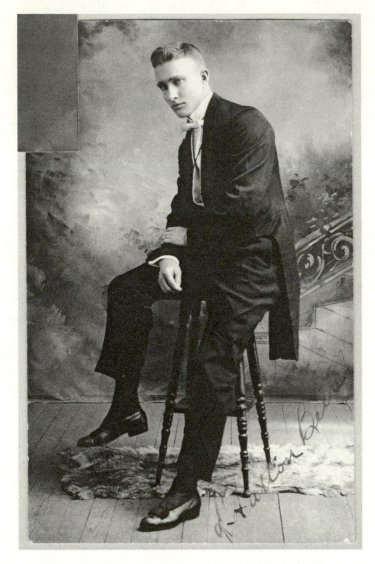

FIGURE 1.1. Luther Hutton Bellah Jr., circa 1920. Robert N. Bellah personal papers (RBPP), courtesy of Jennifer Bellah Maguire and the Robert and Melanie Bellah Estate, Berkeley, CA.

protect the southern border from armed incursions on June 18, 1916, Bellah rushed to volunteer at the conscription office in Oklahoma City. After a brief period of training, Hutton and seven Hollis buddies were assigned to the hospital corps of the "Oklasodak brigade" and then sent to San Benito, Texas. They soon discovered that military life was nothing like advertised: serving as the second line behind regular troops, their unit never had a chance to meet the enemy, and spent months repeating a tedious routine of drill, exercise, and marches. What neither Hutton nor his fellow guardsmen knew at the time was that their days at the border would be crucial not only for improving military training, but also for renewing technical equipment, assessing tactical problems, and devising novel organizational schemes. When the United States declared war on Germany on April 6, 1917, its soldiers were ready for combat.[2]

And into combat they went. Early in August, Hutton Bellah and a Hollis friend from their days on the southern border, Mott Keys, were recalled and assigned to the hospital corps of the newly constituted 36th Texas-Oklahoma Division. They were sent to Camp Bowie for a year of extra training and then crossed the Atlantic to serve on the 111th Sanitary Train in the Tonnerre area of north-central France. Hutton's savoir faire and his command of the German language made him a precious asset for communicating with and gathering information from war prisoners—an assignment he carried out with commitment and pride well into the fall of 1919. After being discharged with the rank of sergeant, Bellah joined the American Legion and Scottish-rite Freemasons, as his father, his grandfather, and many of his forebears had done before him.[3]

The problem was that Hutton was back in Hollis for the third time in six years—and for the third time he started to look for an escape route. In September 1920 he took the momentous decision to attend the University of Oklahoma and left for Norman, never to return home. Founded seven years earlier by Harold Harvey Herbert, the School of Journalism aimed at blending traditional liberal arts education with the most advanced instruction in the burgeoning fields of publishing, editing, and advertising. As part of his training as a reporter, Hutton was at first entrusted with the sports column of a student newspaper, the *Oklahoma Weekly*, but his sharp articles and remarkable editorial skills soon earned him a number of highly visible positions: sports editor for both the *Oklahoma Daily* and the *Sooner* university annual, director of the funding drive for the new athletic stadium, and publicity manager for the whole university.[4]

In a few months, Hutton had found his calling and the scene to pursue it. Popularity and honors followed: together with Keys and Mex, the Boston terrier they had found at the Texas border in 1916, he was tapped by a number of elite cliques, including the Kappa Sigma fraternity and the Dark Deep Mystery Club, a secret society whose members were selected from among the most brilliant undergraduates. Born as a prankster group in 1907, the DDMC had somehow evolved into a masked vigilante posse enforcing basic rules of decency on campus, and had been banned from the university premises owing to its questionable practices and alleged proximity to the Ku Klux Klan—a circumstance that did not prevent Hutton, Mott, and Mex from enjoying the company of their fellow clubmen. For all his popularity, however, Bellah was far from being the most renowned member of the trio: as the first official mascot of the Sooners football team, little Mex had become "the most famous dog in Oklahoma"—when he died in 1928 classes were suspended and businesses were closed to allow the whole town to attend the funeral.[5]

As graduation approached, in the spring of 1922 Hutton's outstanding scholarly achievements earned him induction into the local Pe-et and the national Phi Beta Kappa honor societies. Shortly after the award ceremonies, he rushed to Texas to join Lillian Neelly, a psychology student he had first met as an assistant editor for the 1922 *Sooner*. Born in Fayetteville, Arkansas, on September 14, 1900, Lillian came from a long lineage of landowners and merchants of English descent whose wealth came from a string of fortunate investments in the Dardanelle-Mount Nebo area, eighty miles northwest of Little Rock, Arkansas. The couple married at the Neelly estate in Dallas on June 21, 1922, and then moved to a small house one mile north of the University of Oklahoma campus, where Hutton had been appointed assistant professor at the School of Journalism. In less than two years the student had become a teacher.[6]

I

Before long Hutton grew tired of the slow pace of academic life—he had the most ambitious plans for himself, and mentoring would-be journalists was not among them. In the summer of 1924 he and Lillian moved to the small town of Altus in Southwest Oklahoma and took control of a local weekly magazine, the *Times-Democrat*, with the ultimate goal of turning it into an influential state-level newspaper. When Luther Hutton Bellah III was born in Altus on February 23, 1927, his indefatigable father had already accomplished the objective of daily publication and was rapidly marching toward professional and personal success.

Hutton's dreams were an almost perfect reflection of the unbounded optimism of pre-1929 America. The early 1920s had been a time of rapid technological and social transformation, as the diffusion of electricity, mass-produced automobiles, sound cinema, radio, and television changed the habits and the imaginary of the average American. A sense of a continual improvement of

FIGURE 1.2. Lillian Bellah (née Neelly) with baby Luther Hutton
Bellah III, 1927. (RBPP)

material conditions spread among the citizenry, and the nation's leaders and
popular magazines endlessly praised the pursuit of economic success and the
benefits of hard work and commitment. As a steady flow of consumer goods
swept the country from sea to sea, presidential nominee Herbert C. Hoover
announced at the 1928 Republican National Convention that for the first time
in history the human race was rapidly approaching "the final triumph over
poverty."[7]

A fierce opponent of Hoover and his political ideas, Hutton nonetheless shared the candidate's confidence in unlimited scientific and technological progress. From the columns of the *Times-Democrat* he campaigned with equal passion for the establishment of a modern sewage system in Altus, the renovation of the city's schools, and the building of its first hotel. His daily feature, titled "SnapShots," was a mixed bag of news, anecdotes, and commentary, which often included what he called "Today's Pome," a short satirical composition made of "a bit of advice here, a caustic remark there, a jingle yonder and a bromide hither." Thanks to his success and savoir faire, in early 1929 Hutton was appointed chairman of the advertising committee of the Altus Chamber of Commerce, a task force aimed at attracting investment for the improvement of local business. Even in Southwest Oklahoma progress seemed inevitable.[8]

As far as state and national politics were concerned, Hutton often took unpopular stances. In the spring of 1928, for example, the *Times-Democrat* supported New York governor Al Smith's bid for the Democratic nomination in the presidential elections, in the face of the well-known hostility of the local Ku Klux Klan. In spite of repeated personal attacks, Hutton blasted the "insidious intolerance" of the Klan and its damaging influence on mainstream Freemasonry, and denounced anti-Catholic rhetoric as "something that should never be injected in American politics." After Smith obtained the nomination at the Democratic National Convention, Hutton worked tirelessly for his election, hoping for "a triumph of the common people over the hosts of privilege and plunder." Four months later, his grace and composure upon Hoover's landslide victory in the presidential elections were congratulated by his political friends and foes all over the state.[9]

Hutton's big break seemed to come in March 1929, right after a heated press campaign had ousted governor Henry S. Johnston for "general incompetence." The *Times-Democrat* was one of the first papers to congratulate the new incumbent, William J. Holloway, with its usual hopeful tones: "Again thank God for Bill Holloway," Hutton wrote in his editorial, "This is the man. He will do it if it is at all possible. He realizes the responsibilities before him and his many years of service to the state as a legislator, as lieutenant governor and as acting governor peculiarly fits him for the work of the next twenty-two months." When Holloway offered him a job as his private secretary, however, Hutton declined: being "a newspaper man and not a politician," he had "lots of things" to care about—Altus, Jackson County, the *Times-Democrat*, and the State Press Association, of which he had just been appointed executive vice-president.[10]

The last but in no sense least important item of Hutton's list of things to care about was his small family of three. Given his almost complete amalgam of public and private life, it was no surprise that "the missus" and "Snaps III"—as his wife and child were affectionately nicknamed—had been a staple of "Snap-Shots" since its early days. Whether he was welcoming a new puppy or encountering his first defeats, baby Hutton III was depicted as a miniature of his bright and resolute father: "The wee sma' lad is sporting his first real black eye—result of a mix-up with the concrete sidewalk in which he came off second best. But the boy is not daunted by a little thing like losing to a concrete walk board. . . . He gets up and tries again."[11] Readers also got the occasional photo of Snaps III along with the news of his progress:

TODAY'S POME

The wee sma' boy attempts to talk.
There is incessant chatter.
But what he says we do not know
And it really doesn't matter,
The missus claims to understand
The little fellow's mutters—
But we are rather of the mind
That this infant sputters.[12]

By January 1929 Hutton III's involvement in the busy professional life of his father was almost complete: wearing the "white duck coverall with 'Snaps III' on the front and 'Times-Democrat' on the back" he had been given for Christmas by Hutton's business partner, Harrington C. Wimberly, the twenty-three-month-old baby would joyously run around screaming "Dadee go to work Times Democrack! Dadee go to work Times Democrack!" whenever he saw his father wearing his overcoat.[13]

To his readers' surprise, in the summer of 1929 Hutton sold his shares to media mogul Eugene C. Pulliam and passed on the editorship of the *Altus Times-Democrat* to Wimberly. In his last "SnapShots," published on July 21, 1929, he looked back at his five years as a publisher-editor with a tone reminiscent of Harold Herbert's project of combining the craft of journalism and sophisticated managerial skills: "I believe that I have proved that a newspaper can have a mind of its own," Hutton wrote, "that the editor can speak right out in meeting, as it were, and at the same time operate a successful business. Too many newspaper men are prone to let the almighty dollar influence their every action and refrain from having an opinion contrary to the popular one," he added, "I have never let such things dictate and have taken my stand as I thought right regardless of the popularity of it." One day later, Wimberly paid homage to his longtime friend in the last "SnapShots" instalment ever. He described Hutton Bellah as "one of the hardest working men" he had ever met, a decent and free newsman who had bowed "to no clique or klan, recognizing no restraint when expressing opinions." Soon, he added, "some good town in Oklahoma" would get "a fighting editor who [would] put some real life into its newspaper." Wimberly was right: although Hutton did not know yet what the future would bring, he had no intention of leaving Oklahoma or the publishing business.

Whatever the plans were at the time, the Black Tuesday of October 29, 1929, shattered them all. The Bellahs lost over $35,000 in the stock market crash, and set out to move to Los Angeles to rejoin Lillian's relatives and look for a new start.[14]

II

Moving from a small town in rural Oklahoma to Southern California was nothing less than a shocking jump into modernity. A metropolis of 1.2 million inhabitants, Los Angeles in the 1920s had become the fastest growing urban area in the United States, thanks to the arrival of thousands of immigrants attracted by the promise of unlimited economic opportunity and a world-famous climate. A steady flow of capital and a booming real estate market reshaped the urban landscape: oil fields were excavated just a few miles from downtown, while the rise of Hollywood as the latest epitome of the American frontier prompted the building of new hotels, shopping districts, and theaters. As tourists flooded in, Los Angeles cleaned up its slums and adorned itself with architectural gems: the Pasadena Rose Bowl was completed in 1922, the Public Library in 1926, and the Hollywood Bowl in 1929.[15]

With a cars-per-resident ratio thrice the national average, the City of Angels also led America's motorization. The multiplication of private vehicles carrying commuters back and forth from the ever-expanding suburbs fostered the creation of a complex system of high-speed superhighways—a far cry from the deserted roads where Hutton's tires would get punctured three times during the 140-mile trip from Altus to Oklahoma City. The development of the Major Traffic Street Plans of the 1920s fostered in turn the creation of a number of new business districts. A couple of miles down the road from the condo on Queen Anne Place where the Bellahs first settled down, for example, visionary developer A. W. Ross was turning a hitherto unpaved portion of Wilshire Boulevard into the so-called Miracle Mile, a commercial stretch designed to attract motorized consumers using modern retail and advertising techniques. As one of the many "boosters and shamans" of the 1920s, Ross contributed to transforming Southern California into a magical place where anything seemed possible. "The future is yours," wrote Bruce Bliven in 1927, "And the past? There isn't any."[16]

In theory, Los Angeles was the best place to be for a bright and dynamic young man—the materialization of that blend of progress and freedom that Luther Hutton Bellah Jr. had always longed for. At the same time, its size and complexity might have seemed too wide a sea to someone who was used to swimming in a pond. Although he received good offers from a number of newspapers, on December 28, 1929, Hutton disappeared. But in spite of the grim content of the few letters he sent Lillian, who soon discovered she was pregnant again, he had no intention of killing himself: he first headed to New York City, where he started introducing himself as William A. Lee, the last remaining scion of a historic Southern family. During a vacation in Cuba he met one Miss Catherine R. Blythe and followed her to Chicago, where they got engaged. On April 18, 1930, five days before their wedding, he fled to Madison, Wisconsin, where he got engaged again, this time to a young music teacher, Edna Louise Schatz. The couple married in Rockford, Illinois, on July 17, 1930, and then moved to Yuma, where Lee, sticking to his Altus pattern, bought a local newspaper and made himself a name as an entrepreneur.[17]

Things, however, were far from settled. Early in 1931, Bill Lee was approached by an Altus acquaintance who questioned his identity. Investigations had been started by Harrington Wimberly after he had spotted some familiar lingo, such as Hutton's trademark "the missus," in the editorial column of the *Arizona Sentinel*. At about the same time, Lee had been writing to a millionaire friend, Lew Wentz, asking for a loan to rescue his new journal from financial disaster. The prospect of being identified as Hutton Bellah and then tried for bigamy was the proverbial straw that broke the camel's back. In a crescendo of fear and anxiety, on April 6, 1931, Bellah/Lee shot himself in the head while Edna was doing chores in the room next door—"I can't go on," he wrote in his suicide note, "I am sorry. I am not all bad." Contacted by Wimberly, Lillian Bellah traveled to Arizona with her sister to identify the body—"I am positive that is my husband" was all she said. After a vigil ceremony in Yuma, Molly Emaline Jones took the remains of her disgraced son back to the Bellah-Scott-Jones clan's big white house in Saint Jo, Texas, where there was a solemn funeral paid for by Wentz. Neither Lillian nor Edna was among the hundreds of people who attended the ceremony.[18]

Soon after her husband's death, Lillian had little Hutton III's name changed to Robert Neely Bellah.[19] "Bob," as everybody called him, grew up in the Mid-Wilshire neighborhood in Los Angeles with his mother and sister, Hallie Virginia, born on May 12, 1930, under the stern authority of Lillian's older sister, Elizabeth, and her doctor husband, Clifford A. Wright. Born in 1882, "Uncle Clifford" worked as the senior attending physician at the Psychoendocrine Clinic of the Los Angeles County General Hospital and an associate professor of clinical medicine at the College for Medical Evangelists in Loma Linda. The clinic, which Wright had helped found, was a free public institution devoted to the scientific study of cases that showed both psychotic and endocrine gland symptoms. In particular, Wright's clinical research focused on homosexuality as a natural condition due to congenital imbalances of masculine and feminine hormones. His late-1930s articles on the subject were strongly criticized by Alfred C. Kinsey, then a taxonomist known for his work on gall wasps, and led him to the study of human sexuality. An old-style Presbyterian matron, "Aunt Bessie" supported her husband as a member of the State Board of the Woman's Auxiliary to the California Medical Association and the one-time chair of its Los Angeles chapter. In spite of their close-knit relations, the members of the Wright-Neely-Bellah clan held opposite political persuasions: while Clifford and Bessie were staunch supporters of free capitalism and the Republican Party, Lillian remained true to Hutton's Southern Democrat roots without properly being on the left.[20]

At the time of his third birthday on February 23, 1930, little Bob had been waiting in vain for his father to come home from his "long trip" and help him cut his cake. He was finally told of Hutton's death a couple of years later, at a time when the effects of the Great Depression were sorely testing the City of Angels and its sparkling image as the capital of unlimited opportunity. Wages fell rapidly as tens of thousands of immigrant agricultural workers flooded the fields of Southern California, and class and ethnic confrontations became a permanent feature of the metropolitan landscape. By June 1934 one-fourth of all Californians depended on some form of public assistance, and one-third of these lived around Los Angeles County. After the Dust Bowl of the mid-1930s, the flow of indigent families from the Great Plains and the Southwest became so intense that in 1937 the so-called Anti-Okie Law was passed to prevent further immigration. In the meantime, affluent Anglos had moved to the suburbs to shun the arrival of undesired ethnic minorities and the decadence of old business districts.[21]

The times were trying, but Lillian had the money from her husband's generous life insurance and a little help from the Wrights to support her family without being forced to get a job. Walking in Hutton's footsteps, Bob soon developed a consuming passion for reading difficult books and penning short stories, poems, plays, and even faux newspapers. In a short autobiography written at the age of ten, he declared his love of history and geography, his distaste for spelling and Chinese food, and his ultimate plan "to make the world a better place to live in." Lillian took great pride in the academic achievements of her children, and regularly did parent-teacher association work for their schools. She also kept strong ties with former students from the University of Oklahoma, and enjoyed the occasional trip across the Mexican border, while Bob and Hallie stayed with Aunt Bessie and Uncle Cliff. Bob's favorite time of year was the summer, when he spent his time swimming and riding horses at camp.[22]

As the 1930s came to an end, Lillian Bellah took a job as a wedding director at the Shatto Chapel of the First Congregational Church of Los Angeles, where she arranged ceremonies, decorations, and parties. Following his mother, Bob started attending Sunday school at the huge gothic building completed in 1932 at the intersection of South Commonwealth Avenue and Sixth Street. There he developed a strong interest in politics, thanks to a young minister who taught a radical reading of the Old Testament books of Amos and Hosea. Struck by the power of the Social Gospel, Bob turned into a passionate New Deal Democrat. As the most learned and the only male member of the family, he had already acquired a position of advantage vis-à-vis his mother and sister: not only could he do whatever he wanted whenever he wanted, but Lillian had developed such an intense dependency upon him that a teenage rebellion became almost unthinkable. After graduating from the John Burroughs Junior High School with the highest of honors, Bob was ready for the next step: Los Angeles High, the oldest and most revered public secondary school in Southern California.[23]

III

Robert Bellah enrolled at LA High in the winter of 1942. By that time the Wall Street Crash had become a distant memory: massive public undertakings such as the Arroyo Seco Parkway and the Colorado River Project had boosted the

FIGURE 1.3. Robert N. Bellah as a teenager, early 1940s. (RBPP)

Californian economy and, with it, the Republican Party—the elective affinity between the ethos of suburbia and Hoover's progressivism made sure that the New Deal would never win the hearts, or the votes, of white middle-class Angelenos. The time of symbolic reflection on the American Dream initiated by Black Tuesday was over, and the City of Angels had emerged once again as the capital of glamour and fun. Contrary to the dark predictions of forced citizens like Bertolt Brecht, Thomas Mann, or Theodor Adorno, the metropolis thrived as the living illustration of "California as pleasure principle," a place where all were allegedly granted the possibility of conducting a life of pure enjoyment without ever having to justify themselves. To the dispassionate observer, in 1942 Los Angeles looked "beautiful but dumb, an Attica minus the intellect," a metropolis that "lacked ambition and generosity of spirit," a "screwy" place where unadjusted people would live in a "utopia touched by sadness."[24]

To the eyes of fifteen-year-old Bob Bellah, Los Angeles was not at all beautiful, just dumb. A typical "brain," nerdy student, Bob did not really care about the judgment of his far-too-different peers—he took pride in the fact that his Saturday nights at the Los Angeles Philharmonic and the Hollywood Bowl, where he worked as an usher in order to attend classical music performances for free, were as far as could be from an average night out in Southern California. At school he befriended mostly Jewish students, with whom he shared an interest in liberal politics, the writings of Karl Marx, symphonic music, opera, and poetry; he also became an avid reader of the novels of Thomas Wolfe and Arnold Bennett, which he had found in the old trunk where his father had once kept his revolver. Unlike most Americans, who thought that the war would change little of their everyday lives, Bellah was an enthusiastic interventionist and closely followed the unfolding of tragic events in Europe, devouring dailies and periodicals.[25]

Walking in Hutton's footsteps, in the fall of 1944 Bob became the editor of the school newspaper, the *Blue and White*. For six months he performed his task smoothly and responsibly, publishing all kind of serious and facetious news and paying scrupulous attention to even the smallest detail. In his weekly column—"Inside L.A."—he addressed local political and ethical problems, such as the adjustment of first-year students and the correct functioning of the merit system, but also the pros and cons of student government, in which he himself participated as an officer in a number of councils and committees. As the 1944 presidential election approached, Bob started to deal with more general issues in a way reminiscent of his father's political columns in the *Altus Times-Democrat*. His editorial of October 23, 1944, for example, offered a poignant portrait of his generation: "Born out of depression, we had just arrived in junior high when the world went to war," he wrote. "The United States has been into war ever since we came to L.A. [High]. We cannot remember back to when there was no war." The consequences were appalling: "We may have become so used to war that we consider it inevitable." He warned, "we must fight against that attitude and prepare to accept a reality we have never known peace—peace which was denied us by some leaders of the past generation. They betrayed us and they betrayed our brothers and friends fighting on foreign soil."[26]

FIGURE 1.4. The staff of the *Blue and White*, including Melanie Hyman (*far left*) and Robert Bellah (*middle*). (*1945 Yearbook*, Los Angeles High School)

Bellah's interest in political and ethical matters suffused the articles he wrote in the wake of his graduation in December 1944. While admitting that his attempts to improve the school had not been entirely effective, Bob praised "the beginning or widening of a movement for a more liberal and democratic system here."[27] He also commended the ethos of unceasing self-improvement of LA High and called for its renewal: "Every term we are faced with the challenge of continuing and enlarging this spirit," he exhorted his fellow students. "Its price, like that of liberty, is eternal vigilance. If we allow the small groups to come first, if we give our loyalty first to them and then to the school, the whole basis of the greatness of L.A. [High] is gone. That the whole is more important than any of its parts must be our doctrine."[28]

Bellah's inspired collectivism was, to say the least, exaggerated. His teenage years in Los Angeles had made him into a competitive individualist determined to excel and lead in each and any situation. If these traits made him into a veritable replica of his father, Bob lacked Hutton's grace and savoir faire—he had explicitly wanted his photo to be published at the top of his column to accentuate his "you may despise me, but I'm right here in your face" attitude. He had to be a winner, and this required him to keep his feelings and doubts about himself locked inside, where no one could see them. Thus, when he met with his LA High counsellor he had only two ideas in mind: he wanted to get into the best college he could afford and put as much distance as possible between himself and shallow Southern California. Harvard seemed to be a natural solution, and Bob was so sure he could do it that he decided to apply there and nowhere else. In her letter of recommendation, Professor Mary Howell praised his ability to articulate complex ideas, his deep social concern, and "the courage of [his] well considered convictions," but remained silent on his blatant superiority complex. The wager was successful, and Bob was accepted as a member of the Harvard Class of '48 on a generous scholarship.[29]

For 150 years, the Bellahs had unfailingly headed west. Looking for a better life, they had become merchants and explorers in South Carolina, planters and slave owners in Tennessee, physicians in Arkansas, and Freemasons in Texas. They had found and lost a fortune in Oklahoma and resettled in Los Angeles in hope and pain. Now Robert Neelly Bellah, formerly known as Luther Hutton Bellah III, was leaving home to move back to the East Coast, albeit to a place that was miles away, both geographically and culturally, from the shores of Sullivan's Island where his ancestor, William Ballagh from County Antrim in Northern Ireland, had first set foot in 1692 with a hundred pounds in his sack. Things were about to change, and dramatically so.[30]

2

A Writer and a Teacher

UNITED STATES EAST COAST, 1945–1950

ON A WARM WINTER AFTERNOON, Robert N. Bellah waved an emotional goodbye to Lillian and Hallie and boarded the Union Pacific *Challenger* streamliner. After short breaks in San Bernardino and Las Vegas, the train devoured the frozen plains of Utah, Wyoming, Nebraska, and Iowa and finally stopped in that "horribly dull, dirty and repelling city," Chicago. There Bob switched trains to head to Boston's South Station, where he arrived five days after his eighteenth birthday and one day before his hero, Franklin Delano Roosevelt, would report about the talks at Yalta in front of a Congress shocked by his evident physical decay. It had been a comfortable trip, blessed with delicious, if expensive, food and pleasing companions. Rambling over the snow that covered Beacon Hill's irregular cobblestones, Bellah felt as though he had landed on a different planet—a world that bore no resemblance to the flat concrete sidewalks of the sunny and shallow Los Angeles of his childhood.

In fact, Bob had learned something important during his first solo trip across the country: average people were not *that* fascinating, even outside boring Southern California. The young navy trainee sitting across the aisle on the *New England States*, for example, had shown no interest in Bob, busy as he was playing cards with his friends. And the three women Bellah had met and befriended on the *Challenger*—a navy wife with her three-year-old daughter, a Catholic coast guard officer who had often attended Lillian's First Congregational Church during its Bach Festival, and the aged ex-housemaid who had been traveling across the United States to visit her children—were pleasant and kind, but definitely "simple" and "not bright." Once again, Bob felt that he had been cast in a different mold: it was not by chance that he was heading east to get the best college education an American could dream of. His grades had been excellent, and he had shown his mother, teachers, and schoolmates that he could deliver, whether as the editor of the *Blue and White*, an officer in the Boy's Council, or a commencement speaker. After a light lunch in Boston, Robert Bellah left his bags at the station baggage claim and hopped on the first streetcar to Cambridge, Massachusetts, in a state of tense but excited anticipation.[1]

I

When Bob Bellah first walked through the gates of Harvard Yard on February 28, 1945, American higher education was bringing to completion a radical transformation rooted in the so-called "three revolutions" of the late nineteenth century: the establishment of land-grant colleges, the rise of collegiate culture, and faculty professionalization. The creation of state-supported institutions of higher learning via the Morrill Acts of 1862 and 1890 expanded college enrolment and supported the development of agriculture, engineering, journalism, and teacher education. At the same time, the emergence of a new collegiate culture "presumed to produce character, 'manliness,' and subsequent success in the business world" boosted and dignified peer-to-peer relations, extracurricular activities, and student-run organizations on campus. Though not a land-grant college, Hutton's and Lillian's alma mater, the University of Oklahoma, was a typical example of this novel combination of practically oriented instruction and buoyant undergraduate life.[2]

Last but not least, scholarly inquiry became more professional through a process of generalization and standardization of the ways and the ethos of scientific inquiry. The center of gravity of faculty work shifted from the education of undergraduates to the production of knowledge and the training of new generations of scientists-to-be. The creation of research-oriented universities such as Johns Hopkins and Clark; the establishment of the University of Chicago; and the reform of Yale, Harvard, and Columbia institutionalized a culture centered on scholarly autonomy, research opportunities, and the judgment of like-minded peers at the expense of existing local and denominational networks. Modern disciplines became increasingly separated thanks to the creation of scientific journals and selective professional organizations—such as the American Historical Association (1884), the American Sociological Society (1905), the American Association of University Professors (1915), and eventually the American Council of Learned Societies (1919). As a result, during the interwar period American physics, medical science, economics, and psychology led the way in asserting the global supremacy of the United States in the production of knowledge.[3]

In Cambridge the revolution took the form of a pendulum swinging between a research-centered, "German" idea of higher education and an Oxbridge-inspired penchant for collegiate life. Change was started in 1869 by Charles W. Eliot, a scion of one of those business families who had taken control of Boston's institutions the mid-nineteenth century and had established themselves as a metropolitan upper class, the so-called "Boston Brahmins," in the process. A stalwart advocate of a stricter connection between the emerging industrial complex and academic culture, during his forty-year presidency Eliot reinforced professional studies, expanded graduate training, and enabled college students to choose their own courses thanks to a new elective system. His reforms opened Harvard to diversity and conflict, producing what the president complacently called a "collision of views."[4]

Whereas Eliot made Harvard into a self-conscious university meant to turn each student into "something of a scholar," his successor, Boston Brahmin A. Lawrence Lowell, focused on the communal aspects of undergraduate life and their impact on the production of "a well-rounded manhood." Appointed in 1909, he saw the college as a character-making institution aimed at "forming lifelong friendships," "acquiring intellectual tastes," and "the craving of clear and profound thought."[5] The building of freshman dormitories around the Yard in 1914 was the first step of an ambitious program, which reached its culmination some fifteen years later with the creation of an Oxbridge-inspired "house system." Each run by a master and a number of faculty and resident tutors, the houses provided accommodation to the members of the upper classes in a comfortable, stimulating environment. Dining halls, interhouse sports activities, and common rooms with small libraries and record collections were created to reinforce a healthy esprit de corps and shape the character of students. Lowell's swan song before leaving the presidency in 1933 was a stunning personal gift of $1.5 million to create the Society of Fellows as a sort of corrective to the "mass production of mediocrity" and "the scholastic drudgery" of professional graduate programs. Thanks to Lowell's generosity and the leadership of his biochemist friend Lawrence J. Henderson, year after year a small number of exceptionally gifted young men would be chosen by a selected group of faculty members and allowed to be "free to follow their bent, free of academic anxieties" within a socially dense milieu complete with its own headquarters, budget, and rituals.[6]

The birth of the Society was a paradoxical form of recognition of the fact that the pendulum had again swung in the direction of Germany. The main architect of this change of course was Harvard's new president, James Bryant Conant, a renowned chemist who had made himself a name as a staunch opponent of Lowell's policies. Sharing Conant's diagnosis of the university as an "ungainly and fissiparous" institution in desperate need of incisive reform, in 1933 the Corporation picked him with the explicit mission of furthering the prospects of scientific inquiry: the disparate body of schools, departments, laboratories, observatories, museums, and botanical gardens that made up Harvard in the early 1930s had to become a "place of specialized disciplines and world-class scholars, dedicated to the pursuit of truth."[7]

Although actual policies did not always match his rhetoric, Conant considered meritocracy and the Jeffersonian idea of a "natural aristocracy" as the keys to unify Harvard while diversifying its student body, and boost its national vocation. After introducing standardized testing as a novel way for adjudicating admissions, Conant envisioned a system of national scholarships to ensure that talented students from all corners of the United States could come to Cambridge regardless of their means—when Robert Bellah was admitted in 1945, the university was spending an average $800,000 a year in grants and financial aid to students. In a few years the combination of the two policies brought graduates from public high schools to a record high of 57 percent of freshmen, and reversed the traditional sixty/forty proportion of New England natives versus students coming from the rest of the United States.[8]

The values of academic brilliance and strong character also came to inform the recruitment of tenured faculty. Striving to strike a balance between disciplinary autonomy, institutional needs, and scientific renown, Conant created the modern system of ad hoc hiring committees composed of external scholars. In 1939 a limit of eight years was set for the renewal of untenured jobs, which, together with the introduction of the "up or out" rule for assistant professors, provoked the opposition of conservative academics and younger faculty members. By the early 1940s, however, Conant's methods were generally accepted at Harvard and other top American universities. To round off his academic policy, in 1943 he created the Committee on the Objectives of a General Education in a Free Society. Led by the powerful dean of the Faculty of Arts and Sciences, Paul H. Buck, the twelve-man group appropriated $60,000 to devise a comprehensive reform of the "the liberal and humane tradition" of undergraduate instruction.[9]

As an early interventionist and the chairman of the National Defense Research Committee, Conant also made sure that Harvard would give a weighty contribution to the war effort. In the introduction to a booklet for aspiring freshmen printed in July 1943, he described his university as utterly focused on winning the war in close collaboration with the federal government. Not only were one-third of the faculty regularly traveling back and forth to Washington, DC, but everyday life on campus had been altered to accommodate special courses of instruction in radar and statistical sciences, engineering, and military chaplainship for army and navy servicemen. At the beginning of the 1944–1945 spring term, the civilians enrolled at Harvard numbered slightly fewer than two thousand, one-fourth of average prewar numbers and one-half of all army and navy students combined. Writing in January 1945, Conant was firmly convinced that the war experience and the "partial conversion [of colleges and universities] to a purpose alien to their fundamental tasks" would bolster higher education both "internally and in the minds of the American people." From the northern banks of the Charles River the future looked unmistakably bright.[10]

II

Three days after Bellah's arrival, 741 civilians would crowd Harvard's University Hall to register for courses, dorms, and board; of those, only 84 were freshmen at their debut—a small number by any measure. To the young Angeleno, however, statistics were of no interest: Cambridge was ebullient with people to meet, customs to learn, and experiences to deal with. Bob was awed by the imposing redbrick buildings and skeletal trees, fascinated by the quiet character of Harvard Square, amazed by all the "kind, friendly, helpful and above all sympathetic" people he met. Since freshman dormitories on the Yard were occupied by the Reserve Officers' Training Corps, he was directly admitted to Adams, the house then occupying the august complex on Mount Auburn Street that had once served as the base of a young Franklin Delano Roosevelt. At Adams House Bellah was warmly welcomed by a janitor who escorted him to suite A-11, an old-fashioned apartment on the first floor complete with leaded bay windows leaning on to Bow Street, an upright piano, and a decorated fireplace. Bob was stunned: having arrived one day early, not only was he able to choose his own room, but he would enjoy the whole suite for himself for his first night at Harvard. "God is in his heaven," he wrote to his mother that very evening, "and if all is not well with the world, at least all is well with me."[11]

As students started flocking to the house, things got better and better. The home of nonconformists and bohemians, Adams was known for the "casualness and sincerity" of its members, its proximity to the Yard, its delicious food, and the only in-house swimming pool on campus. Classical music came out of every room and Bob, used as he was to Southern California's irritating background of crooners and big bands, reacted with sheer incredulity—"I still can't believe that all this is happening to me."[12] During his first formal dinner with David Mason Little, the master of Adams who also doubled as the university's secretary, and his wife, Bob found that the house and its denizens were also congenial from a political point of view: everybody was "pro-labor, pro-[Henry] Wallace and pro-New Deal." What conquered him, however, was *respect*. "We are Harvard men," he wrote Lillian, "and will be treated as such." That meant no curfew and no drinking rules—not that Bellah was much of a drinker: as he told his mother, he had to familiarize himself with beer in order to fully participate in the master's evening parties.[13]

Bob was literally overwhelmed by the intensity of his new experiences. If his first letter to Lillian included doodles of both Harvard's and Adams's coats of arms and an explanation of the university's motto—"'Veritas' means truth in Latin"—a couple of days later he created his own "official" stationery by adding Harvard stickers and drawings to his correspondence.[14] Writing to his aunts Irma and Bessie, Bob minutely described the various buildings of Adams House and the tunnels running underneath the Yard, explained the mores of student life, and confessed being so "overwhelmed by the ancient traditions" of the university that he could only "gaze in silent wonder."[15] Even the buildings spoke to him: day after day the motto inscribed on the arch of the Class of 1890 Gate to Harvard Yard—"Enter to grow in wisdom, depart better to serve thy country and mankind"—reminded him of the burden he had somehow accepted to carry as a Harvard man. No wonder, then, that his comments on the "good indoctrination course" given to freshmen and his retelling of a documentary depicting a recent graduation ceremony were only apparently ironic:

President Conant, president of Harvard university, is just about the most important man on earth. People around here say his name in hushed awed tones. If even the freshman class is allowed to look at him I am sure half of us will faint from even being so close to THE GREAT MAN. Anyway, the PRESIDENT, in all his splendor, follows the sheriff and is followed by a very insignificant man who is merely Governor [Leverett] Saltonstall of Massachusetts. He is followed by the MEMBERS OF THE CORPORATION. . . . Such a sight they make puts the English coronation to shame.[16]

Outside the classroom life looked just as grand and exciting: chamber music ensembles and the Boston Symphony Orchestra played Harvard once a week, the streets and squares of old Cambridge were thick with bookshops, neighborhood stores, and inexpensive cafeterias, while its cinemas routinely screened European movies. Student groups abounded, and Bellah dreamed about joining a number of extracurricular activities: the Liberal Union, the Philosophy Club, the Government Club, and the Glee Club, which used to perform with the Boston Symphony twice a year. All of this, along with the discovery of Harvard University's contribution to the war effort, intensified his excitement for being right where the action was.[17]

For the first time in his life Bob had found a place that was wholly his own, a milieu he considered fit to nurture the image he had of himself as a passionate, rigorous, highbrow student. Not that everything was ideal; his roommates, for example, fared below his expectations—"They are immature, nonintellectual and interested only in having a good time for a few months before the army gets them," he wrote to Lillian. But he was making a lot of friends during nightly discussions at the Adams dinner hall, and when he wrote his mother that he found Easterners conspicuously amiable and much warmer than Californians, he was in fact expressing his gratitude for finally being among his peers—learned, disciplined, and liberal young men. His, however, was more than a feeling. At Harvard his sense of being part of a natural elite of hardworking, bright men had found the support of a number of like-minded friends and an indomitable institutional mythology—what radical sociologist Alvin W. Gouldner would later call the "Olympus Complex." Bellah was "a Harvard man," *had always been one*, and now was just being treated as such.[18]

Bob's stint in heaven, however, was of short duration. After a mere three weeks in Cambridge, he was deemed fit for general military service and set up to join the army. Though he would not have been able to obtain a deferral, Bellah fully embraced his imminent departure: "Dear mother," he wrote to a much-worried Lillian, "please do not feel bad about this thing. I am really glad to go. I want to play an active part in winning this great war. I want to learn how I will stand up under fire. I want to be in this great citizens' army and see how it works." Professor Cecil E. Fraser, the assistant dean of Harvard Business School and liaison with the armed forces for the university, reassured Lillian about the eventual replacement of Bob's scholarship with the provisions of the GI Bill at the end of his service in the army. In order to be closer to his family, Bellah asked to be inducted in California and headed back to Los Angeles on March 26, 1945.[19]

III

Luckily enough, Bellah never made it to the battlefield. Once in California he was examined again and declared temporarily unfit for service because of his thinness, with a new check-up scheduled for September. He then resolved to remain in Los Angeles with his family, working at the Public Library, reading the news from Europe and the Pacific, and eating truckloads of bananas in order to reach the required weight. The following six months proved to be crucial for the war: on April 12 the sudden death of President Roosevelt opened the doors of the Oval Office to Harry S. Truman; Milano was liberated on April 25 and Germany was defeated two weeks later; Japan signed its unconditional surrender on August 15, after the dropping of atomic bombs on Hiroshima and Nagasaki. When Bob went back to the army physician in September the war was over, but personnel were needed to run the demobilization of some twelve million servicemen. He was thus drafted as a typist at Port MacArthur and then sent to Tilton General Hospital at Fort Dix, not far from Trenton, New Jersey, at the end of April 1946.[20]

As the largest separation office in the nation, Fort Dix marched at an average of seventy thousand servicemen per month on a 24/7 routine—since April 1944 some nine hundred thousand enlisted men and women had already walked through its hallways. Its Tilton General Hospital, where Bellah was employed as a consultant investigating claims about lost or damaged property and small personal injuries caused by military personnel, managed a load of nearly four thousand patients a day. As Bob told Lillian, he found his job fairly interesting, but what he loved the most were the "austere grey-green" of the New Jersey woods and the free time he needed for his studies. Bellah also made a habit of spending his weekends in New York City with his companions in arms; while all other servicemen spent their time on drink, sightseeing, and cheap movies, however, he was determined "to systematically consume the whole vast cultural resources of the great city." In a typical weekend of May 1946, for example, he attended to two Broadway plays (Shakespeare's *Henry IV* starring Lawrence Olivier, and Maxine Wood's political drama *On Whitman Avenue*), a number of Russian and Italian movies, and the Festival of Contemporary American Music at Columbia University.[21]

This frantic cultural schedule confirmed his self-image as a true Harvard man as much as his formal and informal reading. "I have come to feel that the two gifts which I have been given are a certain ability to write and a great thirst for knowledge," Bob told Lillian one month after his arrival at Fort Dix. "I think a man should find out what his talents are in order to choose his life's work. Therefore I think I was meant to be *a writer and a teacher*, and that that is how I can best serve my fellow men and find a useful place in the world. Of course there are many kinds of teachers and many combinations of the two," he concluded, "I have not decided on any of these. But in a general way I know what I must do with my life."[22]

Even if he had not been under enemy fire, Bob had discovered much about himself during his first year in the army. He carried out his duties as a clerk, but he did not really like office work. He enjoyed the company of army comrades, but only as long as their relations were not too tight. He liked to go to the movies, but preferred foreign films to Hollywood blockbusters—in fact, he was so enthusiastic about Roberto Rossellini's *Roma Città Aperta* as to predict the nearing collapse of the American entertainment industry. At nineteen, he thought he had found his calling: just like L. Hutton Bellah Jr., the former assistant professor of journalism whose witty "SnapShots" had bantered the public vices and private virtues of the citizens of Altus, he was going to be a writer and a teacher. Without ever mentioning him, Bob was marking his way in the shadow of his father—who, not by accident, was going to be a haunting presence during the tour of the East Coast he embarked on during his first long-term furlough.[23]

On June 15, 1946, Bellah left Trenton for Washington, DC, where he visited art museums, national monuments, and both branches of Congress. He then moved south to Richmond, Williamsburg, and Charlottesville, and then again to his beloved New York City, where he spent a busy week before going back to Fort Dix. In the nation's capital Bob was a guest of Harrington Wimberly, his father's old business partner, who, besides editing the *Altus Times-Democrat*, had been appointed to the Federal Power Commission. Wimberly had not met "Snaps III" in more than fifteen years, and was truly moved to see how much the young man resembled his father in his face, figure, and manners. Night after night the two would engage in long conversations about the man who, for better or worse, had left his mark on their lives—and Wimberly had only words of admiration for his never-forgotten friend, a "fine, hard-working, fearless man" who had literally succumbed to "the pace he had set for himself."[24]

If Bob was touched, he did not show it. Rather, his letters to Lillian focused on the "surprisingly and shockingly backward state" of Virginia. In Richmond he remained nauseated by the grimy streets and the "revolting odor" exuding from the James River. Way more disgusting, however, was the smell of Jim Crow. As soon as he got off his train, Bob noticed with some consternation that African Americans were not allowed to leave the station from the main hall—something he had neither seen nor imagined possible in Los Angeles or New York City. But it was on public transportation that he had a most revealing experience: "On a bus in Richmond I went to take a seat beside a negro. The only seat left, without thinking anything about it until the horrified glances of the white people indicated to me I was in the *negro* section." He described the situation as "simply appalling" for those who had to endure such brutality, and wondered how people of color could get anything done in the South.[25]

Like many other American leftists, Bellah was going through a difficult but exciting time. During his lengthy talks with Wimberly, he had the chance to explain his well-considered position to a (not very sympathetic) Washington insider: he considered Henry Truman a traitor of Roosevelt's legacy, and hoped for the creation of "a third party, a labour party" led by Claude Pepper or Henry Wallace, a man he considered "the leader of all that is good in the democratic party." Once a New Deal Democrat, Bob was moving further to the left, mainly because of his acquaintance with the works of two thinkers who would deeply influence his outlook—Karl Marx and Friedrich Engels.[26]

Although they never mentioned the word "communism," after the trip to Virginia, Bellah's letters to his relatives became increasingly gloomy and partisan. Echoing his recent readings, Bob called capitalism "desperately wrong" and foresaw the arrival of a new economic crisis that would bring America to the brink of fascism and perhaps to a global conflict. Truman's foreign policy was a major target of Bob's rage. He resented the support given by the US Army to "fascist dictatorships" around the world, and backed Wallace's opposition to the aggressive stance toward Stalin taken by Truman and his secretary of state, James F. Byrne. The United States, he wrote to his mother, had no interest in waging a war against "our great democratic ally, the Soviet Union." Looking at the first intimations of the emerging Cold War, he had no doubts about whose side he was on: "The idea of competition and self interest must give way to the idea of cooperation and human brotherhood. The Soviet Union is showing the way and like it or not the world is following."[27]

This political radicalization also altered Bellah's perception of the military: he now saw the army as "miserable" and "repellent to everything Americans believe in," and looked with concern at his remaining six months of service. The situation only got worse when he was promoted in October 1946: as a barrack sergeant he now had one corporal and thirty privates at his command, a responsibility that took too much time away from his reading and forced him to require "his men" to do all sorts of "stupid things." It was thus a relief when, on November 16, 1946, he was almost unexpectedly discharged.[28]

After a full year in the army, Bellah could not wait to be in Cambridge again. Thanks to his frequent trips to New York City he had created an idiosyncratic vision of the East Coast as a dream palace of cosmopolitan, highbrow cultural life, an imaginary that reinforced his self-conception as a would-be writer and teacher. When he left New Jersey for Los Angeles to discuss with Lillian her intention to start a business as a wedding planner—a project that Bob opposed, given that the ensuing economic crisis would soon wipe out any demand for luxury goods and services—he was older, wiser, and firmer in his commitment than ever.[29]

<h1 style="text-align:center">IV</h1>

When Bellah arrived in Cambridge as a reinstated freshman, Harvard had already undergone a profound change. If in March 1945 the college had been far below its normal capacity, in January 1947 it was exploding with students. Reaching the 1,645 tag, the enrollment for the Class of '50 had been the highest in history—a couple of years earlier, Bob's Class of '48 had counted only 653 new freshmen. This brought the total number of Harvard undergraduates to over 5,000, around 60 percent more than the school's prewar capacity, while the whole university now included more than 12,000 students. Classrooms and houses were packed, but thanks to the previously unseen number of veterans who flocked to Cambridge, attracted by the rich provisions of the so-called GI Bill, the general feeling was one of great excitement.[30]

The Servicemen's Readjustment Act had been signed into law by President Roosevelt on June 22, 1944, after complex political negotiations. It included unemployment benefits, a system of loan guarantees for house buying, and generous provisions for vocational training and higher education of which a total of eight million ex-servicemen took advantage. At a time when Harvard cost $400 a year, the bill offered individual students up to $500 a year for tuition, books, and other fees for a maximum of forty-eight months. To this, the federal government added a stipend proportional to the veteran's familial status. As a single student, for example, Bellah received a monthly allowance of $65; although he needed some additional money from his relatives to meet all his expenses, on the whole the new arrangement was far better than his original scholarship.[31] Besides flooding American institutions of higher education with unprecedented levels of funding, the GI Bill had the effect of suffusing them with what Paul Buck called "the veteran atmosphere": the many Willie Gillises who enrolled after discharge were "older, less unformed, more anxious to put diversion aside and get on with things" than ordinary undergraduates. Their "adult intensity" and no-frills approach ran counter the shallow collegiate culture of the upper classes and slowly pushed higher education in the direction of a more democratic, but also more practical, culture.[32]

During his first stint at Harvard, Bob Bellah had enjoyed only the sweetest fruits of the collegiate revolution, something he was still celebrating in 1947: "It is wonderful how serious and weighty the conversations are around here," he wrote Lillian upon his return to Cambridge, "You sit down to lunch and instead of discussing the latest movies you find yourself involved in a close discussion on Hume's theory of value or was Plato or Aristotle the apotheosis of Greek culture." He now had to start real academic work, albeit in a deeply changed environment. During the 1946 fall term, Harvard College initiated an experimental program inspired by the recommendations of the Committee on the Objectives of a General Education in a Free Society. In its analytical survey of the transformations of American society and education, the committee had looked "for some over-all logic, some strong, not easily broken frame within which both college and school [might] fulfil their at once diversifying and uniting tasks" in full continuity with "the wisdom of the ages" and traditional Western cultural patterns. Its report suggested translating this all-embracing logic into what historian Jamie Cohen-Cole called the "open mind," a mentality based on the shared skills of "honest thinking, clearness of expression, and the habit of gathering and weighing evidence." The Harvard Faculty of Arts and Sciences thus devised an original curriculum according to which freshmen had to choose two elective half-courses in each of "the three cultures"—the natural sciences, the humanities, and the social sciences—before declaring their concentration.[33]

During his four years at college Bellah thus attended classes on modern and contemporary European history, Renaissance art, and the history of philosophy, as well as courses in geology, German, mathematics, and a wide-ranging introduction to the social sciences coordinated by George C. Homans. Bob's ambitious program of supplementing his regular courses with two more classes as an auditor, and maybe an interview to enter the *Harvard Crimson,* was short-lived. He then devised a tight study plan, with the effect of finding himself literally "swamped with work" within a few weeks. Among the authors Bob read in that period were those as diverse as Marx and L. J. Henderson, Aristotle and Herbert Marcuse, Robert Browning, and Alfred North Whitehead.[34]

All in all, Bellah's first year as a regular student was an exciting and at times frightening ride. Although his midterm grades were far from satisfactory—his C in history was the first one he got "for as long as [he could] remember"[35]—his final exams went fairly well, and he was admitted to the Dean's List, never to leave it before graduation. Bob then spent the summer of 1947 in the classroom, leaving the Yard only for the occasional weekend in New York City. His major source of inspiration, however, were two huge introductory courses on the great books of the Western tradition: the first was taught by the initiator of New Criticism, I. A. Richards, and focused on Homer, Plato, and the Old Testament; in the second, literary critic Theodore Spencer surveyed the New Testament, Dante, and Shakespeare. Listening to Richards—"perhaps the greatest living reader in America"—opened up entirely new vistas: "I never really understood before how great [the Old Testament] was and how much meaning there is in it," wrote Bob to his sister. "Read AMOS, for instance, and see how it applies to this country." Later he also audited some lectures by the famed German classicist, Werner Jaeger, on Plato and Aristotle.[36]

As Bob later remarked, no other college in the United States offered undergraduates such outstanding training and personal attention. As pressure, competition, and failure could bring frail students to alcoholism, mental disturbances, or even suicide, Harvard might at times offer a depressing spectacle. That was not the case for Bob: he had a wonderfully supporting family and, in spite of having no time for leisure or diversions, he deeply enjoyed his days at Harvard. In fact, his everyday life in Cambridge was full of occurrences he had no intention of telling his mother or sister about: not only had he sought the assistance of a university psychiatrist to ease his intermittent sense of inadequacy, but early in 1947 he had also joined a small Marxist study group founded in 1930, the John Reed Society, and had openly become a member of the undergraduate branch of the Communist Party–USA. Apart from occasional pickets in support of factory workers or racial equality, the members of the society mostly coordinated public conferences: between 1947 and 1948, they invited economist Vladimir Kazakevich, historians Francis O. Matthiessen and Herbert Aptheker, and sociologist Robert S. Lynd, as well as the noted "kingpin Commie," John Gates.[37]

Although he was mostly interested in discussing Marxism and other philosophical ideas, Bellah had his share in the activities of the John Reed Society: he was its chairman at different times between 1947 and 1949, and took care of its relationships with the Communist Party, the Boston School for Marxist Studies, and the local chapter of the Joint Anti-Fascist Refugee Committee, an organization founded in 1941 to supply relief to Spanish Loyalist refugees. For some time he was also a collegiate editor for *New Foundations*, a student journal published in New York, and contributed to the selling of the *Daily Worker* on campus. Perhaps more importantly, in the John Reed Society and other political groups Bellah found a number of learned, intelligent, and good-humored friends with whom he could truly share his interests: Eli Sagan, Geoffrey White, Staugthon Lynd, Leon Kamin, Perez Zagorin, Joel Rotschild, Dick Reichardt, and John Drake, among others. The improvement of American society, the end of racial discrimination, and the repeal of the Taft-Hartley Act were hot topics of discussion among a group of young men devoted, as it were, "to find[ing] a real way to accomplish the brotherhood of man and work toward the ultimate good of society."[38]

V

At the beginning of the 1947 fall semester Robert Bellah declared his concentration in Social Relations, a new interdisciplinary department that brought clinical and social psychologists, sociologists, and social anthropologists under the same roof. The time was ripe for thinking about what to do next: he intended to be a writer and a teacher, but at the same time he also wanted a measure of financial security. His vague ideas against a career in "the conventional professions" had somehow been reinforced by the weekend he had spent at the summer house of the parents of his good friend Staughton, the famed sociologists Robert and Helen Lynd. His final decision, however, was sealed in December 1947 thanks to an unexpected encounter. Tired of Social Relations' crowded classes, Bellah started thinking of switching his concentration to social anthropology. Inspiration first came from a recently retired Berkeley professor, Alfred Kroeber, whose approach seemed "more tangible if more difficult" than the all-too-theoretical attitude of regular Social Relations faculty. Bob only needed a last push, and he got it from a British scholar who had spent World War Two working for the Office of Strategic Services and was now teaching in Cambridge as an adjunct.[39]

At forty-three, Gregory Bateson was exceptional even for Harvard's standards. The third husband of star anthropologist Margaret Mead, he was equally at ease with biology, mathematics, epistemology, and film analysis, and had been selected as a core participant in the Josiah Macy Foundation Conferences where the new science of cybernetics was being elaborated. In a letter to his sister, Bellah described the anthropologist as "one of the greatest lecturers I have ever heard, not only because of the immense grasp he has of his subject but because of his personal magnetism."[40] He avidly attended Bateson's classes, and made a habit of following him from the lecture hall to the pub, from the graduate seminar to the faculty room. Bob felt thrown into the center of an exciting enterprise: "Bateson is at the very apex of the new social science. The methods and problems on which he and a very few others in the country are working on," he added, thinking of cybernetics, "are going to open up entirely new vistas in our knowledge of social phenomena. You don't know what a thrill it is to be working with a man like that, feeling you are on the verge of startling new discoveries."[41] Unfortunately, their relation lasted only a couple of months: Bateson's teaching and demeanor were anything but appreciated by his colleagues, and his contract was not renewed. If Bellah later resolved that their common work had been too loose to be really effective, in a handful of weeks the British anthropologist had shaped the ideal image of the scholar that would accompany Bob for the rest of his life.[42]

Emboldened by his recent experiences, Bellah wrote his mother about his newly found vocation. Given her troubled story, Lillian had always hoped for her son a future as a doctor, a lawyer, a broker, or perhaps an editor of the *Atlantic Monthly*. On his part, Bob had no interest in money as long as he could do something "important for its own sake" in the particular scholarly realm he had chosen for himself: "The study of anthropology is a new field, one which is growing rapidly, and one [in] which there is much original and important work waiting to be done in. Right now I am terribly interested in the subject and am seriously thinking about devoting my life to it. At all events I will almost surely go into the Academic profession in some field." Bellah knew that Lillian, and all his other relatives, would disapprove of his decision—academic life was hard and social anthropology was a small and peripheral "science." But that was his choice, and he needed his mother's encouragement to succeed. After some weeks of stand-off, Bellah decided to spend the summer with his family in Los Angeles, declining an invitation to spend three weeks at Gregory Bateson's house on Staten Island "for the purpose of studying, reading, and discussion in a casual way." His refusal to join was his last communication with his first mentor.[43]

If during the spring of 1948 he had somehow traveled ahead in time, imagining what his professional future could be, in September Bob jumped back to the late 1920s to meet with the Bellahs of Quanah, Texas. Not only was it his first ever visit to Hutton's places and relatives, but it was a rare chance to speak of his father with people outside his Southern Californian familial circle. And he certainly did. During his first stop in quiet and dusty Altus, Bob visited the

Times-Democrat and met a number of people who praised his father just as Wimberly had done some months before. He was brought to the old homestead in Hollis and then back again to Quanah, where his relatives could not help calling him "Hutton." Besides that, everything was just perfect, from the generous barbecue dinner to the present of his father's old watch, cleaned and repaired for the occasion. Given their reverence for education, the Bellahs considered Bob's visit an extraordinary event and treated the Harvard undergraduate as a Nobel laureate. Bob had the most touching moment with his seventy-two-year-old grandmother, Mollie Emaline Jones: "At one point when she took me aside for a talk she could hardly keep from crying. She told me they always said she was partial to Hutton and she said she guessed she was. She said she was also partial to me and though her other grandchildren were nearer to her she always felt closer to me."[44]

Back at Harvard Bellah threw himself headlong into a host of new classes, among them a big lecture course in dynamic psychology with Henry A. Murray and history of Far Eastern civilizations, also known as "Rice Paddies," taught by Edwin O. Reischauer and John K. Fairbank. He also resumed his hectic cultural life and his contacts with his comrades, with whom he supported Henry Wallace's failed bid for the presidency and oversaw the merger of the John Reed Society and the Harvard Youth for Democracy, another communist group, into John Reed Club. As its first public initiative, the new club sponsored a controversial conference on Marxism and social change by the noted German communist author and politician, Gerhardt Eisler, which Bellah chaired. To his great delight, Bob was "in the groove again."[45]

VI

In the letter announcing his decision to pursue an academic career in social anthropology, Bellah depicted himself as a serial contrarian. No matter what, he told his mother, he would not back down: "I have never quite fitted the pattern; I have always asked questions when the proper thing was to accept answers. It is too late to change now."[46] At first, such rebellion had no immediate consequences other than pushing Bob to enroll in a honors program under the guidance of David F. Aberle, a young anthropologist well entrenched in functionalist circles, in order to be better placed for admission to graduate school. Then, early in August 1949, Bob called his mother on the phone and gave her great news: he was getting married and wanted to fix the best date for his whole family to come to Cambridge and share his joy.[47] If the announcement was a bolt out of the blue, the name of the bride-to-be was not. In fact, as Bob wrote to Aunt Bessie and Uncle Clifford a few days later, he and Melanie Claire Hyman had "known [each other] and been in love for several years."[48]

Melanie was born in New Orleans on May 16, 1928, into a secular Jewish family. Her father, Earl Hyman, was the fifth child of Perl Heiman and Isaac Switatz, a pious observant Jew who worked mainly as a handyman and a cabinetmaker. In 1905 the Switatzes left their home in Odessa, in the Russian Empire, to flee repeated anti-Jewish pogroms. They first moved to Austria, then to Baltimore, and finally to New Orleans, where they changed their name to Hyman. Louisiana had been the destination of three waves of Jewish emigration, starting with Sephardim from Spain, Portugal, and Jamaica in the mid-eighteenth century, followed by liberal German Jews from the Atlantic Seaboard, and finally mass arrivals from Eastern Europe. The social and charitable organizations created by Jews after the Civil War were essential to addressing the adjustment problems of the newcomers—at the price, however, of religious homogeneity and orthodoxy. In the mid-1930s the New Orleans community was described as old, "well satisfied, smug and self-sufficient."[49]

Earl Hyman graduated from the Tulane University School of Medicine in 1924 and worked as an intern in New Jersey and New York. Melanie's mother, Josephine Meyer, was born in New Orleans in 1909 into a family of local entrepreneurs. A couple with a stormy married life, in the mid-1930s the Hymans moved to Los Angeles, where Earl set up a successful private practice as a gynecologist and obstetrician, delivering the children of such well-known celebrities as Kirk Douglas, Natalie Wood, and Burt Reynolds.[50] Melanie grew up in Southern California during wartime as a spirited and committed student, with a consuming passion for classical music, ballet, and sports. Petite and vivacious, she did not shy away from going out dancing with her friends, and was fourteen when she had her first experience with men—in fact, with a boy six years older than she was, who would later become her fiancé. In 1944, shortly before Josephine would give birth to her only sibling, Melanie got to know a tall, skinny boy one year her senior thanks to her journalism teacher at LA High, Margaret Ray, who took the handoff of the editorship of the *Blue and White* as an excuse to introduce the two. Bob and Melanie soon discovered their common love for poetry, classical music, and liberal politics, and resolved to stay in touch after his departure for Cambridge.[51]

Upon completing high school with all grade As "except cooking," in the spring of 1946 Melanie was admitted to the new program in English and creative writing at Stanford University, where she was mentored by the modernist poet and critic Yvor Winters, and had two of her compositions published in the second volume of his edited anthology *Poets of the Pacific*. In 1948 she became a member of the Independent Progressive Party and a founder of the Stanford Students for Wallace group; she also sought unsuccessfully to create a chapter of the National Association for the Advancement of Colored People in Palo Alto. Persuaded that political unity could be created only through "discussion, thought, compromise," she soon came to resent the university's "phoniness" and reactionary atmosphere. Meanwhile, in Cambridge Bob had literally developed an obsession for her. His comrades and friends made fun of his continuous prattle about his far away "sweetheart," and any attempt at matching him with other girls ended in failure. His attitude persisted in spite of the fact that at Stanford Melanie dated other boys, and even found herself on the brink of getting married. Upon breaking up with her fiancé in February 1947, she had other romantic relationships, but also remained interested in Bob and decided against becoming more serious with anyone else.[52]

When Melanie graduated in June 1949 with Phi Beta Kappa honors, Bellah wasted no time and proposed; in a matter of weeks she moved to Cambridge, took a course in publishing procedures at Radcliffe College, found a job at a local press, and set a date for the wedding. Unfortunately, none in their families shared their enthusiasm, albeit for different reasons: while Lillian Bellah anticipated a disaster for her son's career plans, Earl Hyman feared his beloved first child would marry into a family of "disrespectful or anti-Semitic gentiles," a not entirely irrational doubt given Bob's Southern background. Nothing, however, could stop the two young lovers, who resolved to marry as soon as possible—their good friends Frimi Giller and Eli Sagan were getting married on August 7, and they were determined to follow suit. The civil ceremony was officiated by the city clerk of Cambridge on August 17, 1949; neither Bob's nor Melanie's relatives attended the formality or the small party that followed.[53]

Bob and Melanie had created a new home some three thousand miles from Los Angeles. The distance they had placed between themselves and their families, however, was not merely physical, and it took some time for the couple to regain good relations with their parents. In fact, it also took them some time and the help of a good therapist to adjust to their new condition: now in his senior year, Bob started his final blast as a college student and while Melanie did her best to help him, she often became the target of his sudden bursts of anger. Bob's poem "Winter Moon," written for Melanie as their first New Year's Eve as a married couple approached, spoke of the preoccupations raised by the unfinished task of creating a proper family, but also of his deep love for his wife:

FIGURE 2.1. Robert and Melanie Bellah in the early 1950s. (RBPP)

Winter Moon

Though the streets lie bare, the winter
    has well begun
And the last vestiges of decayed snow will not
    be gone before a new fall covers them
And there will be many falls before the
    spring.

But now the moon is a single line
And though the year is dying, the moon
    begins

Our love is that bright line
Must grow to fullness, and as surely
    be renewed.

Knowing this, even the cold prospects of
    naked streets
Cannot chill my heart.[54]

Bob's last year at college was about to begin, and he had to make a decision about graduate school. Was he really going to apply? If so, where would he like to apply? And to which program? Social anthropology seemed to be a logical choice: Bellah had truly enjoyed his thesis work with Aberle, and had developed a good relationship with the doyen of social anthropology at Harvard, Clyde Kluckhohn. At the same time, he could not deny that his sociology classes—including one taught by Samuel A. Stouffer, who had just published his multivolume *Studies in Social Psychology in World War II*, aka *The American Soldier*—had been much more intellectually challenging. Following Aberle's advice, Bob had also taken a course taught by a professor whose abstract and convoluted jargon had failed to impress him during his freshman year, Talcott Parsons. This class, however, was different: the syllabus moved freely from Parsons's unpublished paper on the language of basic social science to the draft of his next book, *The Social System*, tackling "big" theoretical problems in a sparkling dialogical, and often oppositional, way.

Among the many better- or lesser-known authors who made the course's reading list, two stood out as particularly compelling: Émile Durkheim and Max Weber. Parsons had built his first theoretical masterpiece, *The Structure of Social Action*, on the alleged "convergence" between the work of the two European social scientists, who were usually deemed to belong to opposite schools of thought. A noted French intellectual of the Third Republic, Durkheim had promoted the study of social facts as external, impersonal "things" capable of exerting coercion on individual actors, and had imagined societies as complex systems whose parts, from institutions down to the single individual, constantly needed reciprocal integration and harmonization. With his interpretive sociology Weber had taken the exactly opposed route, and focused on the understanding of the subjective meaning that actors attached to their own action. Besides their opposite view of sociology and its object, however, the two European theorists shared a typical nineteenth century evolutive understanding of human history and an inspiring balance of scholarly seriousness and intellectual joy, which was further boosted by Parsons's brilliant and "Socratic" style of teaching.[55]

Thanks to Parsons's big ideas and larger-than-life culture heroes, Bellah could finally revive the exciting sense of discovery that he had twice experienced in his study of Marxism and his Bateson days—in fact, he and Melanie had just been expelled from the Communist Party for their interest in the work of Sigmund Freud, their recourse to psychotherapy, and for "never having been hungry," and had remained, so to speak, intellectually homeless. Parsons's epiphany, however, only added to Bob's confusion. Should he pursue a master's or a doctoral degree? Should he apply to sociology or anthropology? Should he limit himself to Harvard, as he had done at the time of leaving LA High, or consider other universities? David Aberle had no doubts: "There are more boneheads in sociology than in any other field," he said, "but the brightest are the most interesting in any of the social sciences. The average level of intelligence among the anthropologists is much higher, but the best are not as good as the best sociologists. Anthropology has good people, but they don't change the way people think." That was enough for Bob to decide, and not even a spirited tête-à-tête with Kluckhohn could change his mind. In February 1950 he applied to graduate school in sociology at various Ivy League universities. When favorable responses came from Cornell and Harvard, Bellah's choice fell almost naturally on his alma mater. Now, with his finals in sight and a lovely new apartment at 27 Irving Terrace, right behind Harvard's imposing Memorial Hall, things looked rosier than ever.[56]

When Bellah took his Departmental Examination in Social Relations on May 11, 1950, he knew he was not going to change his address for another four years. As expected, his scores were excellent: he graduated summa cum laude, the best in his class. One month later, just like his father and his wife before him, Bob was inducted to Phi Beta Kappa together with ninety-three other seniors. Uniquely among them, however, he received the highest of honors: his BA thesis based on a comparison of kinship structures of seven Athabascan tribes was presented by the Department of Social Relations as its pick for the Harvard Phi Beta Kappa Prize and won it—the first time that the award, instituted in 1935 to honor the best among the best, had been bestowed on a student in the social sciences.[57]

3

Enter Talcott Parsons

CAMBRIDGE, MA, 1950–1953

WINNING THE PHI BETA KAPPA PRIZE filled Robert N. Bellah with a unique sense of pride: not only did it give substance to his self-image as a would-be intellectual, but it also vindicated his decision to marry Melanie—she had supported him through his last year of college, and the success was hers as much as his. And yet the story also had an interesting public side. To understand it, a flashback is needed to 1936, the year of Harvard's party for its three hundredth birthday. The celebrations lasted three weeks and relied on the presence of a star-studded cast of characters, which included President Franklin Delano Roosevelt, Nobel laureates Robert A. Millikan and Arthur Holly Compton, and European masters Carl Gustav Jung, Corrado Gini, and Bronislaw Malinowski. As the university congratulated itself, its social scientists went through a world of trouble to arrange their symposia. The Departments of Government, History, and Economics saturated the intellectual space that in other universities was also shared by anthropology, psychology, and sociology. The latter disciplines fared low in President Conant's judgment, and even the most sympathetic among Harvard's power brokers, such as the physiologist Lawrence J. Henderson, lamented their lack of sound methodological and analytical foundations.[1]

Not that the chairman of the Department of Sociology, Russian émigré Pitirim A. Sorokin, had made any effort to project a positive image of his discipline: when asked to draft a list of "class A sociologists" he would like to invite, he replied with some contempt that there weren't any. But Harvard had always been ambivalent toward sociology. Caught in between the Divinity School and the Department of Economics, instructors in sociology and other faculty members had pleaded for the creation of an autonomous academic unit since the time of the establishment of the first Department of Sociology at the University of Chicago in the early 1890s. In 1905 a businessman from New York, Alfred T. White, pledged a donation for the construction of Emerson Hall on the Harvard Yard, contingent on the creation of a Department of Social Ethics. President Lowell, who saw the new unit with suspicion, refused to add university funds to the existing allowance until the late 1920s, when intense lobbying on the part of economists Edwin F. Gay and Frank W. Taussig set things in motion for the creation of a proper Department of Sociology.[2]

Then at the University of Minnesota, Sorokin had published a number of widely discussed books, including *Contemporary Sociological Theories* and *Social Mobility*. These works reassured the Harvard Corporation about the standing of sociology as an empirical science, and the forty-one-year-old scholar was picked as the first departmental chair at the expense of his British competitor, Leonard T. Hobhouse. The new academic unit began operations in September 1931, just five years before the tercentenary. Besides Sorokin, his associate Carle C. Zimmermann, and former Social Ethics faculty members, the department included a number of nonsociologists as part-time instructors with full voting rights. Soon it became clear that Sorokin's expansive conception of sociology and his lofty attitude were a serious hindrance for the self-defined "Levellers," a group of scholars in their late thirties or early forties who had great plans for the future. Working within a number of interstitial but influential outlets such as Henderson's Pareto Seminar, the Society of Fellows, and the Harvard Fatigue Laboratory, the Levellers envisaged a new conception of social science as a theory-driven, collaborative endeavor that would prove to be much in line with Conant's ideas about the professionalization of scientific research.

After the outbreak of World War Two, the Levellers came to occupy prominent roles in the war effort: psychologists O. Hobart Mowrer and Henry Murray, head of the Harvard Psychological Clinic, worked in the evaluation of candidates for the Office of Strategic Services, while social anthropologist Clyde Kluckhohn codirected the Foreign Morale Analysis Division of the Office of War Information. The involvement of social scientists with the federal government bolstered the prestige of the lesser disciplines, and encouraged the Levellers to advance a wide-ranging plan to reorganize the social sciences at Harvard. Reunited in the Committee on Concentration in the Area of Social Sciences, in 1941 they drafted an ambitious memorandum, "Toward a Common Language for the Area of Social Science." The paper courageously upturned the logical (and academic) relations between the established and the up-and-coming social sciences: clinical and social psychology, sociology, and social anthropology were going to merge into a "basic social science" charged with providing the analytical foundations of the study of particular problems, which had until then remained the turf of history, economics, and government. In support of its epistemic argument, the document envisioned the creation of an academic unit fully devoted to basic social science.[3]

Backed by President Conant and Dean Buck and endowed with $335,000 from the Carnegie Corporation, the Department of Social Relations was approved on February 1, 1946, and opened its doors at the beginning of the following fall term as the home to a "synthesis of socio-cultural and psychological sciences which [was already] widely recognized in the academic world." In the words of its founders, the "recent war greatly accelerated the fusion of research activities" in the common territory of basic social science and a "new discipline" was emerging for the study "of the 'human factor' in a technological and nuclear age." Based in Emerson Hall but dispersed throughout the campus, the interdisciplinary venue included among its faculty former Levellers Kluckhohn and Murray, social psychologist Gordon W. Allport, and the czar of quantitative techniques, Samuel A. Stouffer, as the director of the Laboratory of Social Relations. Among junior faculty were Frederick Mosteller, Jerome Bruner, Freed Bales, Robert White, Alex Inkeles, and Barrington Moore Jr.[4]

I

The first chairman of the Department of Social Relations was a forty-three-year-old former Leveller and a true believer in the promise of basic social science whose name would resonate clear and loud both in the history of sociology and in Bob Bellah's own story: Talcott Parsons. Born in Colorado Springs in 1902, Parsons was the fifth and last child of Mary Augusta Ingersoll and Edward S. Parsons, a Congregational minister, Social Gospel advocate, and one-time president of Marietta College in Ohio. In 1924 he graduated from Amherst College and spent a year at the London School of Economics, where he attended courses by Malinowski, Hobhouse, and Richard Tawney, before moving to Germany's major intellectual center, the University of Heidelberg, as an exchange student. There Parsons was taught by Karl Jaspers, Karl Mannheim, and Alfred Weber, the younger brother of Max Weber, who had died five years earlier and whose name was almost unknown outside Germany. Under their influence he decided to undertake doctoral work on the concept of capitalism in the writings of Weber, Marx, and Werner Sombart. In

Heidelberg he was also introduced to Weber's widow, Marianne, who encouraged him to work on the first English translation of *Die protestantische Ethik und der Geist des Kapitalismus*, thus initiating a major revolution in American and global social science.[5]

In 1927 Parsons obtained an instructorship at the Department of Economics at Harvard, a stronghold of neoclassical theory. As he commingled into this new academic environment, he gradually came to embrace an orthodox understanding of economics, as elaborated by his colleagues Gay, Taussig, and Joseph Schumpeter. Indefatigable and ambitious, Parsons aimed at creating a set of general concepts for sociology similar to that of Newtonian mechanics, which would complement the analytical framework typical of classical economics, based on value, rationality, and supply-and-demand curves. Combined with the naturalistic conception of social science put forward by Henderson in his seminar on Pareto in the early 1930s, this position led Parsons to set for sociology the goal of discovering the uniform laws of social behavior focusing exclusively on one element of human action—common values—that had been neglected by economics and political science, focused respectively on scarcity and power.[6]

The results of Parsons's theoretical efforts were published in 1937 as *The Structure of Social Action*. The book included a long and grueling conceptual introduction followed by four lengthy studies of European social scientists of the past generation—Alfred Marshall, Vilfredo Pareto, Émile Durkheim, and Max Weber. In spite of their different cultural and intellectual origins, the four scholars had independently converged on the idea that human individuals act in the pursuit of goals irreducible to those dictated by biological heredity or economic rationality. Well-adjusted actors, wrote Parsons, customarily act in accordance with the set of values and norms they share with the majority of the members of their society, and find no particular strife in doing so—hence the name of "voluntarism" given to the paradigm. *The Structure* departed from the mainstream of coeval American sociology not only in the centrality attributed to European theorists, but also in its refusal of hard-nosed empiricism and in its image of sociology as a carefully bounded discipline against imperialistic and/or reductionist conceptions of social science.[7]

Thanks to his affiliation to the powerful Henderson circle, in the late 1930s Parsons rapidly gained ascendancy at Harvard as one of the staunchest promoters of theoretical synthesis in the social sciences, an effort that was finally repaid by the institution of Social Relations. In spite of Parsons's excitement and his dedication as the departmental chairman, however, the new organizational arrangement could not supply the unified interdisciplinary framework that the Levellers had optimistically anticipated. To break the stalemate, in 1949 Parsons persuaded the Carnegie Corporation to sponsor a research project focused uniquely on theoretical elaboration and integration. With three collaborators—Harvard anthropologist Richard Sheldon, Chicago sociologist Edward A. Shils, and Berkeley psychologist Edward C. Tolman—he discussed his ideas in a number of seminars held from October 1949 to January 1950. A latent goal of the project was the legitimation of analytical-theoretical inquiry per se and the affirmation of its value as the foundation of social scientific empirical research at Harvard and beyond.[8]

At the time of Bob Bellah's graduation in May 1950, the Department of Social Relations was lagging behind its promise to become America's major hub of theoretical and methodological innovation for the social sciences, and the results of the Carnegie Project were still too woolly to be of help. Winning the Harvard Phi Beta Kappa Prize, Bellah brought grist to Parsons's mill—he proved that Social Relations students could occupy the apex of the academic hierarchy and that basic social science had nothing to be envious of in the more established disciplines. His mastery of analytical tools and his ingenious interpretation of primary data had also shown Parsons his promise as a prospective participant in the intellectual endeavor on which depended nothing less than the scientific coming of age of global social science. It was time to turn the brilliant student into a professional scholar.[9]

II

One key element of the academic revolution had been a profound shift in graduate instruction: the growing influence of organized disciplines pushed graduate schools to standardize their teaching of paradigms and methods, while scholarly journals and abstracting services guaranteed the dissemination of research and contributed to the differentiation of scientific communication from that circulating in the general public sphere. New sources of funding allowed graduate schools to expand the number of advanced students without betraying the principles of scientific excellence. During the interwar period a nationwide competitive system for the allocation of entry slots, financial support, and job opportunities emerged as a key component of a homogenized and professionalized intellectual and scientific landscape.[10]

The new system of graduate instruction also introduced its students to a new model of the scholar. The ideal persona of the "courageous risk-taker with authentic intellectual interests" coalesced during World War Two, when the creation of loosely assembled teams of diverse scientists allowed practical problems to be tackled with unprecedented speed and efficacy. During the postwar era, scholars had to be creative and reliable in the pursuit of their intellectual goals; eager to present their ideas without fear of being criticized; and ready to combine multiple vocabularies to invent new conceptual tools so as to produce sound objective knowledge oriented to the social, political, and practical problems of the day. Opening the 1947–1948 academic year at Columbia University, the historian Jacques Barzun skillfully captured the spirit of the times pointing to President Conant as the embodiment of this "adventurous, even reckless" attitude, committed to the creation of new objects of study, disciplines, and institutions for the sake a more efficient, informed, and democratic society.[11]

The former Levellers who now ruled Social Relations looked like a Baedeker of the open-minded scholar. Ever since the late 1920s, when he had been appointed head of the Harvard Psychological Clinic, Henry Murray had taught innovative subjects, including a massive dose of psychoanalysis, to the enthusiasm of graduate students and the scorn of conservative colleagues. Sam Stouffer had once been described as "the most stimulating and disheveled professor that ever existed"—his lectures and the way he communicated his dedication to the pursuit of knowledge through a thick cloud of cigarette smoke were legendary. The same was true for Clyde Kluckhohn, who led would-be ethnographers in the field with the manners of an explorer, and Gordon Allport, who arranged his seminar on prejudice around "democratic pedagogical groups."[12]

More than any other member of Social Relations, however, Talcott Parsons was described as "a paragon of the virtue of an intellectual." Indefatigable, creative, open to the continuous revision of his ideas, he often provoked the admiration of those who attended his lectures or seminars. His students from the late 1930s—among whom were heavyweights of the postwar social sciences such as Robert K. Merton and Robin M. Williams Jr.—praised his unrelenting dedication to intellectual pursuits, his dramatic appreciation of moments of discovery, his urge to follow suggestions coming from any possible source. And yet his students were not the only ones to be impressed by his feverish pace: at the time of the Carnegie Project, Edward Shils would recount working all day in Parsons's office and then receiving excited phone calls in which his intellectual partner would report the ideas that had come to him in the hour or so since they had parted ways.[13]

The graduate seminar on social mobility first given in 1948–1949 was a prime example of the attitude of senior faculty in Social Relations. Led by Parsons, Stouffer, and Florence Kluckhohn, a small number of students would discuss an ongoing research project on the aspirations of some three thousand junior high school boys in the Boston area. Meeting after meeting, students were exposed to social science in the making as their mentors presented and discussed theoretical hypotheses, unpolished data, and tentative explanations, gradually opening the floor to all participants. This "teaching by example" showed students that nothing was fixed: from concepts to methods, from hypotheses to explanations, everything could be changed if new data or sound arguments pushed the investigators to do so. Students also learned to look at the craft of research as a collective endeavor, one in which different inclinations should be put to the service of a common scientific purpose.[14]

During the seminars and the restricted meetings convened by Parsons with two or three of his closest students in the small departmental library, would-be scholars could participate in the process of discovery and feel empowered by the symmetrical relation they (at least ideally) entertained with their teacher. For those who worked in close contact with him, Talcott Parsons was a human work in progress, constantly busy in remaking his theories through the assimilation of an ever-expanding pool of authors, themes, and disciplines. Not surprisingly, combining this uncommon "theoretical possession" with the professional expectations of 150 doctoral candidates was no easy task. Although most students were sympathetic with Social Relations' general mood, they lamented the sparseness of paradigms and methods, the absence of a clear intellectual direction, and the dim appeal of a graduate degree in social relations in a world dominated by the major disciplines.[15]

As a consequence, between 1949 and 1950 the requirements for obtaining a PhD were adjusted to reflect more conventional models. For candidates to a sociology degree, this included a test of their "mastery of the general field of sociology, its history, its main contemporary theoretical literature, and its methods of research," and special oral examinations. The program also had statistical and foreign language requirements, and a mandatory period of six to nine months of training in the field. In this respect, the majority of graduate students in Social Relations conducted their research close to home, studying ethnic, professional, or religious groups located in the Boston area, while a number of them joined the Comparative Study of Values in Five Cultures, an ambitious project inaugurated by Kluckhohn in 1949. Conducted in what

Kluckhohn considered to be experimental conditions (although they wouldn't be by modern standards) in northwestern New Mexico, the research aimed at comparing the values of five different ethnic groups who shared the same territory and thus the same living conditions; doctoral students contributed to data gathering and analysis, and wrote their dissertations on specific groups, events, or phenomena.[16]

Other graduate students, including would-be anthropologists David M. Schneider and Clifford Geertz, conducted their fieldwork abroad, taking advantage of the new global focus of the United States. In the first decade of the postwar era, the urgent need of a cohort of regional experts able to advance American interests around the world led to the creation of a number of area studies centers offering intensive language study and advanced training in the social sciences. Building on existing networks and institutions, and using the lavish funding provided by the Carnegie Corporation and the Rockefeller and Ford Foundations, such institutes focused on the Middle East, the Far East, Latin America, and Russia, and provided unprecedented traveling opportunities for both established and up-and-coming scholars. The Modjokuto project joined by Geertz and his wife Hildred between 1952 and 1954, for example, was part of a conscious effort to strengthen political and cultural ties between the United States and Indonesia financed by the Ford Foundation, while Schneider's fieldwork on the Pacific island of Yap in the late 1940s was funded by the US Navy through the Coordinated Investigation of Micronesian Anthropology.[17]

III

Sunk into his well-deserved summer vacation in Los Angeles, Bob was barely aware of all this ferment. One year after their wedding, he and Melanie had restored excellent relations with their families, who reaffirmed their moral and financial assistance for the near future. While in California Bellah worked hard to turn his BA thesis into a book, counting on the long-distance support of David Aberle, but he also had time for the beach, the company of his relatives, and the occasional trip to San Francisco. It was a wonderful summer, but Bob had no time to rest on his laurels: back in Cambridge in September 1950 he filed a request for a double PhD program in sociology and Far Eastern languages.[18]

The decision to advance such a demanding proposal was justified by Bellah's belief in the reigning penchant for interdisciplinarity and the complexity

of his chosen topic, the industrialization of Japan in the eighteenth and nineteenth centuries. Bob had first developed an interest in Eastern societies
thanks to the fresh outlook and scholarly passion of the two teachers of the
undergraduate course on the history of East Asia he had taken in the fall of
1948, Edwin O. Reischauer and John K. Fairbank. Born in Japan in 1910, Reischauer had obtained his PhD at Harvard in 1938 and had been teaching at the
Department of Far Eastern Languages ever since. In the early 1940s he directed
a school for intelligence officers in Washington, DC, and acted as a consultant
for the State Department. At a time when the American public was fed with
images of the Japanese as the bestial executors of a totalitarian will to power,
Reischauer encouraged his fellow citizens to appreciate Japanese culture in all
its creativity, complexity, and dignity. On his part, Fairbank had studied in
Beijing and Oxford in the early 1930s and had been hired by Harvard in 1936.
During the war he worked as a representative of the Office of the Coordinator
of Information in Chungking, China, an experience that partially inspired his
1948 bestseller, *The United States and China*.[19]

Although they were both historians by training, after the end of the war
Fairbank and Reischauer jumped on the bandwagon of area studies and devised a new East Asian program based on the marriage of the humanities and
the social sciences. In so doing, they greatly expanded the vision of their common mentor, Serge Elisséeff, who had never accepted the practice "of treating
East Asian languages and cultures as if they belonged to a dead tradition."
Born in Saint Petersburg in 1889, Elisséeff had been the first Occidental to ever
enroll in, and graduate from, the Imperial University of Tokyo. After a tor-
mented career in the Soviet Union, Sweden, and France, in 1934 he was appointed director of the Harvard-Yenching Institute, a transnational foundation
created in 1928 to foster academic cooperation between China and the United
States. At Harvard Elisséeff combined the study of the history, literature, and
arts of China, Japan, and Korea with first-hand knowledge of contemporary
East Asia.[20]

Bellah's plan was accepted on October 25, 1950, and a committee composed
of Parsons, Elisséeff, Reischauer, and anthropologist John C. Pelzel was nominated to supervise the advancement of his schedule, which required the completion of two-thirds of each individual PhD program.[21] There followed a
time of exciting and furious study, which often left Bob "in a state like one
pursued by hounds." The workload was so heavy that he had no time for anything else: no politics, no outings, no New Year's Eve in New York. Even writing Christmas cards would take precious time away from the study of Japanese,

Chinese, history, and sociology. Luckily, Bob had his wife. After a passionate but difficult start, their bond was now stronger than ever. "We came across the letters we wrote that last year before we were married," wrote Melanie to Lillian, whom she now called mother, "and they sounded so superficial compared to how we love and understand each other now. We were each a dream to each other, and it was so fortunate that when the dream came true, it was even better. So often the people one dreams about are a mere reflection of one's own ideals, and turn out to in reality to be far from liveable, or even at all that they were supposed to be."[22]

And yet their marriage was a complex affair. On the one hand, they often behaved, and others generally treated them, as a typical 1950s couple: Bob acted as the breadwinner and Melanie attended to household chores and managed their social and cultural life, which mostly revolved around her husband's occupation. On the other hand, being a Stanford Phi Beta Kappa with a lively interest in classical music, literature, and ballet, Melanie actively rejected the stereotype of the postwar housewife. Not only did she get a part-time job as a secretary at a time when only one American woman out of three worked, but she helped Bob with his book by reading, editing, and typing the manuscript. Apart from working, she took ballet classes and became an active member of the Boston Dance League. She even learned some Japanese, anticipating the time they would spend in the Land of the Rising Sun for Bob's mandatory period of fieldwork, and was soon obsessed by all things Japanese, from art exhibitions and poetry to fittings and furniture.[23]

Melanie's wit and savoir-faire proved to be decisive when the young couple was invited to a party at Parsons's house in Belmont late in February 1951. Six months had passed since the beginning of graduate school, and Bob had been able to observe the chairman of Social Relations from the vantage point of a restricted seminar on social systems. Although he now considered Parsons the best social theorist since Max Weber, his mentor remained shy, distant, and very difficult to talk to—in fact, an older replica of Bellah himself. When the fateful evening finally came Bob and Melanie left their apartment highly anxious that they should make a good impression. Fortunately, the party was packed and the evening went by without a hitch. At some point, Parsons set up a radio in the hall and the younger guests started to tumble and twirl. When the forty-nine-year-old professor asked the wife of a graduate student for a dance, however, as Bob later described it, a wave of embarrassment crossed the room. The song ended, and Parsons did what Bob feared the most: he walked toward Melanie and requested the pleasure of her company. While

Bellah stood frozen against the wall, his sharp, beautiful wife danced and chatted with "the most important living sociologist" in the most natural way. The ice was broken, and all thanks to Melanie.[24]

Parsons's restricted seminar was based on a number of working papers that would later find their way into the main offshoots of the Carnegie Project, *Toward a General Theory of Action* and *The Social System*, both published in 1951. In the long monograph written for the first book, titled "Values, Motives, and Systems of Action," Parsons and Shils introduced a set of five distinctions, the "pattern variables," meant to capture the alternatives faced by individual or institutional actors when relating to other social actors. Should I evaluate my students according to who they are or what they do? Should I treat my children as I treat my customers? Should I show or hide my emotions when interacting with people I do not know? The novelty of the pattern variables resided in the fact that they might be used to describe the actor's orientations on three different levels—personality traits, interactional expectations, and common values—so that each level could vary independently of the others, as when an intimately racist doctor is compelled by her professional deontology to treat all her patients, regardless of their race. Moreover, since the five dichotomies were said to be wholly autonomous, their use suggested that the binaries used by European theorists—Durkheim's mechanical versus organic solidarity or Weber's traditional versus rationalized societies, for example—should be abandoned in favor of more nuanced descriptions of individual phenomena.

The pattern variables returned in the draft chapters of *The Social System*, which also proposed an image of the social world as a multilayered reality where any phenomenon might be observed as either a whole or a complex of related parts. Building on the action-centered approach of *The Structure*, Parsons reworked the problem of social order and stressed that being bound to conformity with reference to a common set of value-orientation standards would advance, rather than reduce, the interests of individual actors. The mimeographs advanced a number of theories on roles, interactions, social differentiation, and the normative regulation of institutions and organizations, distinguishing between a system's structures, functions, and processes.[25]

After much work and reflection, Bellah extracted from the unpublished chapters of *The Social System* a theoretical scheme for his BA thesis. What had been a technical essay on Athabascan nomenclature now focused on the relations between kinship and the internalization of societal values using an eight-variable matrix inspired by the work of a Social Relations former graduate student, Marion Levy Jr. Bellah's theoretically informed comparison of available data on different tribes led to the emergence of causal and functional connections, where specialists like George Murdock and Morris Opler had seen only random factors at work. Amazed by what Bellah had done with his own theoretical tools, Parsons helped to secure the funds needed to publish the thesis as a book. Some time later, he declared Bob's presentation on the value-pattern of Japanese society one of the best he had ever heard. "Keep an eye on him," Parsons told another would-be sociologist, Renée C. Fox, "he's going to go far."[26]

IV

In June 1951, after passing his finals with distinction, Bob took Melanie to New York City, the first time he had visited what once had been his favorite place. Focused as he was on his doctoral work, however, Bellah had little time to spare, even for New York—the study of Eastern languages and his thesis outweighed everything else. Slowly but surely his research was addressing itself to a sociological study of the transition between Tokugawa Japan and the Meiji Restoration.[27] Having shelved his seminar presentation on Japan's value system, Bellah was now pursuing a *much* more ambitious idea: "Nothing less than an Essay on the Economic Ethic of Japan to be a companion to Weber's studies of China, India, and Judaism." In particular, he intended to translate the now famous thesis on the relation between the Protestant ethic and the spirit of capitalism into a hypothesis to be tested through a combination of historical data and original empirical fieldwork in Japan.[28]

Impressed by his thoughtful work and his flawless knowledge of key sociological theorists, in December 1951 Parsons joined forces with Pelzel and Reischauer to recommend Bellah for the Society of Fellows, the elite body with which many members of the interstitial Harvard of the 1930s were now involved. In a formal letter to his old friend Crane Brinton, who chaired the society, Parsons described his student as "a completely outstanding young man" who, "given the adequate opportunity," would become "among the outstanding contributors to the social sciences in his generation." But in spite of his stellar qualifications and the endorsement of a number of figures influential in campus life, Bob was not made a fellow. It was a big blow to his ego, and for decades he would recall the episode as the first time his alma mater had failed him.[29]

Darker clouds, however, were appearing on the horizon. Bob and Melanie's daily life was exhausting: the schedule was tight, money was scarce, and the thesis was still in its embryonic stage. Anxiety soared, and in the spring of 1952 they began looking forward to their trip to Japan as a moment of release that would end all their difficulties. This, in turn, created new strains with their families. As Hallie Bellah started planning her wedding in the summer of 1952, for example, Bob rudely told her that all their savings were needed to finance their year abroad, and they could not afford to fly back home. "I only wish we had some children," wrote Bob in a rather outlandish letter to his mother on July 2, "as it would surely facilitate getting integrated into the community and in a position to carry out the investigations I will be engaged in." Their whole life centred on the completion of the PhD program, and if Bob's mentors described him as "highly competent as a theoretical analyst" but also "a rather shy and difficult person," it was because his maturation as a scholar was absorbing all of his, and Melanie's, energies.[30]

Given this situation, it is hard to overestimate the double blow of November 1952: within a few days of each other, Dwight D. Eisenhower beat Adlai Stevenson in the presidential elections and Bob was denied a passport because of his past membership in the Communist Party. The trip to Japan had to be cancelled and Bellah lost his mind. Not even the publication of *Apache Kinship Systems* a few days after the elections could relieve his anger and pain. In his extreme agitation, he wrote to the *American Sociological Review*, the flagship journal of the American Sociological Society, to protest a biting review of *The Social System* written by Chicago sociologist Ellsworth Faris, which he called "unfair," "undignified," and "personally vituperative." While Bellah had never intended his rant for publication, the episode annoyed Parsons, who had not been informed of the letter and worried that it might damage his own reputation, with the aggravating circumstance that the journal editor was the reviewer's son. Luckily, two fairly apologetic letters to Robert Faris succeeded in closing the incident, and prevented Bellah from making his debut in the sociological field with an awkward breach of academic etiquette.[31]

The impossibility of traveling to Japan created another problem—what Bob should do for his fieldwork—although one that fortunately turned into a precious personal experience and a big professional win. After some bargaining, the department granted Bellah permission to participate in the Harvard Values Study in order to fulfil his obligatory fieldwork. In June 1953 Bob and Melanie moved to Ramah, a small outpost forty-five miles south of Gallup, New Mexico, where they were warmly welcomed by their friends Buzz and Bernice Zelditch. Besides doing some interesting research on the tightly knit Mormon community and befriending some of its liveliest members, the young couple often borrowed the Harvard project jeep to ramble over the pine-covered mountains and the sandstone mesas of the southwestern Colorado Plateau. While he was no fan of ethnographic research, in less than three months Bellah had won the respect of the entire Values Study staff and was asked to write two chapters for their final report, in place of another sociologist, Thomas O'Dea, who had abandoned the project owing to personal problems with Kluckhohn.[32]

No professional achievement, however, could match the sweetest of news: just like her sister-in-law and her friend Frimi Sagan, Melanie was having a baby. Sometime in July 1954 Bob would become a father. He hoped his first child would be a boy.[33]

4

Expectations versus Reality

FROM CAMBRIDGE TO MONTREAL, AND BACK, 1954–1957

ALTHOUGH EXCITED FOR THE LONG-AWAITED NEWS of his imminent fatherhood, Robert N. Bellah still had to turn his sparse musings into a proper dissertation. The basic idea was clear—Japanese religion contained a number of cultural elements that, when properly triggered by Japan's encounter with the West, had independently contributed to the country's industrialization—but its realization was not. Forced by circumstance to be an armchair scholar, in early 1954 Bellah set down the outline of a historical-comparative study of the relationship between religion and the economy in Japan, with China as his countercase. He had now to find the data to validate his hypothesis among the more than three hundred thousand books and documents housed by the Harvard-Yenching Library, one of the finest in the world.

Luckily, Bob had the best of allies: Serge Elisséeff, who had been tutoring him in one-to-one reading sessions for almost a year. Following his counsel, Bellah focused on a religious movement, Shingaku, and its leader Ishida Baigan, who had tried to legitimate the activities and the lifestyle of the merchant classes in a society whose model of virtue was embodied by the frugal, selfless samurai. As he wrote to Lillian on January 24, 1954, Shingaku was also an uncharted territory: "There is nothing in any Western language except one article in German, so it is a chance to get in with a bit of splash." But as he began digging in the Harvard-Yenching collection of Shingaku original texts, Bellah realized that the ancient materials were too numerous and too difficult to master in a short time and decided to focus on the life of Baigan, and use Western scholarly sources to illuminate his other cases.[1]

Documents, however, were only half of the story. The relation between economic action and religious values had to be explained with reference to both Weber's ideas and the current state of sociological theory. Unfortunately, Parsons could be of no help—he had left for a visiting professorship at Cambridge University, and was going to spend the whole academic year 1953–1954 in England. Soon Bellah realized that his search for viable theoretical tools was not producing any appreciable results. All the demons that he had buried in his effort to become a scholar now ran free: How could he be a good parent if he could not even bring his thesis to completion? His deep sense of powerlessness finally pointed to Hutton's suicide: "He may be dead but he is not dead," he wrote in his diary on April 4, 1954, "not so dead there are not whole compressed slate strata of hate against him within me. If I could touch that so deep level of hatred and all the love beneath it and feel them both, the love and the hatred together, then, then, death, where is your victory?" How could he be a good father if he had never had one? This was no ordinary moment of misery. Now Bellah could see that his father's death had disintegrated the solid ground he needed to become a man. Neither Lillian nor Melanie could relieve his pain. He craved for help, but he did not know to what, or whom, he could turn.[2]

Rescue came from, of all people, C. Wright Mills. A sociologist at Columbia University, Mills advocated a critical understanding of the inner connections between everyday life and wider historical processes that was as different from Parsons's systemic naturalism and his optimistic liberal politics as could be. In a short review published in April 1954, titled "IBM Plus Reality Plus Humanism = Sociology," he satirized "Grand Theorists" and "Higher Statisticians" alike, thus anticipating some of the key ideas of his 1959 classic, *The Sociological Imagination*, but he also presented a list of books and authors he rated highly. Among György Lukács, Theodor Adorno, Karl Löwith, and Gunnar Myrdal, one name cropped up that was not often found in sociological literature: "One of the few books I know that really locates Freud's work in a more ample philosophical framework," Mills wrote, "is the wonderful little volume by Paul Tillich, *The Courage to Be*."[3]

Impressed by the title of Tillich's book, Bellah bought and read it immediately. The German theologian, born in 1886, had been dismissed from his post at the University of Frankfurt in 1933 and had soon moved to the Union Theological Seminary in New York upon the invitation of Reinhold Niebuhr. Besides the first volume of *Systematic Theology*, *The Courage to Be*, published in

1952, was his most celebrated achievement. The book advanced an analysis of anxiety defined as the awareness of one's own finitude from three different points of view—existential, spiritual, and moral—and Bob was quick to connect his moment of confusion to what Tillich described as a form of anxiety due to the loss of "an ultimate concern, of a meaning which gives meaning to all meanings." Only an "ethical act in which man affirms his own being in spite of those elements of his existence which conflict with his essential self-affirmation," wrote Tillich, could elude this "universal breakdown of meaning." No secular or political philosophy, however, might nurture this "courage to be," as it depended on the religious experience "of being grasped by the power of being-itself." This was the truth contained in the doctrine of justification by faith: the courage to be was "the courage to accept oneself as accepted in spite of being unacceptable."[4]

Bellah could feel Tillich's gaze upon himself: he was not sure what had made him unacceptable, but he must have done something terrible for his father to have abandoned him at such an early age. This conviction was put into words four months later:

Not the Dead Alone Die
(For my father)

This is the hard thing
To think that you heard my cry
That you stopped and turned on the high
Porch and left with a sight
This is the hard thing.

This is the hard thing
That you knew the depth of my need
I called but you would not heed
The course of my life was decreed
This is the hard thing.

This is the hard thing
That the gun you raised to your head
Lay me as you on my bed
Not only the dead are dead
This is the hard thing.

As shown by the poem, *The Courage to Be* did not solve Bob's problems entirely. Together with Tillich's *The Protestant Era* and *Systematic Theology*, however, the book gave him the tools he needed to face his condition. "I am ready for the ultimate seriousness," Bellah told Lillian on July 23, 1954: he needed courage, and courage needed faith. No need to "believe in the unbelievable," though. In Tillich's hands, he wrote, faith became an *act* in which "death and suffering and anxiety and meaninglessness" were recognized, accepted, and outdone in an intentional act of personal affirmation.[5]

It was perhaps because of his new understanding of faith and courage that Bob decided to take the initiative to befriend another graduate student. Up to that point his new friend's life had been far more adventurous than Bellah's boring route between Cambridge and Los Angeles: he had served in the military during World War Two and had studied abroad. Bob was deeply taken with him, to the point of regularly attending the gym, something he had never done before, to avoid the company of others and secure some extra time with his handsome and athletic friend.

Reflecting upon this particular relationship in his diary, Bob ascribed its "saving, redeeming" character to the fact that he had, for the first time in his life, found a real peer, someone with whom he could grow a symmetrical companionship. Now he understood that bonds could be created between males "without having to win or submit" to the other. He truly enjoyed this time, especially the moments of connection when they engaged in "manly" activities such as swimming, exercising, or playing basketball. More importantly, his friend was not wary of letting his feelings show, something that Bob had prevented himself from doing since he was a child. Bellah's gratitude showed through a poem he wrote for his friend when he left Cambridge one year later:

Salute

There is the mirror, in your face
The brown in your eyes gives back my grey-blue
Your casual masculinity molds my image
And the steel in your hands builds steel in me.

Not that I will ever smile as you smile
Or speak with your voice
Or lift my head as you lift yours
Or ever feel pain or love as you feel it

Even though I may have wanted to

I know now
That what you had to give was not yourself
But the image of your manhood.
You go, and yet you leave me strong.

I silently salute you.

Between May and December 1954 Paul Tillich and this new friend had persuaded Robert Bellah he could accept his own flaws and imperfections and get along with them. At about the same time, Talcott Parsons supplied him with the tools and the drive needed to bring his dissertation to a conclusion.[6]

I

Early in September 1954 Bellah flew to Flagstaff, Arizona, for the final conference of the Harvard Value Study, where a collective discussion of the drafts of chapters for the project's forthcoming books was to take place. As was often the case, Talcott Parsons stole the show with an impassioned talk on his theoretical chapter, "The Relation of Values to Social Systems." Anticipated in the Marshall Lectures given at Cambridge University one year earlier, Parsons's latest breakthrough portrayed the working of all social systems, from face-to-face interactions to whole societies, as subjected to four functional problems: obtaining resources from the external environment, establishing and attaining collective goals, preserving solidarity or coherence among their elements, and maintaining their identity or "latent value pattern." A critical element of the four-function model was its graphic representation as a 2×2 table, where structures and subsystems were analytically differentiated and then connected by arrows depicting the circulation of different resources. This fourfold grid could be iterated *within* each cell, thus allowing multilevel analyses that helped social scientists to focus on (and anticipate the existence of) a whole new range of subjects and processes. Implicit in the model was a clear biological metaphor: with societal evolution, particular structures such as roles, collectivities, and organizations would specialize in performing a single function, so that more advanced social systems would be more complex and internally differentiated than less advanced ones. The "AGIL scheme," named after the initials of the four functional imperatives (L = latent pattern maintenance, I = integration, G = goal attainment, A = adaptation), was born.[7]

The new model was a world-changing gift for Bellah, who immediately recognized its potential as a tool for thinking. He quickly rearranged his historical data according to Parsons's "AGIL logic," and just before Christmas 1954 he submitted a theoretical chapter and a sociological outline of Tokugawa society to his dissertation committee. Writing the rest of the thesis took only a couple of months: at the end of February Bob presented chapters three to five, focused on a substantive and functional analysis of Japanese religion and its relations to the polity and the economy. Combining the pattern variables with a simplified version of the AGIL scheme, Bellah distinguished Japan's "political values," focused on the attainment of collective goals, from America's "economic" stress on the rationalization of means and China's predilection for harmony and rituals. Thanks to the peculiar political orientation of the Japanese upper classes and its propagation during the Tokugawa period, it had been easy to appeal to a general sense of duty to mobilize the population in the pursuit of economic development. Bellah also showed how Shingaku had contributed to spreading the samurai ethos among the urban population and presented an interpretation of the Meiji Restoration as a period of radical institutional change, but one that lacked the defining traits of a bourgeois revolution. The final version of the thesis came to slightly fewer than three hundred double-spaced pages, with Bellah's translation of a eighteenth-century document, *Ishida Sensei Jiseki* (A memoir of our teacher, Ishida), as an appendix.[8]

When he turned in his completed dissertation, Bellah was already thinking beyond it, determined to expand its slim theoretical chapter into a full-fledged framework for the sociological study of religion. The difficulties he had experienced in writing his thesis convinced him that Parsons had always been right: the meanings of empirical and historical data depended on sound conceptual models, which also gave social scientists a common basis to discuss their work with psychologists and humanists. Bob's project was nothing if not ambitious, but it took him only a few weeks to draft a long and complex paper, "Some Suggestions for the Systematic Study of Religion." Adding a dash of Weber and Freud to Parsons and Tillich, Bellah defined "religion" as supplying humans with "ultimate meaning" and managing tensions at the boundary between personalities and the social system—a typical functionalist definition that strongly resonated with coeval works such as J. Milton Yinger's *Religion, Society and the Individual*. From symbols to pathology, no aspect of religion escaped Bellah's AGIL treatment, which sometimes produced virtuoso, if almost incomprehensible, results, as when Bob iterated his 2 × 2 grid four times in order to distinguish 256 types of behavior.[9]

Besides the theoretical intricacies, the new paper had two implications. On the one hand, it aimed at reorienting not only the scientific study of religion, but also the interpretation of its fate in modern societies. Parsons's AGIL scheme was based on the primacy of functional analysis: according to its logic, the four basic functions could be performed by different structures within different systems—for example, socialization, an aspect of the "latent pattern maintenance" function, could be performed by the family or by the school. Applied to religion, this meant that any set of institutions and symbols might function as "a religion" *if* it succeeded in motivating human beings by supplying them with the meaning of "life, the universe, and everything." And thus, according to the logic of the AGIL scheme, the modernist view of secularization as the gradual extinction of religion became a theoretical impossibility: if existing religions were unable to fulfill the function of religion, new symbols, groups, and institutions would emerge to fill the gap.

On the other hand, the paper revealed that Bellah had achieved an extraordinary familiarity with the AGIL paradigm in a short period of time, and his inclination to employ it as a general tool of analysis and adjust the work of other authors, and sometimes reality itself, to its logic when needed. His treatment of Tillich's conception of anxiety is a typical case in point. In *The Courage to Be*, the theologian had attributed existential anxiety to the fear of death, of condemnation, and of meaninglessness. To these three, Bellah added the fear of loneliness in order to reach AGIL's magic number of four and "fulfill the scheme." On top of his general traits of scholarly open-mindedness and a special expertise on Japan, China, and the history of religions, Bellah had planted AGIL and its theoretical logic at the very heart of his scientific mindset. Parsons was so impressed with the paper that he asked Jerry Kaplan, who owned and ran the Free Press, to issue it as a stand-alone volume—Bellah, he wrote in his letter to the publisher, had "carried the conceptual scheme in that area [religion] a long way and worked it out wonderfully."[10]

Bob's first daughter, Thomasin "Tammy" Bellah, was born on July 9, 1954, in the midst of a difficult moment of professional, personal, and familial turmoil. But ten months later Robert Bellah had successfully completed his PhD, had started to reckon with his suicidal father, and had a new friend whom he saw as the brother he'd never had. Above all, he was sharing with Melanie the joy of being a parent—she described how some nights she would tenderly watch her husband reading a book on the couch with baby Tammy sleeping on his chest. To a large extent, this newfound serenity depended on the fact that Bellah had found a job, albeit temporary and quite different from the one he had been dreaming of.[11]

II

Given the general appreciation he and his work had received, Bellah had long taken for granted that he would remain at Harvard, at least for his postdoctoral work. His stint as a member of the Communist Party, however, jeopardized not only his remaining there but also the very conclusion of his graduate studies. Shortly after Tammy's birth, but before going to Arizona for the Value Study conference, Bob had been summoned by McGeorge Bundy to discuss his earlier political activities. The scion of a Boston Brahmin family, the thirty-five-year-old professor of government had been nominated dean of the Faculty of Arts and Sciences in 1953, after losing the office of president to Nathan M. Pusey. Thanks to his intelligence, drive, and ability to control the complex balance of faculty and administrative demands, Bundy had rapidly gained an unrivaled control over the daily operations of the entire university. Soon after his appointment, he had also taken the lead in countering the repeated attacks of militant anticommunists, who had been targeting Harvard academics as the university's high profile made that a perfect ploy to generate publicity. Striking a precarious balance between a secret strategy of appeasement of the FBI and the quiet dismissal of embarrassing untenured faculty, Bundy had reduced institutional harm while projecting a positive image of Harvard as a bulwark of academic freedom.[12]

After a number of controversial incidents, in the spring of 1954 Dean Bundy started to interview former communists—including graduate students Everett Mendelsohn, Sydney James, and Robert Bellah—about their political activities, and encouraged them to comply with Harvard's policy of "full disclosure" if they were asked to collaborate with the FBI or any other public authority. In particular, Bundy told Bob that his fellowship was at risk of not being renewed for his final year of graduate school, to which Bellah replied that he was ready to discuss his past, but declared himself unwilling to talk about others. Bob left Bundy's office in a state of shock; like many others before him, he was trying to find a truthful and morally justifiable path out of a situation that had nothing to do with the present. Luckily (and ironically), his fellowship was paid for by the Harvard-Yenching Institute, whose director had himself been persecuted during the Bolshevik Revolution of 1917. "This is just like Russia," muttered Serge Elisséeff when Bob went to see him in September 1954. "As long as I am here your fellowship is safe." These events, however, prompted the young scholar to actively look for a way to cross the northern border.[13]

One month later Bellah received a letter thick with questions and ideas from Wilfred Cantwell Smith, a professor of comparative religion at McGill University in Montreal. In the correspondence that followed, Bob presented himself as a serious scholar who had devoted his life to the comparative study of cultures and societies. In particular, he had a clear idea of the relation between the social sciences and existing religious communities, which nicely dovetailed with Smith's: "When you say that a science of religion must enable the religions to function better 'by making that functioning self-conscious, and thereby self-critical and self-directing,'" he wrote, "you have closely stated what is for me the very heart of the matter." It was not long before the two had become sufficiently intrigued with each other to set up a meeting in Cambridge.[14]

Born into the Toronto upper class in 1916, Wilfred Cantwell Smith had studied the history of religions at Oxford University before leaving for Southern Asia as a Christian missionary. After seven years in what is now Pakistan, Smith went back to North America to complete his doctoral work at Princeton under the direction of Philip Hitti, a Lebanese scholar with a PhD from Columbia University who had been pioneering Near Eastern studies in the United States since the mid-1930s. He then got a job at the new Faculty of Divinity at McGill University, where he worked hard to set up an institution based on a radical understanding of interfaith dialogue. With an annual budget of $46,000 provided by the Rockefeller Foundation, Smith's Institute of Islamic Studies opened its doors in 1951.[15]

Although the idea of inviting individuals from the Islamic world to quietly reflect on the possibilities of reforming their own tradition from within had been particularly appreciated by his patrons, who saw the institute as an outpost of East-West cultural diplomacy, Smith was no ordinary cold warrior. In a mid-1950s piece titled "The Place of Oriental Studies in a Western University," for example, he argued against the use of the social sciences as a pragmatic tool for training foreign relations technocrats. "The study of a religion is the study of persons," he warned. "Of all branches of human inquiry, hardly any deals with an area so personal as this." As a consequence, "no statement about a religion [should be considered] valid unless [it could] be acknowledged by that religion's believers." Moreover, investigators should enter into an open, cordial dialogue with the holders of other traditions so as to create "an intellectual statement (or history) of the diverse religions of mankind that [would] ideally [do] justice to all of them as well as standing independently."[16]

This general understanding clearly informed Smith's approach to subject dearest to him, Islamic culture and society. During their long chat at Bob's apartment, Smith spoke of the central problem that the rise of modernity created for ancient civilizations: that of finding viable new meanings in the turmoil of radical societal change. Since the *Ummah*, the community of the righteous, was conceived as the embodiment of God's word in history, this task proved to be particularly difficult for Muslims. The decline of Islamic institutions created a spirited resentment toward the West, in particular among the Arabs, who expressed their disgust in the creation of the Muslim Brotherhood and forthright religious propaganda. Smith was, however, hopeful: as declared in his original project for the McGill Institute, all concerned Occidentals should help Muslims to "re-express" their faith and their heritage in an "Islamic Reformation."[17]

Although Smith was only eleven years his senior, Bellah quickly understood that he could be an impassioned and solicitous mentor. The appreciation was mutual, and Bob was soon offered a postdoctoral fellowship in Islamic studies, whose modest stipend could help him further his education by adding a new language and a whole new array of cases to his comparative repertoire. Ignoring an attractive offer from the University of California, Los Angeles, in December 1954 Bellah prepared his application for McGill. In his recommendation John Pelzel described Bob as an exceptionally able and erudite scholar, one who "given normal chances" would surely become "one of the most outstanding social scientists of his generation." He also characterized him as "a very quiet and slow-spoken person. . . . An intensely hard- and effectively-working man, he has one of the most pleasant and relaxed personalities with which I have contact at this university." Not surprisingly, Parsons's letter was a bit colder than Pelzel's: he wanted Bellah to stay at Harvard, and was doing everything he could to have him appointed an instructor in sociology.[18]

When the McGill Institute formally pledged him a fellowship in February 1955, however, Bellah was still confident that he would not leave Cambridge. As expected, two months later he was proposed for an instructorship for the 1955–1956 academic year. Bowing to Bundy's request, Parsons had informed all Social Relations members of Bellah's situation, and the department had unanimously voted to keep him. The dean then summoned Bob for the second time in a year, and said he was going to recommend the appointment to President Pusey and the Corporation; at the same time, he could not assure that the instructorship would be extended for another year if Bellah persisted in his decision not to "name names." When Bob restated his previous position, Bundy invited the young sociologist to consult with the director of the university's Health Services, Dana L. Farnsworth, about his psychological and emotional fitness. The examination was considered necessary because most members of the Harvard Corporation, like many others at the time, equated communism with a mental disorder—Bundy's suggestion was intended to protect the young sociologist from widespread prejudice. Without even waiting for the results of the examination, Bundy forwarded his full endorsement of Bellah's appointment to Pusey, underlining that Bob would have managed any eventual investigation far better than other Harvard associates. Moreover, he invited the president to hire Bellah unconditionally to "strengthen the sense of mutual confidence that now exists, I think, between the Corporation and the Faculty."[19]

In the meantime, Bellah underwent two different examinations. Shortly after his meeting with Bundy, he was contacted by two agents of the FBI, who between April 6 and May 13, 1955, subjected him to three interviews about long-forgotten places, facts, and names. Their questioning was fair and kind, but Bob refused to speak of his former comrades. Early in May he also met with Farnsworth, who interrogated him about his old problems with anxiety and adjustment, and asked a number of intimate questions about homosexuality and whether Bob had "ever engaged in sexual acts for which [he] could be blackmailed." Bellah understood that Farnsworth had received sensitive information from a doctor of the Harvard Psychological Clinic he had seen as an undergraduate, and felt deeply humiliated by his implications. After the ordeal was over, the Corporation's response finally came: upon approving the appointment, President Pusey wrote Parsons and Bundy that "if, during Mr. Bellah's year of service as instructor, he should refuse to testify about any past association with Communists, the Corporation would not look with favor on any proposal for his reappointment." The condition was intolerable; sure of his moral high ground, and appalled by Harvard's "second failure" of him, Bob chose McGill. At the end of the summer he packed the 1941 Oldsmobile sedan he had bought from Sam Huntington for $150 and left for Montreal with Melanie, baby Tammy, and the echo of Talcott Parsons's last words: "This is not the end of it."[20]

III

With the help of Wilfred Smith's secretary, Bob and Melanie found a small condo at 5760 Monkland Avenue, a pleasant shopping street in the residential neighborhood of Notre Dame de Grace, about seven miles west of the McGill campus. Fortunately, the hectic, absorbing life of the Institute of Islamic Studies left them little time to think of Cambridge, their friends, and their past routines. Headquartered at Divinity Hall—a grey collegiate Gothic building complete with oak *boiseries*, stained-glass windows, and a chapel—the institute had been carefully made into a cozy place for its twenty-some "Muslim" and "Western" members. A dense schedule of classes and seminars, a small but growing library, "mandatory" afternoon teas, and Wilfred Smith's ebullient presence made sure that the stay at the institute would be an exacting, and unforgettable, experience.[21]

Following Smith's indications, Bellah enrolled as a master's candidate in Islamic studies and was entrusted to the care of Turkish sociologist Niyazi Berkes, a former student of Louis Wirth's at the University of Chicago, who had left his country in 1952 owing to his left-wing Kemalist political sympathies. Under his direction, Bob learned some Arabic, studied the texts, history, and institutions of Islamic religion, and reinforced his Weberian comparative approach against any residual ambition to conduct empirical fieldwork on contemporary phenomena. In fact, the papers on Islam he wrote at McGill reflect an almost exclusive interest in the historical study of the relationships between religion and politics according to the principles of Parsonian functionalism. The analytical independence of social and cultural systems built into the AGIL scheme, for example, pushed him to reject the "continuity thesis" of coeval Orientalism, according to which Islam was a "coherent civilization" whose various elements expressed "a basically unitary and stable set of core values and beliefs." In a few months, his mentors developed the same high expectations that Parsons and Pelzel had of him—in his 1956 report to the Ford Foundation, Smith called Bellah "the most interesting and probably most promising Western student that we have at this Institute."[22]

But for all his involvement with the life of the institute, Bob's eyes remained fixed on Cambridge. In particular, he kept a steady correspondence with his former graduate school friend, Clifford Geertz. The would-be anthropologist had been in Indonesia from 1952 to 1954 to study the religion of Java and its connection to modernization—the two men's dissertations were variations on the theme of applying the Protestant-ethic thesis to societies left untouched by Weber. After his return from Java, Geertz had been appointed research associate at the MIT Center for International Studies and was working on his thesis, "Religion in Modjokuto," and a host of more practically oriented projects. Before Bob's departure and along with Parsons, the two had constituted a small working group on religion in which Bellah was granted the right to speak first, while the others generally reacted to his carefully phrased memorandums. In November of 1955, for example, Geertz wrote a lengthy review of "Some Suggestions for the Systematic Study of Religion" based on the idea that a full-fledged theory of culture cast "from a rather different angle" was needed before Parsonian tools could be used in the study of cultural phenomena. Such an analytical assessment of meaning and symbols would need, in turn, the "outside support" of the work of philosophers such as Suzanne Langer and Ernst Cassirer.[23]

Encouraged by Geertz's comments, and inspired by his use of the concept of "worldview," in Montreal Bellah hastily wrote a thorough historical-theoretical survey before being forced "to turn his attention to other tasks." In the eighty-five-page paper, titled "Religion in the Process of Cultural Differentiation," he made a distinction between "natural worldviews," defined by their naïve identification of language and reality, and "philosophical worldviews," marked by the dissociation of symbols from their referents. Whereas Bellah indicated the four historical societies of ancient Greece, Israel, India, and China as the seedbeds of a critical understanding of the conventional relationship between language and reality, he saw the distinction between natural and philosophical worldviews as typological rather than historical. "The Philosophical Breakthrough is not a once and for all occurrence," he wrote in a nodal point of his paper. "It occurs wherever and whenever people emerge from the natural worldview into the world of conscious conceptual thought. For many millions it has not occurred even today."[24]

Not surprisingly, the AGIL scheme was everywhere. Bellah first employed it to categorize the various strands of the philosophical worldviews born out of the discovery of a "gap" between man, language, and the truth: for its interest in the physical world and the foundation of being, for example, he placed classical Greece in the A/adaptation cell, while the focus on harmony typical of Chinese culture landed it in the I/integration cell. Second, the AGIL scheme was employed to draw analogies between the peculiarities of the four main civilizations, Freud's theory of mind, and Parsons's functional theory of the nuclear family. Bob also used the model to perform another operation: he grouped the four civilizations using the 2 × 2 matrix but according to different criteria, thus creating alternative, and partially incompatible, classifications. In one version, for example, the transcendence-based societies of Greece and Israel were opposed to immanence-oriented China and India, while according to another version secular societies (Greece and China) were distinguished from religious societies (Israel and India).[25]

In the remainder of the paper Bellah interpreted the emergence of world religions as different attempts at bridging the chasms opened by the philosophical revolution. While occupying fifty typewritten pages, these analyses were sketchy at best, and made no use of any technical vocabulary. This decision depended on a momentous *prise de conscience* that is worth quoting at length:

> In conclusion we must stress again the tentative nature of this paper. It is more in the nature of a survey of the field in order to see what needs to be found out and where would be the most strategic places to look than it is a summary of a comprehensive investigation. To devote monographic attention to all of the points which have been raised is clearly beyond the scope of any one man. Nevertheless it does seem possible to undertake in monographic detail the explication of a number of the crucial problems, such as, for example, the various "philosophical breakthroughs" or "medievalisms." Such a program of rigorous empirical scholarship should in turn both modify and enrich the theoretical apparatus which lies behind this paper. *After two or three decades spent in such labour one might return to the issues set forth here with some greater degree of confidence.*

A conclusion that might have sounded like an unprovoked apology to the ears of an outsider was immediately clear to Geertz and Parsons. It was at the same time a reflection on the reciprocal influence of theory and research, a pledge of allegiance to a very specific sociological school, and a plea for further collective scholarly work. Most of all, it was an explicit formulation of the master plan that Bellah had devised for his life so as to fulfill his "exceptional promise" as a social scientist.[26]

Parsons and Geertz were not the only American colleagues with whom Bellah shared his drafts. Upon reading "Some Suggestions for the Systematic Study of Religion," Columbia sociologist Charles Y. Glock was stunned by Bellah's prowess in conceptual analysis, and asked him to contribute a chapter to a planned reader on American religion. It was a proposal that Bob, although a specialist in Far and Middle Eastern studies, could not refuse, and that was more possible to achieve than it seemed. Some years earlier, after a brief trip to Washington, DC, he had drafted quite a long reading list on American history, which included the work of his former professors Perry Miller and F. O. Matthiesen, and writers like Whitman, Emerson, and Melville. The forty-five-page paper he wrote for Glock used a simplified version of the AGIL scheme to frame the history of the interchange between American society and its churches. While the social system provided the resources and the dynamism needed for the attainment of religious goals, Bellah wrote, religious bodies supplied it with meaning and enthusiasm via periodical moments of spiritual renewal. This was also true for the postwar religious revival, which should "not be interpreted as a mere fad, but [might] be indicative of crucial long-term equilibrating functions which religion [might] play in modern society." Supplementing his functionalist framework with a resounding Tillichian tone, Bellah expressed once again his opposition to the idea of secularization as a mere decline of religion, and depicted the United States as a deeply spiritual and pious society.[27]

Together with Jacob Taubes, a German theologian whom Bob had met before leaving for Montreal, Glock also offered the young sociologist an assistant professorship at Columbia University and the Union Theological Seminary. Bellah had already received similar proposals from Princeton and the University of Washington, but was waiting for an offer from his alma mater as a reparation for the events of a year earlier. In the spring of 1956 Parsons finally presented Bob with an alternative: he could either get a temporary research position at Harvard or spend a year at the "Ford Center" in Palo Alto with him, and perhaps Geertz, to finalize their common work on religion. Entirely sponsored by the Ford Foundation, the Center for Advanced Study in the Behavioral Sciences began in September 1954 as a lavish retreat where creative scholars could enjoy nine to thirteen months of unstructured time to work on their "big ideas," in the company of a class of fifty like-minded peers from different disciplines. The process for offering Bellah a fellowship at the center was initiated by Social Relations' Evon Z. Vogt in February 1955. During the discrete preevaluation conducted by the center's director, Ralph W. Tyler, in the spring of 1955 and then again in the fall of 1956, scholars like Parsons, David Aberle, and Freed Bales unsurprisingly praised Bob's "highly sophisticated level of theoretical analysis," "great intellectual creativity," and "very high promise."[28]

In November Bellah flew to Cambridge to meet with Sir Hamilton A. R. Gibb, a Scottish Arabist who had been Smith's mentor at Oxford and was now the chairman of the Center for Middle Eastern Studies. Created in 1954 under the leadership of historian William L. Langer, a former director of the Office of Strategic Services who also chaired the Harvard Russian Research Center and the Committee for Regional Studies, the institute aimed at educating experts in Middle Eastern matters for service in private industry and the government. Although in 1957 its chair had been given to Gibb, the center was intended to train American professionals and not, as Langer remarked, "to develop Arab philosophers." When Gibb offered him a one-year research fellowship that included almost no teaching commitments, Bob refused all other offers, including a double appointment at McGill University as assistant professor of sociology and Smith's right-hand man. He would bring back his family of four—his second daughter, Jennifer "Jenny" Bellah, was born in Montreal on November 1, 1956—to Cambridge. For two Southern Californians like Bob and Melanie, the continental climate of Eastern Massachusetts was still a dream compared with the freezing cold of *l'hiver québécois*.[29]

5

Becoming an American

FROM CAMBRIDGE TO TOKYO,
AND BACK, 1957–1961

IN MAY 1957 Robert N. Bellah and his family headed back to the United States. Their first summer in Cambridge was hectic, as Melanie and Bob started looking for a new house—after the long Montreal commutes they were determined to find a place not far from Harvard Yard. After some digging around, they bought an old Victorian at 62 Gorham Street, just a fifteen-minute walk from Bob's new office at the Center for Middle Eastern Studies. Surrounded by shady trees in the quiet, working-class, interracial neighborhood of Agassiz, the three-story house was big enough to accommodate Tammy, Jenny, and, hopefully, their long-awaited brother. In a few weeks, Bellah's tiny study was cluttered with the books and reading notes from the course on religion and culture and the restricted seminars given by Paul Tillich, who had been appointed University Professor at Harvard in 1955. As he wrote to Wilfred Smith, he was also auditing classes in Arabic, Greek, and biblical exegesis to prepare for his most cherished project, a comparison of Augustine of Hippo and Al-Ghazzali. Most of his time, however, went into two sociological texts: a small programmatic volume on the sociology of religion for the Free Press and a report on politics and religion in Asia for the Committee on Comparative Politics of the Social Sciences Research Council, a research forum established three years earlier under the chairmanship of political scientist Gabriel A. Almond. Less willingly, Bob had also agreed to take over Parsons's and Gibb's classes while his two mentors were on leave.[1]

This mixed bag of projects reflected Bellah's being suspended between two conflicting approaches to the study of religion, a condition that became increasingly clear as he caught up again with Harvard's buzzing academic life.

His stint in Montreal had coincided with what historian Hunter Heyck has called "the magical year 1956, plus or minus one," a three-year period in which a number of seminal texts appeared in the social sciences—including Parsons and Neil J. Smelser's *Economy and Society*, *A Study of Thinking* by Jerome Bruner and collaborators, W. Ross Ashby's *Introduction to Cybernetics*, and *How the Soviet System Works* by Clyde Kluckhohn and others, along with "Revitalization Movements" by Anthony Wallace, Herbert Simon's "A Behavioral Model of Rational Choice," and Walt Rostow's "The Take-Off into Self-Sustained Growth." Although varied in focus and style, these works marked the ascent of a scientistic, pragmatically oriented conception of social science which almost perfectly dovetailed with the ideas devised at Harvard from the early 1940s.[2]

In fact, the Social Relations bubble was only a refraction of a much wider scientific movement, one that combined a penchant for the construction of formal analytical models; a general notion of complex, hierarchical, and adaptive systems; and an interest in functional analysis and equilibrium-generating mechanisms. The pattern variables, the AGIL scheme, and the other concepts of "structural-functionalism" were but an instance of a larger family of technical tools to think with. While highly intrigued by symbols and language as privileged means for reducing the world's complexity, however, Bellah's colleagues gave little or no attention to religion. Most of the protagonists of the magical year 1956, for example, ignored it, while others embraced a flat definition of secularization as a mere decline of religion. In *How the Soviet System Works*, Kluckhohn and Inkeles concluded that "the main trend strongly [suggested] that religion [would] constantly become less important in the USSR," while Wallace argued that "human affairs around the world seem more and more commonly to be decided without reference to supernatural powers."[3]

In spite of their full participation in this "high modernist" trend of American social science, neither Parsons nor Bellah shared their colleagues' scorn for religion. In a spirited essay published in *Daedalus* in 1958, Parsons explicitly refused the theory of secularization as decline and explained contemporary American values as firmly rooted in the tradition of ascetic Protestantism. On his part, Bellah persisted in the attempt to create a general theory of religion combining Tillich's analysis of the human condition with cybernetic functionalism. In the manuscript of his book on religion he drew an analogy between the "boundary problems" of social systems and the "boundary situations" experienced by stressed individuals. "There is a very real sense," he wrote, choosing his words with thinly disguised irony, "in which science is a luxury whereas religion is a necessity."[4]

While the idea that any social system could somehow find an answer to the functional problem of general meaning making made any deflation of religion impossible, Bob's opposition to his fellow social scientists cut across theoretical quarrels. High modernists typically thought that the social sciences should get as close as possible to the aims and methods of the natural sciences and thus saw the objectification, and sometimes the sheer elimination, of human subjects via mathematical models, games, and simulations as equivalent to scientific maturity. However, at McGill Bellah had learned to combine philological work on ancient texts with Smith's revolutionary practice of creating a symmetrical relation between the scholar and his or her subjects of study. Just as religious symbols and practices could never be reduced to cultural mechanisms, religious people should not be seen as a bunch of backward-minded folk who needed to be shepherded into secularization via carefully planned strategies. As shown by a letter written to his McGill mentor in the fall of 1957, Bellah's preferences were clear: "As for the Center [for Middle Eastern Studies] here I think you are perfectly right," he wrote, "in thinking it no place for a Muslim fresh off the boat. The atmosphere is very impersonal and there is simply no place for the 'nurture' which the [Institute of Islamic Studies] provides. Also of course Western students greatly outnumber Muslims and there are I think no muslims on the staff. I am glad," he concluded, "I got my start in Islamics at IIS partly because it is the next best thing to being in the field."[5]

Luckily, Harvard was rich and articulated enough to spare Bob the choice between cybernetics and humanism—two halves that he soon came to see as entirely, if not easily, compatible. On the side of behavioral science, the Department of Social Relations had celebrated its tenth birthday in February 1957 with a two-day gathering in which Robert K. Merton—the influential "theorist of the middle range" who had been one of Parsons's graduate students in the 1930s before becoming a professor at Tulane and then at Columbia University—participated. Before passing the chair on to a fellow founder, psychologist Robert W. White, Talcott Parsons wrote a final report in which he offered three suggestions for the future: first, the department should maintain, and perhaps increase, its focus on scientific research and the training of social scientists; second, Social Relations should limit itself to basic research, leaving applied work to professional schools and area studies centers; third, the department should remain at the vanguard of American social science, and that meant only the most creative and open-minded scholars should be welcomed into its ranks. In a few years, the arrival of David Riesman and Erik H. Erikson confirmed that the interdisciplinary spirit of Social Relations could still lure some of the best minds around. "We are on the way," Parsons concluded, "but the journey is going to be long and hard, and we are only at its beginning."[6]

On the side of humanities, the financial and institutional consolidation of the Harvard Divinity School had been a priority ever since Nathan M. Pusey had taken the place of James Conant in 1953. "Andover Hall," said the new president during his first public appearance, "is not on the periphery of Harvard University . . . and it cannot be permitted to become so." The hiring of Tillich under Pusey, which Conant had refused while in office, fearing a backlash from the more secularized members of the faculty, had been a signal of the changing tide. Further, in 1956 funds had been offered to establish a more welcoming environment in which good-willed scholars and graduate students from all over the world could teach one another their respective traditions in a spirit of respectful curiosity. Given the similarities between this new "Program on World Religions" and the Institute of Islamic Studies, it was not surprising that Wilfred Cantwell Smith was offered the chair of the new academic unit. Upon Smith's refusal, the post went to his McGill colleague and Bellah's former professor, Robert H. L. Slater, a student of South Asian Buddhism with a long record as a missionary in Burma.[7]

In February 1958 Bob accepted a four-year lectureship at the intersection of all these institutional and intellectual developments. The financial responsibility for his annual salary of $8,500 was shared by the Department of Social Relations, the Center for Middle Eastern Studies, the Program on World Religions, and the newly established Center for East Asian Studies chaired by John Fairbank. Although Bellah's teaching and administrative duties were going to be weighty and time-consuming, his new position placed him exactly at the crossroads of all the major developments of the postwar behavioral sciences. He was in the right place, and among the right people, at the right time.[8]

I

While in Montreal, Bellah had spoken often with the head of the Free Press, Jerry Kaplan, about publishing his thesis. The volume finally saw print in 1957 under the title of *Tokugawa Religion: The Values of Pre-industrial Japan*. Apart from small editorial changes, it reproduced the dissertation as it had been presented in April 1955, with one exception—Bob's discussion of his comparative approach and his justification of the expression "modern industrial societies" to include both capitalist and communist societies under a single category were nowhere to be found. At the same time, the conclusion emphasized the structural and cultural differences between Japan and the West, and sounded like a methodological plea against those American scholars who shared with their Marxist colleagues a penchant for materialistic explanations. "Both the Restoration and the subsequent modernization of Japan," wrote Bellah, "must be seen first in political terms and only secondarily in economic terms. I am insistent on this point because the tendency to regard economic developments as 'basic' and political developments as 'superstructure' is by no means confined to Marxist circles but permeates most current thinking on such matters."[9]

What had happened? Between the dissertation and its book version stood the magic year 1956, and with it the takeoff of modernization theory. As a cultural counterpart to the postwar attempt at affirming American geopolitical and economic hegemony, modernization theory was a combination of traditional Western philosophical ideas, Cold War notions of development, and the scientific principles of high modernism. At its center stood a set of familiar themes: a conception of societies as complex systems that might be steered by adequate equilibrium-seeking mechanisms, usually known as "cybernetics"; a sharp dichotomy between "tradition" and "modernity," where the latter was presented as a nexus of market economy, pluralist democracy, free media of communication, and secularization; and an ambition to employ social science to shepherd the public toward "freedom and progress." Integral to the project was a forceful if often implicit identification of full modernity with an idealized image of the United States, aimed at showing "to the 'emerging countries' that development along liberal, capitalist lines could alleviate poverty and raise living standards at least as fast as revolutionary and Marxist alternatives."[10]

These ideas were developed in a small number of lavishly financed institutions where scientism, positivism, and Americanism became a widely shared common sense. Besides the Congress for Cultural Freedom, initiated in 1950, and the Harvard Department of Social Relations, the network included the MIT Center for International Studies, the Committee for Comparative Politics of the Social Science Research Council, the Columbia University Bureau of Applied Social Research, and various area studies centers. Around 1958, scholars like Edward Shils, David Easton, Lucian Pye, Gabriel Almond, Ithiel De Sola Pool, and Lloyd Fallers also became regulars of the Center for Advanced Studies in the Behavioral Sciences in Palo Alto, where another major outlet of modernization theory, the Chicago Committee for the Comparative Study of New Nations, was devised a couple of years before its establishment in 1960.[11]

FIGURE 5.1. Official Harvard portrait of the newly employed Robert
Bellah, 1958. (Courtesy of Harvard University Archives)

While the general framing of the theory was set in an ideological confrontation with the Soviet Union, a number of exquisitely theoretical problems surfaced. As a junior member of major modernization theory networks, Bellah
was pushed to reflect on two pivotal questions—the relationship between
economic, political, and cultural factors on the one side, and the shape taken
by the process of modernization in different countries on the other. To Bob's
scorn, the answers proposed in the mid-1950s were quite clear: no matter how
articulate, erudite, or anti-Marxist, his colleagues indicated technology and

the economy as the sources of social change, relegating culture to a secondary, if not irrelevant, role. An influential advocate of this position was a former student of Parsons, Marion Levy Jr. Now a professor at Princeton University, in 1952 Levy published a book inspired by a series of seminars in which both David Aberle and John Pelzel had participated, *The Structure of Society*. That same year, he also presented a comparative paper on Chinese and Japanese modernization, which Bob came to know pretty well. While he wrote that "the presence of similar actual patterns but different ideal patterns in a given sphere cannot be without structural implications," Levy's explanations pointed ultimately to structural factors—familial and political systems, class relations, and mobility processes. Four years later, economic historian Walt W. Rostow would speak of the (ir)relevance of religious factors for the emergence of modern dynamic elites in terms that would leave Bellah horrified: while it was "increasingly conventional for economists to pay their respects to the Protestant ethic, . . . allusion to a positive scale of religious or other values conducive to profit-maximising activities is an insufficient sociological basis for this important phenomenon."[12]

Another epochal dilemma had to do with the shape of modernization: Was there a single path to full modernity, or was each social system going to follow its individual trajectory? For most theorists, available data proved the existence of a single, unilinear route comprising a succession of identifiable "stages." Armed with a simplified version of Parsons's pattern variables, they described all traditional societies as marked by the attribution of status according to ascriptive biological givens, such as age, sex, and kinship, and the primacy of moral particularism. In this view, technological advances were singled out as triggering a fixed sequence of economic, political, and cultural shifts, at the end of which stood the example of the United States as a kind of perfectly realized modernity—the kingdom of moral universalism where individuals were evaluated on the basis of performance rather than inherited status. Against this simplistic solution, between 1957 and 1960 Robert Bellah reworked some of the ideas he had first presented in embryonic form in his dissertation and in *Tokugawa Religion*.[13]

To begin with, Bellah argued for the autonomy of culture and religion within a multidimensional sociological framework in which no element could claim "billiard ball priority." Supported by Parsons's latest work, the argument took two different forms. From a theoretical point of view, Bellah maintained a firm allegiance to functionalism—a position that, ironically, most modernization theorists were eager to subscribe to. In a long essay titled "The Myth of the Middle Class in Japan," written with the Harvard historian Albert M. Craig at Bernard Barber's request, Bob explicitly criticized the Marxian bent of much Japanese and American historiography on the Tokugawa to Meiji transition. He also named Ernest Cassirer, Arthur Lovejoy, and Kenneth Burke as his most thought-provoking allies in the study of culture as a symbolic system. More substantively, Bellah's paper on Turkey and Japan, a spin-off of his report for the Committee on Comparative Politics, focused on the role played by religion in advanced societies. In order to maintain their equilibrium, he wrote, modernized societies required an adjustment of the sacred, one that only "a new religious initiative" claiming "religious ultimacy for itself" might bring about.[14]

The dichotomous view of modernization was Bellah's second target: "tradition" and "modernity" were complex phenomena whose relationship couldn't be depicted as a zero-sum game between mutually exclusive alternatives. In his dissertation he had been careful not to exaggerate the relevance of Shingaku; while Baigan had preached an influential reinterpretation of traditional wisdom among Kyoto merchants, he was no Luther, and certainly no Calvin. This emphasis on the difference between Baigan and the Reformers was somehow lost in the print version, but its main point was there: Japan had been able to walk the path of modernization neither against nor in spite of its tradition, but *thanks to it*. More importantly, this was not only a passing stage in the attainment of American-style modernization, but a lasting feature of modernity *à la japonaise*. Tradition and modernity were not objectified alternatives, but extensive, fuzzy categories containing different objects and combinations of elements.[15]

This argument led almost naturally to a third point, the relativization of the West. While unilinear depictions would justify the differences between countries only as different stages of growth or the effect of structural or psychological obstacles to the full deployment of modernization, for Bellah the historical differences between a number of paths would produce rather different modernities. In *Tokugawa Religion* his objects of comparison had been four: Japan, China, Anglo-Saxon countries, and Continental Europe. America, Japan, and China were seen as the carriers of value systems focused on different areas of social life, and their respective conditions were in no sense described as different stages of a single path. Analogously, in "The Myth of the Middle Class in Japan", Tokugawa "feudalism" was first declared irreducible to European experiences and then compared to both traditional and modern-day China and the Abbasid Empire. While there was just one theoretical frame, the specificity of each case ruled out any reduction to a single narrative.[16]

From a methodological point of view, this meant that to understand Japan, China, or any other non-Western country, serious scholars should observe their object from multiple points of view. In particular, thorough familiarity with regional scholarship would help Americans in reducing their own ethnocentric bias. It was not by chance that an up-to-date review of Japanese historiography opened Bellah's rejoinder to the critical remarks on *Tokugawa Religion* that his Social Relations colleague and Parsons's archenemy Barrington Moore Jr. had privately circulated in January 1960. Writing from a materialist point of view, Moore depicted Bob's book as the vehicle of an idyllic picture of pre-modern Japan where class conflict and exploitation were nullified by an indigestible mixture of bourgeois functionalism and Tillichian theology. Against this charge, Bellah lamented once again the nefarious influx of Marxist materialism on the study of Japanese history and invited Moore to update his knowledge of local materials—which, to be sure, he anticipated in the paper to the extent necessary to prove once and for all his first-rate expertise.[17]

Bellah's insistence on the uniqueness of Japan had been reinforced by a long review of *Tokugawa Religion* published in April 1958 by Maruyama Masao, Japan's foremost historian of political thought and a well-known public intellectual. Strongly influenced by German idealism, the forty-four-year-old professor at Tokyo University equated "modernism" with the ability to observe one's own society from a universalist standpoint in order to replace allegedly natural institutions with "vital fictions worked out by actors with some degree of . . . self-consciousness." After the end of the war, Maruyama had urged Japanese intellectuals to form a "community of contrition" and help the full realization of democracy. When Bellah's graduate school peer, Arima Tatsuo, gave him a translation of the review, Bob could not believe his eyes. Among the books on Japan written by Americans, wrote Maruyama, *Tokugawa Religion* "more than many in a long time, [had] aroused [his] appetite and [his] fighting spirit."[18]

As well as praising Bellah's "sophisticated maturity" and "powerful concentration," the Japanese professor criticized his use of Western categories, which hindered a full understanding of historical data. The Weberian concept of rationalization, for example, had been extended to a number of irreducible phenomena, while loyalty to the emperor had been greatly overestimated. In a single stroke, Maruyama could subtly point to the strengths and weaknesses of the book: "The author stands on the cogent position of emphasizing the multiplicity of patterns of modernization in world history," he wrote, "and while recognizing the Japanese idiosyncrasies in the bearers of modernization and the psychological motivation of the ideologies which promoted it, he fails to see how these idiosyncrasies are stamped in the internal structures of 'rationalization' and 'industrialization' themselves." And yet, for all the book's shortcomings, "in the ambition and boldness of his systematization," wrote Maruyama, it was not an exaggeration to say that the thirty-year-old Bellah had succeeded "in wearing the mantle of the late Professor [Ruth] Benedict." As an epiphany, these words helped Bob to finally find the *mondai ishiki*, his own "sense of the problem" in his work on Japan.[19]

II

With the exception of Barrington Moore Jr., at Harvard Bellah was surrounded by a diverse range of people who unfailingly confirmed his self-image as an exceptionally gifted scholar destined to leave a permanent trace in the development of social science. Within the Parsonian circle, he enjoyed a privileged relationship with his old mentor, who from 1958 onward shared with him the sociology of religion course on a peer-to-peer basis. At the Program on World Religions Bellah was daily consulted by Slater, and his relations with Reischauer, Fairbank, and Craig at the Center for East Asian Studies had never been better. While never a close friend, Paul Tillich continued to be a source of intellectual and personal inspiration. During a seminar he even said that the young scholar had reminded him of "the structure of grace in history"—a phrase that made a strong impression on Bellah and those around him. As the icing on the cake, after the meeting Bob was approached by David Riesman. The world-famous author of *The Lonely Crowd*, who had just given his inaugural lecture as the first Henry Ford Professor at Harvard, was impressed by Bob's erudition, his intellectual poise, and what he later called his "purity." It was the beginning of a lifelong friendship, which would also extend to their wives, Melanie and Evey, and their children.[20]

Sometimes, however, Bellah's excellent reputation did him more harm than good. A case in point was the seven-week trip to the Middle East that Sir Hamilton Gibb arranged for him in the spring of 1959. Trying to steer Bob's career in the direction of Islamic studies, the "leading Arabist of the West" offered him a stalwart of the Harvard scholarly landscape: his undergraduate course on Islamic institutions. The trip was meant to complement the young sociologist's armchair knowledge of Islamic societies with some firsthand experience, but also to help him in forging connections with local scholars that could prove pivotal for his professional future. As the preparations for the trip were underway, the *Atlantic Monthly* commissioned from Bellah a full report of his travels, to be published shortly after his return. From Bob's point of view, however, the prospective seven weeks of lonely wandering from Cairo to Istanbul looked like an unwelcome diversion from his study plans. To make things worse, Melanie had just found out that another child was on the way—the long trip would coincide almost perfectly with the fifth and sixth months of her pregnancy. As Bellah got on his first intercontinental flight on May 2, 1959, all he saw was doom and gloom.[21]

Bob wrote Melanie his first letter two days later, after hopping from Boston to Shannon, Ireland, and then again to Cairo through Paris, Geneva, Rome, and Athens. His first trip out of North America was nothing but "stunning and depressing." The capital of Egypt was a filthy, smelly place, crammed with abandoned human corpses, disgusting food, and "short sightedly predatory" shopkeepers. To make things worse, as Bob moved from the Nile Hilton—a magnificent construction "sitting literally surrounded by squalor, yet with an opulence that any sultan would have envied"—to an inexpensive pension, an intestinal bug certified his being in a "backward country."[22] Reluctantly, Bellah set out to begin his academic tour: in a few days he met with scholars from Cairo University, the American University, the Dominican Institute of Oriental Studies, and al-Azhar University, the world-class hub of Sunni culture. Announced by his fame—"Wilfred apparently wrote a very warm commendation of me, calling me the new Max Weber, etc."[23]—he also met with the Canadian ambassador to the United Arab Republic, Arnold Cantwell Smith, who handed him a ticket for the coronation of Coptic Orthodox Pope Cyril VI of Alexandria. "I am rather miserable most of the time," Bob wrote to Melanie after visiting the pyramids and the Sphinx of Giza, which he found smaller than expected and rather unimpressive.[24]

As the trip proceeded Bellah felt increasingly sad and unengaged. On May 21 he flew to Jerusalem, where the Haram esh-Sharif and the Garden of Olives failed to inspire him and local Christians annoyed him with their stubbornness. One week later he reached Beirut, then Damascus, Ankara, and finally Istanbul. Unable to fully enjoy his visits to some of the places he had been dreaming about since he was a Sunday school student, almost midway through this errand into the wilderness Bob wrote Melanie about his loathing of traveling in general. His rant left no doubt as to where his heart and mind were:

Travel is for the young and gay or the old and mouldy. I thoroughly hate it. . . . Things look like their picture and what is the good of the damned place. It is not dirty old Athens with a few pillars lying around which is the meaning of "Athens." Athens is the spirit of Athens as in Aeschylus and Pindar and Plato. Not any damned pile of rocks. I think traveling is very egotistical. The real motive is that no place really exists until *I* have seen it. My presence gives it tangible persistence.

Bellah also added a bittersweet comment about his encounters with scholars and intellectuals, the only part of the trip that he had enjoyed so far: "The only thing is that I am getting a lot out of talking to people. Even that is probably mostly illusion."[25] In the end, the places he found congenial were those that reminded him of Western cities—wide and empty streets, clean hotels, American-style restaurants. "Too bad it's not very Islamic here," he wrote Melanie while in Beirut, "as it would be a good place to spend a year." On his way back to the United States he stopped again in Athens and Rome, where he visited the Acropolis, the Colosseum, and the Vatican. He finally got home on June 15, 1959, after forty-four incredibly long days.[26]

Given the lows he reached during the trip, it was almost miraculous that Bob could even set out to write "The Well of the Past," an articulated sociological travelogue titled after the opening line of Thomas Mann's *Joseph and His Brothers*. To his unknowing reader, Bellah admitted that his experience had been influenced by his own "extensive inner travels": from the white-robed students flocking the courtyard of the Azhar mosque to the "tremendous controlled power" of the statues of Egyptian deities, all his images bore the stamp of a mild orientalism filtered through some very idiosyncratic parallels. "After all," he wrote, "I could not claim that my Southwestern travels [of 1953] were valueless. Indeed there was more than a little to link the two areas together. . . . The latter impression turned out to be accurate for the Transjordanian hills and the country north of Damascus are like nothing so much as the American Southwest; the Arab villages of Jordan and Syria seemed almost images of Hopi villages." At the same time, the paper was also a deeply ambivalent document, one that showed that Bob's approach could be assimilated neither to the works of mainstream modernization theorists nor to the dry geopolitical dispatches routinely published by the *Atlantic Monthly* in the late 1950s. As much as a 25-page essay can be compared to a 460-page book, reading "The Well of the Past" side by side with Daniel Lerner's *The Passing of Traditional Society* might help to highlight the peculiarity of Bellah's positioning within the field of modernization theory.[27]

Published in 1958, *The Passing* was based on a large-scale quantitative study of the impact of the mass media in six Middle Eastern countries, funded by the Department of State as part of an effort to extend American cultural influence overseas. The original fieldwork had been carried out under the supervision of the Bureau of Applied Social Research of Columbia University in the early 1950s. With his secondary analysis, Lerner aimed at understanding how the peoples of the Middle East might "modernize traditional lifeways that no longer 'work[ed]' to their own satisfaction." He mainly saw modernization as a psychological process: being modern meant "learning to dream," becoming "empathic" and "accustomed to change," apprehending the importance of having personal opinions, and participating in the political and cultural life of the nation. Thanks to technological progress and the diffusion of the mass media, seen as "mobility multipliers," the people of the Middle East could finally join modernity—that is, an ideal, perfected version of American society.[28]

The study presented six case studies: Lebanon and Turkey as successfully modernized nations, Jordan and Iran as problematic countries, and Egypt and Syria as societies caught between two worlds. Religion appeared as either an impediment to full modernization or a political tool for mobilizing the masses. Lerner also argued against the existence of Islam as a distinct, identifiable civilization and considered conflicting versions of the Islamic faith as residual, unimportant explanatory factors. In fact, he saw no connection between a weak, almost nonexistent, "Muslim world" and the abstract symbolism needed to meet the challenges of modernization. It is no wonder, then, that *The Passing* contained one of the clearest formulations of the marriage of structural determinism and unilinear evolution that Bellah opposed in his work: "The model of modernization follows an autonomous historical logic," wrote Lerner, "each phase tends to generate the next phase by some mechanism which operates independently of cultural and doctrinal variations."[29]

Although one would expect differences in style and complexity between a weighty tome and a twenty-five-page essay, "The Well of the Past" still reads as remarkably fresh and dynamic compared with *The Passing*. Building on ideas developed in other pieces of work, Bob could confidently write about modernization, the Middle East, and Islam, whilst avoiding excessive objectification. Every actor, group, or culture was an ambivalent, ever-changing subject: Following the lead of Wilfred Cantwell Smith, for example, Bellah described the Arabs as characterized by both a fascination for modernity *and* a deep resentment of the West. Contrary to Lerner's judgment, Egypt showed "a refreshingly discordant collection of ideas," a creative diversity of opinions that Bob had not found in Lebanon or Turkey. As for contemporary Islam, he wrote of secular Muslims who lived religion as a form of personal ethics and praised what he called the Muslim "feeling for the freedom of the individual" as a protection against attempts at creating despotic rule.[30]

In fact, it was when writing of Abrahamic religions that Bob Bellah was at his best in turning commonplace distinctions on their feet—especially at a time when Protestant Neo-orthodoxy and Cold War concerns converged on the idea of a "Judeo-Christian tradition." Describing his experience of biblical sites, Bellah worked out a complex interpretation of the contradictory meaning of images, practices, and objects that unearthed the ambivalent connections of the elements of Near Eastern culture. Bob's Presbyterian sensibility, reinforced by his occasional attendance of Quaker meetings in Cambridge, was horrified by the places of Christian worship. In the Church of the Holy Sepulchre, and even more in the Church of Nativity in Bethlehem, he found a repulsing aesthetic of "formless monstrosity" that was miles away from his idea of what an expression of "the New Testament feeling" should look like. In his understanding, the appearance of holy places was related to a major evolutionary rift, that between idolatry and Semitic monotheism. Abstracting this distinction from linear chronology, Bob gave it a symbolic and genealogical form: the "light of Israel" was carried on by Islam, while Christians were the heathens. As Bob had experienced it in the Holy Land, Christianity was a "backwards culture" with respect to the radical monotheism shared by Islam and Judaism.[31]

More interestingly, Bellah refrained from using Max Weber's depiction of Roman Catholicism as "magic" to indicate Protestantism as a purer Christianity. Rather, he took from "Religion in the Process of Cultural Differentiation" the idea of two alternative evolutionary paths: the one that generated Islam, starting from the Babylonian Empire through the mediation of Israel, and the other going from the Egyptian Empire to Western modernity through Greek rationality. Independent at first sight, the two paths intersected not only in Christianity as an encounter of Jewish law and the Greek mind, but also in the identification of contemporary Judaism with Hellenism—the bête noir of Neo-orthodoxy. Using evocative images in lieu of scientific arguments, in a few pages Bellah reworked the web of historical and symbolical connections between Abrahamic cultures—in no other writing of the period had he been so oriented toward a critical reading of religious signs and meanings.[32]

At the end of 1959 it was pretty clear that Bellah was infinitely more interested in culture and history than were his fellow modernization theorists.
While the latter saw tradition as the antithesis of progress, he found himself
continuously "slipping deep into the well of the past" and its amazing complexity. Staring at the Giza pyramids, the Dura Europos synagogue, or the immense court of the Ibn Tulun mosque, Bob told of a continuity of historical
time that came close to a revelation. The past was a fresh, inexhaustible source
of living symbols, where every step of a complex and discontinuous evolutionary sequence—Ancient Egypt and Mesopotamia, Israel, Hellenism, early
Christianity, and Islam, as well as Western, Asian, and Soviet modernities—
was profoundly connected to every other in a truly mysterious relation. All
Bellah's subsequent work would be marked by an increasing engagement with
the past as a crucial factor for assessing modernization and its peculiar problems of meaning. Moreover, as anticipated at the end of the first version of
"The Well of the Past," Bellah now embraced a decidedly cosmopolitan position: "A sense of mine and thine can never be entirely lost in the realm of
culture," he wrote. "But the sense in which the Parthenon or the Sistine Ceiling
are, as Americans, ours, is already so broad that it is easy for us to imagine the
modern Arab or Japanese feeling they are also theirs. Of course they are. For
the strands are crossing. . . . This is not to say," he concluded, "that there are no
problems of conflicts, or that any easy synthesis is likely to emerge. But it is
clear that no culture can ever look at itself again in self-complacent certainty
as to its unique significance in the life of men."[33]

Due to a change of editorial policy at the *Atlantic Monthly*, "The Well of the
Past" remained unpublished, and Bob's trip to the Middle East quickly faded
from memory as he and Melanie started to set things up for the birth of their
third child. In fact, a small trace of those lost weeks of lonely wandering soon
became part of family culture. On the very first evening of Bob's return from
the trip, as he was "laying down the law" with his family in quite a patriarchal
way, Jenny, who was not even three at the time, yelled out what would soon
become an oft-repeated slogan of resistance against one piece of the past that
Melanie and the girls could easily do without: "Back to Egypt, Daddy!"[34]

III

Abigail "Abby" Bellah was born on September 23, 1959. Although she was a
quiet, serene baby, her appearance caused a twist in the symbiotic relationship
between motherly Tammy and her fiery little sister Jenny, and put their

mother's manic quest for perfectionism at risk. While Melanie learned how to juggle three children of assorted ages and temperaments, Bob moved his study to the third floor to make space for the new baby. Having relocated his office at Andover Hall, he now worked just a five-minute walk from Gorham Street, and could eat lunch with his family several times a week and then stay to study or to help Melanie. With three beautiful daughters, a smart and gorgeous wife, and a job at the very place he called home, only one thing stood between Bob and the full realization of his professional and personal dreams—the Pacific Ocean. For ten years now, Japan had been much more than an object of study: it had been a reverie, a symbol, and sometimes a nightmare. From Elisséeff to Reischauer, from Fairbank to Craig, many people had shared with him stories about the Land of the Rising Sun. It was time to turn their narratives into a real, lived experience.[35]

With the help of Kishimoto Hideo, a professor at Tokyo University he had met at Harvard, Bellah obtained an invitation from Kokugakuin University, a major center for the training of Shintoist priests and one of the first private institutions to be granted the status of university by the Japanese government. After a Fulbright grant and funds from the Harvard-Yenching Institute were secured, in the spring of 1960 the die was cast. In July Bob, Melanie, and their three daughters finally landed in Tokyo, where they found a Japanese-style house complete with tatami floors and futon beds in the neighborhood of Hanazono-chō, not far from the Shinijuku Gyoen Park and the Ni-chōme and Kabukichō entertainment districts. While Tammy and Jenny attended the American Air Force school, Abby stayed home with Melanie and Fusako-San, a nineteen-year-old maid hired to help the Bellahs with the girls and with their spoken Japanese. The fall of 1960 was a time of joyous immersion in a culture that Melanie and Bob had long been dreaming about: they visited every corner of Tokyo and Melanie bought a number of traditional kimonos, which she wore with ease and grace. Late in October the couple visited the old capitals of Kyoto and Nara on their first solo trip after six years of uninterrupted parenting.[36]

Eight years had passed since Bellah had been forced to give up his field-work, and Japan was in the midst of a profound social and political crisis. Its unequivocal alignment with the "Free World" and the emergence of the conservative bloc of big business, state bureaucracy, and the Liberal Democratic Party had gone hand in hand with a booming economy and an emerging culture of mass consumption. After the Communist Party had lost its appeal in the early 1950s, the opposition to the reactionary "1955 system" was represented by the Socialist Party, the Sōhyō union confederation, and sparse groups of intellectuals. When Bellah arrived in Tokyo, a wave of massive demonstrations against the renewal of the Treaty of Mutual Cooperation and Security, signed by the United States and Japan in 1951, had just exhausted its cycle. With his calling to the "Spirit of August 15, 1945," Maruyama Masao had been at the forefront of the protest, whose main achievement was the ousting of Kishi Nobusuke's cabinet on July 19, 1960. In a letter to Parsons, Bellah interpreted the upheaval as an expression of "the frustration of the intellectuals with a government which seems to have a permanent control of the diet but to which they are utterly opposed." What he saw around him was a resurgence of "a real nostalgia for the days when Japan was a major power in the world." His tone swung between preoccupied and patronizing: "At any rate it is clear that the hundred year buildup of the 'Japanese spirit' did not just die on August 15, 1945. It is still around and gets expressed in funny ways."[37]

Bellah was going to dedicate his sabbatical to a book on the history of Japanese modernization based on the long paper written with Albert Craig. He could count on a generous stipend, two research assistants, three language teachers, and the advice of a number of Japanese colleagues, of whom Kishimoto and Maruyama were the most eminent. Among his peers, Bellah enjoyed long talks with sociologist Yanagawa Keiichi, who would later spend a year in Cambridge as a fellow of the Harvard-Yenching Institute, and historian Ikado Fujio, a former student at the University of Chicago who was now employed by the Religious Affairs Section of the Ministry of Education. For all his obsession with Japan, however, Bob remained strongly connected to the United States, in more than one sense. He was often visited by his colleagues—Fairbank, Levy, Reischauer, and Benjamin Schwartz, among others—and his exchanges with Parsons and Slater on scholarly and academic matters remained frequent. Glock pressed him to complete his paper on American religion, a task Bellah found "horribly difficult" to come to terms with. As a Fulbright exchange scholar he was also repeatedly requested to give public talks on the political and cultural relationships between the two allied countries.[38]

Discussing Calvinism and Arminianism with Parsons while polishing the umpteenth version of the Glock paper and drafting the notes for a conference on the first Roman Catholic president of the United States forced Bob to think about the relation between religion and politics in a regime of constitutional separation. In Cambridge such reflections would have been routine scholarly work. Contextualized in a mysterious country where the foreigner was "seldom allowed to forget that he is not Japanese," they had the effect of making Bellah fully conscious of his own Americanism.[39] As shown by the public

FIGURE 5.2. The Bellahs in Japan, 1960–1961. (RBPP)

lectures given at the International Christian University in the spring of 1961, this growing awareness had a profound impact on Bob's outlook. Speaking to an attentive audience of Japanese students and professors, Bellah unfolded a radical interpretation of his homeland as a "*Gesellschaft* society": "I think in America modernization goes all the way down to the roots," he said, "because there is not anything else in America and never was. It is not surface; it is the whole structure, the whole substance of the society itself."[40] In the absence of pre-existing traditions, the founders had created "the only large scale example" of a society built on "the fundamental motives of left-wing Protestantism."[41] Generalized and secularized, the Puritan ethic still constituted the basis of a peculiar mixture of rationality, autonomy, and bureaucracy, which Bellah called, using a Parsonian idiom, "institutionalized individualism."[42]

While its theoretical underpinnings remained unaltered, Bob's position was becoming more and more radical: if American modernity depended on the unique cultural premises of Calvinism, then an almost unbridgeable gap divided it from Japan and other Asian societies. Freed from the straitjacket of Parsons's pattern variables, Bellah could now see that what America and Japan shared was dwarfed by what they did not: a transcendental point of view from which a critique of existing institutions could be issued. In its opposition to "particularism," "universalism" was a poor ersatz for the breakthrough achieved in the encounter of Mosaic religion and Greek philosophy. Immersed as they were in the cosmological myth of an inner connection between nature, society, and the individual, East Asian cultures were not equipped to distinguish "is" from "ought," and thus generate modernity; the only real source of transcendence in Asia—Indian and Chinese Buddhism—had been "submerged" by indigenous traditions at the time of its arrival in Japan. A meaningful response to moderniza-tion could emerge only from a painful process of (re)appropriation of the most radical principles of Buddhism and Western (that is, Christian) culture.

Given these premises, it is not surprising that Bellah turned to the intel-lectual history of the Taishō and Shōwa periods as an inexhaustible repository of failed attempts at "gradually creating a new cultural tradition for Japan" in the face of modernization. In fact, he began focusing on the work, to which Yanagawa Keiichi had introduced him, of a small number of thinkers: historian Ienaga Saburo, whom Bob repeatedly met in Tokyo, and philosophers Miki Kiyoshi and Watsuji Tetsuro. Ienaga's work on the logic of negation and his writings on Shōtoku Taishi and Uchimura Kanzō were illustrative of the titanic difficulties met by Western-educated Japanese scholars in their search for a universalistic ground. The same conundrum emerged from the work of Wat-suji: an authority on European existentialism who had studied with Martin Heidegger in Germany, he had nonetheless campaigned for what he called "the Way of Reverence for the Emperor."[43] Watsuji's postwar reappraisal of his position, according to which Japan should become a "good group member" of the international community, had not changed the basic structure of his think-ing: in fact, he "never finds another standard of value which can transcend the emperor. The fusion of Japan, emperor, society, and individual, which he had held from the early 1920s as the highest good," concluded Bellah, "remained at the core of his thought."[44]

The contrast between Japanese and Western culture could not be sharper. In the 1890s Émile Durkheim had taught that the sacredness of the nation depended on the degree to which it embodied an abstract "ideal of humanity." As Bob would write in a 1962 add-on to his lectures at the International Chris-tian University, the moral value of American experience entirely depended on the upholding of "certain universal principles." His own "loyalty" and appre-ciation of the United States were contingent on the adherence, on the part of his country, to those (modern and revolutionary) values. In a different yet similar way, John F. Kennedy had reasserted the belief that in America "the ultimate sovereignty has been attributed to God," and thus that "the will of the people is not itself the criterion of right and wrong." In a year or so, Bellah would go so far as to scorn any attempt to find such a thing in East Asian cultures: "We are forced to take seriously Weber's argument for the special significance of Protestantism." At the same time, however, he drew a confident parallel between America and Pericles's Athens, according to which the United States could be seen as "the educator of the modern world." It was not by chance that at the end of May 1961 an old teacher and now friend of Bellah who strongly subscribed to both the open vistas of the New Frontier and the ideal of America as a role model for the rest of the world, Edwin O. Reischauer, arrived in Tokyo as the new ambassador to Japan.[45]

6

Time to Leave

CAMBRIDGE, 1961–1967

ON SEPTEMBER 1, 1961, the Bellahs were back in Cambridge. The final balance of their year abroad was decidedly positive. The girls were happy to be home again, but had truly enjoyed their time in Tokyo. Melanie now spoke decent Japanese and could perform a number of traditional dances with some ability. She also came home with unexpected news: in the spring she would give birth to her fourth child. Bob had completed a two-year cycle that had brought him into direct contact with the societies to which he was to devote his scholarly life, and he had been both changed and reaffirmed by his experiences. The Middle Eastern fiasco and his ambivalent days in Japan brought Bellah's Americanism to the surface. At the same time, he found the deepest value of being an American in the possibility of drawing on a revolutionary tradition of criticism that made sure that the nation could always be subjected to higher ethical standards. As he wrote to his friend David Schneider in Chicago, he did believe in God and progress, "but more in God than in progress." Apart from this confident regeneration of his political and moral outlook, another major change had occurred while he was in Tokyo: as soon as he got to Harvard, Bellah took up his duties as an associate professor of sociology and regional studies.[1]

Negotiations on Bellah's tenure had begun early in 1961, one and a half years before the end of his lectureship. Piece by piece, Parsons had assembled a formidable team of Harvard notables to plead the cause of his protégé before the Corporation. Not that Bob was desperate to get a job: he had been offered an associate professorship by the Department of Anthropology and Sociology at the University of California, Los Angeles, where another of Parsons's best students, Harold Garfinkel, was working on a rather mysterious object named

87

"ethnomethodology"; by the East Asian Institute and the Department of Sociology of Columbia University; and by the University of Michigan, home of the oldest interdisciplinary center of Japanese studies in North America. As the icing on the cake, in January 1961 Geertz and Shils offered him a position at the University of Chicago, where he could work with his old graduate school peer in the Committee for the Comparative Study of New Nations. Harvard still being Harvard, Bellah pledged that he would not consider any proposal before things had been settled in Cambridge.[2]

Parsons's attempts were a complete success. On May 24, 1961, his former student—the man he considered "a special modern variant of the older style of universal scholar"—wrote him a very emotional thank you note. Sixteen years after his first walk across the Yard, Robert Bellah had been just notified he had gotten tenure at Harvard. Now he was free to pursue his ambitious projects with the institutional support of the greatest university in the world, in full continuity with the work of his mentor: "I am also pleased that," he wrote, "as far as I am capable of continuing it, the tradition of sociology which you represent will continue at Harvard." From his new position he could clearly feel the burden of the words of Max Weber: "Was ich nicht mache, machen andere [What I don't do, others will do]."[3]

I

What had to be done, besides the careful study of individual cultures and societies, was nothing less than a comprehensive theory of social and cultural evolution—after all, in a letter sent to Pusey in January 1961, Parsons had gone so far as to write that as a general theorist Bellah was "probably *superior* . . . to Robert Merton." The traces of Bob's interest for social change were scattered all through his published and unpublished writings. Moreover, he saw evolutionism as the most important conceptual connection between the two cultural heroes he had inherited from Parsons: Max Weber and Émile Durkheim. In a paper written in 1958 after a full immersion in thousands of pages of untranslated material, Bob had shown the central importance of history for Durkheim to rebuke the allegations of a lack of interest in social change often addressed to structural-functionalism. While no sociological inquiry could claim to be truly scientific without comparing at least two societies over time, he added, meaningful analyses of social change could be issued only when "the facts compared [had] been carefully classified in terms of a systematic and theoretically relevant typology" of the kind that could be found only in Weber's work.[4]

But what did Bellah mean by "evolution"? In a letter to Schneider he defined evolutionism as a theory of societal differentiation, and distinguished it from the mere accumulation of historical facts, which he dubbed "gossip." Most modernization theorists shared a vague idea of unilinear evolution as an alternative to both the cyclical conception of history found in the work of Oswald Spengler and Arnold Toynbee and the idea that social change proceeded via sudden epochal breaks typical of revolutionary Marxism. This diffuse interest in evolutionism depended in part on the resurrection of another intellectual tradition, that of Herbert Spencer, to which Parsons himself had contributed with a preface to the 1961 edition of *The Study of Sociology*. Given his distance from the mainstream of modernization theory, Bellah was not attracted to Spencer. Rather, in order to find a sounder and firmer theoretical basis for evolutionism, in the spring of 1963 he convened a series of seminars with Talcott Parsons and Israeli sociologist Shmuel N. Eisenstadt, who had quite divergent ideas on social change and differentiation.[5]

The article inspired by their passionate exchanges, titled "Religious Evolution," was a summary of everything Bellah had done up to that moment. "Evolution" was defined as a general process "of increasing differentiation and complexity of organization," which made social systems more adaptable, and thus more autonomous, vis-à-vis their environment. Such a process was neither inevitable nor irreversible, and surely did not "follow any single particular course." Bob's refusal to equate evolution with progress was clear: although more-differentiated symbol systems, such as Christianity or Islam, produced "a much more complex relation" to the ultimate conditions of human existence, "everything already exists in some sense in the religious symbol system of the most primitive man." The essay also presented a typology of five stages, defined as "relatively stable crystallizations of roughly the same order of complexity along a number of different dimensions"—that is, religious symbols, actions, and organizations.[6]

The first two stages of religious evolution shared what Bellah had previously called the "natural worldview," or the "cosmological myth"—that is, the idea of a seamless continuity between man, nature, language, and society. In "primitive" religion, symbol systems based on free associations were enacted through participatory rituals to which the whole community contributed— examples were Dinka tribes or the Australian aboriginals studied by Durkheim and Marcel Mauss. Stage two, the "archaic" religion of ancient empires, was characterized by the emergence of social stratification and well-defined gods, often conceived as the ancestors of the ruling classes. Religious rituals evolved into codified worship and sacrifice administered by a sacerdotal class subordinated to political power. In stage three, "historic" religions were based on a radical process of de-mythologization of the world. Now the cosmos was seen as divided into two irreducible realms, mundane and transcendent, that could be reconciled only via the idea of individual "salvation." In Buddhism, Judaism, early Christianity, and Islam the quest for salvation encouraged the emergence of religious communities, which almost everywhere clashed with political elites because of their tendency to criticize existing social arrangements "in terms of standards that the political authorities could not finally control."[7]

The remaining two stages of religious evolution could be understood as a double movement of intensification and collapse of the epochal breakthrough effected by historic religions. Here Bellah's reflections on the peculiarity of the West induced by his travels in the Middle East and Japan resulted in a rather radical view of Protestantism. The fourth stage, "early modern" religion, coincided with the Reformation seen as a "congeries of related cases," in which the collapse of the hierarchies that previously structured both the transcendent and the empirical world led to a profound redefinition of religious symbols, action, and institutions. Salvation became an individual quest that no longer required collective structures, as the intimacy of the relation between God and the believer sanctified everyday life and inner states at the expense of specific communal ritual forms. Social stratification was redefined according to a hierarchy where the elected led voluntarily constituted religious congregations aimed at creating the Kingdom of God on earth.[8]

A fifth stage, "modern" religion, emerged in the eighteenth century as a radical outcome of the Protestant Reformation. The collapse of the rift between transcendence and the mundane world was not followed by the restoration of the unified cosmos of "primitive" religion, but rather by "an infinitely multiplex" world in which life became "an infinite possibility thing." After Immanuel Kant, religion had become not only an intrinsic dimension of the human condition, but also *the* place of individual and collective self-reflexivity. Modern men and women saw the world as the ever-changing scene where their radical, urgent, and continuous questioning took place. The search for ultimate meaning was not going to end: "The analysis of modern man as secular, materialistic, dehumanized and in the deepest sense areligious," Bellah wrote, merging history, social theory, and his own experience, "seems to me fundamentally misguided, for such a judgment is based on standards that cannot adequately gauge the modern temper."[9]

In fact, at the center of modernity stood the self and its uninterrupted re-constitution into ever-newer forms, the emergence of a multidimensional identity capable of doing and redoing itself and the world through symbolic action: "Rather than interpreting these trends as significant of indifference and secularization," wrote Bellah with unusual conviction, "I see in them the increasing acceptance of the notion that each individual must work out his own ultimate solution and the most the church can do is provide him a favorable environment for doing so, without imposing on him a prefabricated set of answers." Such a conclusion sounded too emotional to be merely scholarly work—it was not. Many years after Robert Bellah had lost the sullen God of Presbyterian Sunday school, Paul Tillich had convinced him that true faith was not a "belief in the unbelievable," but rather a mature, reflexive way to relate to one's ultimate concerns. In the quest to give his religious experience an institutional anchorage, Bob had attended the Episcopal Church and the Quakers, but had left both with a profound sense of disconnection. At around the same time, the birth of Harriet "Hally" Bellah on March 1, 1962, had forever laid to rest his wish to have a son, and that had somehow left his final confrontation with the death of his father—"the most poignant moment" in a man's life—in a state of ominous suspension.[10]

II

As a touch of grace in history, a chance for redemption presented itself at the time of sending "Religious Evolution" for publication, as Harvard University accepted Bellah's request to spend the 1964–1965 academic year at the Center for Advanced Studies in the Behavioral Sciences. Bob had been offered the fellowship twice: in 1957, when he had declined to accept his first job at Harvard, and again in 1960, a couple of weeks before leaving for Japan. To make up for these failed opportunities, in December 1962 he wrote to Preston S. Cutler, the center's assistant director, to propose himself as a fellow for the 1964–1965 academic year, a suggestion that was promptly accepted.[11]

Looking for some additional money to support the relocation and expenses of his family of six, in September 1963 Bellah unsuccessfully submitted to the National Institute of Mental Health and the National Science Foundation a research project centered on the study of the cultural and ideological aspects of Japanese modernization in comparative perspective. In fact, wrapping up the book on modern Japanese intellectuals he had started to put together in Tokyo was not his only objective. In Bob's ambitious plan, most of his year in

Palo Alto would be devoted to writing a master treatise, tentatively titled *A Theory of Religion*. Not only would the volume mark his coming of age as a scholar and, hopefully, consecrate him as the premier theoretical sociologist of his generation, it was also going to be the cornerstone of the new cross-disciplinary PhD program in religious studies that Bellah was devising with Wilfred Cantwell Smith. With Slater's retirement approaching, Smith had been called to Harvard as the next director of the Center for the Study of World Religions, and Bob saw his arrival as the first step toward the creation of an independent Department of Religion. As the Levellers had done twenty years earlier, Bellah and Smith would try to give an institutional home to a wide-ranging interdisciplinary project. And as Parsons had done fifteen years earlier, Bob set up to write a theoretical treatise aimed at acquiring a canonical status in the new program. It was not by chance that his former teacher wished him "to make the most of [his] grand opportunity at the [Palo Alto] Center": Bob's "big book" was going to fill a real theoretical gap and function as a bridge between social scientists and humanists.[12]

Once in Palo Alto, the Bellahs rented a big house in Alvarado Row, right on the Stanford campus. The girls truly enjoyed the bike rides, the weather, and the relaxed atmosphere of the West Coast, while Melanie could not believe she was back where she had spent her college days—and this time, she was with Bob! At the Center for Advanced Study, Bellah was assigned office number forty-five; together with the keys came a list of its previous occupants, among which were the father of econometrics Jacob Marshack, economic historian David S. Landes, philosopher of science Ernest Nagel, and sociologists Alvin W. Gouldner, Philip Selznick, and Harold L. Wilensky.

In spite of the pleasant weather, the occasional teach-in against the war in Vietnam, and the interesting conversations he had with Erik H. Erikson, Theodore Mills, Norman O. Brown, Dell Hymes, Buzz Zeldtich, and Neil Smelser, Bellah's sabbatical turned out to be rather unproductive.[13] As anticipated in the center's booklet, fellows would enjoy some "much needed time for contemplation, but also the *Sturm und Drang* of conflict and creation; the discovery of colleagues, and also the discovery of self." For scholars used to the frantic rat race of a top academic department, this free-ranging "intellectual stocktaking" might have its drawbacks—it could bring about "confusion as well as clarity, doubt as well as certainty." These last words were almost prophetic. Hampered by a chaotic reading schedule and distracted by seminars and other commitments, Bellah was unable to draft more than a short preface and a couple of pages of *A Theory of Religion*. Much of his attention was absorbed by the epilogue to a forthcoming volume on religion and modernization in Asia and an entry on the sociology of religion for the *International Encyclopedia of the Social Sciences*, which he considered his major theoretical writing after "Religious Evolution."[14]

In this new paper, Bellah distinguished between rationalistic attempts to demonstrate the falsity of religion and the "irrationalist" tendency to study it as a completely irreducible phenomenon. In their opposition, the two traditions agreed in rejecting the need for theory: while rationalists tried to explain away religion, irrationalists defended its particular nature, but refused explanations. Combining cybernetics with the work of Weber, Freud, and Durkheim, Bellah theorized symbols as control mechanisms that actors interpreted using internalized cultural models, which in turn made human agency into a purposive, autonomous practice. It was thus possible to integrate into social science "the contributions of the humanistic disciplines without abandoning an essentially scientific approach." Erikson's *Young Man Luther*, Kenneth Burke's *Rhetoric of Religion*, and Philip Slater's *Microcosm* were indicated as examples of this new understanding of religion.

A number of critical responses from Burke, Clifford Geertz, and Eli Sagan persuaded Bellah that his theory of religion still lacked a viable assessment of symbol systems: How did religious symbols influence the human psyche or society? How could human beings come directly into contact with the reality represented by and through religious symbols? And how might scholars describe and interpret those relationships from a scientific point of view? In his ongoing conversation with his intellectual partners, Bob was developing a new point of view on religious phenomena, but the end product was still not in sight. His unrest, however, was far from being a purely intellectual matter—it also had professional and personal sides that would soon push him to a radical change.[15]

III

Upon his return from Stanford, Bellah worked closely with Wilfred Cantwell Smith to establish an autonomous Department of Religion at Harvard. Until that moment he had enjoyed multiple affiliations, nurturing his personal inclination to ignore disciplinary boundaries. Now he was trying to create a novel cross-disciplinary venue for the study of religion, one in which scholars could freely collaborate irrespective of their scientific, national, and denominational origins. In this regard, the accord between the two scholars was almost perfect. Responding to a letter in which Bob praised his new book, *The Meaning and End of Religion*, Smith declared his allegiance to a cross-disciplinary project that embraced not only the view of religion as a legitimate academic partner of the humanities—an idea enshrined in Clyde A. Holbrook's influential *Religion: A Humanistic Field*, published in 1963—but also the beginning of the détente between religion and the social sciences. "I have gone through what might almost be regarded in a mild way as *a kind of conversion experience*," wrote Smith, "and now regard myself as a social scientist. . . . So far as I personally am concerned, this particular battle is over—and this particular dichotomy obsolete." Bellah was glad to acknowledge their convergence, and underlined the need to supplement the inductive attitude typical of humanistic scholars with a "systematic deductive approach." He was so adamant about his plan that in June 1965, commenting Alex Inkeles's attempt to dismantle the Department of Social Relations, he told Parsons that he was "tempted to secede [himself] into a new Dept. of Religion."[16]

Bellah's return from Stanford also brought about an apparently minor change in the organization of his everyday life. After his year in Japan, he had set up his office at the so-called "God motel" of the Center for the Study of World Religions, quite distant from Emerson Hall, where Parsons and the Social Relations administration were housed. In 1964 the whole department was reunited in the new Center for the Behavioral Sciences, a fifteen-story white skyscraper designed by Minoru Yamasaki, the Japanese American architect who would later create the World Trade Center towers in New York City. Although the new building was just five hundred yards from World Religions, Bob had to move there along with his colleagues—his new office being on the fifth floor, contiguous with those assigned to Florence Kluckhohn and psychiatrist John P. Spiegel. In spite of the great view he had from his corner windows, in a handful of months he soon learned to hate William James Hall, which he called "something of a madhouse."[17]

The new situation and the impossibility of getting any work done pushed Bellah to think of leaving his alma mater—the first time he seriously considered such an option. Finding a job had never been a problem, and soon he received tempting offers from Michigan and Chicago. In the fall of 1965 Bob and Melanie visited Ann Arbor, but Chicago proved to be more attractive: in a letter to demographer Nathan Keyfitz, Bellah expressed his interest for the University of Chicago Lab School system and listed a number of people who might help to boost his cross-disciplinary plans: "In addition to my talk with you and with whatever administrative officers you think appropriate," he wrote, "I would also like to talk to Professors [Morris] Janowitz and Shils in sociology, Schneider and [Lloyd] Fallers in Anthropology (I understand Cliff Geertz is away), Ho [Ping-Ti] and [Edwin] McClellan in East Asian Studies and [Joseph] Kitagawa in religion."[18]

After Bellah mentioned these offers to his Harvard colleagues, a number of senior staff began to speak with hyperbole of his career at Harvard and academic prowess. In a letter to Parsons, David Riesman called Bob "the ablest, most dedicated, most disinterested, and most universal scholar in the whole university." And to Ezra Vogel and Albert Craig on November 3, 1966, he described Bellah as "our strongest colleague in every sense: as an intellectual, and in terms of erudition and dedication without peer, to say that I reverence him would not be too strong." Parsons's praise of his former student was no less enthusiastic. Both suggested to the Corporation that a full professorship might help in keeping Bellah at Harvard.[19]

In fact, while he was considering academic offers, Bob was also thinking about something completely different—something he did not really care about but that, in the end, would force him to give his career and his life a radical twist he had neither imagined nor desired.

IV

In mid-April 1965, historian Stephen R. Graubard had sent Bellah a letter announcing the convocation of a conference on American religion at the American Academy of Arts and Sciences that October. As the editor of *Daedalus*, the prestigious cross-disciplinary journal published by the academy since 1958, Graubard had organized the conference as the first step toward the publication of a wide-ranging monograph issue on the state and the promise of religion in America. With some hesitation—he mainly saw himself as a specialist on Japan—Bellah accepted the invitation to draft a short memorandum to start the discussion. His drawers were full of unpublished material on the United States, and he quickly assembled the paper combining a summary of the latest version of the Glock chapter with the lecture on John F. Kennedy's inaugural address delivered in Japan in 1961.[20]

The first part of "Heritage and Choice in American Religion" was a catalog of typical Bellah themes—the relationship between meaning and modernization, the importance of the past as a repository of living symbols, and the societal and cultural strains created by technological change. As he had done in previous papers, Bob argued that those who saw Protestantism as a prisoner of the American way of life were just ignoring the historical record: "Before we accept too quickly the critical conclusion that religion in America has been made captive by an alien culture or has been completely 'privatized,'" he wrote, "we should remember to how great an extent that culture is itself a product of the religious tradition and how important for the 'public' sectors of life a stable private sector can be."[21]

To illustrate the point, Bellah shifted to the public dimension of American religious heritage, emphasizing the abstract, inclusive vocabulary used by John Fitzgerald Kennedy when speaking of God during his inaugural. Far from being a violation of the constitutional separation of church and state, Kennedy's words had translated one of America's oldest cultural themes into a language that could be shared by all his fellow citizens. The major difference between the 1961 conference and "Heritage and Choice" was the use in the latter of Rousseau's expression "civil religion" rather than the "religious dimension in political life"—what had been a simple periphrasis was now labeled with a classical phrase. In section three, Bellah pointed to two contemporary cleavages: that between the secularized elites and the religious population, and that between engaged clergymen and passive churchgoers. Here he stood on the side of the "good (repressed) bourgeois": since it was not possible to make the middle class abandon its "irrational anxieties" for the future, Bellah suggested a mobilization of religious heritage, in its private and public dimensions, to elicit a powerful and positive response from "the majority middle strata of the society."[22]

At the conference, this talk of "civil religion" aroused much interest—David Riesman praised the paper and Talcott Parsons immediately incorporated Bob's thesis and vocabulary into his own writings. A second conference on American religion sponsored by the academy and the Church Society for College Work was scheduled for May 14–15, 1966, with Parsons, Harvey Cox, Martin E. Marty, Michael Novak, Daniel Callahan, and Milton Himmelfarb among its participants. In reworking his memorandum, Bellah focused on civil religion, strengthening his thesis and widening the historical perspective. The new paper, "Civil Religion in America," fully reproduced the Kennedy section from "Heritage and Choice," but added new segments on other presidents, the Civil War, and the future of civil religion. "There actually exists alongside of and rather clearly differentiated from the churches," wrote Bob at the very beginning of the paper, "an elaborate and well-institutionalized civil religion in America. This article argues not only that there is such a thing, but also that this religion, or perhaps better, this religious dimension, has its own seriousness and integrity and requires the same care in understanding that any other religion does."[23]

In Bellah's narrative, the constitutional separation of church and state had not hindered the rise of "certain common elements of religious orientation" that had "played a crucial role in the development of American institutions and still [provided] a religious dimension for the whole fabric of American life." Civil religion had taken on its distinctive form during two pivotal moments: the Revolution and the Civil War. While the original American civil religion was distinctively vetero-testamentary, the Civil War had introduced "a new theme of death, sacrifice and rebirth . . . symbolized in the life and death of Lincoln." Bellah saw the late 1960s as a "third time of trial," as America took on the responsibility of leading a world of emerging nations looking for freedom, equality, and happiness. Echoing the words of Henry David Thoreau—"I would remind my countrymen that they are men first, and Americans at the late and convenient hour"—Bob concluded with a deeply prophetic tone: "As Americans, we have been well favored in the world, but it is as men that we will be judged."[24]

Contrary to Bellah's claims, the theme was far from new. A Durkheimian framework to interpret religion in America had been employed in the early 1950s by Robin M. Williams Jr. and Lloyd Warner, whereas the idea of a general "American religion" had been advanced by, among others, Parsons and Seymour Martin Lipset, a well-known political sociologist who had taught at Columbia, Berkeley, and Harvard. What Bob called "American civil religion," however, was neither a generic system of ethics nor Christianity in disguise. Rather, it was an original interpretation of historical events in the light of a special relation between the American people and a transcendent God. "The civil religion at its best," he wrote, "is a genuine apprehension of universal and transcendent religious reality as seen in or, one could almost say, as *revealed through* the experience of the American people." A few years earlier, the idea of a special covenant between God and the United States had been the target of sociologist Will Herberg's successful *Protestant, Catholic, Jew.* Reflecting on the mid-1950s religious boom, Herberg spoke of the "sanctification of the American way of life" as a form of idolatry and of "civic [*sic*] religion" as a consolatory practice: "In this kind of religion it is not man who serves God, but God who is mobilized and made to serve man and his purposes. . . . God is conceived as man's 'omnipotent servant.'" The diagnosis was also paraphrased by Martin E. Marty in *The New Shape of American Religion,* where God appeared as a "comforting and jolly good fellow."[25]

Bellah knew of these studies, but decided to focus on another side of civil religion, the concern that "America be a society as perfectly in accord with the will of God as men can make it." Kennedy's inaugural address indicated *prophetic* civil religion as *the* perspective from which the nation and its leaders could be judged according to the standards of a truly religious morality. At the same time, the American civil religion was "well-institutionalized": it was a text by the nation about the nation interpreted by those who led the nation—a feature that differentiated Bellah's critical, and thus potentially disruptive, idea of civil religion from what Herberg and Marty saw as a sanctification of the American way of life. As for the relationship between the polity, the churches, and the civil religion, in the United States the latter "was able to build up without any bitter struggle with the church powerful symbols of national solidarity and to mobilize deep levels of personal motivation for the attainment of national goals."[26]

Bellah's papers showed both similarities to and differences from his previous work. On the side of continuities, the revolutionary theme of the existence of a higher set of religious values by means of which ordinary national political and social life could, and should, be judged related to Bob's work on Japanese intellectuals and the gap between Western transcendental criticism and Asian cosmological unity. The new paper also echoed his presentation at the 1965 annual meeting of the rechristened American Sociological Association, published in 1968 as "Meaning and Modernization" but written together with "Heritage and Choice." There, the interplay between social change and the need to integrate a viable conception of identity was singled out as a major problem of modernization, one that was not easily solved by any existing religion: "Let me say that 'success' in modernization is always relative and transient," Bellah argued, "because modernization itself is so endlessly subversive of every fixed position, no matter how great an achievement it may have originally been. There are no grounds for complacency that any society has in any final sense 'solved' the problems of meaning and modernization."[27]

The most striking novelty of the *Daedalus* paper was to be found in the attempt to develop a new, jargon-free writing style that could speak to the educated public as well as to academics—if Bellah wanted his bleak critique of American foreign policy, from the Mexican-American War to the ongoing confrontation in Vietnam, to reach a wide, general audience he had to leave Parsons's abstruse language behind. From a historical point of view, the complex relation between religion and politics sketched in "Civil Religion in America" was nowhere to be found in the various versions of the "Glock

paper" of the mid-1950s. At that time, Bellah had credited the Revolution and
the founding of the republic to "secular movements," and had explained the
insertion of the phrase "under God" in the Pledge of Allegiance as a mere
symptom of the postwar religious revival, with no hint at deeper cultural
themes. In general, Bob's increasingly evident interest in the stratified nature
of symbols and his firm belief in the religiosity of all humans called for a
"thicker" understanding of culture that went far beyond Parsons's formal grids
and schemes, and more in the direction of the theory of cultural systems elaborated by Clifford Geertz since the mid-1950s.[28]

V

Contrary to what Talcott Parsons had hoped, the promotion to full professor
was not enough to bring Bellah's frustrations to an end. All of a sudden he felt
that his twenty-year association with Harvard was hindering his intellectual
development and economic possibilities. In particular, Bob was not happy
with his salary. Earning around $17,000 a year, Bellah saw consummate strate-
gists such as Neil Smelser and Seymour Lipset play with offers from different
universities to get a constant flow of new benefits and promotions, and felt
unable to do the same while staying at Harvard. On the intellectual side, he
voiced his strong doubts on the direction taken by Middle Eastern studies after
Gibb's departure in 1964, and although he was growing pessimistic about the
prospect of having a Department of Religion at Harvard he was still convinced
that such an environment would be the best venue to nurture a new breed of
discipline-blind scholars. Additional stress came from teaching, to the point
that Bellah often had nightmarish daydreams about being eaten alive by his
voracious graduate and undergraduate students.[29]

As the last straw, at around the same time he discovered that as soon as he
crossed the borders of his habitual circles his association with Parsons might
become a source of embarrassment. During an informal seminar in Cape Cod,
the famed Canadian sociologist Erving Goffman recounted the difficulties of
getting ahead in the academic profession: how one had to constantly compete
with others to get material published, speak at meetings, and so on. As Bellah
objected that he had never had to go through any of that, Goffman gave him a
grim look and said out loud: "Bob, you didn't *have* to. You were Talcott's fair
haired boy. You never had to compete for anything." Goffman had been rude,
but Bellah knew he was right.[30] Would he accept to remain "Parsons' best
student" forever or would he try to find his own place in the intellectual field?

In the spring of 1966 Bob was approached by sociologist Reinhard Bendix, who brought him a proposal from the University of California at Berkeley: a raise in salary, a reduced teaching load via a Ford Professorship, and the chair of the Center for Japanese and Korean Studies. The Berkeley Department of Sociology and Social Institutions had been established only in 1946 under the chairmanship of Edward W. Strong. Already the home to social science heavyweights like Lipset, Philip Selznick, Robert Nisbet, and social psychologist Tamotsu Shibutani, in 1952 the department dropped the "Social Institutions" tag to welcome the arrival of its new chair from Chicago, Herbert Blumer. With a strong mandate from the campus chancellor, Clark Kerr, Blumer enacted an aggressive recruiting policy that brought to Berkeley stars like Goffman, Kingsley Davis, Leo Löwenthal, Nathan Glazer, and one of Bellah's old acquaintances, sociologist of religion Charles Y. Glock. A case of exceptional success was Neil J. Smelser, a former student at Social Relations who had co-authored *Economy and Society* with Talcott Parsons even before finishing his doctorate. In 1958 Smelser was hired as an assistant professor at Berkeley and rushed into full professorship in four years, editing the *American Sociological Review* and publishing a major book on collective behavior in the meantime. In the mid-1960s, he had been invited to take part in the campus administration during the Free Speech Movement revolt, an episode that, in spite of Smelser's goodwill and skillful maneuvering, created devastating tensions and centrifugal pressure among the sociologists.[31]

Bellah knew of the political discord among his colleagues, but he was also aware of the department's reputation and appreciated its generous offer, which also included a post of adjunct professor at the Berkeley Graduate Theological Union. Founded in 1962 as a consortium of existing Episcopalian, Lutheran, Baptist, and Presbyterian seminars of the Bay Area, the GTU had been created to pool resources and offer stronger graduate programs in biblical studies, ethics, history, and theology. By the time of Bendix's offer, the GTU had grown to include the Unitarian-Universalist seminar and, rather unusually, two Catholic schools. In particular, the Oakland Dominican Theologate had been accepted into the roster before the Second Vatican Council's decree on ecumenicism of November 21, 1964, thus indicating the truly open-ended nature of the communal endeavor. From Bellah's point of view, the GTU might become the perfect venue for continuing the dialogue with theologians and clergy he had started at the Harvard Divinity School and finding students interested in religion—something that the Sociology Department could not, on the whole, assure him.[32]

Academic lures, however, would have been pointless if the year in Palo Alto had not persuaded Melanie and Bob "that life was possible outside of Cambridge, Massachusetts. And not only possible, but even desirable." In particular, nostalgia and sunshine played a large part in the discussions about moving back to California, up to the point that David Riesman observed that he found the Bellahs' longing for the Golden State almost inexplicable. Frankly alarmed at the prospect of losing one of their best faculty members, Social Relations sociologists urged Franklin Ford to act; this time, however, the dean's response was much colder than it had previously been.[33]

To relieve the pressure of a difficult year, the Bellahs decided to spend the month of July in the rural quiet of Martha's Vineyard. Every day they would take long walks, swim together, and travel all over the island to try out its cuisine. Free from pressure, Bellah seemed to regain a measure of happiness and control. He focused his summer reading on analytic psychology with a double goal in mind: finding a good starting point for A Theory of Religion and reflecting upon an approaching milestone. "[Forty] as the turning point into the second half of life," he wrote on July 27, 1966, in the journal he had started to keep track of these epochal personal changes, "Jung: first half is growth of ego; second half is growth of self." Every day was the perfect balance of family life and personal study, with the occasional social gathering—most memorable was one evening at the house of Bob's former Adams housemate, film director Murray Lerner, who showed them a preview of the documentary he had shot at the 1965 Newport Folk Festival. When Bob, Melanie, and the girls got back home on July 31, 1966, "they swore that the next year they'd rent the same house for two months instead of one."[34]

Back in Cambridge, however, Bob found himself still dissatisfied. His diverse readings—Goethe, Stanner, Jeffers, Weinberg, and Thomas Mann—and his new musical crush on Bob Dylan could not stop the whirlwind of reveries and recriminations that occupied most of his time and prevented him getting any work done. Interested in the intersection of individual and collective consciousness, Bellah developed a brief but intense fascination for LSD and group dynamics, which he observed thanks to a controversial undergraduate course, Analysis of Interpersonal Behavior, also known as "Hostility" by students. As envisioned by the social psychologist and Parsons's collaborator Robert Freed Bales, the course invited students to analyze their own ongoing interactions. Each session was facilitated by an instructor who helped participants to interpret their actions and motivational dynamics. All this delicate work took place in a custom-built facility on the thirteenth floor of William James Hall, a "plush, carpeted wombroom" equipped with a one-way mirror that enabled researchers, professionals, and members of Social Relations to monitor the students from an adjacent room.[35]

Listening to tapes of the summer sessions convened by his therapist friend Phil Helfaer, Bellah found the interpersonal dynamics extraordinarily interesting, to the point that he played for some time with the idea of creating a new course, Analysis of Religious Action, based on the self-study of the participants' beliefs, practices, and expressions, and rooted in readings from Freud, Slater, Jung, Hesse, Rieff, and Durkheim. All this intellectual effervescence, however, had no effect on Bob's gloomy mood, whose source was, once again, the sense of rejection engendered by his father's suicide: "37 years of mourning. My relation with [an old friend] is one long grief work," he wrote in his diary. "My optimism, belief in socio-cultural progress and the quest of personal maturity perhaps are compensations for this sense of grief."[36] The mention of his old friend from Harvard was Bob's way of confessing to himself that his own sexual identity was far from settled. Oblique allusions to a childhood memory "of being absorbed by the maleness of grown men in the locker room at the Del Mar Club" in Santa Monica or at "a need for thumb sucking equivalents" brought him to realize that "masculinity cannot be formed in the mirror or in other men. The animal is me."[37]

For all the anxiety and exhaustion, one thing was clear: Bellah was not going to abandon his scholarly goals or the image he had of himself as a top academic destined for the highest of achievements. Moreover, he was not going to be happy with being just another Social Relations big shot: "Is it enough to be Professor X or even Professor Somebody? So desperately comfortable, prosperous and secure, writing clever books covered with inch thick shit like Jerry Bruner or even good sound but finally safe books like Tillich?" The stressful combination of economic, intellectual, and personal discontent pushed Bob to create for himself a mythical image of California as a Promised Land: just as in 1945 he had moved eastward to find a place where he could be born again as a highbrow scholar, now he was considering the possibility of going back as yet another beginning. "Again," wrote his daughter Tammy in her diary, "Professor Bellah thought he would find new freedom in Berkeley, and his wife, who loved California, encouraged the move."[38]

Finally bowing to Melanie's insistence, on March 21, 1967, Bob announced his resignation from Harvard and his acceptance of the Ford Professorship at Berkeley, effective from July 1, 1967. His ambivalence remained, but the very idea of leaving gave him an evident sense of relief. He felt particularly offended by Dean Ford's lack of interest, a circumstance he read as yet another Harvard affront: "To that extent [Ford's indifference] is a defeat; a third (Junior Fellow, Montreal) and last defeat." This, he knew, was no more than an excuse not to take responsibility for a decision that had been wholly his (and Melanie's). Bob felt guilty toward all the individuals who admired and loved him in Cambridge—not only Parsons, Riesman, or the "East Asian people," but also his students, with whom he was developing a genuine and more dialogical relationship. And he felt guilty for his low productivity, to the point that he resolved to stay away from both job offers and academic chores for at least five years.[39]

June 1967 arrived, and Melanie and Bob packed their things, ready to go. Just before leaving, they gave one last luncheon for Helen and Talcott Parsons and Evey and David Riesman in the old Victorian at 62 Gorham Street they had owned for exactly ten years. It was a moving moment of gratitude and friendship that announced a radically new phase of their lives.

7

"Stand Back and See It All"

BERKELEY, 1967–1968

WHEN ROBERT N. BELLAH and his family finally landed in San Francisco on June 23, 1967, the Summer of Love had reached its peak. One week earlier, Janis Joplin's Big Brother and the Holding Company had set fire to the Monterey International Pop Festival together with Jimi Hendrix and the Grateful Dead, and had then moved to Golden Gate Park to celebrate the summer solstice with seventy-five thousand youths with flowers in their hair. To the eyes of the Bellahs, however, the hippies whose daily clashes with the police at the intersection of Haight and Ashbury Streets had turned into an attraction for middle-class tourists looked less exotic than the "friendly idiots" of Orinda, the suburb where the family had temporarily settled. In this conservative enclave beyond the Berkeley hills, their biggest problem was avoiding the umpteenth invitation to join the local bridge club.[1]

Bob and Melanie spent their first summer in the Bay Area looking for a home at a walking distance from campus. The purchase of a solid 1911 three-story house on Mosswood Road, complete with a patio and a breathtaking view of the San Francisco Bay, and the first, uncertain steps into his new academic milieu had a strong impact on Bellah. "We live in a balance between elation to be in California," he wrote in his journal on August 8, 1967, "and anxiety about all the tasks of adjustment." To make the best out of this fresh start he needed a long-term plan: "We have twenty-five or thirty years. They will go quickly, unless I strengthen my defences." Turning every ounce of his passion, weakness, and ambiguity into a creative energy both at work and at home—that was the goal. It is no coincidence that he chose Carl Gustav Jung over Sigmund Freud, the ability to look ahead over the analysis of the past, as his Virgil.[2]

Berkeley seemed the perfect place to experiment with meaning, symbols, and creativity. The city had found itself in a state of excitement ever since the mid-1950s, when Allen Ginsberg had decided to move there. Now that daily protests fired the University of California campus, the general atmosphere of openness attracted old and new leftists from all over the country. Political factions, small magazines, and bohemian communities thrived. Berkeley radicals were particularly active in protesting against the Vietnam War. They soon created a lively cultural scene along Telegraph Avenue, where people from all walks of life came to share music, drugs, and bizarre lifestyles. A mere ten-minute stroll downhill from Mosswood Road, Telegraph was "Berkeley's jewel": an artsy, cosmopolitan, and plural environment where the countercul-ture flourished.[3]

On the other side of Sather Gate, the president of the University of Cali-fornia system, the economist Clark Kerr, was trying to turn his conception of the "multiversity" into a concrete reality. In his Godkin Lectures delivered at Harvard in 1963, he described contemporary American academe as a loosely organized city-state made up of different communities endowed with diverg-ing interests and moral outlooks. Students, faculty, administrators, donors, alumni, and the general public were the actors in an endemic, low-intensity conflict. Lonely at the top, presidents tried to ensure a balanced peace between the many factions, while protecting their embattled institution vis-à-vis the demands of external economic and political forces. Gone were the days of the Eliots and the Conants: presidents should now turn their multiversities into well-managed but chaotic organizations, "quickly responsive to opportunities, readily adaptable to change."[4]

The need to keep academic institutions "as confused as possible for the sake of the preservation of the whole uneasy balance," however, came at a cost. A growing interdependence with the outside world had already changed the cloistered nature of the university into a ragbag of different traditions, pro-grams, and ideologies; scholarly and economic cleavages between scientists and humanists grew wider, and the concretion of governmental and private funding to a small number of excellent universities only deepened the faculty's sense of discomfort. As for students, Kerr anticipated "an incipient revolt": "If the alumni are concerned, the undergraduates are restless," he wrote. "The students find themselves under a blanket of impersonal rules for admission, for scholarship, for examinations, for degrees. . . . The students also want to be treated as distinct individuals." While he acknowledged the difficulties, how-ever, Kerr stood by the multiversity and pointed to a renewed role for the humanities and the social sciences in defining "the good" and in adding a dimension of wisdom to the pursuit of scientific and technical knowledge.[5]

The rise of the multiversity was nowhere more evident than at Berkeley, the oldest and most revered campus of the University of California system. During his stint as the first Berkeley chancellor in the 1950s, Kerr had pursued an ambitious program of renewal. In the wake of the 1949–1951 loyalty oath controversy, he had tried to ease tarnished relationships between members of the faculty of different political persuasions, and had started a wide development plan. Once he became the system's president in 1959, Kerr strengthened his managerial style, ruling through regulations and legal arguments in an increasingly symbiotic partnership with the Board of Regents. In 1960 he contributed to defining the California Master Plan for Higher Education, which led to the establishment of new campuses at San Diego, Irvine, and Santa Cruz, and the creation of closer relations between the various systems of public higher education.[6]

As for collegiate life, Kerr's activism produced divergent results. On the one hand, he had new residences and common facilities built to accommodate the growing student body. On the other, he tried to enforce Rule 17, according to which all political activity should be conducted off campus. As they came back from civil rights campaigning in the South, the students were repeatedly denied permission to organize conferences and political initiatives within the reach of the Berkeley campus, and the revolt exploded. "We have come up against what may emerge as the greatest problem of our nation— depersonalized, unresponsive bureaucracy," proclaimed Mario Savio, somehow echoing Kerr's 1963 prophecy, "The bureaucrats hold history has ended. As a result significant parts of the population both on campus and off are dispossessed, and these dispossessed are not about to accept this a-historical point of view."[7]

Despite their modest outcome, the 1964–1965 student revolts left profound scars on the Department of Sociology. In January 1965 Neil Smelser had been appointed by acting chancellor Martin Meyerson as his assistant for student political activities, an experience he would later describe as "the most educational and exciting of my life." Although one of their most respected members held a key position, or perhaps because of it, Berkeley sociologists clashed on the free speech movement in public and private. In *Commentary*, Nathan Glazer described his disillusionment over the student protest and scolded faculty members who had not withdrawn their support when things had gotten out of hand. Philip Selznick replied that Kerr "lacked a vital theory of the university community" and that both the president and Glazer had failed to truly listen to the students. According to Seymour Martin Lipset, "the indifference to legality shown by serious students [could] threaten the foundations of democratic order if it [became] a model for student political action."[8]

Despite the sometimes gloomy predictions, the free speech revolt brought about profound changes in the approach to higher education of the vast majority of students, as "a passionate concern with morality, clarified by study, documented with facts, and experienced through action—not just term papers— became the activist style of learning." As a result, when Robert Bellah first set foot on the Berkeley campus, he found the "wide-open chaos of the post-Protestant, post-modern era" right in front of him, ready to be embraced.[9]

I

And yet, it took Bob some time to accept Berkeley on its own terms. To that extent, his later description of his leaving Cambridge as the "outward expression of an inward change" was grossly inaccurate, as in the fall of 1967 his transformation had barely begun. Misery and anxiety saturated his days, and one of the main sources of regret was the multiversity itself. Even before meeting with his colleagues and students, Bellah described his new employer as lacking "the high seriousness and intellectual commitment of Harvard." Not that he was reconsidering his decision, but he had a persistent sense of unease that he needed somehow to clear. At the root of these negative emotions stood, once again, the sense of inadequacy that Bob had first felt while writing his dissertation—the terror of not being up to the exceedingly high expectations of his mentors, peers, students, and family trapped him into an exhausting condition of constant self-reproach.[10]

In the fall, a short trip to Japan allowed him to focus on the implications of his recent move to California. What had happened was nothing short of epochal, at least from his own point of view: "It is the second great home leaving, comparable to the earlier one at age 18. I have left mother Harvard, father Parsons, brother ***, and uncle Riesman, as well as assorted more dubious or hostile uncles." As Bob knew, in the Buddhist tradition the act of becoming a monk was called *shukke*—literally, "leaving one's house." Bob had no intention of abandoning his home or family, but he had left his intellectual kin for good, and was now wondering if the rest of his professional life was going to be the lonely stroll of an intellectual orphan—some kind of post-modern errand into the wilderness, without the support that the Puritans had originally found in their tightly knit community.[11]

Gone was the egotism of the forty-year-old eager to jump headlong into the second half of his life: "Who will feed me and how will I work if I am not fed[?] Also since I have few students and no undergraduates, who will I feed?" To counter this feeling Bellah tried out different routines, and compiled long lists of authors who might help him to regain momentum—Lévi-Strauss and Wittgenstein, as well as his beloved Jung, Burke, and Durkheim.[12] As his work on *A Theory of Religion* sank into a "confused greyness," he started musing about bringing together a collection of earlier papers as a way to review his intellectual and personal development so far, and maybe gather new energy for the future: "The idea of a book of essays—retrospect at forty—is gaining in attractiveness," he wrote in his journal, "Perhaps *Religion in Human Action* as a title. With an intellectual autobiography introduction? . . . Should it aim at completeness and include some unpublished papers? Or should it be short and include only the most finished and influential pieces?"[13]

Bob was not alone in suffering from maladjustment. Now thirteen, Tammy resented the move to California, which had forced her into a sudden adolescence. Some years later she described her feelings much as her father would do: "Berkeley hit me like a bomb. It is a fast moving place; it can be wonderful, exciting, stimulating. It can also be, to a naive child, devastating. I was miserably homesick the first year." On her part, Melanie was appalled to see her daughters becoming more and more independent, while her social life was but a pale imitation of the one she had in Cambridge. She had never felt satisfied with being "only" a mother and a housewife, and took the opportunity of the move to the West Coast to put an end to her (exceptionally) "long 1950s." This complex familial and personal situation seriously strained Melanie and Bob's relationship, and they had some unusually bitter fights over the time-consuming and expensive renovations of 10 Mosswood Road. Tension hit Melanie "like an electric storm" and caused a rift between the couple for some time.[14]

Despite all the stress, nobody argued with the plan of settling in the Bay Area or the prospect of staying there indefinitely. After all, their difficulties could be interpreted as the unwanted consequences of the encounter with "the intensity, the immediacy, the openness and the precariousness of an emergent social order."[15] Bob, for example, saw that his agitation was counterbalanced by a feeling of "primordial security" he had not experienced since his early years in Los Angeles. This ambivalence was encapsulated in two short poems he wrote during his first fall in Berkeley:

FIGURE 7.1. Tammy, Jenny (*back row*), Abby, and Hally
(*front row*) in Berkeley, late 1960s. (RBPP)

California

Green November comes in streets misted
With rain, trees heavy with green, bay
For dimming and diffusing light.
I am heavy, green and wet with childhood.

Study Window

So many books here.
The warm comfort of reading
In order to learn.
The scholar looks up:
Clouds on the peak of Tamalpais,
Cold mountain air.[16]

Interestingly, Bellah's inner life had a sudden positive turn on his first trip to
the East Coast. In December 1967 he participated in a conference organized
by the Church Society for College Work, together with some inspiring
individuals—social activist Dorothy Day, psychologist Abraham H. Maslow,

and the founder of the Esalen Institute, Michael Murphy—and lectured at the University of Rochester, where he met with an old friend from his John Reed Society days, historian Perez Zagorin. When he finally got to Cambridge, Bob walked past his old house in Gorham Street and was shocked by its squalor. Moving to California seemed, after all, to have been the right choice. Later that day, a long, uneasy conversation with Phil Helfaer persuaded him it was time to openly face his deep sense of loss and his exhausting impostor syndrome.

"I want perspective," Bellah wrote on his diary upon returning home, "I want to stand back and see it all. To develop 'a self that touches all edges.'"[17] For that he needed a new personal myth and some brand new cultural heroes, whom he found in the "unlikely pair" of a poet and a philosopher—Wallace Stevens and Jean-Jacques Rousseau. Though seemingly ambitious, his program had a serious limitation: Bellah was determined "to know the whole range of human experience in time, space and depth. *Not directly* but through imaginative insight into inner structures and as a *geistes* historian, poet or anthropologist." While the scope of his inquiry was immense, Bob's tools of choice remained books and imagination. Not even being at the very center of the counterculture changed his attitude: everything had to be observed, analyzed, and understood from a safe distance. Direct, unmediated involvement with the world was out of the question.[18]

The ambivalence of Bellah's early Berkeley experience was decisive in pushing him to radicalize his need for a thorough interpretation of the mythical, nonrational substratum of the human condition. His published work proceeded step by step through a number of short pieces connected by the search for systematization. In a survey of contemporary sociology of religion written in 1967, Bob focused on the reciprocal relationship between symbols and experience: "Religion is not simply a reaction to some fixed parameter of human experience, not simply a means to cope with anguish and despair," wrote Bellah, "Rather, religion is a symbolic form that shapes human experience, both cognitive and emotional." Religion was best understood as a form of deep reflexivity triggered, so to speak, by the failure of all other problem-solving devices: "It is not concerned with particular problems as with the problematic nature of man, and with the particular problems, such as death, which most immediately imply that problematic nature." The task of the sociology of religion was to interpret the many symbolic forms through which it related humanity to the ultimate conditions of its existence.[19]

Crucial for Bellah's developing approach was his engagement with the most recent work of his old friend Clifford Geertz. Back in 1955, Cliff had criticized Bob's "Some Suggestions for the Systematic Study of Religion" on the grounds that its understanding of symbolic forms was insufficient to grasp religion's most distinctive element: "In contrast to economics, politics, class, family, and so forth," Geertz had written in his commentary, "and in common with science, art and the like, religion has a peculiarly 'cultural' quality: the symbolic-meaning aspect of religion looms rather large compared to the interaction aspect." Ten years later, he finally published a complex and more detailed version of this early intuition in an essay that was soon to become a classic of twentieth-century social science, "Religion as a Cultural System."[20]

Geertz's experience in the field and his undergraduate training in the humanities had made him sensitive to ordinary-language philosophy, literary criticism, and semiotics, which surfaced again and again in his use of the work of Kenneth Burke, Gilbert Ryle, and Suzanne Langer. Combining all these influences with a distinction between common sense and other symbolic perspectives introduced by the father of phenomenological sociology, Alfred Schütz, Geertz presented a novel definition of religion that underlined the special relationship between symbols, practices, and experiences: "A religion is a system of symbols which acts to establish powerful, pervasive, and long-lasting moods in men by formulating conceptions of a general order of existence and clothing those conceptions with such an aura of factuality that the moods and motivations seem uniquely realistic." Revolutionary as it was, from Bellah's point of view the definition still had a huge problem. What did Cliff intend to say, wrote Bob, reviewing a collection of essays that included Geertz's paper, when he wrote that "the moods and motivations *seem* uniquely realistic"? What was that "seem" about? If he meant that religious symbols and experiences were "less real" than they "seemed," Bellah continued, then Geertz was plainly wrong. Since humans dealt with reality only through symbols, each symbolic perspective possessed its own irreducible kind of truth: "Religion does not 'seem.' *It is.* Or if it seems, then science and common sense equally seem." In no way could social scientists downplay religious symbols, actions, or institutions: as the basic factor of "the deeply unconscious fantasies on which both personality and society are built," religion was an essential part of "the species life of man."[21]

These ideas found a first synthesis in Bellah's "Transcendence in Contemporary Piety," a paper written in the spring of 1968 whose point of departure was not that distant from Geertz's reframing of Schütz's approach. Given their nature as symbolic animals, human beings could participate in reality, creating and recreating it, only by means of their symbolic activity. As "systems of pure terminology," religion and metaphysics were meant to give human symbolism a firm, independent ground, untouched by the limits of reality. Bellah took his insight into the relation between man and nonempirical symbols from an aphorism of Wallace Stevens: "The final belief is to believe in a fiction, which you know to be a fiction, there being nothing else." In fact, as symbols and experience were one, the word "belief" was grossly inadequate: only when symbols were artificially separated from experience might one speak of "belief," but "as part of the experience itself [symbols were] perfectly and impressively real."[22]

Bellah's last step was to refuse to look at the problem of the "truth" of religion from a naturalistic point of view. On the one hand, symbols such as God, Being, Nothingness, or Life were *intrinsically fictive* in that they did not refer to "things" that could be pointed to. On the other hand, they were also *perfectly real*, for they were the only means human beings might employ to create a representation of the world as "an integrated whole" and relate themselves to it. Bellah's theoretical insight called for a radical interpretive approach to the study of religious symbols, directed at understanding the many ways in which systems of pure terminology had been created, used, made, and remade. But it also called for the demise of any disciplinary restriction. Distinguishing theology and the social sciences was now impossible, for they belonged to a "single intellectual universe" that the Enlightenment had unwisely torn into pieces.[23]

II

All of a sudden Bellah was on a roll, and he tried to focus on the theoretical volume on religion that he had left in the drawer for too long. Ideas were blossoming, connections were multiplying, confidence was growing. Bob's student and good friend from Harvard, Andrew Bard Schmookler, moved to Berkeley in May 1968 and the two enjoyed long walks along the fire trails in the hills, relating Andy's research on altered states of consciousness with Bob's ideas on religious symbolism. It was during one of these conversations that Bellah was able to give a name to the "unconscious fantasy" that had dominated his whole life—a reverie that had Luther Hutton Bellah Jr. as its protagonist: "I have the fantasy that if I am a good boy and sit quietly my father will come back and save me." The image of the eternally waiting boy included the other main character of his childhood: "Behind the father fantasy is probably a mother fantasy. How can a starving man be active? How little I ate as a boy and how thin I was! Only after marriage," he concluded, "did I begin to gain." A weak child could not run away—not only was he unable to leave his mother as his father had done, but he would also be at home should daddy come back to rescue him. It was only when ties with Lillian were severed as he formed a new family that Bob could gain weight, a metaphor for all the "supplies" he needed in order to become active and autonomous.[24]

While Bellah was busy coming to grips with his past, "Civil Religion in America" started to enjoy an unexpected success. After its publication, the paper was featured in the *New York Times* and soon became the object of criticism from different quarters. In an early rejoinder to his critics, Bellah redefined the civil religion as "a set of religious beliefs, symbols and rituals growing out of the American historical experience interpreted in the dimension of transcendence" that had emerged as a spontaneous, unplanned social fact. Moreover, although the American civil religion he had written about was "distinctively American," as a general phenomenon civil religion was in no way exclusive to the United States: "It is my conviction that any community of people with a strong sense of its own identity will so interpret its experience."[25]

These early exchanges set the tone of the debate on the American civil religion: the clash over definitions, the perplexity about a solely symbolic analysis, the relationship between description and evaluation. Some social scientists devoted to statistical analysis began work comparing the United States with other societies in order to verify Bellah's theoretical hypotheses, and concluded that "the real locus of the American civil religion [may be] in the minds of intellectual political liberals." Jürgen Moltmann, a German theologian, commented unsympathetically on Bob's political ideals—in his view Christian universalism could be achieved only as "a solidarity with those who are oppressed by the civil religion of a society." On his part, Robert W. Lynn wrote that "few established theologians were more prescient in anticipating the shape of emerging religious concerns than this maverick sociologist."[26]

Maverick or not, Bellah and his work had never raised so much interest. Soon after the paper came out, he began receiving invitations to take part in countless seminars and symposia on the American civil religion in both academic and nonacademic settings. Obviously, all these new engagements greatly reduced the time he could devote to the study of Japan or to *A Theory of Religion*. Once again, an external distraction was diverting him from his major project, contrary to the idea of excellence in scholarly work that he had made his own since his early days in graduate school. At the same time, Bellah had many good reasons to participate in the American civil religion debate. First, the discussion gave him the opportunity to interact with scholars from two disciplinary fields—history and theology—that he found much more interesting and prestigious than late-1960s sociology. And second, his persistent inability to concentrate on his theoretical book pushed him to focus on a more concrete kind of scholarly work, one that he saw as easier to deliver because he was driven by external pressure.[27]

Beyond these academic reasons, however, what was decisive for Bob was his deeply felt, if ambivalent, attachment to his country. While his year in Japan had forced him to recognize how American he was, Kennedy's assassination, the war in Vietnam, and the election of Richard Nixon in November 1968 had increasingly darkened his political outlook and pushed him to take action. Shortly after the first *Daedalus* conference, for example, Bellah wrote to the American ambassador at the United Nations, Arthur J. Goldberg, to call for the inclusion of all the factions of Vietnamese fighters in an extended political negotiation, and warned that "if victory is our aim we can only extend the conflict ultimately to world-wide proportions after which any notion of victory becomes irrelevant."[28]

That, however, was as far as it went. In spite of his self-image as a "political animal," after his experience as a member of the Communist Party Bob had never been inclined to get involved in civic or political activism. Certainly, he would be happy to participate in peaceful demonstrations, but late-1960s Berkeley was more likely to be a theater of violence and urban guerrillas. Bellah felt no connection with these activist groups—for example, he considered the ideas of the Committee of Concerned Asian Scholars "ill-founded," and decided not to contribute to its effort. As for student protests, he'd had his share of disturbance during the so-called Third World Strike, which he'd found particularly annoying. On one occasion, his lecture on Japanese society was interrupted by a noisy group of White graduate students who questioned his legitimacy as a professor of "Yellow Studies." Bob quietly asked them who should be teaching the class, and one of the disrupters indicated an Asian American undergraduate sitting in the front row. When Bellah turned to the student and asked if he knew of Japanese language, history, or literature, he received, quite predictably, three straight *nos*. At that point, the protesters just turned around and left. Some months later a firebomb was exploded during the night at the Center for Japanese and Korean Studies, where Bob kept most of his books. Like many members of the university community, he felt "angry and exhausted, almost shell-shocked" by what he called "our local mishuganah [*sic*] or asshole revolution of Berkeley Trotskyites."[29]

Bellah had no intention, however, of secluding himself in an ivory tower. To the "pettit [*sic*] bourgeois infantile leftism" of his radical students and colleagues, he opposed an understanding of the public academic modeled on the august figure of the founder of sociology, Émile Durkheim. In 1968 Bob had started working on a Durkheim reader for the Heritage of Sociology series edited by Morris Janowitz. The combination of old texts and some hitherto untranslated pieces on civic morality and modern individualism was meant to present the French sociologist as a charismatic thinker "called to hold a mirror to his society, to make conscious its deepest values." At a time when sociologists had elected as their role-model either a watered-down version of the arch-relativist, and sometimes chauvinist, Max Weber or a post-modern enactment of "good ole" revolutionary Karl Marx, Bellah effectively presented Durkheim as the archetype of the impassioned but rigorous civil theologian, one who urged scholars to get politically involved in the ways and with the tools that most characterized them—that is, through writing, speaking, and teaching.[30]

The need to embrace a clear political position was to be tempered by an unfailing sense of responsibility toward those very institutions that allowed creativity and reflexivity to flourish: "There are moments when decisive action will make for us strange bedfellows," wrote Bellah in an editorial for *Theology Today*. "So be it. It is better that we call on Reagan to send in the state police than let the activist burn down the university. Yet on the next day we may find ourselves joining those very activists to demand an immediate end to the immoral war in Vietnam which acts like a destructive acid throughout our entire society." The reference to Vietnam was not casual: Bob had seen so many vigils, fasts, "teach-ins and speak-outs" against the war that he sometimes felt floored by his own ignorance of what was happening beyond the inner motions of his "white psyche." That is why in the fall of 1969 he embarked on a period of intense reading in the history of the women's movement and Afro-American activism—Harry Edwards, Richard Wright, Malcom X, and Martin Luther King Jr. From this moment on, he increasingly saw his involvement in the civil religion debate as his own way to strengthen and renew his commitment as a citizen-academic.[31]

8

"To Put It Bluntly, Religion Is True"

ROME AND CAMBRIDGE, 1968–1969

EARLY IN JULY 1968, Robert N. Bellah went through "a great storm of creativity" in which everything unexpectedly came together in a feverish, dazzling moment of revelation. The catalyst of this sudden burst of insight was a book he had bought a couple of years earlier: Norman O. Brown's *Love's Body*. The volume had been published in 1966 as a sequel to the much acclaimed *Life against Death*, a portrait of the whole of human history based on a psychoanalytical view of man as "the animal which represses himself and which creates culture or society in order to repress himself" in the face of his own death. The only way to escape from a catastrophic condition where civilization and neurosis were fully synonymous consisted in bringing both repression and sublimation to an end and embracing Dionysus—an existence of free play, poetry, and narcissistic fulfilment. In Brown's plea for polymorphous perversity, disparate strands of Western and Eastern wisdom merged in the image of a "resurrected body" pervaded by a new "dialectical imagination."[1]

In expanding the last chapter of *Life against Death*, *Love's Body* effectively trashed it—as Brown would say some time later, the book had been carefully designed to "torpedo *Life against Death*, to destroy it as a position." Starting from the human body as "the measure of all things," the new book preached the dissolution of all distinctions between symbols and reality, so that everything became just a reference mark to something else, there being no self-evident ground of "reality as it is." *Love's Body* could be read as the ultimate mutiny against Freud's reality principle, or perhaps as its disintegration in an endless game of mirrors in which politics, social life, sex, and ultimately the human body itself are swallowed up into indifference or, as Brown would say, "unity."[2]

While one of the key themes of the book was the opposition between Protestant literalism and the prospect of unification of mankind as one resurrected body, Brown was not ready to leave Christianity for good. In his famous 1960 address, "Apocalypse: The Place of Mystery in the Life of the Mind," he had sketched a "Dionysian Christianity, an apocalyptic Christianity, a Christianity of miracles and revelations." Now *Love's Body* offered a synthesis of Christ and Dionysus "in which meaning is not fixed, but ever new and ever changing; in a continuous revelation; by fresh outpouring of the holy spirit." As an intellectual trip, Brown's apocalypse was aimed at annihilating meaning and, ultimately, the world itself: "To restore to words their full significance, as in dreams, as in *Finnegans Wake*, is to reduce them to non-sense," he wrote. "It is a destruction of ordinary language, a victory over the reality-principle; a victory for the god Dionysus; playing with fire, or madness; or speaking with tongues."[3]

The promise of *Love's Body*'s was first realized in its style—a collection of aphorisms, disjointed phrases, and powerful images. From the Bible to Pascal, from Lao Tzu to Hobbes, the book embraced everything and nothing, assuming the semblance of a centerless, unorganized space. Brown invited his readers to get lost within *Love's Body*'s formless labyrinth, to assault it frontally or coast it sideways in order to find their own way in and out of it. "Things are real, unreal, and neither real nor unreal"; God and the world, "mercifully," do not exist, behind the veil there is nothing. The last lines of *Love's Body* clearly stated the point of arrival of Brown's wild journey as an entirely intellectual trip—a particular that was lost in translation when the book started to circulate: "The antinomy between mind and body, word and deed, speech and silence, overcome. Everything is only a metaphor; *there is only poetry*."[4]

When Bellah brought *Love's Body* on his May 1968 trip to the East Coast, the book and its author, popularly known as "Nobby," were already enjoying mass success on campuses across the nation. Along with Herbert Marcuse's *Eros and Civilization* and *One Dimensional Man*, *Love's Body* had inspired or legitimated an amazing number of existential experiments—in which Brown himself certainly would not participate, as he saw his whole project as "a poetical, rather than a literal thing." Professors, on the whole, were less enthusiastic. Most reviewers disparaged Brown's effort as incoherent, pointless, or kitschy, confining it in the province of the grotesque. In the *Partisan Review*, for example, Frederick Crews emphasized the contradictions of *Love's Body* and its "subtle perversion of the whole body of Freudian theory." Like a number of others, he saw some similarity between Brown and Marshall McLuhan in their constant wavering "between scholarship and showmanship." Cultural critic Theodore Roszak dubbed Nobby as "Professor Dionysus" and depicted the book as an "oracular out-pouring" and an "embarrassing exercise in pretentiousness."[5]

In the most famous of all reviews, Marcuse himself expressed his contempt for the disembodied quality of Brown's "de-realization of reality": "the imagery is not enough," he wrote, "it must become saturated with its reality: symbolism must recapture that which it symbolizes. The king must be shown not only as father but as king, that is to say, as master and lord; war and competition and communication must be shown not only as copulation but as war and business and speech." Without the chance to "go back" to the tainted practices from which they first emerged, allegories and metaphors were doomed to turn into either ideologies or consolatory discourses—and thus create further mystification and oppression. In his answer, Nobby laughed at his German friend and repeated his mantra with the grin of a trickster: "From politics to poetry— legislation is not politics, nor philosophy, but poetry."[6]

Bellah read *Love's Body* on the plane to San Francisco and his mind was blown: "It is easy to be haunted, dominated, possessed by the reading—to be fucked by it," he wrote in his diary on July 1, 1968, "But one is also impregnated. And the power of imagination . . . is swelling to phallic ripeness, Creativity is the overcoming of all boundaries, of subject and object, of male and female." During the summer he read the book again and again, together with William Blake and Northrop Frye, who had inspired Brown, and esoteric works of fiction such as John Fowles's *The Magus*. His world was rocking: "I feel enormously stirred up. A great many boundaries are wavering. It seems that there needs to be only a match to the tinder. All kinds of things are ready to come together." Bob's readings in psychoanalysis were finally coming to life as his experiences were turned into deeply personal reflections through a wild assemblage of metaphors.[7]

He first paralleled his favorite occupations to active and passive sexual intercourse: "Giving birth is painful, ejaculation is pleasurable. The intense joy I get from writing, the anxiety, the guilt. The pen is my penis. The problem of phallic masculine adequacy. Sight as copulation. Reading for me as (passive?) intercourse. Deeply pleasurable but receptive, taking in, non-phallic."[8] Bob was now able to see writing and reading, his "two major modes of relating to reality," as extrinsications of his inner masculine and feminine sides—a bold interpretation in the light of his difficulty in writing and his voracious reading habits. In December 1967 Bob had pledged "to know the whole range of human experience in time, space and depth," but had immediately added that he would use his "imaginative insight into inner structures," operating "as a *geistes* historian, poet or anthropologist." Eight months later, through the image of reading and writing as sexual intercourse, he was finally able to nail the intrinsic alienation of his approach to reality.[9]

What was happening to Robert Bellah was so radical and so intense that no one, not even his beloved Andy Schmookler, would understand it. But the die was cast, and Bob found himself wondering how this mind-blowing moment could be announced in professional and academic settings—"Can I tell those people in Rome about it?" At the same time he felt that maybe he would rather seek refuge than exposure: "I am like a pregnant cat—I would like to hide from the world in order to give birth. And there is so much beauty and so much joy, joy, joy." But reading, writing, and perhaps imagining were all he could and would do—the notion of a vicarious sex act with reality was disturbing enough. This reluctance to see it through also fed Bob's persistent hesitancy toward Berkeley. As he wrote in his diary, teaching was much less close to the core of his identity. Although he loved his students and was eager to learn from them, he felt overwhelmed by his introductory course in sociology of religion, which enrolled more than twice as many students as he was used to teaching at Harvard. The main problem, though, was not with quantity: "What strikes me the most," he wrote to David Riesman in the spring of 1968, "is the strong dependency needs of the students. This was not absent at Harvard but these students are far less autonomous than the Harvard undergraduates. . . . I am determined to make them learn something without compromising my own standards. This takes me much time for every single lecture, even though I have given the course for 10 years." Some weeks later he candidly told David Schneider that he still was undecided whether he appreciated Berkeley better than Cambridge—in fact, he confessed that he was "still not sure that anyone should ever move anywhere."[10]

Difficulties notwithstanding, the refurbishment of 10 Mosswood Road was finally done, and Melanie, now forty, was determined to start a new phase of her life. At that point the Protestant establishment called back. On October 14, 1968, Bob's friend Krister Stendhal offered him a newly endowed professorship at the Harvard Divinity School: the Houghton Chair in Theology and Contemporary Change, established for "a theologian who creatively [interpreted, guided, and shaped] the Church's mission in times and fields of change." Excited letters and phone calls from Wilfred Smith, David Riesman, Richard Niebuhr, Alex Inkeles, and Talcott Parsons quickly followed. Caught off guard,

Bellah gave some serious thought to moving back to Cambridge, but eventually turned down the offer. The decision to leave Harvard had been made, and Bob felt it was the right one: not only did he enjoy the freedom from teaching and the exciting climate he had found at Berkeley, but he also wanted to publish "a book or two" to regain for himself the confidence that others seemed to place in him. The fact that Melanie had decided to apply to the University of California School of Law strongly contributed to the decision.[11]

Well before completing "a book or two," however, Bellah listened to his intellectual instinct and decided to unveil his still unpolished ideas in front of a properly constituted audience. Over the course of 1969 Bob had at least two eventful opportunities to act out his new epistemological stance—and both turned out to be experiences that were gloomy and exhilarating at once.

I

Shortly before the offer came from the Harvard Divinity School, Bellah had received a long-awaited letter from Franz Cardinal König and Monsignor Antonio Grumelli of the Secretariat for Non-believers, an office of the Roman Catholic Church instituted in the wake of the Second Vatican Council to extend the mission of the Church to atheists and nonbelievers and enter into some kind of dialogue with them. After a couple of years of groundwork and analysis, the Secretariat had published a document where this unprecedented attempt to approach nonbelievers was defined as "an aspect of the general renewal of the Church, which also [called] for a more positive appreciation of human freedom." The paper also invited social scientists to exchange views with the Vatican, and special attention was given to dialogue with "those Marxists who adhere to Communism," an expression that alluded to scholars from behind the Iron Curtain. In spite of doubts as to the feasibility of such a dialogue, "because of the intimate connection which [Marxists] establish between theory and practice," the document caused quite a stir in conservative circles, where it was read as a capitulation of Catholicism to the Soviet Union.[12]

The Secretariat formally invited Bob to participate in the International Symposium on the Culture of Unbelief, which would take place in Rome in March 1969. Planning for the conference had been going on for months under the aegis of the Vatican, the Berkeley Sociology Department, and the Fondazione Giovanni Agnelli, a research institute established by the Fiat automobile manufacturer in Turin in 1966. The chairman of Berkeley Sociology, Charles Y.

Glock, had offered his university as a likely venue for the meeting, and Bellah as a keynote speaker and perhaps the chairman. In the end, the decision was taken to hold the symposium in Rome and its chair was given to the Austrian sociologist Peter L. Berger. Keynotes by Bellah, Glock, and Thomas Luckmann would function as the springboards of wide-ranging discussions between social scientists and theologians.[13]

The meeting was an unprecedented event. At the inaugural press conference on March 21, 1968, Grumelli said that "this Symposium is the first of its type from every point of view; this is the first time that an attempt is made to approach the religious from a world-wide point of view and from a truly 'ecumenical' interdisciplinary perspective."[14] Aware of the polemics over the 1968 document and wary of losing control of the media, the Secretariat and the Fondazione Agnelli planned everything in great detail. The decision to host the meeting at the Hotel Parco dei Principi, an opulent resort designed by star architect Giò Ponti, was justified by the need to find a "neutral" venue where religion and atheism could be discussed without giving the impression that the organizers would limit or undermine the freedom of the invited scholars.[15] Invitations to top-tier clergy, politicians, and businessmen were issued, and dozens of journalists were admitted to the meeting in order to ensure the widest possible media exposure. The final list of participants included Talcott Parsons, Martin Marty, Jean Danielou, François Houtart, David Martin, Harvey Cox, Samuel Z. Klausner, and Milan Machovec.[16]

The symposium opened on March 22, 1969, at the Jesuit Pontificia Università Gregoriana in front of a crowd of three thousand people that included prelates, Fiat's patron Gianni Agnelli, diplomats, politicians, students, and even some members of the so-called Roman black nobility. After three days of group and plenary sessions, on March 27 Paul VI warmly received the participants in private audience and blessed the collaboration between the Church and social science. A Catholic Pope receiving social scientists, some Protestants and others declaredly Marxists, was big news: the media saw the conference as a success, even if, as Berger later remarked, they erroneously focused on the "dialogue" between theologians and social scientists, while the Secretariat had sought the sociologists' help to identify participants for future dialogues. Scholars praised the relaxed atmosphere—for some a rather surprising experience, given the obscurantist reputation of the Catholic Church—and expressed their hope for the inclusion of intellectuals from other disciplines. Martin Marty spoke of the symposium as "the first probes by Roman Catholicism toward diplomatic recognition of some of its historic enemies."[17]

From Bellah's point of view, the symposium was a puzzling experience. Although he was scheduled as one of the keynote speakers, he decided for a last minute change. In the paper he had circulated three months prior to the conference, "The Historical Background of Unbelief," he wrote of unbelief as a societal problem that had been considered a political crime ever since the times of Plato. And yet, from the nineteenth century onwards—that is, in what he had called the "modern stage of religious evolution"—it had become "genetic to contemporary consciousness" as part of the quest to find one's creed as an individual. In order to understand this momentous change, scholars should start to consider religion as an "embodied truth" that individuals performed and transmitted to others through narratives, images, and practices. This complex innerness would come to light whenever the search for personal identity combined with group membership and solidarity—Black power, the American civil religion, and Kennedy's Peace Corps being only the most recent examples of modern religions. In fact, Bellah added, "the recent outburst of youth in search of social justice, but motivated more by personal values than class resentments, is a kind of vivid surfacing of *a vast value consensus* that has been growing in the modern world and whose actualization youth impatiently demands." In this novel situation the very concept of dialogue was outdated, as Christians should be ready to build "the boundaryless community, the body of man identical with the body of Christ," with any other individual human being, taking for granted that different people would be free to imagine that community in their own way. By way of Bob's paper, Norman O. Brown was going to break into the Vatican.[18]

Radical as it was, the paper was nothing compared with the brief remarks penned by Bob the night before the session. On March 24 he had participated in the boring discussion of Luckmann's presentation and had resolved to change the pace of the conference. Although he anticipated that he would "tread on a tight-rope," he called the meeting in Rome the "christening" of a new stage in the religious history of humanity. Talking of avant-garde minorities who pushed for change, he defined himself and his fellow participants as "too old to speak with much authority about what is happening"—a remark that sounded too similar to Jack Weinberg's famous slogan "Don't trust anyone over thirty" to be palatable to the distinguished audience of churchly and lay academics. The closing of the brief intervention made Bob's colleagues jump on their seats: "We are in a revolutionary situation with respect to both science and religion, reason and faith, dogmas of all kinds are [questioned]. We stand at the verge of a possible reunification of consciousness, not because of the imperialism of science, but because of the realisation of the falling nature of man and the perception of the eschatological possibility of a new being."[19]

This was too much for even the most open-minded social scientists. They had been invited to the symposium to help the Catholic Church find the unbelievers, and now Bellah was proclaiming that belief and unbelief were outdated categories, that social science was merely one way to look at reality, and that hippies were the spearhead of an epochal revolution that he and his fellow conveners were too old to understand. The general reaction to Bellah's words would be keenly captured by Berger in his foreword to the meeting's proceedings, published three years later: "I have grave doubts about Bellah's putative 'reunification of consciousness' (possibly not living in California may be the *Sitz im Leben* of these doubts)." Immediately after Bob's speech, Berger was a bit blunter: "I don't know if the baby is there, but we certainly have the christening sermon."[20]

Respondent Martin Marty praised Bob's decision to introduce the session with a speech that had made him "vulnerable," but focused on the written paper, where he found "a more firm and historical and a little less eschatological grounding." He also underlined the dominance of "operational man" against the avant-garde, which he reduced to a fringe phenomenon. If Marty was a fair player, David Martin was "the wicked witch at this particular christening": he called Bob's speech an existential rant and accused him of turning his Californian experience into a benchmark for assessing modern society—an observation later echoed by Berger in his foreword to the proceedings. Bellah had let his totally unjustified fascination for Berkeley students, those "antinomian, radical subjectivist child heroes of our times," take over his scientific rationality. Berger continued the christening metaphor when giving the floor to a rather laconic Bellah:

> BERGER: I think we are beginning to see what Mr. Bellah's baby looks like, kind of has long hair. I didn't get that impression, that he was specifically thinking of students, but . . . were you thinking of students?
> BELLAH: I don't recognize much of myself in that last portrait.[21]

It was time to listen to Talcott Parsons, who rebuffed almost everything he had read and heard. He noted that the paper belonged to two very different genres, scientific and eschatological, and while he declared himself to be much more optimistic about the nature of man, he poked fun at Bellah's Brownian overtones—"I don't trust my unconscious and I don't trust yours." He also made fun of his former student's understanding of religion as a wild outbreak of the sacred into the routines of daily life: "Mr. Bellah has asserted that religion is grounded in the non-ordinary reality which, sometimes, breaks out into our reality," he said, "I have always thought that religion was the everyday, was the regular, was the aspect of the recurrent and that somehow this breaking out into the unusual was just that, a rather unusual extreme version of it."[22]

Given that they had shared a course in the sociology of religion for almost a decade, Parsons's comments were unexpected—in fact, he was himself quite surprised by the path taken by his former protégé. Some minor critiques later, Parsons launched his last nuke in an ironic reversal of sociological functionalism, modernization theory, and his own public image as a conservative intellectual according to whom everything in America was getting better and better. His words deserve to be quoted at length:

> The notion here that there is an integration of the society around notions of effective moral and political action . . . *I just don't see our current American society as being that integrated.* I am too concerned with the strife and the conflict and the violence that we are facing today in the society to believe that [we are] moving to a point at which there is a joint notion of the moral. I think the problem which is cutting right down through the society is that we don't even know what effective moral and political action is; we can't even agree that we have different interests, people making different decisions, different parts of the community supporting different notions of the moral.

After the break, Luckmann, having noticed how harshly Bellah had been treated by his colleagues, tried to set things straight. He argued that Marty's operational men and Bellah's religious avant-garde were probably the same people, a fact that could not be seen by those who, "in California," were trying to expand their religious consciousness. Thomas O'Dea declared his sympathy for Bellah's opening remarks and agreed that the project of finding a balance between existential problems and "scientific posture" was crucial—and still, Bob's solution was utterly wrong, for it mixed two things that should have remained separate.[23]

In his reply, Bellah expressed some discomfort at the accusation of having "given up" the entire Western tradition of rationality, for he had taken for granted, he said, the necessity of being analytical and empirical. He just wanted to push things a bit further for the simplest of reasons: again and again, he would participate in seminars and panels where he found not "the slightest element of reality." At the same time, he understood he ran the risk of being labeled as an extremist: "I am afraid, in taking a polemical position, that the necessary consequence is that one is immediately classed somehow in the opposite camp whenever one makes a statement which seems critical of any given position." Well aware of the dangerous game he had started, Bellah then replied to some of the critiques: he pleaded for an "integrated personality" in which conscious and unconscious elements would finally be connected, and invited anyone interested in religion to learn not only from theology but also from immediate, lived communal experiences.[24]

Bellah's rant did not go unnoticed. Journalists reported his debated contribution and retrospective accounts stressed the relevance of his ideas, though not agreeing with them. On his part, Bob had gone through an ordeal of sorts, and some of the critiques were not wholly undeserved: the drive of his performance was not matched by the strength of his argument—his distinctions were blurred, his reasoning shaky, his answers tentative. Bob's attempt at positioning had failed to create a recognizable niche for his work. On his way to Berkeley, he stopped at Harvard to give a seminar at the Center for the Study of World Religions, where he spoke of the influence of Vatican political preoccupations on the conference and of the "acrimony and defensiveness of the participants," but also concluded that "the doors are open" between traditionalist and post-traditionalist views of religion.[25]

In the meantime, the reunification of consciousness had gotten slightly out of hand. A few days after his return to Berkeley, Bob found himself in the middle of the Battle for People's Park and was tear-gassed on his way to class. Later, his daughter Tammy described his shock at the attack on Willard Junior High, a school just a couple of blocks south of the park, where she had found refuge during the confrontations between the students and the police. On May 19, 1969, three days after Governor Ronald Reagan declared a state of emergency, Bellah participated in the seminar "Religion and Secularization" with Jay Demerath and, again, Thomas Luckmann at the University of California, Los Angeles. There, he repeated some of the points he had made during the conference on unbelief, but also acknowledged the positive effects of the separation of critical social science and Christian theology. His proposal of a "nonantagonistic differentiation" was more cautious than he had been in Rome; at the same time, the Berkeley revolts echoed in Bellah's call for "the necessity to translate constantly between different scientific and imaginative vocabularies" without pretending to identify reality with one single depiction of it. The Los Angeles piece seemed to be a well-balanced rendition of the ideas that Bob had been developing for some time. In fact, it was crucial enough to become the first section of one of his best-known essays, "Between Religion and Social Science." The second section came from his most (in)famous performance ever.[26]

II

Late in the evening of Saturday October 25, 1969, Robert Bellah convened with sociologist Werner Stark at a joint plenary session of the Society for the Scientific Study of Religion and the American Academy of Religion held at Harvard's Sanders Theater. On the invitation of Samuel Z. Klausner, they were to discuss the relationship between scientific and humanistic approaches to the study of religion. A participant in the Rome conference, Klausner was in his third and final year as the executive secretary of the society, and had asked the speakers to compare different approaches to the study of Christianity in the face of the emerging consensus on the primacy of cognitive rationality. Bellah's speech took instead the direction of a wider critique of the validity and "the viability of an academic enterprise limited to the development of rational knowledge."[27]

As was now customary, Bellah started from the Enlightenment as "the search of the kernel of truth hidden in the falsity of religion—the truth behind the symbols." Marx, Freud, and Durkheim all believed "to be in possession of a truth superior to that of religion," while the only classical sociologist who had not spoken of a hidden truth, Max Weber, "still [managed] to convey the feeling that the scientific observer cannot finally take seriously the beliefs he is studying." In order to understand what religion was really about, however, materialism and reductionism had to be abandoned in favor of *symbolic realism*, "the knowledge that noncognitive and nonscientific symbols are constitutive of human personality and society—*are real in the fullest sense of the word.*" This called for an "interactionist model of social science, or what Talcott Parsons [called] 'action theory,'" where "reality" was seen not as something "out there," but rather as depending on the relationship between subject and object. Bellah's words are worth quoting at length:

> Even a natural scientist selects those aspects of the external world for study which have an inner meaning to him, which reflect some often hidden inner conflict. But this is true of all of us. We must develop multiple schemes of interpretation with respect not only to others but ourselves. We must learn to keep the channels of communication open between the various levels of

consciousness. We must realize with Alfred Schütz that there are multiple realities and that human growth requires the ability to move easily between them and will be blocked by setting up one as a despot to tyrannize over the others.

Among alternative realities, religion was defined as that symbolic complex intended to evoke "the totality which includes subject and object," something that no other symbolic reality could do. In its limited sense, religion had its own validity as a sui generis reality. Or, in Bob's forceful phrase, "To put it bluntly, religion is true."[28]

He was now ready to introduce another devastating thesis: "I believe that those who study religion must have a kind of double vision," as both scientists *and* religious subjects. Besides Wilfried Smith, Richard Niebuhr, and Paul Tillich, Bob pointed to William Butler Yeats and Anaïs Nin as his inspirations, and cited Nobby Brown and Herbert Fingarette—the author of another of Bob's favorite books, *The Self in Transformation*—as "the most vivid illustration of the rapprochement between the language of religion and the language of the scientific analysis of religion." Bob's references and tone were fully intended and could not be misunderstood: it was as though all his reflections, fears, and excitement had coalesced to form an integral vision of the place of religion in the life of man that had once and for all "resolved" his double identity as a social scientist and a humanist. This led inevitably to the climax of the performance: "If this seems to confuse the role of theologian and scientist, of teaching religion and teaching about religion, *then so be it*. The radical split between knowledge and commitment that exists in our culture and in our universities is not ultimately tenable. Differentiation has gone about as far as it can go. *It is time for a new integration.*"[29]

To a large part of the audience it was crystal clear that the intervention was not business as usual. Immediate reactions went from exhilaration to embarrassment to sheer hostility, according to disciplinary or epistemic fault lines. The Yale psychologist James E. Dittes saw the speech as treason on Bob's part: "The delighted applause of the humanists and the angry sense of abandonment expressed by the social scientists suggested that *all* thought they had witnessed the capitulation of social science to humanistic study." The performance was so powerful that some of Bellah's friends felt the need to write him to express their appreciation. Wilfred Cantwell Smith, for example, declared that he "like so many others was not merely enthusiastic but excited," while David Riesman called the speech "magnificent" and added: "Naturally, I'd heard you speak a number of times, but never with such force, brilliance, passion, and magnetism. Here the medium was the message—and of course there was a message too."[30]

At Sanders Theater, Bellah had purposively tried to suggest a revolutionary change of mentality in the study of religion. As he had done in Rome, he took some ideas to the extreme, filling his speech with rhetorical figures and powerful phrases and performing his ideas with the help of his body, voice, and facial expressions. While what he had to say sounded obscure to most, his passion and drive were unmistakable. Certainly, symbolic realism was difficult to assess. Bellah's sense of the confused, and diverse, reactions that his work was eliciting was well expressed in his reply to Smith on November 11, 1969: "Even though the group at Sanders was quite responsive to what I said," he wrote, "I am not sure that all of them were favorable for the right reasons, and many others are very doubtful of the most recent trend of my thinking. This being the case, I am especially grateful for your support and encouragement since I think you are the one of the few people who really knows what I am about these days."[31]

The published version of the paper was accompanied by transcriptions of Klausner and James Burtchaell's original comments, and an additional note by sociologist Benjamin Nelson, who stigmatized Bellah's project as "totalism" and a return to premodern Gnosticism. Klausner warned that "reintroducing a religious vision in the academy would reduce its effectiveness" as an institution focused uniquely on the development of rational knowledge. "My first reaction is quite simply dismay," wrote Bob in his rejoinder. "It is hard for me to understand how my remarks could be taken in ways obviously (to me) not intended." Quoting Victor Turner's *The Ritual Process*, he argued that symbolic realism "simply holds that religious symbols are not primarily social or psychological projection systems . . . but the ways in which persons and societies express their sense of the fundamental nature of reality, of the totality of experience." He was "just" advancing a more adequate, nonantagonistic differentiation between science and religion, in which neither of the two was thought to be necessarily superior to the other.[32]

As a consequence, Bellah remained puzzled at the doubts raised about his disciplinary allegiance to social science. He expressed his dissatisfaction for what he interpreted as unwarranted criticism in a letter to Talcott Parsons: "It is really hard for me to understand why [Nelson] says what he does. His refusal to see that there is any alternative to scientific 'objectivism' except irrational subjectivism baffles me. . . . I can't believe that he doesn't know better. But why attack me like this? . . . I guess you are used to being attacked," he concluded, "but this is a rather new experience for me. I can already see the reviews of my collection of essays." Conceived as a carefully crafted attempt to reposition "Robert Bellah and his work so far," the new book was much more than a mere assemblage of previously published texts. In the rapidly changing intellectual and political environment of the late 1960s, Bob saw all his reference points collapsing one by one—but then not quite.[33]

9

Beyond Borders

BERKELEY, 1969–1971

IN JANUARY 1968 Talcott Parsons added the final touches to his introduction to a volume on the state of American sociology commissioned by the Voice of America. From a purely quantitative point of view, the discipline seemed to thrive. As shown by the twenty-plus chapters of the volume—to which Robert Bellah had contributed a general essay on the sociology of religion—a whole new set of specialties, theories, and methods had emerged. The American Sociological Association had now more than thirteen thousand members, and attendance at annual meetings touched the three thousand mark. And yet, in presenting "at least a partial picture of a rapidly growing and changing discipline," the sixty-five-year-old former Leveller and past chairman of the Harvard Department of Social Relations conceded that sociology still was in its infancy and had not "reached a stage of development . . . where complete objectivity and impartiality can be expected." Clearly, numerical triumph did not translate into scientific success.[1]

It was not the first time Parsons had tried to gauge the progress of his discipline, but his tone and mood had changed dramatically over the years. In his 1945 contribution to a similar volume edited by his colleagues Georges Gurvitch and Wilbert E. Moore, for example, he had written that sociology was "just in the process of emerging into the status of a mature science," adding that his own project of creating a general theory of action was one of the key components of this triumphal march. Thanks to new public and private sources of funding and the dazzling expansion of the academic job market, the members of the American Sociological Society doubled between 1949, when Parsons had been its president, and 1959. While sociologists consolidated their position through intense boundary work and developed solid connections

130

with various branches of the government and the world of business, the organization had been pushed to abandon its original character as a learned society to embrace the model of a professional association.[2]

To examine the growth problems of the discipline and advance sound (and hopefully consensual) solutions, a Committee on the Profession, chaired by the omnipresent Parsons, had been created in 1959—the same year that the American Sociological Society had changed its name to the American Sociological Association to avoid pesky acronyms. In his final report, the Harvard sociologist had praised the emancipation of American sociology from being the work of just "a few outstanding individuals" through the emergence of "a growing body of solidly trained and competent people who provide in the aggregate a cumulative development of knowledge on which their successors can build and which is the most important hallmark of a relatively mature science." At the same time, Parsons had described with an ambivalent mix of pride and concern the new role played by sociologists as consultants and public intellectuals, a novelty he interpreted as a contribution to the "general definition of the situation"—that is, the ideal image that any society has of itself and its collective goals.[3]

Situated where "society's value-commitments and its empirical scientific culture" met, this truly ideological activity threatened to interrupt what Parsons saw as sociology's long march toward scientific respectability. To help his beloved discipline improve its self-reflection, in 1965 he threw himself body and soul into a new venture as the founder and first editor of the quarterly review the *American Sociologist*. In his early columns, Parsons reiterated his concern that the American Sociological Association might become a victim of its own success, especially after the launch of Lyndon B. Johnson's Great Society programs had taken the involvement of sociologists with government to unprecedented levels. To avoid the twin dangers of partisanship and fragmentation, professional codes and norms had to be strictly upheld: "The general situation," wrote Parsons in 1967, "imposes on the academic professional . . . an obligation to differentiate between his commitments in his professional role and his 'private' political position."[4]

The wind, however, was blowing in the opposite direction. Although the statesmen of postwar sociology and the "myth of value-freedom" had been criticized in the late 1950s by C. Wright Mills, Barrington Moore Jr., and Alvin W. Gouldner, it was only after the emergence of unprecedented political scandals at the national level, such as Operation Starlite and the disclosure of Project Camelot, that the opposition assembled to advocate a thorough transformation of disciplinary culture and structures. Between the 1967 and the 1969 meetings of the American Sociological Association, the self-proclaimed Sociology Liberation Movement, comprising mostly White male graduate students from top universities, joined forces with the caucuses of Black and women sociologists to attack the postwar consensus. Among the topics proposed for discussion were the integration of hitherto excluded minorities within panels and associational boards, the relationship between sociology and the political and military-industrial complex, and the possibility of explicitly committing the association to the pursuit of what the critics saw as the pressing political issues of the day—social justice, the rights of minorities, and opposition to the war in Vietnam.[5]

The new generation of radical social scientists was particularly interested in boundary work. What had happened to "sociology"? How should it change? And, most importantly, who had derailed it? Who, in other words, was the enemy? In a famous rant at the 1968 American Sociological Association convention in Boston, an unknown graduate student from Brandeis University, Martin Nicolaus, depicted a fairly clear image of "the type of sociologist who sets the tone and the ethic of the profession": "The honored sociologist, the big-status sociologist, the jet-set sociologist, the fat-contract sociologist, the book-a-year sociologist, the sociologist who always wears the livery—the suit and tie—of his masters" thus being "nothing more or less than a house-servant in the corporate establishment." In Nicolaus's "view from below," everything that Parsons and his older colleagues considered as a step toward scientific maturity was in fact a sign of the discipline's degeneration: "Today's prominent sociologists," wrote Nicolaus in a well-known article published in 1969, "are the direct financial creatures, functionally the house-servants, of the civil, military, and economic sovereignty."[6]

I

As shown by the success of Gouldner's *The Coming Crisis of Western Sociology*, published in 1970, the insurgents found a perfect villain in Talcott Parsons, seen as the embodiment of what they called "the establishment"—the Harvard-Columbia complex and its support troops, also known as "the Sunshine Boys" for "their effort to make capitalism a smooth and streamlined organization of happiness." And yet, as much as Parsons looked like the perfect target for such activism, his grip on American sociology was not as strong as his opponents (and perhaps he himself) thought. True, he held important positions within the association and surely enjoyed great visibility as a (much criticized) theorist. And it was true that many among his former students had very good jobs and had de facto colonized the departments of most Ivy League universities—from Robert Merton and Bernard Barber at Columbia to Robin Williams Jr. at Cornell, and Renée Fox at Barnard College and then at Penn, the list was long. Among Parsons's privileged scions were also less visible individuals who possessed a great deal of power. An example of the latter was Francis X. Sutton, who had been a member of the Society of Fellows while pursuing his PhD in sociology under Parsons in the late 1940s. After a stint at Harvard as an assistant professor, in 1954 he had joined the Ford Foundation as an executive associate in the Behavioral Sciences program, and then became deputy vice-president of the recently created International Division in October 1968—just two months after Nicolaus's "fat-cat sociology" speech in Boston.[7]

At the same time, the spread of Parsons's intellectual influence was hindered by multiple factors. Always absorbed in theoretical reasoning at the highest levels of abstraction and ready to walk any intellectual and scientific path to improve his multilevel theoretical schemes, the "real Talcott Parsons" was an enthusiastic and fascinating scholar whose image did not really match that of the tedious, conservative egghead propagated by Mills and Gouldner. But the pace and complexity of his work ensured that most, if not all, of his associates had serious difficulties in following him in his quest. Most of Parsons's students just stuck to "the theory" as they had learned it at a particular moment of its development—Marion Levy Jr., for example, based much of his teaching and research at Princeton on the version of structural-functionalism he had absorbed in the mid-1940s, and explicitly criticized Parsons's advances in 1959.[8]

And that was not all. As soon as one moved away from the Eastern Seaboard, other academic networks and alternative ways of doing sociology, such as the variable-based and statistical traditions of the universities of Minnesota and Wisconsin, had been left untouched by Parsonian functionalism. The same was true for the heirs of Chicago sociology and symbolic interactionism, whose vindication of the new American welfare state was so different from that put forward by the Sunshine Boys that in 1969 Alvin Gouldner wrote an article chastising Howard S. Becker's plea for a "partisan sociology" as yet another paradoxical attempt at reaching a faux scientific objectivity. Such pluralism meant, first, that not even the fiercest attacks against high modernism and functionalism could stop the wider trend toward market-driven research;

the use of more and more sophisticated, variable-based methods of causal analysis; and the connection between "local" sociologists and "local" problems (and funders). But it also meant that all the emerging theoretical perspectives—including various strands of Marxism, feminism, a heterodox (that is, anti-Parsonian) reading of Max Weber, and ethnomethodology— would soon become the small and unconnected provinces of an increasingly fragmented or, as it is sometimes generously called, "post-paradigmatic" field.[9]

At forty-two, Robert Bellah had no stake in the American Sociological Association and rarely attended its annual or regional meetings, and thus had very little to say about the organizational or professional requests of the protestors. And his peculiar position at the fringes of the disciplinary elite would remain untouched by the upheaval. He was the only product of Parsons's Department of Social Relations who had reached the position of tenured full professor at Harvard before moving to one of the best, and most diverse, departments in the country (and the world). He had benefited from the largesse of the postwar period, but he had never participated in any of the most controversial government-funded research programs. As the holder of a Ford Professorship and the chairman of the Berkeley Center for Japanese and Korean Studies, he continued to enjoy lavish funding and reduced teaching obligations, and undoubtedly sat at the top of the academic hierarchy. At the same time, the slow but inexorable decline of area studies, the subordinate condition of the study of religion within sociology, and his reluctance to take on any office within a professional association made Bob Bellah a well-established, highly respected, but almost powerless member of the top tier of academic sociology.[10]

As for the intellectual side, Bellah would never consider the protesters and their unsophisticated Marxism as real intellectual foes. In this sense, it was not so much the anti-Parsonsian uprising that worried him, but rather the lukewarm reception that established social scientists had given symbolic realism in Rome and at Sanders Theater. The scholars he had addressed at the conference on atheism and his discussants in Cambridge were no iconoclasts. They all belonged to the older generation, and had scolded Bellah for what they had caught in his spirited performances—the few published papers where he had come up with more reflective, although still unpolished, versions of symbolic realism, such as his review of Clifford Geertz's "Religion as a Cultural System" and "Transcendence in Contemporary Piety," were little known. If symbolic realism was to be recognized as proper social science, Bob had to find a way to combine four different exigencies: he had to gain some distance from Parsons without being identified as a hippie, a radical, or a humanist.

Interestingly, he shared this last problem with the two old friends he was experimenting with in the unknown realm of radical symbolic analysis, Geertz and David M. Schneider. The two Social Relations–trained anthropologists, who had both found jobs at the University of Chicago in 1960, were laying the foundations of what would later be designated "interpretive social science." Still in its embryonic stage, the new perspective entailed a refusal of any reduction of symbolic phenomena to biological, economic, psychological, or social factors; an idea of culture as "webs of significance" that man "himself has spun," built on conventional relationships between publicly available symbols rather than on the correlation between symbols and "external reality"; and the positing of a reciprocity of sorts between symbolic life and practical activity that could be understood only in the effects that the perceived reality of symbols exerted on social actors.[11]

As underlined by anthropologist Victor Turner in a review of symbolic studies published in 1975, the interpretive approach was heavily influenced by "microsociology à la Goffman, sociolinguistics, folklore, literary criticism (notably as practiced by Kenneth Burke), and semiotics," and was thus at odds not only with any reductionistic treatment of culture, such as vulgar Marxism, but also with Parsons's own formulaic analyses of patterns of societal values. This meant that any step in the direction of a more thorough consideration of the peculiarities of the symbolic sphere forced Schneider and Geertz to define their relation with their former teacher in scholarly, positional, and even personal terms.[12]

The two anthropologists, however, found a straightforward strategy: they explicitly acknowledged their debt to Parsons and then moved away. In the first footnote to *American Kinship: A Cultural Account*, published in 1968, Schneider portrayed his conception of the symbolic realm as similar to that of his teachers—Clyde Kluckhohn, Alfred L. Kroeber, and Talcott Parsons. But then he added: "I have, however, departed from this tradition in one important respect. I have here attempted to deal with culture as a symbolic system purely in its own terms rather than by systematically relating the symbols to the social and psychological systems, and to the problems of articulating them within the framework of the problem of social action." While paying homage to Social Relations, Schneider was liberating culture from the synthetic role Parsons had given it in his analyses of societal values. The theoretical leap was enormous, but it was also enormously understated.[13]

The path taken by Cliff Geertz was more convoluted, but had the same point of arrival. In the early years of his career, he had published a host of books and articles framed by a strongly Weberian version of modernization theory; just like Bellah, he had an easy command of the nuances of Parsons's AGIL scheme and used it as an implicit tool for thinking. And yet, in the mid-1950s he had already moved toward an appreciation of different types of symbols as connecting individual experiences and cultural codes. "Religion as a Cultural System" introduced an open-ended idea of symbol systems, where particular cases became much more important than general theoretical frameworks for grasping the "elusive" nature of culture. At the same time, Geertz was not going to disavow his old mentor: "In working toward such an expansion of the conceptual envelope in which our studies take place, one can, of course, move in a great number of directions," he wrote in the paper. "For my part, I shall confine my effort to developing what, following Parsons and Shils, I refer to as the cultural dimension of religious analysis." With the publication of *The Interpretation of Cultures* in 1973, Geertz's shift to interpretive anthropology was to become fully public, thus producing the perception of a radical distancing from Parsons that was, in fact, grossly overstated by both critics and sympathizers.[14]

II

Being a sociologist, Bellah occupied a thornier position. While he never identified with functionalism, he was not going to attack Talcott Parsons head-on, especially in a moment when a growing number of what he considered unsophisticated critics were competing to deride his old mentor. Bellah's reluctance, however, was not only due to sentimental reasons: he still admired Parsons and truly found inspiration in his work, as he did in "old school" cybernetics, ego psychology, evolutionism, psychoanalysis, and Protestant theology. As a consequence, his first steps away from his heritage of Social Relations were much more ambivalent than those of the anthropologists. The paper on Japanese culture and religion he submitted in 1969 to the collection that Alex Inkeles and Bernard Barber were assembling to celebrate Parsons's retirement made spare use of the pattern variables; later that year he penned a note to explain the genesis of his old paper "The Systematic Study of Religion" that was quite similar to Schneider's and Geertz's declarations of intent: "Though I have moved away from heavy use of explicitly Parsonian vocabulary," he wrote, "and have shifted some of the emphases that can be discerned in this paper, I consider my subsequent work more a development than a repudiation of Parsonian theory."[15]

This, however, was not enough. Bellah needed a clear path out of confusion, something that would help him leave the intellectual grip of mother Harvard and father Parsons, thus finding his own way to intellectual adulthood. Indeed, Bob needed a transitional object. As defined by psychoanalyst Donald W. Winnicott, this particular object of attachment helps an infant come to terms with the awareness that reality, and in particular the mother, exists independently of the infant, and the feeling of anxiety that may engender. To fulfil their function, transitional objects must surpass the mother in importance, while retaining their symbolic quality: "It is not the object, of course, that is transitional. The object represents the infant's transition from a state of being merged with the mother to a state of being in relation to the mother as something outside and separate."[16] When the shift to autonomy is over, transitional objects lose their very raison d'être, to the point that they are "not forgotten and . . . not mourned," since the relationship infants have with them eventually becomes generalized as a safe area of symbolic mediation between inner and outer reality.[17]

The transitional object had always been there, right at Bob's hand: Norman O. Brown's *Love's Body*. Through Nobby's looking glass, Bellah's work on religious symbols, his interest in literates and poets, and his refusal of disciplinary boundaries could finally be brought into shape. And yet, *Love's Body* remained too radical for the orphan son of Luther Hutton Bellah Jr., the one who had found a new fatherly figure in the high priest of high modernism, Talcott Parsons. Looking for a satisfactory way out of this dilemma, Bob shifted from "some three cornered balance between orgiasticism, mysticism and the Protestant Ethic" to the thorough demolition of Nobby Brown's intentions. As Winnicott would say, transitional objects are cuddled and cared for, but also "excitedly loved and mutilated." This is what happened to *Love's Body* in Bellah's hands: it was glorified, probed, desecrated, and then left behind.[18]

In April 1969, back from the conference in Rome, Bob wrote a piece on *Love's Body* that was eventually published one year later in Mircea Eliade's journal, *History of Religions*. This "strange book review" was his first clear declaration of allegiance to Nobby Brown, with whom he had resumed an epistolary and, when possible, face-to-face relationship. In an attempt to articulate his *personal experience with* the book rather than to summarize it or subject it to scholarly criticism, Bob told the story of his discovery of *Love's Body* on the plane from Massachusetts to California—from his old home to his new home, from his old self to his new self—and declared that one year later he was "still living with the book, teaching with it, absorbing it." Bellah saw *Love's Body* as emerging from the need "to embrace the whole, to break down the walls of academic specialization"—that is, according to his own definition, as a truly religious work. At the same time, Brown's horror of demystification allowed Bob to consider traditions as alternative ways to grasp the human condition, with no single vocabulary providing an ultimate standard for reduction or critique. Against Marcuse, Bellah saw a new understanding of the world as a way to change it, and praised *Love's Body* as the sign that "we are already coming out of the wilderness and beginning to enter our inheritance."[19]

Readers would have had serious trouble recognizing the author of *Tokugawa Religion* and "Civil Religion in America," though not the passionate preacher seen in Rome or at Sanders Theater. Bellah's friends met his new work with mixed reactions. Nobby Brown was obviously moved: "It is hard for me to put into words my reactions to your review of my book," he wrote. "You go so deep so close to the heart of the matter it is too close to my heart: close to that point where all antinomy of word and deed, speech and silence is overcome." Wilfred Smith and Jacob Taubes followed suit, as did David Riesman and his wife Evey. Others were far more critical: Kenneth Burke, who had scorned *Love's Body* in a "mean" (his word) review in the *Nation* in 1967, compared Brown's language to "a piece of clockwork without a ratchet," while Clifford Geertz met Bellah's suggestion "to be a little more Dionysiac" with an eloquent silence.[20]

Whether for or against, however, they all considered Bob's interest in Brown as a personal, more than a scholarly, matter, while some lecture notes of February 11, 1970, showed a different interpretation: "How did I get from T.P. to N.O.B.?" Bellah wrote. "Then I realized how much of what I said that infuriated my commentators [in Rome and Cambridge] was really already in T.P.—but so abstract that nobody understood what it meant. Then I realized that I am a left Parsonian like Marx was a left Hegelian." The next day, Parsons expressed his puzzlement over Bellah's interest in Brown, and Bellah reasserted his basic allegiance to his mentor: "I am convinced however, more than I have been in several years, that I am carrying through to certain kinds of conclusions implications that were already deeply embedded in your work." At the same time, *Love's Body* was crucial to place "the creative role of symbolism" at the center of a new synthesis "between physical organism, social system, personality, and symbol systems"—that is, the four AGIL subsystems of Parsons's general theory of action.[21]

The continuity that Bob saw between the two phases of his work was such that he advanced the most unexpected analogy: "While it would hardly be possible to find a writer more different from Talcott Parsons than Norman O. Brown," he wrote to Parsons himself, "I would be prepared to make the drastic statement that Norman O. Brown is an ecstatic Talcott Parsons." This insight—which was met with another eloquent silence—was worked out in a paper written for a conference on the work of Norman Brown held at the University of North Carolina at Chapel Hill in April 1970, in which Burke also partici-pated. Published in 1971, "Brown in Perspective" became Bellah's second and final study on *Love's Body*.[22]

Contrary to what his opening proviso would imply—"A prosaic commen-tary is not the right response to *Love's Body*"—Bellah was not ready to follow Brown down the path of aphoristic thinking; moreover, he was conscious that his systematic approach was going to bring Nobby's work quite far from its premises. As a consequence, "Bellah on Brown" had an unexpected point of departure: Jerome Bruner's model of cognitive development through three levels of consciousness: enactive (rooted in practice and action), ikonic (built on images), and conceptual (based on conventional language). The model implied that in moving to higher stages of consciousness, earlier stages were not eliminated but maintained in latency—much like Freud's unconscious, all modes of representation continued to influence behavior at any time.[23]

In a risky theoretical move, Bob projected this ontogenetic model onto the human species as a whole and depicted *Love's Body* as an early example of the language needed to connect all forms of consciousness by way of a simultane-ous employment of all three modes of representation. The reunification of mind, feeling, and body made possible by the use of this multilayered language would allow enlightened individuals to "dream while awake" and contribute to a new integration of science and life, religion and spiritual experience, poli-tics and education. The paper ended with two quotes from *Love's Body*, intro-duced by Bellah's very last words on Norman O. Brown: "Perhaps our only choice is between a literal 'end of history' and the transfiguration and rebirth which Brown means by that phrase."[24]

Turning the classic parallel between ontogeny and phylogeny on its head, Bellah connected Jerry Bruner—Cambridge, Harvard, systems, high modernism—with Nobby Brown—California, Berkeley, ecstasy, postmod-ernism. Though only a sketch, this solution remained for a while the capstone not only of Bob's theoretical work, but also of his reflections on how a Brown-inspired symbolic consciousness could be achieved and, even more impor-tantly, taught. Between the late 1960s and early 1970s he spent a disproportion-ate amount of time reflecting on the practice of teaching religion, and even considered dedicating an entire book to it, *The University as a Religious Institution*. Rarely read and almost forgotten, his writings on the matter were a window on the development of symbolic realism as a research program and a personal stance.[25]

III

While Clifford Geertz was often described as annoyed by large classes, Bellah had always had an ambivalent relationship with teaching. At Harvard he resented the stressful demands of too many bright students—as recounted by Melanie, "he would come home at night and say, 'It's killing me, it's killing me.'" Once at Berkeley, he was struck by the effervescence he found at both the university and the Graduate Theological Union, where "a sort of adolescent Leftism" was widespread among both the students and the faculty. Although irritated by the most radical fringes, Bob considered the majority of Berkeley kids to be genuinely interested in living through the late 1960s, and appreciated their exuberant and concerned attitude. Combined with his new approach to religious symbolism, this led to a radical shift in his teaching goals and habits.[26]

The undergraduate course in the sociology of religion that Bellah had taught with Parsons from 1962 to 1966 was a typical Social Relations introduction to the discipline: strong on theory and framed by a vague version of modernization theory. When he first offered the introductory course at Berkeley, Bob taught a simplified version of the Harvard lectures, adding Slater's *Microcosm* to his familiar selection of Durkheim, Weber, Troeltsch, Freud, Parsons, and Geertz. After his encounter with *Love's Body*, however, this format would simply not do. Bob had to leave his past as a professor behind: "I realize that when I started teaching I was a disembodied ghost presenting abstract concepts," he wrote, while now he maintained that "unless you are willing to teach with your whole self, *with everything you have*, you are not really going to teach at all." As an attempt to respond to the crisis of the late 1960s, teaching religion should be considered "a kind of religious discipline" in itself, one that turned belief, pluralism, and criticism into lived experiences. As even the most skeptical among his students were going to discover, Bellah was not afraid "of blurring the boundary line between religion and the teaching of religion."[27]

Major changes were introduced during a 1969 graduate seminar in the sociology of religion. During his first class, Bellah read from Brown's "Apocalypse" and announced that any distinction between scientific and humanistic disciplines was "temporary and inessential." He then presented *Love's Body* alongside its "anti-text," Philip Rieff's *The Triumph of the Therapeutic*, and indicated the main goal of the course: how to (critically) conceive and put into action a nonauthoritarian society and a nonrepressive personality. How could Bob and his students "institutionalize the 'permanent revolution' socially and personally?" Now that the gates of the counterculture were open, Brown's book could find its way into undergraduate classrooms. After asking his students to recount their liminal religious experiences, Bellah introduced Alfred Schütz's dialectic between the world of common sense and alternative realities by way of some poems by Robinson Jeffers. When he proclaimed that "You cannot live in everyday reality all of the time!" the classroom exploded with applause. With his new formula, Bellah intended to help his students to reach what the French philosopher Paul Ricoeur called a "second naïveté." Since humans dealt with reality only through symbols, the positivist pretense to have a direct, unmediated access to reality was as wrong as the radical skepticism of archconstructivism. All symbolic complexes—science, religion, art, ideology, and common sense—had an equally legitimate access to reality.[28]

And yet, the awareness "that every interpretation of reality [was] finally only an interpretation, and not reality itself" could not be learned from the pages of a book. Symbolic realism had to be the result of a dialectical process of personal growth. It had to be made and remade one student at a time. The maturation of second naïveté, in other words, depended on a complex voyage through the primary naïveté of the common believer and the reductionism of rationalist criticism. Students would first come into contact with the most paradoxical, ecstatic religious experiences and, through them, would learn to accept the irruption of the sacred into ordinary reality. Then, with the help of the Holy Trinity of Social Relations—Weber, Freud, and Durkheim—they would learn about symbolic reductionism and move beyond it, into a postcritical apprehension of symbolic innocence. Through a half-semester odyssey students would hopefully develop a "double vision," a "conscious magical thinking," or even a "new, purified animism" that would transcend Bob's old distinction between a natural and a philosophical attitude to reality.[29]

Traditional academic grades did not fit well with the new approach. Bellah invited his students to write their term papers on first-person experiences or "their own symbolic attempts to come to grips with reality." Autobiography, religious and quasi-religious services, altered states of consciousness, and the interpretation of basic symbols soon became the hottest topics among undergraduates. During final examinations students were requested to analyze an iconic symbol such as "ocean, sun, light, tree, mountain" in "its personal, social and transcendental implications," to write about the myths and rituals of the American university, or to trace "the direct and indirect influences of Weber and Durkheim on Slater and Brown." Classical social theory was presented as a Janus-faced key to the attainment of second naïveté: on the one hand, it was Enlightenment social science—antireligious, reductionist, and thus unacceptable. On the other hand, the Lares of Social Relations all showed a backdoor to transcendence: Durkheim's collective effervescence, Freud's unconscious, and Weber's charisma were the harbingers of personal and social novelty, which proved to be refractory to a fully rational analysis.[30]

At the center of Bob's new interpretation of the heritage of classical social theory stood Émile Durkheim. Even if *Tokugawa Religion* was based on a combination of Weberian insight and Parsonian models, Bellah had silently worked on the French sociologist for years. Now he wanted to save Durkheim (and himself) from the deadly embrace of functionalism and make him the major forerunner of interpretive social science—a position that, at the time, was occupied by either Weber or Schütz. A nonreductionist reading of Durkheim's *The Elementary Forms of Religious Life* would provide sociologists with a whole new array of concepts to grasp the relationship between man, community, and transcendence. During his moment of epiphany in July 1968 Bob nailed his interpretation of Durkheim as a proto-symbolic realist in quick strokes:

> Various thoughts for Durkheim introduction: Durkheim as visionary—stress collective effervescence. The difference between society alive and society dead. Durkheim's theories of symbolism. His notions of solidarity and integration. All of this not primarily to be dealt with in Marxist terms but more modern. The form and the *unreadable* in Durkheim. The vital glowing image of society. Mother? Apparently no father—no fuhrer-prinzip [sic]. "Society" *gives* almost everything. Is his definition of God literalist? Or symbolic? Elementary Forms as central. The other selections as eluminating [sic] it.[31]

These points made their way into the introduction to Bellah's edited collection, *Émile Durkheim on Morality and Society*, written in early 1970. Here, Bob argued that the mainstream reading of the *Elementary Forms* as reducing religion to a projection of society was based on a gross theoretical mistake. Since Durkheim had defined "society" as "a set of ideas and sentiments," when he spoke of morality and religion as mirroring society he was in fact speaking of a relation between two different but mutually constitutive sets of symbols. In other words, if society was seen as a *conscience collective*, myths and rituals did "not merely give an intellectual conception of society, *they [created] it*" in a two-way process that only a deep hermeneutics of societal and religious symbols could uncover. Durkheim had repeatedly been on the verge of "discovering" the autonomous creative force of religious symbolism—that is, of discovering symbolic realism.[32]

Bellah's complex and contradictory image of the French founder of sociology was the crucible where his Brownesque idea of religious symbolism, his need to combine systematic analysis with personal experience, his concept of civil religion, and his view of the engaged scholar could be molded into a single, original *prise de position*. It also was yet another way to generate some distance from Parsons without fully rejecting him. It was not by chance that Bellah sent Morris Janowitz the first draft of his introduction to the Heritage of Sociology collection of Durkheim's texts on July 6, 1970, the very same day he was given notice that he'd won the Harbison Award for Gifted Teaching, a $10,000 grant from the Danforth Foundation he could freely use in the furtherance of his academic interests and career. In fact, the combination of Bob's theoretical insights and radical teaching experiences was a better illustration of his scholarly and personal condition than his first collection of essays, *Beyond Belief*.[33]

IV

The idea of a volume of essays as a "retrospect at forty" had kept Bellah busy during his first fall in Berkeley, when everything else was proceeding so slowly that he saw no other way out of his intellectual paralysis. Its first tentative title, *Religion in Human Action*, came from Bellah's oldest theoretical article, published in 1958, and was clearly indebted to Talcott Parsons. In 1969 Bob approached different publishers as he began selecting the papers for the book, which was eventually published by Harper and Row in 1970 as *Beyond Belief: Essays on Religion in a Post-Traditional World*. It included sixteen chapters carefully arranged as a hypertextual illustration of the first fifteen years of Bob's scholarly career. Introduced by an autobiographical essay, *Beyond Belief* included three parts—"Theoretical Foundations," "Religion in the Modernization Process," and "Religion in Modern Society"—each opened by a short preamble, while each chapter had a footnote detailing its context and place in Bellah's development.[34]

According to its dust jacket, the collection presented "the new ground for the interpretation of religion that men in a variety of disciplines [had] moved toward for decades," as related to "the author's self-conscious search for personal meaning." In fact, the *fil rouge* of the book's lengthy introduction was Bob's personal journey from Altus to Berkeley. "I am very uncomfortable with the balance between revealing and concealing," he wrote in his diary in October 1969, "and will probably redo [the introduction] by drawing the blinds quite a bit further down." What found its way onto the printed page was a larger-than-life narrative of his shift from the "Harvard complex" to the "Berkeley complex," whose end results were symbolic realism, postmodernism, an expanded consciousness, and the refusal of "any political totalism"—an amalgam that would bring Robert Bellah to embrace "the playful radicalism of Norman O. Brown" and a "politics of the imagination, a politics of religion," whatever that meant.[35]

Bob's focus on the subjective side of his work was far from being mere sentimentalism. The last essay of the book, "Between Religion and Social Science"—a collation of the 1969 Los Angeles conference and the Sanders Theater speech—pointed to the intersection of theory and experience as the very epistemic foundation of symbolic realism. In a sense, *Beyond Belief* aimed at being *in itself* an exemplar of the integral relationship between scholarly and personal life on which symbolic realism was built: "The chapters of this book must stand finally on their own merits, on the cogency of their arguments and the clarity with which they order the empirical data," wrote Bob in the introduction. "But the experience out of which they come, which I have tried to discuss in this introduction, is not irrelevant to them and if they succeed it will be not only because they contain convincing arguments but by their capacity to order the common experience. They are attempts to find patterns of meaning in a world where all the great overarching systems of belief, conservative and radical, have lost their viability. These essays," he concluded, "are expressions of 'belief,' in Wallace Stevens' words, 'without belief, beyond belief.'"[36]

As a novel approach to the study of religion, symbolic realism also needed a newly conceived institutional environment. In the wake of his Sanders Theater speech, Bellah proposed to recast the positivistic study of religion into a new, independent field of research and reflection, which he simply (and perhaps incautiously) named "Religion." The new field would thrive thanks to the reform of departments of religion as transdisciplinary havens where religious orthodoxy, secularist critique, and symbolic realism would develop together in a double dialectical relationship. Social science could then perform a crucial function vis-à-vis the search of ultimate meaning: "Social science may soon play the role that traditionally philosophy filled: that is, to provide the intellectual tools for religious self-reflection"—the echoes of the failed Harvard project of the mid-1960s were loud and clear.[37]

No matter how carefully planned it was, *Beyond Belief* was anything but a compact, coherent cultural object. It had neither the simplicity of Parsons's collections of essays nor the perspicuity of Geertz's *The Interpretation of Cultures*, which would be published in 1973. In part, this was because, unbeknownst to its readers, *Beyond Belief* was a proxy for a book that had still to be written. Its structure reflected Bellah's past projects for *A Theory of Religion*: the theoretical introduction—now shrunk down to "Religious Evolution" and the 1968 *Encyclopedia* entry—and two parts on the modernization process and modern society. With respect to the original project, lost was the detailed elaboration of a multidimensional approach to religion, as were the analyses of premodern stages of religious evolution. Moreover, the early writings on symbolic realism were included in part three, *as though* they were analyses of empirical phenomena rather than theoretical arguments aimed at changing the way in which social scientists saw religious phenomena. This choice came from Bellah's view of post-modernity as a hyper-reflexive stage in which the comprehension of the effects of the new symbolic consciousness would surely change all existing relationships between forms of knowledge.

In fact, the grandiosity of Bob's wager was tamed by the complexity of the book, which also pushed most reviewers to approach *Beyond Belief* with a sense of mild puzzlement. In the *American Journal of Sociology*, for example, Andrew M. Greeley called Bellah a Parsonian and a Weberian, "one willing to push . . . to logical conclusions which neither of his two masters seem to have reached." This was Bob's own interpretation of his progress as a theorist, but also one that downplayed the novelty of his contribution and somehow neglected his attempt at distancing himself from his mentor, whose presence was felt by most commentators. Other reviewers focused on Bellah's account of his own progress as a scholar; Michael R. Brendle deemed the introduction "superb" and praised the essays as "expanded expressions of that [individual] search." Certainly, Bob's vision of the sociology of religion as a way of finding oneself had wider implications in that it highlighted "the subjective nature of *all* contributions of sociology of religion."[38]

This interest in subjectivity was echoed by Samuel S. Hill in the *Journal of the American Academy of Religion*. Hill singled out Bellah and Geertz as the most influential scholars in the study of religion and spoke of Bob's "uniqueness" in taking a wide array of roles: "In addition to being social scientist, phenomenologist, and historian of religious-philosophical ideas . . . , he is humanist, poet, mystic, and theologian." Hill also praised Bellah's open-mindedness: "No one should be surprised that his program sometimes meets with savage rejection. Yet, so intelligent, humane, and thoughtful a student of culture must be listened to. I have to conclude that he is a prophet." Bob's insistence on his subjectivity had apparently taken the lead over the attempt at reforming the discipline: as he would soon discover, in the early 1970s the sociology of religion was not ready to accept too radical a conception of interpretive social science.[39]

10

Twilight of the God

FROM BERKELEY TO PRINCETON,
AND BACK, 1970–1973

BOOSTED BY THE IMMEDIATE SUCCESS of *Beyond Belief*, Robert N. Bellah's career reached new heights. His status as one of the most famous sociologists of religion in the country earned him an uninterrupted flow of speaking engagements on East Asian, American, and "religious" matters, especially in front of nonacademic audiences. The "disembodied ghost" had finally become a full-blooded human being. Berkeley undergraduates acknowledged Bob's dedication and rewarded him with moving expressions of gratitude: his sociology of religion course was packed, students even squatting on the floor, mesmerized and intoxicated as he cast "poetry, mysticism, essay and diagram" in a "sweet convergence, a radiant amalgam, in a hitherto unimagined crucible."[1] Something unexpected happened on the occasion of his forty-fifth birthday on February 23, 1972. "Before I left Daddy called to tell me and Mommy," recounted Tammy in her diary, "about how his students had surprised and touched him at the end of the class by singing 'Happy Birthday.' Never before had that happened to Daddy (he never told anybody), and it was really very lovely."[2]

Bellah's passionate approach also made him a respected mentor to graduate students at both the Department of Sociology and the Graduate Theological Union—who, in this period, included Jeffrey Alexander, Ann Swidler, Harlan Stelmach, and Robert Wuthnow. Besides the inner circle of his collaborators, he also had a small coterie of die-hard admirers, mainly coming from the seminary, who sat in his classes just to enjoy his charismatic presence. As twin jewels in his crown of achievements, in the summer of 1971 Bob won one of ten Harbison Awards for Gifted Teaching and its accompanying $10,000 grant, and a year later *Beyond Belief* was nominated for the National Book Award in the section Philosophy and Religion.[3]

Not that everything was perfect, though. Bellah had grown disillusioned with the possibility of establishing a "vigorous program" in religion at Berkeley. While his appointment had originally come with the prospect of transforming the existing major in religious studies into a department, things had not gone as expected and the project was abandoned. Combined with the difficult act of balancing his Harvard-trained, "Protestant" scholarly persona with the new emphasis on experience and irrationality inspired by Nobby Brown, this failure put Bob between a rock and a hard place. On the one hand, his scholarly self saw the loss of scientific credibility and moral standing of the academic system—as effected by clashes between faculty, graduate students, and staff that went back to the days of the free speech movement—as a major threat. Some of his Sociology colleagues had already decided to leave: in 1969 Nathan Glazer moved to Harvard and Erving Goffman to the University of Pennsylvania, while two years later Reinhard Bendix migrated to a quieter, more conservative academic unit, the Berkeley Department of Political Science. Those who remained were split between a leftist "student side," a conservative "faculty side," and a "wishy-washy majority" that included Arthur L. Stinchcombe, Smelser, Glock, Selznick, and Bellah, who consistently joined forces to uphold intellectual rigor and distinction as the prime standard of academic appointments or promotions.[4]

On the other hand, Bob resented the "all-or-nothing" approach of liberal critics of the counterculture, according to whom the only possible reactions to cultural and political radicalism were rejection or surrender. He thought that an attempt should be made to give "the tide" a sound direction—a task he deemed possible via the employment of oxymoronic conceptual tools such as Erich Fromm's "rational feelings" or that "open communication and access between the levels of consciousness" he had outlined in his pieces on *Love's Body*. Against Geertz and Riesman, Bellah retained the optimistic outlook on the counterculture that he had voiced at the Rome conference and in *Beyond Belief*. In practice, though, "directing the tide" proved to be more difficult than expected, both at the university and at home.

To begin with, the relationship between Bob and his beloved Andy Schmookler had broken down. One evening in August 1970, Andy had told him of a "bone-shaking insight" he had had on the nature and meaning of history. Bellah felt highly ambivalent about the revelation—he found the vision of mankind and civilization proposed by his student interesting but also quite distant from his "Calvinist view." Schmookler was on the verge of leaving for Yale, where he had been admitted to the American Studies program, and Bob encouraged him to develop his intuitions within a regular graduate school frame. When Andy came back to Berkeley in the fall of 1971, the Graduate Theological Union granted him permission to form a committee of five established scholars to discuss his dissertation. When the two finally met again in early 1972, Bob accused his former student of trying to bend academic standards to his own idiosyncrasies. Their lunch at Andy's small apartment did not end well—and despite a few brief encounters over the coming decades, their relationship was never repaired. As anticipated by his friend Stanley Kurnik, Bellah's identification with academic institutions remained his "Achille's heel." The impact of the internecine struggles in the Department of Sociology and the many adjustments he had made to the system, as well as his recurring doubts about his own scholarly talent, made deviations intolerable to him and meant he sometimes overreacted.[5]

At home, Melanie's decision to attend law school in the fall of 1969 had created turmoil in the family. The youngest children—Abby and Hally were, respectively, ten and seven years old—resented her decision, but she was determined to embrace a new phase of her life, which included starting a law practice of her own. Around the same time, Tammy's adolescence was becoming a difficult affair. Berkeley in the late 1960s was quite different from wartime Los Angeles: if Bob had not learned how to drink beer before Harvard, and then only to please the master of Adams House, the life of teenagers was now a mayhem of alcohol, drugs, and tense interracial relations. At fifteen, Tammy had somehow inherited her mother's drug-like dependence on being in love, but had also developed an ambivalent Electra complex to her father complete with a love-hate relationship with her identity as a middle-class White girl.[6]

After some bleak episodes, Tammy started attending "Project Community," a weekly therapy group she immediately found rewarding, and then, in the fall of 1970, Other Ways, a seventy-student, open-classroom school created at Berkeley by educational pioneer Herb Kohl "to attract what he termed the 'freaked-out' white, middle-class kids" who were bored with the traditional high school. Jenny had been the first of the Bellah children to enroll at Other Ways, and did her best to discourage her parents: the institute, she told them, was nothing short of a "primitive jungle," and Tammy was too delicate to survive in such an unstructured and stressful environment—a judgment apparently shared by Kohl himself. But Jenny's pleas did not convince Bob and

Melanie, and Tammy began attending the experimental school, whose deseg-
regated student population supplemented regular courses with classes in sea-
manship, urban survival, poetry, photography, guerrilla theater, and Black
economic development.[7]

Up until then, the Bellahs had been quite liberal about the use of drugs, and
had put up with some of Tammy's friends whom they deeply disliked. Nothing, however, had prepared them for the news of the romantic relationship
between their eldest daughter and the director of Other Ways, a fascinating
and authoritarian Black educator who was twice her age. After some heated
discussion, they decided to keep quiet and, to use Bob's phrase, try to "direct
the tide"—they thought they could "guide and support her through this, could
help [her] learn and grow from this bad relationship." In fact, Tammy was trying to somehow process, and go beyond, the uneasy mix of fear and admiration
she felt for her father. Shortly after a meeting with her therapist, who had asked
her to bring Bob along, Tammy recorded the following in her diary: "Today I
dressed all in dark with a black scarf in my hair and went with Daddy to see
Sandy. She asked me if my clothes were symbolic mourning of an end to a
certain relationship with Daddy. I, in a strangely, scrupulously honest mood,
said she could be right. . . . I do not want to face my relationship with my
father. It is the dread idea of incest that scares me," she added, "I do not want
to confront it, I'd rather let it die in my unconscious. But isn't that the root of
my problem with Daddy?"[8]

In late April 1972, Bob and Melanie set out for a three-week trip to Europe,
and agreed with some discomfort to leave Tammy in charge of the house and
her younger sisters. Thanks to his connections to the American Academy of
Arts and Sciences, to which he had been elected in 1967, Bellah had been invited to join in a major scholarly endeavor devised by Stephen Graubard together with the Giovanni Agnelli Foundation and Fabio Luca Cavazza, one
of the founders of the influential publishing house, Il Mulino. Aimed at
launching a transnational dialogue on the history and prospects of Italian
society, the project would result in a volume presenting breakthrough analyses of Italy's cultural, economic, and political problems within a comparative
modernization framework. On top of all this, the Agnelli Foundation would
pay for a trip to Italy for those who would like to know the country first hand.
Although his acquaintance with Italian society was nil, Bellah decided to take
advantage of the occasion in order to extend the scope of his comparative
work on civil religion and spend some time alone with his wife, whose studies
in law were nearing completion. On April 21, 1972, Bob and Melanie

eventually left for Italy, where they traveled widely, meeting with local politicians, intellectuals, and entrepreneurs during the heated campaign for the May 1972 general election.[9]

This succession of positive and negative incidents left Bob Bellah in a familiar state of disarray: the most satisfactory episodes could not balance his growing frustration or the lack of focus that was, once again, hindering the achievement of his many projects. He had intended his first five years at Berkeley to be the time to achieve some major scholarly goals and beef up his scant publications list—among the titles he had planned were the Durkheim reader, the collection of his past essays, a primer titled *Comparative Perspectives on Religion*, and his long-awaited theoretical volume. In correspondence, Bob also mentioned the book on Japanese modernization conceived in 1960 and a reworked version of the Frank L. Weil Memorial Lectures given at the Hebrew Union College/Jewish Institute of Religion in Cincinnati in the fall of 1971, tentatively titled *The Deepest Day: Studies in the Mythic Dimension of American Culture*.[10]

Of all these, in the spring of 1972 only *Beyond Belief* had hit the shelves. As Tammy later wrote in an essay titled "The Search for Freedom," Bob's quest for wholeness had apparently met some unexpected obstacles: "The family had stayed in Berkeley for five years. By the fifth year, Professor Bellah was disillusioned by Berkeley and searching for the next utopia." Once again, he began craving an "outward change," a physical move that "would transport the family into a utopian environment where none of the problems that irritated and bewildered [him] would exist." That magical place was the most prestigious academic institution in the world, the Institute for Advanced Study in Princeton, New Jersey.[11]

I

Surrounded by beautiful woodland, the Institute for Advanced Study had been created in 1930 thanks to a generous donation by New Jersey businessman Louis Bamberger and his sister Caroline Bamberger Fuld. Their acquaintance Abraham Flexner had persuaded them to invest in the creation of an ideal haven for a small number of outstanding scholars. The program was simple: unqualified freedom to undertake one's research, no teaching obligations, and stellar salaries. Besides its permanent faculty, the institute would welcome a varying number of temporary fellows and allow them to pursue their own projects. It opened in 1933, with Flexner taking up administrative responsibilities for its School of Mathematics, which included John von Neumann and Albert

Einstein. By the mid-1930s it had expanded to add a School of Economics and Politics and a School of Humanistic Studies. In 1946 the second director of the institute, Frank Aydelotte, retired and was replaced by the former leader of the Manhattan Project, physicist J. Robert Oppenheimer. In 1948 the Schools of Humanistic Studies and Economics and Politics merged to form the School of Historical Studies, to which Harold Cherniss, George Kennan, and Ernst Kantorowicz would belong. Oppenheimer also appointed some promising young physicists—among them Tsung-Dao Lee and Freeman Dyson—and created an independent School of Natural Sciences in 1966. André Weil, Kurt Gödel, and Armand Borel were among the institute's mathematicians.[12]

Carl Kaysen, a Harvard economist who had been John F. Kennedy's deputy special assistant for national security affairs, became the institute's fourth director in 1966, with the mission to create a full-fledged School of Social Sciences. The main guidelines for the new unit were detailed in a twelve-page document drafted in January 1969, in which two main research areas were laid out: organizational behavior and social evolution. Herbert Simon, James March, and Kenneth Arrow were selected for the first program for their rigorous scientific work on institutions and decision-making processes, while the second program would involve historians and social scientists in an interdisciplinary endeavor aimed at "understanding how social change [took] place and what [determined] its pace and direction." The systematic use of the concepts elaborated by the social sciences in the analysis of modern Western societies and postcolonial nations was seen as a sound new way to tackle timeless questions on the direction and the meaning of history.[13]

Among the individuals listed as paradigmatic of the work that this second interdisciplinary program sought to promote were Geertz, Bellah, Neil Smelser, Shmuel Eisenstadt, Seymour Lipset, David Apter, Gabriel Almond, Edward Shils, Bernard Lewis, Charles Tilly, and Ronald Dore. The document also reported that a sum of $500,000 had been allocated by the Carnegie Corporation and the Russell Sage Foundation to finance an experimental program in social change for the years 1970 and 1971, and a new building to host the new school and to provide some additional space for existing ones. While the project excluded any policy orientation, and "modernization" was nowhere to be found, the list of usual suspects clearly shows that the Harvard-MIT-Chicago network of high modernist behavioral science was alive, kicking, and undergoing a new incarnation.[14]

Psychologists George Miller and R. Duncan Luce, both mentioned in the original plan, were already long-term visiting fellows at the institute before

Clifford Geertz, then at the University of Chicago, was appointed the first permanent social scientist early in 1970. Soon after he got the job, Geertz invited Bellah for lunch in his hometown of San Francisco. Cliff talked effusively about the institute and how exciting it was to be in such a wonderful scholarly place, and Bob expressed his joy at his friend's new condition. When they were leaving the restaurant, however, Geertz suddenly burst out with: "Don't you want to come?" Bellah replied that he had never been asked to go, and Cliff made clear, in his characteristic brusque tone, that he expected his friend Bob to ask *him* if he could go. That was the first time the two discussed the prospect of Bellah joining the institute as a permanent member. Later in 1970 Bellah wrote Geertz a letter expressing his excitement at the prospect of moving to Princeton: "If the Institute position should open up for me that can be a pleasant surprise," he wrote, "but whatever happens I want you to know, as I said in April, that I am very touched that you wanted me." If their hopes for him to join the institute came true, he continued, he would concentrate on the study of Japanese intellectual history and "the psycho-social-symbolic process we call religion in a variety of cultural contexts." The point, though, was that being together again for the first time in years would help them both become better scholars and perhaps even better human beings: "I do think it would be wonderful to work alongside you. We have diverged a bit in recent years but I think that is all the more reason that I would gain from the association. You might help keep me from getting too pompously preachy and I might encourage you to be a little more Dionysiac."[15]

When the English demographer Anthony Wrigley turned down the offer of a permanent position at the institute, Geertz decided it was time to invite Bellah to come for one year, with the prospect of tenure. On November 13, 1970, Bob received a letter from Kaysen offering him a temporary post at the institute for the academic year 1972–1973 and a Stewart Fellowship, a grant that required its recipient to give a seminar in the field of religion at Princeton University. Bellah was baffled: being a Ford Professor allowed him to teach one quarter a year, and teaching "only" one seminar would be no big difference from his ordinary duties—he had expected better conditions for his year at the institute. When he told her, Melanie tried to persuade her husband not to accept the proposal on the grounds that it would not be a real year off; more importantly, she would be leaving law school soon, and was determined to pursue a career as an attorney in California. After some discussion, they decided that Bob should accept Kaysen's offer under reserve, and agreed it was not the right time to tell the children.[16]

During 1971 Bellah and Geertz renewed their scholarly and personal bonds. Thanks to his rising fame in American Studies, Bob had been asked to give the Weil Memorial Lectures in the fall of 1971, an invitation he saw as the perfect chance to develop his interpretive approach using the mythical foundations of the United States as a test case study. The problem was that the framework of symbolic realism was still in embryonic form, its method nonexistent, and Bellah's idea of an American civil religion was highly contested. In September 1971, Bob received from Geertz a draft of "Deep Play: Notes on the Balinese Cockfight," an essay that would soon become a classic of interpretive social science. Reading it only intensified Bellah's state of confusion: "The problem of interpretation is very much in my mind these days," he wrote his friend. "Indirectly suggestions from your paper are influencing my Weil Lectures on the mythical substructure of American culture. I am simply overwhelmed with what I have gotten myself into. I vacillate between being very excited about material and ideas and feeling completely incapable of bringing order to such a vast subject."[17]

As a consequence, Bellah started to look at his stay in Princeton as an occasion to work with Geertz on a method for the interpretive approach to social science. This particular was not lost on David Riesman, who was spending the 1971–1972 academic year at the institute. In a letter written on November 30, 1971, he shared with Bob some of his impressions about the place and its denizens:

About the Institute, I've continued to think about your coming here permanently and believe it is the right decision. You should make use of the rare opportunity to work together with Cliff Geertz—there are so few such opportunities, and we must reject the individualism which does not take such non-kin connections seriously enough. Evey and I were struck that evening at the Geertz's—our first such occasion and our first glimpse of [Hildred Geertz]—how shy Cliff is beneath his brilliance and outgoing quality. You are in some ways shy too, but there is perhaps more iron in you, and you don't have the same inner resistance quite, so far as I can see, that Cliff does when it comes to approaching people. Thus, in a human as well as in an intellectual way you would support and complement each other. This seems to me worth all the rest of the rational arguments one can make one way or the other. Furthermore, I see the two of you together changing the style of at least part of the Institute away from solipsism toward helping younger people, very specific ones, who want to come and work with you the way

Fouad Masrieh is working with Cliff this year. This seems to me an enormously powerful way of teaching which is somewhat less feasible where you have so many other demands on you at Berkeley.

Bob responded that Kaysen had "virtually committed" the second professorship to him, but also that a final decision would have to wait until his visiting appointment the next year. But the rumor took off: Seymour Lipset mentioned it to Riesman, who in turn told Bellah in a letter dated January 4, 1972. Again, Bob replied that there had been no formal invitation and he had not made up his mind on the matter: "I don't have it yet and besides that I don't know what I will do should I get it." He urged Riesman to underline "how very tentative the whole matter [was]."[18]

Apart from merely academic difficulties, Bellah's discretion was dictated by the realization that any talk about going to Princeton would create trouble in the family. On moving to Berkeley, he had solemnly promised his wife and children that they would never move again, not even for a single year. Now he was breaking his vow: "Taking a year away," he repeatedly told Melanie, "is an expected part of my profession!" And the institute in Princeton was the top academic institution in the world, a place where the best minds could find the perfect environment for nurturing their creative, revolutionary work. It was Einstein's place! How could they not understand how important this appointment could be?[19]

Tammy's essay "The Search for Freedom" echoed dinner discussions full of grand dreams, haunting names, and spirited confrontations: "In Princeton he could take up the thread of his private work again. This 'work' gradually took the air of divine importance to him, which he transmitted to the rest of the family. Because of this feeling they shared of the great importance of 'his work' with the potential to be another Einstein," she concluded, "they may have objected to the move but felt deeply guilty for even daring to object." Guilty or not, Tammy had been admitted to the University of California and told her parents she was not going to leave Berkeley. Jenny, Abby, and Hally protested they did not want to go either. On her part, Melanie for some time played with the idea of commuting between Berkeley and Princeton. Unlike her husband, she still believed in the symbolism that had brought them back to California: if the West was "life" and "growth," going back to the East would surely mean "death."[20]

In the end Bob won. Melanie applied for a job as a law clerk for Judge Phillip Forman at the United States Court of Appeals for the Third Circuit in

Trenton, and when she got the post in early December 1971 she began to think of the move as an occasion to start her legal career on the right foot. Plans were made to rent out two floors of 10 Mosswood Road, leaving one floor for Tammy to use when not at school. At that point, the three younger daughters had no alternative but to accept the move to a strange, unknown place that their father described as "the epitome of all good." After all, Tammy wrote, "though they were astute enough to see through some myths," the other members of the family "still viewed him *as almost a god.*" Everything was ready, and late in August of 1972 the Bellahs packed their cases and left California for New Jersey. Two years earlier, Bob had written Kaysen that he looked forward "to a quiet and . . . productive year." Unluckily, it was going to be neither.[21]

II

The early days in Princeton were far from happy. When Tammy visited her family just before the beginning of the fall semester, she found them in a miserable condition—later she would call her trip a *rêve macabre.* The 1928 Dutch Tudor they rented from the institute at 24 Haslet Avenue was filthy, dark, and infested with fleas. Tammy found Melanie "hysterical, crying and screaming all the time," Jenny and Hally acting "wild and bitchy," Abby terribly depressed, and Bob so upset that his eyes were constantly filled with tears. In addition to the discussion group on methodological approaches in the social sciences he convened with Geertz at the institute, Bellah also gave a seminar on religious symbolism at Princeton University as an abridged version of his recent graduate courses; *Love's Body, Beyond Belief,* and Paul Ricoeur's *Freud and Philosophy* were among the required reading, while books by Jung, Langer, Cassirer, Eliade, and Fingarette made the suggested reading list. In line with his new style, Bob repeatedly invited his students to leave reductionistic and strictly analytical approaches behind—a recommendation that sounded utterly out of place away from Berkeley.[22]

When the offer of a permanent appointment was made on September 25, 1972, it triggered two symmetrical reactions. At the institute it alerted those professors of the Schools of Mathematics and Historical Studies who had already constituted a united front against Kaysen's expansion plans and the School of Social Sciences. And at Berkeley, the members of the faculty who saw Bellah as a pivotal figure in religious studies immediately wrote him offering to do whatever was necessary to keep him at the University of California.[23] Neil Smelser sent Bob a touching letter, arguing that the almost absolute freedom allowed by the institute was something one would better consider "at a near-retirement age": scholarship and creativity needed a "friction," he wrote, that was to be found "mainly in the communication with students and colleagues"—a warning echoed by Talcott Parsons, sociologist Hal Wilensky, and theologian John C. Bennett. In mid-October the historian and Bob's personal friend Bill Bouwsma reported that, should he decide to go back to Berkeley, Bob would certainly be proposed as the director of the new program in religious studies.[24]

In the meantime, an ad hoc committee of five external and six internal members had been appointed to assist the faculty in evaluating Bellah's potential as a member of the social science program. Kaysen and Geertz took a leading role in the selection of the external scholars, whose final list included the familiar names of Robert K. Merton and Edward Shils, historian of religion Joseph M. Kitagawa, and Harvard philosopher Stanley Cavell, as well as Bob's old teacher and former ambassador to Japan Edwin O. Reischauer. On their appointment, the committee members received Bellah's curriculum vitae, a list of his major publications, and two documents. The first of these, an unsigned description of the new program in the social sciences, was an updated version of the 1969 document, in which Geertz's (and Bellah's) imprint was clear. Gone was the interest in organizational studies: now the school of social sciences would focus exclusively on the understanding of social change by way of hermeneutical and qualitative methods that cut across the "artificial" boundaries between the analytical social sciences, history, and the humanities.[25]

The second document presented an account of Bellah's work, signed by Geertz. It described the candidate's well-known publications on Japan, Durkheim, and the American civil religion as paradigmatic of the new program's focus on the dynamic relationship between ideas and institutions. Geertz also spoke of their common intellectual project: "I have known and worked with Robert Bellah for 20 years. . . . There is no social scientist in the country for whom I have more respect and no one whom I should more wish to have associate with me in developing our program in the determining years immediately ahead." Two things stood out. First, as anticipated by Riesman, the document implied that Geertz was making an effort to subvert the isolation typical of the institute's professors in order to establish the School of Social Sciences as a true community of scholars. According to this plan, "new criteria were being injected into the selection process—that Bellah be able to work with Geertz, that they together fill a social need for new knowledge in the area of comparative social change, that the new program needed this particular man to succeed." Second, no mention was made of Bob's more recent work on symbolic realism, let alone of his pieces on Norman Brown: given the unusually friendly ad hoc committee, prudence suggested not calling attention to controversial work that might hinder the appointment.[26]

The plan, however, did not work. The meeting of the committee, held on December 3, 1972, was long, bitter, and inconclusive. Doubts over Bellah's originality, his command of philosophical literature, the viability of symbolic realism, and even his judgment in the choice of relevant authors—Ienaga, Watsuji, and, obviously enough, Brown—were voiced by most internal members, a quite antireligious group that was also disturbed by the echo of Bob's flamboyant seminar at Princeton University. The appointment process was proving harder than expected and Bellah suddenly found himself in a stressful situation that, as had happened at Stanford, impaired his ability to focus on his work. In fact, during his first few months at the institute he would only complete his essay for the *Daedalus* project on Italy and start the draft of a paper for a conference on Buddhism. In a letter to Riesman he voiced his uncertainty about joining the institute, but also his confidence in a positive outcome "in spite of all the guff from a few die hards."[27]

What was happening in Princeton was not Bellah's only concern. In mid-December Tammy underwent a few days of hospitalization after taking an overdose of sleeping pills. Bob and Melanie received the news with a mixture of worry and surprise: they had visited their daughter in Berkeley shortly before the incident, and had been persuaded that she was faring well. When she came to Princeton for Christmas, the whole family gathered around Tammy as she reassuringly told them it had a been a momentary lapse of reason that would never happen again. The six of them were finally reunited, the girls were in good spirits, and hopes were growing of a happy ending with regard to Bob's appointment. The situation, however, remained out of focus. Due to Tammy's absence and Melanie's full schedule as a law clerk, for example, the Bellahs were not able to send out their Christmas cards for the first time since Bob's bleakest days as a PhD student; moreover, they discovered they had no copy of Clement Moore's *The Night Before Christmas*, which Bob had always read aloud in his declamatory style on Christmas Eve. This breach of small but cherished family traditions gave the holidays a bittersweet taste— everything was in order, but not quite.[28]

With the new year the hatchet was unburied. As Bellah left for Italy for a conference, the internal members of the ad hoc committee resolved not to support his nomination. Geertz and philosopher Morton White exchanged multiple memos expounding their conflicting views, and presented them to

FIGURE 10.1. David Little and Robert Bellah at the American Civil Religion consultation at Drew University (Madison, NJ), February 22–24, 1973. (People and Events Photograph Collection, Special Collections and Archives, Drew University Library)

their colleagues on January 15, 1973. In two different votes, the faculty rejected Bellah's nomination and resolved that no proposal should be transmitted to the board of trustees. But Kaysen had already decided to back Bob no matter what, and proceeded to forward his nomination to the trustees. After hearing the grievances of part of the faculty, on January 20 the board approved Bellah's appointment, claiming "ultimate responsibility for the conduct of the affairs of the Institute."[29]

Bellah received a formal invitation to join on January 31, 1973. He accepted a couple of weeks later, with a proviso that only Geertz, Kaysen, and a few others should be told. Given the growing tension at the institute, he said, he would commit only for one year in order to help his friends in appointing a fourth professor, and then decide what to do next—an extension of his leave of absence from Berkeley and the offer of a Benjamin Franklin chair at the University of Pennsylvania gave him more than one alternative.[30] In a letter to

Riesman, he compared himself to the main character of a nineteenth-century scandal who had been strenuously defended by his role model, Émile Durkheim: "I don't feel at all good about it and may well return to Berkeley in 1974 if I cannot muster the enthusiasm of playing Captain Dreyfus at the institute for long." Given the atomistic structure of the institute, Riesman replied, Bellah might become an "invisible man" rather than a Dreyfus. Never had he been so wrong. Almost immediately the members of what came to be known as the "dissident majority" mobilized their scholarly networks in a concerted attack against Kaysen and the board of trustees.[31]

At that point, someone thought that the stakes were high enough to justify the use of unprecedented weapons. On March 2, 1973, a long and detailed piece by Israel Shenker, titled "Dispute Splits Advanced Study Institute," appeared on the front page of the *New York Times*.

III

Although Shenker framed the episode as a clash between Kaysen and the permanent faculty, much of his article was devoted to reporting divergent evaluations of Bellah as a scholar. On the side of the dissident majority, Weil deemed Bob's work as "worthless" and said that he had never had "the feeling of so utterly wasting [his] time." White called Bellah's references to philosophical literature "pedestrian and pretentious beyond even the call of journalistic duty," while Ronald Dore, a Japan specialist, and an anonymous "Ford professor at Berkeley" were cited as doubting his standing as a sociologist *tout court*. On the other side, Geertz praised Bob's "extraordinary depth and scholarship," while physicist Freeman Dyson and Yale historian John W. Hall were cited among those who had given an informal positive opinion.

Unexpectedly, the article also quoted the opinions of three external members of the ad hoc committee: according to Shils, Bellah was "one of the foremost sociologists" of the entire international profession; Merton called him "one of the two ablest sociologists of his generation" working on social change; Reischauer, whose judgment was bluntly dismissed by Weil, wrote that no one surpassed Bellah in "breadth-times-depth capacity." Not only had Shenker interviewed some of the faculty members, but he had been granted access to the confidential documents produced during the appointment process. In a second feature published on March 4, Shenker told his readers that the trustees had nominated an internal committee of five to review Kaysen's record. Doubts about the originality of Bellah's work, he added, were receiving "considerable support from colleagues from other institutions." Morton White was said to have drawn an irreverent parallel: Was Bellah the Einstein of sociology? If so, he deserved the appointment. Since he was not, he did not. The article also reported some observations by Bellah himself, who pointed to the fact that no one of his detractors had explained why he was considered unfit.[32]

Soon other national media were spreading the news: the *National Observer* on March 17, *Time* and *Newsweek* on March 19, and *Science* on March 23. An article published in the *Washington Post* on March 11 made no hint of the ongoing battle between the director and the faculty, but reported further comments on Bellah's alleged lack of scholarship. Historian Harold Cherniss had no doubts: "I read Mr. Bellah's works and I have a low opinion of them. Why do I have a low opinion of them? Because they are bad books." The omnipresent Morton White described Bob as follows: "First, his thinking was obscure, he had no great power of analyzing concepts. Second, he was not strong on marshalling evidence. His thinking was fuzzy and lacking in respect." On March 25 the *New York Times* published a third article, which conveyed the feeling that the incident had gotten out of hand.[33]

The subplot was that by appointing less-than-exceptional scholars the institute would lose its supremacy as the world's leading research center. Weil was reported to have said that the institute had not been created to become "a service institution or a RAND corporation," and medieval historian Kenneth M. Setton asked if the School of Social Sciences was to be a respected department or a mere "intellectual coterie of bright people who would be approved by Professors Geertz and Kaysen." Moreover, the dissident majority described itself as fully entitled to evaluate Bellah's work—according to White, "this guy doesn't write in Chinese, in Japanese, or in mathematical symbols we can't understand. This wasn't a case of no spikka da English."[34]

Those who had personal acquaintance with Bob found the situation immediately clear. In the phone calls and letters that flooded in after the first *New York Times* article, a number of unrelated individuals gave remarkably similar interpretations of the incident: the assessment of Bellah's work by the dissident majority was so utterly unbelievable that it could be explained only by reference to some recondite motivation. On March 5, 1973, John K. Fairbank wrote to his former student that "it is obvious . . . that you represent social science in general in the face of a literary-mathematical combine." Three days later Smelser, Bouwsma, Bendix, and other Berkeley scholars sent Bob a worried letter, expressing "admiration and respect for [his] professional accomplishments" as well as their "personal affection." They described the episode as an "unethical breach of academic confidentiality" and invited their colleague to find his way back home.[35]

In a letter dated March 8, 1973, Talcott Parsons wrote that Harvard would never permit appointments to be decided by faculty members incompetent in the nominee's discipline. On the same day he accepted a request by an influential Catholic magazine, *Commonweal*, to write an article in defense of his former student.[36] Among all Bellah's friends, Kenneth Burke unknowingly came closest to the mark, pointing to Bob's intellectual crush on Norman Brown:

> *Beyond Belief* is an exceptionally competent book. EXCEPT
>
> The guy went nerts on what is basically a travesty of religion, in a piece of brilliant quackery of youknow.
>
> If the guy recants that, he should be let in. If he won't recant that, then put him on the academic equivalent of the rack.

At that point, the impact of the scandal on Bellah's reputation was a concern for most of his friends. If sociologist Ezra Vogel wrote that the whole episode should be regarded "more as free publicity than anything else," Riesman's words to Reischauer were much more alarmed: "It is a terrible situation, as I am sure you recognize, for Bob himself."[37]

These sentiments surfaced in many different ways: as published letters, as opinions expressed by noted scholars in the second wave of articles, and, later, in essays by top sociologists. The letters sent to the editor of the *New York Times* by heavyweights the likes of David Apter, C. Vann Woodward, and a group of experts on Japan including Albert M. Craig, H. D. Harootunian, and Henry Rosovsky all declared their esteem for Bellah and condemned the breach of academic confidentiality. In a letter published on March 13, 1973, sociologist Norman F. Washburne described Bellah as a victim of the pretension to evaluate his works without having the pertinent expertise to do so. Surely André Weil had "never had to suffer the indignity of having his works judged by sociologists, since we admit that we aren't competent to do so." Besides disciplinary (in)competence, Washburne also challenged Weil's inappropriate standard of excellence: if the professors at the institute should be "above discussion," then no sociologist could qualify for the job, for good sociological work *had to be* controversial.[38]

Bellah was justifiably disheartened. "Nothing prepared me for the degree of vindictiveness and total callousness of certain members," he said in an interview published in the *Philadelphia Inquirer*. "In the end, you have to ask yourself what it is about the institute that creates such people." Bob was not alone in his judgment—in the same article Geertz was quoted saying that the institute mostly got "thoroughbred and very nervous types. No sanctions exist. In other academic institutions, if a professor does not get along with the dean, he can end up behind the toilet." *Newsweek* described the quarrel as "astonishingly petty," while according to *Time* Bellah's appointment had "aroused that special combination of incandescent anger and pettiness of which large intellects are sometimes capable."[39]

As Merton later wrote to Weil, the breach of academic confidentiality was "unprecedented in American academic history," and it was being condemned from many quarters. This in turn contributed to a general understanding of Bellah being scapegoated in a struggle that had little to do with him and his work. The dissident majority was described as deeply embroiled in a fight for academic power: in order to stop the creation of the new school, it had indulged in reprehensible behavior that might ruin that very scientific establishment it allegedly wanted to protect. On the other side, Carl Kaysen was depicted as a tricky politico engaged in a conspiracy against the faculty. As the controversy heated up, the majority finally questioned his appointment and the very idea of creating a School of Social Sciences. Kaysen also had his share of private fights. Immediately after the first *New York Times* article, for example, Robert K. Merton had been contacted by André Weil, who had suggested he take the appropriate steps to defend his name and his expertise after they had been "misused" by the press. Before answering to Weil, Merton called Kaysen for clarification. Not only had his confidential assessment been made public, it had also been condensed and thus distorted, giving the impression that Merton fully supported Bellah, while he had written a "carefully worded" letter to make sure that at least some of his reservations emerged. The Columbia sociologist asked Kaysen to ensure that nobody would again present a less-than-fair account of his letter—his scientific and scholarly reputation mattered more than the director's generic call to defend the social sciences. Not even this, however, would stop Carl Kaysen. As the spring came he joined forces with Geertz and Bellah and resolved to fight back.[40]

IV

On April 1, 1973, the Bellahs got mixed news from Tammy. Although her headaches were getting worse and friends had noticed her growing sense of disquiet, she wrote that she was finally happy. The spring semester was about to start and she had found the love of her life: Vernon, a Black ex-convict and former heroin addict she had met while looking after her friend Barbara at a rehab center. Tammy also told Bob and Melanie about another relevant novelty: "Yes, I believe in some kind of cosmic God now. It has to do with guardian angels. It may all sound silly to you and it's hard to explain to you in a letter, but I've come to a private belief of my own," she wrote in a rather complex but cheerful letter. "Daddy, you've studied all this, and you must know the joy I'm feeling to be discovering things like this inside of me. But see I had to discover them by myself, you couldn't show me." In closing, she added that she could not believe how badly her father was being treated at Princeton. Ironically, in his public remarks, which Tammy had not read, Morton White had used the same benchmark for outstanding intellect, Albert Einstein, as she had cited in "The Search For Freedom."[41]

On receiving the letter, Bob called Tammy to reassure her about his condition: although the conflict between Kaysen and the dissenting majority was not over, he said, things were moving in the right direction. A few days later he and Geertz circulated a letter among some respected members of academe in which they asked their friends to write in support of the new School of Social Sciences. The attached list of suggestions included the hypothesis of public censure "of the undignified public behavior of some permanent members of the institute." After receiving some encouraging replies, Bellah set out for Dickinson College in Carlisle, Pennsylvania, where he was to give the keynote speech at a symposium on the American civil religion. After all, his reputation seemed intact, and he was ready to hit the road again.[42]

That very night Bob got a phone call with terrible news he was not in the least prepared for: he had to get back to Princeton as soon as possible, Tammy had killed herself. How in the world could the orphaned son of Luther Hutton Bellah Jr. receive a call like that? He had sensed that something was wrong—he had even suggested Melanie go back to California to be closer to Tammy. But this? How could he, how could they all deal with this? Bob left Carlisle and silently drove home, where he found Melanie and the girls in a state of complete disarray. Later that night he told his wife that it all made sense: "I wonder how I could have thought, when my early life was so tragic, that my later life could be so happy? First my father, now my child, it has come full circle."[43]

The morning after—April 13, 1973—on the plane to San Francisco, Bob told Melanie he had decided to go back to California for good after her clerkship in Trenton was finished. Berkeley was the only place where they could express their grief and try to live through it. At home, friends came and went; tears were shed; plans were made; stories were told, retold, and then told again. Eventually Melanie and Bob discovered that, against her their instructions, Tammy had let Vernon, Barbara, and her boyfriend move in to 10 Mosswood Road, as they had fallen back into heroin. Her therapist, Daniel Greenson, told the Bellahs that she had finally resolved to kick them out after they had stolen some items from the house; in fact, he had been worried that Tammy would also use heroin, but had decided not to call her parents to respect her right to privacy and not to compromise her trust in future therapy work.[44]

In all his calm and stoic concentration, Robert Bellah could not help but blame himself. After all, it had been his decision to move to the East Coast, leaving Tammy behind, and she had died from an overdose of pills in his very bed. Now he saw he'd had no idea how bad things were for her, and reflected on his attitude toward his children—maybe such destructive behavior was the only way Tammy could rebel against her parents, who had been so liberal as to leave only extreme options for their children to explore. As he reiterated to his wife and children that none of them would ever comprehend what had happened, Bob began reading his daughter's journals, and came to think that the news of the ongoing fighting in Princeton had prevented Tammy from being open with her parents about her condition out of love and respect for her father. In his formal letter of withdrawal from the institute, written on April 26, he told Carl Kaysen that he thought it possible "that her anxiety about our suffering [had] made it more difficult for her to burden us further with troubles of her own." Since the members of the dissident majority had remained silent, Bellah anticipated any retaliation or schadenfreude on their part with this vague, and perhaps desperate, accusation of complicity.[45]

Bob was not the only one blaming himself for Tammy's death. Melanie had always hated Princeton and now saw the institute as an evil place that had extended its wicked influence over her entire family. Although she was mad at her daughter for what she had done, she found herself unable to express her anger and plunged into a state of deep despair. In her own attempt to understand, Melanie forced herself to talk to people she deeply disliked or considered partly responsible for her daughter's death, such as Vernon, Barbara, and their mothers. Among them, Paulette Goldman, a University of California instructor who had been quite close to Tammy, was a refreshing exception. In her description, Tammy was painfully similar to Bob in his back-breaking impostor syndrome: while she "made the class" and her work had been "a cut above the others," Paulette said, Tammy was constantly terrified of falling short of expectations.[46]

All of a sudden, an idea made its way into Melanie's heart: they would have another baby, a replacement child who would help them start a new life. Bob was shocked by the request. How could they return to normal? *What if it happened again?* He was completely against Melanie in this and wanted rather to focus on the girls, who were living their pain in rather different ways. Abby and Hally could not believe their Tammy-mommy was gone, and felt their life had been ruined—while Abby expressed her sadness quietly, Hally would often run out of the house screaming, while Bob tried to catch her before an accident happened. Having lost "the person she loved most in the world," Jenny was in a state of complete disarray, where good and evil had no more sense or meaning, but still decided to move on with her life—as soon as she graduated high school in spring 1973 she went back to Berkeley, where she lived with a friend for a while before returning to 10 Mosswood Road and settling in the top floor apartment she had shared with her sister. It was in this painful, complex condition that Bob, Melanie, Abby, and Hally left Princeton to move back to the only place they called home. It was July 19, 1973.[47]

11

Breaking Covenants

BERKELEY, 1973–1976

IT TOOK A LONG WHILE for Robert N. Bellah and his family to resume a tolerable routine after Tammy's death. They alternated between a fleeting sense of improvement and the sensation that healing was simply not possible. Overwhelmed by grief but resolved to pass her bar examination, Melanie started reading Tammy's journals with the goal of writing a book about her daughter—a project that, she thought, might have a remedial effect. At the same time, she had not given up her desire for another child. In this she was backed only by Abby, while Bob resolutely opposed the plan: "You still have three children," he would often say. "Try to focus on the good things we have." On her insistence, he agreed to consider the idea only if she accepted undergoing therapy for at least six months—if after that time she had not changed her mind he would comply with her wishes. Taking a year for herself, Jenny studied creative writing at the University of California, danced with the Oakland Ballet Company, and started drafting college applications, while Abby and Hally fluctuated between moments of misery and the desire to live as normal teenagers, as normal as a teenager could be in Berkeley in the early 1970s.[1]

As the Bellahs limped through their *annus horribilis*, America came close to a nervous breakdown. Although Richard Nixon's landslide victory in the elections of November 1972 had been shocking news to many, the new year had aroused some hope as the Supreme Court issued *Roe v. Wade* and the United States signed the Paris Peace Accords. In fact, 1973 marked the conclusion of the 1960s and, with them, the end of the postwar era. The period of unprecedented economic growth came abruptly to a close as the national economy got worse and worse and entered an unforeseen state of recession and stagflation. Inflation jumped to a stunning 6.6 percent in 1973 and the mass entrance of women into the workforce depressed the national productivity rate. As the OPEC embargo of mid-October 1973 clearly demonstrated, the Unites States was becoming increasingly dependent on foreign oil.[2]

In the medium run, the rising distrust in welfare liberalism and the anti-tax backlash that accompanied the crisis would lead to the conservative revolution of the 1980s. In the short run, most Americans concentrated on the unfolding of a sordid story of political espionage and obstruction. As the months went by, it became clear that the break-ins at the Watergate Hotel were but a small part of a larger offensive of dirty tricks, sabotage, and "psywar" targeting the president's political enemies. After a slow start, the scandal gained momentum with the broadcast of the Senate Watergate hearings and the discovery of the White House tapes. When Nixon announced a restructuring of government spending and the launch of tough-on-crime policies in an attempt to consolidate his Sunbelt constituency, his image as a paranoid and ruthless politician had been irreparably set.[3]

The year 1973 was also pivotal for popular culture. Marshall McLuhan depicted the world as both a global village and an all-embracing "whispering gallery," and the first ever reality show, *An American Family*, was aired by the Public Broadcasting Service. From their Princeton living room, Bob, Melanie, and the girls watched with interest and a bit of apprehension the falling apart of the Louds—a suburban Southern Californian family whose five children and affluent lifestyle made them superficially similar to the Bellahs themselves. At about the same time, Andy Warhol turned his *Interview* magazine into a vehicle of camp and nostalgia, while New Hollywood movies like *American Graffiti, Badlands*, and *The Exorcist* conveyed a stifling sense of intergenerational disruption growing out of the void left by absent, distant, or inept fathers. Women, African Americans, homosexuals, and other hitherto excluded groups scorned liberal universalism and created a string of new political movements, which replaced integration with ethnic nationalism and diversity. By 1973 the radicalism of the 1960s had dissolved into a post-modern combination of narcissism and nihilism.[4]

It was with all these facts and figures in mind that Bob finally resolved to speak in public on November 4, 1973, just two days before the assassination of school superintendent Marcus Foster by the Symbionese Liberation Army in Oakland. Asked to deliver the McCall Memorial Lecture at the First Congregational Church in Berkeley—the place where Tammy's funeral had been six months earlier—Bellah addressed his audience with a tone of doom and gloom. "It is winter in America, or so it seems," he began, before listing the bloody standoff at Wounded Knee, Spiro Agnew's quitting, and the Vietnam War as signs of a crisis that was threatening the very existence of the republic.[5]

Speaking not only as an academic but also as "a father and as a citizen," Bellah set out to explore the connection between "personal pain and common pain" and unveil the religious meaning of America's current condition. He told the story of a nation plagued from its very beginning by an exclusivist definition of the national community "that its own universalism does not warrant," but, echoing the many dinner table discussions about Tammy's suicide, warned his audience against "sentimentalization of the experience of the oppressed" and the feeling of "false guilt in idealistic young white people" that was causing so much pain and destruction. Avoiding the self-righteousness typical of lesser critics, he urged his fellow citizens "to look at the abyss, the nothing that is there," starting from the persecution of ethnic, religious, and political minorities that had torn the ideal image of America to pieces.[6]

Many in the audience were moved to tears, and praised Bob's ability to interweave intimate emotions and public concerns. With the title "Reflections on Reality in America" the lecture was published in a small but combative journal edited by the Community for Religious Research and Education, of which Graduate Theological Union student Harlan Stelmach was a member, *Radical Religion*, shortly after Nixon's resignation in August 1974. Its themes, and much of its pitch, were found in other coeval pieces, of which "Religion and Polity in America"—initially written as the introduction to the print version of the Weil Memorial Lectures—was the most eloquent and articulate.[7]

Dismissing his old Parsonian idea of the continuity between Protestantism and individualism, Bellah now saw modernism as "an illegitimate offspring" of Calvinism, and thus separated the symbolic complex of philosophical utilitarianism from the civil religion. It was as if a local version of the distinction between individualistic and communalistic societies, typical of modernization theory, had been found *inside* the most modernized society ever. Again, modernity and tradition were not clear-cut, mutually excluding categories, but complex forms that might come as mixed, or even competing, principles in concrete reality. It was time, Bellah wrote, to fully embrace "the schism in the national soul" and develop "an ability to face the abyss of personal and social nothingness, to see the evil in society, other men and ourselves, and to hate what is evil but not to hate any man including ourselves." While he summoned the sociological tradition, Augustinian theology, symbolism, and mythology as powerful allies against utilitarianism, Bob wrote that a true renewal could be brought about only by a hierophany: "Perhaps only a new eruption of the sacred out of the unconscious depths can show us in immediate experience the source of our ethical vision."[8]

To a well-trained ear these words sounded both familiar and surprising. The theme of religion and America, the scholarly references, and the occasional Brownesque slip were surely typical of Bob's late-1960s and early-1970s work. At the same time, something was new in his approach to the American civil religion. Gone was his prophetic but ultimately hopeful tone. Gone was his confidence in the revolutionary potential of a correctly understood civil religion—an attitude that some critics had misinterpreted as nationalistic triumphalism. Could it be that the ongoing suffering of his family had influenced him so much as to let his personal experiences bias his judgment as a scholar? Or could it be that the bleak political and social events of 1973 had shattered his belief in the self-healing power of America?

What was happening had to do with the unanticipated effects of the success of "Civil Religion in America" as much as with personal and national tragedy. As a committed citizen and a follower of Durkheim's ideal of the public intellectual, Bellah had felt an obligation to accept all the invitations to speak on the American civil religion he could reasonably attend. Soon, however, a loathsome routine emerged: Bob would give a paper, and then somebody would ask a question that he could not answer. For the very first time in his life he was forced to admit his ignorance. Facing this frustrating situation, he did what his impostor syndrome, but also his self-understanding as an exceptional scholar, made him do: he gave himself a crash course in American history and studied, studied, and studied more. This allowed him to develop a deeper and more nuanced assessment of American politics, culture, and religion that brought him away from "Civil Religion in America" and closer to the mainstream of historical research.[9]

The shift was evident as early as 1971. In the second Weil Memorial Lecture, Bellah presented a thorough reversal of his thesis on the connection between the civil religion, Protestant piety, and national consciousness. According to this new interpretation, the civil religion had never been self-sufficient: on all crucial issues, it had been "the churches who [had spoken] with the combined voice of believers and citizens."[10] In "American Civil Religion in the 1970s," a paper first drafted in early 1973 while at the Princeton institute, Bellah embraced Martin Marty's distinction between the civil religion and public theology: while the former should remain "as symbolically open or empty as possible," religious traditions should be able to speak up on public matters from their own specific points of view. In a few years, Bellah had abandoned almost all the ideas advanced in his first essay; still convinced of the historical relevance of the civil religious tradition, he had become increasingly negative about its potential—when he put forward suggestions for the renewal of American society, he now pointed to the role of church religion.[11]

Most of his interlocutors, however, dealt only with "Civil Religion in America," often reduced to a simplified Durkheimian depiction of America's *conscience collective*. As its major—and in fact sole—incarnation, the original 1967 essay had been turned into a milestone that contributed to shaping the symbolic oppositions around which the debate was growing. After all, even if others had reflected upon the same phenomenon, it was Bellah's "conceptual formulation of civil religion [that] stuck when others did not." The noted theologian Herbert Richardson explained his preference for the first article as follows: "Robert Bellah's 1967 essay, 'Civil Religion in America,' has provoked lively discussion; and it should be noted that Bellah has considerably developed his own thinking on this subject over the past seven years. His 1967 essay will serve, however, as a conversation partner to my own discussion, primarily because Bellah's concern there is also with the way political power can be effectively limited and rightly used." At that point, the more Bob diminished the importance of American civil religion vis-à-vis the role played by church religion and utilitarianism, the more the identification of his work with the original civil religion thesis became troublesome.[12]

Another problem with the civil religion debate was its dispersed character: as the disciplinary fields where the discussion was happening turned around different conceptual constellations, Bellah's public image was being defined in divergent, if not contradictory, ways. Sociologists, for example, criticized him for his functionalism, the lack of empirical data, or his value-ladenness, while in history and religious studies the targets were the abstruseness of the civil religion concept and the scant attention given to the evangelical tradition. When Bellah's theses made the mainstream media, the results were similar. An article published in the *New York Times*, for example, described the Religious Education Association convention of 1975 as a confused discussion between the critics and the supporters of the civil religion—hastily defined as "that blending of patriotism and piety manifested when children sing a national hymn that invokes the name of God or a clergyman offers a prayer at the inauguration of a President"—and enrolled Bob in the ranks of the former. Soon the assessment of Bellah's ideas became even more complicated.[13]

I

After much reflection and many attempts at finding the right title, the Weil Memorial Lectures were published by the Seabury Press of New York in February 1975 as *The Broken Covenant: American Civil Religion in Time of Trial*. The three years since the lectures had been delivered in Cincinnati had been the longest of Bob's life. Melanie had successfully passed the California Bar Examination and set out to start her law practice. Abby and Hally had become "two ambivalent sides of a self, all their lives so close to each other, and so competitive; so comforting and so annoying." The heaviest burden had fallen on Jenny, who had left home to attend Bryn Mawr College in Pennsylvania. Having lost her closest sister and far from familial comfort, she fell into serious health problems and nearly starved herself to death. Only during her sophomore year she was able to catch up, and worked hard in both her academic and dance classes, determined to succeed in the challenge of becoming a professional dancer while graduating from college.[14]

As for Bob, he had resumed his teaching at Berkeley, focusing once more on Brown, Weber, and Durkheim, and expanding his graduate syllabus to include classics such as Machiavelli's *Discourses* and Plato's *Laws*. Editing a collection of essays by the Indonesian socialist intellectual and former ambassador to the United States Soedjatmoko, and working with the newly constituted Berkeley Religious Consciousness Group, took most of the time left by the ongoing civil religion debate. At the same time, the flow of job offers and speaking engagements proved that the Bellah affair at Princeton had been rapidly forgotten. Now that the celebrations for the bicentennial were about to start, Seabury Press anticipated a huge success for *The Broken Covenant*.[15]

In the preface to his second major book, Bellah declared his "amateur status as an Americanist, though not, I hope, as an American," and offered his work as an understanding of the political and cultural tradition of the United States according to the methods of historical-interpretive social science. The title encapsulated the idea that the covenant on which America was built had been in pieces from the outset: expanding the argument first presented in "Religion and Polity in America," Bob wrote of a constitutive opposition between the collectivist emphasis of the Puritan and republican ideals and the utilitarian worldview derived from the ideas of classical liberal philosophers Thomas Hobbes and John Locke. He saw the crisis of the mid-1970s as depending on the rampancy of a modern utopianism aimed at achieving "total technical control, of course in the service of the 'freedom' of individual self-interest." This new utilitarianism was neither a child nor a degeneration of the Puritan culture: it was a completely different culture that had been there in America from the very beginning as one of the two embattled halves of the nation's myth of origins.[16]

Within this general framework, the main thesis of *The Broken Covenant* was presented in a ten-page tour de force on the relationship between the civil religion, Protestantism, and "a gradually clarifying American national consciousness" first presented in Cincinnati in 1971 as the second Weil Memorial Lecture. There Bob described the civil religion as a cold, "embalmed" symbolic script that only exceptional individuals had been able to bring to life. As such, it "could hardly have provided the imaginative basis of a national consciousness without which the new nation could easily have shattered into the divisions and fragments that continually threatened it." Luckily enough, Protestant revivalism had often come to the rescue of the civil religion: echoing Martin Marty, Bellah wrote that the American tradition had been handed over "to private interpretation, to the speech of any man—preacher, politician, or poet—who [had] the power to persuade." It was precisely "this dynamic combination of public form and private meaning that [had rendered] the American civil religion so difficult to understand and analyze."[17]

Bellah now saw the bicentennial as an opportunity to recreate the collective effervescence of exceptional moments such as the Great Awakenings and the Civil War. The external covenant protecting negative freedoms had first to be reaffirmed through a renovation of classical civil religion. After that, positive freedom had to be nourished via a critical reappraisal of the collective dimension of the American tradition and the creation of an inclusive, diverse political campaign: "Such a movement would have a political, I believe socialist, side. It would also have an intellectual and a religious side." As a nod to the counterculture and his own Nobby-inspired understanding of a higher form of politics, Bellah wrote that crucial to the whole enterprise was the activation of a flow of ecstatic reason aimed at realizing "a knowledge of the whole." In his conclusion, Bob sketched the contours of a progressive coalition with the mission of creating the political, cultural, and religious bases of a decentralized democratic socialism that would reject utilitarianism without losing its American character.[18]

But *The Broken Covenant* contained much more than a historical genealogy of the (failures of the) civil religion. One of its most consequential features was its symbolic analysis of single moments and episodes in American history, from the landing of the *Arbella* to the killing of Larry Casuse in Gallup, New

Mexico, some three centuries later. Nothing of what Bellah wrote about the history of America would qualify him as a "Sunshine Boy." One example is his interpretation of the myth of "the chosen people," an idea as old as America itself. Bob surveyed many different versions of the myth, but his bottom line was that the United States had been built on a "double crime," the extermination of Indians and slavery, which depended on the failure, on the part White Americans, to take other cultures and races into account and respect them as equals. The point was further analyzed in the fourth chapter, titled "Nativism and Cultural Pluralism in America" and dedicated to the place of those "groups that differed significantly from the majority of early colonists." Here Bellah indicated the Puritan distinction between "saints and sinners" as *the* symbolic blueprint of group relations in America. While it originally had nothing to do with ascriptive groups, "it was not long before certain of the characteristic traits of sinners were projected onto whole groups of people," especially Indians and blacks, who were depicted as "prone to every kind of sinful impulse" and thus subjected to the oppressive control of Whites as "sinner groups."[19]

At the same time, having defined the Puritan roots of American culture as intrinsically solidary and communitarian, Bob interpreted the utilitarian ideal of individual freedom as a twisted development of national culture that had also impacted negatively on the lives of many *White* Americans. In this sense, no social group had been able to protect itself from the rise of a market-driven economy: "There is no point in overlooking the price that white male Americans have paid for their rewards, for they have much to contribute and much to gain from a conception of the meaning of life different from the late American preoccupation with success. But the rewards tarnished though they are, must begin to be shared more widely now."[20]

Only a critical reappraisal of the American cultural and political tradition could put the country back on track. Bellah listed three ways to respond to defeat: the "wordless scream" of the many minorities who had been crushed by White power; the identification with the aggressor, as had happened in the South after the conclusion of the Civil War; and the "attempt to build and maintain some kind of community that will not only aid in physical survival but be a model of human values in stark contrast to the opposing society." The new community, wrote Bob, should be built on a humble and pluralistic reconsideration of national history, but not *against* the dominant social group of which he himself was part. He thus called for a bold practice of crossing internal and external lines: "Experimentation with new cultural and social forms does not stop at the boundary of Western and Biblical culture," he wrote in chapter 4, "Indian America, Africa, and above all Asia are supplying many new possible patterns. . . . Expansive openness is a characteristic of the present situation as is the revival of the past."[21]

Theoretically speaking, Bellah's interpretive shift was deeper than the particulars might reveal. In the most-cited passage of the book—"Today the American civil religion is an empty and broken shell. It was from the beginning an external covenant"—he was not saying that at the time of his 1967 essay the civil religion was still intact, while ten years later it had become an empty shell. Rather, the point was that the civil religion had been a cold system of rules from the very beginning of the American experience. In fact, in *The Broken Covenant* the civil religion was given a walk-on part in a drama where the starring roles were assigned to a very strange cast: John Winthrop, Thomas Hobbes, and Norman O. Brown.[22]

Friends cheered Bob for his accomplishment—after all, he had just turned forty-eight and *The Broken Covenant* was considered by many to be his long-awaited second book. In a letter dated September 27, 1975, Wilfred Cantwell Smith called the volume "a master sermon" and bet on its promise as a political and religious document: "My hopes that [*The Broken Covenant*] will prove an exceptionally significant book are hopes for all of the rest of us, and not merely for you as an author—though of course I deeply hope that you will get for it the recognition and applause that it deserves." David Riesman and Kenneth Burke praised the book, while Duke sociologist Edward A. Tiryakian and theologian John C. Bennett were particularly interested in the contribution that Bob might make to reviving democratic socialism in America.[23]

Not unexpectedly, Talcott Parsons was on a different page. His annoyance about Bob's latest work was not new—in a letter dated February 13, 1974, the seventy-one-year-old sociologist had called "Reflections on Reality in America" a "very powerful and moving document," but had questioned its style and its scorn of "what you and I would both regard as desirable changes." This divergence of opinion led Parsons to tell Bellah that "were you to incorporate the main line of your sermon into a document designed for general circulation and maximum publicity and to solicit signatures to it, my own inclination at the moment would be not to enroll among the signatories of such a document." Implicit in Parsons's words was a negative judgment of the scholarly quality of the paper, which hurt Bellah. Some three months later, Bob finally thanked Parsons for his detailed critique, but held his ground, emphasizing the connections between his interpretation and the sociological tradition of Weber and Durkheim. He also sent Parsons the draft of his introduction to *The*

Broken Covenant—until that moment, he had not even told his old mentor about the book.[24]

Doomsday had to wait until September 10, 1974. The first words of Parsons's long letter were unusual, but at that point fairly predictable: "Quite frankly I was disappointed in the manuscript and I feel that it is not up to the high level of scholarly standards which you have so impressively maintained over a long period." His criticism was threefold. First, bowing to a tradition that went back to Thorstein Veblen's critique of the "profit motive" in American capitalism, Bellah had overstated negative facts and processes. This, in turn, meant that he had not seriously reflected on the relationship between the new liberties of the 1960s and the discipline of the Puritan ideal—a rather ironical comment, if one considers how much Bob had tried to strike a balance between the two ever since his discovery of *Love's Body*. Parsons's second point related to the resignation of Richard Nixon: the happy ending of the Watergate scandal had shown that American society still possessed powerful self-healing mechanisms. Finally, Bob had overlooked the most recent developments in the inclusion of "previously disadvantaged and excluded groups." This probably had to do with his Augustinian view of man, while Parsons interpreted modernization as the secular institutionalization of a religiously grounded ethic. In closing, Parsons wanted to be sure that Bellah knew that his strictures were "deeply felt and meant" and asked him to take his critiques seriously in the final revision of his manuscript.[25]

Apart from the skirmish in Rome some five years earlier, it was the first time that Parsons had questioned Bellah's scholarly qualities and Bob decided not to reply to his harsh criticisms. *The Broken Covenant* was the final result of many hours of reflection and countless papers, conferences, and discussions. As much as he still appreciated the unfailing optimism of his old teacher— "Indeed, if you became pessimistic about America, I think I would feel almost betrayed"—Bob was ready to stand his ground without doubting his own scholarly abilities. It had taken some ten years to kill "father Parsons," but now the liberating homicide was a fait accompli.[26]

II

Even a less rigorous critic than Talcott Parsons would have recognized that *The Broken Covenant* was as different from *Tokugawa Religion* as could be. Gone was the functionalist frame—a feature that some of Bellah's opponents during the Princeton affair had interpreted as a lack of originality. Gone was the turgid

academic prose, replaced by a vivid declamatory style that enhanced the evocative elements of Bob's argument. Also gone was any residual confidence in
modernization, replaced by a lucid perception of the many troubles of American modernity. All these novelties were much appreciated by colleagues and
critics, and the book became a clear success. The sociological profession gave
The Broken Covenant its most sought-after mark of approval: in early September 1976 Bob was notified he had won the Pitirim A. Sorokin Award of the
American Sociological Association for 1976, together with his former Berkeley
colleague Jeffery M. Paige. "Bellah's *The Broken Covenant* is an important contribution by a sociologist to an understanding of American society," read the
official motivation. "In its treatment of civil religion, it both makes concrete
and challenges conventional ideas of secularization in western society. It provides an insightful analysis of the culture in which American sociology, as well
as American society, is embedded and, in so doing, reinforces the recent attention to historical studies within the discipline."[27]

Even more importantly, most reviewers were showing a new approach to
Robert Bellah and his work, for the first time focusing on Bob's style and
persona. In a sense, his participation in the American civil religion debate
and the clamor of the Princeton affair had made him sufficiently well known
to warrant his ascendancy as "an author"—a rather ironic outcome of the
attempt at character assassination by Weil, White, and company. In his review for the *American Journal of Sociology*, Martin Marty explicitly noticed
the gap between the 1967 essay and *The Broken Covenant*—"In the Weil lectures everything is changed"—but then decided to focus on the man rather
than on his work. He described Bob as "a sensitive person whose manner of
living, speaking, and even writing make it impossible for him not to be responsive to change. His antennae are always out, and his nerve endings are
exposed." Benton Johnson's review for *Contemporary Sociology* nailed the
complex relationship between Bob and his old mentor: "By and large, Parsons' analyses of American life have been implicitly optimistic, even Pollyan-
nish, in temper," whereas *The Broken Covenant* sported a dark tone and a
quite un-Parsonian penchant for socialism. For Johnson, Bellah should be
trusted no matter what: "His insights sometimes run ahead of his ability to
make them clear and plausible," but, as "one of a very small number of contemporary pioneers in the sociology of religion," he was "in his prime and
we [could] expect to learn more from him soon." In a similar mood, Yale
historian Sidney E. Ahlstrom compared Bellah to "a skier making a new trail
who releases an alpine avalanche."[28]

At least in some quarters, the relationship between Bellah's image as a scholar and his work had acquired primacy over the content of his ideas—in a sense, his own status had surpassed that of any of his writings. Critics were now trying to interpret his work as a whole, drawing connections and distinctions that he himself had never imagined. His new condition was secured by the symposium "The Sociology of Religion of Robert N. Bellah," published in the *Journal for the Scientific Study of Religion*—the fourth in a series that had previously featured Charles Y. Glock, Andrew M. Greeley, and Joseph H. Fichter. At around the same time another paper, titled "Bellah and His Critics: An Ambiguity in Bellah's Concept of Civil Religion," was published in the *Anglican Theological Review*. Its author, Joan Lockwood, was a former student of Herbert Richardson's and worked as a tutor in religious studies at the University of Toronto. During the civil religion debate, she argued, Bellah had shifted from a normative to an analytical understanding of civil religion, thus revealing "a serious weakness" in his position. As she showed some "proofs" of Bob's "changed concept," Lockwood presented his Durkheimian toolkit as an endorsement of a reductionist conception of religion.[29]

Bellah's reaction was furious and professional at a time. While accusing Lockwood of superficiality, he seriously engaged with her critiques, so as to show how a "true scholar" should work. He first remarked that the distinction between a normative and an analytical frame was "entirely a figment of Lockwood's imagination, or to be more charitable, it [was] an analytical distinction in a theory of hers which [had] very little to do with any thinking" of his. Second, "I do not subscribe to a functional theory and phrases about integrating or unifying society are virtually absent from my discussion of religion." Had Lockwood been careful in reading Bellah's work, she would have found nothing about projection, functionalism, or integration, and she would have seen that his Durkheim was very different from the social-control freak of conventional debates.[30]

Bellah's reply to Lockwood was unusual for someone used to showing a religious respect for academic etiquette, but his new status as an author had brought new problems that he was not ready to confront. If in the first twenty years of his career Bob's intellectual production had been discussed, as it were, piece by piece, now his critics were combining his diverse works in order to unearth an implicit or underlying scheme. And yet, as his publications, courses, and public lectures clearly showed, at least since the mid-1960s Bellah had willingly combined his many sources of inspiration into dialectic arguments in which conceptual opposites would cohabit in an uneasy combination. "I must repeat something that came up in a discussion in Berkeley not long ago," he had joked in 1974 during the question-and-answer session of his first Beatty Lecture in Montreal, "when a student . . . I mean [it was] the first time it ever happened to me . . . accused me of having an unambiguous view of something." All the paradoxes of Bob's writings on civil religion, the complex relationship between realism, critique, and second naïveté in his writings on teaching—the ambivalence and contradiction that had been scorned by the dissident majority at the Princeton institute as signs of poor scholarship—testified to the unresolved character of his thinking. The truth was that there was no hidden structure under the surface of Bellah's work, but only a growing assortment of diverse ideas, paradigms, and analyses that could be systematized only at the price of distortion or simplification.[31]

The tensions created by this new situation shaped most of the writing on America that Bellah published in the late 1970s. In his attempt to reaffirm his new interpretation of civil religion without going back to his original essay, Bob denounced his past ambiguities and introduced not only new concepts and distinctions, but also new interpretations of his historical evidence. In "The Revolution and the Civil Religion," for example, he acknowledged "a certain ambiguity" in his original article, a conflation between what he now termed "general" and "special" civil religion. To illustrate the point, Bob used some of the examples he had given in his original 1967 article, but reallocated them on the two sides of his new dichotomy. In another piece, Bellah repeated for the umpteenth time that his idea of civil religion had nothing to do with consensus or harmony. This understanding of the conflictual relation between a society and its civil religion had been perfectly instantiated by Émile Durkheim during the Dreyfus affair, when the father of sociology had been "willing to put in jeopardy the 'social integration' of France for the sake of defending a form of society worth living in." This disordered piling up of rejoinders, polemics, and new ideas did not produce a neat and convincing theoretical argument and, in the end, only hindered the reception of Bellah's ideas. At the end of 1975, Bob was stuck in the trap of intellectual success: the greater his fame, the less he was able to control the diffusion, reception, and even proliferation of his ideas.[32]

12

Ashes Alone

UNITED STATES OF AMERICA, 1969–1976

IN JANUARY 1976, just before Robert N. Bellah's forty-ninth birthday, the popular magazine *Psychology Today* featured an interview that finally substantiated his new status as a national-level public intellectual. Bob was described as a dedicated, intense scholar who knew that "the yin and the yang, the soft and the hard, private conviction and public" belonged together "in a never ending dance." This penchant for antinomies differentiated Bellah from the hard scientists who had fought him at the Princeton institute—a place of "isolated splendor" to which such "a man of deep passion" surely did not belong. The conversation between Bellah and Sam Keen wandered freely from the meaning of tradition to Bob's religious apprehension of reality, founded on an idea of the sacred as a disruptive force that called all conventional expectations into question, something that kept human beings "from settling into a groove." With his spirited tone, Bellah weaved Émile Durkheim, Abraham Lincoln, and Norman Brown into a gallery of powerful images that anyone could understand. In one remarkably intriguing answer to Keen, he declared that the counterculture of the 1960s should be seen as a true liberation of the emotional and spiritual energies that had been repressed in the 1950s. Maybe, he added, hippies lacked some subtlety in their questioning of American life, but after all it was the fate of prophets to be despised.[1]

To fully understand what Bellah was trying to say it is necessary to go back to the International Symposium on the Culture of Unbelief of 1969. During the discussion on a methodological paper presented by Charles Glock, Bellah had sketched a research design aimed at apprehending the "new situation with respect to man's religiosity." His suggestions were clear: "In this case one would want to seek out strategic groups, voluntary associations of various sorts, spontaneous movements, arising in some respects on the fringe of established society, movements which may or may not have a tinge that would be traditionally considered religious, but in any case think in ways and forms quite different from any traditional formulation." In fact, he added, this kind of group "would not be caught or would be caught in only very tiny percentages in national samples, but may be suggestive of new modes of organization, new cultural forms, which could be very important for the future."[2]

During the 1970–1971 academic year, Glock and Bellah convened a mixed Berkeley–Graduate Theological Union discussion group on the late-1960s counterculture. After a couple of meetings, some students proposed the idea of embarking on a collectively managed research project on new religious movements. Eager to follow the suggestion, Bellah tried to get funding from the Institute for Religious and Social Change at the University of Hawaii, which was at the time sponsoring a similar project, coordinated by his old friend Yanagawa Keiichi, in Japan. When a grant of $125,000 was eventually secured from the Ford Foundation, Bellah and Glock set out to shepherd the diverse group of PhD students, visiting researchers, and activists off the beaten paths of coeval sociology of religion.[3]

Given the differences between Glock's quantitative approach and Bellah's historical-interpretive perspective, the group decided to work on two parallel projects: a broad survey of the San Francisco Bay Area, directed by Berkeley graduate student Robert Wuthnow, and a number of ethnographic studies on countercultural and mainstream religious, quasi-religious, and political groups. The decision was taken to avoid any attempt at debunking the beliefs of the groups under scrutiny, privileging a sympathetic approach to the reporting and interpretation of observational data. This perspective soon led the "Berkeley Religious Consciousness Group" to conclude that the various cases were hardly comparable, for their "big questions" were radically different. One participant even suggested using Gertrude Stein's last words—"What Was the Question?"—as a title for the research report. In 1974 the group flew to Honolulu to meet with their Japanese colleagues for a three-day immersive experience that peaked with a decidedly hippieish hike of the main island by the students.[4]

Eventually titled *The New Religious Consciousness*, the research report was published in the fall of 1976. It included chapters about the Hare Krishna, the Church of Satan, Synanon, and the Healthy-Happy-Holy movement, along with papers on the charismatic renewal of the Catholic Church, Jewish identity in the 1960s, and Berkeley's New Left. The dust jacket presented the book as the first study on the belief system of the American counterculture, from a plurality of points of view—"phenomenological, theological, experiential, sociological, and socio-psychological." While the blurbs on the back cover had been written by scholars whose reputation was beyond question—Talcott Parsons, Seymour Martin Lipset, Peter Berger, Martin Marty, and Harvey Cox—the authors had been allowed to present themselves as they pleased. In a crescendo of extravagance Donald Heinz described himself as "a Lutheran clergyman, . . . a therapist, a carpenter-gardener," Alan Tobey told of his interest in "winemaking, yoga and meditation, Renaissance music, and herbal medicine," and Randy Alfred identified as "a nondirective shaman." As Jeffrey Hadden later wrote, the overall picture only vaguely resembled that of a properly constituted group of social scientists.

Another unusual feature of *The New Religious Consciousness* was that it lacked a consensual finale. Unable to find a synthesis of the many stories and tendencies recounted in the book, each editor wrote his own assessment of the new religious movements. Glock framed the counterculture as a fascinating, but ultimately futile, symptom of the rise of a scientific worldview destined to replace the early modern compromise between God and the individual. The final triumph of the scientific perspective, however, was "inevitable" and the civilizational outcome of the process thus depended on "whether the sciences [would be] able, out of new discoveries, to identify a life purpose to which individuals [might] commit themselves and around which a new social order [might] be built."[5]

From the point of view of the creator of symbolic realism, Glock's belief in the ability of science to provide purpose and meaning should have seemed, at best, a naivety. In his alternative conclusion, Bellah proposed a rather different explanation for the rise of the new religious consciousness. He saw the counterculture as a reaction against the changing balance of power between the two pristine American cultures: "The main cause [of the uprisings] . . . is to be found, from my point of view, in the inability of utilitarian individualism to guarantee a meaningful model of personal and social existence, especially when its alliance with the biblical religion began to give in because of its destruction." Following the early lead of Martin Luther King Jr., the movements of the 1960s had revolted against that unnatural combination and its failures. Bob thus saw the emergence of "a new consciousness of the problem of ends," which took two ill-matched but equally inspired paths: collective action and individualistic escapism. In spite of some successful experiments, however, the 1960s had been a failure: if the New Left had suffered "the weakness verging

on nonexistence of an old Left for it to be the new Left of," much of the religious or quasi-religious counterculture had turned into rescue units for bums
and drop-outs. The reelection of Richard Nixon in 1972 had been the most
worrying substantiation of the victory of that "cynical privatism" on which the
Hobbesian tradition was founded.[6]

What to expect, then? Once again, Bellah's picture was highly ambivalent.
On the one hand, thanks to the positive influence of Zen and other Eastern
traditions, a nondualistic conception of the world had become almost common sense, at least in some quarters. On the other hand, Bob anticipated a
further radicalization of utilitarianism or even an economic catastrophe followed by unseen forms of authoritarianism. A renewal of the American revolutionary spirit would require a paradoxical alliance between the most creative
strands of the counterculture and a biblical religion freed from the deadly
embrace of strategic individualism. The emergence of such a holistic utopian
vision, concluded Bellah, would encourage a mass renewal of the revolutionary spirit of the early republic, thus creating a new, purified and self-limiting
patriotism.[7]

On its publication, *The New Religious Consciousness* was generally praised
for its scope and creativity, but critics argued against the study's methodology
and were split over the contribution of nonprofessional sociologists, as some
lamented the younger researchers' lack of detachment. Writing in 1977, one
reviewer pointed to the rise of conservative evangelicalism as a phenomenon
that seemed to contradict those described in the book, while another attacked
the project using a simple argument: "new religious consciousness" was an
extravagant label for a nonexistent phenomenon, and attributed the blunder
to the unhappy marriage of "Berkeley sociology" and the "rag bag" of "commitment and frivolity" of the late 1960s.[8]

Unable to reproduce in print the enthusiasm and stamina that had pervaded the Berkeley group, *The New Religious Consciousness* looked like an unfinished work, a waypoint on a long journey toward a fuller grasp of the history
of the United States and its contemporary culture. To be sure, Bellah had traveled a long way from "Civil Religion in America," and his reasoning and style
were now sharper and subtler. As reviewers of both *The Broken Covenant* and
The New Religious Consciousness repeated again and again, however, the point
of arrival was not yet in sight, and Bob's status as one of the foremost sociologists of religion in America risked giving him an undeserved pass of sorts. As
Robert Stauffer had warned back in 1975: "My concern is that Bellah's growing
stature does not prevent us from continuing to question, and, when necessary,

strongly criticize the possibly unwarranted assumptions, claims, and hopes which tend to multiply when analysis is couched in faith."[9]

In this unstable tangle of conflicting activities, at least one thing was clear: while both projects dated back to 1970–1971, symbolic realism was nowhere to be found. *The Broken Covenant* did not include any methodological reasoning and its title was much less effective in alluding to symbolic realism than the original suggestions—*The Deepest Day: Studies in the Mythic Dimension of American Culture*, or even *To Avoid the Shipwreck: The Religious Meaning of American History*—had been. In the new book, nobody, not even Bob, had abided by the methodological tenets advanced in "Between Religion and Social Science" and similar essays. After a noisy launch and much discussion, in just five years symbolic realism seemed to have gone underground. But maybe Bellah had elected as a laboratory of symbolic realism one stream of his work that we have neglected for too long.[10]

I

Although he might soon write a sequel to *The Broken Covenant*, said Bellah in an interview published in the *New Review of Books and Religion* in October 1976, he was not going "to get stuck in the American scene forever." After all, he said, he remained "a Japan specialist." As a matter of fact, Bob had chaired the Japanese and Korean Research Center until 1974, and had never stopped teaching classes on Japanese society. He had also carried on attending symposia and conferences on East Asian matters both in the United States and overseas, and convened a study group with Chicago historian Harry D. Harootunian. And yet, by the mid-1970s his engagement with East Asia was just a shadow of what it had been. Upon his arrival at Berkeley, Bob had been at the vanguard of Asian studies; ten years later, Japan was little more than a distraction in a schedule crammed with speaking engagements on American history and religion.[11]

This was not what Bellah had in mind in 1969, when he contributed a short piece titled "Japan, Asia, Religion" to *Sociological Inquiry*. There he described an articulated research plan embracing the general problem of religion, Asian modernization, and the transformation of traditional worldviews in modern Japan. After regretting his inability to coordinate the three elements, Bob described his current work on the Far East as concerned with the reconstruction of Japanese identity vis-à-vis Western modernity on the one side, and the transformation of popular religion and cultural values on the other. The papers he wrote between 1968 and 1971 tried to combine these two lines of work, focusing on the cultural homogeneity of Japanese society, the alternation of moments of openness and closure toward foreign culture and technology, and the juxtaposition between group loyalty and the tradition of submerged transcendence he had found in Ienaga and Watsuji.[12]

Being an intelligent and experienced scholar, Bellah could craft some professionally acceptable pieces, but nothing that matched his past work in subtlety or creativity. As Albert Craig wrote to him on August 20, 1970, Bob's new essay "Transformations in Modern Japanese Thought" broke no new ground and was "a bit flat" if compared with his previous writing on Japan. One theme, however, stood out among the others and was hinted at again and again in different essays after being introduced in "The Japanese Emperor as a Mother Figure." In the short paper, first drafted in 1966 and widely circulated among fellow Japanologist and Berkeley students, Bellah contrasted the authoritarian approach of the *bakufu* model based on patriarchal Confucian precepts with the nurturing and "feminine" power of the emperor. The imperial family, he observed, was said to descend from Amaterasu, the Sun-goddess, who was often depicted as confused, vulnerable, and interested in peacemaking rather than imposing her will on others. Modelled on a weak symbol, the emperor had become an emotionally central "mother figure" who exercised "a powerful motivational attraction even when giving no effective command." The stable emotional base provided by the emperor in the public sphere dovetailed with the support given by actual mothers to their male children and thus legitimated the innovative and aggressive behavior typical of the samurai class that partly explained Japan's rise among nations before and after World War Two.[13]

Aside from the gendered language in which the argument was cast, it is not difficult to see why the paper on the Japanese emperor quickly became a small campus sensation in post-1964 Berkeley: in the image of the emperor purified from the pitfalls of actual Japanese political history, radicals and hippies could find the inspiration for creating new communal organizational forms evoking the image of a successful case of institutionalization of a "gentle" political symbol. Unfortunately though, these "preliminary notes" were never turned into a full-fledged study, and the twelve-page paper was published only in 2003.

Obsessed with the debate on the American civil religion, Bellah was losing touch with the development of area studies—a field where deconstructionism and postcolonial critique were rapidly supplanting old modernization theory (and theorists). The new direction of Japanese studies might have looked appealing to someone who was, in that very moment, preaching his own emancipation from scientism and high modernism. But in the early 1970s, as indicated by small clues scattered throughout his work, Bob had no time to give to his old intellectual love. For example, the first draft of "Baigan and Sorai: Continuities and Discontinuities in Eighteenth-Century Japanese Thought," presented in Chicago in 1974, was introduced by a note anticipating an extended and more scholarly version. When the paper was published some four years later, however, the only visible changes were the deletion of eight lines of text and the replacement of a couple of adjectives.[14]

What, then, about symbolic realism? Maybe, as hypothesized at the end of the previous section, in the 1970s Bellah had seen his work on Japan as the ideal place to experiment with symbolic realism as a radical interpretive methodology for the study of religious and cultural phenomena. After all, here his main topic was intellectuals and religious thinkers—that is, the very actors who created, manipulated, and diffused symbols and ideas; moreover, Japanese intellectual history was a safer niche for theoretical and methodological experimentation than the discussion on the American civil religion. In fact, with the exception of an almost perfunctory hint at the complex nature of political and religious ideologies as neither accurate descriptions of reality nor window dressing aimed at veiling underlying material structures and processes at the very beginning of the emperor paper, nothing could be found in Bellah's essays in Japanese intellectual history that related to symbolic realism. As claimed by anthropologist Amy Borovoy, after 1967 Bellah's work on Japan was mainly a sphere in which he tried out a broader set of questions that he would later develop in his writings on America and civil religion. "Baigan and Sorai," published in 1978, was to be his last major publication on Japan before his 1985 introduction to a new edition of *Tokugawa Religion*, a complex piece of work where he would discuss the shortcomings of 1950s modernization theory and the leading role acquired by Japan in the mid-1980s.[15]

II

Not that Bob needed distractions: the bicentennial had finally come, amid controversy and opposition. The shadow of Watergate still hung over the American public, and President Gerald Ford had not found a viable way to regain the trust of an exhausted citizenry. The attempt to transform the bicentennial into a "patriotic party celebrating (and selling) the virtues" of the nation aroused the protest of minorities, local communities, and leftist grassroots groups, who saw the commemoration as a chance to refresh the "spirit of the Revolution" and create a more inclusive version of "we, the people," rather than a mindless glorification of America. In the end, the federal government renounced its primary role in favor of local committees, public historians, and, especially, businessmen. In fact, the flood of patriotic kitsch, often totally unrelated to 1776, provoked harsh criticism of the commercialization of the event, which the People's Bicentennial Commission, a coalition created by left activist Jeremy Rifkin in 1972, labeled the "Buycentennial sellabration."[16]

In his countless appearances before collegiate, religious, and community audiences, Robert Bellah tried to weave the best legacy of the counterculture with public theology and his socialist interpretation of civil religion, and produced an original brand of left-leaning patriotism that somehow resonated with the one promoted by the People's Bicentennial Commission. Focusing on the risk of self-congratulation and the rise of a nostalgic nationalism that he found completely oblivious to revolutionary ideals, Bellah had little to say about the marketization of the bicentennial. Shortly before the Fourth of July, he addressed the graduating class of the Berkeley Department of Sociology, describing the Declaration of Independence not as "a description of what we are but a test of what we ought to be"—a test, he added, that America had never passed, "not in 1776, not in 1863, not in 1976." The Declaration, and with it the American civil religion, were not the "expression of a bland consensus ideology," but contradictory sets of embattled principles that had, in the past, been the cause of conflict and civil war. Republics, he warned his colleagues and students, were built on virtue, and whenever virtue was ridiculed or forgotten, despotism and authoritarianism would soon replace liberty.[17]

Bellah's tireless wandering from place to place made his name a recurrent feature of newspaper articles and op-eds. An interview published in the *Seattle Times* on April 17, 1976, for example, described him as "lanky, lean," with a "Lincolnesque frame" and presented him as "*the* sociologist of religion in the United States, a scholar able to express academic thoughts in common folkslanguage." An editorial published by the *New York Times* on July 4, 1976, defined "civil religion" as "sociologist Robert Bellah's phrase," and an article published in the *Los Angeles Times* some two weeks later hinted at his writing in order to explain that "people who [attended] bicentennial celebrations or national political conventions [were] taking part in the ritual of what some scholars [were] calling American civil religion."[18]

Fame had its drawbacks, too. Shortly after the Fourth of July, Bob received a letter from atheist *pasionaria* Madalyn Murray O'Hair. In her capacity as the president of the Society of Separationists, O'Hair had been given a newspaper article about Bellah, and asked him to "exchange information" on the idea of civil religion. It had been a busy summer for "the most hated woman in America": as the headquarters of her organization moved to a new location, aptly named the "American Atheist Center," she announced a series of lawsuits aimed at removing religious references from state-related objects and rituals—including the phrases "In God We Trust" from US coins and "under God" from the Pledge of Allegiance. In "Civil Religion in America" Bob had commented on both phrases, which he interpreted as conveying a deeply meaningful truth about the relationship between the American polity and the religious dimension.[19]

Bellah soon wrote back, including copies of his papers on civil religion. It is not hard to imagine O'Hair's disconcert when reading this key passage from the 1967 essay: "In American political theory, sovereignty rests, of course, with the people, but implicitly, and often explicitly, the ultimate sovereignty has been attributed to God. This is the meaning of the motto, 'In God we trust,' as well as the inclusion of the phrase 'under God' in the pledge to the flag. . . . The will of the people is not itself the criterion of right and wrong. There is a higher criterion in terms of which this will can be judged; it is possible that the people may be wrong. The president's obligation extends to the higher criterion." O'Hair's second letter, to which Bellah did not respond, brought criticism of his ideas about the American civil religion to a previously unseen emotional level. Her typical emphatic tone is worth quoting at length:

Robert N. Bellah,

I was shocked, and dismayed—physically reacting to your letter, your essay, and your logic.

It is impossible that such convoluted reasoning could be rewarded by publication in scholarly journals or books of our times. My gawd! We are undone! We can not survive as a nation.

I have been sitting at this typewriter, horrified, trembling, unable to express my reactions, fears, counter-remarks. *You can't mean it.* As I extrapolate one of your ideas after another back to its root idea—I absolutely fill with panic. . . .

My heart is just pounding—I can not write at this point—that is NOT civil religion. My expertise is law, having a Doctorate in jurisprudence. My gawd! 1984 is here. Words are not standardized; they mean what each person wishes them to

mean. You have destroyed by definition, by use of terms, by
innovative utilization of new meaning. How clever! How totally
disasterous [*sic*] for the nation![20]

For all their differences, Robert Bellah and Madalyn Murray O'Hair shared
at least one thing: they were both supporters of James Earl Carter Jr., who had
been nominated as Democratic Party candidate for the 1976 presidential elections in the New York National Convention of July 12–15. Jimmy Carter's
image as a Washington outsider, his emphasis on values and pragmatism, and
his decent persona were a breath of fresh air after the Nixon years and Ford's
failed attempt to regain the trust of the American people. And yet, much as
Bellah appreciated Carter's human decency and passionate public theology,
the candidate's inability to translate his personal piety into a real mobiliza-
tional kind of politics still fell short of Bob's prophetic version of the civil religious tradition.[21]

As a consequence, Bob's keynote speech at the annual meeting of the Society for the Scientific Study of Religion in Philadelphia on October 29, 1976,
titled "Religion and the Legitimation of the American Republic," sounded
more like a grim analysis of the 1976 presidential campaign than a scholarly
review of the first ten years of the American civil religion debate. Bellah depicted the rhetoric of the two candidates as an uneasy balance between the
stale formula of fiscal conservatism and some "vague and listless allusions to
a largely misunderstood past." The failure, however, was not theirs alone: Bob
also called on his fellow students of religion to help America recover "something that has so slipped out of memory as to be almost without a name." He
closed with the words he had repeated again and again in his bicentennial
talks: "It is not a time for self-congratulation. It is a time for sober reflection
about where we have come from and where we may be going."[22]

Stretching things a bit, one may say that in the year of the bicentennial the
Society for the Scientific Study of Religion annual conference looked much
like a Bellah-fest. Not only was Bob asked to give the inaugural keynote, but
The New Religious Consciousness was the object of the only "authors meet critics" gathering, while a special session was devoted to the American civil religion. The Philadelphia meeting, however, gave Bellah something much more
precious than scholarly recognition. It gave him the chance to renew his relationship with a scholar whom the program surprisingly associated with the
University of Pennsylvania, someone Bob had not seen or heard from in two
long years: Talcott Parsons.[23]

After his retirement in 1973, Parsons had gradually loosened his ties with Harvard and its newly formed Department of Sociology chaired by his old foe, George C. Homans. Thanks to his ex-student and friend Renée Fox, he had gotten a part-time teaching position at the Department of Sociology at Penn, and had professionally relocated there. Increasingly marginalized by the dominant cliques of 1970s social science, Parsons had committed himself to a continuous revision of his AGIL-based theoretical work, a highly formalized matter that only a small cohort of devotees would dare to learn and employ. Fortunately, most of these aficionados—sociologists Fox, Victor Lidz, Willy DeCraemer, and Harold Bershady—were at the University of Pennsylvania. With them, Parsons set up a seminar aimed at widening his general theory of action to the philosophical level of the "human condition"; starting in 1974, the group had met regularly when the old man was in town, and occasionally included historian A. Hunter Dupree and even Clifford and Hildred Geertz. At almost the same time, Parsons had his rude confrontation with Bellah over *The Broken Covenant*, which initiated a long period of reciprocal silence.[24]

Then, late in August 1976 Bob learned from his old graduate-school-mate Renée about the Human Condition seminar at Penn and unexpectedly expressed his wish to participate in this highly abstract endeavor—which, at that point, looked much like an attempt to keep the flame of Social Relations alive in a world turned irredeemably hostile. A delighted Talcott Parsons immediately wrote to both Bellah and Fox to convey his intellectual excitement at the prospect of the encounter, which would take place in Philadelphia after the Society for the Scientific Study of Religion meeting. Parsons provided Bob with an updated version of the manuscript on the human condition, which served as the basis for the discussion, and a new paper, "Death in the Western World."[25]

The seminar finally took place on Sunday, October 31, 1976. Parsons and Bellah had last met in person in 1974 and had never explicitly worked out their disagreement over *The Broken Covenant*, but their first encounter was warm and affectionate. A short session was held in the afternoon, focusing mostly on the relations between action and organism and Parsons's new interpretation of Freud. The two had a quick dinner together, in the course of which Parsons informed Bob about his latest theoretical breakthroughs, and then went to bed early. At breakfast the next day, Bellah announced that he had spent the night in a state of sparkling excitement, and went on scribbling his notes directly on the restaurant menu. Once at the department, the seminar members had to move to a fully equipped room to give Bob the blackboard space he needed to work out his insights. In what Parsons would later call "one of the most extraordinary bursts of intellectual creativity I have ever seen,"

Bellah filled blackboard after blackboard with four-function diagrams, comparing how a general religious orientation was reflected in the religions of major civilizations all the way down to Marxism. Contrary to expectations, he had effortlessly immersed himself in a game that he had not played for a decade: Parsonian formalism had never left the deepest structures of his mind, and he could still perform his AGIL act like a pro.[26]

Back in Berkeley, Bellah could write his old mentor that he had been deeply pleased by both the visit and Parsons's new work. He also added that he looked forward "to work[ing] out in detail what [he had presented] so schematically on that Monday morning." Excited by their rapprochement, Parsons sent Bob the draft of "Law as an Intellectual Stepchild," a rather long essay in which he had put on paper, for the first and only time, his critique of *The Broken Covenant*. In the piece, the book was used as a "case study" of "moral absolutism," defined as a critical position that "stresses the importance of common values in the constitution of social systems" and according to which "almost *any* concern for individuality, either religious or moral, or still more in spheres indifferent to morality," is (wrongly, from his own point of view) seen as "religiously and morally suspect." In his critique of American individualism, Bob had willingly focused on one strand of the utilitarian tradition and neglected many of its other scholarly or institutional forms. This narrow, and incomplete, assessment was mainly due to Bellah's "devotion to—and I think personal commitment to—a religiomoral collective ideal," which included what Parsons saw as an overreaction to modernity and rationalization. While he certainly received the draft, Bob decided not to respond to Parsons's request for feedback. To paraphrase a distinction drawn by Erik Erikson he himself had used as a title for a recent paper, Robert Bellah had now realized that he had no need to kill Parsons in order to survive—he was now strong and confident enough to let the critique go without fighting, knowing that this would make him a wiser intellectual, and perhaps even a better human being. On top of that, and in spite of all Bob's reservations, Jimmy Carter's victory on November 2, 1976, looked like a much-awaited sign of hope.[27]

III

A few days after the elections, Bob and his family resolved to have their Thanksgiving dinner at a restaurant.[28] Melanie had been busy with her law practice and declared herself too tired to cook a traditional meal as she had always done. Under the surface, however, reality was simpler and much more painful. The holidays had always been a time of love and closeness, but now, with one child gone and another one at college, Bob and Melanie felt that something vital was missing. It was their third Thanksgiving since Tammy had committed suicide, and in a month they would celebrate their third Christmas without her. Their planned visit to Jenny in Paris, where she was spending her junior year, was not sufficient to soften the pain provoked by the empty chairs. Predictably enough, the dinner at the restaurant turned out to be a complete failure and the four Bellahs drove home in silence and regret. In spite of appearances, their inability to lead an ordinary life showed through a comment that Abby wrote in her diary: "Somehow we couldn't play at being a whole family with its convention and petty institutions. It was a good game but that seemed the final end. . . . It is hard to comprehend how much pain we all feel daily. It should have ended long ago."[29]

And then the inconceivable happened. On December 5, 1976, just ten days after that gloomy night out, the Bellahs' phone rang at half past five in the morning. Before Melanie and Bob could get out of the house, the coroner had knocked on the door and entered the living room to give them the most appalling news: some three hours earlier, Abby and her best friend Lee had been in a car accident while coming home from a night out in San Francisco. Abby had been brought to Herrick Hospital in Downtown Berkeley around a quarter to three in the morning, and declared dead some twenty minutes later. The only relief for Bob and Melanie was when they discovered that Hally, who had been at the party with the girls, had decided to sleepover at a friend's house. When she came home, however, they had to tell her that her beloved sister—her creative, skinny, confident alter ego—had gone. And then they had to call Jenny in Paris and arrange for her to come back to Berkeley. Incredible as it was, it was happening again. Now they were four.

The morning came and Melanie and Bob were given some details of the accident from two empathic policemen. The car had run out of gas while Abby and Lee were cruising down the Berkeley hills, and had crashed at the intersection between Marin and Cragmont Avenues, a couple of miles north of Mosswood Road. Abby had been thrown through the windscreen onto the street, and when the paramedics had arrived some minutes later they found her unconscious and could only take her to the hospital. Lee had been pulled into the back seat—she was severely hurt but her life was not in danger. It was only when Lee recovered, however, that Melanie got to know the whole story. Trying to reach a gas station, the girls had turned off the engine of Bob's car and had coasted down Marin Avenue, a steep road leading from the hills to flatland Berkeley. Abby, who was driving, lacked the strength to operate the power brakes with the engine off, and

Lee had tried to help by pulling the wheel from the passenger's seat. The car had skidded, hit a fence, and then crashed into a telephone pole.

The story left Melanie horrified. Immediately, it was guilt time again. Who was to be charged for Abby's death? Had it been her fault? Had Melanie been a careless mother? Had it been Lee, taking the wheel while Abby was driving? Or was the fault Bob's, who had given the girls permission to use his car that night even though Abby had gotten her driver's license only one month earlier? Three years after Tammy's suicide, which Melanie had always associated with Bob's decision to leave for Princeton, another tragedy had touched her family, and once again she blamed her husband. Bob and Melanie decided to hold the funeral at the chapel of the Pacific School of Religion, and asked father John A. Coleman, SJ, a former student and now a colleague of Bob's, to take care of the ceremony. On Bellah's request to "make it as close to a kind of eucharist as you can," Coleman delivered a moving sermon, weaving words and symbols from Judaism, Christianity, and Buddhism. Hally and Jenny were shattered, the pain so unbearable it left them speechless. Letters, friends, solitude—nothing could help. In the words of Helen and Talcott Parsons, Abby's accidental death was "an event that literally strikes terror in the world."[30]

When Jenny left again for Paris in late December, Hally remained home with her parents. Early in the morning of December 5, 1976, her whole life had changed in a matter of minutes, and while only fourteen she now felt thirty years older. In her journal entry on New Year's Day 1977, she tried to capture her inner turmoil using the words of two books she had recently read, Herman Hesse's *Siddharta* and *Steppenwolf*: "Can you draw the line? Is there one between the real and the unreal, the sane and the insane, the truth and a lie? . . . Life is samsara, full of lust, greed and competition. It's all a game," she concluded. "I am in it and no matter what seems to happen I think I shall remain and without too much doubt I will probably always remain unenlightened, held fast in cycles of samsara, left only myself to contemplate. Screams from the horror pits of life's agonies. My mother was stung too hard for her soft comfortable aura to resist. I am a crusty little outcome of this place and this society I guess but I just get the feeling I wasn't put here to stay or maybe only until a psychopathic god finished experimenting on me. Everything I do is irrelevant and ridiculous."

One night, after taking the sleeping pills that gave her some respite from pain, Melanie asked Bob when the two of them would have permission to die. The eldest child of Luther Hutton Bellah Jr. had no doubts. "When all four of them are dead," said Bob. "'We are sentinels on the wall,' as Plato said. As long as any are living, we must remain for them."[31]

13

"We Create Our Planets
on the Table"

BERKELEY, 1976–1978

THE FIRST HUNDRED DAYS after Abby's death were deeply unsettling for
Robert N. Bellah and the three surviving members of his family. As well as
their obvious sorrow, they were devastated by how different the experience of
loss was when it happened a second time. "The hurt was more than flesh could
bear and yet this time the way was learned," wrote Melanie thirty years later.
"The first death was an unbearable, bewildering outrage, an obscenity done by
fate, unimaginable. Now it was known that such a thing could happen, and yet
it was not known at all that this thing could happen." Their feelings were taking
different routes: this time, Bob kept teaching and traveling, while Melanie
clung to her law practice, and Jenny returned to France to complete her junior
year. As a high school student, it was Hally who was able to give more space
and time to the profound change in her everyday life—she and Abby had been
extremely close and the loss cut to the very essence of her being. Given her
relative freedom from commitments, her parents agreed to the two sisters'
plan to send Hally on a month-long trip through Europe to visit her boyfriend
Peter in London and Jenny in Paris.[1]

On her flight back to Berkeley on April 24, 1977, Hally anticipated being
"tossed back into the same filthy shit hole, the same muddy rut." She was in
fact developing well, moving through her studies at Berkeley High and nurturing a recently discovered talent and passion for dance that would soon become
a vocation. At the same time, for the adults in the family things were moving
faster, and more radically, than they had three years earlier. Having a second
catastrophic tragedy so soon after the first led Melanie and Bob to take stock

of their marital relationship, and this pushed them to immerse themselves more than ever in their individual lives. Focusing on the day-to-day demands of their professional activities was one strategy to relieve the pain of the death of their third-born daughter; psychotherapy was another, and romantic interest for other individuals was a third.[2]

In fact, unbeknownst to most of their friends, some years earlier the Bellahs had agreed to have an open marriage, complete with clear and mutually accepted ground rules. In the late 1950s Melanie had once had a brief, embarrassing affair with a neighbor in Cambridge, but Melanie and Bob had responsibly brought the incident under control. After their arrival in Berkeley, however, something different had happened. During the long and stressful renovations of 10 Mosswood Road, Melanie had initiated a passionate relationship with the contractor, which had, in turn, led her to a profound reflection on her life— what she had achieved so far and what she wanted to do now that the move to California was a fait accompli. Just like her husband, Melanie needed a new start. Hence her decision to enroll in law school with the goal of pursuing a career of her own, but also her need to examine her relationship with Bob. Given how they were influenced by post-Freudian psychoanalysis, both Bellahs had come to see the imperative of strict monogamy as a regressive projection of "the wish for a faithful parent," one that denied the deepest needs of the other. So they agreed to have an open marriage, with two vital and non-negotiable rules to protect their twenty-year partnership: no meaningful family time would be sacrificed and no colleagues of Bob's should be involved.

In the eight years or so between this "constitutional reform" and Abby's death, the agreement had worked, and the couple had been able to maintain a deep, candid, and fulfilling relationship. Melanie had had a number of affairs, of which she would freely speak not only with Bob, but also with Tammy, who would in turn recount her mother's stories to Jenny. Some of her lovers came from Boalt Hall, and at least one of these relationships proved to be lasting, intense, and very satisfactory. When the family moved to Princeton to support Bob's unlucky bid at the Institute for Advanced Studies, Melanie had a liaison with a young colleague, which she discussed at length with sixteen-year-old Jenny, and on their tragic return to Berkeley and the start of her own family law practice she got involved with another lawyer, with whom she maintained a rewarding relationship that continued after Abby's death.[3]

Bob, however, had remained "technically faithful." The adverb, used in a diary entry of January 3, 1970, pointed to the fact that "occasions lacked." As he himself knew, this explanation was only part of the story: far from being a practical problem, Bellah's scant interest in women other than his wife largely resulted from his complex and unresolved attitude toward other men. In fact, while Melanie had experimented widely with relationships of varying intensity and duration, Bob had been content to fantasize about a number of male acquaintances as a way to deal with his deepest desires. Some of these reveries had been so detailed and intense that they rivalled, and at times exceeded, his involvement with Melanie.

All these musings, to be sure, had been a wholly internal affair. While Bob had discussed these longings with his wife for decades—she had laughed loudly when he had asked her if his inclinations toward men might jeopardize their intention to marry—no one else knew of them. Whenever he had felt attracted by other men he had suppressed these sentiments, covering them in a thick wrapping of symbols and metaphors. In this sense, with the announcement that his Dionysus for the masses was nothing more than an intellectual trip, Nobby Brown had legitimated Bellah's inclination to see "reading and writing as [his] two major modes of relating to reality" and validated his general "stand back and see it all" attitude. As 1976 came to its tragic end Robert Bellah remained convinced that "the whole range of human experience" could be grasped "not directly but through imaginative insight into inner structures." No wonder one of his earliest answers to the immense pain caused by Abby's death was to establish an informal reading group on the themes of grief and hope, where he studied the Book of Job together with some of his graduate students.[4]

I

The seminar "Tradition and Interpretation: The Sociology of Culture" that Bellah had started teaching a few weeks prior to the accident and some of the people who attended it were another important source of external support. For a couple of years he had successfully convened a summer workshop on civil religion and American culture, taking advantage of a program of short-term seminars for college teachers started by the National Endowment for the Humanities in 1973. At first Bob had applied to the program to raise money to help pay for Jenny's college tuition at Bryn Mawr, but he had soon found that "teaching teachers [was] the most rewarding kind of teaching," and had thus decided to submit a more ambitious project, a full-year course on interpretive social science. The new seminar picked up the thread of the work done at the Princeton Institute for Advanced Study three years earlier and built on the publication of Clifford Geertz's *The Interpretation of Cultures*, a book that had provoked immediate excitement across disciplinary boundaries.[5]

As was now his habit, Bob recited a poem by Wallace Stevens, "The Planet on the Table," to set the tone of the seminar:

His self and the sun were one
And his poems, although makings of his self,
Were no less makings of the sun.

"We are students of poetry (*poiesis* = making) but we are also makers-poets," he added, pointing to the triangular relation of reality, individuality, and tradition as the foundation of our being in the world. As such, "we create our own planets on the table" out of a condition of radical rootedness that might be analyzed, grasped, and eventually transformed, but never transcended. "Our question," he continued, "is how does the planet get to be on the table, but also, how does the planet on the table change the planet that is not on the table." As anticipated in *The Broken Covenant*, the quest for truth and the pursuit of critique had to start from a specific tradition and then proceed by way of methodic interpretation and renewal—losing one's tradition meant losing both truth and critique. The syllabus reflected some of Bellah's new interests: apart from a small deputation of amicable social scientists—Shils, Eisenstadt, Geertz—it was continental philosophers, from Dilthey and Gadamer to Habermas and Ricoeur, who got the lion's share.[6]

Listening to Bob's inaugural lecture were his colleagues Leo Löwenthal, a member of the Frankfurt School who had been teaching at Berkeley since the late 1950s, and Hubert Dreyfus, a leading Heidegger scholar and critic of artificial intelligence. Among the twelve college teachers from all corners of the United States who had been picked by the National Endowment for the Humanities to attend the seminar, two stood out. The first was William M. Sullivan, "Bill," an assistant professor of philosophy at Allentown College of St. Francis de Sales, Center Valley, Pennsylvania. He had received his PhD in 1971 from Fordham University, a Jesuit school in New York City, with a thesis on the process philosophy of Alfred North Whitehead and the cultural sociology of Max Weber—two typically Parsonian themes, although he had no connection with Bob's old mentor. Given his solid command of moral philosophy and social and political theory, Sullivan now intended to focus on more historical-interpretive work on civic reform movements. For this reason, he had applied to the National Endowment for the Humanities to study with Bellah, whom he knew only as the author of *The Broken Covenant*, rather than

choosing a more philosophical option, such as the seminar "Empiricism, Pragmatism, and Historicism" offered by Richard Rorty at Princeton.[7]

The second notable member of Bellah's seminar was Paul Rabinow, a former student of Geertz's in Chicago who had participated in the original workshop on interpretive social science at the Princeton institute in 1972, and now
taught at the City University of New York. At the time of his arrival at Berkeley,
Rabinow was losing hope of publishing a two-year-old manuscript titled "Situations: Reflections on Fieldwork in Morocco." Inspired by his encounters in
Sefrou in the late 1960s, the young ethnographer had written the book to question the methods of mainstream anthropology and invite his fellows to prob-
lematize their relation with their subjects and informants from a more symmetrical, open-ended point of view. Geertz's take on "Situations" had been
ambivalent: while he had not disliked the manuscript, he was worried that its
epistemic radicalism might hurt Rabinow's career, and had urged his former
student not to publish it as it was.

But Bellah fell in love with the book and made sure that it was accepted for
publication by the University of California Press: the critique of the
detachment-objectivity-authority complex advanced in the manuscript was
music to the ears of the inventor of symbolic realism, who interpreted it as a
clarion call for crossing the boundaries of narrative, poetry, and scholarship.
In a short preface, Bob emphasized "that knowing in the human studies is always emotional and moral as well as intellectual" and attributed to Rabinow
"a degree of being at ease with himself that many of us lack." Thanks to this
episode and the increasingly congenial mood of the seminar, Bellah, Rabinow,
and Sullivan developed a strong intellectual relationship, to the point that Bob
asked his two colleagues-turned-students to take an active part in Abby's funeral service.[8]

Then, in late April 1977, the anthropologist made a jocular comment on
Bill's not-so-obvious homosexuality that threw Bellah into an unexpected
emotional storm. Some days later, eating at a well-known Chinese restaurant
on University Avenue, Bob bluntly told Sullivan that he had felt attracted to
him since they had first met. Although he had no idea of what to do next, he
added, he was ready to offer his young student-colleague his "enormously
strong, almost unconditional love." The news caught Sullivan off guard. For all
the admiration he had for Bob, the idea that there could be anything more than
a friendly mentoring relationship between them had never crossed his mind—
in fact, he had never suspected that Bellah was attracted to men. Now that the
august professor, who had been married for nearly thirty years and had just

lost a daughter in a car accident, had declared his passion, Bill's immediate response was one of confused resistance. It was May 3, 1977. "Me in my black parka, scaring him to death," wrote Bob in his diary almost one year later, recalling their momentous lunch at the "Taiwan."[9]

Things, however, were far from settled. In the coming weeks Sullivan and Bellah began exploring a complex friendship, one in which sentimental, metaphorical, and scholarly elements combined in a multilayered, dynamic constellation. The two spent the summer visiting the Castro and trading books, reading and discussing Armistead Maupin's *San Francisco Chronicle* series "Tales of the City" and Mary Renault's *The Last of the Wine* and *Fire from Heaven*. In fact, it would have been hard to find someone better suited than Bill to provide the complex balance of passion and reflection that Bob hungered for. The two refined intellectuals, steeped in high culture but also separated by a curious set of asymmetries—Bellah was older and more established than Sullivan, but also had no experience of homoerotic relations—subjected their affair to relentless analysis from its very beginning: What was really happening? What kind of desires was their romance responding to? Could they find the key to what was going on in the works of classical and contemporary authors they were so eager to exchange and discuss? There was no doubt that their friendship mapped onto wider or even universal concerns, but which ones, and how? Neither fully realized that they were beginning a relationship that would come to be for each of them, in different ways, among the most significant of their lives.[10]

Driven by Bob's liberated curiosity for homoeroticism, the two slowly developed an element of physical closeness. Although Bob had fantasized for decades about having contact with men, the outcome was, to his great surprise, unimpressive. And yet, besides the lack of bodily fulfilment, the meaning of what was happening was clear: it made Bob feel accepted, it made him the focus of attention of a learned, remarkable, and decent man, and that made him feel good. Around the same time, Bellah found himself at the center of another incident, one that was no less essential for coming to terms with his past.[11]

II

A couple of weeks before the lunch at the "Taiwan" restaurant, the *New York Review of Books* published a commentary on David Riesman and Seymour Lipset's *Education and Politics at Harvard*, in which Columbia historian Sigmund Diamond attacked the commonplace image of Harvard as a bulwark against McCarthyism. In the short piece, Diamond recounted for the first time in print how his stint as a member of the Communist Party in the 1940s had prevented him from getting a job at Harvard in April 1954. After being asked by Dean McGeorge Bundy to collaborate with the authorities, he had refused to name names during an FBI interrogation, and the appointment had been withdrawn. "If Professor Lipset had taken as his motto not *Scio*, I know, but the proud motto of Fustel de Coulanges, *Quaero*, I search," he concluded, "he might had given us something more useful than this complacent, self-congratulatory chronicle." Among the topics proposed by Diamond for further research, one spoke directly to Robert Bellah, who read the piece with obvious interest: "Were graduate students asked about their political beliefs and associations? . . . Until we know that, how can we be sure what Harvard's policy was?"[12]

Up to that moment, Bob had remained silent about his own case—the only exceptions being his hint at McCarthyism in the introduction of *Beyond Belief* and a brief, unreferenced talk with Lipset during the preparation of the book. Paradoxically, his reserve was justified by the same principle that had cost him the instructorship at Harvard in 1955: he would not talk about the doings of others if it might harm them. As recently as 1973 Bellah had declined a request for information from one Roger Meltzer, who was writing his BA thesis on anticommunism at Harvard: "Somehow the truth of that episode should come out and when it does it will differ considerably from the widely accepted version that Harvard stood up to McCarthyism," he wrote in a letter that was later reproduced in the dissertation, "I do not see how I could talk about that period in my life without naming the individuals involved. . . . Since some of them are vulnerable to attack for a great many reasons than my difficulties in the early fifties, I think what I have to say might be used for extraneous ends. It is odd to be in a position of wanting to protect my prosecutors by not naming them," he concluded, "when it was precisely naming people that they originally wanted me to do."[13]

Meltzer's request for information reached Bob early in 1973, after the Paris Peace Accords but before Tammy's death. By then, Pusey and Bundy had both left Harvard for good: the former in 1971 to be appointed president of the Andrew W. Mellon Foundation, the latter in 1961 to become John Fitzgerald Kennedy's special assistant for national security affairs, a job he had relinquished five years later to move to the top of the American establishment—the presidency of the Ford Foundation. Bundy's "vulnerability" depended on the part he had played as Kennedy's advisor for foreign policy as exposed by a recent bestseller, *The Best and the Brightest*. In the book, journalist David Halberstam described the president's team—which had also included a man who in that precise moment was playing a crucial role in Bellah's life, Carl Kaysen—as a small cadre of overconfident men who were often made blind by their brilliance and conceit. A handful of months after Halberstam wrote of Bundy as an arrogant elitist who "always had a single pragmatic answer to a single question, and [who] was wary of philosophies, almost too wary," Bellah thought that his own story would have been too scandalous, even if only for a BA thesis.[14]

Four years later Bob still was of the same opinion, and although he spoke of the *New York Review* article with Melanie and a number of friends, he did not decide to go public until June, when he read McGeorge Bundy's piqued reply to Diamond. Questioning both the historian's factual accuracy and his interpretation of what had happened, the former dean justified himself using what he considered the simplest of reasons: Diamond had been promised an administrative post that had nothing to do with academic freedom. While Bundy had respected the young scholar's "morally superior" position, he had been trying to avoid another scandal, since the one involving physics professor Wendell Furry was at that time far from settled. Bundy now recognized the "obviously agonizing" character of Diamond's situation and the "cruel pressures" exerted on him, but felt no remorse about his own decision.[15]

That was too much. Bellah's appointment as an instructor would have been wholly academic, and still Bundy had treated him just the same as he had Diamond (and Sydney James, a former comrade with whom he had consulted a couple of days earlier). While penning his reply, Bob had the occasion to exchange a couple of phone calls with Bundy himself, who tried to prove his good faith by reading a long letter he had written to Pusey in 1955. "Bob," said Bundy without an ounce of irony, "we're on the same side now." Apart from the pleasure he felt in gaining the upper hand on his former dean, Bellah was unimpressed by the latter's attempt to spin the story and set out to tell it in full detail, siding with Diamond. In a poignant passage, he also revealed how close he still felt to his "adoptive mother": "I owe much to Harvard and my life is indelibly formed by it. It has never occurred to me to reject the institution as a whole and all it stood for, for that would involve among other things a rejection of much of myself. But I know from personal experience," he added, "that Harvard did some terribly wrong things during the McCarthy period and that those things have never been publicly acknowledged." In conclusion, Bellah called for an independent investigation on the matter—the only point on which Bundy agreed in his lofty, condescending rejoinder.[16]

Published in the *New York Review* late in June 1977, Bellah's version of Harvard's record on McCarthyism made the news. Among those who wrote to compliment him were David Riesman, who knew only a partial version of the story; playwright Eric Bentley; activist Fay Stander; and historian Ellen W. Schrecker, who later interviewed him for what would become celebrated volumes on McCarthyism—*No Ivory Tower* (1986) and *Many are the Crimes* (1998). One of the most interesting letters came from James D. Steakley, a gay activist who had recently published a book titled *The Homosexual Emancipation Movement in Germany*. Focusing on the episode in which Harvard psychiatrist Dana Farnsworth (not named in print) had pressed the young sociologist about his sexual preferences, Steakley called attention to the repression of homosexuals in the academy before, during, and after McCarthyism. After praising Bellah for his courage and open-mindedness, he asked him a seemingly innocent question: "What would have happened if you had been a practicing homosexual?"[17]

III

Ironically, when Steakley's letter reached him the effects of Bob's affair with Bill Sullivan were starting to show in many different ways. In the early summer of 1978 the man who had been portrayed as "so much like a college professor he might have been sent over by Central Casting" not only looked more and more like a true Californian—"more informal, more color, more jeans, more plaid"—but was also becoming aware of the needs of that much neglected vehicle of his "mighty brain"—his body. His efforts at gaining weight and his regular training schedule, which included indoor exercise and running along the fire trails above Mosswood Road, soon made him look fresher, younger, and healthier.[18]

Being able to finally live out some of his long-repressed fantasies in the company of a man who truly loved and understood him also had a positive effect on Bob's marriage, which paradoxically became closer as a result. Although her law practice, resuming smoking, and the project of writing a book on Tammy had allowed her to conceal the most obvious signs of her pain, Melanie had been anything but okay. Within a few months she had found herself in a state of inner desolation, which had further been aggravated by a secret attempt before Abby's death to stimulate her fertility that had in fact resulted in menopause, and thus the end of her dream of having a "replacement child." As if this were not enough, the lawsuit she had brought against Tammy's analyst, Daniel Greenson, for what she saw as irresponsible behavior regarding her daughter's suicidal tendencies, had been pending for two years now, and the end was still not in sight.[19]

When Bob told Melanie of his flourishing friendship with Sullivan in the most enthusiastic of tones, she immediately realized what was going on. Thanks to Bill, her husband was finally fulfilling a long-repressed need, and was thus going to create for himself that individual independence she had known for some time thanks to her affairs. Melanie understood the therapeutic value of Bob's romantic liaison with Bill in the face of Abby's death, and its deeper implications for his continuing search for meaning. But she also welcomed it as a much-needed effort to add balance and perspective to their open marriage, something that up to that point had been missing from the equation. For all these reasons, she wanted the two men to find the fulfilment they sought in each other "without having to violate [their] nature." As a consequence, Melanie adopted a positive attitude toward Bill, welcomed him as part of the family, and was supportive of Bob's desire to make Jenny and Hally part of what was going on.[20]

The exploration of the symbolic dimensions of the new makeup of his relational life pushed Bellah to finally deal with another big elephant in the room. After lengthy discussions with Melanie and Bill, on September 13, 1977, Bob wrote one old friend a long letter about his current situation. Announced by a vague phone call, the note spoke of the "rather intense friendship" between Bob and Bill as "a protest against death," one in which Bellah had discovered "new resources of living in [himself] and in others." The letter also pointed to the obvious parallel between Bellah's relationship with Sullivan and his early days with his old friend—although the two individuals, the times, and the dynamics of their relations were worlds apart, Bob could not help but compare them. Without being too explicit, he wrote to his friend that "my friendship with Bill seems to remove some old frustrations and resentments that plagued our friendship and makes me more open toward you." If the kind of "male affection" between them had been comparable to a brotherly relationship, he added, he now had "a kind of son and the kind of childish affection one can have with a son."[21]

If Bellah's words sounded confused, it was because the situation was itself far from clear. Not only was Sullivan a partner *and* the son he had never had, but also a substitute for his old friend and sometimes even for his father. As Bob now understood it, his main attraction toward his younger friend was rooted in his craving for what he called "the One Male" or, better, a peculiar kind of "bigamy, a male spouse that [he] would see almost as much, have almost as much sex with, but just as intensely close to and in love with as M[elanie]." And yet, although he had found Bill and considered him to *be* that One, he still felt an irresistible urge to freely explore whichever direction his now-liberated polymorphous condition would push him.[22]

The words of Norman O. Brown's "Apocalypse" clearly resounded in Bob's mind: "It is not possible to get the blessing without the madness; it is not possible to get the illuminations without the derangement." This time, however, Nobby's symbols and poetry were not enough—Bob remained curious and had decades of lost time to try to make up. Luckily, it was the right moment to do that. He had never been so self-confident before: his newfound physical fitness made him feel bolder and even "intimidating," while the controversy on McCarthyism at Harvard and the ongoing exchange with his old friend—who had been baffled at Bob's revelation and had urged him to stick with Melanie—had boosted his conviction of being on the right track to finally come to terms with his past. "No suffering no progress. No fighting no love. . . . Of course there is risk," he wrote Sullivan on December 9, 1977, "but no risk, no life." A few weeks later, the Ford Professor of Sociology and Comparative Studies at the University of California, Berkeley, got into his car and drove across the Bay. It was February 17, 1978.[23]

IV

Thanks to a unique series of events, for thirty years Bob had always found himself in the right place at the right time. In 1945 he had been made temporarily unfit to join the US Army, and that had saved him from going into combat just before the end of World War Two. His service at Fort Dix from April to November 1946 had allowed him to enroll at the Department of Social Relations, which had not existed at the time of his arrival in Cambridge. When he had to flee Harvard owing to the university's collaboration with the FBI, he was able to obtain a fellowship at the Institute of Islamic Studies at McGill, rather than having to seek nonacademic work as some of his peers were forced to do. Then, his return from Montreal in 1957 coincided not only with the peak of Talcott Parsons's creativity and influence, but also with a massive infusion of public and private research money into the academic system.

Ten years later, his decision to move to Berkeley to change his life had brought him to the heart of the counterculture at the very beginning of the Summer of

Love. Now that he had finally taken his finger off the repress button—a phrase from Tom Wolfe's famous article on the "Me Decade" that perfectly fit his current mood—and had decided to practice "a little promiscuous sex" to "limber himself up," he had the veritable gay mecca of the world a half hour from home.[24]

Ever since that fateful summer of 1967, San Francisco had interested Bob Bellah mainly from two points of view: as the haven for the social and cultural radicalism later portrayed in *The New Religious Consciousness* and as the setting of the not-so-frequent weekends that he would spend with Melanie at festival marketplaces like Ghirardelli Square. In the last ten years, however, the City by the Bay had undergone a number of profound transformations, and its homosexual residents had been at the forefront of most of them. During and after World War Two, the vibrant gay and lesbian scene that had emerged across the bars and nightclubs of the bohemian North Beach and Embarcadero districts at the beginning of the twentieth century had been strengthened by the hundreds of GIs who had been "dishonorably" discharged from the Pacific Theater in the early 1940s and had chosen San Francisco as their new home. In the 1960s, the shift to a tertiary economy based on services, finance, and tourism, and the obvious freedom created by the civil activism of homophile organizations and bar-owners' trade groups attracted a steady inflow of homosexual immigrants from all corners of the United States.[25]

After the Summer of Love, and some time before the iconic Stonewall revolt in New York, things had changed again thanks to the emergence of a groundbreaking gay liberation movement. The speech of San Francisco activist James Foster at the 1972 Democratic National Convention marked a critical moment of political visibility that was followed, four years later and not without difficulty, by the repeal of California sodomy laws through the Consenting Adult Sex Bill, a "homosexual bill of rights" sponsored by future mayors George Moscone and Willie Brown Jr. As each step toward the full legitimation of homosexuality was followed by a reactionary backlash, in the 1970s, gays had to suffer not only hostile political campaigns—such as the drive for the adoption of the so-called "Briggs Initiative" in California in 1977–1978—but also an escalation of police harassment and private violence. These continuing struggles, however, contributed to bringing the community "out of the bars, into the streets" and encouraged a new generation of politically savvy activists—of which Harvey Milk was only the most famous, and tragic, example—to step out.[26]

Bob Bellah's time of experimentation could thus unfold within the context of a vibrant gay population whose dimensions, self-awareness, and creativity were unprecedented in the history of mankind. Early in 1978, San Francisco had between 75,000 and 120,000 homosexual residents—that is, 12–15 percent of all San Franciscans according to even the most conservative calculations. Of these, nearly two-thirds were men, and most of them had moved to the city during the previous eight years. Given these numbers, the community was big enough to seize a number of different districts, each with its own vibe, subculture, and style—"Folsom Street Daddies, Castro Street Boys, Polk Street Queens."[27]

While the Tenderloin was the realm of down-and-out young men and women selling their bodies to make a living, Polk Street catered to an affluent, traditional gay population which had no problem integrating with the bourgeois straight community. Conversely, the formerly Catholic working-class neighborhood of Eureka Valley had evolved into a social experiment of sorts—the Castro. Young men came from all over the United States to experience the thrilling atmosphere of an openly gay environment where the first ever picture-window bars alternated with bookstores, cinemas, and nightclubs fully equipped for casual sexual encounters. Besides its freedom and visibility, this "gilded gay ghetto" offered its denizens a mark of mutual recognition in the distinctive aesthetics of the so-called "Castro clone"—"tight blue jeans, preferably Levi's with button flies, plaid shirts, leather vests or bomber jackets, and boots."[28]

Last but not least, Folsom Street or "South of Market" was the sanctum of leather and macho culture and the home of a more hedonistic lifestyle. As the night fell on the old warehouse district, its clubs and restaurants opened their doors to "serve the unlimited purpose of providing a place for gay men to have unlimited sex" within an encouraging, almost communal atmosphere. In addition to its many bars, South of Market was also dotted with bathhouses—a staple of gay life since the late nineteenth century. At the "tubs," as they were called, male homosexuals had learned to overcome their isolation and develop a sense of pride and self-assurance, while being protected from blackmailing and police harassment. In the late 1970s, popular tubs in San Francisco had names like Ritch Street Health Club, Folsom Street Barracks, or Liberty Baths. Of these, the Club Baths was the largest and possibly the most renowned. Lodged in a former depot a couple of blocks north of Folsom Street, the two-story bathhouse included snack and TV rooms, glory hole booths, private quarters for casual sex, a small porn movie theater, and an orgy room complete with open and bunk beds and a large padded platform. Its dim lightning, the rule that everyone should just wear a white towel, and the paucity of verbal exchanges gave the search for "Mr. Right Now" a dreamy, loose, almost demo-cratic, flavor.[29]

After Sullivan had returned to Philadelphia, Bellah had sometimes strolled around the Castro, either alone or in the company of gay friends—in Decem-ber 1977, for example, he attended a screening of Peter Adair's documentary *The Word is Out* at the Castro Theater with a young acolyte. Now that he was ready for action, South of Market seemed more promising. After a few drinks alone, he drove to the corner of 8th and Howard Street and hesitantly made his way into the blue doors of the Club Baths. "The strange almost surrealist atmosphere of disco music," he noted in the first entry of the journal he com-menced right after his solitary foray, "The towel-clad bodies. The steam room. The callous checking out . . ." Again, Bellah's immediate reaction was one of confusion and distaste. Something was missing, and that something had a name: *love*. Without love, having sex with strangers was not different from watching porn in a movie theater, and Bob wrote that he had no desire or in-tention to try again.[30]

In fact, the Club Baths episode had the effect of boosting Bob's self-confidence: he now felt "centered and outrageous," "free about the whole thing," with no restraints "and very few taboos." The next experiment took place in New York City during a two-day conference convened by the top brass of the Rocke-feller Foundation to discuss the possibility of recreating a value consensus in America after the difficult start of Jimmy Carter's presidency. On the evening of March 28, 1978, Bellah joined Rockefeller's Joel Colton, William Sloane Coffin, Kenneth Boulding, David Halberstam, and the other participants for dinner at the Princeton Club of New York on West 43rd Street. Back at his hotel, he met with "Brad," a "not unintelligent" twenty-four-year-old callboy who gave him his first same-sex orgasm. This more-manageable version of casual sex somehow sweetened Bob's judgment: "Nice to have no involvements," he wrote in his diary as soon as Brad had left the room, "know you will never see him again."[31]

The crucial step had been taken—Bellah had let desire run free, allowing chaos and spontaneity to enter his life without his usual careful consideration. It was not by chance that the involuted, nightmarish dreams about Bill, Hut-ton, and Melanie that had haunted Bob since his visit to the Club Baths stopped right after that later encounter. As he explicitly wrote in his diary, it was as though a period of liminality had been brought to an end by the ap-propriate rite of passage and a new phase of his life had started.[32]

14

Articulating the Real

BERKELEY, 1978–1979

AMONG THE THIRTY or so people who attended the Rockefeller Conference "The Search for Value Consensus in America" was Richard Sharpe, a young executive of the Ford Foundation who would soon play a major part in helping Robert N. Bellah resume his scholarly activity. After the brutal disruption brought about by Abby's death, Bob's evolving friendship with Sullivan and his parallel intimate investigations had greatly diverted him from his academic preoccupations. Major books—Charles Taylor's *Hegel*, Anthony Giddens's *New Rules of Sociological Method*, and E. F. Schumacher's *Small is Beautiful*, to name a few—passed across his desk without impressing him. The only exception was *From Mandeville to Marx*, a finely textured critique of "modern ideology" written by a French anthropologist, Louis Dumont, who had done fieldwork in India and the South of France and was now using his ethnographic experiences to reflect on the whole of Western society and its worldview. Enthusiastic about Dumont's treatment of liberal individualism, in a crisp book review Bellah compared him to Michel Foucault and Claude Lévi-Strauss, a compliment that earned him an invitation to give a seminar at the École des hautes études en sciences sociales in Paris whenever he wanted.[1]

The Dumont episode persuaded Bob that he still had the cultural and reputational capital needed to function as before. Teaching could be done routinely, and as far as conferences were concerned it was not difficult to meet expectations with a minimum of effort. In September 1977, Bellah succeeded in writing a paper for the Inter-Religious Peace Colloquium in Lisbon in less than a week; some months later he put together his thirteen-page speech for the Rockefeller Conference in a single afternoon, and then resolved to write his next interventions on the way to meetings. Interestingly, this had no impact on the reception of his work: his papers were published with little or no editing, and he would constantly receive letters of praise, invitations to further conferences, and interview requests from local and national mass media. For one good year, Bob could focus on his personal life while maintaining a more than acceptable professional façade.[2]

Then, early in May 1978, he received an unexpected phone call from Steven M. Tipton, a Harvard doctoral student he had known for some time. A fifth-generation Californian in his early thirties, Tipton had studied literature, philosophy, and religion at Stanford before entering the Religion and Society program at Harvard in 1971. In Cambridge he attended the courses of some of Bellah's old friends—Evon Vogt, Daniel Bell, James Luther Adams, Wilfred Cantwell Smith—and John Rawls, who was just about to publish *A Theory of Justice*. In 1972 he began a tutorial relationship with Talcott Parsons, in which they discussed the works of Max Weber, Ernst Troeltsch, and others centered on comparative studies of societal evolution.

For his dissertation, Tipton decided to study how ordinary people experienced, grasped, and lived out their morality—how they distinguished right from wrong and how they enacted their understanding in everyday life. Since 1972 he had been traveling between Cambridge and the Bay Area to conduct his fieldwork on three alternative religious movements—Neo-Pentecostal, Zen Buddhist, and Human Potential—which had been joined by young men and women in their attempt "to make moral sense of their lives" after the intense social experimentation, and sometimes the personal disruption, of the 1960s. In seeking to find out how the subjects of his study conceived of what made an act right and a person worthy of praise, Steve asked his interlocutors to spell out "what you go by," and to reflect upon how they enacted their understanding of good character and community. Starting with an apparently straightforward question—"How should we live?"—Tipton's "moral conversations" invited ordinary people to express their vision of the good life and think about its underlying premises and contradictions.[3]

Following Parsons's counsel and introduction to Bellah, in 1974 Steve found the way to Bob's office. Fascinated by the project, Bob took a leading role in mentoring Tipton through his PhD and suggested that he add sociology to the study of religion to complete a joint PhD program. He also introduced him to Ann Swidler, a Harvard assistant professor who had recently gotten her PhD at Berkeley. An undergraduate at Radcliffe College in the mid-1960s under the tutorship of one of Parsons's collaborators, Andrew Effrat, Swidler had spent a year as Seymour Martin Lipset's research assistant before moving to

California in 1967. While writing her dissertation on alternative high schools under the guidance of Arlie Hochschild, she had worked as Bob's teaching assistant during his radical course of 1971–1972, conducting sessions on Durkheim, religious evolution, and the "symbolic resources for liberation and integration in contemporary America." Thanks to Lipset, in 1975 Ann had returned to Harvard to teach sociology and work on her first book, later published as *Organization without Authority*. When Ann finally read a precis of Tipton's thesis she found Bellah's enthusiasm fully justified—it was, to put it simply, the most exciting thing she had ever read. The two soon developed an intense intellectual friendship, which led Swidler to sit on Steve's joint-degree dissertation committee.[4]

Up to that point, Tipton had benefited from the generosity of the Ford Foundation, which had granted him over $20,000 to conduct his multisite comparative research. In the spring of 1978 the dean of the Harvard Divinity School, Krister Stendahl, sent the young sociologist to his friend McGeorge Bundy with the goal of securing some additional funds to complete his thesis and help the school introduce the study of new religious movements into its curriculum. In New York, Steve met with the Committee on Public Policy and Social Organization, a division of the Ford Foundation created in 1973 to finance applied scholarly work on the problems and prospects of modern societies. Its program officer, Richard Sharpe, had long been trying to steer humanists and social scientists toward work on relevant policy issues, but had often been frustrated by the narrowness of "typical discipline-bound scholars."[5]

Fueled by his frustration, Sharpe was looking for a bold research project that might work as a prototype for a new interdisciplinary program, titled "Humanistic Perspectives for Social Problem-Solving." As his main concern regarded the connections between values and community, he saw Tipton's work as the perfect beachhead for a wider expedition into the spiritual and moral crisis of contemporary America. Sharpe urged Steve "to let the weirdos go" and concentrate on those who really mattered—the broad mainstream of the middle class. In one of "those strange moments when grace comes through the Ford Foundation," Sharpe pledged the money needed to get the investigation started.[6]

It was at that point that Tipton called Bellah: while intent on finishing his dissertation, he saw the opportunity to define a broad inquiry into middle-class morality and commitment in terms that Bob could help lead beyond the bounds of solving public policy problems. After a quick discussion with Swidler, the three resolved to create a small research team aimed at proposing a project to Ford to respond to Sharpe's concerns while exceeding his agenda and expectations. They also decided to enlarge the group by bringing in a colleague of Tipton's from Harvard, Richard Madsen. Born in 1941, "Dick" had attended the seminary to become a member of the Maryknoll Fathers and Brothers, a Catholic society of apostolic life. After being ordained in 1968, Madsen was then sent as a missionary to Taiwan, where he also studied sociology and Chinese. Upon his return to the United States, he enrolled in graduate school at Harvard and then left the order in 1973. His PhD dissertation focused on revolutionary asceticism in contemporary China, under the direction of Bob's old friend Ezra Vogel, and used interviews of Chinese émigrés to Hong Kong as a proxy for an ethnography of the transformations of a small peasant village under twenty-five years of Communist rule. Madsen was also well known to Swidler, who recommended him as her substitute when she went back to California for a sabbatical in 1977.[7]

All of a sudden, Bob had a brilliant intuition. Paul Rabinow and Bill Sullivan had been working for some time on a reader—titled *Interpretive Social Science* and eventually published in 1979—that would organize some of the texts used during the 1976 residential seminar to make them available to the wider public. "Let us be clear," they wrote in their introduction, "what we want to understand is not something behind the cultural object, the text, but rather something in front of it. . . . Social structures, cultural objects, can be read also as attempts to cope with existential perplexities, human predicaments, and deep-rooted conflict. . . . They point toward the *aporias* of social existence." Seeing this epistemic program as the perfect complement to the culturalist approach emerging from the discussion of the newly formed group, Bellah suggested his friend for inclusion. The move put Sullivan in a liminal position—he was a perfect stranger to the other three and the only one who had not studied at Harvard with Bob's former colleagues.[8]

What was about to start, however, was far from being yet another mundane academic project, and the general mood of intellectual excitement ensured Bill was rapidly allowed in. After a couple of high-spirited meetings, the five scholars decided to work on a handful of sociological case studies framed by Bellah's historical-theoretical meditations. Taking *The Broken Covenant* and Tipton's dissertation as their points of departure, they nonetheless dedicated most of their attention to Alexis de Tocqueville's *Democracy in America*. In fact, Bellah's 1978 National Endowment for the Humanities summer seminar, formally dedicated to some "important political religious movements of the 17th and 18th centuries, with the writings of significant American religious and political thinkers of that time period, and with the fate of the ideas crystallized in the late 18th century during subsequent American history," focused mostly on what the quintet soon termed "the wisest book ever written on America."[9]

In their reading, Tocqueville's critique of individualism was somehow amplified at the expense of his worries about the excesses of equality. What counted the most, they thought, was the embeddedness of laws and institutions in what the Frenchman called the "mores" or "habits of the heart" of a people. It was the sentiments, "the opinions and practices that created the fabric of society"; these moral and intellectual dispositions were themselves rooted not only in religion, but also in the experiences of political participation and a communal economy. While the small-scale society observed by Tocqueville during his 1831 trip through Jacksonian America could never be revived as such, it might be used as a powerful myth of renewal against the malaises identified in Bellah's 1975 book: unrestrained individualism, economic inequality, political apathy, and towering bureaucracies. "If our mores are the key to our success," Bob wrote in a speech he gave publicly many times between 1978 and 1979, "we might well ask how we can characterize them in the past and what seems to be their present and their future fate."[10]

I

Thanks to the National Endowment for the Humanities, which in the late 1970s had replaced the Ford Foundation as his major funder, the fall of 1978 brought Bellah a one-year sabbatical—the fourth such leave in his career, after the three spent respectively in Tokyo, Palo Alto, and Princeton. The goal of this sabbatical-at-home was very ambitious: to finally bring a number of uncompleted works to their appropriate conclusions under the umbrella title of *Religious Vision and Social Order in Comparative Perspective*. Bob planned to work on three books at the same time: the sequel to *The Broken Covenant*, described as a volume on "the basic understanding of the human condition contained in the several major strands of the American tradition"; a book on how "modern Japanese have attempted to appropriate (or abandon) their past" in their encounter with modernity; and the latest incarnation of his theoretical-comparative book, *The Roots of Religious Consciousness*. "I will show in some detail," wrote Bellah in a request for additional funding addressed to the Rockefeller Foundation, "how constellations of symbolic, personal and social factors vary in primitive, archaic, historic, early modern, and modern contexts." His 1964 essay "Religious Evolution" and a series of lectures given at the

University of California, Santa Barbara, in 1975 were indicated as the initial core of this third manuscript, scheduled for the end of 1979.[11]

Much more than work, however, what interested Bob were the intricacies of his affective, sexual, and relational life. While the evolution of the latter was rather different from what he had imagined, the progression was evident. He now felt the need to make sense of what was happening: how would he integrate the various, ever-changing facets of his personal identity? Would he be able to reconstruct his autonomy from the many episodes of his ongoing emancipation? If he wanted to combine his liberated eros with his relational commitments in terms of spousal love and philia, his energy had to be tamed and channeled. This, however, had be done without exhausting himself in his old routines.

In other words, Bob was entering a moment of *re-articulation*. Coined by one of his favorite philosophers, Eric Voegelin, the idea of "articulation" captured the "process in which human beings form themselves into a society for action," as embodied, for example, in political figures who emerge to act on behalf of the whole of society. Once a human group finds a new way of organizing itself, wrote Voegelin, there begins an interpretive process aimed at creating a "representation"—that is, the set of symbolic images, stories, and myths needed to legitimate collective action as appropriate and binding. The new representation works until a new arrangement is found through a new articulation, and so on.[12]

As far as Bellah's personal life was concerned, a re-articulation could be effected by creating a new relational configuration embracing the new sentiments, practices, and individuals he had gotten to know in the last few months, and then reflecting on the structure itself and its deeper meaning. While he did not immediately give up having casual sex, Bob envisioned a stratified network in which his marriage and "a continuous and close relationship [with a man; that is, Bill Sullivan], psychologically intense with a certain physical closeness" would be surrounded by a handful of caring male friendships—including one with Steve Foster, a young anthropologist to whom he had been introduced by Paul Rabinow—and an even wider circle of less intense relations aimed at fulfilling his "purely physical homoerotic needs."[13]

Solidly settled at the center of this emerging complex, Melanie had long taken an active part in her husband's parallel life: she had encouraged Bob to try the Club Baths, approved of his experiments with casual sex, and pushed him to come out to Jenny and Hally—who had been presented with their father's friendship with Sullivan as extremely profound and positive, and thus

FIGURE 14.1. Robert and Melanie Bellah in the late 1970s. (RBPP)

not open to discussion—and then to a small number of friends, colleagues, and acquaintances. Besides Bill, welcomed as a genuine addition to the family, Melanie also got to know some of Bob's intimate friends, whom she would invite to 10 Mosswood Road, or sometimes out for dinner or tea to chat of their respective experiences—at one point, her involvement was so intense that one of her lovers dubbed Bob "the only bisexual with a manager."[14]

Thanks to Melanie and Bill, Bob was on his way to achieving what, some years earlier, he had dubbed "bigamy"—but, unlike that practiced by his father, in a way that was not built on deception, escape, or exclusion, but rather on the inclusion of a number of different individuals within a diverse affective circle. It was no coincidence that before long Bellah could write Sullivan that his "homoerotic frenzy" was over—"It's not that there is any taboo," he wrote, but "the overloaded compulsiveness of mysterious homoeroticism is largely gone, largely because our love is, finally, so satisfactory." And yet, it was impossible not to hear the echo of an old, and obvious, interrogative—"Am I gay?" From the locker room of the Del Mar Club to the City Hall of Cambridge, Massachusetts, where he and Melanie had married on August 17, 1949, and then again on the shores of the Charles River where he had bidden his friend a silent but painful farewell at the time of his leaving for Montreal, Bob had lost count of the number of times he had asked himself *the* question. The growing complexity of the "bigamy and friends" architecture he had created, coupled with his continual reflection, either alone or with Bill, suggested that the answer could not be a simple yes or no.[15]

II

As Bellah had anticipated at the beginning of his search, any in-depth reflection about his own needs and desires had to begin with Hutton's flight. "I suppose I must have thought it my fault that my father left," he wrote Bill in February 1979, a conviction that had caused him to develop a "deep sense of inadequacy as a man." For nearly fifty years, Bob had longed for someone not only to dissolve this feeling of not being good enough, not being in the right place, but also to help recreate an "archaic," "mythical paradisial *Urzeit*" in which Hutton had not yet abandoned his family. Given the source of his pain, this "someone" had to be a man, but not just any man. He had to be a man whom Bob could like from a physical point of view but also admire as a thinker and befriend as a decent human being. In the despair caused by the death of two daughters within three years, he had found the courage to make a first move toward Bill Sullivan, a young man who perfectly fit the description and who "would understand." Bellah's wager had been successful, and Bill had become "the One Male," able to confirm that Bob was worthy of being loved, to whom he could pledge his unconditional devotion. With time, their relationship had become a unique vehicle for appropriating the positive potentials of a homoerotic friendship—a search for the foundations of a mutual, respectful male romance that was further enriched by their collegial scholarly work.[16]

To be clear, although times had changed and other men who had similarly repressed their homosexuality for decades were ending conventional marriages in droves, not even for a moment had Bellah thought of leaving his wife. As early as November 1977, the two had renewed their fusional vows: asked if she still loved him, Melanie had responded more than positively—"I not only love you," she said, "*I am you.*" Their "bone deep commonality," based on "a shared experience since childhood, on a common being that knows not the boundary of skin," had ultimately been sealed not only by the difficulties they had endured as parents to Thomasin and Abigail, but also by being parents to Jennifer and Harriet, who still needed all their love and care. Given his awareness of the origin of his needs, his unceasing attachment to Melanie, and his ambivalence about his early homoerotic experiences, it was easy for Bob to think that "perhaps genitally [he was] just more heterosexual than [he] thought" and thus, when in need of a label, bisexual. "There is difference between sexual identity and sexual choice," he lectured a friend on December 4, 1977, "I am in identity (and Bill is too) as male as you are. . . . If I am bisexual in my object choice that is just a fact, not confusion."[17]

And yet, at times Bellah could not help but identify as homosexual. This happened mostly when he found himself in more traditionalist or conservative contexts such as Salt Lake City, which he first visited in March 1978 for a conference on Mormonism at Brigham Young University. As he wrote in his diary, there was "something 30 years out of date about Mormon men," whose stress on conventional notions of "marriage and the family" made him "feel like saying that [he was] a faggot and shaking their gentile puritanism." One year later, he experienced a similar impatience during a dinner party hosted by David M. Gillespie, the new dean of San Francisco's Episcopal Grace Cathedral. When the conversation veered on to gay rights Bellah suddenly felt "most uncomfortable, having to talk about 'them' when I was thinking 'us.'" As Melanie scolded him for his reluctance to come out, he replied that explaining his situation would have been too complicated. On yet another occasion, conversely, Bob commented in his journal that he was "taking some grim pleasure in how much [he had] upset" a young male friend with an unexpected advance. "A sort of revenge on the world of straights," he added. "They will have to know we are here whether they like it or not."[18]

But why was Bellah's situation "too complicated"? An interesting point of entry to his feelings is the comments on his own seniority that filled his diary and correspondence. Most of Bob's uneasiness came from his difficulty feeling at home in the very particular gay subculture of late-1970s San Francisco—neither the exhibited masculinity of Castro clones nor the supermacho attitude of South of Market bar life, with its paradoxical combination of highly codified street rituals and impersonal cruising, fitted with Bellah's longing for personal meaning, tender loving, and significant relations. Moreover, in the wake of Harvey Milk's brutal murder after his election to city government, the gay community had embraced an attitude of radical politicization that was somewhat at odds with what Bellah was looking for. Having lost its initial "gay power" orientation—which, incidentally, Milk had never fully shared—the gay liberation movement had transitioned to a novel pride-and-rights combination from which New Leftist concerns for social justice had almost wholly disappeared.[19]

Parallel to this sweeping political shift came a revolution in the practices and meaning of publicly identifying as a gay man. For over a decade now, the phrase "coming out" had been deliberately employed to indicate "a politicized ritual of political avowal" meant to prove one's courage in assuming a clearly demarcated sexual identity—which, in turn, pointed to the conviction that "same-gender sexual attraction was sufficiently salient as a dimension of human experience to form a base for a minority group identity." This then-radical interpretation of the act of coming out also put self-defined bisexuals in a thorny position, as most gay and lesbian activists looked down on them as confused individuals who had "to make up their minds" and choose whose side they were on. The creation of the San Francisco Bisexual Center in 1976, the first of its kind, had only made their residual condition and their lack of recognition more visible than ever.[20]

These cultural and political developments were as remote from Bob's personal history, scholarly ideas, and explicit politics as could be—he was, after all, an affluent White man in his early fifties, raised in the 1930s in a socially conservative family, who had a complex political life as a youth, passing from communism to modernization liberalism, and who now supported social democratic ideas of economic justice and felt a deep respect for those very religious organizations that most gay activists saw as the embodiment of homophobic repression. Even if Bob had sometimes felt an urgent "need to shout [his identity] out from the hometops," the context around him had changed in such a way as to render any public declaration of his newly emancipated, complicated sexual identity almost impossible. This delicate situation, however, did not stop Robert Bellah from turning his inner musings into a universal parable, which eventually found a public, though not particularly visible, expression.[21]

In May 1979, a long interview was published in an Episcopal journal, the *Witness*, in which Bob spoke of the connections between consciousness, sexuality, and power. Before the 1960s, he said, American culture strongly distinguished between women, defined as emotional and incapable of self-discipline, and men, who were stereotypically seen as rational and controlled. For this reason, males had been educated to "reject whatever [they] viewed as feminine" as to develop "a repressive attitude toward [their] physical self." Since the brain-over-body hierarchy within each male individual reflected the social-political hierarchy of men over women, being able to accept the autonomy of women as "total human beings" was a requisite for being able to accept what Bellah called one's "allegedly feminine" side—that is, one's "impulsive and emotional life." The sexual revolution had inaugurated the possibility of a balanced acceptance of inner diversity and antinomy, and thus a more equilibrated personality.[22]

Besides liberating male sexuality from its preoccupation with "dominance and submission," the reappropriation of feminine elements on the part of men might also contribute to break down what Bellah saw as a common attitude toward homosexuality: for middle-class Americans the question "Am I gay?" sounded exactly like "Am I a woman?" and somehow expressed "one of the deepest fears of the traditional American male." From a symbolic point of view, being a homosexual was the same as being a woman—"you don't screw, you get screwed"—so that the mere doubt of having "a little teeny piece of us that's part homosexual" was considered an unbearable threat to one's integrity. To the contrary, Bob concluded, "My own guess is that if less anxiety about homosexuality were possible for the American male, it would probably actually reduce the number of people who choose homosexuality. People wouldn't be caught in that bind of either renouncing it totally or adopting it exclusively. . . . If [homosexual practices] were demystified and accepted as one of the possibilities of human life, it would have less impact. *If some people choose that as their option, OK, but it's not something one needs to get hysterical about.*"[23]

To the eyes of the few who knew of the last twenty-four months of his life, Robert Bellah's *Witness* interview looked incredibly autobiographical. Ten years after his encounter with Norman O. Brown and his first, and failed, attempt at remaking himself, Bob had been sufficiently disinhibited by the force of tragedy to enter a quasi-religious moment of relational and symbolic rearticulation. As he had written in a long-forgotten theoretical article, living through a "boundary situation" could be done only by "giving oneself up to it, responding with one's total personality and with the deepest center of one's being." Two years after the "Taiwan" restaurant incident, Bob had somehow crossed the conventional boundary that divided his unresolved "masculine" side from his repressed "feminine" one by way of a process that paralleled the dialectical sequence of primary naïveté, criticism, and second naïveté of symbolic realism. The point was not to seek a conversion based on a radical rejection of the past, but to integrate a number of contradictory experiences that would illuminate the past and put it at peace, letting one's previous identity come forth changed and strengthened from the process—knowing, as it were, that everything had to be done "without belief, beyond belief."[24]

Slightly past his fifty-second birthday, Robert Bellah was now able, with the crucial help of Melanie and Bill, to put his "real self" into practice. In this sense, after reckoning with his innermost fears and cravings, he had no interest in the definition game—an attitude that went against the grain of contemporaneous gay and lesbian identity politics. Words and labels would not do: as he had written in 1958, those who had been through a boundary situation "can only point to it with more or less misleading symbols and we can understand [them] only if we have in some part experienced what [they have] experienced." Thus, while he had openly rambled the Castro and its cinemas, restaurants, and bars for months, and would later participate in the 1979 Gay Freedom Day parade with thousands of other individuals, Bob found no use whatsoever in a public coming out.[25]

III

In spite of Bellah's continuous work of self-reflection, no single coherent structure was emerging to connect the personal, professional, and political pieces of his existence. At the same time, the shift toward clarity was evident: not only did he become more open in his feelings and personal relations, he also became bolder in his scholarly and political work. In fact, if a common thread could be found to join the scattered pieces of his activity, it was a new willingness to take strong, unabashed positions. As one of the participants in the Rockefeller Conference on Value Consensus in America had commented in private, "Bellah was impressive; he stood his ground; clearly he is one of the deep thinkers of our time and refused to be budged from his depth, nor did he feel the need to apologize for it." In this, Bob was also helped by a number of unexpected events that allowed, and sometimes forced, him to take major steps ahead. Just like Machiavelli's ideal prince, this time he was trying to seize the chances presented by *fortuna* and bring them to a satisfactory completion.[26]

A prime example of Bob's newfound scholarly courage was the research project he envisioned with Tipton, Sullivan, Swidler, and Madsen, titled "The Moral Basis of Social Commitment in America." The final version of the grant proposal, penned in the fall of 1978, pledged nothing less than "an inquiry into the moral health of the American republic," focused on how ideas, opinions, and styles of moral discourse influenced the relation between the private and the public lives of American citizens, and their will and ability to commit to democratic political action. The four younger scholars would each concentrate on one of "four windows onto [their] common problem," grouped into two wide categories: Ann and Steve would study the ideologies of love and psychotherapy, while Dick and Bill would focus on traditional and innovative forms of civic activism and political participation in the public sphere.[27]

In the plan, and later in the addendum they wrote for their prospective funders, the five scholars underlined that they had tried to "find ways to study each system of moral meaning where it might be lived out and elaborated more fully." That meant that they were not preoccupied with finding the average distribution of views among the American population through some representative sample: on the contrary, Bob and his collaborators were looking for places in which their object could be observed in its most extreme forms—where the richness and the failures of moral meaning-making were more intense.[28]

Sociological in nature, the study was also presented as a "historically rooted philosophical inquiry" based on Tipton's method of engaging ordinary individuals in in-depth moral conversations, whose final outcome was going to be "in part a product of ourselves as well as of those to whom we [would] talk." This two-way relationship between the researchers and the subjects of their inquiry, also reminiscent of Rabinow's *Reflections*, was just one of the many collective features of the project. Not only did Bellah write that the group's meetings had been permeated by an "enthusiasm and commitment rare in academic life," but he also indicated a small cadre of distinguished advisors who had accepted a role as an echo chamber of sorts, to clarify the group's ideas and strategies: his old friends Renée Fox and David Riesman; Harvard Divinity School's Ralph Potter, an ethicist whose work on morality and nuclear arms policy helped inspire the taxonomy of "styles of ethical evaluation" in Tipton's dissertation; Harvard psychiatrist Robert Coles, author of the Pulitzer Prize–winning series *Children of Crisis*, whom Bellah met through Steve; and the former secretary of health under Lyndon Johnson and founder of Common Cause John W. Gardner, who had introduced himself to Bob shortly after the Rockefeller Conference in New York. In its authors' intentions, the result was to be as collective and accessible as possible—in fact, in addition to the usual academic publications, the grant request anticipated a jointly authored book addressed to the educated public.[29]

In order to reach this dual goal, Bellah concluded that his prophetic public persona should not cloud the distinctive prospect of "The Moral Basis." In the debate on *The Broken Covenant*, a book that was less than five years old, his work had been repeatedly stereotyped and he had been depicted as an American Jeremiah, the last defender of civil religion in a world gone postmodern—a role that in no way reflected what he thought and what he wanted to do next. If the new project was to have any impact, the slate had to be cleared. And thus Bellah did what successful intellectuals seldom, if ever, do: he dropped all the catchwords that had made him famous and started (pretty much) anew—no version of the research proposal bore trace of either "civil religion" or "symbolic realism." At that point, "The Moral Basis" clearly was the biggest, broadest, and perhaps bravest endeavor in which he had ever been involved.[30]

Be that as it may, this courage paid off. The reviewers for both the Ford Foundation—Peter L. Berger and Daniel Bell—and the National Endowment for the Humanities—Norman Birnbaum and the ubiquitous Riesman—all underscored that studies of the kind proposed by Bellah and his collaborators were all too unusual in American social science, and strongly recommended the project.[31] After a few iterations and adjustments, on May 11, 1979, Bob received a much-awaited call from Sharpe, who announced both the support of the National Endowment for the Humanities and the arrival of a matching grant from the Ford Foundation. Together with additional resources pledged by the Rockefeller Foundation, the total financial backing for the group's proposed three years of research came to $250,000—the biggest sum Bellah had ever come to manage.[32]

Even the best of news, however, was bound to leave a bittersweet taste in Bob's mouth: three days earlier Talcott Parsons had unexpectedly died in Germany. None of his relatives, students, or friends had anticipated such a traumatic event—not even Helen Parsons, who reported that her seventy-six-year-old husband had given a lecture *and* a seminar on the very day of his fatal stroke. By a twist of fate, Parsons's last talks had taken place in the very Munich University building where in 1920 Max Weber had given his last lecture before his death. Like everyone else, Bob was floored. While he had been rather disappointed with his old mentor's most recent work on the United States, he had participated in another seminar with the Penn group shortly before Parsons had to leave for his European trip through France, the Netherlands, Germany, and Great Britain—the occasion being the conferment of a "golden doctorate" at Heidelberg University during a two-day public event in which star social scientists Jürgen Habermas, Niklas Luhmann, and Wolfgang Schluchter would also speak. Just like Cliff Geertz, but with much more enthusiasm than his old friend, Bob had even pledged to write a chapter for the forthcoming book of the Human Condition group.[33]

Bellah could not help but see in the simultaneous occurrence of the two events a sign of his (conclusive, this time) coming of age: "I am for the first time," he wrote to Bill Sullivan, "without my teacher and the sole principal investigator with a major research grant." A quick exchange with Geertz, who still considered his Cambridge years as the most important stage of his intellectual career, was needed to reflect on Parsons's heritage and their actual distance from it. "I sometimes wonder," wrote the anthropologist, "what would have happened if you and Neil [Smelser], and Renée [Fox] and I and a few others had really gone back to Harvard and carried the torch. But I, at least, just couldn't bring myself to do it, and perhaps [Social Relations] was something which really couldn't be maintained." Bellah replied, emphasizing how close "to the heart of what Talcott was talking about" his new research project was, and added that "it will be only our students and not ourselves who finally sift out what of Talcott is going to be continuingly important."[34]

Unlike Geertz, Bellah was able to spell out his feelings during the American Sociological Association memorial session for Parsons, which took place on August 28, 1979, under the chairmanship of another illustrious ex-student, Robert K. Merton. In the hotly anti-Parsonian climate of the late 1970s, Bellah used the words of Wallace Stevens's "Asides on the Oboe" to describe his teacher as "the central man, the human globe, responsive as a mirror with a voice." Parsons might have looked like "the quintessential sociologist's sociologist," Bob said, but his most important teaching resided in his curiosity and unabashed passion for intellectual wandering. He then described the "conception of the four sub-systems of action" and its recent extension to the human condition as a titanic wager on the ability of social science to embrace all reality in a "series of widening circles." The ultimate goal of Parsons's life had been to "integrate, integrate, integrate more and more reality" into his ever-growing theoretical scheme.[35]

Bellah knew how the word "integrate" sounded to the ears of his heterogeneous public—so different an audience from the handful of middle-aged White men who used to run the meetings of the American Sociological Society in the 1950s. For many of his colleagues—and certainly for those who in that very moment were packing a nearby ballroom to salute another eminent social scientist, Herbert Marcuse—"integration" was a four-letter word, and

Talcott Parsons was nothing but a relic from a long-forgotten past. But Bob had no time to think about academic quarrels. He described his mentor's analytical schemes as a set of metaphors from which no social law could be deduced, but one that anticipated an interpretive approach to social science. And then he closed his short speech, turning again to Wallace Stevens, calling Parsons "the man of glass, who in a million diamonds sums us up."[36]

With his impassioned speech Robert Bellah did something that nobody would have dared do in the intellectual climate of the late 1970s: he explicitly reclaimed the intellectual legacy of Talcott Parsons a bare three months after his death. Twelve years had passed since his fateful decision to leave Cambridge for Berkeley, and he had tried to become his own man in every possible way, sometimes even pushing things a bit too far. For those who knew Bob, his words had been no less than a public declaration that Parsons's passing was the closest thing to a father's death he could think of. And since "the death of the father is the death of the son's most religiously significant object," the speech on the floor of the Grand Ballroom of the Sheraton Boston Hotel had been a religious ritual of sorts. With his gaze fixed on his father's rebellious children, Bellah had praised the one who had begotten him, asked forgiveness for his sins, and defiantly claimed his right of primogeniture.[37]

As in an ideal Freudian story, Bob Bellah's wish to follow in Parsons's footsteps was readily satisfied. In the fall of 1979 he was selected to succeed Herbert Blumer, Robert Nisbet, Arthur Stinchcombe, Charles Glock, and Neil Smelser as the chair of the Berkeley Department of Sociology. To be sure, a Talcott Parsons he was not, and the politically charged atmosphere of the department was as distant from the bright optimism of 1950s Social Relations as could be. Bob, however, "took his turn" with the best of intentions. His effort to secure Michael Burawoy's tenure against the conservative wing of the department, and the leading role he took in wooing one of the intellectuals he respected the most, the German philosopher Jürgen Habermas, to accept a chair in sociological theory at the University of California soon became the best examples of his willingness and ability to engage in controversial academic matters in the years to come.[38]

15

On the Edge of the Eighties

BERKELEY, 1979–1983

ROBERT N. BELLAH's newfound self-confidence turned out to be a crucial asset early in July 1979, when he was summoned to 1600 Pennsylvania Avenue by an administration on the verge of a nervous breakdown. Ever since his inauguration in January 1977, Jimmy Carter had seen the country sinking in a quicksand of intractable problems and declining trust. The hopes raised by his electoral promise to leave the ill-fated Nixon-Ford era behind through a blend of political pragmatism and personal integrity had vanished, and he was now seen as an algid and ineffective president. A number of seasoned competitors kept him under siege as domestic economic crises and foreign politics disasters in Iran and Nicaragua unfolded: from Massachusetts senator Ted Kennedy to California governor Jerry Brown and his predecessor, Ronald Reagan, the critics of Carter's soft policies were legion across the political spectrum. As if this were not enough, Jerry Falwell's revamped "I Love America" rallies and the rise of the Religious Right, heralded in June 1979 by the fundamentalist takeover of the Southern Baptist Convention and the creation of Moral Majority, Inc., were dissolving one of the president's most valuable assets—his electoral base of White, conservative, Southern evangelicals.[1]

At the peak of this pyramid of troubles stood the egocentric lifestyle of the "Me Decade" and the resources needed to power it. A net exporter of energy for most of its history, in the 1970s the United States had become the biggest buyer of fossil fuels in the world, and neither Nixon nor Ford had been able to stop the trend. Between 1978 and 1979 the consequences of the Iranian revolution and the hardening of OPEC policies had further exasperated the situation. In May 1979, thousands of vehicles had queued at gas stations all over the country and, as the spring progressed, news of violent episodes multiplied. Worried White House staffers were now explicitly anticipating an explosion of unmanageable disorder. It was, as historian Kevin Mattson put it, as if "below the surface of a society supposedly composed of narcissistic, self-absorbed individuals dancing away their worries in discos across the country there lingered angrier elements that could erupt and tear the nation apart"—in fact, that had been one of Richard Sharpe's key reasons for suggesting "The Moral Basis" project to Tipton, Bellah, and friends.[2]

Understandably, when his aides suggested he address the nation about what *Newsweek* had termed "the Energy Plague," Carter sought to pierce the infamous bubble surrounding American presidents, and asked for the advice of intellectuals, experts, and common citizens. As suggested by his pollster and adviser Pat Caddell, and against the judgment of Vice-President Walter Mondale and much of the White House staff, he thought of switching from his usual policy-oriented language to a moral, even preaching tone. On May 30, 1979, Carter invited a small group of "wise men" for dinner and asked them to give him a novel outlook on the crisis. Among them were Harvard's Daniel Bell, author of *The Cultural Contradictions of Capitalism*; historian Christopher Lasch, whose *Culture of Narcissism* was enjoying unexpected mass success; and the founder of Operation PUSH, reverend Jesse Jackson. The roster was completed by one of Bellah's advisers, Common Cause's John Gardner, and newsmen Bill Moyers, Charles Peters, and Haynes Johnson.[3]

Other crowded encounters followed until July 9, 1979, when Robert Bellah received a call from Carter's special assistant, Anne Wexler, who told him to get to Washington, DC, as soon as possible. At quarter to ten the next morning Bob was at the White House, wondering whether it had not taken the president too long to call him for counsel. The only academic in a diverse group of religious leaders, which included Terence Cardinal Cooke from New York, Claire Randall of the National Council of Churches, pastor Otis Moss Jr., Rabbi Marc Tanenbaum of the American Jewish Committee, and the former president of the Southern Baptist Convention, Jimmy Allen, Bellah was brought to Camp David to meet with Rosalynn and Jimmy Carter, who saluted him, saying "I have been hearing great things about you, Bob." After an opening prayer, the president told his guests about the loneliness of office and the serenity he felt in sharing the table with the unofficially dubbed "God Squad." After hearing a first round of individual statements, he turned to Bellah and looked him in the eyes: "Bob," he said, "What should I say? How much can the American people take?"[4]

Confident and relaxed, the Berkeley professor lectured the president about the antinomies of the current situation, in which the radicalization of individualism was matched by the emergence of new forms of civic commitment. Using the ideas put forth in his article "Human Conditions for a Good Society," which Carter had surely read, Bob advanced the Durkheimian argument that contracts among interest-bearing groups and individuals never work without a solid precontractual basis—in the language of *The Broken Covenant*, external contracts always need to be matched by an internal covenant. Whenever politics becomes a mere henchman to the pursuit of profit, he added, the end result is ineluctable: a war of all against all, and then some form of despotism. Luckily, the American people knew that the crisis was real and the solutions hard to swallow—even if doom and gloom were not what they wanted to hear, they would accept the truth if Carter proved so bold as to take the pulpit as a "teaching president," eager to infuse new life into the traditions of the past.[5]

In a few hours Robert Bellah was back in Berkeley. While he was sure of having done everything he could to honestly advise the president, he had "no great hopes for the outcome." At the same time, having been called to Camp David filled him with pride—as he wrote in his diary, press secretary Jody Powell said that Bob "was one of the reasons for this whole thing (which I took to mean the rethinking of the energy speech into a much deeper and broad ranging thing)." A couple of days later, he invited Paul Rabinow and his wife, Gwen Wright, along with his friend and confidant Steve Tobias, to 10 Mosswood Road to watch Carter's speech. Minute by minute, his guests could feel Bob's anger filling the bright living room overlooking the San Francisco Bay. As he later told a reporter, in the final version of the speech he found "no analysis, no real leadership, just flattery and criticism." The last remnants of his confidence in Jimmy Carter were gone.[6]

Bellah was not going to keep his disappointment for himself. Still furious, at four in the morning he was at his desk drafting a statement for the National Council of Churches in which he called for "a return in part to the simplicity that distinguished the earlier generations," asked (in a section that was cut from the final version) that the burden "be borne fairly by all," and suggested that his fellow Americans turn "the necessity of sacrifice" to their own "moral benefit and the attainment of justice throughout the world." His own personal add-on to the communiqué criticized Carter's analogy between the energy crisis and World War Two: while National Socialism had been "an external evil of proportions unprecedented in human history," in 1979 "if there is an enemy, it is us." For that reason, Bellah called for an extended "national debate on our social and moral problems," one that needed "the fullest and most informed participation of the American people" to succeed. In a widely reprinted interview, titled "A Night at Camp David," he later voiced his irritation at Carter's speech, saying that "the notion that we're going to get through all of this through just harmony and morale is nuts."[7]

I

Robert Bellah was far from being the only critic of the president: Kennedy and Reagan immediately scoffed at Carter's "malaise speech" and capitalized on the subsequent shakeup of his cabinet to launch their respective bids for the presidency. More importantly, the process by which Carter had gotten this disastrous result was somehow symptomatic of a major cultural shift: as the 1980s were about to begin, the role of intellectuals and academics in American society had dramatically changed. As Daniel Bell observed after the May dinner at the White House, not only had the sages in attendance failed to provide the president with useful ideas, but Carter's main interest had been in securing a scholarly blanket for his already-formed political instincts. Gone was the faith in the thaumaturgic powers of expert knowledge that had boosted the postwar rise of high modernism in social science, and the idea of the university as the key institution of the late twentieth and early twenty-first centuries—championed in books like Bell's *The End of Ideology* and rebooted as recently as 1973 in Talcott Parsons's *The American University*—now sounded like a stale old joke. As a result of a number of economic, political, and cultural transformations, the place of those who had once defined themselves as the best and the brightest was being taken by the swift and the raucous.[8]

By the end of 1979 the relaxing of federal legislation concerning the mass media and the introduction of new technologies were exploding the American public sphere into a multitude of niches and bubbles, each dependent on the preferences of its patrons. Communication fragmented around political, social, and lifestyle fault lines, and the tendencies toward cultural polarization that had first emerged during the Cold War and been amplified by the appearance of new collective actors in the late 1960s underwent further radicalization. Public intellectuals became increasingly partisan, prizing ideological coherence and the ability to synthesize simple ideas in easy-to-televise sound-bites over complex analyses and detailed solutions, and this further reduced the chances of even-tempered discussions on the public interest or, God forbid, "common values." In particular, a number of scholars and pundits who in the postwar period had embraced progressive liberalism were now moving to the opposite end of the political spectrum as a reaction to the allegedly catastrophic effects of the New Left's "adversary culture" on the prospects of American civilization.[9]

From the fancy suites of the Heritage Foundation or the American Enterprise Institute and the pages of *Commentary, National Review,* and the *Public Interest,* neoconservative intellectuals and New Right organizers set the tone for the ensuing decade. Their ambitious agenda pointed to a muscular repositioning of the United States at the center of the international scene and a dramatic reduction of federal spending and regulation aimed at demolishing the heritage of the New Deal and of Johnson's Great Society. As always, California was at the vanguard of this political-cultural mutation. Not only had the adoption of Proposition 13 in June 1978 marked the first major victory of the anti-tax movement, but the Golden State also supplied conservatives with an extraordinarily charismatic leader in the person of its former Republican governor. As Carter's opponent in the 1980 presidential election, Ronald Reagan expressed the new Zeitgeist in a last-minute appeal titled "A Vision for America":

> I believe we can embark on a new age of reform in this country and an era of national renewal. An era that will reorder the relationship between citizen and government, that will make government again responsive to people, that will revitalize the values of family, work, and neighborhood and that will restore our private and independent social institutions. . . . That's why I've said throughout this campaign that we must control and limit the growth of federal spending, that we must reduce tax rates to stimulate work and savings and investment. That's why I've said we can relieve labor and business of burdensome, unnecessary regulations and still maintain high standards of environmental and occupational safety. That's why I've said we can reduce the cost of government by eliminating billions lost to waste and fraud in the federal bureaucracy, a problem that is now an unrelenting national scandal.[10]

In addition to radical "neocons," the Reagan coalition included another emerging force, the Christian Right of southern evangelicals and fundamentalists—a constituency whose disgust for the federal government had intensified during Carter's tenure. Artfully coached by New Right strategists, in the late 1970s pastors Jerry Falwell, Pat Robertson, and James Robison succeeded in merging a number of single-issue campaigns against the harms of secular humanism into a tightly packed political agenda, which also included tax cuts, reduced welfare spending, and a revamped anticommunism. New organizations were established to register and marshal prospective evangelical voters, while the creation of Moral Majority, Inc., in June 1979 was a deliberate attempt to lure conservative Catholics and Jews into the movement. Aware of the importance of this voting bloc, Reagan presented himself as a staunch supporter of American traditions and "family values," and sometimes shared the stage with conservative Christians. Having been the object of the anticipatory critique of liberal intellectuals for decades, the coming of the Religious Right was seen as a nearly catastrophic event for the survival of secularism and pluralism in America.[11]

In contrast to many—including his friends Lipset, Shils, and Riesman—Bellah thought that the influence of the Religious Right was greatly exaggerated. As shown in Tipton's dissertation, some of the needs voiced by fundamentalist sects were cogent and justified, but their answers were naive and, ironically, "not conservative enough" when compared with the genuine reinterpretation of American heritage given by Martin Luther King Jr. and the civil rights movement. For this reason, the Religious Right would soon fade away, revealing the true face of the emerging "Amoral Majority"—that is, the supporters of "unrestrained free-market capitalism and radical individualism." For all his irritation with Carter, Bellah anticipated the election of Ronald Reagan as the fortieth president of the United States might lead to a change of regime that would destroy the social and civil achievements of the last five decades. By proposing a new approach to contemporary moral cultures, the collective research project, now rechristened "Habits of the Heart," might contribute to defending the fragile plurivocality of American culture from the excesses of laissez-faire capitalism.[12]

In this sense, Bill Sullivan's theoretical treatise *Reconstructing Public Philosophy* was crucial for defining some of the conceptual categories used by the "Habits group" to imagine ideational and moral alternatives to the hegemony of radical individualism. The manuscript, which was extensively discussed among the five scholars, showed the connections between the "liberal capitalist form of society" and the social-political philosophy found in the work of authors as diverse as John Rawls, Robert Nozick, and Lawrence Kohlberg, who all saw society as merely instrumental to the fulfilment of the desires of abstract, rootless individuals. To repair the damage produced by the antipublic premises of political liberalism, Sullivan pointed to the conceptual resources of civic republicanism—common good, proportional justice, authority, equality as fellowship, and virtue—as the tools needed to build "a sense of civic life as a form of personal self-development." Such a philosophical foundation would in turn encourage a far-reaching transformation in which "the forms of citizenship and of civic association [would be brought] more centrally into the economic sphere."[13]

Needless to say, Bellah fully shared his friend's concerns. Against tax cuts, government reduction, and supply side economics, he started speaking of economic democracy and reforms aimed at giving to workers and employees a measure of control in public and private companies. There remained, however, a clear difference between Bob's and Bill's work. While Sullivan focused on the civic republican tradition and had little to say about organized religion, Bellah also renewed the appeal for a new social movement born from an active "public church" that he had been advancing before and after *The Broken Covenant*. In the fragmented public sphere of the early 1980s, this last move suggested a specious association between Bellah's biblical republicanism and the politics of right-wing evangelicalism. As Falwell's rhetoric could easily be seen as an example of that very idea of the United States as a (White) Christian nation that Bellah had long denounced as an idolatrous interpretation of the American civil religion, nobody would doubt that Bob's ideas occupied the opposite pole of the political spectrum to those of the Moral Majority. At the same time, from the point of view of those Enlightenment fundamentalists he had been chastising for years, the political mobilization of evangelicals was not *that* different from Bellah's call for a stronger public church—after all, Falwell had disowned his infamous 1965 sermon against the civil rights movement to assert that "he and his fellow ministers were now doing exactly what [Martin Luther] King and his fellows had done."[14]

Bellah soon found himself in the crossfire of a new conflict of interpretation of the heritage and prospects of the American experiment: while his critique of unrestrained market individualism firmly placed him on the left, the role he reclaimed for religiously inspired activism put him on a collision course with those liberal humanists who hoped to counteract what they saw as the catastrophic rise of Falwell and his associates with a massive dose of secularism. In retrospect, one might say that the ideational and communicative environment in which Bob issued his call for a renewal of the biblical and republican traditions and their "moral ecology"—a phrase first introduced in *Reconstructing Public Philosophy*—was increasingly being defined by the antagonism of the two outlooks, whose entrenchment would soon lead to the culture wars of the 1980s and 1990s.

For all the difficulty of articulating his ideas within a rapidly polarizing field, Bellah had no intention of embracing the extreme separatist option suggested by Alasdair MacIntyre in *After Virtue,* the book in which he had found "the position towards which [he had] been groping" for some time expressed "with great clarity." A Scottish philosopher who had been moving from the New Left to Trotsky and then to Hegel before coming to a revamped Aristotelianism, MacIntyre had closed his dense philosophical treatise on the evils of "moral emotivism" with an image of unmatched doom and gloom. The paralysis due to the clash of incommensurable moral views, he wrote, was so advanced that nothing could be done to reform existing institutions or effect a substantial change of mind in the direction of the sound-but-impossible answer of neo-Aristotelian teleology. MacIntyre then looked to a small number of "men and women of good will" who would retire into "local forms of community within which civility and the intellectual and moral life can be sustained through the new dark ages which are already upon us."[15]

For all his appreciation of *After Virtue,* Bellah suggested instead a reevaluation of a principled conception of (democratic) hierarchy and virtue, combined with a preference for the institutional form of the "church" and the adoption of prudential judgment against any moral fundamentalism. To avoid any misunderstanding, the duty of those intellectuals who, like Bellah himself, maintained a critical outlook on modernity and its excesses, was not that of defending "order" or "tradition" as abstract, ossified fetishes. On the contrary, they should encourage a dialectical reappropriation of the best heritage of Western philosophy and theology within the general public sphere. While MacIntyre's Godot was "another, doubtless very different, St. Benedict," for Robert N. Bellah the renewal of American society depended once again on creating the preconditions for the encounter of the next Rosa Parks with the next Martin Luther King Jr.[16]

II

The roots and breadth of Bob's enthusiasm for *After Virtue* become fully intelligible when the ideational context of late-1970s moral philosophy and political theory is taken into account. The reading of some exciting new work of Charles Taylor and Joachim Ritter had encouraged Bellah to go back to some old passions of his: Hegel, Plato, and Aristotle. Moreover, through Bill Sullivan he came into contact with younger Aristotelian theorists like Stephen Salkever and Martha Nussbaum and the so-called "republican revival" of J.G.A. Pocock,

Quentin Skinner, and Hannah Pitkin—itself anticipated by the historians and political thinkers upon whom Bellah had built *The Broken Covenant*, such as Gordon Wood, Hannah Arendt, and Sheldon Wolin. With Bellah's slow distancing from the neo-Kantianism of his Parsonian upbringing, Harvard College was taking its revenge on Social Relations.[17]

By pure chance, this "Aristotelian connection" had become Bellah's main theoretical interest at the very time that his old mentor was reflecting upon his allegiance to the opposite camp. Shortly before dying, Parsons had written that the dualistic constructions of Kant's philosophy found an almost perfect parallel in the basic logic of the general theory of action he had been developing since the 1930s. In explaining how Kant's dichotomies could be applied to different theoretical problems, Parsons had explicitly cited symbolic realism as a convincing depiction of the relation between religious symbols and reality "out there." Although rather idiosyncratic, Parsons's reading of symbolic realism was in some ways mirrored in Bob's memorial speech at the 1979 American Sociological Association meeting. Contrary to the impression generated by this ghostly exchange, however, the gulf between Parsons's neo-Kantianism and his student's philosophical position was getting wider, and that was partially because of a strict weaving of theoretical and personal reflection on Bellah's side, which became clear on two very different occasions in the early 1980s.[18]

On September 10, 1982, Bob took part in a session on the legacy of Parsonian action theory at the Annual Meeting of the American Sociological Association, together with Victor Lidz, Aaron Cicourel, Harold Bershady, Karin Knorr, and Jeff Alexander. Much of the discussion centered on two recent articles written by a German sociologist, Richard Münch, according to which "a Kantian 'core' structures the theoretical framework of the general theory of action, and Parsons' theoretical development must be understood as a progressive elaboration and refinement of this central core." While appreciating Münch's thesis, Bellah attacked the very idea of building a general sociology on Kantian premises.[19]

Interestingly, among the many points of entry for his critique, Bob chose the opposition between norm and desire. Parsons's critique of utilitarianism, he said, was in fact based on the acceptance of the "utilitarian *problematic* of practice," in which "desire, even transmuted into interest, can never produce any legitimate normative order." Kant's familiar rift between nature and rationality was mirrored in Durkheim's translation of the categorical imperative into "specific cultural contents," a theoretical trick that had somehow allowed

Parsons to include Freud and Weber—and with them the duality between norm and desire—into the nascent sociological tradition. An alternative tradition, continued Bellah, would take Aristotelian final causality as its starting point, so as to rehabilitate the classical idea of happiness as the telos and measure of a good life. "This means," he said to a public of mostly Parsonian colleagues, "that the norm is inherent in the desire, not radically opposed to it—and that happiness can be the end of practice, indeed must be, but not happiness in the utilitarian sense of pleasure."[20]

How would this alternative social science work? Bellah first pointed to a conceptual change: stop talking of "interests" and "norms," he said, and start using the vocabulary of "practices" and maybe even "virtues." He then pointed to Tocqueville's mores and Hegel's *Sittlichkeit* as prime illustrations of what he had in mind, and hinted at his research group's forthcoming book, *Habits of the Heart*, as an exemplar of this unconventional way of doing sociology. Much had changed since 1969, when Bob had tried to add Norman O. Brown and hermeneutics to the Social Relations tradition, using Jerome Bruner as a bridge to create a "left-Parsonianism" of sorts. Some thirteen years later he was trying to finally disavow his old attempt at combining the insights of different traditions, and was looking for a way to leave Parsons's neo-Kantian dualisms behind and imagine a new sociology built on the Hegelian-Aristotelian motifs of Taylor and MacIntyre.

As shown by the brief, puzzling exchange he had with Michel Foucault one year later, Bellah's theoretical journey was far from concluded. The controversial French intellectual had first been to Berkeley in the spring of 1975 as a guest of literary theorist Leo Bersani, and had taken the chance to enjoy the Folsom Street scene and experiment with LSD with two younger colleagues during a soon-to-be famous trip to Death Valley. After 1979, as his fame grew, Foucault regularly spent part of the year at the University of California, where he entertained intense relations with two scholars whom Bob knew pretty well, Bert Dreyfus and Paul Rabinow. On paper, the two could have been perfect conversational partners: not only were they studying, to use Foucault's vocabulary, the historical regimes of truth in which normative and moral discourses were rooted, but they also shared a burning passion for classical Greek philosophy and its different views of the relations between the individual subject, the aspiration to a good life, and self-reflexive practices—a theme that Foucault had analyzed in his latest courses at the Collège de France and would finally take up in his lectures on "speaking freely" (*parrhesia*) at Berkeley in the fall of 1983.[21]

Up until that moment, Bellah's engagement with Foucault and his work had been sporadic at best. On one side, he had recognized in the French philosopher a "fellow traveler" of sorts in his own quest to discover the relationships between modernity and premodern traditions. On the other side, however, Foucault's combination of epistemic suspicion and political pessimism and his ideas on the relationship between power, desire, and social order seemed too elusive and contradictory to be useful. Bob first voiced his doubts at the 1983 Annual Meeting of the Pacific Division of the American Philosophical Association, where he discussed Charles Taylor's paper, "Foucault on Freedom and Truth." The Canadian philosopher was at the time visiting at Berkeley, and would sometimes discuss with Bob interpretation and the theory of practice. Although appreciative of Foucault's work, Taylor criticized the one-sidedness of his analyses and the Nietzschean idea of the good life as a kind of uprooted self-making. "Can we really step outside the identity we have developed in Western civilization," he said, "to such a degree that we can repudiate all that comes to us from the Christian understanding of the will?" And, then, "granted we really can set this aside, is the resulting 'aesthetic of existence' all that admirable?"[22]

In his remarks, Bellah mostly agreed with Taylor and translated the latter's ideas into the vocabulary of the Habits group, saying that he and his coauthors were "prepared to say that radical American individualism [was] untrue, a systematic falsification of human reality in the service of manipulative power," and that "genuine freedom [always was] the product of a certain kind of discipline, a discipline of shared beliefs and commitments," a civic humanist position he was hesitant to ascribe to the author of *La volonté de savoir*. What Bob was looking for, in sum, was a way to decouple Foucault's sound intuitions on the relations between subjects and practices from what he saw as the unacceptable demise of any notion of the common good. Just a month later, Bellah was able to directly address Foucault during a long conversation, which also included Taylor, Dreyfus, Rabinow, Leo Löwenthal, and Martin Jay. The answer was courteous but rather predictable:

> BELLAH: Discipline can mean coercive control of oneself in the context of relations to others; it can also mean a control of the self by the self, when we say self-discipline. Now, I can accept that one might be justly suspicious of the notion of self-discipline, because it might only mask an illicit kind of control. But, on the other hand, is there any way to distinguish between that self-discipline—well, maybe it's just the same

question as in society as a whole, because without self-discipline there is no person, and yet we must always be suspicious of the legitimacy of any particular claim of self-discipline.

FOUCAULT: I'm not sure that my answer will be very satisfying. I wonder if it's really legitimate to transfer the concepts, the categories, the methods, the analyses we use for the field of society, and for analyzing power relations, to what is the constitution of ourselves, and I mean our relation to ourselves. . . . And although I would say the relation that one has to oneself is not a powerful relation, well sometimes in the ancient ethics people tried to define their own relation to themselves as a power relation: they had to exercise power over their desire in order to exercise power on their family and they had to exercise power on their family in order to exercise power in the city. And the good king and the good father was a real master of himself. I think that was an image.[23]

Bob's theoretical insight was too sketchy to engender a clear *prise de position* on the part of Foucault. Was his "self-discipline" a synonym of that "education of desire" he had outlined in his intervention at the sociologists' meeting? Did it still bear traces of Kantian, Durkheimian, or Parsonian dualisms? Or, again, was it closer to that vaguely defined connection of social commitment and habits of the heart that played a focal role in the new project? As in the case of his interventions in favor of religiously inspired political activism, Bellah's philosophical stance remained caught between two extreme poles: evoking final causality required a resolute shift from "simple hermeneutics" to a substantive conception of the good, and thus the willingness to clearly criticize bad practices—that is, exactly what Foucault's post-Nietzscheanism could not deliver and what symbolic realism had, at least for some time, refused to do. As their book would soon make clear, the solution adopted by the Habits group to solve the dilemma of advancing a neo-Aristotelian point of view in a post-modern world was quite different, but not less interesting—or less uncertain.[24]

III

The flip side of this unfinished intellectual process concerned Bob's inner life. Now that "the purely physical side of homosexuality [had] become demystified," he could engage in alternative ways of reflexivity and self-examination. In addition to meditation, which he would practice mostly while running along the Berkeley fire trails, Bellah commenced an intense therapeutic relationship with the renowned gay analyst, artist, and collector Eli Leon, who suggested that he also attend couple (with Bill) and collective sessions. For the first time in decades Bob found himself "exposed" among a group of people who had no idea of who or what he was. A third source of gratification was physical exercise: the body continued to be a major, and more immediate, source of pleasure. All these advances were signals of Bellah's coming to terms with his relationship with Bill *as it was*: "We have to be able to do for ourselves," he wrote in his diary on August 5, 1979, "what we neurotically expect and hope the other will do for us."[25]

Soon Melanie and Bob succeeded in widening their affective network—which at this point had ceased to have any sexual overtones—and the situation stabilized in a way that everybody found satisfactory most of the time. Bellah's friendship with Bill, which he again described as "an additional marriage," was still growing, losing on the side of compulsion and gaining in depth, affection, and respect. Given this newfound serenity, Lillian Bellah's passing away on May 29, 1980, after more than two years in a retirement home and then a nursing home, had no major impact on Bob, who had met the responsibility of caring for his mother with an increasingly detached attitude—even in the frame of his diligent work of self-reflection, her death went unmentioned in his diary and correspondence.[26]

After a period of renewed interest in Japan due to a number of occasional speaking engagements and the plan to include a comparative chapter at the end of *Habits of the Heart*, in the summer of 1980 Bob started practicing Zen meditation with some regularity. As he later said during a conference on Dōgen at the Tassaraja Zen Mountain Center, the famed Buddhist monastery in the Los Padres National Forest where he had spent some time with either Melanie or Bill, Bellah saw Zen practice as a way to set the individual free from oppressive social relations, but which could be practiced only within a rigidly structured community, the sangha, against any attempt to cast it as yet another spiritual technology in the service of utilitarian individualism. In the same period he also attended, for a brief time and without much enthusiasm, a support group for gay staff and faculty members of the University of California—a minor episode, but one that nonetheless affirmed his willingness to reflect upon himself in different settings. As a result, on August 28, 1980, he could write a diary entry that would have been unthinkable just five years earlier: "Like things have turned out as I wanted, like I am getting what I always wanted. I know that it is hard to accept."[27]

One year later, Bob's process of self-development reached its peak. As antici-pated in their research proposal, the five members of the Habits group assem-bled in Berkeley for two intense months aimed at giving a flying start to the final stage of the process—writing. By then they had a tentative title for their book—*Habits of the Heart. American Mores and the Future of American Democracy*—a thirteen-chapter table of contents, and a well-tested working method. Between 1978 and 1981, the group as a whole had met twice a year, often in Cambridge to make sure that its advisors and other scholars, like Michael Maccoby and Shm-uel Eisenstadt, could join them. Transcripts of pilot interviews had circulated since April 1979, fieldwork had started in the fall of that same year, and the five researchers were already using data from the study in their public lectures in 1980. Between meetings, Bob, who had a project-related secretary at his dis-posal, coordinated the different stages of the fieldwork, circulated books or ar-ticles to read, and distributed his latest theoretical reflections.[28]

As work progressed, the group had seen a curious phenomenon emerging from the interviews given by different people from different classes living in different places: the same concepts and exemplary narratives were used by individuals who self-located at opposite poles of both the right–left and the religious–secular continuums. This had boosted their confidence, but had also alerted their attention to what in the book they would call "vocabularies" or "languages"—that is, how Americans employed the three cultures of utilitar-ian individualism and republican or biblical collectivism—now augmented to four with the addition of "expressive individualism"—as "rhetorical and ideo-logical resources . . . to think about problems of social and political life and the place of the individual in it."[29]

During their two months at Berkeley, the five scholars refined their inter-pretive categories through the examination of selected theoretical themes, communal reading of interview transcripts, and accounts of participant obser-vations and other findings. After, and sometimes during, group sessions, they would split and work alone or in pairs, sometimes along the private/public axis of their research, sometimes according to their personal interests or writ-ing commitments—Ann with Steve and Bill with Dick, but also Bill with Bob, who shared the main responsibility for the theoretical-historical section of the book. At the end of August 1981, eight of their planned thirteen chapters had been drafted fully or in part.[30]

During the group's long, demanding discussions the four younger scholars had the chance to offer their different sensibilities as special assets: Bill Sullivan's capacity to distill his vast theoretical knowledge into original and relatively simple concepts; Steve Tipton's deep thinking and mastery of the method of "moral conversation," which constituted the backbone of the whole empirical endeavor; Dick Madsen's ability to provide vivid and meaningful descriptions, and his brilliance in writing; Ann Swidler's sociological prowess and her constant call not to idealize a past whose existence was, at least, doubtful, as also shown in the work of her husband, Berkeley sociologist Claude Fischer. The atmosphere was so effervescent that the members of the "rather chatty group" soon understood that the only thing that could hold them back was what they were themselves unwilling to contribute. This enthusiastic attitude helped to relieve the tensions that inevitably emerged when two or more of them worked on the same chapter, criticizing, dissecting, and often rewriting what others had drafted with care and commitment.

In all of this, Robert Bellah stood on the command deck, his leadership never showy or authoritarian—in fact, most of the time it was exemplary, in the sense of the word used by Max Weber to describe a prophet whose influence rests on personal example rather than the imposition of norms of behavior. After taking the responsibility of starting each meeting—telling some personal anecdote and setting the agenda for the day—Bob would listen quietly to the others while they developed intuitions, concepts, and implications. In a sense, he had finally found his own way to lead a research group. This was something that did not come from Talcott Parsons, who had usually worked in one-to-one relationships and had been most receptive to ideas that could be integrated into his ever-expanding scheme. It is true that in the early 1970s Bellah had co-led the New Religious Consciousness group with Charles Glock, but the looser character of that project, combined with his working on *The Broken Covenant* and symbolic realism, had ensured that he kept a more distant and "individual" posture. This time, however, Bob's close friendship with Bill and his intense relations with Ann, Dick, and Steve reinforced the collective nature of the project. He could thus "limit" himself to illuminating the wider, general implications of what the others said, while the focus on the four empirical studies prevented the book from becoming yet another "abstract jeremiad" on American culture and society—an outcome that Ann, Steve, Dick, and Bill had pledged to prevent as much as they could.

That summer the management of Bob's crowded, complex, and stratified relationship with Bill proved to be an exhilarating but demanding endeavor, from which, however, emerged an illumination of sorts. Writing in his diary shortly after Sullivan had returned to Philadelphia, Bellah represented their connection as a *kōan*, a Zen puzzle that he had finally decoded from an experiential, rather than cognitive, point of view: "Neither Bill nor I can change. . . . [W]e simply have to accept what is. . . . Not his fault for not giving, not my fault for wanting. . . . [T]here is nothing to be expected. . . . He is not my father or [anyone else]. He does not want to disappoint me. He loves me. He gives me an enormous gift."[31]

In that very moment, the painful, exacting, and rewarding period that had begun with Abby's death and the lunch at the "Taiwan" restaurant entered its final phase. Things were now clear, age-old desires had been demystified, each individual was in his or her place. Determined to follow Bill in "significant change," and increasingly grateful for his good fortune beyond his personal tragedy and pain—"my hands are always full"—Bellah consciously started to shift his vital energy to work and religion. As he noted after a successful meeting of the Habits group with Alasdair MacIntyre in March 1982, Bob needed work to regain its privileged position if his life was to become "an embodiment of truth." The reference was William Butler Yeats's late letter to Lady Elizabeth Pelham: "It seems to me that I have found what I wanted. When I try to pull it all into a phrase I say 'Man can embody truth but he cannot know it.' I must embody it in the completion of my life." For years, wrote Bellah in his diary, he had found joy and satisfaction in his work, and now it was time to be joyous again—the very fact that he had now an idyllic vision of a side of his life that had often been the source of anxiety showed his tremendous progress toward self-clarification. Old fears remained, but the attitude was different: apart from *Habits of the Heart*, which was making Bob happier than he had expected, he knew that he still had a lot to do if he wanted to overcome his fear of writing and finally focus on the theoretical book he had been planning since 1956.[32]

And then came religion. Ever since his Tillichian rapprochement with Christianity in the mid-1950s Bellah had never been consistent in his practice, feeling that no service or community could answer his inner questioning as did the powerful sermons of the German theologian. While in Cambridge, in the late 1950s he had first tried to get involved in the life of an Episcopal parish, and had then moved on to the Society of Friends, for whom he had also taught Sunday school for a while. The failure of both attempts had convinced him to retreat into a silent, uprooted relationship with Christianity. Then, more or less at the time of the beginning of his relationship with Bill Sullivan, Bob became interested in Saint Mark's Episcopal Church, whose Mission Revival–style building sat a few hundred yards from his office at Barrows Hall.

Founded in 1877 by two Berkeley faculty members, Saint Mark's had always entertained a special relationship with the campus community, and was now home to an inclusive and committed body of believers who strongly supported its many social, religious, and cultural activities. Its present rector, Philip A. Getchell, had been a missionary in Brazil and was as much an activist as a pastor—in March 1982 he was one of the signatories of the East Bay Sanctuary Covenant, a revolutionary ecumenical protocol aimed at providing physical refuge, legal assistance, and educational opportunities to asylum seekers from El Salvador, Nicaragua, and other war-torn countries. Although this kind of political engagement was nothing but commendable, from Bob's point of view what now mattered the most was connecting with the ritual life of the church—in 1982 he felt for the first time in his life that he had been truly and fully absorbed in the celebration of the liturgical year.[33]

At the end of July 1983, Robert Bellah ended his term as the chair of the Department of Sociology and set out on his second sabbatical-at-home, this time financed by a Guggenheim Fellowship, to prepare the manuscript of *Habits of the Heart* for publication. As he wrote in his diary on August 22, 1983, leaving his administrative responsibilities was harder than expected, and most of the summer "was taken up with disentangling from the last four years." Unbeknownst to him, that page was going to be his last diary entry. After that, he would never keep a journal again, and the personal side of his correspondence would also dry up considerably. "Spiritual practice and work," read the very last lines of his very last entry, "are the main areas to concentrate on in the coming year." Not that everything was perfect: like all re-articulations, Bellah's remained partial, unfinished, and ever-changing. But a whole life cycle had ended, and he knew it. Echoing a passage from the book he was writing, one might say that, thanks to the members of his small affective community and their loyalty "to shared ideals of what makes life worth living," Bob had gone through the "risky, demanding effort" of self-discovery and had finally become "his own person."[34]

16

The Sociologist's Revenge

UNITED STATES OF AMERICA, 1978–1985

SOON AFTER RONALD REAGAN's triumphal reelection of November 6, 1984, advance copies of *Habits of the Heart: Individualism and Commitment in American Life* were sent by the University of California Press to Robert N. Bellah, his four coauthors, and a number of selected scholars, activists, pundits, and politicians. Seven long years had passed since Richard Sharpe had first suggested to Steve Tipton to shift attention from fringe groups to the mainstream of the American middle class. Seven years in which Bob had been busy traveling his own personal underworld and had finally met himself in the face of the other—seven years in which he had, incredible as it sounded for a man who was now fifty-seven years old, metaphorically left his home only to come back again as someone who was very close to the man he wanted to be. In the meantime, Melanie, Jenny, Hally, and the members of the Habits group had all gone through a number of major changes, which also made their present condition quite different from that of 1978.[1]

Melanie's life had been a vertiginous ride through bliss and misery—as she wrote to Maruyama Masao's wife, Yukari, when their son Takeshi committed suicide in 1984, such tragedies could be endured but never overcome. She fell often prey to an irrational but all-too-human sense of guilt for not having been able to protect her children, and although she underwent long and painful work with therapists and self-help groups, meaninglessness remained a faithful, if unwelcome, companion. There were, however, sources of relief. After amicably parting ways with her office mate, Melanie set up the bottom floor of 10 Mosswood Road as her new workplace, and took some gratification practicing family law and offering her pro bono counsel to exploited women and community causes. During the same period she also committed herself to writing a book about Tammy, in which she detailed the young girl's teenage explorations with drugs and boyfriends and her parents' reactions to her ups and downs, all the way to her suicide and funeral.[2]

Part biography and part memoir, for all the intensive use of Tammy's diaries, letters, and school papers the book still retained a strong Melanie-centric point of view that was disliked and loudly criticized by the other members of the family. Helped by a part-time assistant, Victoria, in June 1981 Melanie was able to submit her manuscript to Harper and Row—the publisher of Bob's *Beyond Belief* and his recent *Varieties of Civil Religion*, a collection of essays edited with sociologist Phillip E. Hammond. When the book was rejected ten months later, she was so upset that the manuscript got lost in a drawer for more than fifteen years. Even more trying was the settlement of the lawsuit she had brought against General Motors after Abby's accident. When the case was finally submitted to court in September 1981, the Bellahs were granted a bitter victory: the automotive company was found guilty for defective brake construction, but 95 percent of the fault for the accident was attributed to Abby as the car's driver. That meant that the check that Melanie received from the manufacturer of the automobile in which her daughter had died only amounted to $376 after all expenses—a rather dreary compensation.[3]

Fortunately, Bob and Melanie's perilous navigation of life was greatly helped by the respective, if different, achievements of Hally and Jenny, who were now older than their beloved sisters had ever been. After graduating in English literature at Bryn Mawr and traveling around Europe on a Thomas J. Watson Fellowship, in 1979 Jenny was admitted to the University of California School of Law, and decided to go back and live with her parents at 10 Mosswood Road. She was soon so absorbed in her studies that she would often spend dinners discussing the law with her mother, causing Bob some annoyance when their conversation veered too much on the esoteric. Sometimes Jenny helped Melanie with her cases, including a displeasing legal action against Neil Smelser, who had been living in the same Mosswood Road complex since the early 1960s and was now trying to sell his property. The litigation, won by the Bellahs, left a permanent scar between the two former wunderkinder of the Parsonian brood, who maintained, from that moment on, a polite but cold relationship.

In September 1980 Hally graduated from high school and left Berkeley for the North Carolina School of the Arts to study classic and modern dance; at about the same time, Jenny's French fiancé, Christian Romon, moved to Berkeley after having completed a doctorate in history at the École des hautes études en sciences sociales in Paris—he and Jenny married in 1981 at the Women's Faculty Club of the University of California. As an undergraduate student, Hally performed at the Jacob's Pillow Festival in July 1981 and got her BFA in 1982, two years earlier than expected. Fulfilling one of her mother's aspirations, she pursued a career as a ballerina and worked with various companies in Los Angeles, New York, and San Francisco, where she became a member of the corps de ballet of the Opera in 1985. At that point, Jenny and Christian had grudgingly decided to move to the "uncivilized and uncultured" metropolis where Bob and Melanie had spent their youth—and where Christian could attend the Graduate School of Management of the University of California, Los Angeles. Having passed the California bar exam, Jenny found employment at Gibson, Dunn, and Crutcher, a legal firm founded in 1890 whose Parisian office would soon allow her and Christian to return to the place where they had first met.[4]

I

The years between 1978 and 1985 were also a time of consolidation and growth for the junior members of the Habits group. The steady progress of their collective project confirmed Sharpe in his conviction that the humanities could give an original contribution to the understanding of contemporary American society, and even suggest solutions to major social and cultural problems. The Ford Foundation thus launched Humanistic Perspectives on Major Contemporary Issues, a new program to sponsor research on social justice and common values through a small number of individual awards. Prominent scholars and literati were asked to nominate young scholars, who would then undergo a rigorous review process. Since the adoption of a comparative-historical method and the willingness to write for an educated lay audience were highly appreciated by the Foundation, and given the involvement of Bellah, Swidler, Tipton, and Sullivan in various review committees, the Habits group easily became the midwife, as well as the first grantee, of the new award.[5]

While fully committed to the collective project, Bill and Steve had also completed their monographs, *Reconstructing Public Philosophy* and *Getting Saved from the Sixties*, while Dick had finished two: *Chen Village* with Anita Chan and Jonathan Unger, and his own *Morality and Power in a Chinese Village*, which won the 1984 C. Wright Mills Award of the Society for the Study of Social Problems. Though conceived at different times and quite dissimilar in object, structure, and style, the four books were clearly influenced by the work of the group in the phrasing of their research questions and the usage of similar conceptual and methodological tools. Together with the four volumes of Jeffrey Alexander's *Theoretical Logic in Sociology*, they all came out of the University of California Press between 1982 and 1984—a fact that filled Bellah with fatherly pride.[6]

Thanks to their solo work, Tipton and Madsen had gotten tenure at Emory University in Atlanta and the University of California, San Diego, while Sullivan had moved back to his alma mater, Philadelphia's La Salle University, as an associate professor of philosophy. Still at Stanford as an assistant professor, Ann Swidler was awarded a Guggenheim Fellowship for the academic year 1982–1983 that she used to finalize both *Habits of the Heart* and the original analytical approach to the study of culture she had been developing for a while. Her essay, titled "Culture in Action," was finally published in 1986. In it, Ann attacked the idea of values as a causal element, and used instead a "tool-kit" metaphor that was quite different from Bob's hermeneutic approach. She saw culture as a repertoire of sorts from which actors draw symbols and practices to construct middle- and long-term "strategies of action." The scope and intensity of the causal impact of culture depends on actors living through "settled" or "unsettled" times—the hypothesis being that the more fluid and dynamic the situation, the more culture becomes refined and explicit, often in the form of an ideology, and thus influences the daily lives of social actors and their "styles" of action.[7]

The first half of the 1980s had been such a period of unsettling transformation, one in which the American people had learned new ways "of organizing individual and collective action, practicing unfamiliar habits" until they had become routine. The United States had changed, albeit not as much as its president had promised in 1980. The ambitious tax-cut plan presented in February 1981 as the centerpiece of the neoconservative revolution had been criticized and obstructed in Congress by liberals and fiscal conservatives alike. It was only after he survived an assassination attempt in March that Reagan had been able to force through the Democrat-controlled House a lesser version of his original bill, in which smaller tax cuts were not matched, as requested by Budget Director David Stockman and other die-hard neocons, by proper spending reductions. Reagan's subsequent attack on social security had been resisted by Democrats, and the intransigent pursuit of supply side economics, combined with an exceptional growth in military spending, entirely financed by federal deficit, had worsened the economic recession. Only in 1983, and mainly thanks to the policies of the Federal Reserve's Paul Volker, a Carter appointee, had the economy started to recover, and Reagan had regained his image as a success.[8]

As for foreign policy, the president's confrontational attitude toward the Soviet Union, famously called the "empire of evil," had projected a tougher, more determined image of America, but had also increased fears of an imminent nuclear showdown, as illustrated by the success of popular dramatizations such as *The Day After* and *Testament* and the rise of the Nuclear Freeze movement. Although Reagan had explicitly stated he wished to avoid nuclear war, in the fall of 1983 his anti-missile-shield project "Star Wars," siting of middle-range nuclear weapons in Western Europe, continued stand-offs with Libya, and the disastrous mission in Lebanon made the prospects for Reagan's "new Cold War" rather grim.

In perfect accord with Swidler's model, all this political and economic turmoil was accompanied by a great deal of symbolic elaboration along old and new ideological fault lines—in this sense, Reagan was clearly succeeding as a teaching president, albeit a strongly partisan one. With his tough but avuncular attitude, the former Hollywood actor had been able to merge politics and culture, making "prosperity patriotic—and transcendent." The 1984 Olympic Games in Los Angeles, the first ever to be paid for entirely by corporate sponsors and television rights, had been made into an almost religious celebration of kitsch and business ambition. And again and again, Reagan employed his black-or-white rhetoric to describe complex social problems such as child abuse, poverty, or drug consumption as straightforward moral evils caused by inexcusable personal choices.[9]

The overall cultural trend, however, veered toward radical, market-driven individualization rather than the imposition of traditional values feared by liberal pundits and scholars. As anticipated by Bellah, the president had never really embraced the desiderata of the Religious Right and had "failed conspicuously to lend his political clout to legislation that might enforce [them]." From his choice of Sandra Day O'Connor as a Supreme Court associate justice to his timid position on constitutional amendments on abortion and school prayer, Reagan had defied the expectations of a sizable portion of his social conservative constituency. The new hyper-individualistic culture had also been reinforced by a flood of seemingly independent developments in pop culture and technology. Since their establishment in the mid-1970s, companies like Microsoft, Apple, and Oracle had revolutionized the way Americans conceived of their working practices and leisure time, renewing the myth of the genial inventor-entrepreneur and legitimating once again the reckless pursuit of wealth and pleasure. The debut of CNN in 1980 and MTV in 1981 was only the harbinger of a vertiginous pluralization of media outlets and thus a multi-plication of the possibilities of choice for the American public.[10]

II

When the first copies of *Habits of the Heart* finally hit the shelves on March 22, 1985, Mikhail Gorbachev had just become the secretary-general of the Soviet Communist Party, patients were taking the first FDA-approved blood tests for AIDS, and USA for Africa's "We Are the World" was topping the singles charts almost everywhere. Full-page ads for the book sported a photograph of the five coauthors, Bill and Ann sitting, Dick, Bob, and Steve standing, all smiling, in a compact group formation. The tagline read "A passionate, sensitive explo-ration of American life," while blurbs from Daniel Bell, philosopher Stephen Toulmin, and Rutgers University political scientist and former activist of SLATE (the University of California, Berkeley, campus political party) Wilson Carey McWilliams described *Habits* as "beautifully written, profoundly medi-tated and morally informed," an "excellent but disturbing book," and "invalu-able as public education and as a contribution to public debate about Ameri-can life and values." Framed by two theoretical-historical meditations, the results of the group's empirical research were arranged in two main sections: part one, dedicated to private life, included chapters on individualism, thera-peutic culture, friendship, love, and marriage, while part two focused on public life, surveyed citizenship, civic and political activism, and a host of competing conceptions of the national community. A clearly normative conclusion, an appendix titled "Social Science as Public Philosophy," and a brief glossary closed the 355-page book, which sold for $16.95.[11]

Instead of presenting the four empirical studies as separate single-authored chapters, materials from all interviews had been mixed and matched in all chapters. Through a long and demanding work of editing, which Bob had taken care of, the whole of the book had finally come out as the joint product of the five authors, whose contributions were acknowledged only as an intri-cate interweaving of writing and rewriting in a footnote on page 331. The cover reported the five names in alphabetical order—here, the fact that the surname of the principal investigator started with a "B" made everything easier—and the appendix underlined the collective nature of their work with words that left no room for the imagination: during their meetings, and especially their summers together, the five scholars had developed "a common culture," and

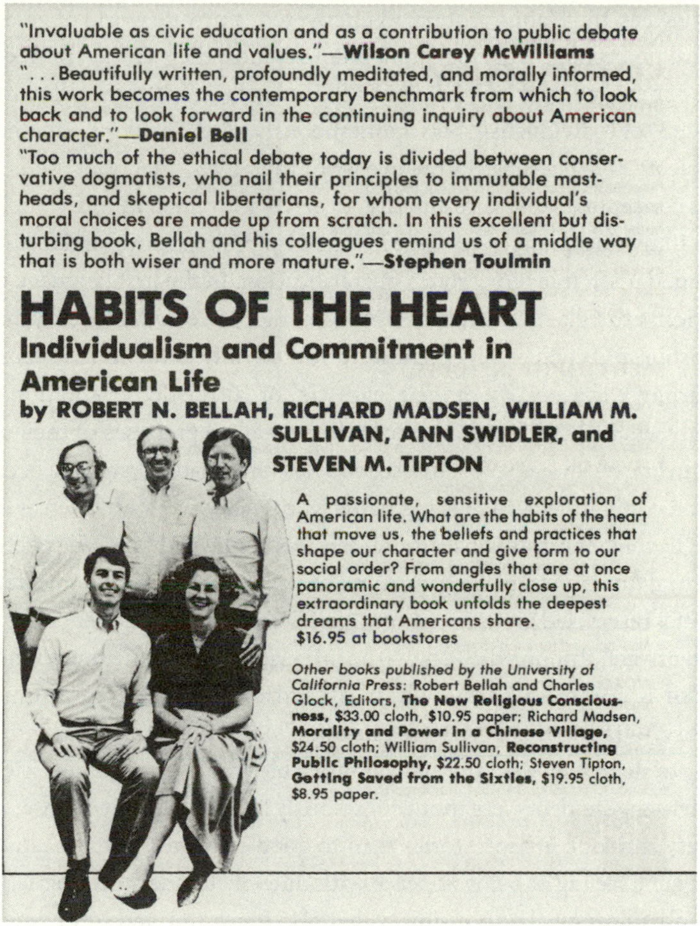

FIGURE 16.1. *Habits of the Heart* advertisement published in the *American Sociological Review*, 1985.

in the process they had strengthened both their common outlook and their individual voices. In other words, the Habits group presented itself as the prime example of a strong collectivity able to nurture individuality and solidarity at the same time.[12]

This self-description, which came at the end of *Habits of the Heart*, was a way to summarize what had been going on for more than three hundred pages. While Bell called it "the contemporary benchmark from which to look back and to look forward in the continuing inquiry on American character," the book might be described as an investigation of a major mismatch between symbols, deeds, and relations. In the words of their White, middle-class interviewees, the Habits group had uncovered "a private world of great intensity and no content whatsoever," a phenomenon they saw as framed by the uneasy coexistence of two different vocabularies. What they called the "first language" of individualism was spontaneously used by their two hundred or so subjects to make sense of the events of their lives, affections, and choices. In this conceptual repertoire, moral action was warranted by individual preferences, individual preferences were justified by "feeling good," and feeling good depended upon transitory states of gratification. In the first language used by Americans to talk about themselves, all choices in terms of work, marriage, friendship, and civic involvement were rooted only in the individual self and its yearnings, irrespective of their "egoistic" or "altruistic" orientation.[13]

Only when pushed to think about the unspoken premises of their answers did some interviewees resort to a second, less articulated, language of community and commitment. In this alternative vocabulary, work was seen as a calling through which the individual's moral self was connected to a wider network of reciprocal functions and exchanges, rather than as a self-centered career. Collectivities resembled inclusive wholes "celebrating the interdependence of public and private" through the (often painful) elaboration of the myths and narratives of a common past—what the authors called "communities of memory"—rather than "lifestyle enclaves," composed of similar individuals willing to share only what they felt comfortable with. And marriage, friendship, and civic engagement were more consciously linked to a shared sense of inherent duty and/or common stories than to good character, psychic satisfaction, or a general feeling of being at peace with oneself. This second language spoke of a sense of personal responsibility that also suggested, and sometimes called for, the deferral of gratification in the pursuit of the long-term commitments inherited from parents, friends, and fellow religionists or activists.[14]

As repeatedly underlined by the Habits group, the first vocabulary was intrinsically unable to articulate the richness of existing social relations: "In the language they use," wrote Bellah and his coauthors, "their lives sound more isolated and arbitrary than, as we have observed them, they actually are." This meant, quite simply, that Americans were just *wrong* when they described their own social life. Framing this gap between social reality and its representation as simply a problem of false consciousness would not capture Bellah's theoretical position, one which had survived intact his decision to drop the label of "symbolic realism." Bob, and with him his coauthors, continued to think that human beings could experience reality only through symbols, whether they be encapsulated in myths, narratives, or theories. As emphasized by Clifford

Geertz, culture is an elusive phenomenon: it is there, but remains unnoticed because all human experience is somehow shaped and impregnated by it. In particular, most actors are unable to see how much their tendencies, words, and practices—their "habits of the heart"—embody the traces of ideas and vocabularies coming from past traditions.[15]

When combined with Bellah's critical stance, this theoretical insight created a paradox of sorts. On the one hand, if human beings can experience reality only through symbols, trying to invalidate a false conscience by showing reality "as it is" would be contradictory at best—and this somehow explained the Habits group's sympathetic stance toward their interviewees, as if they had no other alternative. On the other hand, if relations are not independent of their representations, an erroneous language may have a disastrous impact on how people conduct their lives, for it undermines the social infrastructure itself. Being able to make this last point, however, depends on the conviction of having grasped what social life "is really about," and thus on advancing a very strong truth claim. Although *Habits of the Heart* had been purposely written for educated lay readers, who could easily understand, and perhaps share, a critique of individualism without being troubled by the clash between the hermeneutic and the critical sides of the remnants of symbolic realism, a solution to this theoretical contradiction was necessary and urgent. In fact, it was the veritable engine of the most interesting, and misunderstood, pages of the book.

III

Habits of the Heart presented a twofold solution to the dilemma. On the one hand, the authors framed their study of contemporary practices by way of a historical assessment of the four symbolic sets on which American culture had been built—the "different voices in a common tradition" that, more or less recognizably, echoed through the first and the second language employed by the interviewees. The idea of the four cultures brought the two "halves" of the American tradition first presented in *The Broken Covenant* to a higher level of complexity and refinement. As elaborated by Hobbes and Locke, utilitarian individualism saw "human life as an effort by individuals to maximize their self-interest relative to [some] given ends." Another form of individualism, which the five coauthors called "expressive," came from nineteenth century Romanticism and held that each person "has a unique core of feeling and intuition that should unfold or be expressed if individuality is to be realized." To these two different kinds of individualism, the American heritage opposed two varieties of "social realism," both based on an understanding of groups and societies as phenomena having their own life at least partly independent from that of their members. Within a common "collectivist" understanding, the biblical and the republican versions of this tradition differed in their sources and their emphasis on justice and the public good.[16]

The vital connection between the four traditions and the everyday parlance of common Americans was efficaciously suggested by an initial stylistic artifice. The opening chapter, first penned by Bill and Dick in a sudden burst of creativity, presented four fictitious citizens—Brian Palmer, Margaret Oldham, Joe Gorman, and Wayne Bauer—all trying to find a way to make sense of their everyday life. In chapter 2, written by Bill and Bob, these common Americans were mirrored by four eminent national characters—John Winthrop, Thomas Jefferson, Benjamin Franklin, and Walt Whitman—as the embodiments of biblical and republican holism, on the one hand, and utilitarian and expressive individualism, on the other.[17]

While they underlined the equal foundational role of the four symbolic complexes, and while they repeatedly referred to Tocqueville's idea that political and religious participation might limit the harmful consequences of individualism, the coauthors of *Habits* were in fact advancing an argument situated on a different theoretical level: "There are *truths*," they wrote, "we do not see when we adopt the language of radical individualism." Those who employed the latter not only condemned themselves to a "thin," ungrounded moral life, but also embraced a dangerous misconception of how relations and commitments really worked. In fact, since the very values prized by contemporary Americans—"the sense of the dignity, worth, and moral autonomy of the individual"—were themselves dependent "in a thousand ways on a social, cultural, and institutional context that keeps us afloat *even* when we cannot very well describe it," a mistaken conception of social relations might ultimately impair the pursuit of the American experiment itself. Conversely, those who were more firmly rooted in the second language of biblical and republican ascent had a better understanding of the absence of any "sharp distinction between self and the others" and so of how society really worked and thus could be fostered and maintained.[18]

In a vocabulary reminiscent of Émile Durkheim and Michael Sandel, but also of Bellah's recently republished *Tokugawa Religion*, the Habits group called for the development of "the ability to acknowledge the interconnectedness—one's 'debt to society'—that binds one to others whether one wants to accept it or not [and] the ability to engage in the caring that nurtures that interconnectedness." Such a virtue would then allow common Americans to develop a more realistic vision of human society as "a whole composed of different, but interdependent, groups." This, in turn, might push them to be interested in understanding "the invisible complexity" of contemporary society, starting from the mysterious connections between their comfortable suburban lifeworlds and the sharply differentiated bureaucratic systems of the metropolis. Last but not least, this new awareness of societal complexity as interdependence might generate "a language of the common good" more capable of adjudicating "between conflicting wants and interests" than simply seeking to re-slice the utilitarian pie, maximize individual rights, or refine procedural rules.[19]

This reinterpretation of the classic opposition of individualism and community and the complexity of the main argument of Habits of the Heart were destined to cause some misunderstandings. For example, while Bellah and his coauthors often embodied utilitarian and expressive cultures in the "representative characters" of the manager and the therapist, their grasp of the paradoxical connection of the two kinds of individualism was as far from the clichéd images of narcissism and therapeutic culture circulating in the public sphere as from the rapid sketches of the two champions of modernity advanced in After Virtue. Since professional life now included the manipulation of personal emotions and relations, rational calculation and strategic action had also become the tools for reaching self-fulfillment. This made the average middle-class American anything but self-indulgent, for "the relentless insistence on consciousness and the endless scanning of one's own and others' feelings while making moment-by-moment calculations of the shifting cost/benefit balances is so ascetic in its demands as to be unbearable." From this point of view, therapeutic culture looked like another trick of unfettered capitalism.[20]

Also, for all the preoccupation with individualism, the five authors clearly stated that disowning it "would mean for us to abandon our deepest identity." As their many analyses of the weak interplay between moral languages clearly showed, they were concerned mostly with the unbalance between the four original American cultures—the point was that of restoring the right relation between different levels of understanding, not replacing one hegemony with another. What to do, then? The Habits group explicitly ruled out any possibility of going back to the "good ole days" of Main Street America. Indeed, they described their interviewees' frequent nostalgia for small-town simplicity as a classic example of false consciousness, one that glossed over the narrowness and oppression typical of traditional villages, and whose flawed depiction of contemporary society was unable to grasp differentiation and complexity. This longing for a rosy invented past was, in fact, the antithesis of "a living tradition" as the Habits group conceived of it: an ossified, simplified image of the past versus the continuous reinterpretation and rejuvenation of a rich, plural, and at times conflicting, repertoire of practices, symbols, myths, and narratives.[21]

The solution was, once again, intricate. First of all, the habits of the heart needed to understand how society works, and thus live a meaningful life, could not be simply learned by reading a book. They had to be developed as deeply embodied virtues through regular common practice. To this end, individual and collective actors should begin a wide, inclusive conversation on the common good as a practice of commitment—that is, as an intrinsically rewarding activity that required no external of functional justification to exist. The strength and continuation of this public dialogue, however, depended on the redistribution of material and immaterial resources via an ambitious program of reform, which included an ideal shift from career to vocation, the enactment of workplace democracy, and a boost to participatory politics. In addition to this, forceful actions of economic and substantive justice were also necessary to emancipate American citizens from the alienating effects of a bureaucratized society. Needless to say, the main vehicle of this societal and moral revolution was to be a comprehensive, open social movement that would present itself as "the successor and fulfilment of the Civil Rights Movement."[22]

For all the complexity of the situation described in eleven dense chapters, the final outlook of the Habits group was largely positive: "If there are vast numbers of a selfish, narcissistic 'me generation' in America, we did not find them," they wrote. "Many Americans are devoted to serious, even ascetic, cultivation of the self in the form of a number of disciplines, practices and 'trainings.'" Any solution to the present imbalance between the two languages of American morality should start from this relentless and disciplined quest for meaning. And the only vehicle for finding meaning was shifting the focus of attention from oneself to a common and critical debate about the symbolic, political, and social potential of the many traditions on which America was built. As the authors claimed at the very end of the book, they hoped that a large number of Americans would "join the public discussion by offering interpretations superior to ours that can then receive further discussion."[23]

This solution bore a strong trace of neo-Aristotelianism that probably eluded its own authors. First of all, the empirical research had shown that individualism and democracy were the *endoxa*—that is, the stock of common knowledge—of the American people, and thus the inevitable point of departure of any analysis of the common good. Moreover, since Aristotelian political science shunned the adoption of universalistic moral principles in favor of *phronesis*—that is, the "preparation for informed deliberation in cases where no [definite] answers [to definite questions are] available"—any moral and political solution should emerge at the crossroads between American tradition and specific, concrete situations. In this sense, those who later asked Bellah and his coauthors to render explicit *their* solutions not only failed to understand that for the Habits group the very act of engaging in a discussion would be good *in itself*, but also asked them to act as experts legislating on the lives of others, a position they explicitly refused to occupy. To the contrary, while indicating a general direction and some concrete measures that might help America to remain on the right track, they left the very content of the common good open to the deliberation of an inclusive democratic public. Not surprisingly, the debate on *Habits of the Heart* ignored Aristotle and focused on much more mundane matters.[24]

17

Hitting the Big Time

UNITED STATES OF AMERICA, 1985–1991

AS MUCH AS ROBERT N. BELLAH and his coauthors had anticipated some interest in their book, the immediacy and breadth of its success exceeded all expectations. Paraphrasing Reagan's reelection remarks, the publication of *Habits of the Heart* was the end of nothing—it was the beginning of everything. An article anticipating its contents came out in late January 1985 in the *Los Angeles Times* under the headline "Study Assails Values of the New Right as 'Cancerous,'" a title so misleading that it took Bob some time to understand that it referred to his own book! In his prompt, tongue-in-cheek reply, Bellah tried to defuse any partisan labeling, speaking instead of the centrality of individualism in American culture, and accused Democrats and Republicans alike of being blind in the face of the evident social and ecological limits to the pursuit of individual interests and rights.[1]

Things, however, were moving fast, and in a few days Bob Bellah was approached by a number of liberal politicians and activists looking for advice on "the consequences of radical individualism." Walter Mondale and Tom Hayden each asked for a copy of the book, former governor Jerry Brown paid Bellah a visit at 10 Mosswood Road, and the president of the California State Senate, David Roberti, invited him to address the first Senate Democratic Members Retreat in Palm Springs. Then came a deluge of requests for interviews and public talks from newspapers, think tanks, and associations. Unable to accept them all, Bob tried nonetheless to be as available as possible—he truly believed in the book and its message, and wanted it to circulate to the full. In April 1985 *Habits* was reviewed in both the *New York Times Review of Books* and *Newsweek* within a matter of days. While not uncritical, the two articles praised the volume as "easily the richest and most readable study of

American society since David Riesman's '50s classic, *The Lonely Crowd*," "a kind of moral State of the Union message worthy of Tocqueville himself," and the carrier of a passionate, "grand argument that should at least provoke lively responses," an opinion soon echoed in the *Los Angeles Times* and *US News and World Report*. The word was out.[2]

When *Habits of the Heart* entered course syllabuses all over the United States, the big commercial publisher Harper and Row bought its reprinting rights for $100,000 and also talked with the five authors about putting together a study guide to help college teachers with the book. In November 1985 *Habits* won the *Los Angeles Times* Book Award in the category of Current Interest; five months later, after a day-long three-way tie among finalists in the jury voting, it lost the Pulitzer Prize in General Non-Fiction to J. Anthony Lukas's *Common Ground*, also the winner of the 1985 National Book Award, and Joseph Lelyveld's *Move Your Shadow*. When the paperback version was finally published in 1986, *Habits of the Heart* was launched into the empyrean of sociological bestsellers: "Usually, when I am at a gathering outside of the sociological community," wrote political economist Scott McNall in an article published in 1987, "people look at me blankly when I tell what I do. . . . Lately, however, I have been asked repeatedly by all sorts of people if I've read *Habits* and what I think of it. I've also seen my fellow travelers on airplanes reading the book, and a recent house guest of ours, a California entrepreneur, pronounced the book, 'The most important I've ever read.'"[3]

After the first salvo of articles in newspapers and magazines such as the *Wall Street Journal*, the *Times Literary Supplement*, the *Nation*, the *Christian Century*, and *Commentary*, reviews in scholarly journals started to come out early in 1986. Given the many levels of argument presented in the book and its uncommon theoretical and political positioning, *Habits of the Heart* was described in different and conflicting ways. It was called fashionable *and* untimely, a book that deeply cared for *and* despised the subjects of its research, overly serious *and* "awfully nice," deeply conservative *and* radically leftist. By its admirers, the book was deemed a "monumental and nuanced" analysis of contemporary America that had "very few, if any, equals"; "an ambitious and well-guided effort"; "a literary event"; "intelligent, challenging, provocative, and, despite its diverse parentage, felicitous." Reviewers praised the quality of the writing and the team spirit and evident commitment of the Habits group, and often called the book a sermon.[4]

Not surprisingly, the critics were legion, and pretty pugnacious. *Habits* was attacked first and foremost on methodological grounds. A great many reviewers were not happy with the decision to limit interviews to a (small) aggregate of middle-class White respondents, and saw the book as not representing all American cultures—the *San Francisco Chronicle and Examiner* even expressed its contempt for *Habits* and its sample with an exceedingly strongly worded title, "Kill the Sociologists!" Anticipating this critique, Bob and his coauthors had tried to define the "middle class" as an exquisitely conceptual entity, dissociating it from any concretely identifiable social aggregate. As a "a group that seeks to embody in its own continuous progress and advancement the very meaning of the American project," middle-classness was better understood as the habit of the heart of those who strived for a continuous amelioration of their condition by way of technical means and a bureaucratic logic. The centrality of the middle class, therefore, was not due to its being "simply a 'layer' in a 'system of stratification,'" but rather to its cultural hegemony with respect to the upper and the lower classes, whose members had a more relational understanding of social life. The alternative to it, the authors explicitly but all too sketchily wrote, was represented by the "communities of memory" found among ethnic, religious, and lower class collectivities.[5]

As this uncommon definition of the middle class went almost completely unnoticed, the narrowness of the sampling became an easy target of the reviewers as either a failure or a willed distraction. In this sense, the most devastating critique was penned by Vincent Harding, an African American intellectual who had sometimes shared the podium with Bellah during the American civil religion debate. In a woeful "letter" to the Habits group published in 1987, Harding called the book "fundamentally and sadly flawed" because of the absence of Black, Hispanic, and indigenous voices. From the interviewees to the four exemplary historical figures, everything in *Habits* spoke of Whiteness, and this could mean only that it de facto supported "the old white fantasies that gave Euro-Americans the sole right to define the past, present, and future of the nation." Even Tocqueville, wrote Harding, had pronounced harsher words about slavery than the authors of *Habits*, who had also created a sanitized image of Martin Luther King Jr., to reassure their White readers of their "progressive" sense of inclusiveness. As the only way to supersede this unwarranted representation of America, Harding asked for a rewriting of the book so as to include all those who had been left behind.[6]

Another methodological point that was often raised against *Habits* was that its main philosophical argument sounded too strong, as though it had been cast *before* the beginning of the sociological inquiry. The use of empirical data was deemed as merely decorative, and the book's representative individuals were called "thin," made of "cardboard," or "bloodless abstractions." As summarized by William Kristol, "the interviews are cut and pasted to fit into a clear analytic framework," so that "we do not learn very much from all the stories the interviewees tell. They all amount to Bellah's own." While Robert E. Goodin described the book as "Christopher Lasch meets Vincent Peale, with footnotes," the award for the nastiest comments must go to Andrew M. Greeley, a Catholic priest and sociologist who had been in cordial relations with Bob for at least fifteen years. Professor Greeley gave the book a "D" in methodology, and then described it as "not sociology, not even opinion with which one may agree or disagree, but fundamentalist (in style) evangelism in an academic gown."[7]

The normative argument was also said to be too weak, too woolly, too uncertain to provide real guidance for political or social reform, to the point that one reviewer spoke of "disconnected moralizing." In this sense, the five authors were accused of deceiving themselves—that is, of being unable to see that they were the reflection of the individuals they described in their book—a point made by Harding and the highly respected Penn sociologist E. Digby Baltzell. Between these extremes, *Habits of the Heart* was criticized for almost everything else: for its ideational approach and exclusive cultural focus, for its biased or unscholarly reading of Tocqueville, for its failure to admit or develop its debt to Talcott Parsons and Alasdair McIntyre, for its simplistic image of the biblical and republican traditions, for its flawed genealogy of utilitarian and expressive individualism and the failure to connect them to structural change, and even for its lack of irony.[8]

As for *the* central theoretical point of the book, social realism, only a handful of reviews got the point, while others preferred to comment on the Habits group's all-too-conciliatory critique of individualism. The book, wrote William Grant in the *American Quarterly*, was "a middle-class dialogue with itself, affirming the individualistic tradition, the philosophical and political status quo." Some authors from the left, conversely, tried to bring its argument into new territory. In a masterful essay, for example, the Marxist cultural critic Fredric Jameson showed the book's debt to post-structuralism and its inability to envision a socialist alternative for America, while in the *Monthly Review* Philip Eden commended the scholarship and the deep integrity of *Habits*, and tried to push the discussion in the direction of a more thorough appreciation of the lower-class roots of the civil rights movement.[9]

At the other extreme of the political spectrum, the commentaries published in neoconservative journals were among the worst reviews that Bob had ever had. The Catholic apologist of market society, and former Bellah student at Harvard, Michael Novak accused the Habits group of ignoring how the conservative movement had been voicing the concerns, and championing the solutions, of their book for years. Pointing to Tocqueville's explicit scorn of socialism, he called *Habits* a "profoundly conservative program for the left," and added that as long as Americans remained one of the most active and committed peoples in the world, their lack of a language for expressing social and cultural concerns did not really matter. What had happened, he concluded rhetorically, to his old professor? Where had the man who in the mid-1960s had praised the emergence of modern individualism as the peak of human history gone? As he would remark in more private contexts, Bob Bellah had gone crazy.[10]

Similar concerns had already been expressed by Richard J. Neuhaus in his 1983 review of *Reconstructing Public Philosophy*. While Sullivan presented himself as a left-of-center thinker, he wrote, his vocabulary and arguments were difficult to distinguish from those advanced by "conservatives who define their position more by reference to culture than by reference to economics." In a review of *Habits of the Heart* for the *Public Interest*, Neuhaus wrote that under Sullivan's influence Bellah and his coauthors were now claiming to know the good and the bad of American individualism, and this depended on an outright, if ironic, rejection of Tocqueville's insights about the malaise of equality. This last thread was picked up in William Kristol's review in *Commentary*, which underlined how *Habits* didn't advance a good argument on the ability of the republican and the biblical traditions to reform themselves. Moreover, Kristol found a major flaw in the book's incapacity to see how the four American traditions had recombined during the Reagan era: traditional communitarians were now associated with utilitarian individualists on the neoconservative front, while expressive individualists and progressive communitarians had moved together to the left. Advancing community-inspired proposals outside these all-too-real alignments, the three neocon intellectuals agreed, was tantamount to political suicide. The next five years would prove in every possible way how wrong they were.[11]

I

Aside from its size, the true novelty of the success of *Habits of the Heart* lay in how Robert N. Bellah approached and exploited it. Unlike he had in the past, Bob now took the stance of the public intellectual much more than that of the academic: he paid very slight attention to the attacks of his colleagues and shied away from the most controversial statements advanced in the book. Instead of trying to clarify or revise his work, he strove to create an easily recognizable *prise de position* that could be readily adapted to the multiple and sometimes unpredictable audiences he would encounter in the polarized public sphere of the 1980s.

This new attitude was an outcome of the long and painful learning process begun in the late 1960s, when Bellah had left his comfortable Harvard niche as a Far Eastern specialist to venture into the dangerous territories of general theory and American studies. Academic disputes, he had learned, were often highly ritualized skirmishes producing no conceptual clarification or empirical advancement. In the introduction to *Varieties of Civil Religion*, published in 1980, Bob had written that the American civil religion debate had been "rather sterile, focusing more on form than content, definition than substance." In fact, he was also trying to avoid the deep uneasiness he had felt ten years earlier when his constantly evolving ideas had been dwarfed by simplified, stereotyped, and often "wrong" references to "Civil Religion in America." This time, he would not surrender his energy to his colleagues, but would directly address the lay public.[12]

Bellah's reply to the critics who considered the citizens interviewed in *Habits* too few and homogeneous to warrant generalization was paradigmatic of this new inclination. At another point in his career, he might have answered by theorizing on the middle class as a meaning-making social actor whose cultural hegemony far exceeded its size. Or he might have retrieved a sound intuition from January 1970, when the hectic study of some "necessary, powerful, painful and true" writings on race had convinced him that his being an affluent, highly educated Anglo-Saxon Protestant would never allow him to grasp the trauma and the meaning of being part of an oppressed minority in America. What he could do, he wrote in his journal at the time, was to help by explicating "the white psyche"—for that was his own experience, his own point in which "the personal and the mythical came together." Had Bellah reinterpreted *Habits* as an actualization of his old insight, the book would have looked more one-sided but also more compliant with the imperative of situatedness that was a hallmark of interpretive sociology.[13]

To the contrary, in his interventions on *Habits of the Heart* Bob chose to address only budget strictures or to repeat the mantra that the White middle class was a "strategic point of entry into the study of American culture." In his response to Harding, however, he employed another argument, one that signaled a real gear shift: the minority groups he had met during his travels, he wrote, had almost invariably given positive feedback on the limited focus of the book. Some, for example, had used *Habits* to better understand the mind-set of the majority, while others had employed it to discover whether and how they had been "culturally colonized." Free from the impediments typical of Greeley-style social scientists or Harding-style combative intellectuals, common readers had mirrored themselves in the narrative, the examples, and the rhetoric offered in *Habits*, and this was more important than the book's compliance with the standards of the restricted scholarly sphere.[14]

In other words, Bob Bellah was now mostly focused on *what people were doing* with *Habits of the Heart*. He was happy to hear that a Midwestern home-builder, Perry Bigelow, had been inspired by *Habits* to envision a "culturally sustainable" design for his new developments, or that the superintendent of schools in Eugene, Oregon, had used the book to promote forums on citizenship and character. He was also impatient to exchange views with the faculty of liberal arts colleges, and rejoiced at the news that the Kansas Citizens' Forum, a twelve-person group founded in Topeka in 1986 to discuss *Habits*, would soon organize the "Kansas Habits, Kansas Hope Conference" and then carry on its "Habits Sunday School" for another cycle of collective reading and debate.[15]

To encourage and steer this kind of activity, the Habits group put together *Individualism and Commitment in American Life*, a 475-page sourcebook of scholarly and literary texts. Under the informal editorship of Steve, Bill, and Dick, the compendium included the work of humanists, politicians, social scientists, pastors, novelists, and poets, and enlarged the cast of representative characters to Gwendolyn Brooks, Tillie Olsen, Fritz Perls, Wendell Berry, Norman Mailer, Martin Luther King Jr., and Jesse Jackson. A 13-page guide designed by Gary Hauk and Dick Madsen "to direct discussion with the context of a variety of courses and study groups" was also available upon request from the publisher, Harper and Row. In his brief lead-in, titled "America's Cultural Conversation," Bob tried, once again, to address the accusation of focusing only on the White middle class: "Differences arising from genre, skin color, national origin, religion or language," he argued, "cannot automatically be assumed to correlate with tangible pluralism." Indeed, "if persons different in these respects share the attitudes and practices of the white middle class," as the Habits group had observed, "then no genuine pluralism is involved." Culture and practices trumped social groupings constructed on the basis of seemingly "natural" categories.[16]

Common citizens, however, were not the only target of Bellah's attention—he spoke to political, business, and religious elites as much as he did to local groups and congregations, giving some steam to the doubts of some of his colleagues, who privately spoke of "the elitism lurking behind Bob Bellah's ostensible populism." During his public lectures, Bob would often use one of a few stock speeches created by assembling highly recognizable excerpts from *Habits of the Heart* with the occasional anecdote about inspiring individuals or groups he had met on the road. He would then add a more custom-tailored climax, before finishing with a general note of hope and commitment. At the California Democratic Retreat in Palm Springs, for example, he told state senators that "the Democratic party [needed] to be the party not of gloom and doom or me-too republicanism, but of public responsibility and public happiness," while at the 1986 Annual Conference of the Council on Foundations he stressed the need to make good use of existing, albeit vague, sensibilities to pull privatized individuals into the public sphere.[17]

Lecture after lecture, Bellah learned what worked: subtle distinctions within individualism were soon dropped, and the four American traditions were replaced by Jürgen Habermas's theory of the state and the economy "colonizing" communal "lifeworlds." This new phrasing entailed a significant shift: while the four traditions were different cultural complexes that nonetheless functioned according to a single logic, according to Habermas systems and communities were somehow incompatible, so that the possibility that the lifeworld could "regain control over the systems" was excluded by design, and the only choice was between defending the fort until death and surrender. It was not by chance that, having used this imagery in countless speeches, and after a whole graduate course on the theory of communicative action in 1989, Bellah decided not to make explicit use of Habermas's work in the next book of the Habits group, which was precisely dedicated to "regaining control" of the system and its institutions.[18]

All in all, the first couple of years after the publication of *Habits of the Heart* were challenging but deeply rewarding for Robert Bellah. Through the book his ideas—in fact, the ideas of the Habits group, as he never failed to repeat whether in speaking or writing—had finally reached a general audience. When the *Washington Post* wrote that Democratic Senator Barbara Mikulski had given a copy of *Habits* to the first lady of the Soviet Union during the Gorbachevs' triumphal visit to the United States of December 1987, their success could be considered complete. Moreover, while the book had been harshly criticized by academics, Bellah's new celebrity status brought him a number of alluring job offers from other universities. Determined to keep him at Berkeley, the University of California pledged to supplement Bob's position as a Ford Professor of Sociology and Comparative Studies with a second endowed chair. Thanks to the newly created Maxine J. Elliott professorship, instituted on July 1, 1986, Bellah could now command a sum of up to $50,000 a year for his research needs—an offer that remained unmatched until, and after, his retirement in 1997.[19]

II

One of the most praised and original features of *Habits* was what one reviewer called its "rare and refreshing" attention to religion as both a topic and a general theoretical outlook. Indeed, chapter 9, almost wholly written by Bob, introduced the most memorable character of the book. A young nurse originally interviewed by Steve Tipton, "Sheila Larson" talked about her made-up, individualized faith, which she called "her own little voice," suggesting to her simple precepts like "try to love yourself [and] take care of each other." If Bellah's 1964 essay on religious evolution would have considered "Sheilaism" as a fascinating example of the infinite possibilities opened up by the modern stage of religious evolution, in *Habits* it came out as the epitome of a "personally impoverished and socially impotent" kind of spiritualism upon which nothing could be built—that is, as the perfect religious correlate to the first language of individualism.[20]

To Sheilaism and authoritarian or fundamentalist congregations, the Habits group opposed Bob's thinly disguised Episcopalian parish, rechristened as "St. Stephen's." In their description, the members of this progressive, committed Californian community of memory shared the millennia-long history of Christianity and a structure of reciprocal obligations emerging from communal worship and sacramental life. St. Stephen's stood as an example and a symbol of what could be done: clearly, the second language of biblical "healthy individualism" could emerge only from an eventual activation of those women and men of faith who not only tried to achieve "an intelligent reappropriation [of tradition] illuminated by historical and theological reflection," but who were also eager to participate in national and political life as exemplars of what Martin Marty called the "public church"—mainline Protestants, progressive Jews, and post-conciliar Catholics.[21]

This new version of the argument for religious activism, which Bellah had been championing since the Weil Lectures of 1971, quickly sank into the polemic on the "return to religion" started some ten years earlier by the critics of *The Cultural Contradictions of Capitalism*. As Daniel Bell's book elaborated the classic theme of the weakening of religion as a source of meaning in modern society, its thesis—"What religion can restore is the continuity of generations, returning us to the existential predicaments which are the ground of humility and care for others"—had been interpreted as an unrealistic call to go back to a perfectly integrated, if nonexistent, past. In fact, immediately after his paean to religion, Bell had added that "such a continuity cannot be manufactured, nor a cultural revolution engineered," a point repeated both in his "1978 Foreword" and in an interview published in 1983, where he expressed his preference for "redemptive religions" emerging from lived experience and "based on mediating institutions" in opposition to a forced reenactment of old models.[22]

While the polemic had become stale well before the publication of *Habits of the Heart*, socialist philosopher Barbara Ehrenreich accused the Habits group of being "unbearably patronizing" when advocating "religion for everyone else." As Bellah later noted, Ehrenreich was wrong on all fronts. On the one hand, the members of the Habits group had all been raised within religious communities and were more or less regularly practicing their faith in local congregations, so this was not a case of affluent atheists reviving religion as the opium of the people, as Ehrenreich assumed. On the other hand, it had never come to the Habits group, as it had never come to Bell, to force religion upon anybody. Theirs was an argument in favor of public theology and public philosophy—two expressions that Bellah now used interchangeably to indicate not the esoteric activities of professional thinkers, but rather the emergence of "an area of debate," a humble and open-ended search for a "vision" or a type of "political imagination."[23]

Contrary to Ehrenreich's assumption, practiced religion was becoming more and more central in Bob's life. After 1979, his interest in ecclesiology had grown at the expense of both theology and spirituality. This, in turn, had brought him closer to Catholicism: in 1984 he participated in the drafting process of the American bishops' pastoral letter on the economy, and supported their effort to lobby the US government to avoid armed involvement in Nicaragua. At the same time, his confidence in declaring his own membership of the Episcopal Church and speaking in public as a Christian had visibly grown. Bellah now presented himself as a public philosopher and theologian rooted in a particular faith, one who saw his "ministry" in bringing his "intellectual training to a relationship with my faith in a way that can speak to other people."

As his interest in academic journals waned, he became a contributing editor of the orthodox Catholic *New Oxford Review*, and published regularly in *Commonweal*, Martin Marty's *Christian Century*, the interreligious Jewish progressive journal *Tikkun*, and *Radix*, a Christian cultural magazine edited in Berkeley.[24]

In May 1986, Bob articulated his idea of what being a Christian meant in contemporary America during a lecture given in Tokyo to a largely non-Christian audience. Being a believer, he began, was to be "counter-cultural" in the United States as it was in Japan, for it required individuals to combine private cultivation with public involvement. A Christian life was built on three pillars: the Bible as an intricate text in need of constant study and interpretation; the Church as the community of those who shared the form of life sustained by, and sustaining, the Book; and the Sacraments as the living enactment of the Truth, a way to embody the Word around which all life should be organized. As he revealed in an interview with Leonard Freeman, Bob now considered communal worship as the most enriching moment of his week. Accordingly, when Teruko and Albert M. Craig lost their daughter Sarah in 1992, he sent them a long letter in which he spoke of Tillich, hope, and the mystery of being wholly dependent upon the Grace of God, but also emphasized the value of practice: "I have long since come to think that in religion it is what we do and not what we think that matters," he wrote. "So if sitting helps Al or going to mass helps Teruko, don't worry about whether it is true or not."[25]

In the heated atmosphere of the cultural wars, being a declared religious intellectual caused Bob some trouble. In February 1986, for example, he participated in a meeting on the teaching of ethics in higher education at the University of Michigan, Ann Arbor, where he was also expected to preach at the First Baptist Church. After a rather uneventful speech, Bellah was attacked by a young professor of American history, who put him on a par with Jerry Falwell: "You shouldn't be teaching at the University of California at Berkeley," said the discussant, to the amusement of his largely secular audience. "You should be at Notre Dame or, better yet, Bob Jones University." Ironically, this muscular display of what Bellah had once called "Enlightenment fundamentalism" was oblivious to the fact that Bob's combination of Christian faith and leftist politics would create much more serious problems were he to speak in front of an evangelical or fundamentalist public—indeed, he had never been (and would never be) invited to speak at Bob Jones or Falwell's Liberty University.[26]

At the same time, Bellah's contribution to a forum on Catholicism and American exceptionalism published in the *New Oxford Review* in 1987 showed that he maintained his personal integrity even when writing in conservative venues. Instead of focusing, as requested, on the recent cases of Archbishop Raymond Hunthausen and theologian Charles E. Curran, Bellah employed his few pages to discuss a taboo he held particularly dear—gay marriage. If traditions are to be living organisms, he wrote, the duty of those who have them in custody is to relate them to an ever-changing world instead of freezing them in a particular historical form. In the case of gays, Bob felt that the prohibition of homosexual acts recently reaffirmed by the Vatican had hitherto denied the possibility "that two persons of the same sex [could] love each other, commit themselves to each other, and sustain stable, permanent, and faithful relationships." The Church's obsession with sexual practices, in other words, prevented Catholic homosexuals from entering into what *Habits of the Heart* had celebrated as practices of commitment, love, and care.[27]

As shown by the letters and Bob's reply published in later issues of the *Review*, his ideas on homosexuality were "not in harmony" with the habits of the heart of the journal's readership and editorial team, who obviously knew nothing of his personal story. Little worried by the conflict, Bellah repeated his point framing it in a wider appraisal of the Christian view of the family as a noncontractual, lasting set of reciprocal obligations. Apart from this small bump, however, the road to a growingly intense collaboration between the distinguished Episcopalian author of *Habits of the Heart*, the hierarchy of the Catholic Church, and its more progressive intellectuals was clear and wide, and the 1990s would bring Bellah to appreciate the Church not only as a social actor or a mystical body, but also as the carrier of a specific "imagination," which proved crucial for his own philosophical and political development.[28]

III

It would be wrong to think that with his travels, stock speeches on the malaise of American individualism, and proud assertion of religious identity, Bellah had abdicated scholarly research. Quite the opposite. While he would teach *Habits of the Heart* in his undergraduate classes, in the late 1980s Bob used his graduate courses to tackle more specific theoretical or substantial problems— in fact, as his graduate seminars focused, over the years, on Hegel, the relation of sociology and theology, Max Weber, George Herbert Mead, and Habermas's *Theory of Communicative Action*, "specific" is no more than a euphemism.[29]

It was during the graduate course of 1989 that the drafts of some chapters from the new collective endeavor of the Habits group were first presented.

Given their growing fame, Bob and his coauthors had easily gotten a four-year extension of the original "Moral Basis" grant from the National Endowment for the Humanities and had immediately started working on the sequel to *Habits of the Heart*, this time dedicated to the analysis American institutions. Their prospective volume had soon been optioned by a commercial press, New York City's Random House, whose astronomical advance of $250,000 they split rigorously in equal parts. Work proceeded apace: in the spring of 1987 the new project had a working title, "The Good Society," a tentative table of contents, and some drafted sections. Two years later Bob could circulate to his rather skeptical students no fewer than six complete chapters.[30]

While the Habits group was busy working on its second book, the intellectual climate at the intersection of social science and public philosophy was rapidly changing. A handful of months before *Habits* came out, philosopher Michael Sandel had first used the adjective "communitarian" to present *Liberalism and Its Critics*, a reader including selections from Charles Taylor, Alasdair MacIntyre, Michael Walzer, Peter Berger, Michael Oakeshott, and Hannah Arendt. In his introduction, Sandel described the "growing challenge" of "communitarian critics" inspired by Aristotle, Hegel, and civic republicanism against utilitarianism, libertarianism, and neo-Kantian liberalism. Before long, Princeton philosopher Amy Gutmann attacked this "new" communitarianism on the grounds that any revival of the civic republican tradition would bring back majoritarian rule and, as she called it, "Salem." Fed by liberals, who defended their philosophy of individual rights from what they perceived as untimely, misguided, or even authoritarian alternatives, the polemic gained steam and the perimeter of communitarianism was thus expanded retroactively to include the five authors of *Habits of the Heart*.[31]

The first to call the work of the Habits group "communitarian" was Christopher Lasch, one of the few intellectuals who used the label as an accolade rather than an insult. An early enthusiast of *Habits*, the author of *The Culture of Narcissism* was repeatedly asked to review it, and finally had a highly appreciative piece published in the progressive journal *In These Times*.[32] On April 26, 1985, Lasch dedicated his keynote speech before the Iowa Sociological Association to a perceptive reading of the book, which stressed the connection between Ronald Reagan's rugged individualism and the critique of expressivism advanced by the Habits group. In particular, he showed how the "two languages thesis" transcended both "values talk" and the "cult of the small community" through an imaginative recovery of the idea of tradition as an ongoing conversation introduced by the German philosopher Hans-Georg

Gadamer—a point much appreciated by Bellah, who wrote to Lasch that he had "understood us better than we have understood ourselves." In 1986, when a heavily rewritten version of the paper was published, the cultural historian could confidently assert that "no other book [had] done so much [as *Habits*] to bring the communitarian critique of liberalism to general attention."[33]

At that point, however, the ideological landscape was shifting in an unexpected, or perhaps all-too-expected, direction. Between Reagan's second inaugural and the publication of *Habits of the Heart*, a group of "New Democrats" had created the Democratic Leadership Council, a centrist caucus aimed at recapturing the vote of the White middle class. Wooing the latter through its patent dissatisfaction with both parties, the council acted as though the end of ideology had to be brought inside the Democratic party against its "old" liberal elites, among whom were some of Bellah's favorites, like Jesse Jackson and Mario Cuomo. A crucial step in this march toward the center of the political spectrum was *The Politics of Evasion*, a document presented at the Council's 1989 annual meeting by a professor of public affairs at the University of Maryland, William A. Galston. The paper described old-guard liberals as living in denial of reality: a new centrist approach was needed on the part of the next Democratic nominee, who would win the presidential election only if he succeeded in conveying "a clear understanding of, and identification with, the social values and moral sentiments of average Americans."[34]

Later in 1989 Galston met with Amitai Etzioni, a sociologist from George Washington University who had hitherto been extraneous to the debate between liberals and communitarians. Once dubbed "the everything expert" by *Time* magazine, Etzioni had taught at Columbia University for twenty years and had briefly served as an advisor to Jimmy Carter. In 1982 the *Washington Post* had described him as "frightened by the Moral Majority's proposals, but equally frightened by the exaltation of the individual he sees in 'this laissez-faire conservatism . . . which says we should all be raring-to-go individuals, and which in the process does not maintain the ethical foundation which is the essential underpinning of any civil society.'" Etzioni had spelled out his ideas for "rebuilding America" in an aptly titled book, *An Immodest Agenda*, and in *The Moral Dimension*, a critique of neoclassical economics from the standpoint of what he called "socio-economics."[35]

Galvanized by their meeting, Galston and Etzioni convened a small group of scholars to discuss principles and concrete policy proposals. The group included Berkeley sociologist Philip Selznick; political theorists Benjamin Barber, Jane Mansbridge, and Thomas Spragens; Harvard Law School's Mary Ann

Glendon; and, from the Habits group, Bill Sullivan, whom Etzioni later described as a "soft-spoken, modest and solid philosopher."[36] The first outcome of the Etzioni–Galston connection was a quarterly journal, the *Responsive Community*, whose editorial board included public intellectuals such as James Fishkin, Jean Elshtain, Nathan Glazer, Martha Nussbaum, and, for the first time since his stint as a collegiate editor of *New Foundations* in the late 1940s, Bob Bellah.

The original group issued the "Responsive Communitarian Platform" in November 1991—that is, one year before the 1992 presidential election. Among its signatories were intellectuals, politicians, and activists of disparate persuasions: David Riesman, John W. Gardner, Betty Friedan, Raul Yzaguirre, Enola Aird, Harvey Cox, Albert Hirschman, Richard John Neuhaus, Francis Fukuyama, Orlando Patterson, Adlai Stevens, and, obviously enough, Sullivan and Bellah.[37] At the center of the document stood the need to balance individual rights with a renewed sense of social responsibility, the latter to be learned, and practiced, in the context of an empowered civil society founded on "moral education and character formation." The manifesto explicitly repudiated a winner-take-all conception of majority rule—one of the bogeymen of liberal critics of communitarianism. Calling instead for direct participation, the platform advanced a number of policy suggestions on parental leave, domestic disarmament, national and local civil service, and campaign financing.[38]

As an alternative to the culture wars of the late 1980s, communitarianism resonated with the evolving zeitgeist of the post-Reagan era—years later Etzioni wrote that the movement's core group, in which he included Bill Sullivan, gave more than eight hundred "public lectures, press interviews, radio call-in shows, TV appearances, and briefings of public leaders" from 1991 to 2000. Indeed, the fall of the Berlin Wall in December 1989 and the impending collapse of the Soviet Union presented the United States and its forty-first president, George H. W. Bush, not only with the opportunity to create a "new world order," but also to rethink some of the domestic excesses of the previous eight years. While upholding Reagan's "tough on crime" agenda and high defense spending, in his inaugural address Bush pledged "to make kinder the face of the nation and gentler the face of the world," and talked of volunteer work as "a thousand points of light . . . that are spread like stars throughout the Nation, doing good," thus embracing in some ways a community-oriented rhetoric. It looked as though communitarianism, which just a few years earlier had been dubbed "a fat but attractive kid," was now running fast against the "well trained, lean athlete" of rugged individualism.[39]

Although Etzioni had retrospectively enrolled the authors of *Habits of the Heart* in the communitarian movement in an article published in the *Washington Post* on January 20, 1991, Bellah's stance was far more ambivalent than it appeared there. He had easily understood that the appeal to a new "vital center" amounted to a shift toward the right of the political spectrum, which also entailed a clear reluctance to criticize the American middle class—a development he found rather unpalatable. This clearly emerged from the singular web of assonances and tensions between Bellah's contribution to a *New Republic* symposium on the 1992 presidential election, written in April 1991, and a famous discourse given by the Democratic Leadership Council chairman, Arkansas governor William Jefferson Clinton, a few weeks later. Repeating the counsel he had given President Carter at Camp David, Bob suggested that the next Democratic nominee should, "for once, tell the truth." This meant, quite simply, "to throw away the 'search for the center,'" and tell Americans that they had "gotten exactly the government [they] deserved. It is time," he added, "to examine our values and our institutions and make some fundamental changes in them."[40]

Interestingly, Clinton used the same vocabulary when he said that the nation needed "at least one party that is not afraid to tell the people the truth." His truth, however, was miles away from Bob's: the next Democratic nominee, he continued, had to campaign on "a message that touches everybody, that makes sense to everybody, that goes beyond the stale orthodoxies of left and right, one that resonates with the real concerns of ordinary Americans, with their hopes and their fears." The "very burdened middle class" he was speaking to was undoubtedly better than the elites who (mis)represented it, and had already transcended outdated oppositions in the direction of a new pragmatic language: "Our new choice plainly rejects the old categories and false alternatives they impose," he announced. "Is what I just said to you liberal or conservative? The truth is, it is both, and it is different." Again, while Clinton's rhetoric echoed the very conclusion of *Habits of the Heart*, its final destination was located at some distance from the book's Promised Land.[41]

18

Looking for the Good Society

UNITED STATES OF AMERICA, 1991–1992

ON SEPTEMBER 19, 1991, Robert N. Bellah and Ann Swidler took part in a sober party organized at the Graduate Theological Union to celebrate the launch of *The Good Society*. A blend of hope and concern filled the air: six years after the publication of *Habits of the Heart*, the new book had to find its way within the new intellectual and political climate that its predecessor had contributed to creating—and which had, in turn, much changed the perception of the work of the Habits group. The book's richness and subtlety had been almost completely lost in the dramatization of the debate between liberals and communitarians, which had translated its nuanced portrayal of America's four cultural traditions into a forthright critique of utilitarian individualism by a small "communitarian community" of scholars. Not only, then, was *Habits* by itself a tough act to follow, but the *Habits* of 1991 was nothing like the *Habits* of 1985.[1]

Distorted or not, the ideas advanced in the first book remained *the* point of reference for *The Good Society*, if only because its ideal readers were those individuals who had recognized and scrutinized themselves in the mirror of *Habits of the Heart*. This in turn presented the group with a number of challenges, some related to content and some to style. The new project left cultural analysis behind to focus on *institutions*—the very object that an American whose first language was that of moral individualism found hard to perceive, let alone comprehend. Indeed, *The Good Society* repeatedly decried a sort of culturally acquired blindness toward institutions as socially patterned ways of doing things. The latter, the Habits group told its public of concerned citizens, not only impinge on individual action from without, but also structure and influence it from within. Although "we live through institutions," most of us are unable to recognize them—the parallel with the asymmetry between the rich relational lives of the protagonists of *Habits* and their inability to fully live through them was clear.[2]

In the book, this mismatch between social relations and their description took the form of a particular cultural lag. After the rise of corporate and governmental organizations in the mid-nineteenth century, the apparently coherent version of John Locke's liberalism from which the early phase of the expansion of the United States had gotten most of its steam was now hopelessly inadequate to make sense of society. Where a Lockean would see individual autonomy and a natural harmony of interests, the Habits group saw connectedness and interdependence on a number of local, national, and international levels. Where a Lockean would see free enterprise and self-regulating markets, the Habits group saw an increasingly opaque government, whose interventionism was nonetheless essential for the economy to function. After the end of World War Two, the urgency of creating a covert governmental structure to counter Stalin's alleged might intensified these tendencies, as public and private organizations became less and less accountable.[3]

This cultural lag was itself a product of "the everyday practices of work, school, and politics" of the 1950s, which had trained Americans to think of themselves as consumers in the market and claimants in the political arena. "In our great desire to free the individual for happiness," the Habits group wrote, "we Americans have tried to make a social world that would serve the self." And yet, this ambitious plan had failed: "The folly of trying to operate with Lockean principles in an un-Lockean world" produced predatory corporations, rising inequalities, and sinking performativity in the globalized economy. While American capitalism suffered for its inability to see beyond the short term, all other institutions from federal and state government to the family and the educational system were being colonized by the logic of the market, as cost-benefit analysis, zero-based budgeting, divorce *à la carte*, and the transformation of universities into centers of professional training gained the upper hand over public-oriented policies, charters, and habits.[4]

Given the book's focus on institutions, finding the right style for *The Good Society* was no easy task. Model individuals similar to those presented in *Habits* could be used only in the first chapter, which starkly pictured a number of ordinary Americans expressing their dismay about institutions and their inner workings. All other chapters, each devoted to one social sphere, needed powerful images to put immaterial relational patterns into words—metaphors similar to the imaginative interpretation of the Monopoly boardgame presented in the chapter on political economy. Instead of potent analogies, however, the rest of the book followed a rather standard pattern: a historical account of the development of one institutional area, a diagnosis of its current decline, and a few concrete proposals for improvement. Together with its highly normative title, this tripartite structure gave *The Good Society* a rather preachy tone—in a sense, Bellah was back to the jeremiad, even if his criticism targeted invisible institutions and impersonal systems rather than particular social ills and groups.[5]

Stylistic problems notwithstanding, *The Good Society* was at the same time bolder and weaker than *Habits*. On the side of boldness, the group pressed on against the idea that the solution of social problems should be left to experts and their technological tricks. Second, Bellah and his coauthors also accepted some of the critiques leveled at their treatment of minorities in *Habits*, and made women, the underclass, and African Americans an integral part of the book—Jesse Jackson, for example, appeared on page 14 as an embodiment of the promise and the failure of Bob's beloved civil rights movement. Third, the book depicted the end of the Cold War as not only a half-victory, for the Soviet Union had largely defeated itself, but also a risky circumstance, should Americans unwisely think that yet another "American century" was about to begin. Fourth, the language was sometimes bleaker than that of *Habits*— "Americans fool themselves when they think they can strengthen democracy by weakening government" was a sentence that would have been out of place in the first book.[6]

Last but not least, *The Good Society* was *much* bolder than *Habits* in the policy proposals it advanced to fix the mismatch between Lockean ideas and un-Lockean institutions. If economic participation, substantive justice, and a sense of having a "calling" to one's job came straight from the first book, the plan for a new body of laws on the public purpose of corporations, the request to outlaw campaign advertising on radio and television and limit private money to candidates (and perhaps replace them with public contributions), together with the application of the principle of subsidiarity at every governmental level from city to global, were all new. In accord with the group's culturalist approach and their conviction that the common good could emerge only from a revamped public discussion, all these proposals were little more than sketches. Even with these strictures, and even if Bob and his coauthors continued to address their message to those "reflexive strata" of the White upper middle class portrayed in *Habits*, the tone was undoubtedly more radical than that of the first book.[7]

At the same time, *The Good Society* was looser than *Habits*, and its seven chapters were more diverse in tone and style than those of its predecessor, with some of them using historical and "macro" data and others almost wholly built on individual interviews or anecdotes—Tipton's chapter on religion, for example, made liberal use of his conversations with church activists, pastors, and theologians, while Madsen's chapter on international relations, focused mostly on the defeat of postwar liberalism and modernization theory, was based on the experiences of Ford Foundation officers, missionaries, and radical academics who had devoted their lives to the study of the Far East.

The book, and in particular its appendix, also sported a clear penchant for a number of public intellectuals from the early twentieth century—Walter Lippman, John Dewey, John Courtney Murray, Karl Polanyi, and especially H. Richard Niebuhr, who replaced his much more dramatic brother, Reinhold Niebuhr. Neglecting more contemporary thinkers had a double performative effect. On the one hand, it diverted the reader's attention from the continuing dispute on communitarianism, its ideas and its policy suggestions—although, as even a quick comparison would show, the similarities between *The Good Society* and the Responsive Communitarian Platform were many and substantial. On the other hand, it pointed back to a time when harsh intellectual and political confrontations—such as those between Dewey and Lippman—were made possible by the existence of a modicum of consensus on basic principles: "Argument involved disagreement, but to disagree is to share enough in common to have something to disagree about."[8]

In the context of the culture wars of the early 1990s, when the common ground between political adversaries and intellectual foes was getting thinner by the hour, it was vital to avoid having one's ideas labeled, as that would condemn them to a measure of typecasting that was probably unprecedented in America during peacetime. As shown by the early reviews of *The Good Society*, however, Bob, Bill, Ann, Steve, and Dick had been both too optimistic and too pessimistic at the same time.

I

Given all of the differences between *Habits of the Heart* and *The Good Society*, the response to the new book was ambivalent to say the least. Almost all reviews cited *Habits* at least once—a predictable but significant difference with respect to six years earlier, when Bellah's past work had almost been ignored. Even when they praised the book for its timeliness in raising a series of crucial questions in an election year, critics expressed their longing for the group's "prodigious gifts for interpreting everyday speech," which were "seldom exercised" in *The Good Society*. They also portrayed *Habits* as *the* book that had given 1980s leftists a reason to be proud of being American during the Reagan era, implying that *The Good Society* had failed to follow suit. Some readers compared the two efforts with respect to style, with *Habits*—the sentimental, critical, almost pop-sociological sensation—clearly winning over the colder, turgid *Good Society*. All in all, most reviewers saw the latter as "good but less lively" than *Habits* and criticized the inadequacies of its historical and empirical data—in this last regard, the new book was variously described as "thinly documented," "mushy," or even "bland and vague."[9]

The reaction of professional sociologists was harsher than it had been toward *Habits of the Heart*. For starters, this time the *American Journal of Sociology*, *Social Forces*, and the *Journal for the Scientific Study of Religion* followed the lead of the *American Sociological Review* and just ignored *The Good Society*. This silence, however, may have been an asset for the book, for when the reviews came in, they were anything but positive. In a symposium published in *Contemporary Sociology*, Steven Lukes described Bellah and his coauthors as "Durkheimians" in search of a "thick consensus," and cast doubts upon their view of the sociologist as a "lay preacher." A few pages later, Frances Fox Piven compared *The Good Society* to a verbose seminar crippled by its almost complete neglect of power dynamics. Talking about institutions without pointing to potential sites of conflict, wrote Piven, was "frivolous," as would be asking for more political participation without a thorough analysis of the likely disappointment that ineffective commitment would produce in the underclass.[10]

A number of commentators also expressed their discontent at the vapidity of the book's policy proposals. Indeed, Bob and his coauthors had tried to anticipate such critiques in the conclusion, organized as both a summary and a final reframing of their argument. Quoting the work of Eugene Rochberg-Halton and Mihaly Csikszentmihalyi on "the flow," that condition of full involvement in which individuals can truly unleash their potential, the Habits group defined the ability to pay attention as a general virtue of sorts. Attention and interconnectedness, they wrote, go hand in hand. "Warm," caring families, for example, were the most conducive to civic engagement, although present familial arrangements needed to be changed toward a more a balanced division of labor between men and women. In another poignant passage, the five authors stressed the importance of being rooted in one physical and social locale within a general understanding of the relationships between different institutions, inspired by the Catholic principle of subsidiarity—"higher-level associations such as the state should never replace what lower-lever associations can do effectively," and they should empower the latter to better do their job.[11]

The most obvious and dangerous form of "distraction" was represented by the belief that "the value of persons is determined by how much money they make," which the Habits group contrasted with the classical ideal of "cultivation" as a practice of care, attention, and interconnectedness. It was crucial, then, to find "a social and environmental balance, a recovery of meaning and purpose in our lives together, giving attention to the natural and cultural endowment" for the benefit of future generations. In its final appeal for a "politics of generativity," the Habits group combined some of its intuitions with the hopeful spirit of one of the giants of the post-Soviet era—the dissident writer Václav Havel, who had spent years in prison under the Communist regime and was now the first president of free Czechoslovakia.[12]

The Habits group saw no shortcut to the end: as argued by Walter Lippman in 1937, the "higher law" of the good society was "a progressive discovery of men striving to civilize themselves, and . . . its scope and implications are a gradual revelation that is by no means completed." This in turn, required not only a moment of massive self-education on the part of ordinary citizens and the creation of new kinds of interpersonal trust, but also a radical reframing of "what human happiness really is." When combined with the policy proposals sketched in the book, this position looked neither tepid nor moderate. In fact, as written by the president of the Carnegie Council on Ethics and International Relations, Robert J. Myers, "to accomplish the institutional reform" required by Bellah and his coauthors, "nothing short of *creating a new man*, or at minimum, raising the human consciousness to new levels of insight and action" was needed. The problem, for Myers, was that such a societal and anthropological revolution could be brought about only by an exceptionally charismatic leader.[13]

While somewhat critical, Myers maintained a fair tone and, most of all, a positive interest in *The Good Society* and the ideas of its authors—an interest that was later confirmed when he participated in one of the summer institutes organized by Bellah and his colleagues at the Berkeley Graduate Theological Union. The main problem with Myers's review, however, was the company it kept. As a part of a "double-barreled action" deliberately aimed at striking the Habits group, the paper was published in the journal *Society* together with a straightforward attack written by Andrew Greeley, whose 1985 review of *Habits* had been remarkably critical of the work of the group. Described by the editor and publisher of *Society*, Irving L. Horowitz, as "biting, satirical, and, above all, sociological," to the eyes of those who loved or respected Bob's work the review just looked "vicious."[14]

Greeley first went back to *Habits of the Heart* and presented a number of sociological indicators that seemed to challenge some of the empirical arguments advanced in the book. Doing sociology with figures collected "from faculty coffee tables and feature pieces in the elite national media," he joked, was a rather pleasant endeavor, but it was something that proper social scientists could not afford to do. The Chicago sociologist then equated this "sociology without data" to *The Good Society*'s "sociology without colleagues"—from his point of view, the new book displayed a "deliberately mushy" scholarship guilty of ignoring the best available empirical research on its themes and subjects. Citing a number of sociological authorities whose absence, in his opinion, brought discredit to the book, Greeley identified Bellah's secret as "a combination of intellectual brilliance and deep moral concern. If you have these characteristics," he concluded with one last jab, "who needs data!"[15]

II

In all their brutality and malice, Greeley's words on *The Good Society* were by no means typical. Graceful reviews abounded—chiefly, but not only, in mainstream print media. In the *New York Times*, for example, the prominent African American philosopher and activist Cornel West rated the new book as superior to *Habits*, an opinion shared by Corey Blake in *Tikkun*. Historian David B. Danbom confessed he had read the book nodding in agreement and feeling guilty for his own neglect of institutions, while feminist rabbi Susan Schnur wrote in *USA Today* that *The Good Society* contained a "vast, invigorating load of ideas" that, if properly disseminated, might "change the course of our country." Thanks to this good publicity and a well-orchestrated campaign, the book enjoyed a great deal of exposure. As its best known author, Bellah again became the object of countless invitations to give lectures. Helped by Melanie, who assisted him to free up some of his time for study and reflection, Bob started to charge sensibly higher speaking fees than before—a circumstance which, combined with a string of wise investments and a raise in salary from the University of California, gave him an unprecedented measure of affluence.[16]

Flattering and profitable as it seemed, such a hectic schedule had its drawbacks. On the one hand, in the mid- to late 1980s nonstop traveling had sometimes brought the members of the Habits group to the brink of exhaustion—a situation that this time they would have rather avoided. On the other hand, a change in pace and scope was also needed for theoretical reasons: "Genuine moral conversation," wrote Steve Tipton in 1986, did "indeed require a circle of persons small enough and possessed of enough time and learning to permit an equal and alternating balance of participation in turning a topic around and around." Besides public lecturing, then, the campaign for the new book might profit from the creation of face-to-face settings. As to the ideal participants in this small, intimate endeavor, *The Good Society* contained a clear indication: "One of the purposes of this book," read the appendix, "is to generate a lively dialogue among different types of institutions and to cultivate the practical . . . reason that would make it possible." In other words, the Habits group should do its best to target the top and intermediate echelons of public and private organizations.[17]

With this idea in mind, in August 1989—that is, a good two years before the publication of *The Good Society*—Bellah had written to Jeanne Knoerle at the Lilly Endowment to submit a three-year project aimed at amplifying the impact of the book. In partnership with the Graduate Theological Union and its Center for Ethics and Social Policy, now chaired by Harlan Stelmach, the Habits group would organize a yearly conference aimed at governmental, civic, and religious leaders, and then a summer school "designed to help those who would teach classes or lead discussion groups" using *The Good Society* and *Habits of the Heart*. The project was going to be the swan song for the group: a "round three" was out of question, added Bellah, but this small example of commitment and (temporary) institution building was what their next book was all about. Money was needed to implement such a complex plan, and the group's final request amounted, all told, to $337,800.[18]

The Lilly Endowment, which had already awarded the Habits group a grant for the research and writing of *The Good Society*, had responded positively and had soon provided nearly $350,000 for the program. After a long period of preparation, the first Good Society Summer Institute took place at the Church Divinity School of the Pacific in July 1991, with twenty-one fellows selected among sixty aspirants. The participants included academics, clergymen, activists, administrators, and educators, many of whom already had some connection with one or more members of the Habits group. Armed with a bound copy of the galleys of *The Good Society*, they spent most of their time and meals together, as is customary with summer schools. Formal morning classes alternated with informal discussions—especially between the "students," for the

Habits group also taught an afternoon course at the nearby New College Berkeley. Despite the tight schedule, a strong esprit de corps matured among the participants, who were inspired to compose a song to the tune of "The Battle Hymn of the Republic" and perform it on their last night in Berkeley for the entertainment of their teachers:

Mine eyes have seen the vision of the Good Society,
I got it at a conference at UC Berkeley.
There were Bellah, Madsen, Swidler, Tipton, Sullivan in sling
They all kept talking on.

Glory, glory institutions
Get to know their convolutions
Conversation, transformation
We all kept talking on.

They taught us we should learn to love our Niebuhr as our self.
And take Dewey, Peirce, and Lippman down from off the dusty shelf.
And throw away the Locke upon the Habits of our Heart
They all kept talking on.

Glory, glory institutions
Get to know their convolutions
Conversation, transformation
We all kept talking on.

We've got problems in the church and in the university.
And the market's made an awful mess of home and polity.
And unless we rediscover real sustainability—
We'll just keep talking on.

Glory, glory institutions
Get to know their convolutions
Conversation, transformation
The vision marches on.[19]

The first conference, held in November 1991 under the title "Sources of Public Philosophy in America," was also a success. Among the group of invited participants were Larry Rasmussen of the National Council of Churches; the dean of the Fuller Seminary in Pasadena, Richard Mouw; Michael Lerner from *Tikkun*; and the founder of the Institute for the Study of Civic Values and now

FIGURE 18.1. Ann Swidler, Richard Madsen, Robert Bellah, Steven Tipton, and William Sullivan at the first Good Society Fall Conference, Berkeley, November 1991. (RBPP)

director of the City of Philadelphia's Office of Housing and Community De-velopment, Edward Schwartz. The overall tone was far more academic than that of the Summer Institute: Eugene Rochberg-Halton spoke of the para-doxes of antifoundationalism, Christopher Lasch compared communitarian-ism with the American populist tradition, and Cornel West dug deep into the controversy between Walter Lippman and John Dewey. In the most spirited of the three speeches, West also told the Habits group that in their second book "the gestures are there but they are not concretely fleshed out"; at the same time, he agreed with their idea that the most important duty of intel-lectuals was to prepare the public, as Bob also repeated at the conference, for the next Rosa Parks.[20]

West's second suggestion, that of "working with the elites in place," was also all-important. It echoed a recent piece where Bellah interpreted the rise of Ross Perot's populism as still another example of American anti-institutionalism—or even, borrowing from Harold Bloom's recent book on American religion, of self-centered gnosticism. Since a society without elites was a sociological impossibility, wrote Bob, critical intellectuals should focus, among other goals, on turning selfish oligarchies into a proper "establishment" oriented to the common good. In this sense, the Summer Institute and the Fall Conference gave the Habits group a chance to (try to) steer the dissemination of their ideas, and allowed them to reach a small cadre of opinion leaders who could later spread their message to wider audiences. As shown by the letters published in the first issue of the *Good Society Newsletter*, the project seemed to be on the right track.[21]

III

As agreed by all participants, the opening meeting of the first Good Society Summer Institute was captured on film by a renowned crew, that of Bill Moyers's production company. Born in Texas in 1934, Moyers had studied journalism and theology before becoming a Baptist minister and a top aide of Senator Lyndon B. Johnson, and then a deputy director of the Peace Corps. After Kennedy's assassination, he had been called to the White House as a special assistant to the new president and later his chief of staff and press secretary. In 1967 Moyers clashed with Johnson about the Vietnam War and started a career in journalism, first as the publisher of *Newsday* and then as a successful television personality, authoring productions like *The Bill Moyers Journal, The Power of Myth*, and documentaries for CBS and PBS.[22]

An early enthusiast of *The Broken Covenant*, Moyers had made ample use of *Habits of the Heart* in his late-1980s speaking engagements and had at some point consulted with Bellah about adapting the book for television. Indeed, in 1987 the Jessie Ball duPont Fund awarded a matching grant of $375,000 to the Episcopal Radio and Television Foundation for the purpose of drafting a script and a budget for the *Habits* documentary. An old friend from Bob's days as an undergraduate at Harvard, Murray Lerner, was put in charge of the production. When an additional $40,000 came from Emory University, the Academy Award–winning director started shooting a first batch of interviews with Bob, Steve Tipton, and some of the therapists consulted for *Habits*. When Lerner pulled out, the project was entirely taken up by Moyers and writer-producer Megan Coswell.[23]

At around the same time, Bill Moyers also shot a long conversation with Bellah, which was aired on September 27, 1988, as an episode of *A World of Ideas*—a well-known PBS series, which also featured sociologists Peter L. Berger and William Julius Wilson, philosophers Martha Nussbaum and John Searle, communitarian law professor Mary Ann Glendon, writers Isaac Asimov and Tom Wolfe, and the famed pediatrician T. Berry Brazelton, who coincidentally had taken care of the four Bellah girls in Cambridge some thirty years earlier. "How can we give interdependence," began Bob, "a moral meaning? Interdependence without moral meaning is terrifying." In an edited transcript of the interview published in 1989, Bellah singled out Jesse Jackson as the prime instance of a politician who could speak truthfully of otherwise neglected problems. When asked to spell out what all Americans had in common, Bellah pointed to "the belief in the inherent dignity and value of the individual," but also warned that such ideals could be achieved only through participation in a vital community. "I may be a foolish idealistic, or overly optimistic," he concluded, "but I think there is a growing consensus about some of the most important things"—nuclear disarmament, environmental issues, and the defense of human rights.[24]

Ultimately based on *The Good Society* and titled after it, the documentary was aired in the summer of 1992 as part of the *Listening to America* series: from the economy to the protection of natural resources, from racial injustice to political charisma, Moyers tackled "some questions and problems that get ignored in the course of a political year," alternating the stories of common people and the commentary of academics, journalists, and politicians. The report focused on the search for the common good in two iconic American cities, Atlanta and Los Angeles, in two sixty-minute episodes. The footage of the first meeting of the Good Society Summer Institute was used as a general introduction, and brief exchanges between Moyers and Robert Bellah closed both segments. While the documentary was mostly inspired by the new book—"To move America forward," said the journalist, "we have to work together to reform the institutions that provide us with our common ground"— the spotlight mostly fell on grassroots and third-sector organizations, rather than the corporations, local government, and educational institutions that constituted the focus of *The Good Society*.[25]

Following this general inspiration, the first episode featured the stories of ministers and realtors collaborating with the Atlanta City government and an interview with former president Jimmy Carter about his volunteer work on behalf of the poor. The second episode moved to the sunny place where Bob had languished before being born again in Cambridge, and where his daughter Jenny was now enjoying a successful career as a corporate lawyer. If *The Good Society* had depicted Los Angeles as the epitome of the regional metropolis, it was now shown in its slow recovery from the wounds of the Rodney King riots of April 1992. From Korean businessmen and African American activists to

Hispanic Catholic priests, most of the citizens featured in the documentary belonged to racial minorities. Whites, however, had their poignant moments, as when psychologist Bob Lupton and his wife told about their decision to leave the suburbs and move back to Atlanta, some years earlier: "We were as fearful of the inner city as any suburban family would be," Lupton said, "scared to death that it would be a harmful thing for our children. The reality," he concluded, "has been is that it's the most—it's the richest experience we could give our boys."

The documentary's last soundbite was classic Bellah: "I'll tell you this, and this maybe also sound a bit preachy," Bob said in the best of his prophetic tones, "but I believe it. That is, *we are standing under judgment.* The way of life that we have embarked upon is so destructive of the environment, of the lives of a large number of people on this planet, of the lives of many people in our own society, that it cannot long continue. There's something out there, I think, called a 'moral law' that does operate, maybe not always quite as quickly and as evenly as we would like, but the price for ignoring it is going to be a heavy price. We're already paying it," he concluded, "We've seen the signs of what we're paying right now."[26]

The two *Good Society* episodes were aired on August 4 and 11, 1992—that is, right between the Democratic and the Republican national conventions. Given all Bob's apocalypticism and distaste for centrism, his message still resonated more with Clinton's acceptance speech of July 16, 1992—"We will build an American community again"—than with Pat Buchanan's incendiary tirade at the Republican National Convention. While Bellah considered it important that nobody had "an absolute blueprint [of a good society] that they [could] slam down and say, 'This is it. Take it or leave it,'" Buchanan saw the country devastated by a religious war that could be won only by restoring the order of tradition—plus, obviously enough, free market capitalism. "It is a cultural war, as critical to the kind of nation we shall be as was the Cold War itself," he said in his famous speech, "for this war is for the soul of America." While Robert Bellah appreciated that most Americans wanted "to strengthen the family," Buchanan depicted Bill and Hillary Clinton as a radicals who saw marriage as slavery and supported abortion on demand and free gay marriage. And so on, and on, and on.[27]

Campaigning on what he called "a dynamic but centrist progressive movement of new ideas rooted in traditional American values," and thanks to Ross Perot's successful bid, Bill Clinton won the election of November 3, 1992, and soon appointed the author of "The Politics of Evasion" and cofounder of the communitarian movement, William A. Galston, as his deputy assistant for domestic policy. As the president-elect's speechwriters set out to prepare his inaugural discourse, they slipped a photocopy of "Civil Religion in America" into their briefing book and attentively studied what Robert Bellah had written about the use of religious language in presidential addresses. Thirty years and seven presidents had passed since Bob had given his conference on John F. Kennedy in Tokyo, and while he was not wholly displeased with the outcome of the elections, he knew that he still had a lot of work to do.[28]

19

Time to Leave Again

UNITED STATES OF AMERICA, 1993–2000

MUCH MORE INTERESTED in the practical work inspired by *The Good Society* than in scholarly book reviews, in the early 1990s Robert N. Bellah enjoyed a moment of passionate institutional commitment. The second Good Society Summer Institute was made particularly intense by a distinguished roster of participants—among whom where the president of Concordia College, Paul J. Dovre; the executive director of the Ohio Humanities Council, Oliver Jones; the president of the San Francisco Zen Center, Michael Wenger; and the Franciscan friar and civil rights activist, Louis Vitale. To accommodate and make the best out of such a "power group," the five *Habits* authors took a step back, presenting themselves as "resonance persons"—meaning they were mostly responding to the participants rather than teaching, and the latter did most of the work themselves—and allowing their guests to almost fully manage the week's agenda. The second Fall Conference, dedicated to the emerging world order after the fall of the Soviet Union, aptly held in Berkeley at Halloween 1992, featured some illustrious friends: Daniel Bell, Charles Taylor, and Jean Elshtain.[1]

One year later, another good group of fellows, among them Robert Myers, animated the third Summer Institute. As Bellah wrote to Lilly's Jeanne Knoerle in his final report, this time the Habits group had decided to adopt a more didactic attitude—two years after its publication, it was clear that *The Good Society* was anything but an easy book, and a working knowledge of it could not be taken for granted. The third and final Fall Conference, held in Berkeley on November 13–14, 1993, took up the theme of Bob's own chapter, "Society as Educator." It featured the University of Chicago literary critic Wayne C. Booth, the Pulitzer Prize–nominee author Richard Rodriguez, and the

FIGURE 19.1. Charles Taylor, Robert Bellah, and Daniel Bell at the second Good Society Fall Conference, Berkeley, November 1992. (Courtesy of Graduate Theological Union, Berkeley)

professor of journalism and recent recipient of a MacArthur "genius" grant Michael Schudson. The three-year project had been a success, and the Habits group had had more than one occasion to consider the unforeseen implications of their own work. It was no wonder that, although the possibility of writing a third book had been ruled out, Bob asked for a small extension grant to make sure that he could meet regularly with Dick, Bill, Ann, and Steve to study and reflect together in the coming years.[2]

The early to mid-1990s were also a time of ceaseless traveling and lecturing for Robert Bellah—a "never ending tour" of sorts, whose peak was the invitation from Cardinal Joseph Bernardin to address a plenum of eight hundred Catholic priests from the Archdiocese of Chicago on the theme of "being the Church in America today."[3] By this time, *Habits of the Heart* had firmly regained a central position in most of Bob's speeches. The first book remained vastly more popular than *The Good Society*—as reported in an article based on 1995 data, the difference in sales figures was staggering. Having sold between four and five hundred thousand copies, *Habits* was paired with bestsellers such as Richard Sennett's *The Fall of the Public Man* (published in 1967), Seymour Lipset's *Political Man* (1960), and William Ryan's *Blaming the Victim* (1971).

Only three books written by sociologists had fared better: David Riesman's *The Lonely Crowd* (1951), which sat unmatched at the top, Elliot Liebow's *Tally's Corner* (1967), and Philip Slater's *The Pursuit of Loneliness* (1970). Lower down the list, in three years *The Good Society* had sold "only" seventy thousand copies, similar to volume one of Immanuel Wallerstein's *The Modern World-System* (1974). The "Bible of communitarianism," Etzioni's *The Spirit of Community* reached the twenty-five thousand mark only some decades later.[4]

While Bellah focused mostly on speaking to lay audiences, he also took a leading role in responding to academic critiques. Over the years, his exchanges with Herbert J. Gans, Mark E. Warren, Catherine Zuckert, and Bruce Frohnen testified to his resolve to tackle and rectify what he considered to be careless or biased readings of his solo and collective work. Not that others would always accept his ripostes: while Gans "made good" by citing *Habits* as a prime example of public sociology in his presidential address at the 1989 Meeting of the American Sociological Association, Warren and Zuckert rebuffed Bellah's critiques in print, and Frohnen reproduced his acrimonious attack in his 1996 book, *The New Communitarians and the Crisis of Liberalism*, followed up by another very negative article on Bellah's interpretation of Alexis de Tocqueville one year later. In this realm, Bob's activism and his capacity to remember critiques proved prodigious, as when he cited Greeley's *Society* review essay in a letter written in 1995 to Jeffrey Alexander to censure the latter's assessment of *Habits* as "not only utopian but a bit sociologically naive."[5]

More than individual commentaries, however, what mattered the most was the now routine identification of the Habits group with Etzioni's communitarianism.[6] As stated in *The Good Society* and then in the introduction to the 1996 paperback edition of *Habits of the Heart*, Bellah and his coauthors were miles away from a simplistic understanding of community as either an assemblage of face-to-face relations or a perfectly consensual collectivity—two positions that, in fact, Etzioni did not embrace. Furthermore, they also suffered from the association between the movement and Clinton's growing moderatism, especially after Newt Gingrich's triumph in the 1994 midterm election, when Republicans seized control of the House for the first time in forty years and the president adapted to the new situation by moving further to the right.[7]

If Bob had kept a wait-and-see, but not entirely confident, stance toward Clinton, as the president's first term approached an end he saw no real novelty with respect to policy or, more importantly, compared with the outlook of Clinton's two Republican predecessors. One month before the 1996 election,

Bellah asked the *New York Review of Books* to publish a letter that he and some of his fellow Berkeley sociologists had sent to the president earlier that year, lamenting the end of Aid to Families with Dependent Children. The new act, they said, was "one of the most regressive pieces of legislation passed by any developed society since World War Two," so that a "reform of this so-called reform, which Senator [Daniel P.] Moynihan rightly called 'welfare repeal'" was now needed. The conclusion was pure old-style Bellah:

> Our civic tradition has emphasized that we are all members of a common society. Our labor tradition has called us to solidarity with our fellow work-ers. Our religious tradition has told us that we are members of the same body. All this you seem to have forgotten. You have succumbed to a posi-tion which is politically popular and which resonates with the worst aspect of our individualistic culture and have thereby abandoned your role as a democratic leader.[8]

At this point Bob was quite disillusioned: for all the Clintons' prattle about community, the hegemony of utilitarian individualism was untarnished. In fact, as he wrote in a short article published in *Pacific Church News*, "Mr. Clinton's action in signing [the welfare reform had] destroyed any enthusiasm I might have had for his re-election." In the end, however, he resolved to vote for him— instead of Ralph Nader, a decision he later regretted—and when Clinton was reelected Bellah's outlook became even darker. He now saw no barrier to the triumph of unfettered capitalism, and repeatedly expressed his concern for the distressing condition of public health care and education, as well as for Clin-ton's erratic foreign policy. By mid-1997, Bob would openly speak of his "con-tinuing moral outrage" at the president's policies and even, in writing to his friend Shmuel Eisenstadt, of his hatred for America—a year later he wrote that he was "about to give up on the American project, if I haven't already."[9]

I

Bellah's dissatisfaction with the everyday maneuverings of the Clinton era arose from a general rethinking of the connections between politics, culture, and religion in America that took him far away from his established, and best-known, positions. This general reassessment had started with *The Good Society* itself—a book that with a bit of a stretch might be read as a lament on the decline of mainline Protestantism. The chapter on religion illustrated the chal-lenges of bureaucratized church and para-church organizations vis-à-vis the religious needs of their members, to which evangelical communities seemed to be far more attentive. More generally, the book pointed to the decadence of the revered postwar-era symbols and institutions—civil rights liberalism, progressive American exceptionalism, and high modernist social science—built on the culture of old-line Protestantism. Besides being a clear departure from *Habits of the Heart*, where mainstream churches were seen as *the* example of a healthy community of memory, this development also foreshadowed a more radical turn—nothing less than the denunciation of the calamitous consequences of the Protestant Reformation for the history of mankind.[10]

The introduction to the 1996 paperback edition of *Habits of the Heart*, aptly titled "The House Divided," was a major step in the same direction—and one of the most explicit and candid attempts at self-criticism of Bellah's career. Instead of celebrating the successes of the Habits group or bragging about the apparent validation of their work in Robert Putnam's recent article "Bowling Alone," the essay highlighted three major faults in the original book. First of all, and contrary to their expectations, Bob and his coauthors conceded the nearly absolute victory of neocapitalism. In the tenth chapter of *Habits*, they had "suggested that the impasse between welfare liberalism and its countermovement, neocapitalism, was coming to an end and two alternatives, the administered society and economic democracy, were looming on the scene." Now they had to admit that neocapitalism had "been able to turn even its policy failures into ideological successes," and no new general view of society was in sight.[11]

This in turn pushed the group to move beyond the first book's exclusive focus on the languages of the middle class. Using a tripartite understanding of social stratification introduced by Clinton's secretary of labor, the economist Robert Reich, they first redescribed most of their original interviewees as lesser members of a "deracinated elite" who had lost any sense of obligation toward wider society and related to it only through a "predatory attitude." At the opposite end of the social spectrum, the impoverished underclass suffered from reduced public services, moral shaming, and residential segregation—a combination that almost forced its members to become selfish and bellicose. Squeezed between the two extremes stood the "anxious class," composed of those for whom "uncertainty about the economic future [was] so pervasive that concern for individual survival [threatened] to replace social solidarity." No wonder that former moderates were becoming the easy prey of those conservative demagogues who pointed to what they disparagingly called "welfare queens" as their nemesis.[12]

In one way or another, then, neocapitalism was pushing individuals from all classes to adopt an instrumental attitude toward their fellow citizens and shared institutions—a rather grim perspective for the authors of *The Good Society*. How could America abandon this rather dangerous path? Given the country's far-reaching structural problems, an "increase in devotion to community" or a new wave of voluntarism might in fact create additional problems, especially if combined with existing patterns of residential segregation. In *Habits of the Heart*, Bob and his coauthors had called for a recovery of the biblical and the republican traditions as a bulwark against the excesses of individualism. Ten years later their hopeful exhortation could not be reiterated, for the group now saw even these cultures as containing at least some of the seeds of ruthless American individualism—the antipolitical strands of ascetic Protestantism and the small-world republicanism of the farmer being among the principal suspects. A new symbolic understanding of the relation between individuals and society was needed.[13] But where to find it?

After the publication of "The House Divided," Bellah focused his attention on the individualistic strands of early Protestantism, for two main reasons. On the one hand, he simply wanted, as always, to understand. He then reread Ernst Troeltsch's work on the Protestant sects through the lenses of Georg Jellinek's genealogy of human rights, Shmuel Eisenstadt's reflections on modernity and heterodoxy, and Seymour Martin Lipset's recent account of the United States as the only modern nation born of a sectarian cultural matrix. On the other hand, Bob's involvement in the life of the Episcopal Church grew steadily and this made him more and more interested in the sacramental and the ecclesiological aspects of church life. These ideas and experiences found a first arrangement in Bellah's keynote address to the 1997 Annual Meeting of the American Academy of Religion, titled "Is There a Common American Culture?"—easily one of his most powerful and significant pieces.[14]

Instead of a precarious balance of a plurality of traditions, Bellah now saw a homogeneous, monolingual, and single-minded culture, carried "by the market and the state and by their agencies of socialization: television and education." The name of such monoculture was, obviously enough, utilitarian individualism. As a distinctly Anglo-American trait, it came from a distant past, albeit not from the place where the Habits group had first located it. "Now I am ready to admit," said Bob, "that we, and Tocqueville, *were probably wrong.*" While the Frenchman had justly written that he could "see the whole destiny of America contained in the first Puritan who landed on those shores," he, and Bellah with him, had picked the wrong guy. Forget John Winthrop and his city on a hill: America's common culture was better understood as a secular development of Roger Williams's "absolute centrality of religious freedom," extended to the point of including "any seriously held conviction whatever" into the sacredness of individual conscience—in this sense, Sheilaism was the final and predictable outcome of, and not a deviation from, the development of (at least a certain branch of) Protestantism.[15]

Once morphed into the radical individualism of market morality, however, this common culture had reduced the human person to just another means for the accumulation of wealth and power. "Roger Williams," Bob remarked, "was a moral genius but a sociological catastrophe," whose inability to envision a positive-sum game between solidarity and individual freedom was reflected in the anti-institutional bent of utilitarian individualism described in *The Good Society*. Against all odds, however, Bellah's outlook was not completely negative: "I still believe that there are places in the churches, and even nooks and crannies in the universities, to which we might look," he concluded. "But the hour is late and the problems mount. In this hour of need in our strange republic, it is up to us to teach the truth as we discern it."[16]

As Bob wrote to his former student, Harlan Stelmach, "Is There a Common American Culture?" was to be read as "a not so oblique attack on race-baiting and gender baiting." Twelve years after *Habits*, he still believed that the real conundrum lay at the intersection of class and culture, a point that contemporary identity movements were not keen to understand: "If corporate America had wanted," he added in his letter, "to pay people on the left to get bogged down in arguments on race, gender and sexual orientation so no one will oppose the fact that they are bleeding the country white they couldn't have done a better job." Affluent Whites like himself should learn that under the alleged triumph of neocapitalist freedom, modernity's iron cage was stronger than ever, and would be broken only by more civic engagement and more democracy. This, in turn, could be done only if the upper and middle classes understood the theological roots of their peculiar way of (un)thinking society, make amends, and start anew. The point of no return of a blanket critique of the Protestant Reformation was just a step away.[17]

To launch his final attack, Bob went back to Clifford Geertz's "Religion as a Cultural System" and one of its most Parsonian metaphors—that of culture as a repository of information similar to DNA. Combined with a "dangerous analogy" taken from Noam Chomsky, Geertz's idea of a "model for" allowed Bellah to describe sectarian Protestantism as the "deep cultural code" in which the transient symbols, myths, and partitions of American culture were rooted.

This dominant matrix was everywhere—all Americans were in fact Protestants in their worship of the sacredness of individual conscience. The conversion of this theological individualism into a secular economic ideology, in turn, might be seen as a radical development of two of the pillars of Protestant theology: the absolute transcendence of God, which had pushed the Creator out of this world and replaced Him with the self; and the exclusive relationship between the believer and Jesus, whose personal intervention needed no collective mediation, and thus no church.[18]

As made explicit in "Flaws in the Protestant Code," a powerful speech on the theological roots of American individualism read in front of several audiences in the late 1990s and finally published in 2000, Bellah's solution depended more on his evolving ecclesiology than on social realism. The keys to a badly needed "genetic reengineering" of the deep code of American culture were thus a new (in fact, old) conception of the church as the Body of Christ, rather than a collection of individuals, and its sacramental enactment through the Eucharist. Small wonder that "Flaws" ended with the suggestion to pay attention to what his "fellow sociologist and a Catholic priest" (and *Habits* hater) Andrew Greeley had called the "Catholic imagination"—a plea that was even more forcefully made in a version of the article, titled "Religion and the Shape of National Culture," published in the Catholic magazine *America*.[19]

In spite of his explicit refusal to reject Protestantism *tout court*—"Is not this very talk a kind of Evangelical sermon?" he asked at the end of "Flaws"—it was clear that Bob Bellah's stance toward it had changed very much since the hopeful assessment of the modern religious multiverse advanced in his 1964 essay "Religious Evolution." As he wrote to his radical theologian friend Stanley Hauerwas, "at this point I think the Reformation was a mistake, though a necessary one." The mistake would not end, he added, "until the Roman church [would adopt] a conciliar not a monarchical form of polity." In the meantime, as he repeatedly said, being a faithful and committed member of the Episcopal church was the closest he could get to becoming a Catholic.[20]

II

Read in front of a huge, sympathetic audience on November 22, 1997, "Is There a Common American Culture?" had been framed by the American Academy of Religion to mark two important events: Robert Bellah's seventieth birthday and his retirement from the University of California. Unlike many of his colleagues, Bob had in fact tried to keep celebrations to a minimum. Bowing to his explicit request, only three individuals had been allowed to take the floor at the official farewell party, held at the Bancroft Hotel on May 2, 1997: Ann Swidler, Michael Burawoy, and John A. Coleman—the dozen former or current graduate students who had asked to speak had to content themselves with wine and cheese. As the chair of the Department of Sociology, Burawoy awarded Bob the highest honor of the University of California, the Berkeley Citation, and emphasized how difficult it was to agree with him for more than one minute, "as his own thoughts speed on, like a spaceship forever changing its orbit, circling around one planet before moving to the next." On the same wavelength, Swidler spoke of Bellah's constitutive ambivalences as embodying "contradictions that remain always in play, never reconciled," and quoted William Blake's famous letter to Thomas Butts to describe him:

> Twofold always. May God us keep
> From single vision and Newton's sleep.[21]

Swidler knew what she was talking about. A few days earlier she had attended another party, that given for the end of Bellah's farewell graduate seminar the "Protestant Ethic in Historical Perspective," which they had taught together. For fourteen weeks the two scholars had renewed their knowledge and interpretation of the "enthralling" work of Max Weber in dialogue with their students and a number of books and papers by Shmuel Eisenstadt, Michael Walzer, Phil Gorski, and Michael Mann. For the first time in years Bellah had had the time and the freedom to seriously go back to his own cultural hero, and the outcome was electrifying: "The seminar on Weber's sociology of religion with Ann during my last semester of teaching was a godsend," he wrote to sociologist Ron Jepperson, "I thought I knew Weber! But he is really inexhaustible, and he has new answers when you bring him new questions."[22]

It was as if Bellah had met an old friend and had discovered how much they both had changed, for the better, over the years. At the peak of his enthusiasm, he then wrote a paper on Weber's concept of "world-denying love," which he sent, following Swidler's advice, to the *American Sociological Review*—the flagship journal of the American Sociological Association, where "Religious Evolution" had been published thirty-three years earlier. The editor's request to revise and resubmit the article following the suggestions of two anonymous readers took Bob by surprise and almost scandalized him. "I do feel like a prophet without honor in my own discipline," he told Ann when the *Journal of the American Academy of Religion* accepted the article exactly as it was.[23]

Irrespective of his retirement and his distance from 1990s sociology, in the fall of 1997 Bellah was busier than ever: he was still directing a handful of dissertations, planned two collections of his essays on Japan and America, accepted various writing commitments and even thought about writing a "small book on *The Uses of Sociology* to defend the notion of public sociology or social science as public philosophy." He also found himself swamped by a host of time-consuming activities: writing blurbs and recommendation letters, responding to the mass media, and unsuccessfully planning a "Bellah chair" at the Graduate Theological Union. Moreover, as he and Melanie had no intention of leaving Berkeley for Santa Monica or New Haven, he also took time to refuse job offers from various organizations and universities.[24]

In order to concentrate on his reading and writing, Bob decided to free up his schedule. The primary cog in the system was directing all requests for engagements to Melanie, who explicitly assumed the role of gatekeeper and intellectual property manager for her husband. She refused to allow supplicants to make their case to him directly, and reduced his travel agenda through a number of hard-to-meet requests: now Bellah would accept only five long-distance engagements a year, would require two first-class round-trip tickets (one for Melanie), and would charge between $5,000 and $10,000 for a formal speech and $500 for any additional event. Despite these strictures, in 1998 Bob and Melanie travelled to Belgium, Brazil, and Italy, where he spoke at a seminar of the CISL Catholic trade union and then enjoyed a private visit to the Sistine and Pauline Chapels in the Apostolic Palace in Vatican City.[25]

As mentioned above, one could not invite Bob Bellah without providing tickets and accommodation for Melanie, who lived through the late 1990s alternating serious health problems with moments of great happiness. In 1997 she was diagnosed with breast cancer, which was treated via a combination of surgery and chemotherapy. Often tired and in need of special care, two years later Melanie decided to end her legal practice for good and concentrate on helping Bob and his work. That same year she experienced some closure with regard to the death of her first-born daughter, when she finally managed to publish her massive work on Tammy—the book's moderate circulation, in turn, encouraged Melanie to continue working on a second manuscript, this time dedicated to "Abby and her sisters." Last in this string of meaningful personal events, on August 17, 1999, Bob and Melanie celebrated their fiftieth wedding anniversary, renewing their vows in a touching religious ceremony held at the Women's Faculty Club of the University of California, which also featured a well-rehearsed ballroom pas de deux by the seventy-two-year-old scholar and his still-beautiful bride.[26]

As the new millennium began, three events came to symbolize the end of yet another cycle and the beginning of the final phase of Bob's life. In January Hally announced that her plans "to head back to the old homestead" were moving quickly. Since 1991 she had been living in Berlin, where she was a member of the Komische Oper ballet company for some years, had married a German IT engineer, Andreas Guther, and had given birth to Philip in 1995 and twins Melanie and Alissa in 1997. When Hally and her family of five finally established themselves in the Bay Area in June 2000, the Bellahs had to undergo a period of reciprocal relational adjustment, which also involved Jenny, who had had her share of turmoil in the preceding years. After their son Paul was born in 1989, she and Christian Romon had gone through a period of stress and had decided to separate. Bob and Melanie had a close relation with Christian and tried their best to "talk the divorce out" and find a way to reconcile the two, but in the end the separation had proven to be inevitable. Around the same time, Jenny had also undergone a tough ordeal in trying to become a partner of the law firm where she had been working since 1983—a process that had ended happily in November 1991, ensuring her professional prestige and financial security in quite a difficult moment for the national economy. In 1997 she had remarried—to Stephen Maguire—and shortly thereafter given birth to a daughter, Melissa, whom Melanie and Bob had seen frequently either in Berkeley or Los Angeles.[27]

The arrival of "the Germans" and the subsequent reshuffling of familial relations, however, was far from being the most demanding event of the summer of 2000: early in July, Bellah was asked by the Department of Sociology to vacate his office in a few weeks to make room for a recently-hired faculty member. Annoyed at his virtual eviction and having to organize his accumulations of thirty years at such short notice, Bob was outraged when some hundreds of books he had carefully arranged as a gift to the university's Bancroft Library were moved elsewhere without him being present. The nasty altercation that followed created a rift between him and the department, which was only resolved with reciprocal apologies in March 2001.[28] At the very same time, Bellah also had a momentary collision with Bill Sullivan about the state of their friendship. The philosopher, who was now in his mid-fifties, had moved to the Bay Area in 1999 to take a position as senior scholar at the Carnegie Foundation for the Advancement of Teaching, where he was to expand the case for a new ethics of professionalism first advanced in his 1995 book

Work and Integrity. Some twenty years after the most intense phase of their relationship, this unprecedented geographical closeness and the profound changes affecting both their lives required a renegotiation of the basic dynamics between them.[29]

All these momentous changes forced Bob to think about the last few years and the fact that a new articulation was emerging that he had to understand and somehow adapt to. Although dealing with friends and family had sometimes left him distracted or even exhausted, the "Kafkaesque" separation from the department where he had spent most of his professional life had made him feel worse than ever. "Fifty years of my life is being relived in these few days," he wrote Bill, while moving his books and things out of the office, "I feel the department has declared me dead. . . . My office is just a holocaust." In fact, on reflection he understood that his daughters, Bill, and even Ann Swidler—whose new book, *Talk of Love*, took a theoretical stance that Bob felt quite distant from his own—all loved and respected him, but also shared, more or less vocally, what Bill had recently told him: "I'm not unhappy to have been able to become more of my own person in several dimensions as I've gotten older." Each of them had now a personal agenda and an established network of relations and affections, and Bob understood that he had to relinquish his desire to keep connected with everything and start focusing, once again, on Melanie and himself.[30]

Fortunately, a welcome and delightful distraction was around the corner. As the exceptional epilogue to an absorbing and rocky three-year period, in the fall of 2000 Bob Bellah was invited by the outgoing president of the United States to receive one of the highest honors an American intellectual could receive.

III

It appeared that Bill Clinton was much fonder of Robert Bellah than Bob was of the president's centrist policies and sexual scandals: he had read *Habits of the Heart* and *The Good Society*, and rumor had it that the First Lady had once had a copy of the latter flown to Switzerland for her to look through before a speech. It was no surprise, then, that when he saw Bellah's name on the list of the nominees for the National Humanities Medals for the year 2000, the president approved it wholeheartedly. Like Allan Bloom, Martin Marty, and Bill Moyers, but no other sociologist before him, Bob was going to be given America's scholarly lifetime achievement award.[31]

The ceremony took place in Washington, DC, on December 20, 2000—a cloudy and chilly day just a month before George W. Bush's inauguration. Bob and Melanie were escorted by their lifelong friends Eli and Frimi Sagan, plus Jenny with her husband Stephen and children Paul and Melissa, Hally with her son Philip, and Ann Swidler on behalf of the Habits group. After a meet-and-greet session with the president and the First Lady in a huge pavilion arranged for the occasion on the White House South Lawn, the guests were driven to nearby Constitution Hall, where Hillary Clinton introduced her husband as the president who had done most for the arts and humanities, and for whom this was "not just a ceremonial duty, but a habit of the heart, Professor Bellah." Then Bill Clinton called Bob on stage and read a formula that summarized fifty years of work in a handful of phrases:

> If there is a common critique of the social sciences, it is that their leading voices talk often to each other, but only rarely to the rest of us. This has never been the case with Robert Bellah. For decades now, he has been raising issues at the very heart of our national identity—and rejecting the easy answers. Like Alexis de Tocqueville, whose legacy he has studied, Robert Bellah understands the tension between two of America's core values: individuality and community. His studies on the moral and religious underpinnings of American civic life have helped us to know better who we are as a people, and where we are headed as a nation.

At that point, however, Clinton ad-libbed to thank the old Berkeley professor: "Through some very difficult periods of our nation's life," he said, Bellah "has reminded us that for all our enshrinement of individuality we can't make the most of our individual lives unless we first are devoted to our shared community. Thank you, Robert Bellah, for priceless gifts."[32]

During the ceremony—described by television producer Judy Crichton as "the last hurrah for geriatric lefties"—medals were also awarded to Nobel Prize–winner Toni Morrison, activist pastor Will D. Campbell, painter and critic David C. Driskell, and the legendary music producer Quincy Jones, while Barbra Streisand, Maya Angelou, Mikhail Baryshnikov, and Claes Oldenburg were among the recipients of the National Medal of Arts. Later that night, the Bellahs returned to the White House pavilion for the black-tie gala. Amid sparkling Christmas decorations and delicious entrées, Bob was seated at the president's table together with historian Garry Wills, television personality Martha Stewart, and fine arts patron Lewis Manilow. Just before the end of the dinner, Clinton came closer and told the seventy-three-year-old

FIGURE 19.2. *Left to right*: Eli and Frimi Sagan, Stephen Maguire holding his daughter Melissa, Paul Romon (in front), Ann Swidler, President Bill Clinton, Robert and Melanie Bellah, Hillary Rodham Clinton, Jennifer Bellah Maguire (with Philip Guther in front), Hally Bellah-Guther, and William R. Ferris, Washington, DC, December 20, 2000. (RBPP)

sociologist that his work had truly been crucial for both Hillary and himself—"no bullshit," he added. As much as Bob was touched by this display of attention, a couple of days later he could not help closing the narrative of his great night at the White House thanking his collaborators from the Habits group: "I hope," he wrote, "that you feel that some of my 'glory' belongs to you."[33]

Two decades had passed since Robert Neelly Bellah had first become involved in what he had recently called "the best thing that has happened to me during my entire academic career." Three years into retirement he was still holding a mirror to himself, his family and friends, and the whole American people, and would not easily relinquish his critical but hopeful inclination. And yet, his eyes were turned in a completely different direction: leaving the West and its hard-fought modernity behind, Bob embarked on his last journey, a journey that would bring him back to where he started. Back to where his heart had always been—"the shoreless sea of the comparative history of religion."[34]

20

Between Religion and Evolution

NORTH AMERICA, 1955–2004

DURING HIS SPEECH for Robert N. Bellah's retirement in May 1997, Michael Burawoy made what might sound a rather curious comment: "Bob Bellah is that rare scholar," he said, "whose star is always rising. He retires while still in his intellectual youth, his greatest works yet to come." What was he talking about? What kind of book might ever trump *Habits of the Heart*? What could surpass the still much cited and debated "Civil Religion in America"? Burawoy nailed his point with a poetic analogy: "With childlike animation, arms a-flying, [Bellah] talks with great anticipation of returning to the path from which he was diverted, returning to the study of the great Religions in the millennium Before Christ."[1]

As all the party guests knew, Burawoy was talking of what Bob deemed his "lifelong obsession with One Big Idea"—his original plan to write "the first good book in the sociology of religion since Max Weber," as he used to tell his closest students at Harvard in the early 1960s. Six months after the party, Bellah revealed to the much larger audience of the American Academy of Religion that at seventy he saw his scholarly career, rich and fulfilling as it had been, as a long detour away from his life's work, and explicitly announced that his major book was "yet to be written." In fact he had already resumed his old intellectual passion, and by 1997 had been working on it, on and off, for five years. In a research plan submitted to the Department of Sociology soon after the publication of *The Good Society*, he had described his "next (and perhaps last) major project" as going back to "the whole development of human religiousness in sociological perspective" after a thirty-three-year hiatus. Observing that his work on civil religion had been heavily Durkheimian, he announced his new/old project as an attempt to pull together and rethink what the Weberian tradition had to say about religion and modernity.[2]

While Bob prepared his return to Max Weber, he knew that his drawers were packed with the aborted attempts at writing his "big book"—attempts that had first marched on two parallel paths but had at some point taken a completely different turn. Papers like "Some Suggestions for the Systematic Study of Religion" (written in 1955) and "The Place of Religion in Human Action" (1957) had introduced a framework for the study of religion built on Tillich's theological understanding of religion with Parsons's systems theory. Another set of articles had instead tackled the Weberian problem of the relation between religion and historical change, comparing various individual cases. "Religion in the Process of Cultural Differentiation" (1955), "Some Thoughts on a Typology of Religion" (1958), "Religious Evolution" (1963), and the epilogue to *Religion and Progress in Modern Asia* (1964) were sketchier on the conceptual side, but contained a great deal of historical data awaiting a deeper and fuller interpretation.

In the mid-1960s, Bellah conceived of his book as the confluence of these two streams of research. During his sabbatical at the Stanford Center, for example, he drafted a table of contents that clearly showed this duality: part one, "The Structure of Religious Action," borrowed the title of Parsons's first book, while part two looked like an expanded version of his then-recent article on religious evolution. In his brief preface, Bob described the volume as "an effort to advance the theoretical understanding of religion," a task that neither the "orthodox of whatever persuasion" nor the "social scientific technician, mesmerized by the hardware of science" could accomplish because of their shared "attitude of glib condescension." Seriousness, openness, and empathy were the intellectual virtues needed to bring such a monster project to conclusion. Warning his readers about the likely effects of such an effort—"Awareness changes outlook and behavior," he wrote—Bellah concluded with the following proviso: "I am deliberately setting my sight as wide as possible, not in order to solve all problems but in order to discern where the problems are." Given this promising start, it was a painful denouement to the cherished gift of a year away that he could not write more than a dozen of pages of *A Theory of Religion* while at Stanford.[3]

The complex period that followed his return to Cambridge led Bellah to entirely rethink his plans. On the one hand, he had resolved to leave Harvard precisely because he did not want to grow old writing "good sound but finally safe books" as the umpteenth "Professor Somebody" from Social Relations. In fact, after the decision was taken, Bob believed that moving to the West Coast would help him with the book: "Perhaps," he noted in his diary in a

moment of unrealistic optimism, "I will write it at a white heat in a few weeks."
On the other hand, the birth of symbolic realism relocated the project on a
different level of scientific reasoning: if between 1955 and 1967 Bellah was aim-
ing at creating a theoretical framework for the sociological study of religion, he
was now talking of religion not as an object of study, but as a symbolic complex
provided with the unique capacity to represent certain aspects of the human
condition that science would never grasp. The metaphor was clear: "When we
look at something with the naked eye and then with a telescope," Bob wrote in
a brand new notebook, titled "Mes Pensées," "we have not moved from objective investigation to subjectivity. We have employed two 'ways of seeing' but
the truth gained from one is not 'objective' nor is the other 'subjective.'" Any
absolute, whether scientific, religious, or political, was obsolete.[4]

This theoretical discourse, aimed at understanding "religion" as a peculiar
form of consciousness that was both alternative and complementary to science, was further sharpened by Bellah's intellectual fascination with Norman
Brown, to the point that at least once he played with the idea of embracing
Nobby's fragmented literary style. "Perhaps the first half of the religion book
could be written aphoristically," he wrote in his diary in November 1968, "Like
Love's Body though with more continuity. This might help with the problem
of where to begin. One can begin everywhere." Bob even planned to integrate
some of his journal entries into A Theory of Religion, thus resolving "the problem of the academic style" and securing "the necessary density" for the book.
In listing the titles of his chapters (Experience, Body, Personality, Society,
Symbolism, Transcendence), he noted that "somehow the need for a historical
introductory chapter seems less necessary"—a remark that would have been
unthinkable just a couple of years earlier.[5]

At the same time, he added, "the aphorism isn't enough." Bellah's book had
to be complex and multilayered: "There must be a great epic poem, a narrative,
a journey—which will not only point to the Way but actually get people
started on it." And to get "on the Way" an idea of history as an intelligible process, one in which evolution could be understood as directional but not necessary unfolding, was needed. "Religious Evolution" had just stated the question,
and its allusions to the possibility of regression and the fact that "all earlier
stages [continue] to coexist with and often within later ones" looked more like
concessions to the prevailing antievolutionist climate than fine-grained theoretical principles. Speaking of historical religions, Bellah had hinted at a "mort-
gage" imposed on subsequent stages "by the historical circumstances of their
origins," an idea first introduced by Eric Voegelin in his Order and History. In

both cases, however, the relationship between earlier and later stages was external and almost wholly inconsequential to the analysis.[6]

Eventually, *Love's Body* enabled Bob to envision human evolution as a stratified spiral of sorts: "Evolution not as unilinear but as involuted," he wrote in his diary in July 1968, "adding more circuits. *Nothing is lost.* Stages are in one sense never outgrown or abandoned[,] only reorganized. An apparent abandonment is a repression. Thus a complex arrangement of phases. The capacity to open communication with earlier (deeper) levels," he concluded, "may *increase* at higher levels." Bellah was translating Brown's conception of history as an eternal return of society-induced neurosis into an insight on the history of the species as a chaotic repository of symbols, practices, and institutions. And the secret was that later, more complex stages efficaciously *increased* the likeness of retrieving earlier stages and communicating with them.[7]

I

Bellah first refined his "nothing is lost" insight using Jerry Bruner's evolutionary theory of consciousness and representation: "The totally bodily mode of relating to reality is never lost," he wrote in "Brown in Perspective" (1971), "and everything that happens even to the most conceptually sophisticated human being is rich with ikonic and fantasy meaning, even though he may be totally unaware of them." No wonder that in the summer of 1971 he showed a certain confidence about his project: "It seems to me that it is now possible for *the first time in several centuries*," he wrote in a new draft of his preface, "to write a book which is at the same time religious, a contribution to religious thought, and a contribution to the scientific understanding of religion." Again at the center of his reflection were religious symbols, seen as "images of images, or of classes of images or of relations between images" that allowed humans to experience reality "not in pieces but as a whole." Combining Geertz's latest work with Parsons's multifaceted view of the human condition, Bellah underlined the connections between bodies, perception, feelings, and symbols, to the point of writing that "religious forms are part of culture and thus ultimately of biology." He finally came up with a tentative definition that was highly reminiscent of the one found in "Religion as a Cultural System," but with a radical, almost mystical twist that might severely reduce its appeal to social scientists:

Religion is a world where one tries to discover the plot of the whole thing. Or perhaps better to live that plot, as an individual or a group, through a symbolic form which seems most adequately to express it. Perhaps "plot" is too verbal a word. The symbolic form may be a physical gesture as in the silent sitting of the Zen monk. Religion is also about the nothing from which all worlds come and the silence into which they go.[8]

This is where Bellah was at the end of 1971, when the American religion debate and the success of *Beyond Belief* diverted his attention from his theoretical project. His next major attempt at retrieving the latter, a bundle of three papers titled "The Roots of Religious Consciousness" and read in Montreal in the spring of 1974, expanded the experiential side of his latest insights, starting from the collapse of the idea of progress typical of the postwar era. "Under these circumstances," ironized Bob during the first lecture, "it is perhaps worth considering whether we might have something to learn from those very backward, ignorant and unscientific pre-modern societies that we have until yesterday despised." Past civilizations might tell contemporary men and women something crucial they had unlearned in the pursuit of wealth, power, and rationality. Using a Durkheimian trope, Bellah located the greatest achievement of "primitive" religion in its alternation of profane daily life and sacred moments of ritual effervescence—of *communitas*, as Victor Turner had called it—in which society might remake and nourish itself by "reducing men to their common human essentials and reasserting the fundamental community that is their most basic truth."[9]

Making light of a comment about the impossibility of connecting to "primitive" religions he had made once in the early 1960s, Bellah commended the counterculture for its attempt to restate the value of "non-conceptual representation and non-ordinary consciousness" as critical elements of human life that modernity had sought to annihilate in the name of science and technical rationality. The use of hallucinogenic drugs, the great rock festivals, and the liberation of sexual desire were all more authentic, and successful, ways to regain that fusion of subject and object that less complex societies had put at the heart of their social life than "the commonest form of collective effervescence in middle class American society"—the cocktail party.[10]

Ultimately, said Bellah in 1974, the destiny of the counterculture was doomed by its inability to recognize that human societies need both moments—sacred and profane, *communitas* and structure, homogeneity and difference. Moreover, "the be-ins and the love-ins dissolved no structure at all," for the rational and bureaucratized institutions of modernity were too robust and massive to be disturbed, let alone remade, by small spontaneous flashes of rupture. The 1960s, Bellah said, had crashed against political and corporate organizations "like flowers thrown against a granite wall," and had soon devolved into escapism, cynicism, or even something worse. Where to look, then, for a redemptive way out of the inhuman constraints of modern society? Bob's answer was clear: in the "more trenchant criticism of the world of everyday life" undertaken by "Judaism, Platonism, Christianity, Islam, Hinduism, Buddhism, Confucianism, and Taoism."[11]

For all their differences, these historical religions shared one common trait: they translated the basic function of religion—"challenging man's tendency to become totally preoccupied with the world of everyday and to imagine that the problems of this world can be solved entirely in its own terms"—into a symbolism of radical negation that provided "a point of leverage, a fulcrum of criticism, which kept the world of everyday, the ongoing structures of economic and political power, contingent, open, lacking in automatic self-legitimation." Instead of periodically dissolving the structures of daily life through participatory rituals, the prophets of Israel, Buddha, and Jesus had opened the possibility of submitting them to sustained critique in the light of some transcendental principle. Moreover, some historical religions had institutionalized monasticism as a (consciously incomplete) intimation of *communitas* in the midst of the profane world. Today, concluded Bellah, their trenchant admonishments would be seen as an aberration, but only because modern society, with its "stress on competition for status and advancement, what some call *our meritocracy*," was itself built on pride, "the chief of all the sins."[12] The third and final lecture focused on the contemporary situation and was characteristically more cautious than the first two. Its most powerful section contained a sketch of a theoretical model based on an insight typical of symbolic realism: "To argue . . . not only for the utility but also for *the truth* of a variety of religions is to take a post-modern position, one that is only possible after having gone through the fires of the modern criticism of religion."[13]

For all its hesitancy, "The Roots of Religious Consciousness" was Bellah's major step forward after "Religious Evolution." After the start of the "Moral Basis of Social Commitment in America" project in 1978, Bob turned his undergraduate course in the sociology of religion into a veritable theoretical laboratory. Following the lead of Clifford Geertz, he started from Alfred Schütz's idea of multiple realities, and then distinguished the world of everyday life, also defined as Abraham Maslow's "D(eficiency) cognition," from the alternative worlds of ecstatic, religious, or artistic experience as "B(eing) cognition." Religion, in this understanding, was a symbolic alternative to common sense in which "the Whole" could be made immediately present to experience. Bellah then presented Bruner's four types of consciousness and connected them to various theories of symbols and religion—those of Mircea Eliade, Paul Ricoeur, William James, and even Carl Gustav Jung. He then introduced his "fundamentally Hegelian" evolutionary scheme to discuss "primitive" and historical religions, the Reformation, and the American case, ending with a critique of the rift between religious traditions and the ethos of modernity.[14]

Together with "The Roots of Religious Consciousness," the course was essential to keep Bellah connected to religious evolution through the intense twenty years between Tammy's suicide and the last *Good Society* summer school. The end result was pretty uneven. On the one hand, the lectures presented a detailed conceptual scheme built on non-Parsonian sources and in-depth comparative analyses of historic religions. On the other hand, almost completely lacking was a serious consideration of archaic religions, while the study of less complex societies was limited to Australian aboriginals. Moreover, in all these "oral publications" politico-moral reflections still prevailed over sound scholarly arguments. Bob's various attempts at getting the work done through a dedicated National Endowment for the Humanities grant in 1978, a historical-comparative analysis of different civilizations published in 1980, and a slightly revised version of "The Roots of Religious Consciousness" given in public in 1985 all foundered against his time-consuming commitments as a public intellectual.[15]

Parallel to the development of his general theoretical scheme, Bellah continued to entertain the idea of saying one final word on symbolic realism. In the late 1970s, his work in this area grew in dialogue with two young sociologists of religion, Thomas Robbins and Dick Anthony, who had tried to employ symbolic realism in their study of the so-called Jesus Freaks, and had found it wanting from a methodological point of view. In 1975 they had participated in the Bellah symposium in the *Journal for the Scientific Study of Religion*, suggesting that at the heart of symbolic realism stood a "deep structuralist" understanding of religion similar to Chomskyan linguistics and Claude Levi-Strauss's theory of myth. After a number of friendly exchanges, the three had the idea of collecting the ongoing discussion in a volume, whose tentative table of contents was finally produced by Anthony early in 1977 under the title *On Religion and Social Science*. The book proposal underscored that symbolic realism still was at the stage of "intuitive assumptions" and its methodological and epistemic standing needed clarification vis-à-vis symbolic interactionism, phenomenology, and ethnomethodology.[16]

In 1978 Bob sent Anthony the ninth and last chapter of *On Religion and Social Science*, titled "Symbolic Realism: Structuralism or Hermeneutics?" In the twenty-four-page paper, symbolic realism was once again framed as an interpretive development of some of the ideas introduced by Parsons and Tillich, and defined as "an extraordinary self-consciousness about tradition, both its inescapability and its problematic character." Being a symbolic realist meant being aware that the horizon of meaning drawn by one's tradition might be observed, understood, and maybe transformed, but never transcended in full. In the paper Bellah also commented on the famous phrase—"To put it bluntly, religion is true"—that had shocked half of his Sanders Theater audience almost ten years earlier. Arguing for a third way between relativism and dogmatism, Bob spoke of religion as "a valid effort more or less successful to discern the truth about the whole of existence," whose "truthfulness" depended more on "the quality of the transformed life" of its practitioners than on its beliefs mirroring external reality.[17]

In closing, Bellah characterized symbolic realism as a "dialectic of return" to tradition after the icy but healthy shower of modern criticism. Pointing to Ricoeur, Hans-Georg Gadamer, and Michel Foucault as the three scholars he felt closest to in his search for the connection between modernity and premodern traditions, Bellah positioned his project within the field of postmodern interpretive philosophy. In the end, the dialogical book remained unpublished, and all of Bellah's later attempts at discussing foundational matters—such as "Social Science as Moral Inquiry" (1981) and the appendix to *Habits of the Heart*—marched on the Aristotelian and then Hegelian tracks typical of his work in the 1980s.[18]

II

Given the popular success of *Habits* and *The Good Society*, Bellah was able to go back to religious evolution only in 1993. At that point, however, he faced enormous intellectual and practical problems. He had always thought of the book as his scholarly masterpiece, the magnum opus that would remain as the testimony to his brilliance, erudition, and commitment to understanding humanity—after all, Parsons had compared Bob favorably to Robert Merton, while Wilfred Smith had called him "the new Max Weber." Proud of himself, but also scared to death by these stellar expectations, Bellah had always been exceedingly serious about his book. In the dense paper on religion and cultural differentiation written before he got started at McGill, for example, he had prescribed himself a thirty-year "program of rigorous empirical scholarship," after which he might well return to theoretical issues "with some greater degree of confidence." As seen from 1993, the plan had been a beautiful failure: overwhelmed by the American civil religion debate and then by his long stint as a member of the Habits group, Bellah had spent his last thirty years in what he would often call his "Babylonian captivity to American Studies." If he wanted his life's work to be a sociological treatise in the great tradition, he had to replicate what he had done in the late 1960s, when he had given himself a crash course in American history and politics in order to fully participate in the discussion ignited by his essay on civil religion.[19]

As he approached what looked to be a long period of apprenticeship, Robert Bellah saw that between 1955 and 1995 the scholarship on psychological, social, and cultural evolution had exploded in quantitative and qualitative terms. For an avid reader like him, this was both a blessing and a curse. Now that he felt "like a child in a candy shop having the time to plough through" countless delicious volumes he had not yet had the chance to read, he was aware that all previous attempts at writing his magnum opus had failed for lack of discipline and an external deadline. Age and time were also pressing concerns: anything could be just around the corner, and seeing longtime academic friends battling Alzheimer's had been a wake-up call, if such a thing were ever necessary. Together with Melanie, who acted as a prod and a gatekeeper, Bob established a number of rules that would help him to concentrate on *Religious Evolution*: he further reduced his long-distance speaking engagements to three a year; he decided to focus on one chapter at a time until it reached a publishable form, "so there will be no work for my survivors if I don't live to finish"; and he resolved to start from the book's theoretical section, which might incorporate much of the work done in the prior two decades. Thanks to these self-impositions, by January 1999 Bellah had drafted a prologue and two chapters, the first mostly reproducing the theoretical lectures of his undergraduate course, complete with examples and all, and the second summarizing human evolution from the Paleolithic to historical societies, relying on anthropological and sociological sources.[20]

And yet, mindfulness alone would not suffice. To bring such an immense endeavor to conclusion Bob needed the help of others. Shortly after retirement, he started looking for grant money to pay for at least one knowledgeable research assistant to help in harvesting and arranging the vast amount of material he felt he had to read and digest, but even that was not enough.[21] The uniqueness of the situation demanded a unique strategy—something midway between Bellah's old hyperindividualistic style of work and the intense but unrepeatable experience of the Habits group. What to do? The solution was to try "to learn a lot about quite a few things," and then to seek the advice of "the real specialists," who might read drafted chapters and tell Bob if he was "crazy or not."[22] Luckily, Bellah could count on a wide, dedicated network, which included former students like Anna Sun and Yang Xiao, Marc Garcelon, Phil Gorski, Stephen Tobias, John Maguire, Arvind Rajagopal, and Richard Wood; old friends like Eli Sagan, Donald Levine, Victor Lidz, Charles Taylor, and Renée Fox; local colleagues like David Keightley, George Lakoff, Johanna Nichols, and Norman Gottwald; and last but not least, the junior members of the Habits group pledged part of their annual meeting to commenting on Bob's ongoing work.[23]

And yet, if he was to attain the extraordinary quality he was striving for, Bellah had to further enlarge the scope of his research. In the late 1990s he became acquainted with the latest developments in evolutionary biology and psychology, and by the early 2000s he had developed a certain disdain for "evolutionary" attempts—such as Pascal Boyer's *Religion Explained* or Scott Atran's *In Gods We Trust*—to explain away religion as an adaptive trick of the human mind or even a "brain module." Not only was Boyer's work reductionistic from a theoretical point of view, it also displayed an unacceptable ignorance about historical and sociological research on religion and, in the last instance, a poor understanding of "religion" as a human phenomenon. As he later explained in a blog published in *The Immanent Frame*, Bellah found these books "shockingly shallow, based on tertiary sources that only [repeated] tired clichés or on novel claims that [had] not been adequately evaluated." *Religious Evolution* was going to be the opposite: not only would Bellah discuss each historical case at length, using as many original texts as he could read and the most reliable translations and commentary from all relevant disciplines, but he would also integrate all cutting-edge research in evolutionary biology and psychology—a task that he set aside for a later moment.[24]

This "new" approach also required that Bellah's circle of consultants be enlarged well beyond its actual boundaries. Luckily, he could now count on another product of the Cold War, one that had been expanding exponentially for nearly half a century—the internet. For Bob, who had made the transition from the typewriter to the computer only in 1987, this was a momentous shift in communicative habits. Exploiting the possibilities opened by e-mail technology, he was able to "make friends on the web," establishing working relations with distant specialists, some of whom he never met in person:

Geoffrey Samuel, Brian K. Smith, Louise Lamphere, David Sloan Wilson, Maureen Schwarz, Terrence Deacon, Walter Brueggemann, Christopher Boehm, and Jon D. Levenson, among others. Bellah's first e-mail to the evolutionary psychologist Merlin Donald, sent in September 2004, was typical of his approach:

> Dear Professor Donald:
>
> I have been reading your work for several years and have greatly profited from it. I am engaged in a major reconnaissance of religious evolution from the paleolithic to the present. I first used your work extensively in a long chapter on tribal religion. Since then I have written chapters on religion in chiefdoms and in archaic (Bronze Age) societies. I am just beginning to write on the axial age, the first millennium B.C. Before turning to the case of ancient Israel, I wrote a 28 page introduction trying to say what is axial about the axial age, where your work is crucial. Since I go back over my whole argument briefly in this piece, as well as introducing your theoretic stage more than I have before, it offers the best overall picture of how I am using your work and so I am sending it along in case you are interested. I am sure you are very busy and may well not have time for this. I am sent more than I can ever read or ever asked for.
>
> Whether or not you have time to glance at this, I want you to know how extremely helpful your work has been. I have also introduced it to a number of people who were not familiar with it. I looked at your website (which is where I got your e-mail address) and saw no new book, but a number of articles that I will read. I have read a great deal in "evolutionary psychology" and related fields, but for a cultural/sociological historian yours is by far the most helpful.[25]

Among the nodes of Robert Bellah's expanding network, one was different from any other: his old friend Shmuel Noah Eisenstadt. Born in Warsaw, Poland, in 1923, Eisenstadt had moved to Palestine at twelve, and had gotten his PhD at the Hebrew University of Jerusalem under the mentorship of Martin Buber, who left him the chair of the Department of Sociology in 1951. After meeting Edward Shils at the London School of Economics, he had become a regular of high modernist circles, and had cohosted the 1963 Harvard seminar where Bob had first presented "Religious Evolution." In the 1970s, Eisenstadt had shifted "from a functional paradigm of systemic modernity to an idealistic paradigm of civilizational traditionality" inspired by the work of Max Weber, of whom he was generally considered the most distinguished successor. A wide-ranging reevaluation of modernization theory, first sketched in his 1989 Tanner Lectures at Berkeley, had brought him to hypothesize a variety of paths toward modernity and, as a consequence, a number of instantiations of the latter's basic principles, thus giving birth to his felicitous image of "multiple modernities."[26]

Apart from their ongoing conversation, Bellah also found Eisenstadt crucial as the animator of a small but combative network of scholars committed to bringing to sociological fruition the controversial concept of the "axial age" (*Achsenzeit*) coined by the German philosopher Karl Jaspers in his 1949 book *The Origin and Goal of History*, with the explicit goal of creating a post-Hegelian philosophy of history. A close friend of Max and Alfred Weber's, and a teacher of Talcott Parsons's in Heidelberg, Jaspers sought to locate the historical period in which "Man, as we know him today, came into being," in order to find a truly ecumenical counterpart to what Jesus Christ's birth had been for the West. He then situated this "axis of global history" around 500 BCE, and indicated the wider period between 800 and 200 BCE as the time when Confucius and Laozi in China; Buddha in India and Zarathustra in Iran; Elijah, Isaiah, and Jeremiah in Palestine; and Homer, Parmenides, and Plato in Greece had "launched a struggle against the myth," making man "conscious of Being as a whole, of himself and his limitations." As a result, "consciousness became once more conscious of itself, thinking became its own object," thus subjecting taken-for-granted customs and ideas to examination and critique. While this epochal breakthrough had failed to influence the majority of the population, and had thus become the fixation of a restricted elite, Jaspers saw the ideas and the practices established during the axial age as a fresh source of moral inspiration.[27]

With the beginning of the Cold War and the rise of high modernism in the social sciences the idea of the axial age had somehow disappeared, only to briefly reappear in 1975 in an issue of *Daedalus* titled "Wisdom, Revelation and Doubt: Perspectives on the First Millennium B.C.," edited by the Harvard sinologist Benjamin I. Schwartz. Then, in his pioneering 1982 essay "The Axial Age: The Emergence of Transcendental Visions and the Rise of the Clerics," Eisenstadt had turned Jaspers's idea into a tool for comparative sociological analysis, one that emphasized the parallels between civilizations and the continuities between tradition and modernity in an abrupt change of direction with respect to modernization theory. The Israeli sociologist defined the axial age as the appearance of a metaphysical rift between a transcendental and a mundane order, and focused on the emergence of a clerical elite specialized in "bridging the gap" as a power group connected with, but independent from, political and military rulers. Although from different positions, scholars like J. C. Heesterman, Johann Arnason, Garry Runciman, Yehuda Elkana, Björn Wittrock, Jan Assmann, and Peter Machinist were all participating in Eisenstadt's well-funded collective project, of which an edited collection of essays, *The Origins and Diversity of Axial Age Civilizations*, had been the first visible outcome.[28]

Although he had never employed the expression in print, something similar to the axial age had been at the center of Bellah's work since his early papers on evolution and cultural differentiation. "We are engaged in a common enterprise," he wrote to Eisenstadt in March 1999, "even if our emphases are sometimes different." All he had to do was stop talking about "historic religions," take up the new lingo, and cast for himself a recognizable position in the ongoing debate.[29]

III

What Bellah created after 1997 was an almost militaristic mobilization against the volume of his prospective reading, the passing of time, and the sustained attention of the external world, where his standing as a public intellectual had not been reduced by his retirement. Apart from being much in demand, it was Bob himself who found it difficult to keep his focus on *Religious Evolution*—after all, he was still the person whose "antennae are always out" and whose "nerve endings are exposed." Among his most cherished distractions were, again, theology—which he mostly discussed with Stanley Hauerwas, John Coleman, and a former student, John Maguire—and American politics. For all his dissatisfaction with Bill Clinton's centrism, Bob saw the elections of November 7, 2000, as an epoch-making confrontation, and staunchly supported Al Gore against that almost perfect embodiment of the derailing of the American dream, George W. Bush.[30]

The contested election result and its unexpected finale absorbed Bellah's attention for months, in a crescendo of frustration that he shared above all with two former students, Samuel C. Porter and Marc Garcelon, who also acted as his main connection to the surge against Bush's lame victory. Just a month before his seventy-fourth birthday, Bob was among the five thousand protesters who crowded San Francisco's Civic Center Plaza with Bill Sullivan and Melanie, whose handmade sign read "An Appointed President?" If the events of the first half of 2001 only reinforced his disdain for "the ignorance and stupidity" at the top of the US government, after the Sbarro restaurant suicide bombing in Jerusalem Bellah started to worry for the emerging world disorder and its likely consequences on his everyday life. On August 11, 2001, he ultimately abandoned Eisenstadt's plan to have him give the Martin Buber Lecture at the Hebrew University in December and then fly to Vienna for a crowded conference on the axial age.[31]

Neither Bellah nor Eisenstadt, however, was prepared for the unimaginable. When Jenny called to wake them up earlier than usual on September 11, 2001, Bob and Melanie rushed downstairs to watch incredulously the images of the terrorist attacks against the World Trade Center and the Pentagon. "I am afraid I can't even be angry," Bob wrote to Porter a few hours later. "There is so much evil in the world and so much of it that is our fault that it is hardly surprising that it should come to our shores." Worse still, their "cowboy president" was not up to the task: Bush's pledge to "rid the world of evil" during his speech of September 14 projected what Bob called "shades of Bin Laden" and anticipated further disasters. No wonder that when a journalist called on him to comment upon Bush's words, Bellah replied with a sigh: "I suggested how unlikely it is that we can 'rid the world of evil.' [The reporter] said, 'I can't even rid my own neighborhood of evil,' and I replied, 'I can't even rid my own heart of evil.'"[32]

In October Bob accepted Hauerwas's proposal to contribute to a 9/11 special issue of the *South Atlantic Quarterly*. Titled "Seventy-Five Years," his piece was finally published in the spring of 2002 along with essays by Jean Baudrillard, Wendell Berry, Frederic Jameson, and Slavoj Žižek. In eleven dense pages, Bellah combined national history and personal memoir, comparing the recent trauma to the worst military catastrophes of his lifetime—Pearl Harbor and the Vietnam War. Bob's language had rarely been so harsh: "It would seem that the United States, now engaged in a 'war on terrorism,'" he wrote, reminding his readers of the bombings of Dresden, Berlin, Hiroshima, and Nagasaki, "not so long ago perpetrated the greatest acts of terrorism in human history." Combined with the many coups orchestrated by the CIA around the world over the last fifty years and the massacres waged before Bob was born—the genocide of American Indians, the enslavement of Africans, the Spanish-American War, and the invasion of the Philippines—all these historical facts pointed to the same conclusion: war after war, the United States had become indistinguishable from its "evil" enemies. Past was the time when America might pretend to be the chosen land, now it was "just one more 'homeland' among the nations."[33]

At about the same time, Bellah produced a triptych of more scholarly works showing how America maintained an exceptionalism of sorts. The three pieces were each related to a special occasion—so special that Bob was not able to say no. Late in 1999 he received the papers that the rest of the Habits group had collected for the book meant to celebrate his retirement, to which he was asked to write an epilogue. Although he started working on the piece in the year 2000, the writing took longer than expected and tallied with the composition of one of his deepest works ever—the lengthy introduction to *Imagining Japan: The Japanese Tradition and Its Modern Interpretation*. While Bob had been planning to collect his essays on Japan for twenty years, the publication of Eisenstadt's *Japanese Civilization* in 1996 and his own involvement in a symposium held in Kyoto in 2000 for the 270th anniversary of the founding of Sekimon Shingaku had pushed him to finally sit down and catch up with the last thirty years of scholarship on his first scholarly subject—an exacting task that occupied him for most of 2000 and 2001. The third essay, titled "God, Nation, and Self in America," was written for the proceedings of a conference held in New York City to celebrate the 100th anniversary of the birth of Talcott Parsons, at which Bob did not personally appear.[34]

Common to the three pieces was the definitive adoption of the vocabulary of a civilizational analysis based on the idea of the axial age. Following Eisenstadt's lead, Bellah interpreted Japan as a "non-axial" civilization, one whose tribal and archaic premises had persisted, through various reformulations, since time immemorial. "The Japanese," wrote Bob in a poignant passage, "have been aware of axial principles, have understood them thoroughly, and yet have rejected them" thanks to an extraordinary ability "to use the axial against the axial" and retain their own archaic matrix. This same pattern emerged in politics, where an original model of "galactic polity" underlay Japan's modern statehood; in religion, where Buddhism and Confucianism had been transformed by, and absorbed into, the archaic heritage of Shinto and rural magical rituals; and in the sphere of personal life, where the self remained embedded in social groups of different sizes and orientations. The uniqueness of Japan lay in its being completely "modern" without having undergone any axial breakthrough.[35]

Armed with this new version of his old grasp of Japanese culture and society, Bellah turned his attention to the United States, which Eisenstadt saw as the epitome of an axial civilization. To the contrary, Bob paralleled Japan's pre-axial fusion of people and government through its divine emperor with the post-axial refusal of God and nation typical of the United States: the gap and thus the tension between ultimate truth and social reality—that is, the axial foundations of prophetic civil religion—had been collapsed in the belief that the Kingdom of God had been realized on Earth as *America*, the nation destined to redeem the rest of the world. As anticipated in Bellah's late-1990s articles, this declension of the possibility of moral criticism had always been present "in germ" in the particular brand of Christianity brought from Europe by the very first colonists. The belief in a realized eschatology had obvious effects: manifest destiny, George W. Bush's claim to rid the world of evil— "Apparently what even God has not succeeded in doing," wrote Bellah in an article published in *Commonweal* in 2002, "America will accomplish"—and the eventual rise of a self-righteous global empire. To reverse this demonic drift, the American people should embrace once again the prophetic dimension of axial religions and recognize that the United States was "only another tired version of the city of man." Given this conclusion, it is no wonder that in "God, Nation, and Self in America" Bob described *The Broken Covenant* as "still far too close to Parsons' own view of American society," a view from which he had moved "ever farther over the passing years."[36]

21

"This Big House on the Hill"

BERKELEY, 2005–2010

AFTER THE LONG HIATUS caused by the emotional disruption of 9/11 and his hard work on *Imagining Japan*, Robert N. Bellah swiftly recommitted himself to religious evolution. Resuming a conversation that had been running, on and off, for four years, in February 2002 he told the legendary editor of the University of Chicago Press, Douglas Mitchell, that "with great good luck" his volume might be ready by the end of 2003. That was, to say the least, wishful thinking: Bob closed his third chapter on tribal religion in December 2002, and then spent the whole of 2003 writing a long, two-part suite on archaic societies and the intimations of the axial break. The fall of 2003 went by in a heartbeat while Bob tried to make sense of ancient Egypt, and it was only in the spring of 2004 that he was able to repay his enormous debt to pre-axial societies and focus on the real tour de force of the book, which was to include one extended monograph for each of the four "axial cases"—Israel, Greece, China, and India.[1]

At this point, Bob had resigned himself to the fact that it would take almost a year to complete each chapter. "It is the cases that take me so long," he wrote Mitchell in March 2004, "as I need to read so extensively to get a 'feel' for the quality of the material." A $22,500 individual scholarship awarded by the John Templeton Foundation made him confident about the future and reinforced his intention to work on a triptych: the present "big book," now tentatively titled *Religion in Human Evolution: From the Paleolithic to the Axial Age*; then a "short" 250-page volume where he would summarize the whole story up to the present, to be called *The Well of the Past: The Evolution of Religion*—a hint to Thomas Mann that went back to Bob's Middle Eastern trip of 1959; and finally a "quite exciting" third volume stretching from Rome and early Christianity to modernity, and including, along the way, "a major treatment of Islam," Mahāyāna Buddhism, and the Reformation. Needless to say, Mitchell was enthusiastic about the extended project and declared himself "almost stupefied at the thought that what [he was] reading [was] a 'draft.'"[2]

For all the time he was spending reading about individual cases, however, Bellah still lacked a general assessment of the axial age. All his recent papers made use of the new conceptual jargon, but the idea of the emergence of dual metaphysics or transcendence was not that different from what he had written in his 1964 essay—in a sense, he had just relabeled as "axial" what he had earlier called "historical." As he abandoned archaic societies, Bob resolved that the first half of his sixth chapter, otherwise dedicated to ancient Israel, was the place for a more explicit and detailed *prise de position*—a task he found "intrinsically exciting." When the German sociologist Hans Joas suggested that the *Archives européennes de sociologie* might publish the piece as a stand-alone article, Bob set off to pen his first contribution to the debate.[3]

While the essay copiously cited Jaspers, Voegelin, and Arnaldo Momigliano, its real target was what Shmuel Eisenstadt called the "axial age roadshow," the small group of contemporary scholars whose discussion on the concept of the axial age was open and lively. First came the definition of the axial break as such—as the title of Bellah's article read, "What Is Axial about the Axial Age?" Second, should the term "axial" be used to indicate either a unique historical event or an abstraction—that is, something that might happen again and again in history? The third and final point—the relationship between the axial break and human evolution—was the most delicate, as no member of the Eisenstadt circle embraced an evolutionary model. In other words, Bellah had to carve for himself an original position within a well-structured debate while keeping intact, or at least recognizable, his original insight on religious evolution. Luckily, early in 2002 Bob had discovered the work of Merlin Donald on the coevolution of culture and cognition, whose stages paralleled Jerry Bruner's model of consciousness he had been using since the late 1960s.[4]

According to Donald, human culture evolved through four stages. The first, "episodic culture" defined as the knowledge needed to act properly within a specific situation, is shared by apes and humans. Conversely, "mimetic culture"—"the ability to produce conscious, self-initiated, representational acts that are intentional but not linguistic"—might be understood as fully typical of humans. A third step occurred thanks to the invention of language and its "natural product," narrative form. During the Paleolithic, "mythic culture" emerged as the effort to embrace all aspects of life within a "unified, collectively held system of explanatory and regulative metaphors." The last great cognitive transition had been made possible by the creation of writing and its two by-products—external memory storage and theory construction, defined as the ability to think analytically. While Bruner spoke of a sequence of enactive, iconic, and symbolic representation leading to a "paradigmatic" mode of thought, Donald saw "theoretic culture" as finally transcending the biological hardware of the human mind, and also producing the possibility of going back and forth through the whole sequence of cognitive steps.[5]

Combining his own version of Donald's model with the most recent advances of Eisenstadt's network, Bellah identified the axial age with the beginnings of a particular kind of theory, what historian of science Yehuda Elkana called "second-order thinking"—that is, "the attempt to understand how rational exposition is possible and can be defended." Not only did geometric proof advance some mathematical truths, it also included an explanation of the reason why they should be trusted as "true." For Bellah, it was precisely the extension of the logic of demonstration to cosmology and religion to produce the concept of transcendence, and with it a radical cultural shift. "Because transcendental realms are not subject to disproof the way scientific theories are," he wrote, "they inevitably require a new form of narrative, that is, a new form of myth." As "the capacity to examine critically the very foundations of cosmological, ethical and political order," second-order thinking required not only a new repertory of stories but also a novel logic for understanding and assessing their truth claims. This ultimately gave rise to the idea of a gap between this world and the other—a kind of unfathomable mystery that could, however, be symbolized and argued for—a new kind of religious action oriented to salvation and novel institutional forms.[6]

As for evolution, Bob's point was clear: since the emergence of each new stage depended on the capacities developed during the previous ones, general accounts *had* to be framed in evolutionary terms. "What Is Axial?" also introduced a principle that Bellah had first envisioned in the late 1960s—"Nothing is ever lost." Hinting at the work of sociologist Randall Collins on ritual, he emphasized the importance of considering evolution as a spiral in which previous stages are continuously made and remade: "Humans are still episodic, mimetic, and mythic creatures," he wrote, "although, as in earlier transitions, the emergence of a new form of cultural cognition eventually involves reorganization of the earlier forms." In particular, social forms and structures were never really overcome: "Just as the face-to-face rituals of tribal society continue in disguised form among us," he added, "so the unity of political and religious power . . . reappears continually in societies that have experienced the axial 'breakthrough.'" For this and other reasons, and notwithstanding all the differences between the individual cases, the expression "axial age" should be reserved for a bundle of specific historical events, so that any typological usage of the term was out of the question, at least for Bellah.[7]

I

"What Is Axial?" was published in 2005. It came a good fifty years after Bellah had first sketched his lifelong study plan, and thus fifty-one years after his dramatic clash with McGeorge Bundy about his past as a Communist. When the story of that confrontation had first emerged in 1977, Bellah and Bundy had both asked Harvard University to open its archives to independent researchers, a request that President Derek Bok had turned down, citing the university's "50-year rule" for disclosing administrative records. Published works about the McCarthy era and academic institutions such as Elizabeth Schrecker's *No Ivory Tower* and Sigmund Diamond's *Compromised Campus* had relied mostly on interviews and other sources. Kai Bird's 1998 biography of McGeorge Bundy, who had died two years earlier, had presented a rather critical judgment of Harvard's record during McCarthyism. After subjecting Bird's book to close review, in November 1998 *Harvard Magazine* published a letter by Bundy's former assistant dean: "McGeorge Bundy, Nathan Pusey, and Harvard University," wrote psychologist Edward L. Pattullo, rejecting any allegation, "acted wisely and bravely during those sad times, and deserve honor for helping to turn the tide, rather than the opprobrium Bird offers." In a short reply, Robert Bellah summarized his own case once again, but in the absence of original records he could conclude only that "in 2004–05, if I am still alive, I will be interested to get at the bottom of this matter."[8]

Sixteen years later Bob was ready for his rendezvous with history. In June 2004 he wrote to the dean of the Harvard Faculty of Arts and Sciences, historian William C. Kirby, and three months later he finally received a big envelope from the Harvard University Archives. There he found some documents he already knew of, but also a number of items he had never seen before. Among the latter was a six-page memo from the Department of Social Relations to the Faculty Advisory Committee on Academic Freedom and Tenure, in which Talcott Parsons had made Bellah's case in a forceful, uncompromising way. Bob knew that Parsons had supported him, but his mentor had never been explicit about the form and content of that particular document. Not only was Bob persuaded that Bundy had "tried very hard to get [him] appointed in 1955 without the deadly proviso" imposed by the Corporation, but he was full of admiration for Parsons's "formidable civic mood."[9]

The new evidence had to be made public as soon as possible, not only to set the record straight on 1950s Harvard, but also as a warning in the heated atmosphere of post–Patriot Act America, which Bellah considered as "a time of national anxiety not entirely dissimilar to the McCarthy period." He then decided to send a new letter to the *New York Review of Books* to supplement and correct the story he had told twenty-seven years earlier. "Although Bundy is not here to defend himself," he wrote, "his claim to have supported my appointment in the period in question, a claim I doubted in 1977, is confirmed by the records I have now received"—a discovery that had not changed his judgement of the Harvard administration as "spineless" and its policy as "a discreet collaboration with McCarthyism with the primary concern to avoid criticism." Instead of acting as an example of principled resolution for weaker or lesser institutions, his alma mater had decided to cower under the fear of criticism, and this was not worthy of its spirit, which Bob found "not in President Pusey, Dean Bundy, or the Harvard Corporation but in Talcott Parsons and other faculty members like him."[10]

After the letter was published in February 2005, Bellah received a steady flow of letters and e-mails from individuals known and unknown, who praised his courage, civility, and unrelenting determination. Among his correspondents were some long-lost friends: Leon Kamin, who later sent the *New York Review* a letter detailing his own story, and Staughton Lynd, who had hitherto thought that Bob had died! To Bellah's dismay, however, not a word came from Harvard University. Determined to leave no stone unturned, in August he wrote to Theda Skocpol, a sociologist who had just been nominated dean of the Graduate School of Arts and Sciences, to ask if she knew of any faculty member interested in studying the university's conduct during McCarthyism. In her prompt and apologetic answer, Skocpol remarked that her Harvard colleagues had too much to worry about with the present-day turmoil raised by President Lawrence Summers in January with his comments on the presence of women in science to be seriously interested in historical research about McCarthyism and the Cold War.[11]

At the time of his second *New York Review* letter Bellah was also putting the final touches to another, albeit singular, act of self-historicization—his third collection of essays. While he had first planned an anthology of his work on America in the late 1970s, in the early 2000s the project had grown to embrace the many sides of his eclectic production, from oldies like "Civil Religion in America," "The Five Religions of Modern Italy," and "Religious Evolution" to a number of more recent essays on the United States (including "Is There a Common American Culture?" and "Flaws in the Protestant Code"), academic life, and even sermons. After some bargaining, cutting, and editing by Steve Tipton, *The Robert Bellah Reader* was published by Duke University Press in 2006, following a similar collection of Stanley Hauerwas's writings by five years. Its twenty-eight chapters were introduced by a new autobiographical piece, à la *Beyond Belief*, in which, however, the *fil rouge* connecting the various stages of Bob's intellectual journey was not his sense of loss or the search for a politics of the imagination, but rather his unabating passion for religion and evolution—a slight exaggeration, which nonetheless announced his forthcoming masterpiece.[12]

The publication of the *Reader* almost coincided with Bob's eightieth birthday and thus became the occasion "to pay tribute to his scholarship and life," as announced in the newsletter of the American Sociological Association. Reviewers called Bellah the Louis Armstrong and the Tiger Woods of the sociology of religion, and praised him for his "firm grasp on the most important aspect of the human enterprise: the search for meaning in a world where meaning is complex and elusive." The book was also celebrated in the *Chronicle of Higher Education* with a symposium titled "One of Sociology's Most Influential Scholars," featuring essays by Jean Bethke Elshtain, Alan Wolfe, and Wilfred McClay. Among Bob's friends, Renée Fox wrote to compliment him for "the cauterizing way in which you have dealt with false dichotomies" and "the links you have forged between the cognitive, affective, moral, mythic, and religious dimensions of our individual and our collective lives." And yet, for all the accolades he received, one was sorely missing—the review Clifford Geertz was writing at the time of his passing on October 30, 2006.[13]

After the death of Talcott Parsons, the exchanges between Cliff and Bob had been characteristically sparse, but their mutual admiration and sense of deep and unending friendship had never faded. In 2001 Bellah had nominated Geertz for the National Medal for the Humanities, justifying his choice with the simplest of reasons: Cliff was "arguably the most important living cultural anthropologist (Levi-Strauss is the other possibility)." Even if he had always been an anti-evolutionist, Geertz's judgment mattered, and he was among the first to be sent the drafts of "Seventy-Five Years," "What Is Axial?" and finally the *Reader*'s introduction. "You have maintained a much steadier course through 'everything' than I have," Cliff wrote back, "but the main hedgehog/fox, half-full/half-empty contrast between us remains more or less intact." Bellah, to be sure, was the hedgehog drinking from a half-full glass—although, as he often repeated, his One Big Idea contained many. "I myself wonder," Geertz continued, "whether the narrativist approach is really compatible with 'evolutionary psychology' and the like as you think. But that's what makes horse races, and natural selection, and it will be good to see you develop all this out into the full form you are working on."[14]

"In any case," ended Geertz's letter, "keep in touch. We are bound by common memories, common debts . . ." In fact, more than one year passed before Bob found out that Cliff had been seriously ill and wrote to his wife, Karen Blu, to ask about his old brother in arms. It was October 23, 2006. One week later the anthropologist died of heart failure after a long and difficult period in hospital. Among the things he had left unfinished was a piece on the *Bellah Reader* for the *New York Review of Books*, in which religious evolution was deemed to be the "underlying pulse and metric" of everything Bob had done. As hard as the death of Clifford Geertz hit Robert Bellah, he still harbored such a distaste for the Princeton institute that he resolved not to make the cross-country trek to attend his friend's funeral. As painful as it was, it was a decision he felt entitled to make.[15]

II

Among the reasons why Bob had tried so hard to uncover the truth about Harvard's conduct during the McCarthy era was his sense of a looming catastrophe. After four years of George W. Bush, 9/11, the Patriot Act and the Homeland Security Act, the war in Afghanistan, and the invasion of Iraq, Bellah saw the 2004 presidential elections as a plebiscite between civility and barbarism—during the Democratic primary he first backed Wesley Clark, then Howard Dean, then again Clark, and finally John Kerry, following a single principle: "Whoever can beat W!" His shock at Bush's reelection was such that he told Sam Porter he would stop reading newspapers other than the *San Francisco Chronicle* and watching TV news altogether. While this self-seclusion was more imagined than real, it was also true that he had reached a turning point that needed all his energy and attention—his first two "axial cases," Israel and Greece.[16]

As Bob started to circulate drafts of the final chapters, the Habits group discussed the idea of merging the two preoccupations, scholarly and political, organizing a major conference on the inability of Western liberalism to face the many "eruptions of profoundly destabilizing political, economic, and religious conflict" of the mid-2000s. In a grant request sent to the Rockefeller Foundation in August 2006, Richard Madsen wrote that "the strains upon the emerging global civilization" might produce a "civilizational breakdown" that could be solved only by "new social and cultural breakthroughs, [and] perhaps even a new axial age." The plan was simple: the group would contact a number of leading social thinkers—the attached list included Jürgen Habermas, Charles Taylor, Hans Joas, David Martin, José Casanova, Rebecca Chopp, and Randall Collins—and send them the drafts of Bob's axial chapters as a common background. Then, during a four-day retreat at the Foundation's Center in Bellagio, Italy, on Lake Como, they would "challenge each participant to show how they might move from their analyses of breakdown to realistic visions of breakthrough."[17]

Late in 2006, the Rockefeller Foundation declined the project, and the Habits group set out to find another sponsor—an immediate candidate was the John Templeton Foundation, which had just renewed Bellah's grant for three more years. As his work on the book progressed, Bob discussed with Hans Joas the possibility of relocating the conference to Erfurt, Germany. The two had first met when Berkeley had offered Joas a professorial position in 1998, and had maintained a steady, and growing, intellectual relationship ever since. Widely known for his work on pragmatism and his twin theoretical treatises, *The Creativity of Action* and *The Genesis of Values*, in 2002 Joas had moved from the Free University of Berlin to the University of Erfurt as the director of the Max Weber Center for Advanced Cultural and Social Studies. In *Braucht der Mensch Religion?*, originally published in 2004 and later translated as *Do We Need Religion?*, he had praised Bellah as the one contemporary scholar who had gotten the closest to a grand synthesis in the sociology of religion analogous to those of Weber and Durkheim. The good thing about Bellah's evolutionary approach, he added, was that it turned "the questions posed by the sociologist of religion . . . into religious questions," helping social scientists to avoid both "religiously irrelevant sociology of religion and cryptotheology." No wonder he looked at the publication of Bob's big book with a blend of scholarly involvement and admiration.[18]

Thanks to Hans Joas and the financial help of the John Templeton Foundation, in the spring of 2007 things got going for the Erfurt conference, which was then scheduled for July 2008—that is, ten years after Bob and Melanie's last major European visit. At Joas's suggestion, in the fall Yehuda Elkana invited Bellah to extend his trip to Budapest in order to participate in the 38th World

Congress of the International Institute of Sociology, a venerable organization whose president, Björn Wittrock, was a key member of the axial age network. When the Bellahs finally left for Vienna late in June 2008, the final section of *Religion in Human Evolution* was still far from complete. Between 2005 and 2007 Bob had drafted the chapters on Greece and China in a state of scholarly excitement, sent them to Yang Xiao, Bill Sullivan, and classicists Ian Morris and Anthony Long, and rewrote entire sections following their suggestions. When the invitations went out for the Erfurt conference, however, he was still struggling with India. The delay was due not only to the fact it was the axial case he knew least about, but also to the time spent polishing the piece he would read in Europe, a position paper of sorts, which he also saw as a likely conclusion to his first volume.[19]

At the International Institute of Sociology meeting, Bob Bellah spoke at the plenary, titled "Historical Sociology and Political Theology," chaired by Wittrock and animated by Joas, political theorist Rajeev Bhargava, and philosopher Hent de Vries, but also attended a number of other sessions, mostly those in which Eisenstadt or other members of the axial age roadshow were presenting. Only once did Bob deviate from this routine, and it was to hear a paper on the unanticipated consequences of his own success as the author of "Civil Religion in America" in the rather amazing (for him) and frightening (for the author) double role of subject and critic. The presenter was myself, and I had been working on Bellah's intellectual biography for a couple of years. After a first round of research at the Yale Center for Cultural Sociology and the Harvard University Archives, in the summer of 2007 I had spent a month in Berkeley and had interviewed Bob using the many references found in the papers of Talcott Parsons as a guide and compass. Mining the rich correspondence between teacher and student, I had also uncovered a few clues about some early essays on American religion and had persuaded Bellah to look for them. To his great surprise, the eighty-year old sociologist had found the long-forgotten papers on American religion he had written for Charles Glock in the mid-1950s buried in a drawer, and he agreed to publish them with commentaries by noted scholars in the field.[20]

While there had been a great many articles, comments, and encyclopedia entries on Robert Bellah and his work, it was the first time that someone had undertaken the project of writing an entire book on him—a circumstance that made Bob both proud and curious. As he wrote, recommending me for a fellowship in 2007, "I think it is an advantage for the work Matteo wants to do that he is an Italian, educated in a system quite different from ours. It gives him a distance and a lack of prejudice," he concluded, "that will allow him to see things that American scholars might miss." On their last night in Budapest, Bob, Melanie, and I raised a glass to the completion of the two books, with the promise to meet again in Erfurt in a week.[21]

III

Soon after the conclusion of the Institute meeting, Robert Bellah left Budapest for the lovely Thuringian capital of Erfurt, right in the geographical heart of Germany. Like the tiny towns that surround it—Gotha, Jena, Weimar—Erfurt has a long, intricate history. The conference was to be held in the Barocksaal of the Thüringer Staatskanzlei, the same place where Johann Wolfgang von Goethe had met with the emperor of the French, Napoleon Bonaparte, in 1808. Moreover, the building lies midway between the Erfurter Dom, where Martin Luther had been ordained in 1507, and the birthplace of the legendary social scientist, and Bob Bellah's personal hero, Max Weber.

Two hundred years after the fateful meeting between two men who had played a major role in the creation of modern Europe, expectations for the three-day symposium "The Axial Age and Its Consequences for Subsequent History and the Present" were nothing if not grand. "We cannot assume that the universal aspirations [of the axial age] were 'good' and the particularistic concerns 'bad,'" read the presentation prepared by Joas and Bellah. "Human culture always needs 'a local habitation and a place.' The question is, how were these tensions resolved, fruitfully or unfruitfully, and how can our understanding of this early emergence of the problem help us understand it in its present forms?" One press release highlighted the connection between axial age studies and contemporary concerns, and bore an outright attack on the work of an old acquaintance, one who had sold Bob a junk Oldsmobile sedan some fifty-three years earlier: "For the present day, characterized by wide social and cultural transformations, it is particularly important to return to the cultural roots of the axial age and trace different paths to 'multiple modernities,' especially in order to understand and criticize theses such as those of [Samuel P.] Huntington's 'Clash of Civilizations.'"[22]

In a very literal sense, Bellah and Joas had succeeded in convening most of Bob's conversational partners in a single place for an extended face-to-face discussion: Jürgen Habermas, Charles Taylor, and Merlin Donald would share the table with Eisenstadt, Wittrock, and Johann Arnason, but also with the great Egyptologist Jan Assmann, anthropologist Gananath Obeyesekere, sinologist

Heiner Roetz, and sociologist Garry Runciman, whose work recurred in Bob's draft chapters. David Martin, José Casanova, Matthias Jung, Manussos Marangudakis, and the four *Habits* coauthors were also on the list, to encourage an interdisciplinary and lively discussion. Apart from the members of the axial age roadshow, Habermas and Taylor could be counted among the "believers," while Roetz had interpreted Confucius's illumination as a "logical possibility of a sequential evolution" by way of a "phylogenetic adaptation of Lawrence Kohlberg's cognitive-developmental theory," which might bring to mind Bellah's merger of Bruner and Donald.[23]

And yet, at least one-third of the speakers explicitly questioned the validity of the concept of the axial age, and some had even more controversial claims to make. Assmann, for instance, had always been skeptical of Jaspers's thesis, and related monotheism—an invention of the axial breakthrough—to the beginnings of religious violence. Even more problematic was Runciman, the highest-profile proponent of neo-Darwinian evolutionism in sociology, who would soon call the axial age a typical example of the "fallacy of elective affinity" and "the product more of Jaspers' own existential philosophy than of the selective affinities in the world whose distinctive cultures and societies evolved as they did." Given such a distinguished and varied roster of thinkers, the excitement of the few invited members of the public was palpable.[24]

In his role of co-organizer of the meeting and its *primus inter pares*, Bob presented his "The Heritage of the Axial Age: Resource or Burden" at the only public event, held at a small, unadorned church usually employed by the Catholic Theological Faculty of the University as a seminar room and oratory. Read at dusk on the first day of the conference, the short paper marked a milestone in Bellah's assessment of the axial enigma and its consequences. In "What Is Axial?" he stressed how each breakthrough had been followed by a breakdown, but reaffirmed his hope in a qualified recovery of axial insights. In an important conference given in Berkeley in January 2007, "All Religions Are Cousins," he added that while all known religions "developed out of common roots"— that is, Donald's mimetic and mythic cultures—with the emergence of theory a new "level of generality" was created where "we can begin to discern analogies, not just in form but of content, between the [axial] traditions." In Erfurt his critique took the next step: just as in *The Broken Covenant* he had found the germs of utilitarian individualism at the roots of American culture, now it was the very essence of the axial age to go on trial. And the prime suspect was, rather unexpectedly, Aristotle.[25]

At the heart of Bellah's argument stood a detailed discussion of Plato inspired by *Spectacles of Truth in Classical Greek Philosophy*, a recent book by a Stanford classicist whose name had first been brought up by Ian Morris: Andrea Wilson Nightingale. While originally the word *theoria* had been used to describe the custom of sending an envoy to a faraway religious festival in order to report back to his fellow countrymen about it, wrote Nightingale, in *The Republic* Socrates used it to define philosophy as "loving the spectacle of truth." The Parable of the Cave, dense in visual metaphors of light and sight, was mostly meant to explain how, for Plato, "seeing the good" would occasion nothing less than an existential conversion on the part of the philosopher: "The experience of vision [was] utterly transformative; one [became] a different person as a result." In Plato's philosophy and in Buddhism, introduced by Bob as his countercase, such an awakening had given rise to visions of an alternative world, which also allowed, and pushed, utopian intellectuals to distance themselves from existing social arrangements.[26]

Detachment and disengagement, however, could also point in another direction—to the abandonment of any moral stance and rather to "look simply at what will be useful, what can make the powerful and exploitative even more so." Examples of such a deflection abounded in China and India, but not in Ancient Israel and, at least apparently, not in Greece. In fact, in addition to those Sophists who had famously equated justice with the advantage of the stronger, Aristotle, although not "an amoralist" himself, had gone a long way toward "severing the link between wisdom (*sophia*) and moral judgement (*phronesis*), though many (including me) have tried to see a link." Distinguishing "useless" contemplation from his proto-sociological, and thus nonutopian, analysis of existing forms of government, Aristotle had split *theoria* in two, opening the way to what Bob saw as the fragmentation of modern culture and the legitimation of utilitarianism as a general approach to the world.[27]

Twenty-three centuries later, Bellah told his public with the tone of a preacher, the heritage of the long-gone axial age had become an ambivalent burden: on the one hand, the abstract quality of theoretical culture made it difficult to transform its ethical imperatives into morally relevant practices without falling prey to sheer instrumental reason; on the other hand, the heightened reflexivity and the asceticism of the axial renouncers might be the only way out of the ecological and cultural crisis of modernity. The axial age "has given us the great tool of criticism. How will we use it?" As the small church burst into applause, Habermas stood up from the first row, embraced Bob, and whispered in his ear: "We've always been at one."[28]

The rest of the meeting passed in a rather egalitarian and convivial spirit, with all the speakers sitting together at a very long table. Because of its classic one-paper-per-participant format, the conference ended up with contributors more showing off their academic prowess than exchanging ideas with one another, as most seemed content to represent themselves according to their usual self-image and broke little new ground. As reported by *Die Zeit*, however, the partisans of the axial age were repeatedly challenged by their critics, and many participants shared Bob's "uncomfortable suspicion . . . that the axial age [had] set the wrong course and that its legacy [was] a burden." Other than some lively skirmishes between Bellah and Assmann, and Habermas and Taylor, papers were read, discussions ensued, and the meeting came safely to its almost natural conclusion—the awarding of an honorary doctorate from the University of Erfurt to a visibly moved Robert Bellah.[29]

If the conference had been a success, another tremendous joy was waiting for Bob and Melanie back home: on August 28, 2008, Barack Hussein Obama, the young senator from Chicago who had won the Democratic primary in June, accepted the nomination as his party's presidential candidate. In an article published in *Commonweal* five months earlier, Bob had expressed his preference for his fellow Harvard alumnus over Hillary Clinton, even if the latter had read *Habits of the Heart* and *The Good Society* and would certainly try to put into practice some of the suggestions advanced in those books. "Like no one since Franklin Roosevelt," Obama had stirred Bellah's political hopes for his understanding of "our political tradition, how it has been distorted in recent years, and how we can return to it at its best." Despite understandable doubts about his lack of experience and inclination to compromise, Bellah saw in Obama "a grandeur and a hope" that made him "want to give him the chance to lead our country."[30]

Not surprisingly, in the fall Bob and Melanie followed the campaign with "more obsessiveness" than they would have liked, a tension that found a happy release on November 4: "Last night was delirious," wrote Bob to Anna Sun and Yang Xiao, who had moved to Gambier, Ohio, some years earlier, "Today I am in shock, not yet quite believing what happened. How exciting being in Ohio, and how different from four years ago [when Bush had carried the state with a 2.1 percent margin]. When I heard CNN declare Ohio for Obama I knew it was all over and gave out a shout." Incredible as it seemed, the United States now had a "real person" and a "grown-up" as its president, something that Bob had lost hope of seeing again during his lifetime. He considered Obama's ability to bring back the best of the American political tradition to his fellow citizens something that the United States had longed for since the tragic death of Abraham Lincoln. With the critical detachment of an axial denouncer, Bellah was not afraid to take a clear stand on the most divisive issues of the past campaign: "Obama would never speak like the Rev. Jeremiah Wright," he blogged eight days before the inauguration, "but he knows, as any serious American knows, that Jeremiah Wright was telling the truth, even if not the whole truth, and that denial of the terrible side of our history is no more healthy for us than it would be for Germany or Japan."[31]

IV

Because of the ceremonial occasion and Bellah's forceful performance, the reinterpretation of Aristotle and his place in the development of Western culture advanced at the Erfurt Brunnenkirche went somehow unnoticed. True, Plato had been one of Bob's earliest influences, and the old claim by I. A. Richards that he had jotted down in his 1947 journal with reference to the *Republic*—"some books are lifetime books"—had never ceased to exert a powerful influence on him. After sixty years and countless readings of that momentous dialogue, Bellah remained fascinated by the "sheer beauty" of Plato's system and still saw the *Republic* as "the greatest philosophical work ever written." At the same time, since his self-identification as an Aristotelian was well known before and after *Habits of the Heart*, his disavowal of the Stagirite was no less than a revolution. To put it bluntly, Aristotle now seemed to play the role in Bellah's intellectual landscape that had hitherto been occupied by Thomas Hobbes.[32]

Like all revolutions, however, Bob's new understanding of Aristotle would reclaim its own bloodbath in the form of an irrecoverable rupture with the man who had been his "shadow editor" for ten years. University of Chicago Press's Doug Mitchell and Bellah had been discussing the "big book" since it was just an idea, and their exchanges had been, on the whole, deep and encouraging. Moreover, when tragedy had hit Mitchell and his wife Christine, Bob had been at their side, having passed through the same horrific situation twice. Early in July 2004, the Mitchells had to face the untimely death of their son, a talented painter and graffiti artist. "Nothing replaces those who have gone," wrote Bob to Doug a few days after the incident, "We have found that there is no 'closure,' no 'moving on,' as the clichés of the day have it. . . . All I can say is that time lessens, never eliminates, the pain, and there is much still to live for." In the following months Melanie sent the Mitchells her books on

Tammy and Abby, and Bob discussed with Doug the Bellahs' inability to ever visit the graves of their daughters.[33]

Sharing the greatest of pains strengthened the bond between Bellah and Mitchell, and became an object of conversation parallel to the more scholarly discussions of Bob's growing body of drafted chapters. In December 2006, upon reading a new section on ancient Greece, Doug told the sociologist that his reflexivity was "something of a marvel to watch in action," but also suggested some additional readings to clarify what he saw as Bellah's too-sketchy treatment of Aristotle. The brief exchange of e-mails that followed highlighted not only Mitchell's deep knowledge of classical philosophy, but also his ability to direct Bob's attention to recent work that could be of some use—in this case, Eugene Garver's *Confronting Aristotle's Ethics*. In a later e-mail, Bellah said he was happy for Mitchell's help in making sense of what he saw as a "disturbing problem"—namely, "how far *sophia* for Aristotle is cut off from ethics," an appreciative comment he repeated also to Bill Sullivan. Seven months later, Bellah shared with Mitchell his satisfaction at having reached his first real milestone: "Even if I die tomorrow, I think there is a book there. It would have been pathetic if it had to end with only the Israel and Greece chapters completed— so Eurocentric! Not that I'm planning to die," he concluded, "Just that I think the completion of the China chapter is a kind of landmark."[34]

With this "mission accomplished" badge on his lapel, Bob set out to work on India and his Erfurt presentation. After he came back from Europe, it took another good year to finally resume his correspondence with Mitchell. In July 2009 Bob was winding up the first draft of *Religion in Human Evolution*, and felt ready to discuss the possibility of a contract for both his book and the collection of the Erfurt papers he would coedit with Hans Joas. At that point, something happened that neither Bellah nor Mitchell had anticipated. Doug read "The Heritage of the Axial Age" and then sent Bob a long, articulate reply. After a number of positive remarks, he cast his doubt on Bellah's "Platonist" denunciation of the Sophists, and then added: "Even more clichéd is to blame the sorry state of Western thought, running off tracks, on Aristotle." From Mitchell's point of view, Bellah's parallel between the Stagirite and Machiavellian theories of power was a "major distortion of Aristotle." "Sorry," he continued, "but I was taught to regard this way of treating texts and ideas (and the history of ideas) as intellectually dishonest. I speak here, not incidentally, as a committed Platonist. But I was imbued many years ago with the conviction that monism and the reduction of concepts, methods, and doctrines other than your own to irrelevancy or to error to be pernicious. . . . And I think it's possible to be a pluralist and a Platonist, simultaneously. But I suppose you could say this is merely my credo, and you have yours."[35]

At the heart of this rather unexpected critique was a difference in method and sensibility that came from afar. As a student of the famed Chicago philosopher Richard McKeon, Mitchell had been trained in a rigorous method aimed at understanding the relationship between philosophical texts and their social environment, on the one side, and promoting constructive communication between different (and apparently irreducible) systems of thought, on the other. The lexicon employed by Mitchell in his e-mails clearly showed that McKeon's famous "semantic matrix" was to him what the AGIL scheme had been (and maybe still was) to Bellah: a powerful heuristic device through which the world and its descriptions made sense. From this perspective, derived from a creative reinterpretation of a "problematic" tradition to which Aristotle, Aquinas, William James, and John Dewey all belonged, Bellah's account of the emergence of theory and his penchant for Platonic dialectics looked like the outcome of a "developmental" and far too "unitary" approach.[36]

Although he knew all of this—or perhaps because he knew it all too well—Bob was appalled. The editor's concluding praise for his "creativity, intelligence, and moral urgency" could do nothing to soothe the pain caused by what the eighty-two-year-old sociologist saw as "shockingly unfair" language. He first answered the e-mail trying to make his case on methodological grounds: "My main subject was the deep source of 'theory'" or, better, "the moment when the archaic becomes the axial, when theory in a way that begins to resemble what we mean by it first appears." He thus justified his focus on Plato according to this principle—"the main point about Aristotle is that he did not invent the new use of *theoria*, Plato did." At the same time, it was also true that Aristotle separated *phronesis, sophia, techne,* and politics—a claim that Mitchell would not contest, but to which he attached a fairly different (that is, positive) meaning. Despite making this argument, however, Bellah felt that the relationship between author and editor had been severely wounded, and wondered whether or not to continue his work with Mitchell.[37]

Had it happened at an earlier stage of the writing process, the exchange might have taken a rather different path. Bellah would have underlined that even if his treatment of the emergence of theory in Greece had been tilted toward (his beloved) Plato, in its entirety the book was a paean for pluralism—in fact, when *Religion in Human Evolution* came out, his judgment on the role of Aristotle in encouraging the separation of theory and ethics was softer than in the original Erfurt piece. Moreover, as he had written in 2006, "for volume II [of *Religion*], Aristotle will be essential, and not only for the West but for Islam"—a suggestion that Mitchell had embraced. In 2009, however, *Religion in Human Evolution* was close to completion and the prospects of writing a sequel were almost nil—especially if Bob stuck to his project of focusing on a shorter compendium on modernity and evolution. There was no time or energy left for a thorough treatment of Aristotle.[38]

Mitchell's complex and well-argued reply included a couple of points that deeply surprised the sociologist. Doug first called the axial age "an entirely Platonic myth," so that claiming a special status for Plato within an explanation of its emergence was, at best, a circular argument; he then suggested that to reconstruct and explain the development of human culture he would seek analogies in the arts rather than the natural sciences. To Bob's ear, the remarks sounded like a disavowal of the two main ideas upon which his book (and, in fact, the research work that had occupied him, on and off, for fifty years)— evolution and the axial age. That was too much. Mitchell wrote his e-mail on July 25, 2009, a Saturday. On Monday Bellah called Lindsay Waters, the humanities editor at Harvard University Press who he had first met in 2006 as an internal reviewer of Charles Taylor's *A Secular Age*, to see if he would consider looking at his drafted chapters. A few hours later Waters responded positively: "I do hope you will let me publish your book."[39]

"I am 82 years old and have been attacked over the years by many people for many things," wrote Bellah in his farewell e-mail to Mitchell, "but it was in your message that I was attacked for being intellectually dishonest for the first time. For a scholar I cannot think of a worse crime. I don't know why you would want to edit a book you thought is intellectually dishonest." Even more importantly, he added, "since evolution and the axial age are probably the two most central ideas in my book[,] I don't see how you can edit a book with which you lack sympathy on these ideas." After a collaboration of eleven years and the sharing of such a tragic moment as the loss of a child, it was a painful decision to break with Mitchell, who later apologized and declared that he continued to believe in the book and in Bellah's "reorientation of the way we regard the relation of past to future." The die, however, was cast: *Religion in Human Evolution* would be published in Cambridge, Massachusetts. Sixty years had passed since Bob had got his hands on the first copies of *Apache Kinship Systems*. It was time to go back home.[40]

V

In May 2010, Bellah sent Waters the manuscript of *Religion in Human Evolution: From the Paleolithic to the Axial Age.* The final version included an expanded conclusion that combined the Erfurt paper with new ideas developed in dialogue with the biopsychologist Gordon Burghardt, whose book *The Genesis of Animal Play* supported, and in fact inspired, what Bellah had written on the transition from episodic and mimetic culture, and allowed him to connect human religion to deeper evolutionary processes. Had Bob been younger, these new developments would have required a major rethinking of his whole argument. In lieu of such a radical move, he had nonetheless rewritten the second chapter from scratch. The original text, drafted in 1997–1998, had employed standard social scientific literature—mainly Michael Mann's *Sources of Social Power*, Jared Diamond's *Guns, Germs, and Steel*, and Marshall Sahlins's *Stone Age Economics*—to summarize the evolution of mankind over the last two million years. The new version was completed in February 2010 and began *far* earlier—that is, from the Big Bang and the appearance of life on Earth. This radical shift, which erased from the book almost any reference to sociological theories of evolution and social change, reflected a widening of Bob's reading and scholarly contacts, itself motivated by his plan to relate natural, social, and cultural evolution in a general sense of universal connection, according to which "we, as modern humans trying to understand this human practice we call religion, need to situate ourselves in the broadest context we can."[41]

The widening scope of *Religion in Human Evolution* could also be read as an unconscious attempt to bring the heritage of the Department of Social Relations to a higher level of complexity. In his writings on the human condition, Talcott Parsons had represented reality as an unlimited succession of levels and layers, each emerging from "simpler" ones and then giving rise to more and more complexity. In much the same vein, Bellah claimed that biological, psychological, social, and cultural structures all contributed to create new capacities from which further change continuously emerged in an endless sequence. Given this framework, religion as a distinctive sphere of symbols, practices, and institutions drew on capacities developed elsewhere and, at the same time, shaped the other orders of reality. Contrary to what some critics would later maintain, the burden of the evolutionary mechanism never fell entirely upon "the biological" or "the genus *Homo*"—to the contrary, Bellah's second chapter accentuated the interplay between the theoretical and narrative registers, as well as the internally pluralistic character of the book as a whole.[42]

Upon receiving the draft, Waters promptly sent it out to anonymous readers. Bob, however, had no time to think about the incoming reviews: he had to take care of Melanie, whose health had seriously declined in the last couple of years. In addition to the unwanted side-effects of the many operations—some medical, some aesthetic—she had undergone since the mid-1990s, her arthritis and back pain had worsened with age, and she had begun to make heavy use of opioid painkillers. In spite of her intermittent medical problems, Melanie had been able to enjoy a rich cultural life at home and outside, but also the coda of her twenty-year intense romance with a charming, married lover. Moreover, she had happily traveled with Bob to Europe in the summer of 2008, where she attended both the Budapest and Erfurt meetings. In November 2008 Melanie underwent an elective surgery that quickly developed into toxic shock, which triggered major organ collapse and brought her close to death. She had to be hospitalized for a full month to treat the infection, and only at the end of December was she allowed to go back to 10 Mosswood Road. In July 2009, shortly before their sixtieth anniversary, she underwent two knee-replacement operations that did not entirely restore her ability to walk.[43]

None of these difficulties, however, prevented her from being a dependable presence during the writing of *Religion in Human Evolution*, which she read step by step, as she had done with all of her husband's work for six decades. Even in her most painful moments, Melanie would assure Bob she was fine and would push him to continue writing his book. In April 2010 the two shared the joy of seeing the finished manuscript, and a couple of months later they read together the various reviews coming from Harvard University Press. One response, in particular, almost made them cry when it called Bob's manuscript "a towering achievement, a triumphant example of a monumental project that would have simply been impossible without a lifetime of deep knowledge and wisdom." All past obstacles, delays, and defeats, but also the loyalty, love, and beauty that Melanie had unfailingly given her husband, had finally resulted in the major accomplishment they had hoped it would be.[44]

Later that summer, however, Melanie's health took a stark turn for the worse. After a two-week stay in intensive care failed to restore her to health, she was sent home for palliative care—no further curative treatment would be provided. On the morning of September 2, 2010, she was carried to 10 Mosswood Road to spend her remaining time with Bob. A hospital bed arranged in the sunny, peaceful living room let Melanie happily look out at the extraordinary vista of Berkeley, the Bay, and San Francisco that she had contemplated so many times, with so many different feelings, over the last forty-three years. After a freshly squeezed orange juice and a light meal, she fell asleep, never to wake up again. Jeremiah had lost his Elizabeth Taylor.[45]

Over the next few days Robert Bellah had almost no time to mourn Melanie—and Shmuel Eisenstadt, who had died on the very same day—busy as he was organizing her funeral at his Episcopal parish, as she had requested. "It is a virtual Mozart concert with a sermon I wrote but won't be delivering," he wrote to Anna Sun and Yang Xiao, explaining that Melanie had asked for the ceremony to be centered around the "Ruhe sanft, mein holdes Leben" aria from the *Zaide*. Bob's notes, read by the pastor, climaxed with a question: Why did Melanie explicitly ask for a Christian funeral if she "was born Jewish and never wanted to convert to Christianity as she saw that as a betrayal of a heritage of suffering"? The answer was simple. Thanks to Paul Tillich's theology of the cross and the experience of artistic masterpieces such as Michelangelo's *Pietà*, the *Descent from the Cross* of Roger Van der Weyden, Bach's *St. Matthew Passion*, and Mozart's *Requiem*, she had developed an emotional participation in the suffering of Christ and an idiosyncratic image of the end. "Melanie's idea of the Resurrection was not some special act for her sake," the notes concluded, "but the great reconciliation of all the endless suffering of life on this earth in the love that overcomes all pain. She had no easy hope, but she had a very big hope."[46]

In the next few days, Bob felt, for the very first time, the void left by the physical absence of his wife: "I do work on feeling that she is still in some way present, but it's not the same as having her in the room," he wrote Sam Porter on September 30, "knowing I could reach out and touch her if I wanted to." After more than sixty years together, Bellah was not even sure that what he had lost could be called "love," if love meant having a relationship with "an other": "Melanie and I had reached the state where there was very little boundary between us," he wrote in another e-mail sent that same day. "We just weren't quite sure where one left off and the other began. . . . Maybe I am idealizing, but I do think we had moved just a bit beyond the old Protestant individualism . . . , not, I think, by submerging the self, just by not holding onto it so tightly." Now that Melanie was gone, no one could ever replace her.[47]

And yet, he concluded, "at sunset I can still see that the world is beautiful. That's one reason I don't want to give up this big house on the hill—because of the views." The other reason was that he had a task to bring to conclusion.

It was from his home office at 10 Mosswood Road that Bellah checked the copyedited manuscript and sent it back to Waters in February 2011. There he read and revised 750 pages of proofs in April, while also working on the introduction of the Erfurt conference collection, which would be published by Harvard University Press in 2012. There he received the blurbs provided by Jürgen Habermas, Randall Collins, and Hans Joas, and there he gave the green light to the final version of the cover and its solemn portrayal of the pyramids of Giza—a nonsectarian, if ironic, choice for a book whose culmination was in the axial age. Bob's entire adult life had been leading toward this moment. The quest was over.[48]

22

Nothing Is Ever Lost

FROM BERKELEY TO THE WORLD, 2011–2013

LATE IN JULY 2011, Robert N. Bellah found his first copy of *Religion in Human Evolution* on the doorstep of 10 Mosswood Road. As he unboxed the superbly produced volume, Bob ran his finger over the dedication to Melanie before stopping on the first of three epigraphs—Thomas Mann's "Very deep is the well of the past." For all his sense of fulfilment, the eighty-four-year-old scholar could not suppress a lingering anxiety. Sure, he had done his homework, with all the necessary care, but how much interest could such an unusual book raise? What would the critics say? Would his sixty-year career end in fireworks, disaster, or just silence? The American Sociological Association, for example, had turned down the proposal of an author-meets-critics session at its August annual meeting on the grounds that it was too late to add it to the program. Conversely, the high turnout at Bob's recent talk at the sociology colloquium at Berkeley and the success of his interview released on the *Atlantic*'s website looked like good omens. Also appreciated was an e-mail from Doug Mitchell, among the first to receive the book: in praising "the very distinguished thing," his former editor depicted the reading as a transformative journey: "Freedom is the achievement of your inquiry . . . and, as the reader realizes the potential in himself that your narrative adumbrates . . . , freedom is achieved by the reader."[1] What, then, was to be found in this huge book, complete with stellar blurbs from Yang Xiao, Hans Joas, and then Jürgen Habermas and Charles Taylor—that is, the contemporary champions of the Kantian and Hegelian traditions?

First of all, the readers would get their hands on a piece of work that was a dialectical recapitulation of everything Bellah had done up to that moment and, at the same time, something incomparable to anything he had ever published. At least from the point of view of breadth and articulation, nothing of what Bob had done before might have predicted such an accomplishment: its 746 pages made *Religion* comparable to the sum of *Habits of the Heart* and *The Good Society*—it was thrice the size of *Tokugawa Religion* and four times longer than *The Broken Covenant*. Second, for an academic treatise published by a top university press, at times the book looked rather peculiar. As if the creative process had the same importance as the final outcome, Bellah offered a singular mise-en-scène of his reflexive "axial" oscillations between truth claims and "the grounds for thinking them true," adding to his arguments and case studies detailed analyses of the reliability of primary and secondary sources, together with evaluations of different translations of ancient religious texts and the rationale for excluding specific historical examples—all operations that are normally consigned to ponderous but hidden endnotes. Using an expression from an author who was perhaps closer to Bellah than it seems, Cornelius Castoriadis, one might say that in *Religion in Human Evolution* "the walls of the building are displayed one after the other as they are erected, surrounded by the remains of scaffolding, piles of sand and rocks, odds and ends of wooden supports and dirty trowels."[2]

More importantly, instead of being presented as standard scholarly craft, the process was portrayed as a personal quest. After twenty-six years happily spent as a member of a group—a fact that he was never tired of repeating— now it was Bellah's voice speaking, with all his idiosyncrasies as a scholar and a human being. Again and again, the author of *Religion in Human Evolution* described himself in the act of reading, thinking, or "looking for friends in history," an expression taken from Mencius that somehow made his sources into real conversational partners. In fact, Bob was everywhere. Citing a chapter of Stuart Kaufmann's *Reinventing the Sacred* titled "Breaking the Galilean Spell," for example, he added a rather outlandish remark—"I in my ignorance thought [it] was going to be a criticism of Jesus" rather than of Galileo Galilei. In a note to the preface, he wrote that he "cannot quite forgive Cliff [Geertz] for dying at the age of 80 and thus not being able to read and respond to what I have written." Again, when introducing his fourth and final chapter on the axial age Bellah declared his "trepidation" and told his readers that if he had possessed "what one might call graduate student competence" on Israel, China, and Greece, he had begun his survey of Indian history and religion "at the freshman level, without a knowledge of the major texts in translation or the major secondary works either." The culmination of this the-author-is-present moral tale was to be found in the conclusion, where Bellah admitted that his recent discovery of the importance of play should have prompted him to rewrite the entire book, a luxury he just could not afford.[3]

Why did Bob use such an intimate (and sometimes self-deprecating) register—one that might sound insincere, pharisaic, or just out of place in an academic treatise? Speaking of himself was nothing new: his deeply personal introductions to *Beyond Belief*, *The Broken Covenant*, and, more recently, *The Robert Bellah Reader* were well known, and had already been justified in theoretical terms in the 1970s. Here, however, his story was inextricably intertwined with the rest of the book. As Bellah would later remark, *Religion* was both his autobiography and the autobiography of the human race—as if the subjective and the objective spirit could be brought together in a single frame.

To put it another way, *Bob was the book and the book was Bob*, but not in any sentimental or purely "subjective" way. A hint at the grounds of what can be seen as an implicit epistemic principle came in the conclusion, where Bellah wrote about the alternation of study and reflection typical of scholarly routines. Juxtaposing the work of Mihály Csíkszentmihályi and Abraham Maslow to Alison Gopnik's distinction between "lantern" and "spotlight" consciousness, he wrote:

> Those engaged in demanding intellectual work, scientists and scholars, often have the experience of flow when all is going well in their work. But there are occasions when all does not go well, when facts turn up that don't fit one's expectations, contradictions appear in arguments that had seemed coherent. Then one must stop the flow and think about what is going on. It is then, I would argue, that we engage in "second-order thinking," thinking about thinking, to try to clarify our problems and find a way to deal with them.[4]

When he applied this double movement of being caught in the flow and then actively using detached reason to solve problems and contradictions to axial-age sages, however, Bob added a crucial dimension. "Experiences of *theoria*," he wrote, "provide an insight into reality so deep that the whole empirical world is called into question," thus activating the possibility of criticizing actual forms of life via the translation of the ineffable experience itself into images and metaphors. In other words, what might seem a detached, "cold" activity of the intellect—casting arguments, evaluating proofs, and reflecting on the grounds of credibility itself—in fact had its roots in the incandescent event of seeing "the world with different eyes" that forever changed the life of the sages and drove them to create the small, tight communities of practitioners needed to transmit their teachings to later generations.[5]

While Bellah did not explicitly write about his own conversion, it was clear that he did not regard such experiences as a thing of the past—as the professionalization of philosophical and theological activity would pretend. As a consequence, he had to find a way to guide his readers through something that would trigger an experience, and his choice fell almost inevitably on the abundant use of narratives—including his own—in addition to analytical arguments. When Bob called his book "a history of histories, a story of stories" and argued that his case studies would "tell just enough, I hope, to help the reader, if only for a moment, *actually experience* what living in those worlds might be like," he was going back to a very old insight. As he wrote in his diary on November 23, 1968, "there must be a great epic poem, a narrative, a journey—which will not only point to the Way but actually get people started on it." Just like the myths and the parables conceived by the axial sages to convey their moments of epiphany, *Religion* tried to encourage "an effort to live again those moments that belong to us in the depths of our present" in the remembrance of those archaic gods and tribal spirits that any human individual had already met as a member of the human species—an image that came close to a Hegel-meets-Jung-meets-Nobby cocktail party.[6]

And yet, the choice of writing such a conceptual-cum-narrative work was also rooted in Bellah's major theoretical point. As anticipated in "What Is Axial?" and often repeated in the book, the emergence of theoretical culture did not simply obliterate mythic and mimetic cultures, but produced a new "hybrid system" where, as Bellah's mantra went, "nothing is ever lost." Paralleling the general insight, *Religion in Human Evolution* combined theory and narrative in the attempt to create a hybrid cultural object that depended upon the dialectical return of theory to mythical forms after a long period of haughty seclusion and a briefer moment of self-reflective despair. In a sense, Bob was making the paradoxical argument that arguments can never be enough. The final result was what could be called a post-post-modern myth—a novel system of explanatory and regulative metaphors for grasping the past, the present, and the future, rooted in "religion" but acted out within, and by, "science." As with any myth, the embrace of multiple metanarratives carried its own practical truth, that of becoming, in Herbert Fingarette's words, "naive but undogmatic." And if paradoxes were not enough, the myth was itself built on the quintessentially modern metanarrative of evolution as the only paradigm that might connect the natural and social sciences to the concerns of humanistic culture.[7]

I

Just like the connection of religion and evolution, the idea of creating an ultimate interdisciplinary cross-pollination of the "three cultures" came from
afar—not only from the Harvard Department of Social Relations, but also
from the long-forgotten presentation of the "Program in Social Change"
penned by Bob and Cliff Geertz at the time of the Bellah affair at Princeton.
There, their conception of interpretive social science had been related to a
number of classical questions: "How institutions, ideas, attitudes, and feelings
evolve and change; why some changes are slow and evolutionary, some rapid,
revolutionary and violent; why some new cultures and new religions remain
the possession of a few and others spread across large parts of the world are
puzzles which have always excited the curiosity and speculation of historians
and philosophers of history. Only in the last generation," they added, "has the
systematic application of the concepts of the social sciences—especially those
of sociology, anthropology, psychology, economics, and demography—begun
to provide the analytical tools for a systematic attack on these problems."[8]

Written in 1972, the plan might well have been used as a blurb for *Religion
in Human Evolution*. Among other things, the new book offered itself as a
border-crossing cultural object built on the fruitful collision of different theories, narratives, and perspectives—an echo of the old Sanders Theater exhortation to "develop multiple schemas of interpretation with respect not only to
others but ourselves." What reviewers would later call Bellah's eclecticism was
in fact a plural (and pluralistic) framework designed to tackle a number of
intricate problems without reducing their ambivalence—to reflect upon contradictions through contradictions. In this sense, the absence of a univocal
demarcation of key concepts like "religion" and the "axial age" was the outcome of a conscious, principled choice: both objects were so elusive, so diverse, so unstable that a definitional straitjacket would have destroyed the
whole enterprise and, probably, the objects themselves.[9]

For example, Bellah candidly declared that his goal with respect to "religion" was to understand "what religion is and what religion does and then
worry about its consequences for the world of daily life"—as Max Weber
would say, the definition would come at the end, and maybe would not come
at all. From Bob's point of view this choice was inevitable. In October 2011, as
he saw early book reviews, Bellah wrote to Arvind Rajagopal that "by giving
an evolutionary (even perhaps in Foucault's sense a genealogical) account of

religion I can avoid all the terminological chaos. If religion is rooted in the body (body-mind-world continuum) as far back as animal play," he added, "and then with mimetic culture becomes ritual, elaborated richly when mythic culture is added so that it concerns 'the general order of existence' (Levi-Strauss' statement that myth must understand everything to explain anything), and then in the axial age brings in a critical/transcendent perspective while reorganizing but not abandoning the mimetic and mythic, then the whole debate over the term 'religion' falls apart." Almost two years later, in one of his last e-mails to his former student, he repeated the point, discussing Hent de Vries's *Religion: Beyond a Concept*: "Someone in that book quotes Nietzsche as saying that you can't have a definition of something that is historical. I couldn't agree more. My definition is not Geertz or Durkheim but *my whole book, all the cases.*"[10]

Just like Virgil in Dante's *Commedia*, Cliff appeared at the beginning of the book with his (in)famous "godless" definition of religion "to get things started." And yet, in the first chapter Geertz's ideas were already placed side by side not only with Durkheim's but also with some long-rehearsed reflections on religion as a Schützian nonordinary reality, Maslow's types of cognition, and Bruner's modes of consciousness, as well as some Wallace Stevens and Václav Havel. The result was still another version of Bellah's recipe for understanding religion in its symbolic, practical, and institutional elements: "There are some common human experiential potentialities that have recognizable similarities, but are inchoate until given shape by symbolic form. Once so shaped, their similarities are always qualified: the differences may be crucial. . . . In short," he concluded, "we cannot disentangle raw experience from cultural form. Nevertheless we can see them as equally essential, like the Aristotelian notions of matter and form, and do not have to choose one approach as primary."[11]

The analysis of "religion *in* human evolution" was then introduced as the study of how religio-cultural configurations had influenced, and had in turn been influenced by, the evolution of humankind through the rise and consolidation of new capabilities that did not necessarily bring an adaptive improvement. In order to accomplish such a grueling task, Bellah employed an enlarged conceptual toolkit that included, besides the types of religious consciousness extracted from Bruner's work on ontogeny and Donald's phylogenetic evolutionary scheme, the distinction between two inclinations common to all mammals, nurturance and dominance, as well as Bellah's own classification of tribal, archaic, and axial societies. The ensuing pattern of resonances was so plural and multidimensional that formal parallels might

engender some confusion. The repeated use of triadic distinctions, for example, threatened to obscure the fact that Bob's three societal stages all came after
the invention of language, and thus after the rise of Donald's mythic culture,
so that half of the story told by the evolutionary psychologist came before the
"real" beginning of the book.[12]

The same was true for what most readers and critics saw as the high point of
Religion in Human Evolution—Bellah's interpretation of the axial age. Having
introduced "play" as a crucial capacity for the creation of a distinctively human
culture, Bellah had slightly modified the evolutionary sequence leading from
our prehuman ancestors to the axial breakthrough. As a "useless" activity detached from the struggle for life typical of ordinary existence, he wrote following Gordon Burghardt, play created those temporary "relaxed spaces" whence
ritual practices and, later, "religion" emerged. Such spaces and rites were nonetheless different in different stages: in archaic societies the participatory rituals
à la Durkheim, which maintained a strong resemblance to extended and inclusive play, typical of tribal societies, evolved in the direction of a class-based
double split. On the one hand, the king and the priestly class monopolized the
worship of the gods who had supplanted the old powerful beings, while warring
elites found their moments of relaxation in hunting, tournaments, and sports;
on the other hand, common people had their own religious festivals where
playfulness was often performed in the guise of a ritual of reversal.[13]

In general, the emergence of hierarchical empires depended on the ritual-
based capacity to command attention on the duality of god and king, which
was, in itself, the necessary cultural and structural premise of the next step. All
axial breakthroughs were in fact born of the question that now introduced
chapter 6: "Who is the (true) king, the one who really reflects divine justice?"—as Bellah would often repeat, no king, no axial age. At this point, however, things got immensely complicated. The definition of the axial turn as the
generalization of "theory as second-order thinking" to all cultural
matters—that is, not only to mathematics and logic, but also to religion and
cosmology—remained unchanged. At the same time, as with "religion," too
precise a definition put at risk the appreciation of individual cases. Bellah
wanted to avoid the facile strategy of electing one of the four societies as the
paradigm of the axial age and then using it as a yardstick to comprehend and
evaluate the others—something that Donald had done by electing ancient
Greece as *the* instantiation of theoretical culture. One strategy, then, was applying second-order thinking to itself by supplementing the 2005 definition
with a number of qualifications, ambivalences, and doubts.[14]

Another strategy had to do with form and structure. After a slightly amended version of "What Is Axial?," chapter 6 introduced the axial turn by way of ancient Israel—that is, the one case where theory "narrowly defined" was nowhere to be found. Instead of analysis, logic, and reflexivity, Israel had invented the Scriptures as a book embodying a religion, but a book that was almost wholly narrative in character. At the same time, the "new models of reality" narrated in the Hebrew Scriptures "involved such a fundamental re-thinking of religious and political assumptions that they had a powerful theo-retic dimension"—an idea that echoed Bellah's old definition of the American civil religion as "a genuine apprehension of universal and transcendent reli-gious reality . . . as revealed through the experience of the American people." Mutatis mutandis, this was also true not only for the book of Deuteronomy, which reached its full critical power through rhetoric rather than logic, but also for the many legal arguments between Israel and Yahweh recounted in the Scriptures. While theory had been said to be the defining feature of the axial break, the story of ancient Israel showed that there could be (at least) one axial break without theory.[15]

At this point, Bellah's strategy can be appreciated in all its post-post-modern singularity: if the four axial cases were so different that they could not be seen "as versions of a single breakthrough," any general definition became a mere placeholder—in a sense, Bob had turned Eisenstadt's abstract, "eventless his-torical narrative" on its head, getting closer, once again, to Geertz's qualms about generalizations. "In our quest to understand what makes the axial age axial," he wrote at the end of his Israel chapter, "we will need to look, surely, at the emergence of theory wherever it arises, but we must also look at the pos-sible transformation of older cultural forms into new configurations, and the social consequences of such transformations."[16]

The search thus moved to locating what I would call each case's unique way of giving the axial turn an incarnation, or, to put it otherwise, its "axial shade." And so, if for Israel the axial shade was a "narrative theology" contained in a written text uprooting religion from its spatial and temporal context, in Greece it was the tragedians and Heraclitus who first had a glimpse of axiality through poetic form, and then it was thanks to Parmenides's early arguments that Pla-to's heroic attempt to reconstruct the whole hybrid system—and, in a sense, the whole culture of humanity—could gain steam. Confucius's axial shade took the shape of a this-worldly transcendence pushing all human beings to take care of their selves by internalizing ritually defined habits, not bereft of an implicit, and sometimes explicit, criticism of actual social forms. Last but not least, the origins of the Indian breakthrough could be found in the "great speculative soteriology" of the Upanishads, whose axial shade was the creation of a new repertoire of metaphors aimed at replacing ritual performance with the possession of esoteric knowledge as the main vehicle of salvation. This first step, built on rhetoric rather than rational argument, was later brought to completion by the revolutionary ideal of the "equality of all human beings in their capacity to follow the Path" typical of Buddhism—which was soon re-absorbed by Brahmanism and forced somehow to migrate to China and Southeast Asia, and finally crushed and remade in the pre-axial culture grinder of Japan.[17]

II

As soon as the book was out in September 2011, reviews started popping up like mushrooms. Twenty years had passed since the publication of *The Good Society* and everything had changed: in the mid-2000s a new user-driven version of the internet, the so-called Web 2.0, had exploded with blogs, podcasts, social networks, and e-commerce websites complete with customer reviews. Before the end of December, Bob's big book had sold eight thousand copies in traditional format, and friends around the world were negotiating translations in a number of languages. On top of this communicative oversupply, the invention of portable e-readers also opened previously unseen possibilities for diffusing ponderous and expensive volumes such as Bellah's—the digital version of *Religion in Human Evolution* sold for half the price of the cloth-bound volume. In what came out as the widest scholarly debate on a work by Robert Bellah *ever*, the encounter between a book that was entirely academic but also entirely personal and the gaze of the other was, understandably but painfully, only in part satisfactory.[18]

Besides calling *Religion* Bellah's magnum opus, most commentators used adjectives such as epic, unique, majestic, immense, fascinating, magisterial, and monumental. The breadth of the book and the erudition of its author pushed more than one reviewer to speak of a "grand narrative" that also projected an image of Bellah as a titanic scholarly figure. Philosopher Eduardo Mendieta spoke of Bob's "long, paradigm-shaping career in the sociology of religion" and his "profound sense of humility and ecumenism," while others praised his style and his evident enthusiasm in writing the book. In an earnest review, the winner of the 1996 Pulitzer Prize for biography, Jack Miles, called Bellah "a glad learner," a phrase echoed by sociologist Jeff Guhin in a passage whose grace touched Bob himself: "Yet it is Bellah's aesthetic sense," he wrote, "that is most remarkable: nothing human is alien to him, and the book often feels like a walk through the world's largest museum, every room an opportunity for another gasp of joy." For Charles Mathewes, comparing Nicholas Wade's *The Faith Instinct* to Bellah's book was "a bit like comparing a comic strip to a Rembrandt."[19]

This magniloquent praise often went hand in hand with an evident uneasiness, as though *Religion in Human Evolution* defied categorization and thus a balanced judgement. As always happened with the work of Robert Bellah, the pack of unbelievers was led by sociologists. In the most visible of all reviews, Alan Wolfe asked rhetorically what a well-known adversary of evolutionism, Cliff Geertz, would have said of the book. "I never thought," he added in his *New York Times* piece, "I would read a book in the sociology of religion that contained a discussion of prokaryotes and eukaryotes. Now I have." For Wolfe, and others, neither the discussion of the biological bases of evolution nor the use of Donald's work really pushed Bellah's argument forward, while the lack of a proper discussion of sociological theories risked reducing the impact of the book on the social sciences. According to David Martin, for example, "the fairy lights of biological terminology add nothing in principle to the modalities of sociological understanding." In the *American Journal of Sociology*, David Smilde concentrated on some of the dualities on which the book was constructed, a theme that was later developed with remarkable finesse by the philosopher of mind Nathaniel Barrett.[20]

A number of reviews also spoke of Bellah's most haunting insight: "Nothing is ever lost." Anticipated in "What Is Axial?," in the book the idea was perfected not only via an extension of the Bruner/Donald syndrome, but also, and more cogently, through the concept of "conserved core processes" coined by biologists Marc Kirschner and John Gerhardt—the idea that basic processes developed by simple forms of life are passed on to more complex organisms as evolution proceeds. "Perhaps," wrote Bellah, jumping from the level of cellular biology to that of macro-societal formations, "each [stage of cultural evolution] is a 'conserved core process,' never lost even though reorganized in the light of new core processes, each promoting variation, adaptive and innovative, but each essential to cultural integrity. That comes close," he concluded, "to stating the central argument of this book." Most reviewers appreciated Bob's insight and compared it to various literary or philosophical traditions—from "Faulknerian" to "Romantic." Not all critics were sold: some saw "a tinge of mysticism" in the slogan, while others considered it a deus ex machina coming to the rescue of Bob's shaky framework. "If [nothing is ever lost] is true," said Martin Riesebrodt, "what do the often-repeated passages in Bellah's book, in which he confesses that we have so much to learn from tribal and other societies, actually mean?"[21]

In a sense, for all the superficial praise and the analogies of Bellah to Durkheim, Weber, or even Hegel, the encounter between the time of Bob's self, the time of the world, and the time of religious symbols and practices that might spring from the pages of the book was delayed, to say the least. "As I read *Religion in Human Evolution*," wrote a particularly curious reviewer, "I kept wondering what had proven so compelling in this task as to hold Bellah's sustained and intense devotion for thirteen years and more, at a season in his life when his doorposts are hung with laurels and the clatter of time's chariot interferes with other, more cherished sounds. It is hard to keep the creative flame alive." Although reviewers observed it as yet another academic product, and thus praised or criticized it according to what such a thing should be, *Religion* was anything but an exclusively scholarly book, and not only for its size or the richness of its theoretical and historical material. It was, *by design*, a much more personal and consciously multitudinous work of love and intelligence rooted in Bob's intimate involvement in intellectual and normative questions—a work whose deep scholarly concerns depended on its author being just so, and not on academic conventions. No wonder that, as had happened so many times during his career, Robert Bellah showed a rather thin skin toward what he saw as unwarranted critiques.[22]

Entering into dialogue with the philosophers, psychologists, and scholars of religion assembled in the symposium hosted by the journal *Religion, Brain, and Behavior*, for example, he opened his rejoinder saying that "reading the six papers, one might wonder if they deal with the same book," an observation soon echoed in his harsh conclusion: "One thing you will not find in my book: that religion is always a good thing. I used to begin my course on the sociology of religion by saying to the students that religion is responsible for some of the noblest things humans have ever done and some of the worst. If you don't see that in my book then you haven't read it." And yet it was the richness and the uniqueness of his work that called for opposing judgments and unexpected readings, some of which, like Johann Arnason's double review, underlined its structural ambivalence. On the one hand, wrote the Icelandic sociologist, focusing on Bellah's treatment of the axial age, the four cases were irreducible to a single definition; on the other hand, most of the concepts employed came from generalizing single instances—"utopia" from Greece, the "renouncer" from India, the "moral upstart" from Socrates, and so on. "Bellah," wrote Arnason, "does not so much overcome the paradox [of the unity and plurality of the axial turn] as turn it around" without forcing it into a number of neat pigeonholes. As with the elephant of the Buddhist parable evoked by Karl Morrison, observers each saw in *Religion* what they wanted, or what they were able, to see.[23]

Almost all of the authors of reviews, articles, and blogs read *Religion in Human Evolution* as a purely "theoretical" cultural object, sometimes noticing the presence of stories, but mostly failing to see how Bellah was trying to forge a post-post-modern myth. In fact, even a brief reflection on the book as a self-referential piece of work would have unveiled one last paradox. If it was to be fully true to its maxim "nothing is ever lost," *Religion* could not be content with being just a theoretical treatise or a mythical narrative—it should also include, as far as possible, embodiment and enactment. Clues about the mimetic dimension of working with symbols abounded, as when Bellah wrote about the travelling performers who in the sixth century BCE wandered through Greece reciting Homeric epics. These long-forgotten actors and singers, he said, bore the responsibility of making the *Iliad* and the *Odyssey* become real for their audiences—just like, a hundred years later, the tragedies staged during the City Dionysia festival and Socrates's own philosophical performances. And yet, since the printed page could in no way capture the mimetic, *Religion in Human Evolution* had to be completed from without. Robert Bellah had to turn himself into a traveling bard.[24]

III

Far from being a routine book tour, then, lecturing about *Religion in Human Evolution* was an integral constituent of Robert Bellah's endeavor: it was the book itself and its post-post-modern myth that drove Bob to give himself—and thus his old age, his fading energy, and all the troubles of traveling—to performing his commitment to evolution and religious pluralism within the relaxed fields of scholarly conferences and seminars.[25]

Not that speaking in front of audiences big and small had ever been a problem for him—it was something he loved to do and had excelled at for his entire life. This time, however, the stakes were higher. Bellah was eighty-four, and knew that it would not be much longer that he would be able to cope with the extensive trips and prolonged interactions he had been used to. Being alone, he could not even enjoy Melanie's help or her company—in fact, he sorely missed her every single day. At the same time, he approached this new, and probably last, book tour with a heightened awareness of the relationship between his work and the need to perform it and, within the latter, between lecturing and interacting with the public and his colleagues, especially those who promised to be critical with a constructive, forward-looking attitude. For this last reason—and not without an obvious feeling of personal gratification and the relief that traveling gave him from his constant longing for his wife— he accepted a dozen mid- and long-distance speaking engagements that took him to Philadelphia, New York City, New Haven, and Seattle, but also to Europe and Asia.[26]

All these trips were hugely successful, each bringing its own blessing to what soon become a farewell tour of sorts, one in which Bellah visited a number of strongly symbolic places, and said goodbye to some old and new friends. In October 2011, for example, he gave a seminar at the University of Chicago at the invitation of Hans Joas. It was the first time he had been away from home since Melanie's death, and he greatly enjoyed the occasion, which he also saw as completing "a kind of a circle" of his life—as reported in the book, his 1964 paper on religious evolution had first been read in Chicago in the presence of a very skeptical Clifford Geertz. One year later, his trip to Tokyo was the opportunity to revisit a great city he knew fairly well, but also to pay homage to his beloved teacher and friend, Maruyama Masao, sixteen years after his passing. Soon after his Tokyo trip, Bellah went to China for the first time in his life as a guest of his ex-student Tu Weiming, a former Harvard professor and leading neo-Confucian philosopher who now headed the Beijing Center for Advanced Study.[27]

Using words that Bob later deemed "almost apocalyptical," Tu called the visit "profoundly significant for the academic, intellectual, and social spheres of China. It will be the first time that a truly ecumenical thinker and public intellectual thinker from the US engages in a series of edifying conversations with some of the most brilliant minds in Cultural China." The most significant event in which Bellah took part during his eighteen-day stay between October and November 2011 was the Beijing Forum, an international academic showcase founded seven years earlier to promote "the harmony of civilizations and prosperity for all." The general theme of the meeting—"Tradition and Modernity, Transition and Transformation"—sounded like a recapitulation of Bellah's lifework. In his inaugural keynote at the Diaoyutai State Guest house, titled "What Changes Very Fast and What Doesn't Change," he remarked that while technological and scientific advances had been running at dazzling

FIGURE 22.1. Robert Bellah and Jenny Bellah Maguire visiting the Forbidden City, Beijing, November 2011. (RBPP)

speed for at least two hundred years, "if we look at our moral resources today, we will find that they draw on traditions of the axial age." The point was that, although they "may seem a million miles away" from one another, the world's major philosophical and religious traditions shared a number of similar principles and inspirations, among them that the equality of all human beings was paramount, that might be recovered through scholarly work and lay goodwill: "None of the great traditions, surely not the Biblical and the Confucian, can be affirmed without critical reappropriation—they have so often been distorted throughout history. Yet," he concluded, "they provide what modernity doesn't, the outline of ways of living that are intrinsically good and not merely means to wealth and power."[28]

Bob's trip to China was made happier by the presence of his daughter, Jenny, who accompanied him on both his many academic engagements and his sightseeing tours, sharing with him what was his first international trip since Melanie's death. They visited the Forbidden City and Tiananmen Square—with its "horrifying" portrait of Mao Zedong—and, together with *Habits of the*

Heart's Dick Madsen, enjoyed the Longevity Hill and the Kunming Lake at the beautiful Summer Palace. Other professional engagements included a lively dialogue on axial age civilizations convened by Tu at the University of Beijing, and a number of meetings and seminars with Chinese colleagues and graduate students. One month later, Bob went back to Asia to give a paper on global civil religion at a conference hosted by the City University of Hong Kong—a sign that he had finally made peace with one of his most famous concepts, the same one he had tried to free himself from thirty years earlier. Bellah's public lectures were widely covered by Chinese state-run mass media, but also by the *New York Times*, where journalist Didi Kirsten Tatlow interviewed Bob about his "exhilarating trips to China" and the necessity to break "Mao's spell" via an updated version of the "true ethical standards" of traditional Confucianism.[29]

In between the two expeditions to China, Bellah stopped in San Francisco for his second American Academy of Religion celebration in fourteen years. On November 20, 2011, a good thousand people crowded the grand ballroom of the Marriott Marquis Hotel to hear Bob exchange views on his new book with indologist Wendy Doniger, historian Luke Timothy Johnson, and the venerated Jonathan Z. Smith. A formidable comparativist from the University of Chicago, twenty-five years earlier Smith had trashed Bellah's 1964 essay on religious evolution, calling it "relatively unsophisticated" and filled with "irresponsibly crude formulations." It was for this very reason that Bob had suggested that the organizer, his former Graduate Theological Union colleague Mark Juergensmeyer, invite Smith, not only to share with him "the agony as well as the delight of doing comparative work," but also, as he said during his reply, because he "did not want a choir of angels on this panel." Contrary to expectations, in San Francisco Smith called *Religion* "a damned good read," emphasized the discontinuities between it and the old article, and praised "the boldness and fruitfulness of its connections and comparisons." Smith's words touched Bellah, who duly expressed his admiration for the historian, and later observed that such an imprimatur from a scholar who had always been seen as "an opponent of 'pietism' in religious studies" meant that from now on it was OK for "those who want[ed] to keep religious studies secular" to use *Religion in Human Evolution* in their courses and seminars.[30]

One year later, Bellah flew to Germany for a felicitous trip of the university towns of Freiburg im Breisgau and Heidelberg, and I joined him to collect some memories and help him with stations, hotels, and universities. Apart from the crowded public lectures and the seminars and interviews with graduate students, Bellah also used his trip to visit some particularly meaning-ful places for the first time in his life. In Freiburg, for example, he and I were brought by Hans Joas on a long streetcar ride to visit the grave of one of the most influential philosophers of the twentieth century, Edmund Husserl. In the small, sunny church cemetery, Bob's fit-over shades and perennial bucket hat could not conceal his emotion at being in the presence of the mortal re-mains of the author of the *Cartesian Meditations* and *The Crisis of European Sciences and Transcendental Phenomenology*.[31]

In damp and cold Heidelberg, Bellah and I were welcomed by the director of the local Deutsch-Americanische Institut, Jakob Köllhofer, who led us to the City Castle to enjoy a breathtaking view of the Neckar River, the old uni-versity town, and the house where Max Weber used to live and where Talcott Parsons had talked with his widow, Marianne, about translating *The Protestant Ethic and the Spirit of Capitalism*. "Have I ever told you," Bob asked his com-panions, "that I am just three hands from Weber?" "What does that mean?" I asked. "It means that my hand has shaken Talcott's hand, which had shaken Marianne's hand who had obviously shaken Max Weber's. That makes me three hands from Weber!" "And so," I laughed, reaching out for Bellah's hand, "now I am four hands from uncle Max!"

Later that evening Bellah lectured in the same hall of the Deutsch-Americanische Institut where Parsons had given one of his last public talks before his death in Munich. Alone on the small stage, the eighty-five-year-old scholar was introduced by Köllhofer as "a man of some rarity" whose new work, *Religion in Human Evolution*, he had read with a growing "feeling of re-naissance." The closing of the conference, a long quote from a conversation between Zixia and Sima Niu taken from the *Analects* of Confucius, perfectly captured the mood of the German trip: "I have heard this: life and death are decreed by fate, riches and honors are allotted by Heaven. Since a virtuous person behaves with reverence and diligence, treating people with deference and courtesy, all within the Four Seas are his brothers. How could a virtuous person," concluded Bellah, "ever complain that he has no brothers?"[32]

Not all encounters were as rewarding, though. Early in December 2012, Bel-lah participated in a two-day symposium on his book convened by the con-servative ecumenical journal *First Things*, and generously funded by the John Templeton Foundation. While he had his former student and now Yale profes-sor Phil Gorski to back him up, he felt "very nervous" to be in such com-pany—a feeling that grew when he received the papers of his commenters, who attacked the book's "impossible pluralism" and "meta-relativism," and

commented on the conflict between the alleged triumphalism of Bob's universal history and Christian theology. For all his interest in dialogue with intellectuals who were far from him ideologically, Bellah sometimes felt overtly
misinterpreted, as when the director of the Thomistic Institute in Rome,
Thomas Joseph White OP, called *Religion in Human Evolution* "the greatest
work of liberal Protestant theology ever"—a charge Bob gently deflected citing
Paul Tillich's critique of the "Protestant principle" by way of "Catholic substance." As later recounted by Rusty Reno, the seminar reached its climax
when Bellah defiantly asked his conservative Christian audience: "Can one
believe in more than one religion?" Needless to say, not one of the participants
shared his clear, staunch "Yes!"—the fruit of fifty years of lived life and scholarly reflection upon the place of religions in human evolution.[33]

IV

Robert Bellah, however, was already working on something else—something
that, as not even he then knew, was hinted at by the austere, dark shot of the
pyramids of Giza featured on the cover of *Religion in Human Evolution*. Originally taken by Italian photographer Paolo Pellegrin in 2006, the photograph
had been cropped just enough to eliminate a small white car—a veritable
metaphor of modernity—heading toward the monumental complex. Between
the pyramids, however, the contemporary city of Cairo remained in plain
sight, as a reminder of the fact that Bellah's journey was only apparently over.
In fact, as he had said in his *Atlantic* interview, "the world is full of questions
and we can't take anything for granted, because the more we know, the more
questions are raised."[34] The new—and the old—question was: How did modernity, and more specifically "the modern project," fare when framed within
human evolution?

While he did not explicitly make the connection, Bob's homecoming to
modernity could be seen as still another version of the return to the Cave on
the part of Plato's enlightened philosopher. As he had told readers in his tribal
religion chapter, since he was a social anthropology undergraduate Bellah had
been convinced that understanding modern society required serious comparative work. As shown by *Tokugawa Religion*, he first considered that the comparative study of different paths of modernization might be sufficient. But soon he
moved to a wider consideration of the history of religions—and its connection
with social evolution in general. As stated in "Religion in the Process of Cultural
Differentiation," a true insight on the nature of contemporary society could

arise only from extended travels beyond the borders of modernity itself—only by escaping the Cave to drink from the bottomless well of the past.

In this sense, the thirty years of his "Babylonian captivity" trying to interpret America on its own terms might be read as a study of the Cave from within. Not that Bob hadn't tried to catch a glimpse of the light that he imagined to shine outside—"The Roots of Religious Consciousness" was his strongest effort to do that. But, perhaps as a connected critic of his own society, he was never able to really break the chains until after he retired. Though with moments of longing for his previous life, he had now spent thirteen years away from the Cave and the time had come to go back. In fact, well before the publication of *Religion in Human Evolution* he had received another small grant from the John Templeton Foundation to start working on a new volume, yet one that was to be quite different from the recapitulative book he had planned in 2004. Since his temporal horizon had ineluctably shortened, Bob anticipated writing an "extended essay" whose tentative title, *The Modern Project in the Light of Human Evolution*, contained a clear gesture toward Habermas's idea of modernity as an "unfinished project."

In spite having spent his whole life reflecting on modernity, Bellah found the modern project difficult to frame—if he had learned anything working on *Religion*, it was that definitions are almost impossible to nail. Luckily, he had a lot of material to draw from. Since 2005, he had considered his conferences and speaking engagements as a way to pursue a study of modernity in parallel to the writing of *Religion in Human Evolution*. A recurring theme of these works was what might be termed the attempt, typical of "the last 2000 years," to disentangle theory from narrative and ritual. As anticipated in the Erfurt paper and, with additional qualification, the conclusion of *Religion*, Bob saw the isolation of cognitive knowledge from ethical and practical considerations, which possibly originated with Aristotle himself, as a foolish move fraught with devastating consequences. "My own deepest fear," Bob wrote to Rajagopal in 2013, "is that the whole project of modernity is suicidal, leading to global ruin." At the same time, since "nothing is ever lost," such disembedding could perhaps be reversed through a vigorous recovery of the insights and practices of past traditions—this was the practical aim of a scholarly ponderous work such as *Religion in Human Evolution*.[35]

In this sense, the steps ahead had been presented in an important diptych of lectures read at the Berkeley Center for Japanese Studies in April 2007. In "Confronting Modernity: Maruyama Masao, Jürgen Habermas, and Charles Taylor," Bellah rambled through the lives and the ideas of three of his most

esteemed intellectual friends to translate his ethical take on the axial tradition, which he had expressed in the clearest way in his final report for the
John Templeton Foundation on May 4, 2007: "There is an impulse toward
universality, so that, while the four axial cultures are indeed different, they
can begin to interpret each other's quest for universality in terms of their
own similar quest." Likewise, the three great intellectuals of the twentieth
century confronted the same juggernaut of modernity from three different
points of view, each rooted in personal experiences and a particular civilizational culture. If Maruyama and Habermas were motivated by the basic concern of creating a democratic society built on universal norms and ethical
individualism, the German philosopher could draw heavily from a national
tradition in which this issue had been thoroughly, and sometimes painfully,
examined. For Bellah, however, only Taylor the Hegelian had understood
that a capital problem lay in the foolish attempt to sever the umbilical cord
with the past, typical of modernity and not alien to Habermas's revamped
Kantianism.[36]

At the same time, wrote Bellah, the task of recovering the deep resources
of human culture was "a daunting and difficult process. To presume that those
resources are readily at hand is a fallacy that will blind us to the seriousness of
our tasks." Certainly, the great axial traditions could be a guide in restoring an
ethical understanding of individual, collective, and global action for the common good, but the history of the last two centuries stood as a sinister warning
against any triumphalism.[37]

In fact, the axial heritage was not at all absent from the modern understanding of the right and the good, for its basic values and intuitions, and its thirst
for radical critique of existing social arrangements, had been converted into a
series of "promissory notes," as Björn Wittrock had called them, that modernity had not yet been able to pay. Promissory notes "can be long postponed,"
Bellah wrote, "but where they are denied too long there will be a high price to
be paid." Not only did detours or regressions from the main path remain possible, but the contradictory nature of modernity itself might put the whole
project at risk. In the past various forms of fascism had hindered the realization
of radical egalitarianism. Now neoliberalism threatened to destroy not only
the individual and collective right to a good life, but also the whole planet in
the process. In its ethical form, Bellah concluded, modernity "is not some
inevitable wave of the future. It is a partial and precarious achievement at best,
in the midst of continuous conflict between the various tendencies of the
modern age and the spiritual wasteland it threatens to create."[38]

What, then, of *The Modern Project in Light of Human Evolution*? Late in July 2012, just in time for the annual meeting of the Habits group, Bellah finished drafting two very different papers, whose titles hinted at one of his favorite pieces of humanistic culture, Goethe's *Faust*. In the short "Prelude in the Theater," he framed his next book as the attempt to question the modern condition on three foundational issues: "What kind of universe do we live in? What is the good life for human beings? Why do the good die young and the wicked flourish?" While these questions had been interrelated for most of the history of humanity, the book would explore the emergence of "a world where physics and ethics have basically no relation to each other" and its likely consequences. In this vein, the ninety-two-page "Prologue in Heaven (or Hell)" presented a quick ride through Western culture in an attempt to understand "the background of cultural modernity from as far back as we can reasonably go with literary sources" to the point of separation of the cognitive and the ethical.[39]

Interestingly, both the cast of actors and the shape of their connections had strong ties to the general education courses attended by Bob as a Harvard undergraduate sixty-five years earlier: framed within the classical theme of "Jerusalem and Athens," the prologue started from the bright light of creation of the book of Genesis, and compared Plato to Moses and Plotinus to Augustine. At this point, with an obvious change of pace, Bellah introduced four pairs of authors in a rhetorical allusion reflecting his hope of reconnecting the mythical and the theoretical: Aquinas and Dante, Calvin and Milton, Kant and Goethe, Tolstoy and Weber. While for the first three duos Bob dedicated twice as many pages to the poets as to the theoreticians, he clearly privileged Max Weber over Tolstoy. It was Bellah's own cultural hero, in fact, who embodied the contradictions and the hopes of the archetypal modern man in his life as well as in his ideas. Torn between the ethics of conviction and the ethics of responsibility, undecided between rigorous specialization and unbound creativity, Bellah's Weber was the mirror in which the author of *The Modern Project* could easily see his own image.[40]

Bob admitted the prologue was a "rather rambling effort" on which "considerable more work [needed] to be done." In spite of this confession, the Habits group responded in a decidedly negative way. Most of their critiques focused on Bellah's use of Lars von Trier's 2011 film *Melancholia* as a cue for his concluding parable on the prospects of an ecological catastrophe. Instead of deleting the reference, as suggested by his friends, Bob wrote a new conclusion to the prologue in which the space dedicated to *Melancholia* was doubled to better explain why he saw it as a meaningful depiction of the contemporary condition. Submerged in its quiet, unrealistic depiction of the end of the world, von Trier's film nonetheless responded to Steven Weinberg's question about the meaning of the universe that Bellah had used as one of his epigraphs: "If the world ends with people who genuinely love each other taking care of each other," wrote Bob, then the universe "has a point that somehow qualifies the long history of suffering that went before. . . . In von Trier's film the bright light of creation is extinguished and we are back in the primordial darkness. . . . My story now has a beginning, a middle, and an end."[41]

V

In March 2013 Bellah spoke at Notre Dame for the very first time and attended a crowded banquet together with the university's highest dignitaries. Nothing, however, could match his next major speech. Early in May 2013 Bob flew to Cambridge, Massachusetts, to give the 40th Paul Tillich Memorial Lecture. The invitation from William Crout, Tillich's translator and the initiator of the lecture series, came at just the right moment. Even before the publication of *Religion in Human Evolution* Bellah had told Bill Sullivan about his idea for still another book as "an effort to write the theology of the concrete spirit that Tillich didn't live to write, that would be Christian theology in a context of the acceptance of multiple religions." The plan came directly from the idea that the difference among axial traditions "is so important to us because what the Buddhists know and what the Hindus know are things that Christians often don't fully know. They're not entirely missing in our tradition, but we are helped to understand more about our own faith if we open ourselves to others." As Bob knew, the lecture had been carefully planned as a ceremonial occasion, and more than eighty people had signed up to participate in the formal dinner in his honor. Everything had to be perfect.[42]

To fuel the writing process, Bellah went back to his favorite form of play: he reread all the books by Tillich he owned and then some new ones, including *The Socialist Decision*, a less-known work written in 1933. Delivered in the austere setting of the Harvard Memorial Church, the Tillich Lecture showed Robert Neelly Bellah at his best: biting, dramatic, and ultimately hopeful. The German theologian came across, perhaps more than usual, as a "friend in history," a living individual with whom Bob talked and interacted as if he were (still) walking down Francis Street. In *The Socialist Decision* Bellah found a scheme of religious history going all the way from primordial myths of origin to Kantian autonomy, through Jewish propheticism and Christianity. In spite of its sketchy nature, Tillich's story harmonized with Bob's "nothing is ever lost" principle to the effect that the myth of origin, particularistic and limited as it was in its many incarnations, could never be entirely eclipsed. It perpetually returned, especially as a connection between things, acts, and spirit—that is, as sacrament.[43]

These preoccupations with modernity and capitalism, which were in large part Bob's own, led to a critique of the distinction between autonomy and heteronomy in the direction of Tillich's trademark "theonomy" as a foundation for a post-Marxist kind of socialism. The point where all of these considerations converged was classic Bellah: the risk of turning Kantian ethics into utilitarianism and the perils of a Protestant principle untempered with Catholic substance—that is, the sacramental trace of the myth of origin needed to keep modern men and women connected to their past and, through it, to "the presence of the divine in everything finite." Neglecting the embodiment of Being in sacraments, said Bellah, meant denying "the natural as sacred," and thus thinking of the world "as something only to be manipulated and exploited." Bob, however, refused to close his lecture with an image of ecological catastrophe: "Preaching doom," he proclaimed, "leads to cynicism and despair, not corrective action." To the contrary, he found in Tillich's notion of *kairos*— the promise of something new in history that nonetheless comes "always too late or too early"—the right, hopeful message with which to conclude. "Don't worry about too late or too early," Bellah said as the audience burst into well-deserved applause, "the *kairos* is now, always now. It is now that we are called to hope and to act."[44]

After his memorable lecture, Bellah dined with a small crowd of Harvard faculty and dignitaries, which included two very old friends, the renowned theologians Harvey Cox and Preston Williams. Harvard still loved him, a lot. But did he still love his alma mater? As a *theoros* of old, Bellah had left home to attend a festival in a place that he knew all too well. As soon as he got back to California he had to tell his fellows all about it. "My feelings about Harvard are very ambivalent," he told Rajagopal, an idea he later elaborated in a long telephone call with Jenny. In an almost physical, visual sense Bob told his daughter of his joy and sense of pride at being back in Cambridge as a such distinguished guest, and also of his pleasure in meeting with old and new friends, including his Harvard University Press editor Lindsay Waters. But he also told her of the clear memory of having felt oppressed under a "lower sky"—to be set on an almost inevitable intellectual and professional path in the shadow of the great man Talcott Parsons. All in all, he concluded, "I ended up feeling very glad I came to Berkeley at the age of forty."[45]

What Bob did not know but clearly feared was that his walk to the Memorial Chapel would be his last across Harvard Yard. In fact, as soon as he got back home he started to arrange things for another testing, but decidedly less joyous, appointment. For fifteen years he had been suffering aortic stenosis, a condition he kept under constant low-key monitoring even in the absence of symptoms or complications. Early in 2013, a routine screening made clear his clinical picture had worsened, and his cardiologist advised him that without surgery he had only one or two years to live. Bellah then agreed to have his aortic valve replaced, a routine operation, which, as he told a restricted circle of friends, had a success ratio of 97–98 percent. At the same time, he asked for a six-month moratorium to be able to complete his travel plan, and especially to honor his appointment with the ghost of Paul Tillich at Harvard.[46]

After some preliminary tests in June 2013, the decision was taken to perform a traditional, invasive operation. On July 29, 2013, Bob woke up very early—he had to be at the Oakland Alta Bates Summit Medical Center at five thirty that morning—took the bag of books prepared to counter this "pesky interruption of his work," locked the door of 10 Mosswood Road, and hopped in the car, where his usual driver, Felix, was waiting for him. He had said a not-so-easy but hopeful goodbye to Jenny and Hally, and everything had been taken care of. Ready for what could be his last trip, Bob remained confident that he might be home in a week to host the planned meeting of the Habits group in his living room: "The assistant said I am in better health than many 56 year olds that they see and she thinks I will not need rehab," he wrote to his four comrades on July 25, 2013. "I think all day at Barrows [Hall, where the Berkeley Department of Sociology is housed] would surely be too hard, but if you were here and I should get too tired, I could always go upstairs and you could stay as long as you want."[47]

"About death," he had told his friends a few days earlier, "I have no anxiety, no need to cling to life. I am not saying I don't care. I choose life and hope I have a chance for a few more years, but I am quite resigned to whatever happens. My native stoicism, plus a dose of philosophical Stoicism and Zen, help me to deal with this possibility quite calmly." And then again, writing to Sam Porter: "As for eternal life, that is now. If we don't see eternity in a grain of sand, when will we ever see it[?]" The Christian belief of the resurrection of the flesh, especially in its bourgeois American adaptation of being reunited with dead friends and relatives, was of no interest to him: "If thinking one will rejoin one's loved ones helps bear the pain of death then I'm all for it. I have to look elsewhere, and, with Heraclitus, declare that life and death are one."[48]

As expected, the surgery went pretty well. Bob woke up and was soon out of intensive care. After he called his daughters and closest friends to give them the good news, he put his hands on a book and started to read. And then, a little more than twenty-four hours after the operation, his heart failed and he was no more. It was July 30, 2013.

Epilogue
The Joy of a Serious Life

IS IT POSSIBLE to encapsulate the many lives of Robert Neelly Bellah—born Luther Hutton Bellah III in Altus, Oklahoma—in a single image, one that might convey a synthesis of such a deeply ambivalent, dialectical individual and his way of being in the world? I see no other way than by pointing to one last apparent contradiction, what I call the joy of a serious life. Bellah's synthesis in his own life of gravity, passion, and play stems from his understanding of the human condition and his radical openness to both novelty and the universal. In its scholarly incarnation, Bellah's joyful seriousness was manifest in an incessant curiosity about the boundless creativity of the human race.

Robert Bellah lived the joy of a serious life to its fullest. Besides the many times he joked about studying and writing as his most cherished sources of enjoyment, he gave one last example of this life philosophy in an e-mail he sent to his *Habits of the Heart* coauthors in July of 2013. In this note, sent just a week before his heart surgery, Bellah professed optimism about the outcome, suggesting that the group meet a week after the procedure. Then he added, "just in case I'm not around to tell you later, I must report on another book that has blown me out of the water." He was speaking of Peter Sloterdijk's *You Must Change Your Life*, which I had urged him to read because I thought it could be crucial for his own research on modernity in the light of human evolution. Bellah was past eighty-six and had only a few days left before the operation he would not long survive. The words he used to describe his experience are worth quoting at length:

> It is a long book, over 450 pages. I liked the book though remained ambivalent until the last chapter, containing 10 pages beginning at p. 442. But when I read those ten pages they descended on me like tongues of fire. The last two pages swept me completely away and it took me nearly an hour to

FIGURE E.1. Robert Bellah in the Alte Aula of Heidelberg University, Germany, November 12, 2012. (AF)

recover. I just sat there overcome. I see now that the whole book was leading up to those last pages, yet I didn't expect them. Those pages express exactly what I want to do in my next book, though giving me lots more ammunition. Sloterdijk talks about the practices we will need to meet the ecological Armageddon, about how they are impossible, but the whole of human history is about attaining the impossible. We should not dwell on doom and gloom but on the greatest challenge our species has ever met and how tremendously exciting it will be to meet it. It was like a giant explosion for me, but not a destructive one, rather a global fireworks display that suddenly shed light on everything.[1]

Study and poetry, seriousness and joy. According to the Italian theorist Giorgio Agamben, the word "study" goes back to a root signifying "a crash, the shock of impact." Studying and being enraptured are one: "Those who study are in the situation of people who have received a shock and are stupefied by what has struck them, unable to grasp it and at the same time powerless to leave hold." But what might provoke this state of inebriation? The fact that, through the "long hours spent roaming through books, when every fragment, every codex, every initial encounter seems to open a new path, immediately left aside at the next encounter," the scholar has learned not only that study cannot have a proper end, but also that it does not desire one. For this reason, I would add, studying is not work, but a joyful combination of intransigence and passion—itself based on the realization that the wavering between discovery and loss ends only with "the moment of death, when what had seemed a finished work reveals itself as mere study." I cannot think of a better way to summarize the life of Robert Bellah.[2]

Or maybe I can. On November, 12, 2012, I was with Bob Bellah and Bill Sullivan on a tour of the old town of Heidelberg together with some German graduate students. Halfway into the walk, we were brought to the Alte Aula of Heidelberg University, the oldest in the country and one of the oldest in the world, beating Harvard by a neat two and a half centuries. Once all guests had taken a seat, the tour guide recounted a story she had told a thousand times before. "Maybe you know that a famous sociologist, Max Weber," she said, "used to teach here." We all nodded as Bob said: "Yes, I know." The tour guide continued: "And maybe you've heard that Weber's most famous book is called *The Protestant Ethic and the Spirit of Capitalism*." And we all said: "Yes, we know." The lady then summarized Weber's work with some difficulty. The graduate students giggled and nudged, making fun of her. Clad in a modest waterproof jacket, Robert Neelly Bellah listened in perfect silence, chin in hand, as if he had never heard of Max Weber before.

NOTES

The abbreviation RNB is used for Robert Neely Bellah throughout the notes.

Preface

1. A video recording of the November 20, 2011, session can be found at American Academy of Religion "A Conversation with Robert Bellah on 'Religion in Human Evolution' SD," YouTube, July 7, 2015, https://www.youtube.com/watch?v=bduUUtnPUgI. Matteo Bortolini to Robert Neelly Bellah (RNB), November 22, 2011, author's files (AF). I attended both Bellah's speech and the party afterwards.

2. I am here paraphrasing K. Moore, *Disrupting Science*, 190ff.

3. *Habits of the Heart* was the result of a collaborative effort between Bellah and four younger colleagues: William M. Sullivan, Ann Swidler, Richard Madsen, and Steven M. Tipton. On the political patterns of the 1990s see Gorski, *American Covenant*, especially ch. 7.

4. Adelman, *Worldly Philosopher*, 14, 656; Geertz, *Local Knowledge*, 19ff. (quote 20).

5. RNB to Stanley Hauerwas, April 16, 1998, RBPP.

6. Stevens, *Letters*, entry of June 20, 1899, p. 27.

7. MP-1967–1968, entry titled "Preface" (summer 1971), my italics.

8. "Robert N. Bellah in Conversation with Michael Lerner," September 13, 2012, transcribed and edited by S. C. Porter, Robert N. Bellah website, accessed November 22, 2020, http://www.robertbellah.com/interviews.html, italics modified; Joas, "Conversation with Robert Bellah."

9. RNB and Keen, "Civil Religion," 65; RNB, "Place of Religion," 153.

10. William Butler Yeats's letter to Lady Elizabeth Pelham was one of Bellah's citation classics from the 1970s onwards.

11. Although this book was written by a sociologist, it is not a sociological book, but a narrative of Robert Bellah's life. At the same time, experts in the sociology of ideas will be able to detect a "hidden theoretical framework," which is quite similar to that employed by Charles Camic in *Veblen*.

Chapter One

1. According to Lovick P. Bellah (*Register of the Bellah Family*, 84), Luther Hutton Bellah Jr. was born on June 19, 1895, while more reliable sources report March 19, 1896. "Bellah's Relatives Keep Death Watch at St. Jo Uncle's Home," *Wichita Daily Times*, April 12, 1931; Luther Hutton

Bellah's obituary, *McCurtain Gazette*, December 6, 1939; "B.Y.P.U. Program April 28," *Hollis Post-Herald*, April 28, 1912; "Commencement Exercises of The Hollis High School," *Hollis Post-Herald*, May 29, 1913; "Hollis Boys to Try for the Naval Academy," *Hollis Post-Herald*, May 22, 1913; "Took Examination at Oklahoma City," *Hollis Post-Herald*, June 12, 1913; News section, *Hollis Post-Herald*, December 4, 1913. Local newspapers have been retrieved from http://gateway.okhistory.org. See also Sylvia Hudson and Zen Stinchcomb, "Hollis," *The Encyclopedia of Oklahoma History and Culture*, https://www.okhistory.org/publications/enc/entry.php?entry=HO014; Linda D. Wilson, "Harmon County," *The Encyclopedia of Oklahoma History and Culture*, https://www.okhistory.org/publications/enc/entry.php?entry=HA026; and John D. Heisch, "Old Greer County," *The Encyclopedia of Oklahoma History and Culture*, https://www.okhistory.org/publications/enc/entry.php?entry=OL002, all accessed November 22, 2020.

2. "Hollis Boys to the Front," *Hollis Post-Herald*, June 29, 1916; "At Home Once More," *Hollis Post-Herald*, February 22, 1917; *Oklasodak*, October 4, 1916, 8; L. White, *Panthers to Arrowheads*, ch. 1; Luther Bellah, "Mex: A Memory," 138; C. Harris and Sadler *Great Call-Up*.

3. "Hollis Furnishes One-Third of Quato [sic]," *Hollis Post-Herald*, August 15, 1917; "Letter from Hutton Bellah at Camp Bowie," *Hollis Post-Herald*, October 31, 1917; "Bellah Served under Wichita Doctor in War," and "Former Editor at Altus, Okla., Dead," both in *Wichita Daily Times*, April 7, 1931. Notice of Bellah's Masonic ties comes from the *Harmon County Tribune*, November 20, 1919. United States War Department, Application for Military Headstone, May 16, 1932.

4. D. Levy, *University of Oklahoma*; Harp, *Sooner Story*. "This Week and Next Will Witness Departure of Fifty or More Harmon County Young People to Take Up College Work. Oklahoma University Most Favored," *Hollis Post-Herald*, September 9, 1920; "Hollis Young People at Different Colleges," *Hollis Post-Herald*, December 1, 1921; "Marriages Column. Bellah-Neelly," *Norman Transcript*, June 25, 1922; *Oklahoma Weekly*, December 16, 1920; "Gets Publicity Job," *Oklahoma Weekly*, December 22, 1921; "Stadium Dope," *Oklahoma Weekly*, January 19, 1922.

5. Luther Bellah, "Mex: A Memory"; D. Levy, *University of Oklahoma*, 1:60–64; Dozier, *Oklahoma Football Encyclopedia*, 83–84; Trotter, *I Love Oklahoma*.

6. "Sixteen Form Senior Phi Beta Kappa List," *Oklahoma Weekly*, April 6, 1922; "Pledges to University Honorary Fraternities," *Oklahoma Weekly*, May 18, 1922. See also Gittinger, *University of Oklahoma*, 69. Information on John R. Neely from the *Biographical and Historical Memoirs of Western Arkansas* (Chicago: Goodspeed Publishers, 1891) can be found at "Yell County, AR—John R. Neely—Bio," USGenWeb Archives, accessed November 22, 2020, http://files.usgwarchives.net/ar/yell/bios/neellyjr.txt.

7. See "Altus Times-Democrat: History," Oklahoma Historical Society, accessed November 22, 2020, http://gateway.okhistory.org/explore/collections/ALTUST/; Hearn, *American Dream*; quote Kennedy, *Freedom from Fear*, 10.

8. "SnapShots," *Altus Times-Democrat*, January 6, 1928 and July 13, 1928; "Altus Civic Head Names Committees," *Altus Times-Democrat*, February 6, 1929. For the *Altus Times-Democrat* see Google news, https://news.google.com/newspapers?nid=LpWf3qrnWeoC.

9. "SnapShots," *Altus Times-Democrat*, January 25, 1928 (first two quotes); April 12, 1928; July 1, 1928; November 6, 1928 (third quote); November 7, 1928; November 9, 1928. In fact, after the 1928 elections Bellah also received a host of rude letters, to which he responded in print. See "SnapShots," *Altus Times-Democrat*, November 13, 1928; C. Alexander, *Ku Klux Klan*, 25ff., 162ff.

10. "President of State Editors," 363. "SnapShots," *Altus Times-Democrat*, March 21, 1929; March 24, 1929; March 25, 1929. See also Hopkins, "Harry B. Rutledge"; Hanson, "William Judson Holloway," 36–37.

11. "SnapShots," *Altus Times-Democrat*, March 6, 1928.

12. "SnapShots," *Altus Times-Democrat*, May 4, 1928.

13. "SnapShots," *Altus Times-Democrat*, January 7, 1929; Snaps III's photo was published on May 6, 1928.

14. $35,000 in 1929 roughly corresponds to $530,000 in 2020 (all inflation calculations made via https://www.bls.gov/data/inflation_calculator.htm). "SnapShots," *Altus Times-Democrat*, July 21, 1929; July 22, 1929; "W. A. Lee Identified by Wife as Bellah: Blames Act on Mental Troubles," *Yuma Morning Star*, April 8, 1931; Harral, "Portrait of a Sooner," 281; "President of State Editors," 363.

15. In 1930 Altus had a population of 8,439, and the whole State of Oklahoma of 2,396,040 (US Department of Commerce, *Fifteenth Census*, 571, 541). See also Starr, *Endangered Dreams, Dream Endures*, and *Material Dreams*, 66ff., 83, 99–100, 111–15, 168; Cuff, *Provisional City*, 102–17.

16. Starr, *Material Dreams*, 70–71 (Bliven quote 70), 128–30; Bottles, *Los Angeles and the Automobile*, 93, 113–15; Roderick, *Wilshire Boulevard*, 121ff.; M. Davis, *City of Quartz*, 24ff.

17. It is not clear if Hutton knew that Lillian was pregnant. The suicide note was left in the hope that Lillian and Snaps III could live on Hutton's life insurance. Since no evidence of his death was found at that time, however, the insurance money was not paid. "Luther Hutton Bellah"; "Bellah's Suicide Ends Year of Waiting by Chicago Woman Left on Eve of Wedding Day," *Wichita Daily News*, April 18, 1931; "Lee Identified by Wife as Bellah."

18. "Bellah's Relatives Keep Death Watch at St. Jo Uncle's Home," *Wichita Daily Times*, April 12, 1931; "Body Is Identified by Widow on Arrival from Los Angeles: Burial to Be at St. Jo, Texas," *Wichita Daily Times*, April 7, 1931; "Hutton Bellah Asked but Failed to Await Aid from His Friend," *Wichita Daily News*, April 8, 1931. The *Altus Times-Democrat*'s coverage of Hutton's suicide was particularly limited.

19. According to family lore, Lillian decided to change Hutton III's name after a fortune teller advised her to do so in order to avoid bad luck (Hally Bellah-Guther, June 3, 2018, AF). Since elementary school records from June 1933 bear the name "Bob Bellah," the name was changed shortly after Hutton's suicide. M. Bellah, *Tammy*, 395.

20. Kenen, "Who Counts," 197–218; Advisory Board for Medical Specialties, *Directory of Medical Specialists* (1942), 138; *California Medical Association Bulletin* 52, no. 1 (January 1940).

21. NJ 1969–1979, entry of February 9, 1979. Starr, *Endangered Dreams*, 67–69; Bottles, *Los Angeles and the Automobile*, 212ff.; Cuff, *Provisional City*, 34ff.; Wecter, *Age of the Great Depression*, 175, 183.

22. RNB, "My Autobiography," handwritten paper, 2 pp., Robert Bellah's report cards for the 1933–1935 school years, RBPP. "Magazine Is Passed Around," 195; "In the Mail . . . ," 2.

23. "Calling the Roll of Sooner Classes," 57. Bellah delivered a speech titled "A Plan for the Future" at the school's graduation exercises on January 29, 1942. John Burroughs Junior High School, *Graduations Exercises*, leaflet, January 29, 1942; RNB to Lillian Bellah, May 30, 1947; RNB to Lillian Bellah, April 28, 1948; RNB to Robert Blauner, January 12, 1998; all RBPP. RNB, *Beyond Belief*, xii; RNB, interview, AF.

24. FBI files on RNB, 100–24924, December 31, 1947. Davis, *City of Quartz*; Starr, *Endangered Dreams*, 198, 222, 318, 321, 340ff.; Hearn, *American Dream*, 49, 57–67, 113, 149–51, 192; Starr, *Dream Endures*, 4ff., 20–23, 196–97 (quotes), 285ff., 342ff., 392–94, 260ff.; Starr, *Embattled Dreams*, 33, 66ff., 196–98, 322.

25. RNB, "Inside L.A." *Blue and White*, November 6, 1944. RNB to Alissa and Melanie Guther, May 7, 2007, RBPP. RNB to Samuel C. Porter, September 19, 2005, SPPP. RNB to Matteo Bortolini, March 3, 2008; RNB to Matteo Bortolini, July 10, 2008; both AF. M. Bellah, *Tammy*, 35, 58.

26. RNB, "Inside L.A." *Blue and White*, September 18, 1944; October 9, 1944; September 25, 1944; October 16, 1944; November 20, 1944; December 4, 1944; October 2, 1944; January 15, 1945; October 23, 1944; November 27, 1944; October 30, 1944. At the time, Los Angeles High enrolled slightly fewer than three thousand students. "Roosevelt Carries L.A. Student Vote; Governor Dewey Favored by Faculty," *Blue and White*, November 6, 1944. M. Bellah, *Tammy*, 590.

27. RNB, "Inside L.A." *Blue and White*, November 13, 1944.

28. RNB, "Inside L.A." *Blue and White*, December 11, 1944. For what follows, see RNB to Lillian Bellah, February 26, 1945; RNB to Lillian Bellah, February 28, 1945; both RBPP. A later self-interpretation of Bellah's high-school persona can be found in PR-1954, entry of December 30, 1954.

29. Mary D. Howell to the Committee on Scholarships at Harvard, n.d. [late 1944], RBPP. In the mid-1940s only 4% of all Harvard students came from the Far West. Buck, *General Education*, 183–84. On Bellah's obsession for winning, see RNB to Phil Helfaer, March, 26, 1978; William Sullivan to RNB, April 4, 1978; both RBPP. NJ 1969–1979, entry of February 12, 1979. RNB, interview, AF.

30. Webb, *Born Fighting*; Lovick Bellah, *Register of the Bellah Family*.

Chapter Two

1. RNB to Lillian Bellah, February 26, 1945; RNB to Lillian Bellah, February 28, 1945; both RBPP.

2. Geiger, *History of American Higher Education*, 532ff., 546 (quote); Mattingly, *American Academic Cultures*.

3. Jencks and Riesman, *Academic Revolution*, 13–20; Freeland, *Academe's Golden Age*, 49ff.; Geiger, *History of American Higher Education*, 528ff.; Mattingly, *American Academic Cultures*, 94; Cohen-Cole, *Open Mind*, 68ff.

4. Kerr, *Uses of the University*, 14ff.; Freeland, *Academe's Golden Age*, 20ff.; Mattingly, *American Academic Cultures*, 116ff., 256 ff.; Karabel, *Chosen*, 40ff. (Eliot quote 45); Story, *Harvard*, 173ff.; Isaac, *Working Knowledge*, 37ff., 47ff.

5. Lowell cited in Karabel, *Chosen*, 46–47; Lowell, "Dormitories and College Life"; Mattingly, *American Academic Cultures*, 168; Synnott, *Half-Opened Door*, 34ff.; Jencks and Riesman, *Academic Revolution*, 734.

6. Jencks and Riesman, *Academic Revolution*, 743–47; Isaac, *Working Knowledge*, 52ff.; *War-Time Program at Harvard*, 8, 12; *What about Harvard?* "The Society of Fellows," *Harvard Crimson*,

January 10, 1933; John P. Demos, "Society of Fellows," *Harvard Crimson*, May 9, 1957; Homans and Bailey, "Society of Fellows at Harvard," 91 (quotes); Isaac, *Working Knowledge*, 54–55, 69–72.

7. Isaac, *Working Knowledge*, 32; Keller and Keller, *Making Harvard Modern*, 6

8. Karabel, *Half-Opened Door*, 139–41, 150–51, 166ff., 175–79; Freeland, *Academe's Golden Age*, 52–54; S. Lipset, "Political Controversies at Harvard," 153; Conant, "President's Report"; Hershberg, *James B. Conant*, 66ff., 78–79.

9. Hershberg, *James B. Conant*, 79–80, 104–10; Keller and Keller, *Making Harvard Modern*, 64ff.; James B. Conant, introduction to Buck, *General Education*, viii.

10. Conant, "President's Report," 15–17.

11. RNB to Lillian Bellah, February 28, 1945, RBPP. Harvard University, *Official Register*, 45 (1948): 115; "College to Admit 116 Men into Spring Term Class of '48," *Harvard Crimson*, January 19, 1945; "Term Enrollment Sinks to Year's Low of 741," *Harvard Crimson*, March 6, 1945; Hanford, "College"; Lant, *Our Harvard*.

12. RNB to Lillian Bellah, February 28, 1945; RNB to Lillian Bellah, March 3, 1945; both RBPP.

13. RNB to Lillian Bellah, March 3, 1945 (quotes); RNB to Irma Hesser, March 4, 1945; both RBPP. General information about residential life in Adams House, 1930– (30-G-4), HUA, HUD 3119, folder: General Directory 1940s; "Adams' Food Best . . . ,"*Harvard Crimson*, March 26, 1948; "Adams Presents Good Food, Pool, Location Near to Yard," *Harvard Crimson*, March 24, 1950; Jencks and Riesman, *Academic Revolution*, 753–54.

14. RNB to Lillian Bellah, February 28, 1945, RBPP.

15. RNB to Bessie Wright, n.d. [early March 1945], RBPP; see also RNB to Irma Hesser, March 4, 1945, RBPP.

16. RNB to Lillian Bellah, March 5, 1945, RBPP.

17. RNB to Lillian Bellah, March 12, 1945; RNB to William Sullivan, n.d. [March 2002]; both RBPP. See also Harvard University, *Official Register*, 45 (1948): 57ff.; "Calendar of Introductory Meetings," *Harvard Crimson*, February 27, 1945.

18. RNB to Lillian Bellah, March 3, 1945 (quote); RNB to Lillian Bellah, March 5, 1945; RNB to Lillian Bellah, March 14, 1945; all RBPP.

19. Select Service System, Certificate of Fitness for Robert N. Bellah, March 20, 1945; RNB to Lillian Bellah, March 3, 1945; RNB to Lillian Bellah, [March 23?], 1945; Cecil Fraser to Lillian Bellah, March 24, 1945; all RBPP.

20. RNB to Matteo Bortolini, July 10, 2012, AF. William S. Banks to commanding officer, Medical Detachment, Tilton General Hospital, June 13, 1946, RBPP. FBI files on RNB, 100–20265 JAS, August 31, 1950. RNB to Willian Cantwell Smith, October 13, 1954, MUA, 1996–0025.01 #621. Sparrow, *History of Personnel Demobilization*, 21–22.

21. William S. Banks to commanding officer, Medical Detachment, Tilton General Hospital, June 13, 1946; RNB to Lillian Bellah, May 1, 1946; both RBPP. Kelly, *History of Fort Dix*.

22. RNB to Lillian Bellah, May 24, 1946, RBPP.

23. RNB to Lillian Bellah, April 21, 1946; RNB to Lillian Bellah, May 21, 1946; RNB to Lillian Bellah, May 24, 1946; all RBPP.

24. RNB to Lillian Bellah, June 18, 1946; RNB to Lillian Bellah, June 29, 1946; both RBPP.

25. RNB to Lillian Bellah, June 29, 1946, RBPP.

26. RNB to Lillian Bellah, September 27, 1946, RBPP.

27. RNB to Lillian Bellah, July 4, 1946 (quotes); RNB to Lillian Bellah, June 29, 1946; RNB to Lillian Bellah, July 7, 1946; RNB to Lillian Bellah, July 13, 1946; RNB to Lillian Bellah, September 19, 1946; RNB to Lillian Bellah, September 27, 1946; all RBPP. RNB, interview; RNB to Matteo Bortolini, July 10, 2012; both AF.

28. RNB to Lillian Bellah, September 12, 1946 (quotes); RNB to Lillian Bellah, October 17, 1946; RNB to Lillian Bellah, October 20, 1946; RNB to Hallie Bellah, October 25, 1946; RNB to Lillian Bellah, November 16, 1946; Special Orders #149, extract, June 24, 1946; all RBPP.

29. RNB to Lillian Bellah, August 12, 1946; RNB to Lillian Bellah, September 19, 1946; RNB to Lillian Bellah, October 20, 1946; RNB to Lillian Bellah, November 17, 1946; all RBPP.

30. Harvard University, *Official Register*, 46 (1949): 9, 170. On the GI Bill, see Bennett, *When Dreams Came True*; Mettler, *Soldiers to Citizens*, 6–7.

31. $500 in 1947 roughly corresponds to $5,800 in 2020. RNB to Lillian Bellah, October 23, 1946; RNB to Lillian Bellah, January 30, 1947; RNB to Clifford Wright, January 31, 1947; all RBPP. See also Harvard University, *Official Register*, 46 (1949): 135. A poll taken among veterans in March 1947 calculated that living expenses for single students amounted to $101 a month ("Poll Finds Veteran Expenses Well Above Government Pay," *Harvard Crimson*, March 28, 1947). In a letter to Lillian Bellah dated April 4, 1947 (RBPP), Bob added another $230 per term for living expenses.

32. Geertz, *After the Fact*, 99; D. Clark, "Two Joes Meet"; Harvard University, *Official Register*, 46 (1949): 10, 37; *Veterans Administration Guidance Center*; Karabel, *Half-Opened Door*, 181ff.; Keller and Keller, *Making Harvard Modern*, 34ff.; Mettler, *Soldiers to Citizens*, 7; Bennett, *When Dreams Came True*, 238–41; Mattingly, *American Academic Cultures*, 280ff. Later that year, Bob told his mother that he had no friends among the members of Harvard final clubs. RNB to Lillian Bellah, September 12, 1947, RBPP.

33. RNB to Lillian Bellah, February 2, 1947; RNB to Lillian Bellah, February 5, 1947; both RBPP. Buck, *General Education*, 40 ("some over-all logic"), 190 ("honest thinking"), 53–76; Conant, introduction to Harvard University, *Official Register*, 45 (1948): 11ff.; Cohen-Cole, *Open Mind*, 20ff.; Harvard University, *Official Register*, 45 (1948): 34ff.

34. Syllabus for "Social and Psychological Foundations of Behavior" in HUA, HUC 8582.4.1, syllabi, course outlines, and reading lists in social relations, 1946–1973, box 1/8. See also RNB to Lillian Bellah, January 23, 1947; RNB to Lillian Bellah, February 22, 1947; RNB to Lillian Bellah, March 13, 1947; RNB to Lillian Bellah, April 4, 1947; RNB to Lillian Bellah, November 24, 1947. all RBPP. A dense fifty-page diary of Bellah's intellectual and political experiences (N-1947) is kept in his personal papers. Given the internal organization of this journal, however, it is nearly impossible to distinguish between notes taken during lectures, discussions, and study, and Bellah's own elaborations.

35. RNB to Lillian Bellah, March 25, 1947, RBPP.

36. Harvard College, Office of the Registrar, May 1, 1950, HUA, UAV 801.2235, social relations, general exams and thesis grades 1947–1955. According to the "Memorandum on Concentrators and Honors in Social Relations" drafted by Henry W. Riecken in November 1949, only 1.8% of social relations seniors made group I of the Dean's List—a list of the 2% best students in the college—in 1949 (HUA, UAV 801.2005 social relations, box 1, minutes 1946–1951). RNB

to Lillian Bellah, May 4, 1947; RNB to Lillian Bellah, May 30, 1947; RNB to Lillian Bellah, June 13, 1947; RNB to Lillian Bellah, July 7, 1947; Delmar Leighton to Lillian Bellah, June 20, 1947; Delmar Leighton to Lillian Bellah, September 19, 1947; RNB to Lillian Bellah, November 24, 1947 (quotes); RNB to John Witte, November 1, 2005; all RBPP.

37. RNB to Lillian Bellah, February 8, 1948; RNB to Lillian Bellah, March 14, 1948; both RBPP. Diamond, *Compromised Campus*, 29–39. McGeorge Bundy to Nathan Pusey, April 27, 1955, HUA, UAI 5.169, records of President Pusey, box 89, "Bellah Case, 1956–1957." FBI files on RNB, May 26, 1955. "Communists: The Top Twelve," *Time*, August 2, 1948.

38. Bellah's quote from FBI files on RNB, May 26, 1955. RNB, "'Veritas' at Harvard"; RNB, interview, AF; FBI files on RNB, November 11, 1947; FBI files on RNB, January 10, 1948; FBI files on RNB, August 31, 1948; Victor Grossman to Matteo Bortolini, January 10, 2018; Staughton Lynd to Matteo Bortolini, June 14, 2017; both AF. Grossman, *Crossing the River*, 31ff.; S. Lipset, "Political Controversies at Harvard," 179ff.; Schrecker, *No Ivory Tower*; Lynd and Lynd, *Stepping Stones*.

39. RNB to Lillian Bellah, January 23, 1947; RNB to Lillian Bellah, August 8, 1947; both RBPP. In 1947–1948 concentrators in social relations were around 10% of the total number of Harvard College affiliates, while students who chose anthropology were slightly less than 1%. The highest numbers of concentrators were in economics (16.6%), government (15.5%), and English (10.3%). T. Kroeber, *Alfred Kroeber*, 206ff.

40. RNB to Hallie Bellah, February 8, 1948, RBPP.

41. RNB to Lillian Bellah, March 21, 1948, RBPP.

42. RNB to Lillian Bellah, December 8, 1947; RNB to Hallie Bellah, December 20, 1947; RNB to Hallie Bellah, February 2, 1948; RNB to Lillian Bellah, April 28, 1948; all RBPP. D. Lipset, *Gregory Bateson*, 177–79.

43. RNB to Lillian Bellah, April 19, 1948; RNB to Lillian Bellah, April 28, 1948; RNB to Lillian Bellah, n.d. [spring 1948]; all RBPP. To my knowledge Bellah never resumed his relationship with Bateson after 1948, and has never mentioned it in print.

44. RNB to Lillian Bellah, September 18, 1948, RBPP. Bellah never visited Altus again in his life: RNB to Matteo Bortolini, May 27, 2008, AF.

45. RNB to Lillian Bellah, October 8, 1948 (quote); RNB to Lillian Bellah, n.d. [fall 1948]; RNB to Lillian Bellah, November 16, 1948; RNB to Lillian Bellah, December 21, 1948; RNB to Lillian Bellah, January 23, 1949; RNB to Lillian Bellah, April 27, 1950; all RBPP. "HYD, Reed Group Merge: New Club Backs Eisler Talk," *Harvard Crimson*, February 16, 1949; "Lecture by Eisler Overflows Hall; No Jokes This Time," *Harvard Crimson*, February 23, 1949; S. Lipset, "Political Controversies at Harvard," 182; RNB, "'Veritas' at Harvard"; RNB, interview, AF.

46. RNB to Lillian Bellah, n.d. [spring 1948], RBPP.

47. RNB to Lillian Bellah, April 27, 1950, RBPP.

48. RNB to Bessie and Clifford Wright, August 16, 1949, RBPP.

49. Feibelman, *New Orleans Jewish Community*, 70ff., 110ff., 87ff., 130ff., 133–34.

50. Information about Melanie's family comes mostly from "Descendants of Sam Oscar Heiman," November 29, 2014, http://photos.geni.com/p13/51/6a/83/12/5344483d0228fc20/descendantreport_original.pdf; Jennifer Bellah Maguire to Matteo Bortolini, July 8, 2018, AF. Advisory Board for Medical Specialties, *Directory of Medical Specialists*, 3: 329.

51. When fully grown, Bellah peaked at nearly six foot three, while Melanie was under five foot two. Jennifer Bellah Maguire to Matteo Bortolini, July 8, 2018; Jennifer Bellah Maguire to Matteo Bortolini, January 2, 2020; both AF. RNB, "Notes about Melanie for Phil Brochard's Memorial Sermon," September 2010, RBPP.

52. M. Bellah, "Unity Takes Opinion"; "On Your Dial-880-," *Stanford Daily*, October 25, 1948. Melanie Bellah to David Riesman, January 5, 1969, DRP, HUGFP 99.12, box 1. Winters, *Poets of the Pacific*. RNB to Hallie Bellah, September 22, 1946; RNB to Lillian Bellah, April 20, 1947; RNB to Lillian and Hallie Bellah, May 12, 1947; RNB to Lillian Bellah, February 22, 1947; all RBPP. Staughton Lynd to Matteo Bortolini, June 14, 2017, AF.

53. M. Bellah, *Tammy*, 621. Eli Sagan, interview, AF. Bob and Melanie spent $30 (comparable to $325 in 2020) for their wedding party and documents. RNB to Lillian and Hallie Bellah, May 13, 1952; RNB to Bessie and Clifford Wright, August 16, 1949; both RBPP.

54. The poem comes from P-1949–1954 and is signed "For Melanie, December 31, 1949." M. Bellah, *Abby and Her Sisters*, 183.

55. "Syllabus, Social Relations 130, Institutional Structure, Spring Term 1950," HUA, HUC 8582.4.1, "Syllabi, Course Outlines and Reading Lists in SR 1946–1973." Accessible introductions to Weber and Durkheim can be found in J. Alexander and Smith, *Cambridge Companion to Durkheim*, and S. Turner, *Cambridge Companion to Weber*.

56. RNB to Clifford Geertz, November 26, 2002, CGP; RNB, interview, AF. On Kluckhohn, see Schneider, *Schneider on Schneider*, 79–81. RNB to Robert Blauner, n.d. [summer 2001]; RNB to Lillian Bellah, April 3, 1950; RNB to Lillian Bellah, March 3, 1950; all RBPP.

57. Social Relations, general exams and thesis grades 1947–1955, HUA, UAV 801.2235; DSR, "Recommendations for Degrees," Report of the Committee on Undergraduate Education, May 21, 1950, HUA, UAV 801.2205, box 1. "Brooks Addresses 94 New PBK Members," *Harvard Crimson*, June 20, 1950. Of the seven Phi Beta Kappa Prizes awarded between 1935 and 1949, three went to dissertations in history and classics, two in legal studies, and one each in mathematics and philosophy. RNB, *Apache Kinship Systems*.

Chapter Three

1. Isaac, *Working Knowledge*, 55ff.; "Harvard Tercentenary Celebrations."

2. Isaac, *Working Knowledge*, 52–59; Buxton, "Snakes and Ladders," 42; Nichols, "Establishment of Sociology at Harvard," 202–7; Johnston, "Sorokin and Parsons at Harvard" and *Pitirim A. Sorokin*; Stouffer, *Behavioral Sciences at Harvard*, 6.

3. Isaac, *Working Knowledge*, 161–64, 174; Buxton, "Snakes and Ladders," 41; Cot, "1930s North American Creative Community," 134; Camic, "Talcott Parsons," xxxviii; Engerman, *Know Your Enemy*, 43ff.; "Social Science," 395ff.; and "Rise and Fall"; Cohen-Cole, *Open Mind*, 79–85; Isaac, *Working Knowledge*, 164ff.; Brick, *Transcending Capitalism*, 140ff.

4. Allport and Boring, "Psychology and Social Relations," 119–20 (quotes); Triplet, "Harvard Psychology"; McAdams, foreword to *Explorations in Personality*; Pettigrew, "Gordon Willard Allport"; Nicholson, *Inventing Personality*; Toby, "Samuel A. Stouffer"; W. Taylor, Fischer, and Vogt, *Culture and Life*; Homans, *Coming to My Senses*.

5. Camic, "Talcott Parsons," xvii–xxiii; Scaff, *Max Weber in America*, 213–19.

6. Camic, "Talcott Parsons," xxxi, li–lii, lviii; and "Three Departments," 1004–12, 1026.

7. J. Alexander, *Theoretical Logic in Sociology*, 4:8ff.; Camic, "*Structure* after 50 Years" and "Utilitarians Revisited"; Owens, "Producing Parsons' Reputation." See also the chapters by Camic, George Steinmetz, and Andrew Abbott in Calhoun, *Sociology in America*.

8. "Laboratory of Social Relations Report for the First Five Years, 1946–1951," 1951, 21–22, HUA, HUF 801.5151 (HUA 37-E-3); Cohen-Cole, *Open Mind*, 88ff.

9. In a memo written in 1958, Robert W. White indicated 1951 as the end of "the exciting intellectual climate of the Department." See Robert W. White, "Memo to Permanent Members," April 9, 1958, HUA, UAV 801.2241.

10. Geiger, *Research and Relevant Knowledge*, 219–23; Berelson, *Graduate Education*, 25ff.

11. Barzun, "Scholar Is an Institution"; R. Davis, "Guidance of Graduate Students"; Wilson, *Academic Man*, 90–91; Stouffer, *Behavioral Sciences at Harvard*, 51, 56, 296, 299; Guetzkow et al., "What Is Originality," 206. A thorough analysis is presented in Cohen-Cole, *Open Mind*, which I closely follow. On the concept of "scholarly persona" see Paul, "Sources of the Self"; Isaac, "Tool Shock."

12. McAdams, foreword to *Explorations in Personality*; Toby, "Samuel A. Stouffer," 135–36 (quote); Hauser, "Samuel Andrew Stouffer," 36; Pettigrew, "Gordon Willard Allport"; Vidich, *With a Critical Eye*; F. Cherry, "Nature of Prejudice."

13. Shils, *Fragment of a Sociological Autobiography*, 86. Merton, "Remembering the Young Talcott Parsons"; Riley, "Talcott Parsons"; R. Williams, "Talcott Parsons"; Smelser, "On Collaborating with Talcott Parsons"; Renée Fox, *In the Field*; M. U. Martel, and M. Shields, "A Contemporaneous Ancestor: Testimonials from Parsons' Retirement Banquet (May 18, 1973)," TPP, HUGFP 42.8.8, alphabetical correspondence, 1965–1979, box 12.

14. Parsons, "Graduate Training in Social Relations," 152; "Laboratory of Social Relations Report for the First Five Years, 1946–1951," 1951, 19–20, HUA, HUF 801.5151 (HUA 37-E-3); Edward Tiryakian, interview, AF. The seminar and the way it was conducted were favorably evaluated by students: see "Report on the Dept.: Replies to a Questionnaire Sent to Ph.D's from 1950–1954," 1956: 63–67, HUA, UAV. 801. 2457.

15. The expression "possession" is taken from Renée Fox, *In the Field*, 72. The combined number of graduate students in the Department of Social Relations is found in Parsons, "Graduate Training in Social Relations," 150. See also the brief attached to "Report on the Dept.: Replies to a Questionnaire."

16. See Parsons, "Graduate Training in Social Relations"; "Harvard University and Radcliffe College: Department of Social Relations," pamphlet, n.d. [spring 1950], HUA, UAV 801.2005, DSR, box 1, "Minutes 1946–1951," book minutes 1950–51. Vogt and Albert, *People of Rimrock*; Power, "Harvard Study of Values"; Isaac, "Epistemic Design."

17. Szanton, *Politics of Knowledge*; Solovey, *Shaky Foundations*; Parmar, *Foundations of the American Century*, 37ff.; Rohde, *Armed with Expertise*; Price, *Cold War Anthropology*, 376; Schneider, *Schneider on Schneider*; Geertz, *After the Fact*; Suleski, *Fairbank Center*.

18. David Aberle to RNB, June 23, 1950, HUA, UAV 801.2010, box 3, folder "Aberle, David F. 49–50"; Melanie Bellah to Bessie and Clifford Wright, September 23, 1950, RBPP; RNB, "Research Chronicle: Tokugawa Religion," 164–65.

19. Packard, *Edwin Reischauer*, 41–54, 58–63, 1–3; Dower, *War without Mercy*; Evans, *John Fairbank*, 49ff., 74ff., 106ff.; Suleski, *Fairbank Center*, 12–14.

20. Reischauer and Fairbank "Understanding the Far East," 121–23; Packard, *Edwin Reis-chauer*, 36 (quote); Evans, *John Fairbank*, 57ff.; Reischauer, "Serge Elisséeff"; Suleski, *Fairbank Center*; Fan, *Harvard-Yenching Institute*.

21. DSR, Committee for Higher Degrees, minutes of meetings of October, 4, 1950, and October 25, 1950; both in HAU, UAV 801.2005, DSR, box 1, book minutes 1950–51; Francis M. Rogers to Gordon W. Allport, October 23, 1950, in HUA, UAV 801.2010, box 6; DSR, "Graduate Students: Admissions for 1950–51," June 7, 1950, HUA, UAV 801.2010, box 6; Geertz, *After the Fact* and "Shifting Aims, Moving Target"; Cossu, "Clifford Geertz"; Parsons, "Clyde Kluck-hohn," 35; Buxton and Nichols, "Talcott Parsons," 6, 9–11; Parsons "Graduate Training in Social Relations," 154. Melanie Bellah to Bessie and Clifford Wright, September 23, 1950, RBPP.

22. Melanie Bellah to Lillian Bellah, December 30, 1951 (pursued by hounds quote); Melanie Bellah to Lillian Bellah, September 23, 1950; both RBPP. See also RNB to Lillian Bellah, May 19, 1952; RNB to Lillian Bellah, May 11, 1950; Melanie Bellah to Lillian Bellah, October 22, 1950; Melanie Bellah to Lillian Bellah, December 5, 1950; Melanie Bellah to Lillian Bellah, December 18, 1950; RNB to Lillian Bellah, December 18, 1950; RNB to Lillian Bellah, December 29, 1950; RNB to Lillian and Hallie Bellah, May 13, 1951; Melanie Bellah to Lillian Bellah, June 3, 1951; RNB to Lillian Bellah, September 7, 1951; RNB to Lillian and Hallie Bellah, February 3, 1952; RNB to Lillian Bellah, May 3, 1952; all RBPP.

23. As an example of how people tended to focus on Bob as the breadwinner, for their second wedding anniversary Earl Hyman gave the young couple a bespoke suit for Bob. Melanie Bellah to Lillian Bellah, June 3, 1951; RNB to Lillian Bellah, January 4, 1953; RNB to Lillian Bellah, November 24, 1953; RNB to Lillian Bellah, December 1, 1953; all RBPP. During Bob's graduate school years, the Bellahs lived on five sources of income: Bob's fellowships from the Harvard-Yenching Institute (1951–1952, 1952–1953, 1954–1955) and the Social Science Research Council (1953–1954), ranging from $1,500 to $3,000 a year; Melanie's salary; a small donation of $300 a year given by the Sagan Foundation; a contribution of $1,000 given by California to its student citizens after 1951; and small gifts from their families. Robert Bellah's application for a fellowship to Harvard-Yenching Institute, December 12, 1952; Robert Bellah's application for a fellowship to Harvard-Yenching Institute, February 7, 1954; both RBPP; Robert Bellah's application for a fellowship to the SSRC, December 1952, HUA, UAV 801.2010, box 10, folder "B, 1952–53." RNB to Lillian Bellah, April 20, 1951; RNB to Lillian Bellah, September 7, 1951; Serge Elisséeff to RNB, April 1, 1953; RNB to Serge Elisséeff, April 4, 1953; Serge Elisséeff to RNB, April 1, 1954; RNB to Serge Elisséeff, April 2, 1954; Melanie Bellah to Lillian Bellah, December 18, 1950; Melanie Bel-lah to Lillian Bellah, December 18, 1950; RNB to Lillian Bellah, December 29, 1950; RNB to Lillian Bellah, March 18, 1951; RNB to Lillian Bellah, April 20, 1951; all RBPP. Jennifer Bellah Maguire to Matteo Bortolini, January 2, 2020, AF.

24. RNB to Lillian Bellah, February 26, 1951, RBPP.

25. In October 1949 Parsons had already drafted half of *The Social System*, which was then rewritten several times. Jeremiah Kaplan to Talcott Parsons, October 5, 1949; Talcott Parsons to Jeremiah Kaplan, October 7, 1949; Talcott Parsons to Jeremiah Kaplan, October 21, 1949; Talcott Parsons to Jeremiah Kaplan, March 2, 1951; all TPP, HUGFP 42.8.4, box 17, folder "The Free Press—Jerry Kaplan 1947–1949." Parsons and Shils, *General Theory of Action*, 56ff., 76ff.; Parsons, *Social System*, 38ff., 24; Isaac, "Theorist at Work," 307ff.

26. RNB, *Apache Kinship Systems*, 1–11, 133–35, 82–107; M. W. Smith, review of *Apache Kinship Systems*, 14; Eggan, review of *Apache Kinship Systems*. RNB to Lillian and Hallie Bellah, May 13, 1951; Melanie Bellah to Lillian Bellah, June 3, 1951 (quote); RNB to Lillian Bellah, June 19, 1951; Melanie Bellah to Lillian Bellah, December 30, 1951; Melanie Bellah to Lillian Bellah, June 13, 1952; RNB to Lillian Bellah, November 11, 1952; all RBPP.

27. RNB to Lillian Bellah, June 19, 1951, RBPP. Department of Social Relations Committee of Higher Degrees, minutes of June 13, 1951, HUA, UAV 801.2005, box 1, book minutes 1950–51. N-1951–1952, entries of August 20 and 21, 1951.

28. For Bellah's sparse ideas about his thesis, see N-1951–1952, entries of August 20, 1951; November 19, 1951; February 14, 1952; June 27, 1952. RNB, "Research Chronicle: Tokugawa Religion," 168–73 (quote 168). Bellah's exam for the Social Relations 164 course (sociology of religion), RBPP.

29. Talcott Parsons to Crane Brinton, December 14, 1951, HUA, UAV 801.2010, box 9, folder "Society of Fellows 1951–52"; minutes of Social Relations departmental meeting, January 22, 1952, HUA, UAV 801.2005, box 2, minutes 1951–56, book minutes 1952–51; RNB to Talcott Parsons, March 31, 1952, HUA, UAV 801.2010, box 7, folder "B 1951–52." For Bellah's retrospective interpretation of the episode, see NJ-1965–1969, entry of April 8, 1967. "Interstitial" Harvard refers to the informal interdisciplinary groups that were able to steer the institution outside of formal organs. See Isaac, *Working Knowledge*, ch. 1.

30. In the end, Bob and Melanie were able attend Hallie's wedding, probably thanks to some financial help on Earl Hyman's part. RNB to Lillian Bellah, May 3, 1952; RNB to Lillian Bellah, May 13, 1952; RNB to Lillian Bellah, May 19, 1952; Melanie Bellah to Lillian Bellah, June 13, 1952; RNB to Lillian Bellah, July 2, 1952; all RBPP. Talcott Parsons to Elbridge Sibley, "Recommendation letter for Robert N. Bellah," March 28, 1953, HUA, UAV 801.2010, box 10, folder "B 1952–53."

31. Bellah, "Research Chronicle: Tokugawa Religion," 174. RNB to Lillian Bellah, November 11, 1952; Bellah's draft of the letter to Robert E. L. Faris, n.d. [late January 1953]; Robert E. L. Faris to RNB, February 24, 1953; RNB to Robert E. L. Faris, February 27, 1953; Robert E. L. Faris to RNB, March 6, 1953; all RBPP. RNB, interview, AF.

32. Of the fifty-plus researchers who worked on the project between 1949 and 1954, only eight were included as writers in the first draft of the final report. Given Bellah's serendipitous and marginal involvement in the project, the request to write two chapters shows the high status he had achieved at Social Relations while still a doctoral student. Upon his return to Cambridge in the fall of 1953, Bob wrote a long report on the Mormons of Ramah and drafted a second paper on the religious systems of the five cultures; the former remained unpublished, but the latter achieved print in 1966. "Extract from Departmental Records," March 13, 1953, HUA, UAV 801.2010, box 12, folder "Values Study"; "Recommendations for Special Examinations in Sociology," HUA, UAV 801.2005, box 2, book minutes 1952–53. Detailed prospectuses for the books and of Bellah's chapters dated May 6, 1954, can be found in the Robert Redfield-Ford Foundation Cultural Studies Papers, box 7, Special Collections Research Center, University of Chicago. RNB to Lillian Bellah, May 6, 1953; RNB to Lillian Bellah, June 21, 1953; Melanie Bellah to Lillian Bellah, August 17, 1953; RNB to Lillian Bellah, September 20, 1953; RNB to Lillian Bellah, November 24, 1953; Evon Z. Vogt to RNB, November 26, 1995; RNB to Renée Fox, November 10,

2004; all RBPP. RNB, "The Mormons of Rimrock," unpublished paper, RBPP, 34; RNB, "Notes on a Middle Eastern Journey," unpublished paper, RBPP, 1–2.

33. This is how Melanie Bellah later explained Bob's desire: "Since Bob's father had died when he was quite young and he had no brother, he did hope for a son." Bob's preferences were well known in the family, as witnessed by this page of an autobiographical essay written by Tammy in 1972 and cited by Melanie: "Another sister, Harriet, was born when I was in second grade. I know that my parents had the dream of a son and with every daughter their dream died. But four seemed enough so my family has been essentially female." M. Bellah, *Tammy*, 22. Hallie Bellah to Lillian Bellah, November 20, 1953; RNB to Lillian Bellah, November 24, 1953; RNB to Lillian Bellah, December 1, 1953; all RBPP.

Chapter Four

1. RNB to Lillian Bellah, January 24, 1954, RBPP. RNB, "Research Chronicle: Tokugawa Religion," 175–77.

2. RNB to Yenching Institute, February 7, 1954; Bellah's dissertation prospectus, March–April 1954; both RBPP. Bellah, "Research Chronicle: Tokugawa Religion," 179–80. PR-1954, entries of April 4, 1954; April 21, 1954; April 22, 1954; April 23, 1954; April 24, 1954; April 29, 1954.

3. Mills, *Power, Politics and People*, 574; Geary, *Radical Ambition*, 168ff.

4. P. Tillich, *Courage to Be*, 35ff., 46ff., 3, 163–64; H. Tillich, *From Time to Time*; Finstuen, *Original Sin*.

5. Poem dated September 1954, in P-1949–1954. RNB to Lillian Bellah, July 23, 1954, contained in PR-1954 (perhaps not sent). P. Tillich, *Courage to Be*, 171ff.

6. P-1949–1954, entry of December 30, 1954, narrating events that happened between May 4, 1954, and the following fall. The poem, which was never shown to Bellah's friend, is reproduced in RNB to William Sullivan, December 11, 1977, RBPP. See also RNB to William Sullivan, October 22, 1977; RNB to William Sullivan, October 25, 1977; both RBPP.

7. A precis of Parsons's presentation and subsequent discussion can be found at pages 69–74 in E. Z. Vogt and E. M. Albert, "MEMORANDUM," October 27, 1954, 79 pp., TPP, HUGFP 42.25, folder "Flagstaff Values Study Conference." Parsons and Smelser, *Economy and Society*; Smelser, "Marshall Lectures."

8. RNB, "Religion and Society in Tokugawa Japan" and "Research Chronicle: Tokugawa Religion," 182ff. DSR, Committee for Higher Degrees, February 28, 1995; Talcott Parsons to Florence Kluckhohn, May 9, 1955. The thesis was accepted on May 9, 1955, and the discussion was waived. Talcott Parsons to Francis M. Rogers, May 9, 1955. All documents HUA, UAV 801.2010, box 15, folder "Graduate School, Harvard 1954–55."

9. The piece was published only in 1970, in RNB, *Beyond Belief*, 260–88. On Tillich's influence, see Mews, "Paul Tillich"; Murphey, "Scientific Study of Religion," 153ff.

10. Tillich, *Courage to Be*, 41; RNB, *Beyond Belief*, 282ff. Talcott Parsons to Jeremiah Kaplan, September 16, 1955, TPP, HUGFP 15.2, folder "Publishers—Free Press 1955–56."

11. M. Bellah, *Tammy*, 6–7.

12. Talcott Parsons to Elbridge Sibley, March 28, 1953, HUA, UAV 801.2010, box 10, DSR, correspondence etc., 1952–1953 A–D, folder "B," 1952–1953. Schrecker, *No Ivory Tower*, 203, 241ff.;

Diamond, *Compromised Campus*, 24ff., 40–41; Bird, *Color of Truth*, 125–33; Keller and Keller, *Making Harvard Modern*, 189ff., 203ff.

13. RNB, "'Veritas' at Harvard." RNB to R.B.Y. Scott, September 25, 1954, MUA, 1996–0025.01 #621.

14. RNB to Wilfred Cantwell Smith, October 13, 1954; Wilfred Cantwell Smith to RNB, October 23, 1954; RNB to Wilfred Cantwell Smith, November 1, 1954 (quote); Wilfred Cantwell Smith to RNB, November 6, 1954; all MUA, 1996–0025.01 #621.

15. After an initial five-year grant, in 1955 the Rockefeller Foundation awarded the institute a long-term endowment of $500,000. The very same year, the Ford Foundation included the institute in its Foreign Area Fellowships for American students; in 1957 it added to the original allowance funds for bringing Muslim students to McGill. Cracknell, "Introductory Essay"; Lockman, *Field Notes*, 11ff., 73ff. Wilfred Cantwell Smith to F. Cyril James, July 12, 1955; Secretary of Ford Foundation to F. Cyril James, July 28, 1955; both MUA, 0000–00865.01#139. Webster, *Fire and the Full Moon*, 92–93.

16. W. Smith, "Place of Oriental Studies," 107–8, and "Comparative Religion," 34–38, 42, 54.

17. W. Smith, *Islam in Modern History*, 97, 18–20, 32, 89ff., 41, 55ff., 93ff., 123ff., 105ff., 300.

18. Wilfred Cantwell Smith to RNB, November 27, 1954; R.B.Y. Scott to Wilfred Cantwell Smith, November 6, 1954; both MUA, 1996–0025.01 #621. RNB to Talcott Parsons, December 14, 1954, HUA, UAV 801.2010, box 14 "1953–54—1954–55." John C. Pelzel to the dean of the Faculty of Graduate Studies and Research, McGill University, December 17, 1954; Talcott Parsons to the dean of the Faculty of Graduate Studies and Research, McGill University, December 22, 1954; both MUA, 1996–0025.01 #621. During the departmental meeting of December 7, 1954 (one week before Bob asked Parsons for a letter of recommendation for McGill), Bellah's name was discussed along with those of David Bordua and Morris Zelditch, but no final decision was taken. Talcott Parsons to Harvard University Appointment Office, "Reference for Robert Bellah for H.U. Appointment Office," December 8, 1954, HUA, UAV 801.2010, box 14, folder "B 1954–55"; Talcott Parsons to McGeorge Bundy, April 18, 1955; Talcott Parsons to McGeorge Bundy, May 11, 1955; both HUA, UAV 801.2010, box 17, folder "Bundy-Appointments, Staff 1955–56."

19. Bundy's letter to Pusey is cited and quoted in RNB, "McCarthyism at Harvard."

20. RNB, "'Veritas' at Harvard" and "McCarthyism at Harvard" (quotes). Dana Farnsworth to McGeorge Bundy, May 13, 1955, HUA, UAV 801.2010, box 17, folder "Bundy-Appointments, staff 1955–56"; RNB to Lillian Bellah, January 24, 1954, RBPP. Wilfred Cantwell Smith to RNB, February 25, 1955; RNB to Wilfred Cantwell Smith, March 9, 1955; RNB to Wilfred Cantwell Smith, April 10, 1955; RNB to Wilfred Cantwell Smith, May 17, 1955; all MUA, 1996–0025.01 #621.

21. Webster, *Fire and the Full Moon*, 95ff.; Adams, "Institute of Islamic Studies." RNB to Lillian Bellah, October 17, 1955; M. Bellah, *Tammy*, 7–8; RNB to Lillian Bellah, December 1, 1953; all RBPP. J. M. Laval to RNB, September 26, 1955, MUA, 1996–0025.01 #621.

22. Bellah sat at least seven exams in the MA program, always topping his class (MUA 0000–0865.01#170). Four undated papers have survived from his days at the institute: "Muhammad as a Statesman and Social Reformer" (31 pp.), "Sufism and Its Political Implications" (17 pp.), "Faith, in the Commentary of Al-Taftazani" (12 pp.), and "Legalism and Traditionalism" (13 pp.); all RBPP. On the "continuity thesis," see Lockman, *Contending Visions*, 103ff. (quote at 106). RNB to Institute for Islamic Studies, January 1, 1956, MUA, 1996–0025.01 #621; William

Cantwell Smith to Joseph M. McDaniel Jr., November 16, 1956, MUA, 0000–00865.01#139 (final Smith quote). Dinçşahin, *State and Intellectuals in Turkey*, 97ff. William Cantwell Smith to Joseph M. McDaniel, Jr., June 16, 1956, MUA, 0000–00865.01#139; William Cantwell Smith to F.J.S. Thomson, June 15, 1956, MUA, 1996–0025.01 #621. Bob's monthly stipend of C$300 (roughly corresponding to $2,100 in 2020) was paid two-thirds by the Rockefeller endowment and the remaining one-third by the Ford Foundation grant. D. C. Bain to I. M. Stickler, March 13, 1957, MUA, 0000–00865.01#139.

23. RNB to Talcott Parsons, November 14, 1955; Talcott Parsons to RNB, December 6, 1955; RNB to Talcott Parsons, December 11, 1955; Talcott Parsons to RNB, December 15, 1955; RNB to Talcott Parsons, January 10, 1956; Talcott Parsons to RNB, January 17, 1956; all TPP, HUGFP 15.2, box 5. Clifford Geertz, "Comments on Bellah's Paper on the Typology of Religion (Addressed to Professor Parsons)," unpublished paper, 20 pp., RBPP, 20, 2–4. Cossu, "Clifford Geertz."

24. RNB, "Religion in the Process of Cultural Differentiation," unpublished paper, 85 pp., 2nd version, RBPP, 1–3, 7–9, 49.

25. RNB, 21–23, 29–33.

26. RNB, 85, my italics.

27. N-1951–1952, entry of June 27, 1952. Glock, "Sociology of Religion"; Glock and Stark, *Religion and Society in Tension*, 170; RNB, "Religion in America," unpublished paper, 45 pp., RBPP, 16, 39.

28. Columbia offered Bellah an entry salary of $6,700 a year ($63,000 in 2020). Jerry Muller to Matteo Bortolini, July 8, 2018, AF. RNB to Talcott Parsons, May 21, 1956; Talcott Parsons to RNB, May 31, 1956; RNB to Talcott Parsons, June 7, 1956; all TPP, HUGFP 15.2, box 5. Evon Z. Vogt to Ralph W. Tyler, February 21, 1955; David F. Aberle to Ralph W. Tyler, April 11, 1955; Talcott Parsons to Ralph W. Tyler, July 26, 1955; "Bellah, Robert, Card #2"; all SUA. Tyler, "Study Center for Behavioral Scientists"; Crowther-Heyck, "Patrons of the Revolution," 439ff.; Bessner, *Democracy in Exile*, 178ff.

29. Lockman, *Contending Visions*, 134–35; Babai, "Fifty-Year Odyssey," 4–8; Khalil, *America's Dream Palace*, 147ff., 156–57 (Langer quote 157). Talcott Parsons to RNB, December 20, 1956, RBPP. Wilfred Cantwell Smith to F. Cyril James, October 18, 1956; William A. Westley to F. Cyril James, March 5, 1957; Wilfred Cantwell Smith to F. Cyril James, March 5, 1957; F. Cyril James to Wilfred Cantwell Smith, March 11, 1957; all MUA, 1996–0025.01 #621. Ralph W. Tyler to RNB, February 25, 1957; RNB to Ralph W. Tyler, March 14, 1957; Ralph W. Tyler to RNB, March 19, 1957; all SUA.

Chapter Five

1. RNB to Wilfred Cantwell Smith, n.d. [around October 1, 1957], MUA, 1996–0025.01 #621, folder "Robert N. Bellah." RNB to Talcott Parsons, October 21, 1957; Talcott Parsons to RNB, October 28, 1957 (both TPP, HUGFP 15.2, box 5), where Bellah also speaks of a request from Robert K. Merton and Harcourt Brace to write a handbook on the sociology of religion. Robert W. White to McGeorge Bundy, September 23, 1957, HUA, UAV 801.2010, box 20. M. Bellah, *Abby and Her Sisters*, 7ff., and *Tammy*, 11ff.; Gilman, *Mandarins of the Future*; Crout, "Paul Tillich"; Calí, *Paul Tillich First-Hand*. RNB to George Wright, December 8, 1997, RBPP.

2. Heyck, *Age of System*, 9; Calhoun, *Sociology in America*; S. Turner, *American Sociology*.

3. Heyck, *Age of System*, 10–11, 18ff., 129, 145–46, 178ff.; Allport, *Individual and His Religion*, v, 1; Bauer, Inkeles, and Kluckhohn, *How the Soviet System Works*, 163; Wallace, "Revitalization Movements," 277.

4. Parsons, "Pattern of Religious Organization," 67–68, 77ff.; RNB, "Place of Religion," 152.

5. RNB to Wilfred Cantwell Smith, n.d. [around October 1, 1957], 1996–0025.01 #621, folder "Robert N. Bellah."

6. Talcott Parsons, "Report of the Chairman on the First Decade: 1946–1956," in *Department and Laboratory of Social Relations: The First Decade 1946–1956* (Harvard University), HUA, HUF 801.4156.2, 69–73 (quote 73). Riesman (in 1957) and Erikson (in 1960) were hired directly by McGeorge Bundy and given the freedom to choose their department, and they picked Social Relations. P. L. Schmidt, "Towards a History of the Department of Social Relations, Harvard University, 1946–1972" (unpublished BA honors thesis, Department of Psychology and Social Relations, Harvard University), HUA, HU 92.78.769. Freeland, *Academia's Golden Age*, 146ff., 161ff.; Keller and Keller, *Making Harvard Modern*, 189ff.

7. Keller and Keller, *Making Harvard Modern*, 175ff., 265ff.; Freeland, *Academia's Golden Age*, 138ff.; Darrow, "Harvard Way"; Reynolds, "Later Years," Pusey's quote 228; Carman and Dodgson, *Community and Colloquy*, 13–20. Some correspondence between Slater and Bellah is on record at HUA, UAV 880.10, box 5.

8. RNB to Talcott Parsons, January 8, 1958; Talcott Parsons to RNB, January 31, 1958; RNB to Talcott Parsons, February 27, 1958; Talcott Parsons to RNB, March 4, 1958; all TPP, HUGFP 15.2, box 5. Robert White to Douglas Horton, February 6, 1958, HUA, UAV 801.2010, box 10. Suleski, *Fairbank Center*, 11–16, 22–23; Deptula and Hess, *Edwin O. Reischauer Institute*, 42–43; Lockman, *Field Notes*, 147ff., 135; Khalil, *America's Dream Palace*, 165ff.; Evans, *John Fairbank*, 199–203.

9. RNB, "Religion and Society in Tokugawa Japan," 3–5, and *Tokugawa Religion*, 192–95, 185. Talcott Parsons to Jeremiah Kaplan, September 16, 1955; Talcott Parsons to Jeremiah Kaplan, May 10, 1956; Jeremiah Kaplan to Talcott Parsons, May 14, 1956; RNB to Talcott Parsons, May 21, 1956; Jeremiah Kaplan to Talcott Parsons, October 17, 1956; all TPP, HUGFP 15.2, box 20.

10. Latham, *Modernization as Ideology*, 4, 22, 28 (quotes); Gilman, *Mandarins of the Future*, 101–2; Ekbladh, *Great American Mission*; Knöbl, "Theories that Won't Pass Away," 96–107.

11. Bijan Warner, "Dialogical History and the History of a Dialogue: Three Visions of the Committee for the Comparative Study of New Nations at the University of Chicago," unpublished paper, 2011, Warner's personal files.

12. M. Levy, " Modernization of China and Japan," 168; Rostow, "Take-Off into Self-Sustained Growth," 42.

13. Gilman, *Mandarins of the Future*, 4. 66, 132ff., 151; Knöbl, "Theories that Won't Pass Away," 97–98; RNB, "Introduction to the Paperback Edition," xii, xviii.

14. RNB and Albert M. Craig, "The Myth of the Middle Class in Japan," unpublished paper, 1959–1960, 134 pp. divided into different batches, RBPP, R22b. RNB, "Religion and Society in Tokugawa Japan," 15–16; *Tokugawa Religion*; "Durkheim and History"; "Religious Aspects of Modernization," quotes 2, 5. A. Kroeber and Parsons, "Concepts of Culture"; Gilman, *Mandarins of the Future*, 143ff.; Knöbl, "Theories that Won't Pass Away," 99–100. Barber's book was never published, and Bellah and Craig left their paper unpublished.

15. RNB, "Religion and Society in Tokugawa Japan," 16–17; RNB and Craig, "Myth of the Middle Class in Japan," 10, 13, 33–35.

16. RNB, *Tokugawa Religion*, 3–5; RNB and Craig, "Myth of the Middle Class in Japan," 9; Maruyama, review of *Tokugawa Religion*, unpublished translation by Arima Tatsuo, 48 pp. (original Japanese version in *Kokka Gakkai Zassi 72*), RBPP, 46.

17. Barrington Moore Jr., "Notes on R. N. Bellah, TOKUGAWA RELIGION and on Some Blind Spots in Modern Social Theory," unpublished paper, 1960, 17 pp.; Barrington Moore Jr., "Epilogue," unpublished paper, 1960, 3 pp.; RNB, "Rejoinder to B. Moore, Jr., Notes on R. N. Bellah, *Tokugawa Religion*, etc.," unpublished paper, 1960, 17 pp.; all CGP, box 146, folder 2. Hans Joas to Matteo Bortolini, February 27, 2020, AF. See also Dennis Smith, *Barrington Moore*.

18. Barshay, *Social Sciences in Modern Japan*, 197ff. (quote 213); Koschmann, "Intellectuals and Politics"; Dower, "Sizing Up," 9ff. Maruyama's review was used as an afterword to the Japanese translation of *Tokugawa Religion*, published in 1962.

19. Maruyama, review of *Tokugawa Religion*, 3, 39–41, 42–43, 46, 48.

20. RNB to Talcott Parsons, October 25, 1957; Talcott Parsons to RNB, October 28, 1957; RNB to Talcott Parsons, February 27, 1958; all TPP, HUGFP 15.2, box 5. Fred E. Arnold, "Tillich Asks that Protestantism Give Basis for 'Social Criticism,'" *Harvard Crimson*, December 12, 1958; RNB, "Words for Paul Tillich," (Tillich quote 16). David Riesman to Robert White, April 13, 1961, DRP. "Riesman Talks Today," *Harvard Crimson*, December 9, 1958.

21. RNB to Melanie Bellah, May 9, 1959, RBPP.

22. RNB to Melanie Bellah, May 3, 1959; RNB to Melanie Bellah, May 4, 1959 (quotes); both RBPP.

23. RNB to Melanie Bellah, May 12, 1959, RBPP.

24. RNB to Melanie Bellah, May 5, 1959; RNB to Melanie Bellah, May 6, 1959 (quote);RNB to Melanie Bellah, May 7, 1959; RNB to Melanie Bellah, May 8, 1959; all RBPP. Arnold C. Smith was "sometimes portrayed as Canada's equivalent to George Kennan" for his fierce anticommunism. He would soon become the first secretary-general of the Commonwealth. Webster, *Fire and the Full Moon*, 95,

25. RNB to Melanie Bellah, May 29, 1959—this letter was sent to Melanie on the twenty-fifth day of Bellah's trip. In earlier letters he had expressed interest in his colleagues and some satisfaction about most of the meetings. See, for example, RNB to Melanie Bellah, May 25, 1959: "After all I knew what a Roman column looks like before I came. The main value is talking to people and there I have really learned a lot." RNB to Melanie Bellah, May 21, 1959; RNB to Melanie Bellah, May 24, 1959; all letters RBPP.

26. RNB to Melanie Bellah, May 27, 1959; RNB to Melanie Bellah, May 26, 1959 (quote); both RBPP.

27. The full aphorism reads: "Very deep is the well of the past. Should we not call it bottomless?" The two surviving drafts of the paper are slightly different: a first version of twenty-seven pages was condensed in a shorter one, of twenty-five pages. Here I focus on the first version: RNB, "Notes from a Middle Eastern Journey," unpublished paper, 27 pp., RBPP (quotes 1–2).

28. Lerner, *Passing of Traditional Society*, vii, 47ff., 57ff., 70ff., 411ff. (quotes 44, 49–50, 52–53). Shah, *Production of Modernization*.

29. See Lerner, *Passing of Traditional Society*, 61 (quote), 239, 170–72, 185–87, 404–8.

30. RNB, "Notes from a Middle Eastern Journey," 5–6.

31. RNB, 15 ("formless monstrosity"), 16, 17. RNB to Wilfred Cantwell Smith, n.d. [October 1957], MUA 1996–0025.01 #621, folder "Robert N. Bellah." Silk, "Judeo-Christian Tradition in America"; D. Moore, *G.I. Jews*.

32. RNB, "Notes from a Middle Eastern Journey," 12, 17.

33. RNB, "Religious Tradition and Historical Change," "Religious Situation in the Far East," and "Notes from a Middle Eastern Journey," 24–25 (quotes). Bellah's position was not far from that advanced by anthropologist Robert Redfield, who he had at least met once in Flagstaff in 1954. I have not been able to find correspondence between the two. Sackley, "Cosmopolitanism."

34. M. Bellah, *Tammy*, 13; Jennifer Bellah Maguire to Matteo Bortolini, February 19, 2018, AF.

35. M. Bellah, *Tammy*, 13–15, and, *Abby and Her Sisters*, 30ff.

36. Edwin O. Reischauer to Conference Board of Associated Councils, September 28, 1959; Yukitada Sasaki to Edwin O. Reischauer, April 19, 1960; both HUA UAV 344-HUA, UAV 382.95.1. RNB to Talcott Parsons September 3, 1960; RNB to Talcott Parsons, November 1, 1960; both TPP, HUGFP 15.4, box 4. RNB to Robert Slater, August 5, 1960; Robert Slater to RNB, August 11, 1960; both HUA, UAV 880.10, box 5. RNB to Frimi and Eli Sagan, September 8, 2010, RBPP.

37. RNB to Talcott Parsons, September 3, 1960, TPP, HUGFP 15.4, box 4. On Japan after 1952 see Koschmann, "Intellectuals and Politics"; A. Gordon, *Modern History of Japan*.

38. RNB to Talcott Parsons, November 1, 1960; RNB to Talcott Parsons, May 24, 1961; both TPP, HUGFP 15.4, box 4. RNB, "Remembrance of Professor Yanagawa Keiichi," manuscript, 2 pp., RBPP; Woodard, "Hideo Kishimoto," 103–5; Swyngedouw, "Ikado Fujio" and "In Memoriam Yanagawa Keiichi."

39. RNB, "Japan's Cultural Identity," 114 (quote). RNB to Charles Glock, October 1, 1960, RBPP. RNB to Talcott Parsons, September 3, 1960; RNB to Talcott Parsons, November 1, 1960; both TPP, HUGFP 15.4, box 4.

40. RNB, "Values and Social Change," 22.

41. RNB, 21.

42. RNB, 15–26, 21–22, 27 (quote). Parsons, "Christianity and Modern Industrial Society," discussed in RNB to Talcott Parsons, March 23, 1959, TPP.

43. RNB, "Japan's Cultural Identity," 121.

44. RNB, "Ienaga Saburo," 113, 91; *Tokugawa Religion*, 1; "Religious Situation in the Far East," 113; "Japan's Cultural Identity," 121, 123, 135 (quotes).

45. RNB, "Durkheim and History," 460; "Values and Social Change," 28–29 ("certain universal principles" and "educator of the modern world" 28); "Some Reflections on the Protestant Ethic" ("forced to take seriously Weber's argument" 57); "American Religion since World War I," unpublished paper, 1961, 14 pp., RBPP. Packard, *Edwin Reischauer*, 153ff. RNB to Talcott Parsons, May 24, 1961, TPP.

Chapter Six

1. M. Bellah, *Abby and Her Sisters*, 6, and *Tammy*, 20. RNB to David Schneider, July 22, 1961, DSP. RNB to Robert Slater, May 5, 1961, HUA, UAV 880.10, box 5.

2. RNB to Talcott Parsons, November 1, 1960; RNB to Talcott Parsons, January 10, 1961; Talcott Parsons to RNB, January 24, 1961; all TPP, HUGFP 15.4, box 4.

3. RNB to Talcott Parsons, May 24, 1961, RBPP. RNB, review of *The Religion of India*, Weber quote 733. Parsons's description of Bellah as "a special modern variant of the older style of universal scholar" is contained in a 1961 letter to President Pusey cited in Bortolini and Cossu, "In the Field," 339.

4. RNB, "Values and Social Change," 15, and "Durkheim and History," 451 and n. 30. RNB to David Schneider, June 9, 1960, DSP. Parsons's letter to Pusey is cited in Bortolini, "Trap of Intellectual Success," 194n12.

5. RNB to David Schneider, July 22, 1961; David Schneider to RNB, July 27, 1961; both DSP. Quote from RNB, "Religion in the Process of Cultural Differentiation," unpublished paper, 85 pp., 2nd version, RBPP, 83. Parsons, introduction to *The Study of Sociology*.

6. RNB, "Religious Evolution," 21–25. Bellah's article was published together with Parsons's "Evolutionary Universals in Society" and Eisenstadt's "Social Change, Differentiation and Evolution" in the *American Sociological Review*, at the time edited by Neil Smelser.

7. RNB, "Religious Evolution," 25–35.

8. RNB, 36–39.

9. RNB, 40.

10. RNB, "Father and Son in Christianity," 90 ("most poignant moment"); RNB, "Religious Evolution," 43–44 (other quotes). RNB to Wilfred Cantwell Smith, n.d. [around October 1, 1957], MUA 1996–0025.01 #621, folder "Robert N. Bellah". On Hally's birth and Bellah's disappointment, see M. Bellah *Tammy*, 22–23, and chapter 4, note 33, above.

11. Preston S. Cutler to RNB, May 16, 1960; RNB to Preston S. Cutler, June 7, 1960; Preston S. Cutler to RNB, June 14, 1960; RNB to Preston S. Cutler, December 1, 1962; Ralph W. Tyler to RNB, December 10, 1962; RNB to Ralph W. Tyler, January 15, 1963; Ralph W. Tyler to RNB, January 21, 1963; RNB to Ralph W. Tyler, July 18, 1963; Ralph W. Tyler to RNB, July 25, 1963; RNB to Ralph W. Tyler, September 30, 1963; Carl R. Brewer to RNB, March 20, 1964; RNB to Ralph W. Tyler, April 11, 1964; Robert L. Hall to Preston S. Cutler, April 29, 1964; all SUA. Roger Brown to Franklin Ford, December 23, 1963, HUA, UAV 801.2011, box 1.

12. RNB, application to the National Institute of Mental Health, September 29, 1963; RNB, "Inventory of Professional Interests," July 31, 1964; both SUA. RNB to Wilfred Cantwell Smith, January 6, 1963; RNB to Wilfred Cantwell Smith, February 9, 1963; Wilfred Cantwell Smith to RNB, March 16, 1963; all MUA, 1996–0025.01 #621, folder "Robert N. Bellah." Talcott Parsons to RNB, August 19, 1964, TPP, HUFGP 15.4, box 4. Darrow, "Harvard Way"; Carman and Dodgson, *Community and Colloquy*.

13. Norman O. Brown to RNB, n.d. [spring 1968], RBPP. In 1964–1965 the temporary fellows numbered forty: fifteen of them came from Ivy League universities, and of these seven came from Harvard (Bob included). See 1964–1965 booklet, Center for Advanced Study in the Behavioral Sciences, RBPP. M. Bellah, *Tammy*, 34–37. On May 17, 1965, Bellah participated in the Stanford Vietnam Day teach-in, together with Erikson and others. RNB to Talcott Parsons, November 20, 1964, TPP, HUGFP 15.4, box 4. The program for the teach-in can be found at "Stanford Vietnam Day Official Program," April Third Movement website, accessed November 22, 2020, http://www.a3mreunion.org/archive/1965-1966/65-66/files_1965-1966/66 _Stanford_VietnamDay.pdf. Bellah also spoke at a Vietnam War–related teach-in at Harvard

shortly after his return from Palo Alto. Victor Lidz to Matteo Bortolini, June 2018, AF. Talcott Parsons to Neil Smelser, November 30, 1964, TPP, HUGFP 42.8.8. RNB to Talcott Parsons, December 11, 1964; Talcott Parsons to RNB, January 9, 1965; both TPP, HUGFP 15.4, box 4. Ray F. Kibler III, "Interview of Robert N. Bellah," in "Remembering Theological Education at the Graduate Theological Union in the 1960s Oral History," GTU 98-5-01, Graduate Theological Union Archives, Berkeley, CA, 1994.

14. Quotes from 1964–1965 booklet, Center for Advanced Study in the Behavioral Sciences, RBPP. RNB, *Religion and Progress in Modern Asia*. P. A. Pardue to RNB, n.d. [April 1965]; Dean Hoge to RNB, April 1, 1965; James Peacock to RNB, May 2, 1965; all RBPP.

15. RNB, "Religion, Sociology Of," 4–10. Clifford Geertz to RNB, April 9, 1965; RNB to Philip Slater, December 12, 1964; Philip Slater to RNB, January 13, 1965; M. Brewster Smith to RNB, March 5, 1965; Eli Sagan to RNB, April 14, 1965; Kenneth Burke to RNB, April 29, 1965; all RBPP.

16. Wilfred Cantwell Smith to RNB, November 28, 1964; Wilfred Cantwell Smith to RNB, December 12, 1964 (quote); RNB to Wilfred Cantwell Smith, December 24, 1964; all HUA, UAV 880.10, box 5; my italics. W. Smith, "Excerpt." RNB to Talcott Parsons, June 5, 1965, TPP, HUGFP 15.4, box 4. Holbrook, *Religion*; Hart, *University Gets Religion*, 194ff.

17. The $6 million William James Hall was considered an imposing symbol of the growing importance of the behavioral sciences at Harvard. "Social Relations Directory, Fall term 1959–60," HUF 801.4005. Robert Bellah, interview, AF. Floor plans for William James Hall are on record in the "Department of Social Relations Annual Report, 1964–65," UAV 801.2005, box 4. RNB to David Riesman, August 11, 1966, DRP, HUGFP 99.12, box 1 (quote).

18. RNB to Nathan Keyfitz, November 1, 1965, RBPP.

19. Riesman's letters are cited in Bortolini, "Trap of Intellectual Success," 194n12.

20. Stephen R. Graubard to RNB, April 20, 1965, RBPP. According to Graubard, *Daedalus* at that time had a print run of thirty-eight thousand.

21. RNB, "Heritage and Choice," 5–6, 19 (quote).

22. RNB, "American Religion since World War I," unpublished paper, RBPP, 6; RNB, "Heritage and Choice," 15–19.

23. Parsons, "Religion in a Modern Pluralistic Society," 134. Bortolini, "Before Civil Religion," 19. Quote from RNB, "Civil Religion in America," 168; Cogley, "Scholars Agree," 21.

24. RNB, "Civil Religion in America," 171, 177, 183–185.

25. Bellah, 12. R. Williams, *American Society*; Warner, *American Life*; S. Lipset, *First New Nation*; Parsons, "Christianity and Modern Industrial Society"; Herberg, *Protestant, Catholic, Jew*, 268; Marty, *New Shape of American Religion*, 39–40.

26. RNB, "Civil Religion in America," 186, 181.

27. RNB, "Meaning and Modernization," 67, 73.

28. RNB, "Religion in America," unpublished paper, RBPP, 12–13.

29. RNB to Parsons, November 25, 1966, TPP, HUGFP 15.4, box 3. Talcott Parsons to RNB, January 1, 1965; RNB to Talcott Parsons, February 6, 1965; both TPP, HUGFP 15.4, box 4.

30. NJ-1965–1969, entry of June 24, 1968; M. Bellah, *Abby and her Sisters*, 8. On the Goffman incident, see RNB, interview, AF (Goffman quote); Rajagopal, "Talcott Parsons' Favorite Student"; Hartzell and Sasscer, *Study of Religion on Campus*.

31. RNB, interview, AF. Ernst B. Haas to RNB, June 9, 1970; John Henry Raleigh to RNB, August 18, 1970; both RBPP. $21,000 in 1966 roughly corresponds to $167,000 in 2020. L. Lewis,

"On Subjective and Objective Rankings"; VanAntwerpen, "Resisting Sociology's Seductive Name"; Smelser, "Sociological and Interdisciplinary Adventures" and *Theory of Collective Behavior*.

32. Graduate Theological Union, *First Twenty Years*; Berling, "Theological Consortia"; Pearson, "Religious Studies at Berkeley."

33. Kibler, "Interview of Robert N. Bellah," 2 (quote). Bellah had been complaining about Massachusetts weather ever since his first days at Harvard, and had been fantasizing about going back to the West Coast for graduate work. RNB to Lillian Bellah, July 19, 1947; RNB to Lillian Bellah, n.d. [summer 1947]; RNB to Lillian Bellah, February 22, 1950; Melanie Bellah to Bessie Wright, May 22, 1950; all RBPP. NJ-1965–1969, entry of April 8, 1967. M. Bellah, *Tammy*, 47–51.

34. NJ-1965–1969, entries of "June"; July 26, 1966; July 27, 1966; July 29, 1966. M. Bellah, *Tammy*, 47 ("rent the same house"; Jennifer Bellah Maguire to Matteo Bortolini, September 23, 2017, AF.

35. Dexter Dunphy to Matteo Bortolini, September 17, 2017, AF. Stephen D. Lerner, "Social Relations 120 Experience Distorted by Rampant Rumours of 'Casualty Cases,'" *Harvard Crimson*, September 26, 1966 (quote); Robert E. Smith, "Students Rename Traditional Courses," *Harvard Crimson*, April 20, 1962.

36. NJ-1965–1969, entry of August 15, 1966.

37. NJ-1965–1969, entries of August 12, August 13, August 15, and August 16, 1966; August 17, 1966 (quotes, in order, August 13, 15, 16); August 18, 1966. RNB to William Sullivan, February 4, 1978, RBPP.

38. NJ-1965–1969, entry of August 7, 1966. Tammy's diary is cited in M. Bellah, *Tammy*, 52–53. See chapter 9 for Martin Nicolaus's speech at the 1968 annual meeting of the American Sociological Association and its resonance with Bellah's diary entry.

39. NJ-1965–1969, entries of April 8, 1967; April 18, 1967. David Riesman to RNB, June 30, 1967, DRP, HUGFP 99.12, box 1. Parsons saw Bellah's departure (and Smelser's coeval refusal to go back to Harvard) as a personal tragedy: Talcott Parsons to Shmuel Eisenstadt, July 17, 1967, TPP, HUGFP 42.8.8, box 5, folder "Eisenstadt, S. N."

Chapter Seven

1. RNB to Wilfred Cantwell Smith, June 11, 1967, HUA, UAV 880.10, box 5. M. Bellah, *Tammy*, 57; Hally Bellah-Guther to Matteo Bortolini, August 24, 2017, AF. NJ-1965–1969, entries of August 8, 1967; August 11, 1967. Gair, *American Counterculture*; Rorabaugh, *Berkeley at War*, 143ff.

2. RNB to David Riesman, December 11, 1967, RBPP. NJ-1965–1969, entries of August 8, 1967; August 11, 1967; August 13, 1967.

3. Otten, *University Authority*, 168ff.; Wollenberg, *Berkeley*, 129ff.; Rorabaugh, *Berkeley at War*, 15ff., 110ff., 129.

4. Kerr, *Uses of the University*, 70.

5. Kerr, *Uses of the University*, 14–15, 18, 77–78, 93.

6. Kerr, *Gold and the Blue*; Otten, *University Authority*, 159ff.

7. Kerr, *Gold and the Blue*, 95ff., 128ff.; Otten, *University Authority*, 161–62, 169; Savio, "End to History," 216–17; Rorabaugh, *Berkeley at War*, 19ff.

8. Smelser, *Reflections*, 12, 55; Glazer "What Happened at Berkeley"; Selznick, "Reply to Glazer"; Wolin and Schaar, *Berkeley Rebellion and Beyond*, 39; Rorabaugh, *Berkeley at War*, 46–47; S. Lipset and Seabury, "Lesson of Berkeley," 349. RNB to Talcott Parsons, November 20, 1964; RNB to Talcott Parsons, December 11, 1964, HUGFP 15.4, box 4; both TPP.

9. Otten, *University Authority*, 180–82 ("passionate concern" 182); RNB, *Beyond Belief*, xvii.

10. RNB, *Beyond Belief*, xvii ("outward expression"). NJ-1965–1969, entries of August 25, 1967 ("high seriousness"); October 8, 1967.

11. NJ-1965–1969, entry of October 26, 1967.

12. NJ-1965–1969, entries of October 26, 1967 (quote); October 28, 1967.

13. NJ-1965–1969, entries of October 31, 1967 (quotes); November 13, 1967.

14. Tammy cited in M. Bellah, *Tammy*, 57. NJ-1965–1969, entry of November 7, 1967 ("electric storm"). Jennifer Bellah Maguire to Matteo Bortolini, September 23, 2017; Jennifer Bellah Maguire to Matteo Bortolini, January 2, 2020; both AF.

15. RNB, *Beyond Belief*, xvii. RNB to David Riesman, December 11, 1967, DRP, HUGFP 99.12, box 1.

16. P-1967–1970, 1–2. NJ-1965–1969, entry of November 3, 1967.

17. NJ-1965–1969, entry of December 7, 1967.

18. RNB to Talcott Parsons, November 28, 1967, TPP, HUGFP 42.8.8, box 3. NJ-1965–1969, entry of December, 20, 1967 (quote; my italics). The phrase "a self that touches all edges" comes from Wallace Stevens's *A Rabbit as King of the Ghosts*, cited in RNB, "Transcendence in Contemporary Piety," 200.

19. RNB, "Sociology of Religion," 216–17.

20. Clifford Geertz, "Comments on Bellah's Paper on the Typology of Religion (addressed to Professor Parsons)," unpublished paper, 20 pp., RBPP, 1. Cossu, "Clifford Geertz."

21. Geertz, "Religion as a Cultural System," 90; RNB, review of part 2 of *The Religious Situation*, 291. See also Dean Hoge to RNB, April 1, 1965; Clifford Geertz to RNB, July 30, 1968; both RBPP.

22. RNB, "Transcendence in Contemporary Piety," 200–204; Stevens, *Opus Posthumous*, 163. Friends immediately understood the importance of "Transcendence." Wilfred Smith called it "a very major statement," and wrote to Bob that "that book [i.e., *A Theory of Religion*], and the getting of it written, become the more significant." Wilfred Cantwell Smith to RNB, November 28, 1968, HUA, UAV 880.10, box 5; NJ-1965–1969, entry of June 23, 1968.

23. RNB, "Transcendence in Contemporary Piety," 206.

24. Andrew Bard Schmookler to Matteo Bortolini, May 15, 2009, AF. RNB to David Riesman, June 25, 1968; David Riesman to RNB, June 28, 1968; both DRP, HUGFP 99.12, box 1. Quotes from NJ-1965–1969, entry of June 24, 1968.

25. Fiske, "Religion," E9; Lipsitz, "If, as Verba Says"; RNB, "Response," 389–92 (quotes 389).

26. C. Cherry, "Two American Sacred Ceremonies"; Pepper, "Religion and Evolution"; Thomas and Flippen, "American Civil Religion," 223 ("real locus" quote); Moltmann, "Political Theology," 15; Lynn, "Civil Catechetics," 7–8.

27. NJ-1969–1979, entries of July 14, 1969; October 11, 1969. Kathan and Fuchs-Kreimer, "Civil Religion in America," 541–50.

28. RNB to Arthur J. Goldberg, December 31, 1965, RBPP.

29. NJ-1965–1969, entries of July 1, 1968; January 1, 1970 ("political animal"). Brick, *Age of Contradiction*; Dickstein, *Gates of Eden*; Rorabaugh, *Berkeley at War*, 161. RNB to David Riesman, June 29, 1970, DRP, HUGFP 99.12, box 1. RNB to Stanley Kurnik, September 23, 1969, RBPP ("mishuganah"). RNB, "Is There a Common American Culture?" 62, and "New Consciousness," 81ff.

30. RNB to Stanley Kurnik, September 23, 1969, RBPP; RNB, introduction to *On Morality and Society*, x, xxxvii. See also RNB to Talcott Parsons, February 25, 1970, TPP, HUGFP 42.8.8, box 3.

31. RNB, "Guest Editorial," 369–70; RNB, "Vietnam, Japan, America," transcript of a speech given at Committee of Concerned Asian Scholars meeting, Grace Cathedral, San Francisco, November 10, 1969, RBPP ("teach-ins" and "white psyche"). NJ-1969–1979, entries of January 1, 1970; January, 3, 1970.

Chapter Eight

1. NJ-1965–1969, entry of July 1, 1968; other quotes from N. Brown, *Life against Death*, 9, 307, 318. Greenham, *Resurrection of the Body*; Dickstein, *Double Agent* and *Gates of Eden*.

2. Keen, "Norman O. Brown's Body," 45 ("torpedo" quote). Other quotes from N. Brown, *Love's Body* 193, 233.

3. First quote from N. Brown, *Apocalypse and/or Metamorphosis*, 6; other quotes from N. Brown, *Love's Body*, 221, 196, 258–59. See also Dickstein, *Gates of Eden*, 81ff.

4. N. Brown, *Love's Body*, quotes 261 and 266, my italics. N. Brown, *Life against Death*; Greenham, *Resurrection of the Body*, 98ff.

5. Brown quote from Keen, "Norman O. Brown's Body," 46. Roszak, "Professor Dionysus"; Crews, "Love in the Western World," 277, 280; Allyn, *Make Love, Not War*, 200; Roszak, *Making of a Counter Culture*; Brophy, "Demolish the Ego," 3; Dickstein, *Gates of Eden*, 85.

6. Marcuse, "Love Mystified," 177, 180–181; N. Brown, "Reply to Herbert Marcuse," 83.

7. NJ-1965–1969, entry of July 1, 1968.

8. NJ-1965–1969, entry of July 4, 1968.

9. NJ-1965–1969, entry December, 20, 1967; my italics.

10. NJ-1965–1969, entry of July 1, 1968. RNB to David Riesman, April 21, 1968, DRP, HUGFP 99.12, box 1. RNB to David Schneider, July 26, 1968, DSP.

11. Krister Stendhal to RNB, October 14, 1968, HUA, UAV 880.10, box 5. RNB to Wilfred Cantwell Smith, October 28, 1968, HUA, UAV 880.10, box 5. RNB to Talcott Parsons, October 25, 1968; RNB to Parsons December 2, 1968; both TPP, HUGFP 42.8.8, box 3. Melanie Bellah to David Riesman, December 8, 1968; RNB to David Riesman, December 8, 1968; RNB to David Riesman, January 9, 1968; all DRP, HUGFP 99.12, box 1.

12. *L'osservatore romano*, weekly edition in English, October 10, 1968, 6. Published in English as Secretariatus pro non credentibus, *On Dialogue with Non-believers*.

13. Franz König to RNB, October 2, 1968, RBPP. "Visita del sottosegretario in Canada e USA," *Bollettino del Segretariato per i non-credenti* 2 (1968): 28–29. "Simposium internazionale," memo, Fondazione Agnelli, February 5, 1968; "Colloquio con Monsignor Antonio Grumelli," memo, Fondazione Agnelli, April 4, 1968; both FGA.

14. Antonio Grumelli to Ubaldo Scassellati, May 15, 1968; "Visita di Mons. Grumelli il 19 Luglio 1968," memo, Fondazione Agnelli, July 19, 1968; Ubaldo Scassellati to Franz König,

October 14, 1968; Franz König to Ubaldo Scassellati, October 17, 1968; all FGA. Quote from Phelan, "Report on the Discussions," 55–56.

15. "Peter Berger," memo, Fondazione Agnelli, January 30, 1969, FGA. The original letter of invitation stated that the symposium would take place at "the Papal Residence of Castel Gandolfo in Rome." Franz König to RNB, October 2, 1968, RBPP.

16. Among the scholars who figured in various hypothetical lists were: N. J. Demerath, James Dittes, Clifford Geertz, Jürgen Habermas, Gerhard Lenski, and Raimundo Panikkar. Bourdieu and Nissiotis did not make the conference. Memo, Fondazione Agnelli, early March 1969, FGA. "The Symposium Seen through the Eyes of the Press," *Supplemento al Bollettino del Segretariato per i non-credenti* 6 (1968). In his ironic review, Philip Rieff wrote that "the real meat and drink of the symposium, its inner erotic meaning, must have been the mass media." Rieff, review of *The Culture of Unbelief,* 505.

17. Berger, foreword to *The Culture of Unbelief,* ix; Marty, "Sociologists' Religion under Glass." "Reactions of Participants and Observers," mimeo, Secretariat for Non-believers, Vatican City, July 10, 1969; Rocco Caporale to Ubaldo Scassellati, April 17, 1969; Rocco Caporale to Ubaldo Scassellati, April 30, 1969; M. Abrate to Rocco Caporale, April 30, 1969; Donald Cutler to Ubaldo Scassellati, May 19, 1969; all FGA. Paul VI's speech is available at "Address of Paul VI to the Participants in the Symposium on 'The Culture of Unbelief'" (March 27, 1969), The Holy See, Paul VI, accessed November 22, 2020, http://w2.vatican.va/content/paul-vi/en/speeches /1969/march/documents/hf_p-vi_spe_19690327_cultura-non-credenza.html.

18. RNB, *Beyond Belief,* 216–21, 226–28, my italics. Forty years later, Harvey Cox called Bellah's paper "the most memorable paper at the meeting" and "a prophetic statement," foreshadowing the dismissal of secularization theory. Cox, *Future of Faith,* 219.

19. "Conferenza internazionale sull'ateismo. Seduta del 25 marzo 1969," full transcript, Fondazione Giovanni Agnelli, April 1969, 4, 6, FGA. Handwritten notes for Bellah's speech are kept in RBPP.

20. Berger, foreword to *The Culture of Unbelief,* xiii. "Conferenza internazionale sull'ateismo," 7.

21. "Conferenza internazionale sull'ateismo," 8–11, 19–20, 22–23.

22. "Conferenza internazionale sull'ateismo," 22–23, 28.

23. "Conferenza internazionale sull'ateismo," 31, 42, 49, 53. Talcott Parsons to RNB, March 16, 1970; Talcott Parsons to RNB, November 9, 1971; both TPP, HUGFP 42.8.8, box 3.

24. "Conferenza internazionale sull'ateismo," quotes 65 and 68. RNB, "Dynamics of Worship," 53–69.

25. RNB, "Remarks for 15 Apr. 69, Cambridge" ("acrimony and defensiveness") and "Remarks for 16 Apr. 1969, Cambridge" ("doors are open"), handwritten notes, RBPP. RNB to Wilfred Cantwell Smith, December 5, 1968; Wilfred Cantwell Smith to Antonio Grumelli, April 18, 1969; both HUA, UAV 880.10. At about the same time, Bellah was contacted again by Stendhal, who asked him to reconsider his refusal of the Houghton chair. See "Current Activities and Publication Plans," n.d. [November 1969], RBPP.

26. Wolin and Schaar, *Berkeley Rebellion and Beyond;* Rorabaugh, *Berkeley at War;* M. Bellah, *Tammy,* 117–18; RNB, *Beyond Belief,* 246 (quotes).

27. Klausner, "Scientific and Humanistic Study," 100 (quote); Stark, "Humanistic and Scientific Knowledge," 168. Samuel Klausner to Matteo Bortolini, August 18, 2008, AF.

28. RNB, "Christianity and Symbolic Realism," 90 ("kernel of truth"), 91 ("noncognitive and nonscientific symbols"), 93–94 (block quote), 93 ("bluntly"). At the very beginning of one of the classics of sociology, *The Elementary Forms of Religious Life*, Émile Durkheim wrote that "In reality, then, there are no false religions" (4). In all the difference there is between an affirmation and a double negation, Bellah looked not *that* far from his predecessor.

29. RNB, "Christianity and Symbolic Realism," 95 ("double vision" and "most vivid"), 96 ("confuse the role"), my italics.

30. Dittes, "Confessing Away the Soul," 22; Benton Johnson, review of *The Broken Covenant*; Yates, review of *Religious Aesthetics*; Miles, review of *Religion in Human Evolution*. Wilfred Cantwell Smith to RNB, March 6, 1970, HUA, UAV 880.10, box 5. David Riesman to RNB, October 27, 1969, DRP, HUGFP 99.12, box 1.

31. RNB to Wilfred Cantwell Smith, November 11, 1969, RBPP.

32. Klausner, "Scientific and Humanistic Study," 106; Nelson, "Sociology of Religion," 109. RNB to Talcott Parsons, February 12, 1970, TPP, HUGFP 42.8.8, box 3.

33. RNB to Talcott Parsons, December 2, 1970, TPP. In a shorter letter to Thomas O'Dea written on the same day, Bellah said: "I am afraid I got a bit more aggravated than I should have by the whole thing" (Thomas O'Dea Papers, Brigham Young University, MSS 1417, box 1, folder 14). Other friends had found the paper very interesting (Robert Jay Lifton to RNB, January 16, 1970, RBPP), while Norman Brown had attacked it "from the left" (RNB to Talcott Parsons, February 25, 1970, TPP, HUGFP 42.8.8, box 3).

Chapter Nine

1. Parsons, introduction to *American Sociology*, ix.

2. Parsons, "Present Position and Prospects," 42; Simpson and Simpson, "Transformation." Rhoades, *History of the American Sociological Association*, 47ff.

3. Parsons, "Some Problems," 548, 551, 552–53 (quotes), 554–55, 557.

4. Parsons, "The Editor's Column" (1966), 184ff., and "The Editor's Column" (1967), 64.

5. Gouldner, *For Sociology*; Sica and Turner, *Disobedient Generation*; Oppenheimer, Murray, and Levine, *Radical Sociologists*; Calhoun, *Sociology in America*, esp. chs. 10–14 and 17. Militant groups emerged in other disciplines: the Radical Caucus in Anthropology and the Caucus for New Political Science were formed during their respective associations' 1967 annual meetings, while the Committee of Concerned Asian Scholars and the Union for Radical Political Economics were founded in 1968. McAdams, foreword to *Explorations in Personality*; Novick, *That Noble Dream*; K. Moore, *Disrupting Science*; Brick, *Age of Contradiction*, esp. chs. 7 and 8.

6. Dusky Smith, "Sunshine Boys"; Nicolaus, "Fat-Cat Sociology" (quotes from the 1968 convention at 155) and "Professional Organization of Sociology" (1969 article quote at 89); Carol Brown, "Radical Activism in Sociology"; Flacks, "Sociology Liberation Movement."

7. Gouldner, *Coming Crisis of Western Sociology*. Korom, "Prestige Elite in Sociology"; Sutton, "Ford Foundation: The Early Years" and "Ford Foundation's Transatlantic Role." Quote about the Sunshine Boys from Dusky Smith, "Sunshine Boys," 29.

8. M. Levy, *Structure of Society*. Ogles, Levy, and Parsons, "Culture and Social Systems."

9. With time the elite of the American Sociological Association would co-opt at least part of its opposition via the creation of a number of "sections" representing new interests and new

specialties. A quick look at the list of the past presidents of the association shows that the vast network that Nicholas C. Mullins called "standard American sociology" maintained control of the apical position well into the 1980s, with only one exception. Those who suffered the most in the late-1960s/early-1970s revolt were perhaps those graduate students or assistant professors in their early thirties who had been identified with either Parsons or "the establishment," and found it increasingly difficult to find a job in a rapidly shrinking academic market. S. Turner, *American Sociology*, chs. 3 and 4. With all its limits, the book by Nicholas C. Mullins *Theories and Theory Groups* remains unmatched as an assessment of scholarly networks in the 1950s and the 1960s. "Presidents," American Sociological Association, accessed November 22, 2020, https://www.asanet.org/about/governance-and-leadership/council/presidents.

10. J. Brown and Gilmartin, "Sociology Today"; Szanton, *Politics of Knowledge*; Wallerstein, "Unintended Consequences." On Bellah's lack of academic power, see Renée Fox, *In the Field*, 201ff.

11. Schneider, *Schneider on Schneider*, 73–78; Geertz, *After the Fact* and *Interpretation of Cultures*, quotes at 4–5, 90ff. Handler, "Interview with Clifford Geertz," 608; Shepherd, "Religion and the Social Sciences"; Karcher, Balswick, and Robinson, "Empiricism." Segal, *Religion and the Social Sciences*; J. Alexander, *Twenty Lectures*, 111ff., 219; Rabinow and Sullivan, *Interpretive Social Science*.

12. V. Turner, "Symbolic Studies," 150.

13. Schneider, *American Kinship*, 1n; Kroeber and Parsons, "Concepts of Culture"; Schneider, *Schneider on Schneider*, 82ff.

14. Geertz, "Religion as a Cultural System," 89. Cossu, "Clifford Geertz."

15. RNB, *Beyond Belief*, 260; Barber and Inkeles, *Stability and Social Change*. The book also included papers by Geertz, Smelser, Eisenstadt, and Shils. David Schneider expressed his willingness to join his friends, but was somehow not accepted. RNB to David Schneider, January 8, 1970, DSP.

16. Winnicott, *Playing and Reality*, 19–20.

17. Winnicot, 7.

18. NJ-1965–1969, entries of July 1, 1968 (quote); September 18, 1968; September 26, 1968. Winnicott, 3, 12–14, 19–20, 7 (quote), 18.

19. RNB, *Beyond Belief*, 230–36. MP-1967–1973, entry of December 1968.

20. Norman O. Brown to RNB, June 10, 1969 (quote); Norman O. Brown to RNB, June 15, 1970; Stanley Kurnik to RNB, October 4, 1969; Jacob Taubes to RNB, March 17, 1971; all RBPP. Wilfred Cantwell Smith to RNB, June 17, 1969, HUA, UAV 880.10, box 5. David Riesman to RNB, October 27, 1969; David Riesman to RNB, June 12, 1970; both DRP, HUGFP 99.12, box 1. Kenneth Burke to RNB, September 29, 1969 (quote); Kenneth Burke to RNB, July 28, 1970; Kenneth Burke to RNB, January 31, 1974; all RBPP. RNB to Clifford Geertz, October 1, 1970 (quote); Clifford Geertz to RNB, October 22, 1970; both CGP, box 103, folder 2.

21. RNB, "Sociology 146—Sociology of Religion—Winter 1970," lecture notes, February 11, 1970, RBPP. Talcott Parsons to RNB, February 12, 1970; RNB to Talcott Parsons, February 25, 1970; both TPP, HUGFP 42.8.8, box 3.

22. Talcott Parsons to RNB, February 12, 1970; RNB to Talcott Parsons, February 25, 1970 (quotes); both TPP, HUGFP 42.8.8, box 3. Other participants in the conference were John Chernoff, Donald H. Johnson, SJ, and John Kwang-Han Hsu. John Chernoff to Matteo Bortolini, November 6, 2017, AF. Bellah's "Evil and the American Ethos" represented the (quite

unstable) conceptual bridge between his work on Norman Brown and that on the American civil religion (esp. at 188ff.).

23. RNB, "Brown in Perspective," 450–51.

24. RNB, 456, 458.

25. NJ-1965–1969, entry of May 31, 1969.

26. M. Bellah, *Abby and Her Sisters*, 8. Kibler, "Interview of Robert N. Bellah" and Ray F. Kibler III, "Interview of Charles Y. Glock," in "Remembering Theological Education at the Graduate Theological Union in the 1960s Oral History," GTU 98-5-01, Graduate Theological Union Archives, 1994. RNB to David Riesman, July 30, 1970, DRP, HUGFP 99.12, box 1.

27. RNB, "Confessions," quotes at 232–33, my italics. "SocRel 111. Sociology of Religion," syllabuses and lecture notes from 1958–1959 to 1965–1966, RBPP.

28. Quotes from "Sociology 146—Sociology of Religion—Winter 1970," lecture notes, January 12, 1970, RBPP. See also "Syllabus and Course Notes Sociology 246, 1969," RBPP. MP-1967–1968, undated entry titled "Symbols and Experience." NJ-1969–1979, entries of July 1, 1968; January 4, 1969; January 9, 1969. Robert Wuthnow to Matteo Bortolini, August 22, 2012; Tom Piazza to Matteo Bortolini, August 22, 2012; both AF.

29. RNB, "New Religious Consciousness and the Secular University," 17; "Religion in the University," 14, 17; *Beyond Belief*, 214; "Brown in Perspective," 453 (quotes).

30. RNB "Confessions," 231–32; RNB, "Christianity and Symbolic Realism." Joe Morganti to RNB, January 9, 1973, RBPP. Quotes from "Sociology 146—Sociology of Religion—Winter 1970," notes and final examination, Thursday, March 19, 1970, RBPP. See also "Sociology 146—Sociology of Religion—Winter 1972," notes, RBPP. RNB, *Beyond Belief*, 239–40.

31. NJ-1965–1969, entry of July 4, 1969. Bellah worked on this idea for a long time. Robert Slater to RNB, October 25, 1960, HUA, UAV 880.10, box 5.

32. RNB, introduction to *On Morality and Society*, xlii, xxxv, l–li, lii, my italics. Edward Shils to RNB, November 30, 1972, RBPP. Robert K. Merton to Carl Kaysen, December 9, 1972, published as Bortolini, "Document 4." In an essay on *The Elementary Forms of Religious Life* published in 1973, Parsons wrote that Bellah's introduction made it clear "that Bellah [stood] virtually alone in not only the profundity of his understanding of Durkheim's theoretical thinking . . . but also in his positive use of Durkheim's insights in his own work." Parsons, "Durkheim on Religion Revisited," 229.

33. University of California, "Professor Robert N. Bellah." RNB to David Riesman, July 7, 1971, DRP, HUGFP 99.12, box 1. Morris Janowitz to RNB, August 3, 1971, RBPP. The sum is roughly equivalent to $67,000 in 2020.

34. Donald Cutler to RNB, February 26, 1969, Andover Seminar Archives, Beacon Press, records, 1935–1988, box 32, folder: Bellah, Robert N./Tokugawa Religion/correspondence. NJ-1965–1969, entries of October 28, 1967; October 30, 1967; November 13, 1967.

35. RNB, *Beyond Belief*, xvii, 257. NJ-1969–1979, entry of October 11, 1969. Unfortunately, no previous draft of the introduction has been kept.

36. RNB, *Beyond Belief*, xxi. In the short self-presentation for the Agnelli Foundation he had written just a handful of months before the Sanders Theater performance, Bellah described the sociology of religion as voluntarily blind to the richness of both the humanities *and* its own classical tradition. The first paragraph is worth quoting at length: "Perhaps 'Work in Flux' would be a better heading than 'Work in Progress.' At the moment, and perhaps not unrelated to my

recent move [to Berkeley], I feel intellectually unsettled, dissatisfied with existing assumptions in my field, and doubtful that 'sociology of religion' is really a field at all. At a time where there is more vitality and excitement in the area of religion than there has been in several generations, why is 'sociology of religion' so dull?" Published as RNB, "Japan, Asia, Religion," 93.

37. RNB, *Beyond Belief*, x, 191 (quote). For context see Hart, *University Gets Religion*.

38. Greeley, review of *Beyond Belief*, 754; James W. Gladden, review of *Beyond Belief*, 733; Brendle, review of *Beyond Belief*, 222–23.

39. Hill, review of *Beyond Belief*.

Chapter Ten

1. Joe Morganti to RNB, January 9, 1973, RBPP.

2. Terence Loughran to RNB, October 29, 1971; RNB to Stanley Kurnik, October 23, 1969; RNB to David Riesman, June 29, 1970; all RBPP. Tammy cited in M. Bellah, *Tammy*, 303–4. RNB to Talcott Parsons, November 5, 1971, TPP, HUGFP 42.8.8, box 3. Erikson, "Sociology," 331; RNB, "Liturgy and Experience" and "No Direction Home."

3. Jeffrey Stout to Matteo Bortolini, August 22, 2012; Robert Wuthnow to Matteo Bortolini, August 22, 2012; Jeffrey Alexander to Matteo Bortolini, September 11, 2012; Harlan Stelmach to Matteo Bortolini, November 2, 2012; William Wetherall to Matteo Bortolini, August 11, 2017; Ann Swidler, interview; all AF. The 1972 National Book Award was won by Martin E. Marty, *Righteous Empire*. John Rawls's *A Theory of Justice* also made the finalists' list. See "Beyond Belief Essays on Religion in a Post-traditionalist World," National Book Foundation, accessed November 22, 2020, https://www.nationalbook.org/books/beyond-belief-essays-on-religion-in-a-post-tradtionalist-world/.

4. Smelser, *Neil Smelser*, 265ff.; Duster, *Oral History*, 115, 122, 130; Burawoy and VanAntwerpen, "Berkeley Sociology," 14. RNB to Wilfred Cantwell Smith, June 26, 1969, HUA, UAV 880.10, box 5. RNB to David Riesman, February 3, 1971, DRP, HUGFP 99.12, box 1.

5. Andrew Bard Schmookler to Matteo Bortolini, May 15, 2009; Andrew Bard Schmookler to Matteo Bortolini, September 6, 2020; RNB to Matteo Bortolini, August 11, 2009; all AF. An abridged version of the 1,600-page dissertation discussed in 1977 was published as Schmookler, *Parable of the Tribes* in 1984. Stanley Kurnik to RNB, October 4, 1969, RBPP. "It Is Not a Question of the Right to Express Unpopular Political Views," *Campus Report, University of California Berkeley* 3 (1971).

6. Jennifer Bellah Maguire to Matteo Bortolini, January 2, 2020, AF. M. Bellah, *Tammy*, 134, 147, 175–76, 186, 302–7.

7. Jennifer Bellah Maguire to Matteo Bortolini, August 9, 2019, AF. M. Bellah, *Tammy*, 169ff., 193. A romanticized narrative of Herb Kohl's work can be found in Cynthia Brown, *Refusing Racism*, 126ff. *Hearings before the Select Committee on Equal Educational Opportunity of the United States Senate*, 92nd Congress (1971), First Session on Equal Educational Opportunity, Part 9A, 4560–61.

8. M. Bellah, *Tammy*, 198, 427–28. Tammy's diary entry (of February 25, 1972), is cited on p. 307. Jennifer Bellah Maguire to Matteo Bortolini, January 2, 2020, AF. RNB to Clifford Geertz, October 1, 1970, CGP, box 103, folder 2.

9. RNB to David Riesman, April 18, 1972, DRP, HUGFP 99.8, box 5. M. Bellah, *Tammy*, 337ff. On the trip to Italy, see Stephen Graubard to RNB, March 1, 1972, RBPP. The book was published as Cavazza and Graubard, *Il caso italiano*. Among the many intellectuals Bellah met in Italy were philosophers Norberto Bobbio and Gustavo Bontadini, historians Giuseppe Alberigo and Pietro Scoppola, sociologists Silvano Burgalassi and Danilo Dolci, and activist Franco Alasia. "Italia Apr–May 72," trip notes, 100 pp., RBPP.

10. In the fifteen years between 1952 and 1967, Bellah had published two books, one edited volume, seventeen articles or book chapters, and nine book reviews. His friend Clifford Geertz had published five books, one edited volume, twenty-four articles or book chapters, and twelve book reviews between 1955 and 1967. NJ-1965–1969, entries of April 8, 1967; April 18, 1967. RNB to Clifford Geertz, October 1, 1970, and November 3, 1970, CGP, box 103, folder 2; RNB to Wilfred Cantwell Smith, December 29, 1971, HUA, UAV 880.10, box 5.

11. Tammy cited in M. Bellah, *Tammy*, 356–57.

12. The institute's schools correspond to academic departments. Regis, *Who Got Einstein's Office?*; Batterson, *Pursuit of Genius*; Arntzenius, *Institute for Advanced Study*.

13. "A New Program in the Social Sciences: Needs and Opportunities," Institute of Advanced Studies Princeton, 1969, 3–8 (quote at 4), CGP, box 102, folder 12.

14. "A New Program in the Social Sciences: Needs and Opportunities." At the time, the School of Mathematics included nine professors and sixty visiting fellows; the School of Natural Sciences five professors and thirty visiting fellows; the School of Historical Studies nine professors and forty visiting fellows. Kaysen, *Report of the Director*.

15. Robert K. Merton was a member of the committee recommending Geertz's appointment. Carl Kaysen to Robert Merton, January 28, 1970; Robert Merton to Carl Kaysen, February 2, 1970, cited in Bortolini, "'Bellah Affair' at Princeton," 8. RNB to Clifford Geertz, October 1, 1970, CGP, box 103, folder 2. In a letter to Parsons dated September 6, 1972 (TPP, HUGFP 42.8.8, box 3), Bellah wrote that "Cliff [had] spoken of the possibility of my coming here permanently almost from the time he came himself."

16. Anthony Wrigley to Matteo Bortolini, December 24, 2008, AF. David Riesman to RNB, October 7, 1971, DRP, HUGFP 99.8, box 5. Carl Kaysen to RNB, November 13, 1971; RNB to Carl Kaysen, November 30, 1971; both CGP, box 103, folder 2. M. Bellah, *Abby and Her Sisters*, 22ff.

17. RNB to Clifford Geertz, September 29, 1971, CGP, box 36, folder 6.

18. David Riesman to RNB, November 30, 1971; RNB to David Riesman, December 14, 1971; RNB to David Riesman, February 29, 1972; all RBPP. Talcott Parsons to RNB, August 31, 1972; RNB to Talcott Parsons, September 6, 1972; both TPP, HUGFP 42.8.8, box 3.

19. M. Bellah, *Abby and Her Sisters*, 14.

20. Tammy Bellah, "The Search for Freedom," cited in M. Bellah, *Tammy*, 357, 359; M. Bellah, *Abby and Her Sisters*, 14.

21. RNB to David Riesman, December 14, 1971, DRP, HUGFP 99.8, box 5. RNB to Talcott Parsons, September 6, 1972, TPP, HUGFP 42.8.8, box 3. M. Bellah, *Tammy*, 355–57, my italics. RNB to Carl Kaysen, November 30, 1970, CGP, box 103, folder 2.

22. Tammy cited in M. Bellah, *Tammy*, 363. The temporary members of the social sciences program included David Apter, Pierre Bourdieu, Clive Kessler, Bruce Mazlish, Nancy Munn,

James T. Siegel, Peter Hopkinson Smith, Aristide Zolberg, Albert O. Hirschman, and Paul Rabinow. Institute for Advanced Study, *Community of Scholars*. Jeffrey Stout to Matteo Bortolini, August 22, 2012, AF.

23. M. White, *Philosopher's Story*, 289–91, 296–97; Goldstein, *Incompleteness*, 241ff. David Riesman to RNB, November 29, 1972; RNB to David Riesman, December 20, 1972; both DRP, HUGFP 99.8, box 5. Sanford Elberg to RNB, September 29, 1972; Neil Smelser to RNB, October 2, 1972; Delmer Brown to RNB, October 5, 1972; Delmer Brown to RNB, November 29, 1972; all RBPP.

24. Neil Smelser to RNB, October 16, 1972; Harold Wilensky to RNB, October 19, 1972; Natalie Zemon Davis to RNB, October 8, 1972; John C. Bennett to RNB, December 12, 1972; William Bouwsma to RNB, October 15, 1972; all RBPP. Talcott Parsons to RNB, November 25, 1972 (but dictated on October 23, 1972), TPP, HUGFP 42.8.8, box 3. An offer also came from Harvard. Wilfred Cantwell Smith to RNB, November 10, 1972, HUA, UAV 880.10, box 5. David Riesman to RNB, November 29, 1972, DRP, HUGFP 99.8, box 5.

25. The list of the five external members appears in the official invitation to join the committee (sent out by Kaysen on November 6, 1972; reproduced in Bortolini, "'Bellah Affair' at Princeton," 22–23). Kaysen did not seek advice from Talcott Parsons, for the latter's style of work "did not appeal" to him (Carl Kaysen, interview, AF). M. White, *Philosopher's Story*, 297–98.

26. Geertz, "Work of Robert N. Bellah," 27. L. Jones, "Bad Days on Mount Olympus."

27. M. White, *Religion*, 85–97, and *Philosopher's Story*, 160, 299. Freeman Dyson to Faculty, Institute for Advanced Study, January 24, 1973, RBPP. RNB to David Riesman, December 12, 1972, DRP. RNB to Talcott Parsons, December 21, 1972, TPP, HUGFP 42.8.8, box 3.

28. M. Bellah, *Tammy*, 396ff., 403ff.

29. The vote of the institute permanent faculty was "13 against, 8 for, and 3 abstentions" (M. White, *Philosopher's Story*, 302). Harold F. Linder to the Members of the Faculty, Institute for Advanced Study Princeton, January 20, 1973, TPP, HUGFP 42.8.8, box 7. Harold F. Linder, "Memorandum to the Faculty," Institute for Advanced Study, Princeton, January 30, 1973, TPP, HUGFP 42.8.8, box 7.

30. The appointment was going to be effective from July 1, 1973, with an annual salary of $37,000 (roughly $216,000 in 2020). Carl Kaysen to RNB, January 31, 1973, TPP, HUGFP 42.8.8, box 2. Carl Kaysen to Faculty, Institute for Advanced Study, February 14, 1973, RBPP. RNB to David Riesman, February 19, 1973, DRP, HUGFP 99.8, box 5. RNB to Talcott Parsons, March 12, 1973, TPP, HUGFP 42.8.4, box 12. RNB, interview, AF; Renée Fox to Matteo Bortolini, October 8, 2009, AF.

31. RNB to David Riesman, February 19, 1973; David Riesman to RNB, February 26, 1973; both DRP, HUGFP 99.8, box 5. André Weil, draft of a letter to fellow mathematicians, January 29, 1973, sent to Robert Merton, cited in Bortolini, "'Bellah Affair' at Princeton," 10. Weil and his allies also tried to drag the temporary members of the program in social change into the discussion, as shown by a letter addressed to them by Clifford Geertz (February 2, 1973, RBPP).

32. The expression "dissident majority" was used in Shenker, "Dispute Splits Advanced Study Institute"; see also Shenker, "Institute for Advanced Learning Meets." After his evaluation had been made public, Ronald Dore wrote to Bellah, attaching his original letter to Deane Montgomery and

denouncing the breach of confidentiality. Ronald Dore to RNB, March 14, 1973, RBPP. In a letter to the *Atlantic Monthly* White explicitly stated that he had no part in giving Shenker the confidential materials that had made their way into print. M. White, letter to the editor.

33. "Membership Dispute Divides Institute for Advanced Study," *Harvard Crimson*, March 3, 1973; "Kaysen Cancels Kennedy School Godkin Series," *Harvard Crimson*, March 9, 1973; Shapley, "Institute for Advanced Study"; Chapman, "Battle of Princeton" (Cherniss and White quotes).

34. Footlick, "Thunderbolts on Olympus"; Shapley, "Institute for Advanced Study"; Shenker, "Opposing Sides Dig In" (Weil quote) and "Dispute Splits Advanced Study Institute" (White and Setton quotes).

35. M. Bellah, *Tammy*, 454ff.; John Fairbank to RNB, March 5, 1973; Neil Smelser et al. to RNB, March 8, 1973; Randy Alfred et al. to RNB, n.d. [March 1973]; all RBPP.

36. Talcott Parsons to RNB, March 8, 1973, TPP, HUGFP 42.8.8, box 3. Raymond A. Schroth to Talcott Parsons, March 8, 1973; Talcott Parsons to Raymond Schroth, March 14, 1973, TPP, HUGFP 42.45.4, box 7.

37. Two days later Burke would send Bellah a note to apologize for the tone of his first letter: "Helndamnaysh, please forgive me for that stupid letter I wrote you. . . . I have vast respect for the scope and subtlety of your knowledge. And if there's any notion of mustering a lot of your colleagues who would sign a statement in your behalf, know that I'd eagerly join." Kenneth Burke to RNB, March 2, 1973; Kenneth Burke to RNB, March 4, 1973; Ezra Vogel to RNB, March 2, 1973; all RBPP. David Riesman's letter to Reischauer is cited in Bortolini, "'Bellah Affair' at Princeton," 15.

38. Thomas C. Smith et al., letter to the editor, *New York Times*, March 7, 1973; David Apter, letter to the editor, *New York Times*, March 7, 1973; both RBPP. In a letter published by the *New York Times* on March 13, 1973, Woodward made a striking analogy between the Institute faculty and the students who had occupied the office of the president of Harvard University in 1969— an episode that, ironically, White would narrate with great disdain in *A Philosopher's Story* (262–73). On March 12, 1973, the noted feminist sociologist Jessie Bernard wrote to the editor of the American Sociological Association newsletter urging a public statement in Bob's defense using a familiar argument: "If Bellah's peers believe his work to be outstanding, that should be sufficient accreditation. Certainly the judgment of mathematicians should not be given equal credence." Jessie Bernard, letter to the editor, *Footnotes*, March 12, 1973 (cited in Bortolini, "'Bellah Affair' at Princeton," 17). The letter was eventually published in the May issue of *Footnotes*. William Jay Peck to Carl Kaysen, March 8, 1973, RBPP: "The comparison should be with Galileo, not with Einstein. Dr. Bellah's originality goes against the grain of current orthodoxy in just the same way in which Galileo's was threatening to the ecclesiastical hierarchy of his day."

39. Bellah's quotes from "Ivory Tower Tempest," 48 (*Time*); Conaway, "Infighting in the Ivory Tower," 23; Footlick, "Thunderbolts on Olympus," 60 (*Newsweek*); Chapman, "Battle of Princeton."

40. André Weil to Robert Merton, March 3, 1973; transcript of a telephone call between Robert Merton and Carl Kaysen, March 5, 1973; Robert Merton to Carl Kaysen, March 11, 1973; Robert K. Merton to André Weil, March 11, 1973; Edward Shils to Robert Merton, May 29, 1973; all cited in Bortolini, "'Bellah Affair' at Princeton," *passim*. "Ivory Tower Tempest"; Shenker, "Opposing Sides Dig In"; Chapman, "Battle of Princeton"; Shenker, "Dispute Splits Advanced Study Institute"; Shapley, "Institute for Advanced Study," 1211.

41. Tammy Bellah to her parents, cited in M. Bellah, *Tammy*, 498. RNB to Carl Kaysen, April 26, 1973, RBPP. Bob had been shown Tammy's essay, and had somehow accepted both his daughter's feelings and her critical remarks (M. Bellah, *Tammy*, 357–58).

42. RNB to Talcott Parsons, April 6, 1973, with attachment titled "Suggestions for Letter of Trustees" dated April 5, 1973; both RBPP. Talcott Parsons to the board of trustees, April 24, 1973, TPP, HUGFP 42.8.8, box 3. *Dickinsonian* of April 6, 1973, p. 9, reproduced in "Dickinsonian, April 6, 1973," Dickinson College Archives and Special Collections, accessed November 22, 2019, http://archives.dickinson.edu/dickinsonian/dickinsonian-april-6-1973. M. Bellah, *Tammy*, 653, 538ff., integrated with personal communications from Jenny Bellah Maguire and Hally Bellah-Guther, AF.

43. M. Bellah, *Tammy*, 538.

44. M. Bellah, 547, 581.

45. RNB to David Schneider, July 3, 1973, DSP. M. Bellah, *Tammy*, 583, 608–9. RNB to Carl Kaysen, April 26, 1973, RBPP. On April 28, 1973, the Institute's board of trustees issued a resolution expressing its condolences to Bellah and reaffirming its confidence in his appointment.

46. M. Bellah, *Tammy*, 683.

47. M. Bellah, *Tammy*, 583, 694, 72–76, 683, quote at 720. RNB to David Schneider, July 3, 1973, DSP. For obvious reasons, Bellah did not attend Talcott Parsons's retirement banquet in Cambridge on May 18, 1973.

Chapter Eleven

1. M. Bellah, *Abby and Her Sisters*, 88ff., 97ff., 215 (quote), 104. RNB to David Riesman, November 12, 1973; RNB to David Riesman, January 4, 1974; RNB to David Riesman, January 16, 1974; Jenny Bellah to David Riesman, February 17, 1974; Jenny Bellah to David Riesman, June 8, 1974; all DRP, HUGFP 99.8, box 5.

2. Borstelmann, *1970s*, 53, 60; Berkowitz, *Something Happened*, 55, 58–61; Shulman, *Seventies*, 8; Stein, *Pivotal Decade*; Kruse and Zelizer, *Fault Lines*.

3. Killen, *1973 Nervous Breakdown*, 205ff., 233ff.; Shulman, *Seventies*, 27ff., 35ff., 43ff.

4. Killen, *1973 Nervous Breakdown*, 59ff., 81ff.; Borstelmann, *1970s*, 64ff.; Shulman, *Seventies*, 53ff., 78ff.

5. RNB, "Reflections on Reality," 38.

6. Quotes from the lecture in RNB, "Reflections on Reality," 39, 44–48; M. Bellah, *Abby and Her Sisters*, 88–89. In January 1974 Bellah was determined to use the McCall Memorial Lecture as the epilogue of his forthcoming book on American civil religion. RNB, "Preface, Contents," unpublished document, 4 pp., January 1974, RBPP.

7. Dick Eakin to RNB, November 11, 1973; Jean May to RNB, November 11, 1973; Henry May to RNB, November 11, 1973; Browne Barr to RNB, November 11, 1973; Bill Bouwsma to RNB, December 14, 1973; Kenneth Burke to RNB, January 31, 1974; all RBPP. M. Bellah, *Tammy*, 548ff. Harlan Stelmach to Matteo Bortolini, November 9, 2012, AF.

8. RNB, "Religion and Polity in America,", 107–12.

9. RNB, interview, AF. See also Cully, "Robert Bellah and Civil Religion," 5.

10. This is reproduced word for word in RNB, *Broken Covenant*, 45–46. Copies of voice recordings of Bellah's Weil lectures can be found at the American Jewish Archives in Cincinnati.

11. RNB, "American Civil Religion in the 1970's," 258–59. The paper was first presented at an interdisciplinary conference on civil religion held at Drew University in Madison, New Jersey, in February 1973—that is, in the midst of the Bellah affair at Princeton. It was then published in *American Civil Religion*, a collection edited by Russell E. Richey and Donald Jones, in 1974.

12. Sweet, review of *American Civil Religion*," 547; Richardson, "Civil Religion in Theological Perspective," 164–65. Upon drafting the paper from which the quote is taken, Richardson wrote a letter to Bellah: "I think your proposals have been so frequently misunderstood that they have not been fairly evaluated." Herbert Richardson to RNB, September 6, 1973, RBPP.

13. H. Bowden, "Historian's Response"; Fenn, "Bellah and the New Orthodoxy"; Wimberley et al., "Civil Religious Dimension"; Tanenbaum, "Civil Religion"; Novak, "America as Religion"; Blau, "Educators Weigh a 'Civil Religion,'" 8 (quote).

14. Seabury Press was an Episcopalian publisher that specialized in religious texts. The first tentative title for the book had been *The Deepest Day*, a phrase taken from the American poet Hart Crane. Another proposed title had been *To Avoid this Shipwreck: The Religious Meaning of American History*, a citation from John Winthrop's Arbella sermon. The penultimate title was *The Broken Covenant: Religion and Polity in America*. Geertz, "Work of Robert N. Bellah." RNB, "Preface, Contents." RNB to David Riesman, January 29, 1974; RNB to David Riesman, May 22, 1974; both DRP, HUGFP 99.8, box 5. M. Bellah, *Abby and Her Sisters*, 86ff., 102ff., 244, the quote on Abby and Hally is on 165.

15. The Soedjatmoko volume, prepared for the University of California Press, was never published. Bellah's personal records contain a ten-page introduction to the book where he praised Soedjatmoko and commented upon his ideas about modernization. See Paul J. Braisted to RNB, September 14, 1974; Paul J. Braisted to RNB, December 2, 1974; both RBPP. "Sociology 146—Sociology of Religion—Winter 1974"; "Sociology 246—Sociology of Religion—Winter 1975"; both RBPP.

16. RNB, *Broken Covenant*, vii–viii nn. 1, 2, 17–24, xiii. Between 1973 and 1974 Bellah gave the Furfey Lecture at the Catholic University of America and the Beatty Lectures at McGill University. In March 1974 he was notified by David Riesman of an opening at the Center for the Study of Democratic Institutions that had been founded by Robert M. Hutchins in Santa Barbara. David Riesman to RNB, March 6, 1974; RNB to David Riesman, March 12, 1974; David Riesman to Malcom Moos, March 19, 1974; David Riesman to Harvey Wheeler, April 23, 1974; all DRP, HUGFP 99.8, box 5. Bellah eventually gave the first Irving F. Laucks Lectures in Santa Barbara on April 8–9, 1974, but never moved to the center. *The Institute of Religious Studies Bulletin*, University of California, Santa Barbara, February 1974. Benjamin Nelson to Talcott Parsons, April 24, 1974, TPP, HUGFP 42.8.8, box 10. Charles J. Adams to RNB, February 1, 1974; Thomas A. Metzger to RNB, June 4, 1974; John S. Hadsell to RNB, September 3, 1974; all RBPP. On the expectations concerning *The Broken Covenant*, see Frank Oveis to RNB, December 10, 1975, RBPP.

17. Document attached to F. Reid Isaac to David Riesman, September 9, 1974, DRP, HUGFP 99.8, box 5.

18. RNB, *Broken Covenant*, 151–53, 53, quotes 162 and 171. In 1974, the *Nation* published a version of chapter 5 of *The Broken Covenant* as its lead article, under the title "Roots of the American Taboo (on Socialism)." When former US congressman Charles O. Porter asked him

about the kind of response he got, Bellah replied: "Just yesterday I learned that a colleague of mine in the Forestry Department, of all places, has bought bulk copies of my article and is distributing it to his friends. . . . I myself feel that it is perhaps possible at last to break the taboo on the word socialism. . . . I am, however, quite undoctrinaire about these things and believe that a broad coalition of people who feel the necessity to make structural changes in our economic institutions is possible, even without consensus on all points." RNB to Charles O. Porter, March 14, 1975, SPPP.

19. RNB, *Broken Covenant*, 37, 43, 50ff., 87, 101ff.; quotes 55 and 80 ("double crime"), 87 ("groups that differed"), 101 ("saints and sinners" and "prone to every kind").

20. RNB, 83.

21. RNB, 146, 110–11.

22. RNB, 37, 55, 80–83, 112ff., 142 (quote).

23. Wilfred Cantwell Smith to RNB, September 27, 1975; Kenneth Burke to RNB, January 31, 1974; Edward Tiryakian to RNB, December 9, 1974; John C. Bennett to RNB, March 24, 1975; all RBPP. David Riesman to RNB, December 12, 1973; David Riesman to RNB, September 17, 1974; both DRP, HUGFP 99.8, box 5.

24. RNB to David Riesman, February 20, 1974, DRP, HUGFP 99.8, box 5. Talcott Parsons to RNB, February 13, 1974; RNB to Talcott Parsons, May 29, 1974; Talcott Parsons to RNB, June 28, 1974; all TPP, HUGFP 42.8.8, box 3.

25. Talcott Parsons to RNB, September 10, 1974, TPP, HUGFP 42.8.8, box 3. Interestingly, Bellah had given a presentation on "The Future of Augustinian Sociology" at Harvard on April 23, 1974. The subtitle of that talk ("From Augustine to Parsons, or, Reason and Revelation in Sociology") speaks of a side project that Bellah did not pursue further. Scattered notes for the conference are included in RBPP.

26. Talcott Parsons to Renée Fox, November 12, 1976, TPP, HUGFP 42.8.8, box 5. RNB to Talcott Parsons, May 29, 1974, TPP, HUGFP 42.8.8, box 3 (quote). RNB to David Riesman, October 1, 1974; David Riesman to RNB, October 21, 1974; both DRP, HUGFP 99.8, box 5. Parsons, "Law as an Intellectual Stepchild."

27. Barbara Laslett to RNB, August 30, 1976, RBPP (official motivation attached). The prize committee included Laslett as its chair, Bennet Berger, Jessie Bernard, Norman Birnbaum, Egon Bittner, Judith Blake Davis, Robert Friedrichs, Robert W. Hodge, and Louis Schneider. Diego de los Rios to Matteo Bortolini, August 12, 2012; Norman Birnbaum to Matteo Bortolini, September 10, 2009; both AF.

28. See reviews of *The Broken Covenant* by Marty, Johnson, Steiner, Robertson, and D. Jones; Ahlstrom, review of *Beyond Belief* and *The Broken Covenant*; Mulder, "Bicentennial Book Band."

29. Hadden, "Editor's Introduction," 386; Lockwood, "Bellah and His Critics," 396, 408–10.

30. RNB, "Rejoinder to Lockwood," 417–18.

31. An audio file of Bellah's lecture can be found on the McGill University website, at https://www.mcgill.ca/beatty/files/beatty/at7164_bellah_part_2_4.mp3 (accessed November 22, 2020). See also the transcript included in RNB, "Religion and the Future," 42–43, and the transcript of the discussion following the delivery of the paper "The New Religious Consciousness and the Secular University," 1974; both RBPP.

32. RNB, "Revolution and the Civil Religion" and "Religion and Legitimation."

Chapter Twelve

1. Keen and Harris, "Elegance of Math;" RNB and Keen, "Civil Religion." In 1976, *Psychology Today* circulated 1,026,872 copies a month. Lewenstein, "Was there Really," 32.

2. "Conferenza internazionale sull'ateismo. Sedute del 26 marzo 1969," full transcript, mimeo, Fondazione Giovanni Agnelli, April 1969, FGA, 92–94.

3. Glock and RNB, *New Religious Consciousness*; Wuthnow, *Consciousness Reformation*, ix. Hadden, "Editor's Introduction"; Kibler, "Interview of Charles Y. Glock," 4. Additional information comes from e-mails sent by some of the participants in the project: Robert Wuthnow (August 22, 2012); Randy Alfred (August 24, 2012); Harlan Stelmach (November 2, 2012); James Wolfe (September 3, 2012); Tom Piazza (August 22, 2012); and from Glock's unpublished autobiography; all AF. Yanagawa, "From a Science of 'Behavior,'" 289.

4. Glock and RNB, *New Religious Consciousness*, xiii–xiv.

5. Glock, "Consciousness among Contemporary Youth," 366.

6. RNB, "New Religious Consciousness and the Crisis in Modernity," 338–39, 342–43, and "New Consciousness," 84.

7. RNB, "New Religious Consciousness and the Crisis in Modernity," 347–48, 352.

8. Wallis, review of *The New Religious Consciousness*, 472.

9. Robbins, "Old Wine in New Bottles," 310; reviews of *The New Religious Consciousness* by Roof (94–95), Wallis, Moberg, and Elwood; Stauffer, "Bellah's Civil Religion," 394.

10. In note 13 to chapter 1 Bellah cited the works of Ricoeur and Eliade as evocative efforts to link symbol, myth, and reflective thought. RNB, *Broken Covenant*, 165.

11. Maruyama Masao to RNB, September 20, 1975, RBPP. Najita and Scheiner, *Japanese Thought*, vii. Among the mandatory readings for Bellah's "Japanese Society" course were "Religious Evolution" (1964) and *Tokugawa Religion* (republished in 1970), Ruth Benedict's *Chrysanthemum and the Sword* (1946), Ezra Vogel's *Japan's New Middle Class* (1963), Nakane Chie's *Japanese Society* (1972), and Takeshi Ishida's *Japanese Society* (1971). See "Sociology 165—Japanese Society—Winter 1969"; "Sociology 1965—Japanese Society—Winter 1971"; "Sociology 165—Japanese Society—Winter 1975," all RBPP. Bellah's last full course on Japan was given in 1975.

12. RNB, "Japan, Asia, Religion." RNB, "Shinto and Modernization"; RNB, "Transformations in Modern Japanese Thought," unpublished paper, 21 pp., RBPP; RNB, "Intellectual and Society in Japan," 89–115.

13. Albert Craig to RNB, August 20, 1970, RBPP.

14. Compare the published version with its first draft, in RBPP. RNB, "Baigan and Sorai." Bolitho, "Tokugawa Japan."

15. RNB, "Baigan and Sorai," 143–44. Borovoy, "Dialogues."

16. T. Gordon, *Spirit of 1976*, 3; Capozzola, "Makes You Want to Believe," 29–45.

17. RNB, "Civil Religion and the Bicentennial"; RNB, "Sociology Graduation Address, June 18, 1976," RBPP.

18. Ruppert, "Fundamental Question" (*Seattle Times*), A6; A. Lewis, "System" (*New York Times*), SM7; Dart, "U.S. 'Civil Religion'" (*Los Angeles Times*), A25.

19. Le Beau, *Atheist*, 251.

20. Quotes from RNB, "Civil Religion in America," 171. Madalyn Murray O'Hair to RNB, July 13, 1976; Madalyn Murray O'Hair to RNB, August 17, 1976; both RBPP.

21. "Atheist Leader Endorses Carter for President," *Minden Press-Herald* (Minden, LA), October 26, 1976, 3. Mieczowski, *Gerald Ford*, 325ff.; Bloodworth, "Jimmy Carter's 1976 Presidential Campaign"; Shulman, *Seventies*, 121ff.

22. RNB, "Religion and Legitimation," quotes at 182, 188.

23. Society for the Scientific Study of Religion program, accessed August 4, 2018 (now discontinued), http://rra.hartsem.edu/sssr/SSSR/PROGRAMS/76.html.

24. In an undated letter to Parsons, Fox and Lidz wrote about the possibility of Bellah writing a chapter of proposed (but never published) book coauthored by the members of the seminar: "9. religion and general theory in the action sciences—R.N.B. Bob has promised to adapt a part of his work-in-progress on the sociology of religion to the concerns of the human condition group, but we hope to get from him a general 'response,' as a sociologist of religion and cybernetician, to the involvement of human condition concerns in sociological theory." The letter also hinted at the possibility of Hildred and Clifford Geertz writing a chapter on anthropology. Renée Fox and Victor Lidz to Talcott Parsons, n.d. [fall 1976], TPP, HUGFP 42.8.8, box 5. Renée Fox, "Talcott Parsons, My Teacher," 401ff.

25. I was not able to locate any letter between Parsons and Bellah from September 9, 1974, to September 3, 1976.

26. Talcott Parsons to RNB, November 29, 1976; Talcott Parsons to Harold Berhsady, November 5, 1976; Talcott Parsons to RNB, January 14, 1977; Talcott Parsons to RNB, June 29, 1977; all TPP, HUGFP 42.8.8, box 3. Talcott Parsons to Renée Fox, November 12, 1976; Renée Fox to Talcott Parsons, November 25, 1976; both TPP, HUGFP 42.8.8, box 5. Talcott Parsons to Neil Smelser, May 4, 1977, TPP, HUGFP 42.8.8, box 12.

27. RNB to Talcott Parsons, November 17, 1976; Talcott Parsons to RNB, November 29, 1976; Talcott Parsons to RNB, June 29, 1977; RNB to Talcott Parsons, July 14, 1977; all TPP, HUGFP 42.8.8, box 3. Talcott Parsons to Renée Fox, December 12, 1976, TPP, HUGFP 42.8.8, box 5. RNB, "To Kill and Survive"; Parsons, "Law as an Intellectual Stepchild," 44–47.

28. In this section I mostly follow M. Bellah, *Abby and Her Sisters*, 187–220, with additions from Jennifer Bellah Maguire and Hally Bellah-Guther, AF.

29. Abby's diary entry of November 25, 1976 (Thanksgiving Day), cited in M. Bellah, *Abby and Her Sisters*, 184–85. RNB to Talcott Parsons, November 17, 1976, TPP, HUGFP 42.8.8, box 3.

30. Coleman, SJ, "Remembering Robert N. Bellah." Talcott Parsons to RNB, December 6, 1976, RBPP.

31. Hally's diary entry of January 1, 1977, cited in M. Bellah, *Abby and Her Sisters*, 220, 210.

Chapter Thirteen

1. M. Bellah, *Abby and Her Sisters*, 201 (quote), 219–25. Still today, Jenny recalls the visit as an opportunity to bond with Hally and share with her a deep connection to Paris and the lasting relationships she had formed there.

2. Hally's diary cited in M. Bellah, 224.

3. On Melanie's parallel love life, see Jennifer Bellah Maguire to Matteo Bortolini, January 2, 2020, AF. For Robert Bellah's early reflections on his open marriage, see NJ-1969–1979, entry of January 3, 1970.

4. NJ-1969–1979, entry of January 3, 1970; NJ-1965–1969, entries of December 7, 1967 ("stand back"); December, 20, 1967 ("whole range"); July 4, 1968 ("reading and writing"). Wilfred Cantwell Smith to RNB, January 8, 1977, RBPP.

5. RNB to Clifford Geertz, June 22, 1976, RBPP. M. Bellah, *Abby and Her Sisters*, 111. RNB to David Riesman, June 27, 1974; David Riesman to RNB, July 2, 1974; both DRP, HUGFP 99.8, box 5. On the National Endowment for the Humanities, see S. Miller, *Excellence and Equity*.

6. RNB, "Teaching Notes," December 1, 1976, RBPP.

7. Other participants included Alfred Balitzer, Shigeo Kanda, and David McCloskey, while Alan Wolfe and Raymond Pratt had applied unsuccessfully. "Minutes of the Thirty-Sixth Meeting of the National Council on the Humanities, May 15–16, 1975," available to download from the National Endowment for the Humanities website, https://neh.dspacedirect.org/handle /11215/2745; see also grant number FS-10190-76, Regents of the University of California, Berkeley/Robert N. Bellah, Civil Religion in America, National Endowment for the Humanities website, https://securegrants.neh.gov/publicquery/main.aspx?f=1&gn=FS-10190–76 (both accessed November 22, 2019). Raymond B. Pratt to Irving L. Horowitz, May 10, 1976, HTPA. William Sullivan, interviews, AF.

8. Rabinow, *Accompaniment*, 50–51; RNB, foreword to Rabinow, *Reflections on Fieldwork in Morocco*, xxxi; Paul Rabinow, interview, AF. Grant Barnes to Clifford Geertz, October 15, 1976; Clifford Geertz to Grant Barnes, November 8, 1976; both CGP.

9. RNB to [anon.], September 13, 1977; RNB to William Sullivan, August 16, 1977; RNB to William Sullivan, September 20, 1977; RNB to William Sullivan, October 22, 1977 ("unconditional love"); all RBPP. NJ-1969–1979, entries of February 19, 1978 ("black parka"); February 25, 1978.

10. NJ 1969–1979, entry of March 5, 1978. RNB to William Sullivan, August 16, 1977; William Sullivan to RNB, August 17, 1977; William Sullivan to RNB, September 25, 1977; RNB to William Sullivan, October 22, 1977; RNB to William Sullivan, November 14, 1977; RNB to William Sullivan, December 18, 1977; RNB to Phil Helfaer, March 26, 1978; all RBPP. Other authors discussed by Bellah and Sullivan at the time were Aldous Huxley (*The Island*) and the medieval monk Aelred of Rievaulx (*De spirituali amicitia*).

11. RNB to William Sullivan, September 7, 1977; Paul Rabinow to RNB, September 18, 1977; RNB to Paul Rabinow, September 23–24, 1977; all RBPP.

12. Quotes from Diamond, "Veritas at Harvard." Diamond, *Compromised Campus*, 17ff.; Schrecker, *No Ivory Tower*, 259ff.

13. RNB, *Beyond Belief*, xv; Roger Meltzer, "A Touch of the Tarbrush," Harvard College, April 1973, HUA, HU 92.73.566, 24.

14. Halberstam, *Best and the Brightest*, ch. 4.

15. Bundy, "Exchange on 'Veritas at Harvard'"; Schrecker, *No Ivory Tower*, ch. 7.

16. RNB, "'Veritas' at Harvard" ("I owe much to Harvard"). Sydney James to RNB, May 20, 1977; Robert Silvers to RNB, May 31, 1977; McGeorge Bundy to RNB, June 3, 1977 ("we're on the same side"); Sidney James to RNB, June 8, 1977; McGeorge Bundy to Robert Silvers, June 9, 1977; McGeorge Bundy to RNB, June 27, 1977; RNB to Albert Craig, October 3, 1977; RNB to *Harvard Magazine*, November 19, 1998; all RBPP. Bundy's letter to Pusey is detailed in chapter 4, above.

17. Woodward, "Incomplete Candor," 7. Eric Bentley to RNB, June 30, 1977; Ellen W. Schrecker to RNB, July 5, 1977; Ellen W. Schrecker to RNB, September 7, 1977; Fay Stander to RNB, July 8, 1977; Norbert Wily to RNB, July 24, 1977; Franziska Heberle to RNB, August 1, 1977; Laurence Veysey to RNB, August 30, 1977; James Steakley to RNB, July 8, 1977; Ellen W. Schrecker to RNB, August 25, 1998; all RBPP.

18. Ruppert, "Fundamental Question," A6 ("so much like a college professor"). RNB to William Sullivan, August 21, 1977; RNB to [anon.], September 13, 1977 ("more informal"); RNB to William Sullivan, September 20, 1977; RNB to William Sullivan, September 22, 1977; RNB to William Sullivan, March 30, 1978 ("mighty brain'); all RBPP.

19. M. Bellah, *Abby and Her Sisters*, 236ff. The lawsuit (Bellah v. Greenson, 81 Cal. App.3d 614 [1978]) was presented in 1975, and ended in 1978 in favor of Greenson. M. Bellah, *Tammy*, 601ff., 683.

20. Jennifer Bellah Maguire to Matteo Bortolini, August 9, 2019, AF.

21. See RNB to [anon.], September 13, 1977, RBPP.

22. RNB to William Sullivan, September 7, 1977; RNB to William Sullivan, September 29, 1977; RNB to Paul Rabinow, September 23–24, 1977; RNB to William Sullivan, November 14, 1977 (quote); all RBPP. The need to continuously reflect on what was happening is also shown by the fact that Bellah kept carbon copies of his own letters to Sullivan and Rabinow between 1977 and 1981.

23. N. Brown, *Apocalypse and/or Metamorphosis*, 2–3. RNB to William Sullivan, October 8, 1977; RNB to William Sullivan, October 22, 1977; [anon.] to RNB, n.d. [October 1977]; RNB to William Sullivan, October 25, 1977; RNB to William Sullivan, November 14, 1977; RNB to William Sullivan, November 21, 1977; RNB to William Sullivan, December 9, 1977; RNB to William Sullivan, February 11, 1978; RNB to Phil Helfaer, March 26, 1978; all RBPP.

24. Robert Bellah had first hinted at casual sex in a letter to William Sullivan dated September 29, 1977, RBPP.

25. Boyd, *Wide Open Town*; Shilts, *Mayor of Castro Street*, 51–62; Sides, *Erotic City*, 30ff., 83ff.

26. Sides, *Erotic City*, 90ff., 135ff., 153ff.; Armstrong, *Forging Gay Identities*, 125–30; FitzGerald, *Cities on a Hill*, 42ff.; Roberts, "Plight of Gay Visibility."

27. Stewart, *Folsom Street Blues*, 29–40; Godfrey, *Neighborhoods in Transition*, 117; Sides, *Erotic City*, 97ff.; FitzGerald, *Cities on a Hill*, 27, 32ff.

28. Boyd, "San Francisco's Castro District"; FitzGerald, *Cities on a Hill*, 34, 54 (quotes); Helquist, "Beyond the Baths."

29. Sides, *Erotic City*, 104 ("unlimited purpose"); FitzGerald, *Cities on a Hill*, 33; Rofes, *Walking Tour of South of Market*; Disman, "San Francisco Bathhouse Battles," 74.

30. NJ 1969–1979, entry of February 19, 1978. RNB to William Sullivan, December 9, 1977; RNB to William Sullivan, February 23, 1978; RNB to Phil Helfaer, March 26, 1978; all RBPP.

31. NJ 1969–1979, entry of March 28, 1978.

32. NJ 1969–1979, entries of February 19, 1978; March 12, 1978; March 26, 1978; March 28, 1978; March 29, 1978. RNB to Phil Helfaer, March 26, 1978; RNB to William Sullivan, March 30, 1978; both RBPP. Rockefeller Foundation, *Search for a Value Consensus*. Harry Smith to John Colton, January 12, 1978, and attached documents, RFR, administration, program and policy,

SG 3.1 and SG 3.2 (AF 112), subgroup 2, series 911, box 12, folder "Value Consensus Conference, Supplementary Materials, 1977–1978."

Chapter Fourteen

1. RNB to William Sullivan, August 21, 1977; RNB to William Sullivan, September 20, 1977; Paul Rabinow to RNB, n.d. [October 1977]; RNB to William Sullivan, February 4, 1978; Louis Dumont to RNB, May 11, 1978; all RBPP. NJ 1969–1979, entry of April 2, 1978. RNB, "Read Any Good Books Lately," 13.

2. RNB to William Sullivan, September 20, 1977; RNB to William Sullivan, September 22, 1977; RNB to William Sullivan, September 29, 1977; RNB to William Sullivan, April 23, 1978; all RBPP. NJ 1969–1979, entries of March 19, 1978; March 10, 1979. RNB to Joel Colton, March 10, 1978; Thomas Lawford to Joel Colton, March 30, 1978; Adele Simmons to Joel Colton and Lydia Bronte, March 30, 1978; all RFR, administration, program and policy, SG 3.1 and SG 3.2 (AF 112), subgroup 2, series 911, box 12, folder "Value Consensus Conference, 1977–1978." Sidney Mead to RNB, May 14, 1977; Wilfred Cantwell Smith to RNB, October 17, 1977; both RBPP. David Riesman to RNB, June 9, 1977; David Riesman to RNB, June 30, 1978; both DRP, HUGFP 99.16, box 8. Early in 1977 Bellah also worked with Susan Garfield on a proposal to make a series of documentaries on religion for the KQED public television of Northern California, although the proposal did not receive funding. Clifford Geertz to Jill Butterfield, June 27, 1977; RNB to Clifford Geertz, July 18, 1977; both CGP.

3. Tipton, *Getting Saved from the Sixties*, xiii–xvi.

4. "Sociology 146—Sociology of Religion—Winter 1972," RBPP. Swidler, *Organization without Authority*; Tipton, *Getting Saved from the Sixties*, xvii.

5. "A Report to the Trustees. Committee on Public Policy and Social Organization," September 1979, OFRS, series I: Chronological Correspondence, box 1, folder "September 1979" (quote); Richard Sharpe to Robert McKenzie, February 22, 1978, OFRS, series I: Chronological Correspondence, box 1, folder "February 1978." Richard Sharpe to Marion Coleen, July 13, 1978; Richard Sharpe to Philip Marcus, July 20, 1978; both FFR, International Division, Education and Public Policy Division, office files of Richard Sharpe (AF 557), series I: Chronological Correspondence, box 1, folder "July 1978"; Richard Sharpe to Harold Howe II, August 14, 1978, OFRS, series I: Chronological Correspondence, box 1, folder "August 1978."

6. RNB, "Interview with Robert Bellah," 120. A small grant of $1,762 was awarded to Tipton in May 1978. Richard Sharpe, "Minutes from [PPSO] Meeting of May 18, 1978," May 22, 1978, OFRS, series I: Chronological Correspondence, box 1, folder "May 1978." On Sharpe's projects see Richard Sharpe to members of the Committee on Public Policy and Social Organization, November 9, 1978, OFRS, series I: Chronological Correspondence, box 1, folder "November 1978."

7. RNB to Albert Craig, May 14, 1978, RBPP. Madsen, *Morality and Power*; Chan, Madsen, and Unger, *Chen Village*.

8. Rabinow and Sullivan, *Interpretive Social Science*, 4, 12. RNB to William Sullivan, September 29, 1977; William Sullivan to RNB, November 9, 1977; both RBPP.

9. A first planning grant of $3,300 was given by the Ford Foundation to get the project started. "Minutes from Meeting of June 15, 1978," June 19, 1978, OFRS, series I: Chronological

Correspondence, box 1, folder "June 1978"; Richard Sharpe to RNB, July 20, 1978, OFRS, series I: Chronological Correspondence, box 1, folder "July 1978." For information about the 1978 NEH summer seminar (the last one ever convened by Bellah), see grant number FS-10584-76, Regents of the University of California, Berkeley/Robert N. Bellah, Civil Religion in America, National Endowment for the Humanities website, accessed November 22, 2020, https://securegrants .neh.gov/publicquery/main.aspx?f=1&gn=FS-10584–76.

10. RNB, "Human Conditions," 8–11.

11. Grant number AF-12198-78, Regents of the University of California, Berkeley/Robert N. Bellah, Religious Vision and Social Order in Comparative Perspective, National Endowment for the Humanities website, accessed November 22, 2020, https://securegrants.neh.gov /publicquery/main.aspx?f=1&gn=AF-12198–78. RFR, general correspondence, RG 2, 1971–1980 (AF 401), subgroup 1977: General Correspondence, series 1977/200: United States, reel 13, folder "Bellah, Robert N." (quotes).

12. In fact, as his sabbatical turned out to be an almost complete fiasco, Bob wrote in his diary on February 4, 1979, that "body and sex [were finally] getting theirs after years of tyranny of the mind." NJ 1969–1979, entries of February 20, 1978; February 22, 1978; February 23, 1978; February 25, 1978; February 26, 1978; February 4, 1979; July 29, 1979. Eric Voegelin, *Modernity without Restraint*, 116ff. (quote 117).

13. RNB to William Sullivan, April 23, 1978, RBPP.

14. NJ 1969–1979, entries of February 19, 1978 (quote); February 20, 1978; February 22, 1978; February 23, 1978; February 25, 1978; February 26, 1978; February 4, 1979; February 8, 1979; February 12, 1979. RNB to William Sullivan, February 26, 1978; RNB to William Sullivan, March 30, 1978; RNB to William Sullivan, April 23, 1978; RNB to William Sullivan, May 6, 1978; RNB to [anon.], May 14, 1978; Steve Foster to RNB, August 1978; Steve Foster to RNB, September 1978; Steve Foster to RNB, October 24–25, 1978; RNB to William Sullivan, October 31, 1978; RNB to William Sullivan, February 20, 1979; RNB to William Sullivan, March 6, 1979; all RBPP. Steve Foster, interview; Stephen Tobias to Matteo Bortolini, May 23, 2019; both AF.

15. RNB to William Sullivan, September 29, 1977; RNB to William Sullivan, November 14, 1977; RNB to William Sullivan, May 13, 1978; RNB to William Sullivan, February 5, 1979; RNB to William Sullivan, February 11, 1979; RNB to William Sullivan, February 15, 1979; RNB to William Sullivan, March 14, 1979; RNB to William Sullivan, March 25, 1979 ("any taboo"); RNB to William Sullivan, April 26, 1979 ("homoerotic frenzy"); all RBPP. NJ 1969–1979, entries of February 25, 1978; February 4, 1979; March 10, 1979; March 13, 1979; April 26, 1979; April 2, 1978; March 10, 1979. JNL 1979–1983, entry of August 31, 1980.

16. RNB to William Sullivan, February 15, 1979, RBPP ("I suppose"). NJ 1969–1979, entry of February 9, 1979 (*"Urzeit"*). RNB to William Sullivan, February 5, 1979, RBPP (other quotes).

17. RNB to Paul Rabinow, September 23–24, 1977; RNB to William Sullivan, November 14, 1977 (*"I am you"*); RNB to [anon.], December 4, 1977 ("sexual identity and sexual choice"); RNB to William Sullivan, February 11, 1978; all RBPP. NJ 1969–1979, entry of April 2, 1978 ("shared experience since childhood").

18. NJ 1969–1979, entries of March 12, 1978 ("30 years out of date"); April 29, 1979; May 1, 1979 ("grim pleasure"). RNB to William Sullivan, February 6, 1979 ("most uncomfortable"); William Sullivan to RNB, February 11, 1979; both RBPP.

19. RNB to William Sullivan, November 14, 1977; RNB to William Sullivan, December 4, 1977; RNB to William Sullivan, February 15, 1979; RNB to William Sullivan, March 6, 1979; all RBPP. NJ 1969–1979, entries of February 18, 1978; February 25, 1978. RNB to Steve Foster, October 24–29, 1979, courtesy of Steve Foster. In an interview published in 1985, Bellah defined the San Francisco gay community as "an extreme example of a hedonistic, individualistic, privatized group of people," and "an extreme example of something that claims to be a community but absolutely it isn't." RNB, "Interview with Robert Bellah," 136. On the history of the San Francisco gay community, see FitzGerald, *Cities on a Hill*, 55–56; Shilts, *Mayor of Castro Street*, 115ff.; J. Miller, *Passions of Michel Foucault*, 253; Armstrong, *Forging Gay Identities*, 82–93, 115–16, 121.

20. Miller, *Passions of Michel Foucault*, 255 ("politicized ritual"); Armstrong *Forging Gay Identities*, 61–64, 67–68, 225 ("same-gender sexual attraction" at 67). In his diary and correspondence, Bellah repeatedly used the phrase "coming out" in its old meaning of one's first same-sex sexual experience (referring to Brad). NJ 1969–1979, entries of March 28, 1978; February 4, 1979. RNB to William Sullivan, March 30, 1978, RBPP. Sides, *Erotic City*, 120 ("make up their minds"); Dworkin, "Bisexual Histories in San Francisco."

21. JNL 1979–1983, entry of August 31, 1980.

22. Hoehl, "Interview with Robert Bellah," 7–9.

23. Hoehl, "Interview with Robert Bellah," 13, my italics. The interview developed ideas first voiced in Bellah's earlier conversation with Ed Newman broadcast by NBC on September 17, 1978 (TV script, September 17, 1978, RBPP).

24. RNB, "Place of Religion," 153. See also chapters 8 and 9, above.

25. RNB to William Sullivan, April 26, 1979, RBPP. Given that Sullivan was employed at a small Catholic college, their relationship was also kept private for instrumental reasons. RNB to Steve Foster, October 24–29, 1979, courtesy of Steve Foster.

26. William Bennett to Joel Colton, March 31, 1978, RFR, administration, program and policy, SG 3.1 and SG 3.2 (AF 112), subgroup 2, series 911, box 12, folder "Value Consensus Conference, 1977–1978."

27. Robert N. Bellah, Richard Madsen, William M. Sullivan, Ann Swidler, and Steven M. Tipton, "Revised. Description of Project: The Moral Basis of Social Commitment in America," 1978, Graduate Theological Union Archives, Center for the Study of New Religious Movements Collections, 1977–1983, box 6, folder 18, pp. 2–4.

28. R. Bellah et al., "Revised. Description of Project," 2–4.

29. R. Bellah et al. "Revised. Description of Project," 7 (quotes). William Sullivan to RNB, October 9, 1978; RNB to William Sullivan, October 31, 1978; William Sullivan to RNB, November 24, 1978; RNB to Research Group and Advisory Group, March 20, 1979; all RBPP. David Riesman was particularly active in advising the group. David Riesman to RNB, September 11, 1978; David Riesman to Richard Madsen, September 12, 1978; David Riesman to RNB, September 27, 1978; David Riesman to RNB, April 2, 1979; David Riesman to RNB, April 4, 1979; David Riesman to RNB, April 9, 1979; David Riesman to RNB and Steven M. Tipton, April 9, 1979; David Riesman to RNB, May 2, 1979; all DRP, HUGFP 99.16, box 8. David Riesman to RNB and colleagues, September 15, 1978; David Riesman to Steven Titpon, September 15, 1978; both REEL. John Gardner to RNB, April 11, 1978, RBPP.

30. Bellah's last use of the term "civil religion" was R. Bellah and Hammond, *Varieties of Civil Religion*, while his chapter in R. Bellah and Greenspahn, *Uncivil Religion*, was way beyond it.

31. The four evaluators had all been cited in the research project as likely participants to the group's encounters. RNB to Richard Sharpe, September 1, 1978; Norman Birnbaum to Richard Sharpe, October 18, 1978; Peter Berger to Richard Sharpe, October 20, 1978; Daniel Bell to Richard Sharpe, October 30, 1978; RNB to Richard Sharpe, November 1, 1978; Jason Hall (NEH) to RNB, March 5, 1979; RNB to Jason Hall, April 16, 1979; RNB to Richard Sharpe, April 20, 1979; RNB to Richard Sharpe, April 26, 1979; RNB to Richard Sharpe, May 11, 1979; RNB, Richard Madsen, William M. Sullivan, Ann Swidler, and Steven M. Tipton, "Addendum to Description of Project, The Moral Basis of Social Commitment in America"; all REEL.

32. $250,000 in 1980 roughly corresponds to $785,000 in 2020. RNB to Richard Sharpe, May 11, 1979; Richard Sharpe, "Minutes of the [PPSO] Meeting of May 15, 1979," May 21, 1979; both FFR, Grants Them-Tw (FA732H), reel 4642, folder "The Regents of the University of California, 1979–1984." For the NEH grant, see grant number RO-*1457-79, Regents of the University of California, Berkeley/Robert N. Bellah, The Moral Basis of Social Commitment in America, accessed November 22, 2020, https://securegrants.neh.gov/publicquery/main.aspx ?f=1&gn=RO-*1457–79. Officers from the various organizations had been in contact since the very beginning: Richard Sharpe to Philip Marcus, November 28, 1978; Richard Sharpe, "Minutes from [PPSO] Meeting of November 16, 1978," November 27, 1978; both OFRS, series I: Chronological Correspondence, box 1, folder "November 1978."

33. On Parsons's death, see Renée Fox, "Talcott Parsons, My Teacher." On his trip to Germany, see documents collected in TPP, HUGFP 42.8.8, box 6. Renée Fox to Talcott Parsons, December 10, 1978; Renée Fox and Victor Lidz to Talcott Parsons, n.d. [fall 1978]; both TPP, HUGFP 42.8.8, box 5. See also NJ 1969–1979, entries of March 5, 1978; March 19, 1978. Harold Bershady to Talcott Parsons, October 5, 1978, TPP; William Sullivan to RNB, November 24, 1978, RBPP.

34. RNB to William Sullivan, May 11, 1979; Clifford Geertz to RNB, May 16, 1979; RNB to Clifford Geertz, July 31, 1979; Victor Lidz to RNB, August 11, 1979; all RBPP.

35. RNB, "World Is the World," 60–62. Speakers at the ASA memorial session for Parsons included Robin M. Williams Jr., Jesse R. Pitts, and John W. Riley Jr.

36. RNB, 60–62.

37. RNB, "Father and Son in Christianity," 90. In a letter to Renée Fox (August 22, 1997, RBPP), Bellah confessed that "perhaps there was a sibling rivalry with Neil [Smelser], whom I felt Talcott [Parsons] always preferred, and whose work was closer in style to Talcott's than mine was."

38. In 1981 Berkeley ranked fourth among sociology departments in America, before Harvard but after Chicago, Wisconsin, and Michigan. Burris, "Academic Caste System." RNB to Albert H. Bowker, April 20, 1977, RBPP. RNB, interview, AF. NJ 1969–1979, entry of October 8, 1979; Alessandro Ferrara to Matteo Bortolini, July 9, 2019, AF; Burawoy, "Antinomian Marxist." A former student of Theodor Adorno and Max Horkheimer, in the late 1970s Habermas was the foremost heir of the Frankfurt School, whose critical tradition he kept alive as the director of the Max Planck Institute for the Study of Living Conditions in the Scientific and Technological World in Starnberg. Way before his coming to Berkeley as a visiting professor in January 1980, Bellah informed Habermas about the opening of a senior chair in sociological theory and urged him to seriously consider the opportunity. Embroiled in a prolonged organizational battle at the Starnberg Institute and dismayed by the vicious attacks of conservative politicians

and academic administrators at the University of Munich, the German philosopher formally applied for the job and gave a detailed job talk at the Department of Sociology, to which the University of California replied pledging him the best conditions allowed by its statutes. In spite of painful conflicts with his colleagues, in October 1980 Habermas decided not to leave his country and finally declined the offer as he made ready for the next, and final, step of his career—his resignation from the Max Planck Institute and subsequent return to Frankfurt. Müller-Doohm, *Habermas*, ch. 6. Alessandro Ferrara to Matteo Bortolini, May 11, 2019; RNB, interview; both AF.

Chapter Fifteen

1. All unreferenced information in this chapter comes from interviews with RNB, Madsen, Swidler, Tipton, and Sullivan conducted in 2007, checked and augmented through e-mail exchanges in 2019 (AF). FitzGerald, *Evangelicals*; Kruse and Zelizer, *Fault Lines*, 98ff.; Jenkins, *Decade of Nightmares*, 108ff.

2. Mattson, *What the Heck*, 11; Berkowitz, *Something Happened*, 61ff.

3. NJ 1969–1979, entry of July 13, 1979. RNB, "Notes for Camp David, 10 July 1979"; RNB, "Morality and the American Future: Human Conditions for a Good Society," draft, 1979; both RBPP. Raeside, "Night at Camp David." Horowitz, *Anxieties of Affluence*, 236ff., and *Jimmy Carter*, 48ff., 140ff.; Mattson, *What the Heck*, 89ff.

4. NJ 1969–1979, entry of July 13, 1979.

5. NJ 1969–1979, entries of July 13, 1979; July 16, 1979.

6. "Who in the World Is Robert Bellah?" undated news profile, RBPP.

7. NJ 1969–1979, entry of July 17, 1979. "Religious Leaders' Response to President Carter's Speech," July 16, 1979; RNB, "Supplementary Statement to NCC et alia, Statement of 16 July 1979," both RBPP. Raeside, "Night at Camp David," 157.

8. Mattson, *What the Heck*, 167ff.; Horowitz, *Jimmy Carter*, 120ff.; Bell, *End of Ideology*, 404ff.; Parsons and Platt, *American University*, 278ff.

9. Kruse and Zelizer, *Fault Lines*, 135ff.; Hartman, *War for the Soul*, 21–34; Melzer et al., *Public Intellectual*.

10. Ronald Reagan, "Election Eve Address 'A Vision for America,'" (November 3, 1980), National Archives, Ronald Reagan Presidential Library and Museum, accessed November 22, 2020, https://www.reaganlibrary.gov/archives/speech/election-eve-address-vision-america; Kruse and Zelizer, *Fault Lines*, 96ff.; Hartman, *War for the Soul*, 41ff.

11. FitzGerald, *Evangelicals*; Hartman, *War for the Soul*, 70–101; Kruse and Zelizer, *Fault Lines*, 88ff.; D. Williams, *God's Own Party*, 167ff.; Shields, "Framing the Christian Right."

12. RNB, "Discerning Old and New Imperatives," 15 (quotes), and "Biblical Religion and Social Sciences." Bellah had already depicted Reagan as "the archetypal liberal" in "Commentary and Proposed Agenda," 356. As late as October 29, 1984—that is, one week before Reagan's landslide reelection—Bellah would take a condescending stance toward evangelicals, expressing his hope for their democratic coming of age. RNB, "Toward Clarity," 393.

13. Sullivan, *Reconstructing Public Philosophy*, xi ("liberal capitalist form"), 156–57 (other quotes); R. Bellah and Sullivan, "Democratic Culture," 46.

14. Sullivan, *Reconstructing Public Philosophy*, 205–6. RNB, "Preface," draft for the Japanese translation of *The Broken Covenant* (*Yaburareta Keiyaku*), 6 pp., RBPP. Quote from FitzGerald, *Evangelicals*, 287.

15. RNB to Jürgen Habermas, July 20, 1981 ("the position"); Jürgen Habermas to RNB, September 14, 1981; both RBPP. MacIntyre, *After Virtue*, 263 (other quotes); Sullivan, *Reconstructing Public Philosophy*, 76–77.

16. Sullivan and Bellah, "American Values"; RNB, "Cultural Vision"; "Bellah and Audience, Lecture I," and "Bellah and Audience, Lecture II," November 9–10, 1982, transcripts; both RBPP. Godot quote from MacIntyre, *After Virtue*, 263. Bellah spoke explicitly of MacIntyre's "solution" in a series of three unpublished conferences under the title "Christian and Citizen: Social Responsibility in Times of Confusion," n.d., RBPP.

17. Wallach, "Contemporary Aristotelianism"; Sunstein, "Beyond the Republican Revival."

18. In the introduction to his last collection of essays, published in 1978, Parsons had remarked that "whatever other philosophical positions [might] be possible, [he had] explicitly taken one in the Kantian tradition," according to which the basic epistemic and moral categories came "from outside" with respect to human perceptions, and were thus irreducible to them. Parsons, *Action Theory*, 5 (quote), 340ff.

19. Münch, "Talcott Parsons," 709.

20. RNB, "ASA Action Theory Panel 10/9/1982," handwritten notes, RBPP.

21. Macey, *Lives of Michel Foucault*, 338–40, 430–35; more cautiously, J. Miller, *Passions of Michel Foucault*; Wade, *Foucault in California*.

22. Bellah and Taylor had known each other for some time: Charles Taylor to RNB, April 23, 1982, RBPP. NJ-1969–1979, entries of April 28, 1979; July 16, 1979. Charles Taylor to Matteo Bortolini, September 3, 2019, AF. C. Taylor, "Foucault on Freedom and Truth," quotes at 181. RNB, "Symbolic Realism: Structuralism or Hermeneutics?" unpublished paper, RBPP, 20.

23. RNB, "Comments on Charles Taylor's 'Foucault on Freedom and Truth,'" unpublished paper, March 25, 1983, RBPP. The dialogue comes from "Transcript of a Conversation between Michel Foucault, Robert Bellah, Martin Jay, Leo Löwenthal, Charles Taylor, Paul Rabinow, and Hubert Dreyfus, Berkeley, April 21, 1983," Fonds Foucault, Institut mémoires de l'édition contemporaine, D250(7)*, 16–17.

24. Salkever, "Aristotle's Social Science."

25. NJ 1969–1979, entries of May 3, 1978 ("demystified" quote); July 4, 1979; July 13, 1979. JNL 1979–1983, entries of July 29, 1979; August 3, 1979; August 5, 1979; October 8, 1979. RNB to Steve Foster, October 24–29, 1979, courtesy of Steve Foster. On Eli Leon, see Roberta Smith, "Eli Leon, 82, Dies; Champion of African-American Quilt Makers," *New York Times*, March 23, 2018, https://www.nytimes.com/2018/03/23/obituaries/eli-leon-82-dies-champion-of-african-american-quilt-makers.html.

26. JNL 1979–1983, entries of August 28, 1980; August 31, 1980; February 16, 1981; February 17, 1981; March 26, 1981. RNB to William Sullivan, February 16, 1981; William Sullivan to RNB, June 15, 1983; William Sullivan to RNB, June 21, 1983; William Sullivan to RNB, June 16, 1984; William Sullivan to Robert and Melanie Bellah, n.d. [August, 1984]; all RBPP. On Lillian Bellah, see NJ 1969–1979, entries of February 8, 1979; February 18, 1979; Jennifer Bellah Maguire to Matteo Bortolini, July 22, 2019; Hally Bellah-Guther to Matteo Bortolini, July 23, 2019; both AF.

27. "Syllabus—SOC 290, American Culture, Society and Character," RBPP. JNL 1979–1983, entries of August 28, 1980; December 26, 1980; October 2, 1981. RNB to Richard Baker Roshi, October 13, 1981, RBPP. The UC Berkeley gay support group had been created by philosopher Bruce Vermazen and others in the winter of 1978 during the heated discussions on the Briggs Initiative. See Bruce Vermazen, "UCB Gay History, circa Late 1970s/Early 1980s," LavenderCal, accessed November 22, 2020, https://lavendercal.berkeley.edu/ucb-gay-history-circa-late-1970searly-1980s. The circumstance has been confirmed by Vermazen, David Kirp, and Leonard Johnson by e-mail, May 5–17, 2019, AF.

28. David Riesman to Ann Swidler, April 9, 1979; RNB to Research Group and Advisory Committee, October 25, 1979; David Riesman to RNB, November 6, 1979; David Riesman to RNB, November 19, 1979; David Riesman to Michael Maccoby, November 19, 1979; all DRP, HUGFP 99.16, box 8. William Sullivan to RNB, September 25, 1977; RNB to William Sullivan, September 26, 1977; William Sullivan to RNB, October 5, 1977; all RBPP. See "Syllabus—SOC 290, American Culture, Society and Character," RBPP. All documents pertaining to relations between the Ford Foundation and the Habits group are filed in REEL.

29. Compare R. Bellah, Richard Madsen, William M. Sullivan, Ann Swidler, and Steven M. Tipton, "Revised. Description of Project: The Moral Basis of Social Commitment in America," 1978, Graduate Theological Union Archives, Center for the Study of New Religious Movements Collections, 1977–1983, box 6, folder 18; RNB to National Endowment for the Arts Grants Office, December 9, 1980, REEL (quote).

30. RNB to Marian Coolen, April 5, 1982, REEL.

31. JNL 1979–1983, entry of August 28, 1981.

32. JNL 1979–1983, entries of August 28, 1981 ("hands are always full"); October 2, 1981; March 14, 1982; April 1, 1982 (Yeats quote); April 13, 1982; August 30, 1982. Yeats's letter was later quoted in RNB, "How I Teach," 197–98.

33. Saint Mark's would later be cited in chapter 9 of *Habits of the Heart* as Saint Stephen's (see chapter 17, below). RNB, "Finding the Church"; RNB, "Interview with Philip Getchell, March 22, 1984," RBPP; Kat Jerman, "Berkeley's Sanctuary Movement: Historical Essay," FoundSF, accessed November 22, 2020, http://www.foundsf.org/index.php?title=Berkeley%27s_Sanctuary_Movement.

34. JNL-1979–1983, entries of October 8, 1979; August 22, 1983. William Sullivan to RNB, November 7, 1983, RBPP. R. Bellah et al., *Habits of the Heart*, xi, 252. RNB to Steve Foster, April 29, 1982, courtesy of Steve Foster. RNB, "Interview with Robert Bellah," 121–22.

Chapter Sixteen

1. All unreferenced information in this chapter comes from interviews with Bellah, Madsen, Swidler, Tipton, and Sullivan conducted in 2007, and checked and augmented through e-mail exchanges in 2019 (AF). Interest in the book had also been expressed by the university presses of Harvard, Yale, and Chicago, and the Boston Unitarian publisher, Beacon Press. In the end, and despite a few problems with the editorial board, the five coauthors opted for the University of California Press for its proximity to home and the enthusiasm of the editor, Jim Clark. RNB to Marion Coleen, June 27, 1984, REEL. Brian O'Connell to Russel Edgerton, January 28, 1985;

William Sullivan to RNB, March 18, 1985; both RBPP. J. Clark and Gabowitsch, "Sociologists and Their Publishers."

2. Melanie's letter of December 29, 1984, is mentioned in Maruyama Yukari to Melanie Bellah, January 19, 1985 (in Japanese, transl. February 25, 1985); Maruyama Masao to Robert and Melanie Bellah, February 11, 1985; both RBPP. Victoria Lanakila Generao, personal communication, February 3, 2018; Jennifer Bellah Maguire to Matteo Bortolini, July 23, 2019; both AF.

3. M. Bellah, *Abby and Her Sisters*, 237ff., 227–33. RNB to Phil Helfaer, March 26, 1978, RBPP. RNB to Steve Foster, April 29, 1982, courtesy of Steve Foster. JNL 1979–1983, entries of September 13, 1980; March 27, 1981; March 28, 1981; August 28, 1981; October 2, 1981; March 14, 1982; May 11, 1982.

4. JNL 1979–1983, entry of September 13, 1980. RNB to Clifford Geertz, July 31, 1979, CGP. RNB to Steve Foster, October 24–29, 1979 courtesy of Steve Foster. M. Bellah, *Abby and Her Sisters*, 238. Hally Bellah Guther to Matteo Bortolini, July 23, 2019; Jennifer Bellah Maguire to Matteo Bortolini, July 23, 2019; both AF.

5. Richard Sharpe to Members of CPPSO, January 18, 1979, and attached documents, OFRS, series I: Chronological Correspondence, box 1, folder "January 1979." Richard Sharpe to Messrs. Bell, Sutton, Bresner, Carmichael, and Hines, March 6, 1979; Richard Sharpe to Ann Swidler, March 6, 1979; Richard Sharpe to Steven M. Tipton, March 6, 1979; Richard Sharpe to William Sullivan, March 6, 1979; all OFRS, series I: Chronological Correspondence, box 1, folder "March 1979."

6. Compare the beginning of Tipton's book—"Each of us holds ideas of right and wrong. We ground them in our experience of life and through them we make sense of the experience"—to the first page of Madsen's—"What is a good society? What is a good person? How should a good person act in view of the fact that the society he lives in is inevitably imperfect?"—and the first lines of *Habits of the Heart*—"How ought we to live? How do we think about how we live? Who are we, as Americans? What is our character?" Madsen also made use of Potter's classification of styles of ethical evaluation as reworked by Tipton in his dissertation. Tipton, *Getting Saved from the Sixties*; Madsen, *Morality and Power*; R. Bellah et al., *Habits of the Heart*; Alexander, *Theoretical Logic in Sociology*. JNL 1979–1983, entry of September 12, 1980.

7. Ann Swidler to Matteo Bortolini, September 21, 2019, AF. Swidler, "Culture in Action."

8. Swidler, "Culture in Action," 278 (quote). Troy, *Morning in America*; Jenkins, *Decade of Nightmares*; Kruse and Zelizer, *Fault Lines*; Hartman, *War for the Soul*.

9. Troy, *Morning in America*, 4.

10. RNB, "Legitimation Processes," 91.

11. Ad published in the *American Sociological Review* 50 (1985): x (see figure 16.1).

12. R. Bellah et al., *Habits of the Heart*, 307.

13. As remarked by reviewers, the book's main points are often reiterated in different chapters. In what follows I will give references for some of their occurrences. R. Bellah et al., 57ff., 75–76, 107–8, 130.

14. R. Bellah et al., 66–69, 72 ("celebrating the interdependence"), 73, 93, 100–3, 107–8, 130, 153 ("communities of memory" and "lifestyle enclaves"), 162, 175, 281–82. (Page numbers of these exact quotes are noted here, but the concepts and phrases are repeated on the other pages listed.)

15. RNB, "Cultural Vision," 502; R. Bellah et al., *Habits of the Heart*, ix, 20–21 ("In the language they use," 21). Geertz, *Interpretation of Cultures* and *Local Knowledge*.

16. The definitions of the four traditions are spelled out in the book's glossary. R. Bellah et al., *Habits of the Heart*, 333–36.

17. The best explanation of this point is given in Tipton, "Moral Languages," 166ff.

18. R. Bellah et al., *Habits of the Heart*, 37–39, 84 (quotes), 143, 101, 235–37, 251, my italics. I am implicitly adopting the conceptualization of the continuum of scientific thought introduced in J. Alexander, *Theoretical Logic in Sociology*, 1:2ff.

19. R. Bellah et al., *Habits of the Heart*, 194 ("ability to acknowledge"), 195, 207 (other quotes), 208. In 1985 a new edition of *Tokugawa Religion* was published with a changed subtitle, *The Cultural Roots of Modern Japan* (New York: Free Press). In his "Introduction to the Paperback Edition," Bellah criticized modernization theory and recounted how Maruyama's review had pushed him to change his mind on the Weberian analogy between the Protestant ethic and that elaborated by Japanese religious movements. *Habits* was never mentioned, as Bellah's more substantive preoccupations focused on unlimited growth, the power of experts, and a need to go back to a more harmonious understanding of the relationship between human society and nature.

20. R. Bellah et al., *Habits of the Heart*, 124–28, 139 (quote).

21. R. Bellah et al., 142 ("abandon our deepest identity"), 83, 140 ("living tradition"), 283.

22. R. Bellah et al., ch. 11, *passim*, quote 286.

23. R. Bellah et al., 290, 307.

24. Salkever, *Finding the Mean*, 74–81, quote at 4.

Chapter Seventeen

1. What follows is based on an analysis of seventy-five reviews and essays on *Habits of the Heart* published between 1985 and 1987, not all of which have been cited, plus some later articles. Roark, "Study Assails Values"; RNB, "Is Individualism Out of Control" and "Reading and Misreading."

2. RNB, "Interview with Robert Bellah," 121–22. David Roberti to RNB, February 13, 1985; Nathan Gardels to RNB, March 18, 1985; Clifford Green to RNB, May 31, 1985; all RBPP. Steinfels, "Up from Individualism" ("grand argument"); Woodward, "American Self" ("easily the richest" and "State of the Union"); Champlin, review of *Habits of the Heart*; Sanoff, "Individualism."

3. McDowell, "Harper's Wins Rights"; McNall, "Is Democracy Possible?" 167–68. Steven M. Tipton to Matteo Bortolini, October 2, 2019, AF.

4. Reviews of *Habits of the Heart* by Baltzell and by Marty; Riker, "Learning to Love"; reviews of *Habits of the Heart* by Ehrenreich ("awfully nice") and by Everist; Vree, "Diagnosing America's Troubled Ethos" ("monumental"); reviews of *Habits of the Heart* by Richard Fox ("very few" at 185), Guseman ("ambitious and well-guided" at 134), Tiryakian ("literary event" at 171), Simons ("intelligent, challenging" at 187), and Hunter; Martin, "Searching for the Agorà"; Novak, "Habits"; McNall, "Is Democracy Possible?"

5. Reviews of *Habits of the Heart* by Ehrenreich and by M. Brewster Smith; Johnsen, "Reaffirming Bedrock Civic Values." R. Bellah et al., *Habits of the Heart*, 151–52.

6. Harding, "Toward a Darkly Radiant Vision," 67 ("fundamentally"), 74 ("old white fantasies"), 76, 79–81.

7. Ingham, review of *Habits of the Heart* ("thin" at 294); Steinfels, "Up from Individualism" ("cardboard"); Grant, "Individualism" ("bloodless") at 315; Kristol, "Beyond Individualism?" 77–78; Goodin, review of *Habits of the Heart*, 431; Greeley, review of *Habits of the Heart*; Lieberson, "Einstein, Renoir, and Greeley," 6.

8. Weinstein, "Disconnected Moralizing"; Neuhaus, "Habits of the (Academic) Heart"; Baltzell, review of *Habits of the Heart*, 802; Peacock, "America as a Cultural System"; Warsford, review of *Habits of the Heart*; Burtt, "Communitarian Ethics"; S. Brown, "Breaking the Habits"; Potter, "Qualms of a Believer"; Johnsen, "Reaffirming Bedrock Civic Values."

9. Wolfe, "Is Sociology Dangerous?"; Neuhaus, "Habits of the (Academic) Heart"; Grant, "Individualism," 318; Jameson, "On *Habits of the Heart*"; Eden, "Cancer of Self-Interest."

10. Novak, "Habits." RNB, "Transforming American Culture," 15.

11. Neuhaus, review of *Reconstructing Public Philosophy* by W. M. Sullivan, 435, and "Habits of the (Academic) Heart," 101–2; Kristol, "Beyond Individualism?" 80.

12. RNB, introduction to *Varieties of Civil Religion*, vii, and "Comment"; Mathisen, "Twenty Years after Bellah."

13. NJ-1969–1979, entry of January 3, 1970. Sullivan, "After Foundationalism," 38–40. This fine essay, which makes no mention of *Habits*, might be seen as a reflection on some of the book's philosophical underpinnings.

14. Sullivan, "After Foundationalism," 41; RNB, "Idea of Practices in *Habits*," 269–70. Certainly, Bellah's was not the only way to respond to this critique: Steve Tipton, for example, launched himself into a passionate and eloquent explanation of *Habits'* sampling choices and methodological tools in his response to a symposium on the book published in *Soundings* ("Moral Languages"). For other reactions to *Habits*, see Martin Paley to RNB, October 30, 1985; Edward Tiryakian to RNB, October 27, 1986; James Callaway to RNB, December 4, 1986; Paul D. Hanson to RNB, June 21, 1988; Joseph H. Fichter to RNB, June 29, 1988; Robert Heilbroner to RNB, October 6, 1989; all RBPP.

15. On Bigelow, see Bigelow Homes's website: http://www.bigelowspeeches.com/ (accessed November 22, 2020); RNB, "Social Science as Public Philosophy," 23; RNB, "Teaching *Habits*," handwritten notes, Woorster, October 12, 1986, RBPP.

16. RNB, "America's Cultural Conversation," 6. William Sullivan to RNB, January 2, 1986; Janet Goldstein to RNB, June 17, 1987; Larry Hedges to RNB, February 2, 1988; all RBPP. Steven M. Tipton to Matteo Bortolini, October 2, 2019, AF.

17. Since Bellah's personal organizers have not been preserved, it is difficult to indicate the precise number of his speaking engagements. A rough count of the dated papers from conferences indicates at least thirty-two speaking engagements and forty-two days of travel in 1985, forty-seven in 1986 (fifty-seven days), and thirty-three in 1987 (forty-seven days). RNB, "Palm Springs 28 Feb 85," handwritten notes; RNB, "Private Philanthropy and Moral Leadership," Council on Foundations Annual Conferences, Kansas City, April 14, 1986; both RBPP. The "ostensible populism" quote comes from Irving L. Horowitz to Donald McDonald, September 15, 1986, HTPA. Neuhaus, "Robert Bellah and Social Democracy."

18. RNB, "Social Science as Public Philosophy," reporting a seminar held at the Center for the Study of Democratic Institutions, University of California, Santa Barbara, on February 21, 1986, RBPP. RNB, "Language," 233. R. Bellah et al., *Good Society*, 291–92 (quote).

19. Ira Michael Heyman to RNB, May 20, 1986; Ira Michael Heyman to RNB, April 16, 1987; Barbara A. Mikulski to RNB, January 5, 1988; Neil R. Grabois to RNB, December 8, 1988; all RBPP. RNB, interview, AF. Hilzenrath. "Raisa's Woman to Women Chat"; Taubman, *Gorbachev.*

20. M. Brewster Smith, review of *Habits of the Heart*; Steinfels, "Up from Individualism"; R. Bellah et al., *Habits of the Heart*, 221, 227; RNB, "On Wilfred Smith and George Lindbeck," unpublished paper, circa 1985, RBPP.

21. R. Bellah et al., *Habits of the Heart*, 237ff., quotes at 237. The very conclusion of *Habits* also hinted at Tillich's "structure of grace in history" and spoke of poverty as "the truth of our condition" in a rather Gospel-inspired finale (295).

22. Bell, *Cultural Contradictions of Capitalism*, 30, xxviii; Urban, "Conversation with Daniel Bell," 18. See Rieder and Wiley, review of *The Cultural Contradictions of Capitalism*; Touraine, "What Is Daniel Bell Afraid Of?"

23. Ehrenreich, review of *Habits of the Heart*. Bellah's testimony to the National Conference of Catholic Bishops, written on May 21, 1984, was published as "Economics and the Theology of Work." RNB, "Transforming American Culture," 13, and "Public Philosophy," 93–94 ("area of debate" quotes).

24. Clapp, "Habits of the Heart," 20 (quote); "Robert Bellah Talks," 16–17, 36–37.

25. RNB, "Living a Christian Life," International Christian University, Mitaka, Tokyo, May 26,1986; RNB, "Transcript of an Interview" *Trinity News* 33 (1986); RNB to Albert and Teruko Craig, February 9, 1992; all RBPP.

26. RNB, "Can You Recite Your Creed?" 7. RNB, "Values of the University," handwritten notes, Ann Arbor, February 7–8, 1986; RNB, "Conflicting Roles of the Intellectual Today, or, What Am I Doing Here on Good Friday?" unpublished paper, Berkeley, April 5, 1996 ("shouldn't be teaching"); both RBPP.

27. RNB, contribution to "Symposium on Roman Catholicism"; RNB, "Church as the Context"; letters to the editor, *New Oxford Review* 54 (1987).

28. Guhin, "Robert Bellah's Catholic Imagination," 126–45. Peter Rosazza to RNB, December 15, 1987; Edmond L. Browning to RNB, September 27, 1990; both RBPP.

29. "Syllabus, Sociology 112, Sociology of Religion," fall 1986 (very similar to the undergraduate courses of 1989 and 1991); "Syllabus, Sociology 202, Hegel," fall 1985; "Syllabus, Sociology 280I, Sociology and Theology," spring 1987, taught with John A. Coleman, SJ; "Syllabus, Sociology 202, Sociological Theory: G. H. Mead," fall 1987; "Syllabus, Sociology 202B, Contemporary Sociological Theory: Habermas," spring 1989; "Syllabus, Sociology 280I, Sociology of Religion," fall 1991 (graduate course on Hegel and Weber); all RBPP.

30. $250,000 in 1986 roughly corresponds to $590,000 in 2020. William Sullivan to RNB, October 3, 1986; William Sullivan to RNB, May 2, 1987; both RBPP. On the NEH grant, see grant number RO-20711-84, Regents of the University of California, Berkeley/Robert N. Bellah, *The Moral Basis of Social Commitment in America*, National Endowment for the Humanities, accessed November 22, 2020, https://securegrants.neh.gov/publicquery/main.aspx?f=1&gn =RO-20711–84. RNB, interview, AF. Bellah's students were not impressed: their comments were, on the whole, that the new book was "unconvincing" and "poorly written." Hagen Finley to RNB, November 27, 1989; "Syllabus and Course Notes Sociology 202B-1, Contemporary Sociological Theory: Interpretive Sociology, 1989"; both RBPP.

31. Sandel, *Liberalism and Its Critics*, 5–7; Guttman, "Communitarian Critics of Liberalism."

32. Robert Frenier to Christopher Lasch, January 14, 1985; Phyllis Killen to Christopher Lasch, January 28, 1985; Christopher Lasch to Phyllis Killen, February 17, 1985; Christopher Lasch to Robert Frenier, March 10, 1985; RNB to Christopher Lasch, March 21, 1985; Beverly Roberts Gaventa to Christopher Lasch, April 29, 1985; Christopher Lasch to RNB, May 22, 1985; Christopher Lasch to RNB, July 18, 1985; Christopher Lasch, "Individualism, Community, and Public Covenant," Cedar Rapids, April 26, 1985; all CLP, box 25, folder 32. RNB to Christopher Lasch, June 10, 1985, CLP, box 7, folder 13. Paul M. Hirsch to Christopher Lasch, October 27, 1985, CLP, box 7, folder 13.

33. The appreciative piece is Lasch, "Search for Meaning." Keynote speech quotes in C. Lasch, "Individualism, Community, and Public Conversation," unpublished keynote, Iowa Sociological Association, Cedar Rapids, April 25/26, 1985, 22 pp., CLP, quotes 10–11. Quote from 1986 paper in Lasch, "Communitarian Critique of Liberalism," 174. Selznick, "Idea of a Communitarian Morality"; Spohn, "Virtue and American Culture."

34. Velasco, *Centrist Rhetoric*, 19–20; quote from Galston and Kamarck, *Politics of Evasion*, 18.

35. Lardner, "Amitai Etzioni Prescribes" (*Washington Post* quote); "Behavior: The Everything Expert," *Time*, February 17, 1975; Maxa, "Sociologist at the White House?"; Etzioni, *My Brother's Keeper*, 194–95, 199ff.

36. Etzioni, *My Brother's Keeper*, 205.

37. Etzioni, 219ff.

38. Etzioni, 231ff.

39. Troy, *Morning in America*, 298ff.; Patterson, *Restless Giant*, 238ff.; Kruse and Zelizer, *Fault Lines*, 185ff.; Etzioni, *My Brother's Keeper*, 247–48. Bellah harshly criticized Bush's exploitation of voluntary organizations in DeParle, "'Thousand Points.'" The analogy of communitarianism as a "fat kid" comes from Daniel Callahan to RNB, December 28, 1987, RBPP. "Inaugural Address of George Bush" (January 20, 1989), Avalon Project, Yale Law School, Lillian Goldman Law Library, accessed November 22, 2020, https://avalon.law.yale.edu/20th_century/bush.asp.

40. RNB, "Symposium." Among other participants in the symposium were Daniel Bell, Patrick Caddell, Barbara Ehrenreich, John Kenneth Galbraith, Jim Hightower, Jay McInerney, Charles Peters, Michael Walzer, and filmmaker extraordinaire, Frederick Wiseman, whose one-word intervention read: "Pray." RNB to Hendrik Hertzberg, April, 18, 1991, RBPP.

41. In contrast with the insistence on a public conversation as a good in itself in *Habits*, Clinton's centrist rhetoric "reveals itself to depend on an imagined public that exists *beyond* rhetorical controversy, rather than one that exists *through* rhetorical controversy." Velasco, *Centrist Rhetoric*, 37–43, 51 (Clinton quotes at 37 and 39); Clinton, *My Life*, ch. 25; R. Bellah et al., *Habits of the Heart*, 296. It should be noticed that no commentator related *Habits* to the Democratic Leadership Council at the time.

Chapter Eighteen

1. RNB to Jeanne Knoerle, August 12, 1992, CESP, box 4, ff 3, 97-5-2. Examples of distortions of *Habits* in the press are Holland, "Cardinal Urges Work"; Wycliff, "Critic of Academia."

2. R. Bellah et al., *Good Society*, 4–5, 302, 10–16.

3. R. Bellah et al., 71–72, 37, 79, 114ff., 223ff., 265–66.

4. R. Bellah et al., 61, 85, 101–2.

5. Jendrysik, *Modern Jeremiahs*, 22ff. Some reviewers of *The Good Society* remarked on the shift in tone: Preston, "Paradise Lost," 429; Goodrich, "Philosophical Tuneup," 13; Ryan, "Disunited States," 28.

6. R. Bellah et al., *Good Society*, 9, 15, 306, 220ff., 133. In its second book the Habits group was also able to confront the legacy of Talcott Parsons, and even used the expression "American civil religion," albeit only in passing (165, 215).

7. R. Bellah et al., 107ff., 142ff., 282–83. Other policy suggestions can be found at 176ff., 246–50.

8. R. Bellah et al., 300.

9. Horwitt, "Democratic Vistas"; West, "Struggle for America's Soul"; Woodward, "Looking Past Number One." Preston, "Paradise Lost," 429 ("prodigious gifts" and "thinly documented"); Ryan, "Disunited States," 28, 30 ("mushy" and "bland"); Blake, "Keep the Faith," 75; Hauerwas, "Communitarian Lament" ("less lively"); Scialabba, "Of Politics and Platitudes."

10. Lukes, "Rhetoric of Thick Consensus," 425; Piven, "Exhortation Is Not a Strategy."

11. R. Bellah et al., *The Good Society*, conclusion, *passim* (quote 262).

12. R. Bellah et al., 264, 271.

13. The quote from Lippman's *The Good Society* can be found in R. Bellah et al., 280. Myers, "Good Society Redux," 72–73.

14. As shown by private correspondence, Horowitz knew that what he was going publish would be particularly brutal. Robert J. Myers to Irving L. Horowitz, October 2, 1991; Irving L. Horowitz to Robert J. Myers, October 7, 1991; Robert J. Myers to Irving L. Horowitz, January 27, 1992; Irving L. Horowitz to Robert J. Myers, February 1, 1992; Irving L. Horowitz to Andrew M. Greeley, February 27, 1992 ("biting"); Irving L. Horowitz to Andrew M. Greeley, May 5, 1992 ("double-barreled"); Claude Fischer to Irving L. Horowitz, May 13, 1992 ("vicious"); Irving L. Horowitz to Claude Fischer, June 3, 1992; Irving L. Horowitz to Andrew M. Greeley, August 29, 1992; all HTPA.

15. Greeley, "Habits of the Head," 78, 76, 80.

16. West, "Struggle for America's Soul"; Blake, "Keep the Faith"; Danbom, review of *The Good Society*, 1260; Schnur, "Good Society." Irving L. Horowitz to Paul Roazen, August 12, 1991, HTPA. Jeanne Knoerle to RNB, May 13, 1992, CESP, box 4, ff 4, 97-5-2. John A. Coleman, SJ, to RNB, September 9, 1991 (*The Good Society* "is much better than *Habits*"); David Riesman to RNB, November 1991; John W. Gardner to RNB, December 3, 1991; Harold Ellington to RNB, February 19, 1996; all RBPP. RNB to Jeanne Knoerle, December 7, 1990, CESP, box 4, ff 3, 97-5-2. Jennifer Bellah Maguire, personal communication, December 6, 2019, AF.

17. R. Bellah et al., *Good Society*, 292; Tipton, "Moral Languages," 179. RNB, "Research Plans," August 14, 1992, Department of Sociology, University of California, Berkeley, RBPP.

18. RNB to Jeanne Knoerle, August 26, 1989, CESP, box 4, ff 3, 97-5-2.

19. Lilly Endowment to GTU, n.d. [fall 1989], CESP, box 4, ff 3, 97-5-2. RNB to Jeanne Knoerle, December 7, 1990; RNB to Jeanne Knoerle, August 12, 1991; both CESP, box 4, ff 3, 97-5-2. RNB to Jeanne Knoerle, October 28, 1991, CESP, box 4, ff 3, 97-5-2. $350,000 in 1990 roughly

corresponds to $690,000 in 2020. Documents relating to the first Good Society Summer Institute and the lyrics to the song can be found in CESP, box 4, ff 5, 97-5-2. Donald S. Nesti to Matteo Bortolini, October 27, 2019; Michael Wenger to Matteo Bortolini, October 29, 2019; both AF.

20. RNB to Jeanne Knoerle, October 28, 1991, CESP, box 4, ff 3, 97-5-2. The Institute for the Study of Civic Values was one of the groups studied by Bill Sullivan during the first project and was positively featured in *Habits of the Heart*. The full transcripts of the three speeches can be found at CESP, box 4, ff 7, 97-5-2; West, "Struggle for America's Soul," 13.

21. See the "letters" section of *Good Society Newsletter* 1 (1992), Graduate Theological Union; RNB, "Elite Failure" (quote). Walter Brueggeman to RNB, May 20, 1991; William McDonald to RNB, June 8, 1992; Hans Joas to RNB, August 25, 1992; Robert Dodson to RNB, December 8, 1992; Dolores R. Leckey to RNB, December 6, 1994; all RBPP.

22. Swartz, "Mythic Rise."

23. In the late 1980s *The Broken Covenant* still remained Moyer's favorite Bellah book. Harlan Stelmach, "Civil Religion in the Interfaith Context of Northern California," revised paper from presentation at the Pacific Coast Theological Society meeting, November 6, 2004, Pacific Coast Theological Society, accessed November 22, 2020, http://www.pcts.org/meetings/stelmach.civil.religion.html. George C. Bedell to Bill Moyers, January 22, 1987, RBPP. "Episcopal Group May Produce 'Habits of the Heart,'" *Episcopal News Service*, September 15, 1988, https://episcopalarchives.org/cgi-bin/ENS/ENSpress_release.pl?pr_number=88194E. Steven M. Tipton to Matteo Bortolini, October 7, 2019, AF.

24. "Robert Bellah, Sociologist," in Moyers, *World of Ideas*, 279, 280, 283, 287. A transcript and videoclip of the broadcast of the interview can be found at PBS, "Robert Bellah—A World of Ideas—September 27, 1988," Bill Moyers Journal, accessed November 22, 2020, http://www.pbs.org/moyers/journal/archives/bellahwoi_flash.html.

25. All episodes can be found at "Listening to America," Moyers on Democracy, accessed November 22, 2020, https://billmoyers.com/series/listening-america-1992/.

26. Transcripts of the two episodes of the documentary, from which all following quotes are taken, can be found at "The Good Society (Part One)," Moyers on Democracy, August 4, 1992, https://billmoyers.com/content/good-society-part-one/, and "The Good Society (Part Two)," Moyers on Democracy, August 11, 1992, https://billmoyers.com/content/good-society-part-two/. R. Bellah et al., *Good Society*, 266–72; RNB, "Necessity of Opportunity."

27. G. Bowden, review of "The Good Society" by Bill Moyers. Hartman, *War for the Soul*, 171ff.; Clinton, "Vision for America." Pat Buchanan, "Address to the Republican National Convention" (August 17, 1992), Voices of Democracy, accessed November 22, 2020, https://voicesofdemocracy.umd.edu/buchanan-culture-war-speech-speech-text/.

28. Patterson, *Restless Giant*, 248ff.; Kruse and Zelizer, *Fault Lines*, 199ff.; Clinton, *My Life*, ch. 25 (quote); Galston, "Point of View." Carter Wilkie, "Lessons from a Reading of Inaugural Addresses," December 18, 1992, 6. The photocopy of "Civil Religion" was included in a memo to George Stephanopulos that is contained in C. Wilkie and D. Kusnet (eds.), *Briefing Book on Inaugural Address* (Little Rock, December 23, 1992), Clinton Presidential Library (OA/ID number: 4273), speechwriting files of Carter Wilkie, Clinton Presidential Records: White House Staff and Office Files, box 2.

Chapter Nineteen

1. RNB to Jeanne Knoerle, May 6, 1992; Jeanne Knoerle to RNB, May 13, 1992; RNB to Jeanne Knoerle, October 13, 1992; all CESP, box 4, ff 4, 97-5-2. Paul Dovre to Matteo Bortolini, October 23, 2019, AF. From this chapter on, most of the correspondence cited or quoted comes from printouts of e-mails originally kept by Robert Bellah in his home office (i.e., *not* e-mails recovered from his computer).

2. RNB to Jeanne Knoerle, April 29, 1993; RNB to Jeanne Knoerle, December 30, 1993; both CESP, box 4, ff 4, 97-5-2. Barry Stingers to Jeanne Knoerle, January 27, 1994; Jeanne Knoerle to Barry Stingers, February 16, 1994; both CESP, box 4, ff 3, 97-5-2. Lynne Jerome, "Taming the Giant: Searching for New Models of International Cooperation," *Good Society Newsletter* 2 (1993), Graduate Theological Union. "The Good Society, 3rd Conference, 11/1993," CESP, box 4, ff 18, 97-5-2.

3. RNB to Jeanne Knoerle, May 6, 1992; RNB to Jeanne Knoerle, October 13, 1992; both CESP, box 4, ff 4, 97-5-2. The text of Bellah's strongly theological address is on record in RBPP, together with the nine-page transcript of an interview with Dick Westley dated June 22, 1992, in which Bellah recounts the episode.

4. Gans, "Best-Sellers by Sociologists." While up-to-date figures for the Harper paperback could not be obtained, in July 2019 the Press Publicity office of the University of California Press estimated the total sales of their versions of *Habits* (1985 hardback plus 1996 and 2007 paperbacks) at around 120,000 copies (e-mail, July 12, 2019, AF). Etzioni, *My Brother's Keeper*, 239.

5. Gans, *Middle American Individualism*. Herbert J. Gans to RNB, January 26, 1989, RBPP. Gans, "Sociology in America." Bellah's correspondence with Frohen was published in the *Political Science Reviewer* (22 [1993]: 403–10). Frohnen, *New Communitarians*, and "Does Robert Bellah Care." Reviews by Warren and Zuckert, Bellah's rejoinder, and their answers, were published in two issues of the *Newsletter of PEGS* (2 [1992]). Theory Search Committee, March 31, 1995; RNB to Jeffrey C. Alexander, April 5, 1995; both RBPP.

6. As shown by Bellah's glowing blurb for *The Spirit of Community*, the group maintained a cordial relationship with Amitai Etzioni. Amitai Etzioni to RNB, July 18, 1996; RNB to Annette Bevier, October 21, 1996; RNB to the *New Yorker*, March 31, 1997; RNB to Kent P. Schwirian, August 19, 1997; RNB to Frederick Bird, November 3, 1998; RNB to Shmuel Eisenstadt, December 2, 1998; all RBPP. RNB, "Community Properly Understood." In April 1996, together with Harriet Zuckerman and Peter M. Blau, Bellah was also elected to the American Philosophical Society, the learned society founded by Benjamin Franklin in Philadelphia in 1743. American Philosophical Society to RNB, April 26, 1996; Chang-Lin Tien to RNB, May 17, 1996; Carol T. Christ to RNB, May 24, 1996; Richard C. Atkinson to RNB, July 29, 1996; all RBPP.

7. Etzioni, "Is Bill Clinton a Communitarian?"; Stiehm, "Community and Communitarians." Patterson, *Restless Giant*, 330ff.; J. Harris, *Survivor*, ch. 14.

8. RNB, "Clinton and Welfare." The letter was also signed by sixteen Berkeley sociologists, including Ann Swidler, Michael Burawoy, Arlie Hochschild, Todd Gitlin, and Loïc Wacquant. R. Bellah and Adams, "Beforecare"; RNB, "Outrageous Thoughts"; R. Bellah and Adams, "Strong Institutions, Good Cities."

9. RNB, "'Reforming' the Welfare Act" (*Pacific Church News* quote). RNB to Donald W. Shriver Jr., August 26, 1997; RNB to Shmuel Eisenstadt, August 5, 1997; RNB to Stanley Hauerwas, April 16, 1998; RNB to Normal K. Gottwald, February 7, 1997; RNB to Shmuel Eisenstadt, February 12, 1998 ("about to give up"); Melanie and RNB to Patrick Moynihan, April 15, 1998; RNB to the editor of *Commonweal*, June 19, 1998; RNB to Shmuel Eisenstadt, May 26, 1999; all RBPP. RNB to Samuel Porter, April 6, 2000; RNB to Samuel Porter, August 29, 2001; both SPPP.

10. R. Bellah et al., *Good Society*, 187ff., 234–35.

11. R. Bellah et al., "House Divided," 262–70, xii, xxiii–xxiv, xxvi (quotes), xxix. RNB to Habits group, "Memo on New Intro for *Habits*," October 24, 1995, RBPP.

12. R. Bellah et al., "House Divided," xii, xxxi, xiv–xv. RNB to Shmuel Eisenstadt, January 23, 1998; RNB to Habits group, May 28, 2000; both RBPP. "The House Divided" was strongly criticized by sociologist Brad Lowell Stone in a Greeley-style paper, "Statist Communitarianism."

13. R. Bellah et al., "House Divided," viii–x. RNB to Nina Eliasoph, n.d. [early 1997], RBPP.

14. RNB to Shmuel Eisenstadt, October 13, 1997; RNB to Richard D. McCall, October 14, 1997; RNB to Margaret Miles, n.d. [December 1997]; all RBPP. RNB, "Is There a Common American Culture?"

15. RNB, "Is There a Common American Culture?" 322, 323 (quoting from *Democracy in America*), 324, 327, my italics.

16. RNB, 329–32 ("moral genius" at 329, "still believe that there are places" at 332).

17. William Dean to RNB, November 20, 1997; Laura Gottwald to RNB, November 26, 1997; RNB to Harlan Stelmach, November 29, 1997; RNB to Michael J. Sandel, January 28, 1998; RNB to Rebecca Parker, July 30, 1998; RNB to Michael Hout, November 9, 1998; RNB to Robert M. Hertzberg, December 15, 1998; all RBPP.

18. RNB, "Flaws in the Protestant Code," 335, 339–40.

19. RNB, 343–45; Guhin, "Robert Bellah's Catholic Imagination," 135ff.

20. RNB, "Flaws in the Protestant Code," 348. RNB to Stanley Hauerwas, April 16, 1998, RBPP.

21. RNB to Shmuel Eisenstadt, March 6, 1997; Michael Burawoy, "On the Occasion of Robert Bellah's Retirement," unpublished paper; Ann Swidler, "Remarks for Bob Bellah's Retirement Party," unpublished paper; RNB, "Bob's Response to Talks at Retirement Party, Bancroft Hotel, Berkeley, May 2, 1997," unpublished paper; all RBPP. Swidler was not able to be present and entrusted her short address to Arlie Hochschild.

22. RNB to Ronald L. Jepperson, August 27, 1997, RBPP.

23. Jeff Weintraub to RNB, October 19, 1996; RNB to William Sullivan, May 1, 1997; RNB to Garrett E. Paul, May 22, 1997; RNB to Dirk Kaesler, June 14, 1997; RNB to Shmuel Eisenstadt, June 18, 1997; RNB to Ronald L. Jepperson, August 27, 1997; RNB to Gordon Clanton, August 28, 1997; RNB to Ann Swidler, April 15, 1998; RNB to Stanley Hauerwas, April 16, 1998; RNB to Charles Camic and Franklin Wilson, August 29, 2000; all RBPP. Apart from brief papers published in *Current Sociology* (1987), *Theory and Society* (1992), and *International Sociology* (1997), it took Bellah forty years after "Religious Evolution" to publish a full original article in a scholarly journal of sociology.

24. RNB, "Research Plans," August 14, 1992, Department of Sociology, University of California, Berkeley, RBPP.

25. RNB to Renée Fox, September 24, 1999; Francesca Cancian to RNB, October 16, 1995; Harry B. Adams to RNB, November 2, 1995; Evon Z. Vogt to RNB, November 26, 1995; RNB to Susan S. Phillips, January 11, 1997; RNB to Garrett E. Paul, May 22, 1997; RNB to Martin E. Marty, July 2, 1997; RNB to Frederic B. Burnham, July 26, 1997; RNB to Eugenia Bowman, September 6, 1997; RNB to John A. Coleman, SJ, October 14, 1997; RNB to Glenn R. Bucher, n.d. [December 1997]; RNB to Mary Jane Mann, January 15, 1998; RNB to William L. Sachs, August 26, 1998; RNB to Paul Sheehan, September 7, 1998; RNB to Frederick Bird, November 3, 1998; RNB to Alex Inkeles, n.d. [December 2000]; Lisa Freedman to Melanie Bellah, February 12, 2001; RNB to Jennifer McDowell, July 23, 2001; all RBPP. On the Italian trip, see also RNB to Federico D'Agostino, July 1, 1998; RNB to Achille Cardinal Silvestrini, July 1, 1998; RNB to Joseph Dunne, September 12, 1998; Shikei Koyama to RNB, April 9, 2001; all RBPP. Some of Bellah's ideas for his post-retirement work can be found in "Research Plans," August 14, 1992, Department of Sociology, University of California, Berkeley, RBPP. "The Robert N. Bellah Chair in Sociology of Religion in the Center for Ethics and Social Policy at the Graduate Theological Union," 6 pp., CESP, box 1, folder 8.

26. RNB to Nina Eliasoph, n.d. [1997]; William Sullivan to RNB, March 5, 1997; RNB to James Faubion, June 26, 1997; RNB to James Stockinger, November 26, 1997; RNB to Shmuel Eisenstadt, December 8, 1997; RNB to Kim Hays, January 15, 1998; Yi-Tsi Feuerwerker to Melanie Bellah, April 3, 1999; RNB to Yi-Tsi Feuerwerker, April 3, 1999; RNB to Wilfred and Muriel Cantwell Smith, June 2, 1999; RNB to Shmuel Eisenstadt, August 24, 1999; Melanie Bellah to Tom Southern, February 26, 2000; all RBPP.

27. Hally Bellah-Guther to RNB, January 1, 2000; RNB to William Sullivan, July 21, 2000; Jennifer Bellah Maguire to RNB, n.d. [summer 2000]; RNB to Jennifer Bellah Maguire, n.d. [summer 2000]; RNB to Jennifer Bellah Maguire, June 16, 2000; Melanie Bellah to Hally Bellah-Guther, August 22, 2000; Melanie Bellah to Hally Bellah-Guther, September 4, 2000; Hally Bellah-Guther to Melanie Bellah, September 5, 2000; Melanie Bellah to Hally Bellah-Guther, September 5, 2000; all RBPP. Jennifer Bellah Maguire to Matteo Bortolini, December 16, 2019; Jennifer Bellah Maguire to Matteo Bortolini, December 30, 2019; both AF.

28. Peter Evans to RNB, July 1, 2000; RNB to Peter Evans, July 8, 2000; Michael Burawoy to RNB, July 12, 2000; RNB to Michael Burawoy, July 12, 2000; RNB to Sue Thur, July 24, 2000; RNB to Peter Evans, July 25, 2000; RNB to Michael Burawoy, September 6, 2000; Michael Burawoy to RNB, September 7, 2000; Michael Burawoy to RNB, December 13, 2000; RNB to Michael Burawoy, December 14, 2000; Frank Carothers to RNB, December 18, 2000; The Regents of the University of California to RNB, December 18, 2000; Frank Carothers to RNB, January 3, 2001; RNB to Peter B. Howard, January 3, 2001; RNB to Michael Burawoy, February 4, 2001; Michael Burawoy to RNB, February 5, 2001; Sue Thur to RNB, March 9, 2001; RNB to Sue Thur, March 14, 2001; all RBPP.

29. Sullivan, *Work and Integrity*. While their intimate relationship was long gone, Bellah and Sullivan had continued to celebrate May 3 as the source of joy and community. William Sullivan to RNB, May 3, 1995; William Sullivan to RNB, May 3, 1996; both RBPP. On Sullivan's move to San Francisco, see William Sullivan to RNB, June 29, 1999; RNB to William Sullivan, July 23, 2000; RNB to William Sullivan, July 24, 2000; William Sullivan to RNB, July 23, 2000; RNB to William Sullivan, August 1, 2000; William Sullivan to RNB, August 3, 2000; all RBPP.

30. RNB to William Sullivan, August 13, 2000; RNB to William Sullivan, July 18, 2000 ("Fifty years of my life"); RNB to Frank Carothers, July 26, 2000; William Sullivan to RNB, August 12, 2000 ("I'm not unhappy"); RNB to Ann Swidler, November 1, 2000; Ann Swidler to RNB, November 2, 2000; all RBPP. Swidler, *Talk of Love*.

31. The National Humanities Medal was established in 1997, and was preceded by a similar award, the Charles Frankel Prize, awarded from 1988 to 1996. See the "Awards & Honors" page on the National Endowment for the Humanities website (accessed November 22, 2020), https://www.neh.gov/our-work/awards-honors.

32. Official records of the ceremony and the White House dinner are available online at the Clinton Digital Library: https://clinton.presidentiallibraries.us/. Hillary and Bill Clinton's speeches can be watched online at Clintonlibrary42, "2000 Arts & Humanities Awards Presentation," YouTube, July 25, 2013, https://www.youtube.com/watch?v=hzPswhDZTqQ (Bellah's bit starts at 49:00).

33. RNB to Habits group, January 15, 2001, RBPP.

34. During the presidential campaign of 2016, Hillary Clinton was still recommending *Habits of the Heart*—"that wonderful old sociological work that was led by Robert Bellah"—as "really helpful" to understand "what is unique about the American experience." Ezra Klein, "The Vox Conversation: Hillary Clinton" (June 22, 2016), *Vox*, accessed November 22, 2020, https://www.vox.com/a/hillary-clinton-interview. RNB to Jennifer Bellah Maguire, December 2, 2000; Jennifer Bellah Maguire to RNB, December 3, 2000; RNB to Habits group, December 27, 2000; RNB to John F. Maguire, January 2, 2001; RNB to Daniel Bell, January 3, 2001; RNB to Habits group, January 15, 2001; RNB to Hideo Sato, June 25, 2001; RNB to William E. Johnston Jr., August 27, 1997; all RBPP.

Chapter Twenty

1. Michael Burawoy, "On the Occasion of Robert Bellah's Retirement," unpublished paper, RBPP. In this and the next two chapters I will present the ideation and the writing of *Religion in Human Evolution* as a long, intricate process going back to the 1950s. As I will introduce its various elements one by one, the reader will not find any full or "tidy" summary of the book. I am fully aware that this choice may give a slightly chaotic picture of Bellah's last ten years, but I also think that any attempt to reduce such a complex and idiosyncratic work to a three- or five-page précis would be offensive for both the book and the reader's intelligence.

2. RNB to Clifford Geertz, September 8, 2004 ("One Big Idea"); Clifford Geertz to RNB, January 5, 2005; both CGP, box 36, folder 8-Bellah. Victor Lidz to Matteo Bortolini, August 2020, AF ("first good book"). RNB, "Nov 24, 1997, Session on RNB," handwritten notes, November 24, 1997 ("yet to be written"); RNB, "Research Plans," August 14, 1992, Department of Sociology, University of California, Berkeley ("major project"); both RBPP.

3. RNB, "Preface: *A Theory of Religion*," unpublished paper, 1964, RBPP, 1–3.

4. NJ-1965–1969, entries of August 7, 1966 ("Professor Somebody"); August 15, 1966; April 7, 1967 ("at a white heat"). MP-1967–1968, entry "Nov 68" ("Mes Pensées" quote).

5. NJ-1965–1969, entry of November 23, 1968.

6. RNB, "Religious Evolution," 24.

7. NJ-1965–1969, entries of July 1, 1968; July 4, 1968 (quotes), italics modified.

8. RNB, "Brown in Perspective," 453–55. MP-1967–1968, entry titled "Preface," n.d. [summer 1971], my italics; entry titled "Symbols and Experience," n.d.

9. RNB, "The Roots of Religious Consciousness: I, Primitive Religion," unpublished paper, 20 pp., 1974–1985, 2; "The Roots of Religious Consciousness: II, Historic Religion," unpublished paper, 24 pp., 1974–1985, 1; both RBPP. *Bulletin of the University of California* 22, March 18, 1974. An audio recording of the first lecture is available at "Robert Bellah—1974: Relevance of Man's Religious Experience," McGill University, Beatty Lecture Archive, accessed November 22, 2020, https://www.mcgill.ca/beatty/digital-archive/past-lectures/robert-bellah.

10. RNB, "Roots of Religious Consciousness: I," 13 ("non-conceptual"), 14a ("cocktail party").

11. RNB, 15. The list of historic religions is taken from RNB, "Roots of Religious Consciousness: II," 2 (3), deletions were made in 1985 to the 1974 text. The original 1974 lectures included a section on Plato and Socrates that was later deleted.

12. RNB, "Roots of Religious Consciousness: II," 5, 7, 16, my italics.

13. RNB, "The Roots of Religious Consciousness: III, The Contemporary Situation," unpublished paper, 19 pp., 1974–1985, RBPP, 3–4, my italics.

14. "Sociology 146—Sociology of Religion" and "Sociology 112—Sociology of Religion," from 1976 to 1996, RBPP. In what follows, I will refer to Samuel C. Porter's detailed lecture notes of Bellah's Sociology 146, Winter 1980. Bellah described this course in "How I Teach," 193–203 (quotes at 194).

15. On the NEH grant, see grant number AF-12198-78, Regents of the University of California, Berkeley/Robert N. Bellah, *Religious Vision and Social Order in Comparative Perspective*, National Endowment for the Humanities, accessed November 22, 2020, https://securegrants .neh.gov/publicquery/main.aspx?f=1&gn=AF-12198-78. R. Bellah and Hammond, *Varieties of Civil Religion*.

16. Robbins, Anthony, and Curtis, "Limits of Symbolic Realism"; RNB, "Comment on 'The Limits of Symbolic Realism'"; Robbins, Anthony, and Curtis, "Reply to Bellah"; Anthony and Robbins, "Symbolic Realism to Structuralism" (all these papers were meant to be included in the collective book). Dick Anthony to RNB, December 13, 1974; Dick Anthony to RNB, December 11, 1975; both RBPP. Dick Anthony, RNB, Thomas Robbins, "Prospectus. On Religion and Social Science: A Non Reductionistic Approach to the Study of Religion (working title)," unpublished paper, 9 pp., circa 1977, Graduate Theological Union Archives, Center for the Study of New Religious Movements Collections, 1977–1983, series 1: Office and Working Files, 1977–1983, box 4, folder 30.

17. RNB, "Symbolic Realism: Structuralism or Hermeneutics?," unpublished paper, 24 pp., circa 1978, RBPP, quotes at 19, 17, 10, 11.

18. In the mid-1990s Anthony and Bellah reprised their correspondence, and discussed the possibility of publishing an updated version of their coauthored book. See RNB to Matteo Bortolini, July 23, 2009, AF.

19. RNB to Melanie Bellah, May 12, 1959, RBPP ("new Max Weber"). In January 1995, the remaining $3,000 from the *Good Society* Lilly grant were reallocated to Bellah's new project. Jeanne Knoerle to Barry Stingers, January 24, 1995, CESP, box 4, ff 3, 97-5-2. RNB, "Religion in the Process of Cultural Differentiation," unpublished paper, 85 pp., 2nd version, circa 1955,

RBPP, 85 ("rigorous empirical scholarship"); David Stowe, "The Evolution of Robert Bellah," *Religion in American History* (blog), December 13, 2012, http://usreligion.blogspot.com/2012 /12/the-evolution-of-robert-bellah.html ("Babylonian captivity"); RNB to Wilfred and Muriel Smith, June 2, 1999, RBPP.

20. RNB to Shmuel Eisenstadt, June 24, 1997 ("candy shop"); RNB to Douglas Mitchell, October 15, 1998 ("live to finish"); RNB to Hans Joas, March 10, 1999; RNB to Habits group, July 26, 2000; RNB to Shmuel Eisenstadt, April 1, 2002; RNB to Shmuel Eisenstadt, April 23, 2002; RNB to Shmuel Eisenstadt, May 18, 2002; Richard Wood to RNB, February 12, 2003; RNB to David Delon, August 18, 2003; RNB to Clifford Geertz, September 8, 2004; RNB to Paul Lichterman, December 10, 2004; all RBPP. RNB to Samuel C. Porter, January 23, 1999; RNB to Samuel C. Porter, January 4, 2000; RNB to Samuel C. Porter, January 26, 1999; RNB to Mark A. Shibley, November 8, 2003; Samuel C. Porter to RNB, November 6, 2005; RNB to Samuel C. Porter, November 7, 2005; all SPPP. A file for the original second chapter, titled "Social Evolution I. From the Paleolithic to Historic Society," is on record in RBPP.

21. Scott Nielsen to RNB, August 20, 1997, RBPP. Timothy Doran to Matteo Bortolini, February 20, 2020, AF.

22. RNB, "Where Did Religion Come From?"

23. RNB to Anna Sun and Yang Xiao, December 30, 2002; RNB to Yang Xiao, March 27, 2004; Yang Xiao to RNB, August 14, 2004; RNB to Yang Xiao, July 9, 2006; all YXPP. Yang Xiao to RNB, March 30, 1998; Yang Xiao to RNB, April 13, 1998; Yang Xiao to RNB, October 23, 1998; Yang Xiao to RNB, October 27, 1998; Yang Xiao to RNB, October 30, 1998; RNB to Anna Sun, May 12, 2000; Marc Garcelon to RNB, October 25, 1997; RNB to Marc Garcelon, October 29, 1997; Marc Garcelon to RNB, October 30, 1997; Marc Garcelon to RNB, January 23, 1998; Marc Garcelon to RNB, January 26, 1998; RNB to Marc Garcelon, n.d. [January 1998]; Marc Garcelon to RNB, January 26, 1998; RNB to Philip Gorski, October 3, 1997; Philip Gorski to RNB, June 5, 2001; RNB to Philip Gorski, June 4, 2001; Philip Gorski to RNB, June 6, 2001; Stephen F. Tobias to RNB, September 11, 1998; John Maguire to RNB, October 17, 1998; John Maguire to RNB, April 15, 2005; Arvind Rajagopal to RNB, June 26, 1997; RNB to Arvind Rajagopal, October 15, 1997; Arvind Rajagopal to RNB, n.d. [April 2005]; Richard Wood to RNB, February 12, 2003; RNB to Richard Wood, n.d. [March 2003]; Richard Wood to RNB, March 13, 2003; RNB to Richard Wood, March 13, 2003; RNB to Eli Sagan, December 3, 2002; RNB to Donald N. Levine, August 22, 1997; RNB to Victor Lidz, January 2, 2003; Victor Lidz to RNB, January 2, 2003; RNB to Victor Lidz, January 3, 2003; Charles Taylor to RNB, October 4, 2004; Charles Taylor to RNB, October 23, 2004; RNB to Renée Fox, June 30, 2005; Renée Fox to RNB, July 2, 2005; RNB to Renée Fox, July 2, 2005; Renée Fox to RNB, n.d. [July 2005]; Renée Fox to RNB, September 17, 2006; David Keightley to RNB, April 25, 1998; RNB to David Keightley, March 25, 2004; RNB to Johanna Nichols, March 24, 1998; RNB to Johanna Nichols, n.d. [March, 2003]; Johanna Nichols to RNB, March 21, 2003; RNB to Norman K. Gottwald, February 7, 1997; Norman K. Gottwald to RNB, April 2, 1997; Norman K. Gottwald to RNB, April 7, 1997; Norman K. Gottwald to RNB, May 30, 1997; RNB to Norman K. Gottwald, November 12, 2004; Norman K. Gottwald to RNB, n.d. [November 2004]; RNB to Norman K. Gottwald, December 8, 2004; Norman K. Gottwald to RNB, December 9, 2004; RNB to Norman K. Gottwald, April 4, 2005; Norman K. Gottwald to RNB, n.d. [April 2005]; Steven M. Tipton to RNB, April 11,

1998; William Sullivan to RNB, May 26, 2000; William Sullivan to RNB, November 26, 2002; William Sullivan to RNB, May 30, 2003; all RBPP. Bellah's printed e-mails also include a dozen undated exchanges with Bill Sullivan on Greek and Roman classics (RBPP).

24. RNB, "Where Did Religion Come From?" See the justification of the National Endowment for the Humanities grant number AF-12198-78 (1978–1979), Regents of the University of California, Berkeley/Robert N. Bellah, *Religious Vision and Social Order in Comparative Perspective*, National Endowment for the Humanities, accessed November 22, 2020, https://securegrants.neh.gov/publicquery/main.aspx?f=1&gn=AF-12198-78. RNB to Douglas Mitchell, October 15, 1998; RNB to David Sloane Wilson, October 2, 2003; RNB to Jürgen Habermas, March 2005; all RBPP. RNB to Douglas Mitchell, January 2, 2004, DMPP.

25. RNB to Merlin Donald, September 15, 2004. See also Merlin Donald to RNB, n.d. [September 2004]; RNB to Lenny Moss, April 5, 2005; all RBPP. Abbate, *Inventing the Internet*. RNB, "Where Did Religion Come From?" RNB to Samuel C. Porter, June 22, 2004; RNB to Samuel C. Porter, August 13, 2004; both SPPP. Geoffrey Samuel to RNB, March 27, 2001; RNB to Brian K. Smith, November 26, 2001; RNB to Louise Lamphere, October 4, 2002; Louise Lamphere to RNB, October 9, 2002; RNB to David Sloan Wilson, n.d. [January 2003]; David Sloan Wilson to RNB, January 16, 2003; RNB to David Sloan Wilson, n.d. [May 2003]; David Sloan Wilson to RNB, May 7, 2003; Maureen Schwarz to RNB, January 20, 2003; RNB to Walter Brueggemann, September 1, 2004; Walter Brueggemann to RNB, n.d. [September 2004]; RNB to Walter Brueggemann, September 6, 2004; Walter Brueggemann to RNB, September 9, 2004; RNB to Walter Brueggemann, April 6, 2005; Walter Brueggemann to RNB, May 18, 2005; RNB to Walter Brueggemann, May 19, 2005; RNB to Christopher Boehm, August 25, 2003; Christopher Boehm to RNB, August 26, 2003; all RBPP.

26. Ram, *Israeli Sociology*, 54. RNB to Shmuel Eisenstadt, May 15, 2002; RNB to Shmuel Eisenstadt, July 7, 2002; both RBPP.

27. Jaspers, *Origin and Goal of History*, 2–3.

28. Eisenstadt, *Origins and Diversity*. The network was further strengthened by the project started by Eisenstadt and sociologist Wolfgang Schlucter after their joint winning of the Max Planck Research Award in 1994, with the participation of Björn Wittrock in a trilateral "Erfurt, Jerusalem, and Uppsala" effort. Björn Wittrock to Matteo Bortolini, November 28, 2020, AF.

29. RNB to Shmuel Eisenstadt, March 16, 1999; RNB to Shmuel Eisenstadt, June 24, 1997; RNB to Shmuel Eisenstadt, June 26, 1997; RNB to Shmuel Eisenstadt, August 5, 1997; Shmuel Eisenstadt to RNB, March 23, 1999; all RBPP. RNB to Hans Joas, September 13, 2011, HJPP.

30. Marty, review of *The Broken Covenant*. Stanley Hauerwas to RNB, March 30, 2000; John A. Coleman, SJ, to RNB, February 12, 2001; Mary Ann Donovan to RNB, February 13, 2001; RNB to Michael Slusser, February 25, 2001; Michael Slusser to RNB, February 28, 2001; RNB to Michael Slusser, March 3, 2001; Michael Slusser to RNB, March 12, 2001; RNB to Michael Slusser, March 19, 2001; Michael Slusser to RNB, March 19, 2001; Michael Slusser to RNB, March 20, 2001; Michael Slusser to RNB, May 8, 2001; John A. Coleman, SJ, to RNB, May 8, 2001; all RBPP. RNB to Samuel C. Porter, June 19, 2001, SPPP.

31. Since 2001 Porter has been managing Bellah's pages hosted by the Hartford Institute for Religion Research website (www.robertbellah.com) of Hartford Seminary in Hartford, Connecticut. RNB to Samuel C. Porter, November 17, 2000; RNB to Samuel C. Porter,

December 14, 2000; RNB to Samuel C. Porter, January 22, 2001; RNB to Samuel C. Porter, February 4, 2001; RNB to Samuel C. Porter, February 5, 2001; RNB to Samuel C. Porter, February 7, 2001; RNB to Samuel C. Porter, February 24, 2001; RNB to Samuel C. Porter, March 26, 2001; RNB to Samuel C. Porter, April 4, 2001; RNB to Samuel C. Porter, May 6, 2001; RNB to Samuel C. Porter, May 9, 2001; all SPPP. RNB to Shmuel Eisenstadt, February 16, 2001; RNB to Shmuel Eisenstadt, February 19, 2001; RNB to Shmuel Eisenstadt, June 26, 2001; RNB to Shmuel Eisenstadt, August 11, 2001; RNB to Shmuel Eisenstadt, August 24, 2001; Shmuel Eisenstadt to RNB, September 12, 2001; Shmuel Eisenstadt to RNB, July 11, 2002; all RBPP. The conference was eventually held in December 2001 at the European University Institute in Florence, and its proceedings were published as Arnason, Eisenstadt, and Wittrock, *Axial Civilizations and World History*.

32. RNB to Shmuel Eisenstadt, September 24, 2001; RNB to Shmuel Eisenstadt, October 10, 2001; both RBPP. RNB to Samuel C. Porter, September 11, 2001; RNB to Samuel C. Porter, September 20, 2001; RNB to Samuel C. Porter, September 21, 2001; all SPPP. RNB, "Seventy-Five Years," 260 ("rid the world of evil").

33. RNB, "Seventy-five Years," 255–56, 259. RNB to Samuel C. Porter, September 21, 2001; RNB to Samuel C. Porter, October 3, 2001; both SPPP. RNB to Stanley Hauerwas, November 20, 2001; RNB to Stanley Hauerwas, February 11, 2002; Stanley Hauerwas to RNB, February 27, 2002; all RBPP.

34. In addition to some of his former-students-turned-colleagues—Harvey Cox, Nina Eliasoph, Phil Gorsky, Jeffrey Alexander, John Coleman, and Robert Wuthnow—the batch contained original works by Eisenstadt, Hauerwas, and Charles Taylor. RNB to Samuel C. Porter, January 4, 2000; RNB to Samuel C. Porter, March 19, 2000; RNB to Samuel C. Porter, April 6, 2000; all SPPP. Shmuel Eisenstadt to RNB, February 1, 1998; Shikei Koyama to RNB, July 17, 2000; RNB to Shmuel Eisenstadt, August 21, 2000; RNB to Albert Craig, September 21, 2000; RNB to Renée Fox, January 8, 2001; RNB to Shikei Koyama, March 5, 2001; RNB to Huston Smith, April 9, 2001; RNB to Shikei Koyama, July 4, 2001; RNB to Emiko Ohnuki-Tierney, July 10, 2001; RNB to Sonoda Hidehiro, October 4, 2001; RNB to Reed Malcom, December 18, 2001; Reed Malcom to RNB, December 20, 2001; RNB to Shmuel Eisenstadt, December 22, 2001; William Sullivan to RNB, n.d. [late 2001]; RNB to Shmuel Eisenstadt, February 22, 2002; Renée Fox to RNB, March 8, 2003; RNB to Daniel Bell, August 11, 2003; all RBPP. During the Kyoto symposium, Bellah met with the founder of the Kyocera Corporation, Kazuo Inamori, who invited him to become part of the company's board—a proposal that he accepted. Madsen et al., *Meaning and Modernity*; RNB, *Imagining Japan*; Eisenstadt, *Japanese Civilization*; RNB, "God, Nation, and Self." RNB to Renée Fox and Victor Lidz, April 10, 2003; Renée Fox to RNB, April 15, 2003; both RBPP.

35. RNB, *Imagining Japan*, 4, 32, 7 ("aware of axial principles"), 9 ("galactic polity"), 23 ("axial against the axial"), 59–60. For the roots of this position, see chapter 5, above. The book was published in 2003 to mixed reviews: Vidovic Ferderbar, review of *Imagining Japan*; Nefsky, review of *Imagining Japan*.

36. RNB, *Imagining Japan*, 32–34; RNB, "Epilogue. Meaning and Modernity," 265–66, 275–76; RNB, "New American Empire" (*Commonweal*), 12. RNB to Renée Fox, April 15, 2003, RBPP. Eisenstadt, "Mirror-Image Modernities," 71ff. RNB, "God, Nation, and Self."

Chapter Twenty-One

1. RNB to Shmuel Eisenstadt, October 22, 2001, RBPP. RNB to Douglas Mitchell, October 26, 1998; RNB to Douglas Mitchell, February 18, 2002; Douglas Mitchell to RNB, December 17, 2002; RNB to Douglas Mitchell, November 4, 2003; Douglas Mitchell to RNB, January 1, 2004; RNB to Douglas Mitchell, January 2, 2004; Douglas Mitchell to RNB, January 2, 2004; all DMPP. Samuel C. Porter to RNB, November 6, 2005, SPPP. As early as 1998 Bellah had been approached by the editors of American and foreign publishing houses, but he gave the same answer to all: it would take a long time to finish the book and he was not able to make any serious commitment. Gunnar Schmidt to RNB, February 16, 1999; RNB to Hans Joas, March 10, 1999; RNB to Gunnar Schmidt, March 10, 1999; Stuart Proffitt to RNB, April 28, 1999; Stuart Proffitt to RNB, June 10, 1999; all RBPP. On Mitchell, see Susie Allen, "Press Thrives on Scholarly Collaboration," University of Chicago, February 3, 2014, https://www.uchicago.edu /features/press_thrives_on_scholarly_collaboration/.

2. RNB to Douglas Mitchell, February 18, 2002; RNB to Douglas Mitchell, August 1, 2003; Douglas Mitchell to RNB, August 2, 2003; RNB to Douglas Mitchell, March 25, 2004 ("major treatment of Islam"); RNB to Douglas Mitchell, May 2, 2004; Douglas Mitchell to RNB, May 17, 2004 ("almost stupefied"); all DMPP. RNB to Charles Harper, October 29, 2003; Charles Harper to RNB and Paul Wason, October 29, 2003; RNB to Eli Sagan, March 25, 2004; Patricia Franklin to RNB, April 7, 2004; RNB to Patricia Franklin, April 9, 2004; Patricia Franklin to RNB, 12, 2004; all RBPP.

3. RNB, "Religion: Evolution and Development" and "Epilogue. Meaning and Modernity," 258; Reader, review of *Imagining Japan*. RNB to Douglas Mitchell, May 16, 2005, DMPP ("intrinsically exciting"). Susumu Simazono to RNB, October 20, 2001; RNB to Susumu Simazono, October 25, 2001; Hans Joas to RNB, n.d. [December 2004]; RNB, "Narrative Progress Report for John Templeton Foundation, Grant ID#11248," May 1, 2005; all RBPP.

4. RNB, "What Is Axial," 71. The main theoretical cleavages of the axial age debate are summarized in the introduction to Arnason et al., *Axial Civilizations and World History*; Torpey and Boy, "Inventing the Axial Age"; Flores, "Interview with Stephen J. Mennell" (Eisenstadt quoted by Mennel). RNB to Shmuel Eisenstadt, May 15, 2002; RNB to Shmuel Eisenstadt, July 11, 2002; Johann Arnason to RNB, May 10, 2001; Garry Runciman to RNB, November 3, 2003; RNB to Garry Runciman, November 3, 2003; Garry Runciman to RNB, n.d. [November 2003]; RNB to Peter Machinist, November 24, 2004; Peter Machinist to RNB, November 25, 2004; all RBPP.

5. Donald, *Origins of the Modern Mind*, 149–50, 154–55, 159–60, 168ff., 214, 256ff., 355ff. The different vocabularies of Bruner, Merlin, and Bellah are explained in RNB, *Religion in Human Evolution*, 614n.22.

6. RNB, "What Is Axial," 77, 81, 88.

7. RNB, 72, 78, 83. RNB to Daniel Bell, July 25, 2001; Charles Taylor to RNB, October 4, 2004; Charles Taylor to RNB, October 23, 2004; all RBBP.

8. "Harvard Keeps 1950s Files Confidential," *Harvard Crimson*, December 9, 1977; Pattullo, "Dean Bundy Deals with McCarthyism," 18–20; RNB, "Harvard and McCarthyism," 13.

9. RNB to William C. Kirby, June 7, 2004; RNB to William C. Kirby, June 14, 2004; William C. Kirby to RNB, June 14, 2004; William C. Kirby to RNB, June 14, 2004; William C. Kirby to RNB, September 27, 2004; RNB to William C. Kirby and Sidney Verba, October 19, 2004;

William Sullivan to RNB, October 16, 2004; RNB to William Sullivan, October 16, 2004; Victor Lidz to RNB, November 11, 2004; Renée Fox to RNB, November 11, 2004; RNB to Charles Parsons, November 15, 2004 (quote); Charles Parsons to RNB, November 15, 2004; all RBPP.

10. RNB, "McCarthyism at Harvard." In this book, the content of these documents has been discussed in chapter 4, above.

11. William C. Kirby to RNB, n.d. [November 2004]; Staughton Lynd to RNB, January 26, 2005; Iryne Black to RNB, January 27, 2005; George Mandler to RNB, January 30, 2005; RNB to Roger Bowen, February 1, 2005; R. Taylor Scott to RNB, February 2, 2005; RNB to Robert Silvers, February 5, 2005; Harvey Cox to RNB, February 7, 2005; RNB to Richard Reichard, February 21, 2005; RNB to Leon Kamin, February 26, 2005; Leon Kamin to RNB, February 28, 2005; RNB to William Sloane Coffin, March 15, 2005; RNB to Theda Skocpol, August 18, 2005; Theda Skocpol to RNB, August 18, 2005; RNB to Theda Skocpol, August 19, 2005; all RBPP. Bradley, *Harvard Rules*; Hernandez, "Summer Resigns."

12. Sharon P. Torian to Steven M. Tipton, February 6, 2004; William Sullivan to RNB, July 10, 2004; Renée Fox to RNB, September 11, 2004; Mark Cladis to RNB, October 31, 2004; RNB to Mark Cladis, November 12, 2004; RNB to Steven M. Tipton, May 21, 2005; Steven M. Tipton to RNB, May 21, 2005; all RBPP. RNB to Douglas Mitchell, November 27, 2006; RNB to Douglas Mitchell, December 1, 2006; both DMPP.

13. Shin, "Robert Bellah Honored," 3 ("pay tribute"). Collins, review of *The Robert Bellah Reader*; D. Davis, review of *The Robert Bellah Reader*, 103 ("his firm grasp"); "One of Sociology's Most Influential Scholars," *Chronicle of Higher Education* 53 (2006); Wood, "American Habits"; Lindsay, "Good Habits of Mind." Renée Fox to RNB, November 19, 2006, RBPP.

14. RNB to Daniel Bell, July 25, 2001; RNB to William R. Ferris, June 25, 2001; both RBPP. RNB to Clifford Geertz, September 8, 2004; Clifford Geertz to RNB, January 5, 2005; both CGP, box 36, folder 8-Bellah.

15. RNB to Karen Blu, October 23, 2006; Karen Blu to RNB, October 24, 2006; both RBPP. Clifford Geertz, review of *The Robert Bellah Reader*, ed. R. N. Bellah and S. M. Tipton, unpublished paper, 7 pp., 2006, CGP, box 213, folder 7. RNB, interview; RNB to Matteo Bortolini, November 24, 2006; both AF.

16. RNB to Samuel C. Porter, January 25, 2004; RNB to Samuel C. Porter, October 1, 2004; RNB to Samuel C. Porter, November 6, 2004; RNB to Samuel C. Porter, April 8, 2005; all SPPP. RNB to Patricia B. Franklin, November 1, 2005; RNB to Walter Brueggemann, April 6, 2005; RNB, "Narrative Progress Report for John Templeton Foundation, Grant ID#11248," May 1, 2005; all RBPP. RNB to Douglas Mitchell, January 12, 2005; RNB to Douglas Mitchell, March 27, 2005, DMPP. Upon reading Bellah's chapter on Israel, Eisenstadt suggested publishing it in Hebrew as a small monograph, an idea that enthused the author but was later dropped. Shmuel Eisenstadt to RNB, May 11, 2005, RBPP. RNB to Douglas Mitchell, May 16, 2005, DMPP.

17. Richard Madsen, "Transcendence or Collapse: Social Sources for Moral Order in a Fragmented World," grant application to Rockefeller Foundation, August 1, 2006; RNB to Hans Joas, September 24, 2004; Richard Madsen to Hans Joas, October 3, 2004; Hans Joas to Richard Madsen, October 6, 2004; Charles Taylor to Richard Madsen, October 12, 2005; Richard Madsen to William Sullivan and Robert Bellah, October 12, 2005; William Sullivan to RNB, n.d. [October 2005]; RNB to Paul Wason, November 7, 2005; all RBPP. Hans Joas to Matteo Bortolini, February 26, 2020, AF.

18. RNB to Yang Xiao, January 4, 2007, YXPP. RNB to Paul Wason, November 7, 2005, RBPP. Joas, *Do We Need Religion?* 62.

19. RNB to Douglas Mitchell, December 1, 2006; RNB to Douglas Mitchell, January 25, 2008; both DMPP. RNB to Albert and Yi-Tsi Feuerwerker, June 24, 2007; Yehuda Elkana to RNB, October 31, 2007; Jürgen Habermas to RNB, February 21, 2008; Michael Witzel to RNB, May 20, 2008; all RBPP. RNB to Anna Sun and Yang Xiao, July 4, 2007; Yang Xiao to RNB, July 15, 2007; RNB to Anna Sun and Yang Xiao, January 1, 2008; RNB to Anna Sun and Yang Xiao, October 5, 2008; all YXPP. RNB, "Final Narrative Report for John Templeton Foundation, Grant ID#11248," May 4, 2007, RBPP. Hans Joas to Matteo Bortolini, February 25, 2020, AF.

20. On the 38th World Congress of the International Institute of Sociology, see the program book: *IIS 2008* (International Institute of Sociology, 2008), http://www.swedishcollegium.se/iis/pdf/programme_book.pdf. Matteo Bortolini to RNB, June 12, 2006; RNB to Matteo Bortolini, June 14, 2006; RNB to Matteo Bortolini, June 22, 2006; Matteo Bortolini to RNB, July 4, 2006; Matteo Bortolini to RNB, September 7, 2006; Matteo Bortolini to RNB, January 6, 2007; Matteo Bortolini to John Torpey, December 6, 2007; Matteo Bortolini to RNB, May 27, 2008; Matteo Bortolini to RNB, May 28, 2008; all AF.

21. RNB to Barbara Faedda, November 29, 2007, RBPP. Matteo Bortolini, "Nothing Fails Like Success: Robert N. Bellah before, during, and after the 'Civil Religion Debate,'" unpublished paper, 63 pp., 2008, AF.

22. Quotes translated from https://web.archive.org/web/20100519113858/ http://www2.uni-erfurt.de/maxwe/aktuelles/ss08/axial_age_tagung/project_descript.html; https://idw-online.de/de/news268527 (accessed April 20, 2020, then partially discontinued). Basic information comes from the promotional materials of the conference. I was present at the conference together with my friend and intellectual partner Paolo Costa, who provided me his own narrative of the conference by e-mail, March 2, 2020, AF. Jan Assmann and Heiner Roetz also sent me some memories of the event, AF.

23. Roetz, *Confucian Ethics*, xi, 24ff.

24. Habermas, *Between Naturalism and Religion*; C. Taylor, *Modern Social Imaginaries*, ch. 4; Assmann, *Religion and Cultural Memory*; Runciman, *Cultural and Social Selection*, 202–4, quote at 203–4.

25. RNB, "What Is Axial," 89, and "All Religions Are Cousins."

26. RNB, "The Heritage of the Axial Age: Resource of Burden?" unpublished paper, 2008, RBPP, 7, 9. On Nightingale's book as "a revelation," see RNB to Douglas Mitchell, July 19, 2009, DMPP.

27. RNB, "Heritage of the Axial Age," 12–13.

28. RNB to Douglas Mitchell, July 19, 2009, DMPP.

29. Assheuer, "Kam so die Gewalt in die Welt?" RNB to Hans Joas, October 21, 2011; RNB to Hans Joas, November 22, 2011; both HJPP. The papers from the Erfurt conference were published in 2012 in a book dedicated to the memory of Karl Jaspers. Bellah called the conference "one of the high points" of his life, but he thought the papers were of mixed quality. RNB to Hans Joas, June 24, 2011; RNB to Hans Joas, August 27, 2011; RNB to Hans Joas, September 12, 2011; RNB to Hans Joas, September 17, 2011; Hans Joas to Shanshan Wang, September 22, 2011; RNB to Hans Joas, November 22, 2011; RNB to Michael Higgins (HUP), December 3, 2011; RNB to Shanshan Wang, February 7, 2012; Hans Joas to RNB, February 8, 2012; RNB to Hans Joas, February 8, 2012; RNB to Hans Joas, May 1, 2012; all HJPP.

30. RNB to Anna Sun and Yang Xiao, October 5, 2008, YXPP. RNB, "Yes He Can" (quotes).

31. RNB to Anna Sun and Yang Xiao, October 5, 2008; RNB to Anna Sun and Yang Xiao, November 6, 2008; both YXPP. RNB to Arvind Rajagopal, January 17, 2009, ARPP. RNB, "This Is Our Moment" (blog entry). Tesler and Sears, *Obama's Race*; J. Alexander, *Performance of Politics*; Gorski, *American Covenant*.

32. See N-1947, undated entry, p. 30 ("lifetime books"). RNB, "All Religions Are Cousins," *passim*. RNB to Douglas Mitchell, December 1, 2006, DMPP. Timothy Doran to Matteo Bortolini, February 20, 2020, AF (other quotes).

33. Douglas Mitchell to RNB, January 12, 2005; RNB to Douglas Mitchell, July 5, 2004; Douglas Mitchell to RNB, July 5, 2004; RNB to Douglas Mitchell, January 17, 2005; Douglas Mitchell to RNB, January 18, 2005; RNB to Douglas Mitchell, February 2, 2005; Douglas Mitchell to RNB, February 16, 2005; all DMPP. Zach Goldhammer, "Wyatt's Wall," *South Side Weekly*, May 14, 2014, https://southsideweekly.com/wyatts-wall/.

34. Douglas Mitchell to RNB, March 28, 2005; Douglas Mitchell to RNB, December 1, 2006 ("something of a marvel"); RNB to Douglas Mitchell, December 1, 2006; Douglas Mitchell to RNB, December 5, 2006; RNB to Douglas Mitchell, December 6, 2006; RNB to Douglas Mitchell, December 7, 2006 ("disturbing problem"); RNB to Douglas Mitchell, July 4, 2007 ("if I die tomorrow"); all DMPP. Mitchell would later suggest to Bellah books on what he saw as the recurring distortions in the interpretation of Aristotle: Douglas Mitchell to RNB, April 16, 2007, DMPP. RNB to William Sullivan, July 12, 2006; RNB to William Sullivan, December 17, 2006; both RBPP. RNB to Arvind Rajagopal, February 22, 2011, ARPP. In the end, although Bellah expressed some interest in Garver's book, the latter was not referenced in *Religion in Human Evolution*.

35. RNB to Douglas Mitchell, July 3, 2009; RNB to Douglas Mitchell, July 10, 2009; RNB to Paul Wason, July 10, 2009; Douglas Mitchell to RNB, July 29, 2009; all DMPP.

36. For Mitchell's use of McKeon's categories, see Douglas Mitchell to RNB, December 1, 2006; Douglas Mitchell to RNB, December 5, 2006; Douglas Mitchell to RNB, July 19, 2009; all DMPP. Douglas Mitchell to RNB, July 25, 2009, RBPP. On McKeon, see Mitchell, "Creating Community through Communication"; Z. McKeon, "General Introduction"; R. McKeon, "Philosophic Semantics."

37. Douglas Mitchell to RNB, July 19, 2009 ("creativity, intelligence"); RNB to Douglas Mitchell, July 19, 2009; RNB to Douglas Mitchell, July 20, 2009 (other quotes); all DMPP. Christine Mitchell to Matteo Bortolini, September 10, 2020; Christine Mitchell to Matteo Bortolini, September 11, 2020; William Sullivan to Matteo Bortolini, September 14, 2020; all AF.

38. Douglas Mitchell to RNB, December 1, 2006; RNB to Douglas Mitchell, December 1, 2006; both DMPP. For Bellah's original editorial plan, see the introduction to this chapter, above.

39. RNB to Douglas Mitchell, July 20, 2009, two e-mails; both DMPP. Lindsay Waters to RNB, March 17, 2006; RNB to Lindsay Waters, April 24, 2006; Douglas Mitchell to RNB, July 25, 2009; Lindsay Waters to RNB, July 27, 2009; all RBPP.

40. RNB to Douglas Mitchell, July 28, 2009; Douglas Mitchell to RNB, July 29, 2009; both DMPP. RNB to William Sullivan, July 19, 2009; RNB to William Sullivan, July 25, 2009; William Sullivan to RNB, July 27, 2009; all RBPP.

41. RNB, *Religion in Human Evolution*, 50. Burghardt, *Genesis of Animal Play*. RNB to Gordon Burghardt, February 11, 2010; Gordon Burghardt to RNB, February 11, 2010; RNB to Gordon Burghardt, April 26, 2010; RNB to Gordon Burghardt, April 28, 2010; RNB to Terrence Deacon, May 2010; RNB to Gordon Burghardt, June 29, 2010; RNB to Gordon Burghardt, February 24, 2011; all GBPP.

42. I write "unconsciously" because Bellah himself admitted that the connection was not clear to him at the outset. RNB to Hans Joas, February 16, 2012, HJPP. William Sullivan to RNB, April 20, 2010; Matteo Bortolini to RNB, April 20, 2010; Hans Joas to RNB, May 3, 2010; all RBPP.

43. This section relies heavily on Jennifer Bellah Maguire to Matteo Bortolini, December 29, 2019; Jennifer Bellah Maguire to Matteo Bortolini, February 22, 2020; RNB to Matteo Bortolini, March 27, 2010; all AF. RNB to Douglas Mitchell, July 3, 2009; RNB to Douglas Mitchell, July 6, 2009; both DMPP. RNB to Anna Sun and Yang Xiao, January 2, 2009, YXPP. RNB to Philip J. Ivanohe, June 9, 2009, RBPP. RNB to Arvind Rajagopal, January 9, 2009, ARPP.

44. Lindsay Waters to RNB, July 10, 2020; Merlin Donald to RNB, July 6, 2010; both RBPP. RNB to Arvind Rajagopal, July 6, 2010, ARPP. RNB to Yang Xiao, July 6, 2010, YXPP. Later Bellah discovered that the reviewer was Yang Xiao. The other reviewer was Gordon Burghardt, who continued exchanging critiques and bibliographies with Bellah well into the summer of 2010, encouraging him to make some last-minute changes. RNB to Gordon Burghardt, June 21, 2010; RNB to Gordon Burghardt, June 26, 2010; Gordon Burghardt to RNB, June 27, 2010; RNB to Gordon Burghardt, June 29, 2010; Gordon Burghardt to Lindsay Waters, July 9, 2010; Lindsay Waters to Gordon Burghardt, July 21, 2011; all GBPP.

45. RNB to Matteo Bortolini, September 22, 2010, AF. RNB to Gordon Burghardt, February 24, 2011, GBPP. RNB to Douglas Mitchell, August 26, 2011, DMPP. Obituary for Melanie Bellah, *San Francisco Chronicle*, September 12, 2010. The characterization of Bob and Melanie as "Jeremiah married to Elizabeth Taylor" was made by Ann Swidler during the American Academy of Religion commemorative session for Bellah, November 24, 2013: American Academy of Religion, "Remembering Robert N. Bellah."

46. RNB, "Notes about Melanie for Phil Brochard's Memorial Sermon," All Souls Parish, Berkeley, September 14, 2010.

47. RNB to Samuel C. Porter, September 30, 2010, SPPP.

48. RNB to Samuel C. Porter, September 30, 2010, SPPP (quote). R. Bellah and Joas, *Axial Age and Its Consequences*. RNB to Anna Sun and Yang Xiao, November 1, 2010; RNB to Yang Xiao, April 27, 2011, YXPP. RNB to Arvind Rajagopal, February 15, 2011, ARPP. Lindsay Waters to RNB, May 14, 2011, RBPP. RNB to Hans Joas, April 28, 2011; Hans Joas to RNB, April 28, 2011; RNB to Hans Joas, May 8, 2011; RNB to Lindsay Waters, March 17, 2012; all HJPP. RNB to Matteo Bortolini, April 18, 2011; RNB to Matteo Bortolini, May 8, 2011; both AF.

Chapter Twenty-Two

1. RNB, "Response to Three Readers"; Horn, "Where Does Religion Come From?" RNB to Gordon Burghardt, February 11, 2010; Gordon Burghardt to RNB, August 2, 2011; both GBPP. RNB to Hans Joas, May 23, 2011; Hans Joas to RNB, September 2, 2011; RNB to Hans Joas,

September 2, 2011; all HJPP. RNB to Doug Mitchell, November 27, 2006; RNB to Douglas Mitchell, January 25, 2008; Douglas Mitchell to RNB, August 25, 2011; RNB to Douglas Mitchell, August 26, 2011; all DMPP. Harlan Stelmach to Matteo Bortolini, March 9, 2020, AF.

2. RNB, *Religion in Human Evolution*, 430, 474. Castoriadis, *Imaginary Institution of Society*, 1. RNB to Yang Xiao, May 26, 2011; Yang Xiao to RNB, May 29, 2011; both YXPP.

3. RNB, *Religion in Human Evolution*, xxvii ("friends in history"), 604, 159, 98–99 ("criticism of Jesus"), 111–12, 610n17, 481 ("graduate student competence"), 567. A small sample of the points where Bellah's personal voice comes out: 283, 610n16, 620n20, 628n139, 632n20, 673n92, 692n227, 694n1, 709n2. All through the 1990s and the 2000s Bellah continued to copiously cite *Habits of the Heart* and *The Good Society* in his public conferences, and he always presented himself as just one of five coauthors.

4. RNB, *Religion in Human Evolution*, 592.

5. RNB, 591 (*"theoria"*), 593 ("different eyes").

6. I am not going to speculate about this point, for I have already described a number of moments of "conversion" in Bellah's life that brought him to the point I am recounting here (see chapters 8–9 and 13–15, above). RNB, *Religion in Human Evolution*, 45 ("history of histories"), xvii ("tell just enough"), xxiv ("effort to live again"), my italics. NJ-1965–1969, entry of November 23, 1968.

7. RNB, *Religion in Human Evolution*, 47, 97, 604 ("naive but undogmatic"), and "Reply to My Critics." Bellah's style was completely different from both Shmuel Eisenstadt's "eventless historical narration" and the oracular tone typical of Eric Voegelin's *Order and History*. Marangudakis, "Multiple Modernities," 8; Voegelin, *Order and History*.

8. Kagan, *Three Cultures*; [Geertz and Bellah], "Program in Social Change," 27.

9. RNB, *Beyond Belief*, 254 ("develop multiple schemas"). Stausberg, "Bellah's *Religion in Human Evolution*," 288; Riesebrodt, "Dangerous Evolutions?"

10. RNB, *Religion in Human Evolution*, xxii ("what religion is"), 113. RNB to Arvind Rajagopal, October 2011; RNB to Arvind Rajagopal, July 12, 2013; both ARPP, my italics. Rajagopal, "Interview with Robert Bellah," 7.

11. RNB, *Religion in Human Evolution*, xvii, 12, xviii. Joas, "Conversation with Robert Bellah."

12. RNB, *Religion in Human Evolution*, 221, xviii.

13. RNB, 92, 76, 571–73.

14. RNB, 266.

15. RNB, 283 ("fundamental rethinking"); RNB, *Beyond Belief*, 179 ("genuine apprehension").

16. RNB, *Religion in Human Evolution*, 323 ("In our quest"); Marangudakis, "Multiple Modernities," 8 ("eventless historical narrative").

17. RNB, *Religion in Human Evolution*, 266, 283, 311, 321, 322 ("narrative theology"), 323, 315, 356, 383, 475–80, 512–13, 514 ("speculative soteriology"), 518–19, 531, 542 ("equality"). RNB, "Civil Religion in America," 179, and "Response to Three Readers."

18. What follows is based on an analysis of seventy-seven reviews and essays on *Religion in Human Evolution* published between 2011 and 2014, not all of which have been cited. For a detailed study, see Stausberg, "Bellah's *Religion in Human Evolution*." Hans Joas to RNB, August 10,

2011; RNB to Hans Joas, August 11, 2011; Hans Joas to RNB, March 5, 2012; RNB to Hans Joas, March 5, 2012; RNB to Hans Joas, March 19, 2012; all HJPP. RNB to Matteo Bortolini, July 8, 2009; Matteo Bortolini to RNB, February 21, 2011; both AF. Between 2011 and 2012 the book got eighteen reviews on Amazon.com and fifty-nine on Goodreads.com, most of them good. At the time of writing (late March 2020), *Religion in Human Evolution* has sold fifteen thousand copies in hardback, two thousand in paperback, and another thousand in electronic form (Lindsay Waters to Matteo Bortolini, March 26, 2020, AF). A theoretical case for studying how Web 2.0 impacts on the reception of literary works is made in Santana-Acuña, *Ascent to Glory*.

19. Madsen, "Weber for the 21st Century" ; Wolfe, "Origins of Belief"; Miles, review of *Religion in Human Evolution*, 854; Mendieta, "Religious Origins," 72; Mathewes, "Evolution of Religion"; Guhin, review of *Religion in Human Evolution*, 417. RNB to Hans Joas, May 17, 2013, HJPP.

20. Martin, "What Should We Now Do"; Wolfe, "Origins of Belief"; Smilde, review of *Religion in Human Evolution*; Barrett, "Religion."

21. RNB, *Religion in Human Evolution*, xviii, 64. Mathewes, "Evolution of Religion"; Hann, "Humans and Their Hierarchies," 320; Payne, "Bellah's *Religion in Human Evolution*"; Gould, "Axial Age Religious Commitment"; Riesebrodt, "Dangerous Evolutions?"

22. Morrison, "Holy of Holies," 722; RNB, "Das Ewig-Weibliche". See Ann Swidler's remarks at the commemorative session for Bellah, in American Academy of Religion, "Remembering Robert N. Bellah." I have to thank my friend Paolo Costa, whose image of the encounter of different times went directly from his comments to my page.

23. RNB, "*Religion in Human Evolution* Revisited," 260, 270. Arnason, "Axial Detachment" and "Archaic and the Axial," 149.

24. RNB, *Religion in Human Evolution*, 342, 352ff., 363, 677n148, 702n134. Self-referentiality is the capacity of observers to include themselves as an object of observation. Luhmann, *Introduction to Systems Theory*. Linda Heuman (review of *Religion in Human Evolution*, *Trycicle*, Summer 2012) came close to the interpretation I am advancing here.

25. RNB, *Religion in Human Evolution*, 145. As far as I know, the only one who came close to seeing that Bellah's book needed a mimetic enactment was Doug Mitchell. In the e-mail he sent Bellah upon receiving *Religion in Human Evolution*, Mitchell wrote: "You may think it whimsical or impertinent to bring a movie into a thank-you note, but this year's Cannes Palme d'Or went to a movie that, in my judgment, achieves the highest spiritual vision (fusing emotions, imagination, and will with stunning images and truly great music), and which would enjoy a place in your story if you were to extend it. I'm speaking of Terrence Malick's *The Tree of Life*." After Bellah wrote back saying that Peter Manseau had made the same parallel in his review of *Religion*, Mitchell added: "Now you must see this movie, *The Tree of Life*, which is a virtual enactment, in spiritual terms anyway, of your book." Douglas Mitchell to RNB, August 25, 2011; RNB to Douglas Mitchell, October 16, 2011; Douglas Mitchell to RNB, October 17, 2011; all DMPP. Manseau, "Big Bang."

26. Jakob Köllhofer to RNB, January 17, 2012; RNB to Jakob Köllhofer, January 17, 2012; RNB to Jakob Köllhofer, March 13, 2012; RNB to Hans Joas, March 14, 2012; RNB to Hans Joas, April 4, 2012; RNB to Hans Joas, October 3, 2012; all HJPP. RNB to Arvind Rajagopal, October 27, 2012, ARPP. Marit Trelstad to RNB, August 30, 2011; William Crout to RNB, n.d. [fall 2012]; RNB to W. Scott Green, April 24, 2013; all RBPP.

27. RNB to Hans Joas, April 28, 2011 (quote); Hans Joas to RNB, July 6, 2011; RNB to Hans Joas, July 6, 2011; Hans Joas to RNB, August 18, 2011; RNB to Hans Joas, August 18, 2011; RNB to Hans Joas, October 21, 2011; all HJPP.

28. In 2009 Bellah had refused an invitation to lecture at the City University of Honk Kong on the grounds that Melanie needed care and he would never travel to interesting places without her. Philip Ivanhoe to RNB, June 4, 2009; RNB to Philip Ivanhoe, June 6, 2009; RNB to Yang Xiao, January 14, 2011; Hans Joas to RNB, January 17, 2011; Yang Xiao to RNB, January 18, 2011; RNB to Yang Xiao, January 19, 2011; Philip Ivanhoe to RNB, May 26, 2011; RNB to Yang Xiao, June 13, 2011; RNB to Yang Xiao, June 15, 2011; all YXPP. RNB to Douglas Mitchell, October 16, 2011, DMPP. RNB to Hans Joas, June 1, 2011; Tu Weiming to RNB, June 5, 2011; RNB to Hans Joas, June 5, 2011; RNB to Hans Joas, June 6, 2011; all HJPP. Beijing Forum Brochure, 2015. RNB, "What Changes Very Fast."

29. Arvind Rajagopal to RNB, June 16, 2011; RNB to Arvind Rajagopal, June 17, 2011; RNB to Arvind Rajagopal, October 9, 2011; RNB to Arvind Rajagopal, January 1, 2012; all ARPP. RNB to Hans Joas, November 18, 2011, HJPP. Jennifer Bellah Maguire to Matteo Bortolini, March 8, 2020, AF. "Robert N. Bellah in Conversation with Michael Lerner," transcript by S. C. Porter, Robert N. Bellah website, September 13, 2012, http://www.robertbellah.com/interviews.html. Zhang, "Traditions Deepen Our Grasp"; Tatlow, "Mao's Spell." I should add that my own work on Bellah and the "trap of success" was a catalyst that pushed him to reflect on civil religion and return to use the expression during the last two years of his life, after three decades of silence on the matter. RNB to Matteo Bortolini, April 19, 2010, AF.

30. RNB to Hans Joas, November 22, 2011, HJPP. J. Smith, *To Take Place*, 52, and "Damned Good Read"; RNB, "Response to Three Readers." A video recording of the November 11, 2011, session can be found at American Academy of Religion, "A Conversation with Robert Bellah on *Religion in Human Evolution*," YouTube, July 7, 2015, https://www.youtube.com/watch?v=bduUUtnPUgI.

31. RNB to Hans Joas, December 28, 2011; RNB to Hans Joas, February 12, 2012; RNB to Hans Joas, March 19, 2012; RNB to Hans Joas, June 10, 2012; Hans Joas to RNB, July 17, 2012; RNB to Hans Joas, August 29, 2012; Hans Joas to RNB, August 29, 2012; RNB to Hans Joas, September 10, 2012; RNB to Hans Joas, September 13, 2012; RNB to Hans Joas, October 12, 2012; RNB to Hans Joas, November 20, 2012; RNB to Hans Joas, February 11, 2013; RNB to Hans Joas, February 13, 2013; all HJPP.

32. An audio recording and photos from the conference have been provided by Jakob Köllhofer (e-mail, November 28, 2019, AF). RNB to Hans Joas, August 16, 2012; RNB to Hans Joas, November 20, 2012; both HJPP. RNB, *Religion in Human Evolution*, xxvi–xxvii; RNB, "Religion in Human Evolution," unpublished paper given in Freiburg and Heidelberg, November 8–11, 2012, RBPP.

33. Reno and McClay, *Religion and the Social Sciences*, xiv ("believe in more than one religion"). RNB to Hans Joas, May 8, 2012; RNB to Hans Joas, May 15, 2013; both HJPP. RNB to Arvind Rajagopal, December 15, 2012, ARPP ("very nervous"). Griffiths, "Impossible Pluralism"; T. White, "Sociology as Theology," 34; RNB, "Reply to My Critics," 51.

34. Horn, "Where Does Religion Come From?"

35. RNB to Douglas Mitchell, April 17, 2007, DMPP. RNB to Arvind Rajagopal, January 27, 2013, ARPP. From a theoretical point of view, Bellah had also come to see *The Modern Project* as

carrying out the Parsonian general theory of action "by other means." The insight had actually come from me, in a short piece published in *The Immanent Frame* that described *Religion in Human Evolution* "as an attempt to bring Talcott Parsons' work to a higher level of complexity and explicative power." The point was mainly epistemic, but had repercussions on the whole project: according to Parsons, "reality [was] an almost endless succession of levels and layers, each one emerging from simpler ones . . . and giving rise to more complex ones, which possess new, emerging properties. Likewise," I added, "Bellah's point [was] that biological, psychological, social, and cultural structures combine without any clear causal primacy in creating new capacities upon which further changes build endlessly." Bortolini, "Back to His Roots." RNB to Hans Joas, February 16, 2012, HJPP. RNB to Matteo Bortolini, March 12, 2012, AF.

36. RNB, "Final Narrative Report for John Templeton Foundation, Grant ID#11248," May 4, 2007, RBPP.

37. RNB, 2.

38. RNB, "Two Lectures." The first lecture was later republished in 2010 as "Confronting Modernity: Maruyama Masao, Jürgen Habermas, and Charles Taylor" in the edited volume *Varieties of Secularism in a Secular Age.*

39. RNB, "Prelude in the Theater," unpublished paper, August 2012, 3–4, RBPP. RNB to Hans Joas, July 24, 2012; RNB to Hans Joas, July 24, 2012; RNB to Hans Joas, August 9, 2012; RNB to Hans Joas, August 11, 2012; Hans Joas to RNB, August 13, 2012; all HJPP. From 2008 on Hans Joas was Bellah's key intellectual partner, especially after Bob read, and loved, the manuscript of his *Sacredness of the Person.* Hans Joas to RNB, January 17, 2013; RNB to Hans Joas, July 20, 2013; both HJPP.

40. RNB, "Prologue in Heaven (or Hell)," unpublished paper, April–July 2012, 93 pp., RBPP. RNB to Hans Joas, August 16, 2012, HJPP.

41. RNB, "New Ending to Prologue to Bellah's *The Modern Project*," unpublished paper, 3pp., August 2012, RBPP. As Bellah later explained to Hans Joas, the final version of the book would analyze the rise of modernity in the West during the eighteenth century from both a structural and a cultural point of view, and would surely include a comparison with the history of China. For all his interest in the Athens/Jerusalem syndrome and its civilizational offspring, the last thing he wanted to do was "write one more 'rise of the West' book" (RNB to Hans Joas, July 20, 2013, HJPP). See also RNB to Hans Joas, August 6, 2012; RNB to Hans Joas, August 16, 2012; RNB to Hans Joas, August 25, 2012; all HJPP.

42. RNB to William Sullivan, January 28, 2011; William Crout to RNB, n.d. [fall 2012]; William Crout to RNB, January 14, 2013; William Crout to RNB, January 15, 2013; all RBPP. Joas, "Conversation with Robert Bellah." Corydon Ireland, "Remembering Bill Crout," *Harvard Gazette*, April 9, 2015, https://news.harvard.edu/gazette/story/2015/04/remembering-bill-crout/.

43. RNB, "Paul Tillich and the Challenge of Modernity," unpublished paper, May 6, 2013, RBPP, *passim*. RNB to Hans Joas, April 5, 2013, HJPP. RNB to Matteo Bortolini, April 13, 2013, AF. Mark Juergensmeyer's remarks at the commemorative session for Bellah, November 24, 2013, can be found at American Academy of Religion, "Remembering Robert N. Bellah."

44. On Bellah's unwillingness to play the game of doom and gloom, see his e-mail cited in Miles, review of *Religion in Human Evolution*, 864. Rajagopal, "Interview with Robert Bellah." Quotes from RNB, "Paul Tillich and the Challenge of Modernity."

45. During his stay in Cambridge, Bellah also visited for the last time his old friends Eli and Frimi Sagan, who had recently moved there from New Jersey. William Crout to RNB, December 18, 2012; William Crout to RNB, May 15, 2013; both RBPP. RNB to Hans Joas, May 3, 2013; Hans Joas to RNB, May 4, 2013; both HJPP. RNB to Arvind Rajagopal, May 18, 2013, ARPP (quotes). Jennifer Bellah Maguire to Matteo Bortolini, March 8, 2020; Harvey Cox to Matteo Bortolini, March 31, 2020; Jennifer Bellah Maguire to Matteo Bortolini, April 5, 2020; all AF.

46. RNB to Renée Fox, March 16, 2004, RBPP. RNB to Hans Joas, July 20, 2013, HJPP. RNB to Gordon Burghardt, January 15, 2013, GBPP.

47. RNB to Habits group, July 25, 2013, AF. Among the books that were found in Bellah's study after his death were Bruno Latour's *We Have Never Been Modern*, Ian Morris's *Why the West Rules—For Now*, Thomas A. McCarthy's *Race, Empire, and the Idea of Human Development*, and David Harvey's *The Enigma of Capital*.

48. Joas, "Habits of the Heart"; Madsen, "Robert Bellah: In Memoriam" ("About death"); Bellah's letter to Sam Porter is cited in Wood, "Short Essay." RNB to Arvind Rajagopal, July 17, 2013, ARPP. RNB to Hans Joas, July 20, 2013, HJPP. RNB, notes to Oliver and Alexandria, n.d. [late July 2013]; RNB to Jennifer Bellah Maguire, July 17, 2013; both RBPP. Jennifer Bellah Maguire to Matteo Bortolini, April 5, 2020, AF.

Epilogue

1. RNB to Habits group, July 25, 2013, AF. Bellah would often remark that work was play for him: RNB to Gordon Burghardt, April 28, 2010; RNB to Gordon Burghardt, September 7, 2012; both GBPP.

2. Agamben, *Idea of Prose*, 64–65.

BIBLIOGRAPHY

Archival Sources

AF   Author's files (including interviews, e-mails, personal communications).

ARPP   Arvind Rajagopal personal papers, New York City. Courtesy of Arvind Rajagopal.

CESP   Papers of the Center for Ethics and Social Policy, Graduate Theological Union, Berkeley, CA.

CGP   Clifford Geertz Papers, Special Collections Research Center, University of Chicago.

CLP   Christopher Lasch Papers (D.250), Rare Books, Special Collections, and Preservation, River Campus Libraries, University of Rochester, Rochester, NY. Courtesy of Nell Lasch.

DMPP   Douglas Mitchell personal papers, Chicago. Courtesy of Christine Mitchell.

DRP   David Riesman Papers, Harvard University Archives. Courtesy of Harvard University Archives.

DSP   David M. Schneider Papers, Special Collections Research Center, University of Chicago.

DSR   Department of Social Relations, Harvard University.

FFR   Ford Foundation Records, Rockefeller Archive Center, Sleepy Hollow, NY. Courtesy of Rockefeller Archive Center.

FGA   Giovanni Agnelli Foundation Archives, Torino, Italy. Courtesy of Giovanni Agnelli Foundation.

GBPP   Gordon M. Burghardt personal papers, Knoxville, TN. Courtesy of Gordon Burghardt.

HJPP   Hans Joas personal papers, Berlin, Germany. Courtesy of Hans Joas.

HTPA   Horowitz Transaction Publishers Archives. Excerpts from the Horowitz/Transaction archives (https://libraries.psu.edu/about/collections/horowitz-transaction -publishers-archives) appear with permission of Mary Curtis Horowitz.

HUA   Harvard University Archives, Cambridge, MA. Courtesy of Harvard University Archives.

MUA   Institute of Islamic Studies files, McGill University Archives, Montreal, Canada. Courtesy of McGill University.

OFRS   Office Files of Richard Sharpe (FA 557), International Division, Education and Public Policy Division, FFR.

RBPP   Robert N. Bellah personal papers. Courtesy of Jennifer Bellah Maguire and the Robert and Melanie Bellah Estate, Berkeley, CA.

REEL   Grants Them-Tw (FA732H), Reel 4642, folder "The Regents of the University of Cali-fornia, 1979–1984," FFR.

RFR   Rockefeller Foundation Records, Rockefeller Archive Center, Sleepy Hollow, NY.

SPPP   Samuel C. Porter personal papers, Eugene, OR. Courtesy of Samuel Porter.

SUA   Records of the Center for Advanced Study in the Behavioral Sciences, Administrative Series 1, 1952–1989, Box 54, folder 7, Stanford University Archives, Palo Alto, CA. Courtesy of Stanford University.

TPP   Talcott Parsons Papers, HUA. Courtesy of Charles Parsons and Harvard University Archives.

YXPP   Yang Xiao personal papers, Gambier, OH. Courtesy of Yang Xiao.

Robert N. Bellah's Personal Notebooks (RBPP)

N-1947   "March 1947 to," 50 pp. February 1947–.

P-1949–1954   "Poems," 13 pp. December 30, 1949–September, 1954.

N-1951–1952   "Notes R. B. 1951–1952," 60 pp. August 20, 1951–June 27, 1952.

PR-1954   "Personal Record," 20 pp. April 21, 1954–December 30, 1954.

NJ-1965–1969   "Notes and Journal," 200 pp. March 30, 1965–July 5, 1969.

P-1967–1970   "Poesies," 6 pp. November, 1967–June, 1970.

MP-1967–1968   "Mes Pensées," 49 pp. December, 1967–December, 1968.

NJ-1969–1979   "Notes and Journal," 110 pp. July 15, 1969–July 17, 1979.

JNL-1979–1983   "Journal R. Bellah July 1979–," 65 pp. July 29, 1979–August 22, 1983.

Published Sources

Abbate, Janet. *Inventing the Internet.* Cambridge, MA: MIT Press, 1999.

Adams, Charles J. "The Institute of Islamic Studies." *Canadian Geographical Journal* 65 (1962): 34–36.

Adelman, Jeremy. *Worldly Philosopher.* Princeton, NJ: Princeton University Press, 2013.

Advisory Board for Medical Specialties. *Directory of Medical Specialists.* New York: Columbia University Press, 1942.

———. *Directory of Medical Specialists.* Vol. 3. Chicago: A. N. Marquis, 1946.

Agamben, Giorgio. *Idea of Prose.* Albany, NY: SUNY, 1995.

Ahlstrom, Sydney E. Review of *Beyond Belief* and *The Broken Covenant* by R. N. Bellah. *American Historical Review* 82 (1977): 1057.

Alexander, Charles C. *The Ku Klux Klan in the Southwest.* Lexington: University of Kentucky Press, 1965.

Alexander, Jeffrey C. *The Performance of Politics.* New York: Oxford University Press, 2010.

———. *Theoretical Logic in Sociology.* 4 vols. Berkeley: University of California Press, 1983.

———. *Twenty Lectures.* New York: Columbia University Press, 1987.

Alexander, Jeffrey C., and Philip Smith, eds. *The Cambridge Companion to Durkheim.* Cambridge: Cambridge University Press, 2005.

Allport, Gordon W. *The Individual and His Religion.* New York: Macmillan, 1950.

Allport, Gordon W., and Edwin G. Boring. "Psychology and Social Relations at Harvard University." *American Psychologist* 1 (1946): 119–22.

Allyn, David. *Make Love, Not War*. London: Routledge, 2000.

American Academy of Religion, "Special Topics Forum: Remembering Robert N. Bellah (1927–2013)." SoundCloud, November 24, 2013. https://soundcloud.com/american academyofreligion/special-topics-forum-remembering-robert-n-bellah-1927–2013.

Anthony, Dick, and Thomas Robbins. "From Symbolic Realism to Structuralism." *Journal for the Scientific Study of Religion* 14 (1975): 403–14.

Armstrong, Elizabeth A. *Forging Gay Identities*. Chicago: University of Chicago Press, 2002.

Arnason, Johann P. "The Archaic and the Axial." *Review of Politics* 75 (2013): 143–49.

———. "Axial Detachment: Reflections on Bellah's 'Conclusion.'" *Sociologica* 7 (2013). https://doi.org/10.2383/73708.

Arnason, Johann P., Shmuel N. Eisenstadt, and Björn Wittrock, eds. *Axial Civilizations and World History*. Leiden: Brill, 2005.

Arntzenius, L. G., ed. *Institute for Advanced Study*. Princeton, NJ: Institute for Advanced Study, 2005.

Assheuer, Thomas. "Kam so die Gewalt in die Welt?" *Die Zeit*, October 7, 2008.

Assmann, Jan. *Religion and Cultural Memory*. Stanford, CA: Stanford University Press, 2006.

Babai, Don. "Fifty-Year Odyssey: A Historical Overview of the Center for Middle Eastern Studies." In *Center for Middle Eastern Studies, Harvard University*, edited by D. Babai, 2–49. Cambridge, MA: Harvard University Press, 2004.

Baltzell, E. Digby. Review of *Habits of the Heart* by R. N. Bellah et al. *Social Forces* 64 (1986): 802–4.

Barber, Bernard, and Alex Inkeles, eds. *Stability and Social Change*. Boston: Little, Brown, and Co., 1971.

Barrett, Nathaniel F. "Religion and the Evolution of Meaning: Is Meaning Made or Perceived?" *Religion, Brain, and Behavior* 2 (2012): 225–30.

Barshay, Andrew E. *The Social Sciences in Modern Japan*. Berkeley: University of California Press, 2004.

Barzun, Jacques. "The Scholar Is an Institution." *Journal of Higher Education* 18 (1947): 393–445.

Batterson, Steve. *Pursuit of Genius*. Wellesley, MA: A. K. Peters, 2006.

Bauer, Raymond A., Alex Inkeles, and Clyde Kluckhohn. *How the Soviet System Works*. Cambridge, MA: Harvard University Press, 1956.

Bell, Daniel. *The Cultural Contradictions of Capitalism*. New York: Basic Books, 1978.

———. *The End of Ideology*. Cambridge, MA: Harvard University Press, 1988. First published 1960.

Bellah, Lovick P. *Register of the Bellah Family Descendants of William Ballagh of Charles Town, S. C.* Nashville, 1945.

Bellah, Luther H. "Mex: A Memory." *Sooner Magazine* 2 (1930): 138.

Bellah (Hyman), Melanie. *Abby and Her Sisters*. Berkeley, CA: Celestial Arts, 2002.

———. *Tammy*. Berkeley, CA: Aten, 1999.

———. "Unity Takes Opinion." *Stanford Daily*, April 8, 1948.

Bellah, Robert N. "All Religions Are Cousins." In *Reasonable Perspectives on Religion*, edited by R. Curtis, 47–59. Lanham, MD: Lexington Books, 2010.

———. "American Civil Religion in the 1970's." In Richey and Jones, *American Civil Religion*, 255–72.

———. "America's Cultural Conversation." In *Individualism and Commitment in American Life*, edited by Bellah, R. Madsen, W. M. Sullivan, A. Swidler, and S. M. Tipton, 3–10. New York: Harper and Row, 1987.

———. *Apache Kinship Systems*. Cambridge, MA: Harvard University Press, 1952.

———. "Baigan and Sorai: Continuities and Discontinuities in Eighteenth-Century Japanese Thought." In *Japanese Thought in the Tokugawa Period*, edited by T. Najita and I. Scheiner, 137–52. Chicago: University of Chicago Press, 1978.

———. *Beyond Belief*. New York: Harper and Row, 1970.

———. "Biblical Religion and Social Sciences in the Modern World." *National Institute for Campus Ministers Journal* 6 (1981): 8–22.

———. *The Broken Covenant: American Civil Religion in Time of Trial*. New York: Seabury, 1975.

———. "Brown in Perspective: A Commentary on *Love's Body*." *Soundings* 14 (1971): 450–59.

———. "Can You Recite Your Creed?" *Plumbline* 15 (1987): 4–9.

———. "Christianity and Symbolic Realism." *Journal for the Scientific Study of Religion* 9, (1970): 89–96.

———. "The Church as the Context for the Family." *New Oxford Review* 54 (1987): 6–13.

———. "Civil Religion and the Bicentennial." In *Bicentennial Broadside*, edited by R. Weltge and J. Westerhoff, 6. New York: Department of Publication Services, National Council of Churches, 1975.

———. "Civil Religion in America." In *Beyond Belief*, 168–89. First published in *Daedalus* 96 (1967): 1–21.

———. "Clinton and Welfare." *New York Review of Books*, November 28, 1996.

———. "Comment." *Sociological Analysis* 50 (1989): 147.

———. "Comment on 'The Limits of Symbolic Realism.'" *Journal for the Scientific Study of Religion* 13 (1974): 487–89.

———. "Commentary and Proposed Agenda: The Normative Framework for Pluralism in America." *Soundings* 61 (1978): 355–71.

———. "Community Properly Understood." *Responsive Community* 6 (1996): 49–54.

———. "Confessions of a Former Establishment Fundamentalist." *Theology Today* 28, (1971): 229–33.

———. "Confronting Modernity: Maruyama Masao, Jürgen Habermas, and Charles Taylor." In *Varieties of Secularism in a Secular Age*, edited by M. Warner, C. Calhoun, and J. VanAntwerpen, 32–53. Cambridge, MA: Harvard University Press, 2010.

———. Contribution to "Symposium on Roman Catholicism and 'American Exceptionalism.'" *New Oxford Review* 54 (1987): 5.

———. "Cultural Vision and the Human Future." *Teachers College Record* 82 (1981): 497–506.

———. "Das Ewig-Weibliche: A Reply to Karl Morrison." *Contemporary Sociology* 41 (2012): 733–38.

———. "Discerning Old and New Imperatives in Theological Education." *Theological Education* 19 (1982): 7–29.

———. "Durkheim and History." *American Sociological Review* 24 (1959): 447–61.

———. "The Dynamics of Worship." In *Multi-Media Worship*, edited by M. B. Bloy Jr., 53–69. New York: Seabury, 1969.

———. "Economics and the Theology of Work." *New Oxford Review* 51 (1984): 13–15.

———. "Elite Failure." *Christian Century* 109 (1992): 672–73.

———. "Epilogue. Meaning and Modernity: America and the World." In Madsen et al., *Meaning and Modernity*, 255–76.

———. "Evil and the American Ethos." In *Sanctions for Evil*, edited by N. Sanford and C. Comstock, 177–91. San Francisco: Jossey-Bass, 1971.

———. "Father and Son in Christianity and Confucianism." In *Beyond Belief*, 76–99. First published in *Psychoanalytic Review* 52 (1965): 236–58.

———. "Finding the Church: Post-Traditional Discipleship." *Christian Century* 107 (1990): 1060–64.

———. "Flaws in the Protestant Code: Some Religious Sources of America's Troubles." In R. Bellah and Tipton, *Robert Bellah Reader*, 333–49. First published in *Ethical Perspectives* 7 (2000): 288–99.

———. Foreword to Rabinow, *Reflections on Fieldwork in Morocco*, xxix–xxxiii.

———. "God, Nation, and Self in America: Some Tensions between Parsons and Bellah." In *After Parsons*, edited by Renée C. Fox, Victor M. Lidz, and Harold J. Bershady, 137–47. New York: Russell Sage Foundation, 2005.

———. "Guest Editorial: Christian Realism." *Theology Today* 26 (1970): 367–70.

———. "Harvard and McCarthyism." *Harvard Magazine*, January–February 1998.

———. "Heritage and Choice in American Religion." *Sociologica* 3 (2010). https://doi.org/10.2383/33643. First drafted 1965.

———. "How I Teach the Introductory Course." In *Teaching the Introductory Course in Religious Studies: A Sourcebook*, edited by M. Juergensmeyer, 193–203. Atlanta: Scholars Press, 1990.

———. "Human Conditions for a Good Society." *St. Louis Post-Dispatch*, 100th anniversary ed., March 25, 1979, 8–11.

———. "The Idea of Practices in *Habits*." In *Community in America*, edited by C. H. Reynolds and R. V. Norman, 269–88. Berkeley: University of California Press 1988.

———. "Ienaga Saburo and the Search for Meaning in Modern Japan." In *Imagining Japan*, 78–113. First published in *Changing Japanese Attitudes toward Modernization*, edited by M. Jansen, 369–423 (Princeton, NJ: Princeton University Press, 1965).

———. *Imagining Japan*. Berkeley: University of California Press, 2003.

———. "Intellectual and Society in Japan." In *Imagining Japan*, 150–75. First published in *Daedalus* 101 (1972): 89–115.

———. "Interview with Robert Bellah: Individualism and Commitment in American Life." *Berkeley Journal of Sociology* 30 (1985): 117–41.

———. Introduction to *On Morality and Society*, by E. Durkheim, edited by Bellah, ix–lv. Chicago: University of Chicago Press, 1973.

———. Introduction to R. Bellah and Hammond, *Varieties of Civil Religion*, vii–xv.

———. "Introduction to the Paperback Edition." In *Tokugawa Religion. The Cultural Roots of Modern Japan*, xi–xxi. New York: Free Press, 1985.

———. "Is Individualism Out of Control in America?" *Los Angeles Times*, February 15, 1985.

———. "Is There a Common American Culture? Diversity, Identity and Morality in American Public Life." In R. Bellah and Tipton, *Robert Bellah Reader*, 319–32. First published in *The Power of Religious Publics*, edited by W. H. Swatos Jr. and J. K. Wellman Jr., 53–67, 207–8 (Westport, CT: Praeger, 1998).

———. "Japan, Asia, Religion." *Sociological Inquiry* 39 (1969): 93–95.

———. "Japan's Cultural Identity: Some Reflections on the Work of Watsuji Tetsuro." In *Imagining Japan*, 114–39. First published in the *Journal of Asian Studies* 24 (1965): 573–94.

———. "Language and the Defense of the Native American Life-World." *Church and Society* 79 (1988): 14–26.

———. "Legitimation Processes in Politics and Religion." *Current Sociology* 35 (1987): 89–99.

———. "Liturgy and Experience." In *The Roots of Ritual*, edited by J. D. Shaughnessy, 217–34. Grand Rapids, MI: Eerdmans, 1973.

———. "McCarthyism at Harvard." Letter to the editor. *New York Review of Books* 52 (2005): 42–43.

———. "Meaning and Modernization." In *Beyond Belief*, 64–75. First published in *Religious Studies* 4 (1968): 37–45.

———. "The Necessity of Opportunity and Community in a Good Society." *International Sociology* 12 (1997): 387–93.

———. "The New American Empire." *Commonweal* 129 (2002): 12–14.

———. "The New Consciousness and the Berkeley New Left." In Glock and R. Bellah, *New Religious Consciousness*, 77–92.

———. "New Religious Consciousness and the Crisis in Modernity." In Glock and R. Bellah, *New Religious Consciousness*, 333–52.

———. "The New Religious Consciousness and the Secular University." In *Religion and the Academic Scene*, edited by D. N. Freedman and A. T. Kachel, 1–24. Waterloo, ON: Council on the Study of Religion, 1975.

———. "No Direction Home: Religious Aspects of the American Crisis." In *Search for the Sacred: The New Spiritual Quest*, edited by M. B. Bloy Jr., 65–81. New York: Seabury, 1972.

———. "Outrageous Thoughts on War and Peace." *New Oxford Review* 55 (1993): 15–20.

———. "The Place of Religion in Human Action." *Review of Religion* 22 (1958): 137–54.

———. "Public Philosophy and Public Theology in America Today." In *Civil Religion and Political Theology*, edited by L. S. Rouner, 79–97. Notre Dame, IN: University of Notre Dame Press, 1986.

———. "Read Any Good Books Lately." *California Monthly* 88 (1977): 13.

———. "Reading and Misreading *Habits of the Heart*." *Sociology of Religion* 68 (2007): 189–93.

———. "Reflections on Reality in America." *Radical Religion* 1 (1974): 38–49.

———. "'Reforming' the Welfare Act." *Pacific Church News* 134 (1996): 20–21.

———. "Rejoinder to Lockwood: 'Bellah and His Critics.'" *Anglican Theological Review* 57 (1975): 406–23.

———. "Religion and Legitimation in the American Republic." *Society* 15 (1978): 16–23.

———. "Religion and Polity in America." *Andover Newton Quarterly* 15 (1974): 107–23.

———, ed. *Religion and Progress in Modern Asia*. Glencoe, IL: Free Press, 1965.

————. "Religion and Society in Tokugawa Japan." PhD thesis, Harvard University, April 1955.

————. "Religion and the Future of America." In *Education in a Pluralistic Society*, edited by National Council of Churches of Christ, 29–43. New York: National Council of Churches of Christ, 1975.

————. "Religion: Evolution and Development." In *International Encyclopedia of the Social and Behavioral Sciences*, edited by N. J. Smelser and P. B. Baltes, vol. 19, 13062–66. Oxford: Elsevier, 2001.

————. *Religion in Human Evolution: From the Paleolithic to the Axial Age*. Cambridge, MA: Harvard University Press, 2011.

————. *"Religion in Human Evolution Revisited." Religion, Brain, and Behavior* 2 (2012): 260–70.

————. "Religion in the University: Changing Consciousness, Changing Structures." In *Religion in the Undergraduate Curriculum*, edited by C. Welch, 13–18. Washington, DC: Association of American Colleges, 1972.

————. "Religion, Sociology of." In *Beyond Belief*, 3–19. First published in *International Encyclopedia of the Social Sciences*, edited by D. L. Sills, vol. 13, 406–13 (New York: Macmillan, 1968).

————. "Religious Aspects of Modernization in Turkey and Japan." *American Journal of Sociology* 64 (1958): 1–5.

————. "Religious Evolution." In *Beyond Belief*, 20–50. First published in *American Sociological Review* 29 (1964): 358–74.

————. "The Religious Situation in the Far East." In *Beyond Belief*, 100–13. First published in the *Harvard Divinity Bulletin* 26 (1962).

————. "Religious Tradition and Historical Change." *Transactions of the Institute of Japanese Culture and Classics* 8 (1961): 303–11.

————. "A Reply to My Critics." In Reno and McClay, *Religion and the Social Sciences*, 27–38.

————. "Research Chronicle: Tokugawa Religion." In *Sociologists at Work*, edited by P. E. Hammond, 142–60. New York: Basic Books, 1964.

————. "Response." In *The Religious Situation: 1968*, edited by D. R. Cutler, 388–93. Boston: Beacon, 1968.

————. "A Response to Three Readers." *The Immanent Frame* (blog), February 27, 2012. http://tif.ssrc.org/2012/02/27/a-response-to-three-readers/.

————. Review of part 2 of *The Religious Situation: 1968*, edited by D. R. Cutler. *Journal for the Scientific Study of Religion* 7 (1968): 290–91.

————. Review of *The Religion of India* by Max Weber. *American Sociological Review* 24 (1959): 733.

————. "The Revolution and the Civil Religion." In *Religion and the American Revolution*, edited by J. C. Brauer, 55–73. Philadelphia: Fortress, 1976.

————. "Roots of the American Taboo (on Socialism)." *Nation* 219 (1974): 677–85.

————. "Seventy-Five Years." *South Atlantic Quarterly* 102 (2002): 253–65.

————. "Shinto and Modernization." In *Proceedings, The Second International Conference of Shinto Studies: Theme: Continuity and Change*, 158–62. Tokyo: Kokugakuin University, 1968.

————. "Social Science as Public Philosophy." *Center Magazine* 19 (1986): 8–23.

———. "The Sociology of Religion." In *American Sociology*, edited by T. Parsons, 214–28. New York: Basic Books, 1968.

———. "Some Reflections on the Protestant Ethic Analogy in Asia." In *Beyond Belief*, 53–63. First published in the *Journal of Social Issues* 19 (1963): 52–60.

———. "A Symposium: What Is to Be Done?" *New Republic* 204 (1991): 28.

———. "This Is Our Moment, This Is Our Time." *The Immanent Frame* (blog), January 12, 2009. https://tif.ssrc.org/2009/01/12/this-is-our-moment-this-is-our-time/.

———. "To Kill and Survive or to Die and Become: The Active Life and the Contemplative Life as Ways of Being Adult." In R. Bellah and Tipton, *Robert Bellah Reader*, 81–106. First published in *Daedalus* 105 (1976): 57–77.

———. *Tokugawa Religion: The Values of Pre-industrial Japan*. Glencoe, IL: Free Press, 1957.

———. "Toward Clarity in the Midst of Conflict." *Christianity and Crisis* 44 (1984): 391–93.

———. "Transcendence in Contemporary Piety." In *Beyond Belief*, 196–208. First published in *Transcendence*, edited by H. W. Richardson and D. R. Cutler, 85–97 (Boston: Beacon, 1968).

———. "Transforming American Culture." *Center Magazine* 19 (1986): 2–15.

———. "Two Lectures by Robert N. Bellah: The Maruyama Lecture and Seminar 2007." Occasional Papers no. 5. Center for Japanese Studies, University of California.

———. "Values and Social Change in Modern Japan." Revised version in *Beyond Belief*, 114–45. Original version published in *Asian Cultural Studies* 3 (1963): 13–56.

———. "'Veritas' at Harvard: Another Exchange." *New York Review of Books*, July 14, 1977, 24.

———. "What Changes Very Fast and What Doesn't Change: Explosive Modernity and Abiding Truth." *Journal of Peking University (Philosophy and Social Sciences)* 49, (2012).

———. "What Is Axial about the Axial Age?" *Archives européennes de sociologie* 46 (2005): 69–89.

———. "Where Did Religion Come From?" *The Immanent Frame* (blog), November 2, 2011. http://tif.ssrc.org/2011/11/02/where-did-religion-come-from/.

———. "Words for Paul Tillich." *Harvard Divinity Bulletin* 30 (1966): 15–16.

———. "The World Is the World through Its Theorists: In Memory of Talcott Parsons." *American Sociologist* 15 (1980): 60–62.

———. *Yaburareta Keiyaku*. Tokyo: Miraisha, 1983.

———. "Yes He Can, the Case for Obama." *Commonweal* 135 (2008): 8–9.

Bellah, Robert N., and Christoper Adams. "Beforecare." *Nation* 256 (1993): 378.

———. "Strong Institutions, Good Cities." *Christian Century* 111 (1994): 604–7.

Bellah, Robert N., and Frederick E. Greenspahn, eds. *Uncivil Religion*. New York: Crossroad, 1987.

Bellah, Robert N., and Phillip E. Hammond. *Varieties of Civil Religion*. New York: Harper and Row, 1980.

Bellah, Robert N., and Hans Joas, eds. *The Axial Age and Its Consequences*. Cambridge, MA: Harvard University Press, 2012.

Bellah, Robert N., and Sam Keen. "Civil Religion: The Sacred and the Political in American Life." *Psychology Today* 9 (1976): 58–65.

Bellah, Robert N., Richard Madsen, William M. Sullivan, Ann Swidler, and Steven M. Tipton. *The Good Society*. New York: Alfred A. Knopf, 1991.

————. *Habits of the Heart: Individualism and Commitment in American Life*. Berkeley: University of California Press, 1985.

————. "The House Divided." In *Habits of the Heart*, 2nd ed., vii–xxxix. Berkeley: University of California Press, 1996.

Bellah, Robert N., and William M. Sullivan. "Democratic Culture or Authoritarian Capitalism?" *Society* 18 (1980): 41–50.

Bellah, Robert N., and Steven M. Tipton. *The Robert Bellah Reader*. Durham, NC: Duke University Press, 2006.

Bennett, Michael J. *When Dreams Came True*. Washington, DC: Brassey's, 1996.

Berelson, Bernard. *Graduate Education in the United States*. New York: McGraw-Hill, 1960.

Berger, Peter L. Foreword to *The Culture of Unbelief*, edited by R. Caporale and A. Grumelli, vii–xvi. Berkeley: University of California Press, 1971.

Berkowitz, Edward D. *Something Happened*. New York: Columbia University Press, 2006.

Berling, Judith A. "Theological Consortia: The Creative Space between Church and University." In *Religious Studies, Theological Studies, and the University-Divinity School*, edited by J. Kitagawa, 171–92. Atlanta, GA: Scholars Press, 1992.

Bessner, Daniel. *Democracy in Exile*. Ithaca, NY: Cornell University Press, 2018.

Bird, Kai. *The Color of Truth*. New York: Simon and Schuster, 1998.

Blake, Corey. "Keep the Faith." *Tikkun* 7 (1992): 75–79.

Blau, Eleanor. "Educators Weigh a 'Civil Religion.'" *New York Times*, November 27, 1975.

Bloodworth, J. Jeffrey. "Jimmy Carter's 1976 Presidential Campaign: The Saint, the Sinner, and the Hopeless Dreamer." In *A Companion to Gerald R. Ford and Jimmy Carter*, edited by J. Kaufman, 229–50. Chichester, UK: Wiley Blackwell, 2016.

Bolitho, Harold. "Tokugawa Japan: The Return of the Other?" In *The Postwar Development of Japanese Studies in the Unites States*, edited by H. Hardacre, 85–114. Leiden: Brill, 1998.

Borovoy, Amy. "Dialogues between Area Studies and Social Thought: Robert Bellah's Engagement with Japan." In *The Anthem Companion to Robert N. Bellah*, edited by M. Bortolini, 33–62. London: Anthem, 2019.

Borstelmann, Thomas. *The 1970s*. Princeton: Princeton University Press, 2012.

Bortolini, Matteo. "Back to His Roots." *The Immanent Frame* (blog), March 9, 2012. http://tif.ssrc.org/2012/03/09/back-to-his-roots/.

————. "Before Civil Religion: On Robert N. Bellah's Forgotten Encounters with America, 1955–1965." *Sociologica* 4 (2010). https://doi.org/10.2383/33646.

————. "The 'Bellah Affair' at Princeton: Scholarly Excellence and Academic Freedom in America in the 1970s." *American Sociologist* 42 (2011): 3–33.

———— ed. "Document 4. Robert K. Merton's Letter to Carl Kaysen Containing an Evaluation of Robert N. Bellah's Work (December 9, 1972), 2 Pages." *American Sociologist* 42 (2011): 29–30.

————. "The Trap of Intellectual Success: Robert N. Bellah, the American Civil Religion Debate, and the Sociology of Knowledge." *Theory and Society* 41 (2012): 187–210.

Bortolini, Matteo, and Andrea Cossu. "In the Field but Not of the Field: Clifford Geertz, Robert Bellah, and Interdisciplinary Success." *European Journal of Social Theory* 23 (2020): 328–49.

Bottles, Scott L. *Los Angeles and the Automobile*. Berkeley: University of California Press, 1987.

Bowden, Gary L. Review of "The Good Society" parts 1 and 2 by Bill Moyers. *Canadian Journal of Sociology* 22 (1997): 289–91.

Bowden, Henry W. "An Historian's Response to the Concept of American Civil Religion." *Journal of Church and the State* 17 (1975): 495–505.

Boyd, Nan A. "San Francisco's Castro District: From Gay Liberation to Tourist Destination." *Journal of Tourism and Cultural Change* 9 (2011): 237–48.

———. *Wide Open Town*. Berkeley: University of California Press, 2003.

Bradley, Richard. *Harvard Rules*. New York: Harper Collins, 2005.

Brendle, Michael R. Review of *Sociological Approaches to Religion, The Sociological Interpretation of Religion*, and *Beyond Belief. Sociological Analysis* 31 (1971): 220–23.

Brick, Howard. *Age of Contradiction*. Ithaca, NY: Cornell University Press, 1998.

———. *Transcending Capitalism*. Ithaca, NY: Cornell University Press, 2006.

Brophy, Brigid. "Demolish the Ego." *New York Times*, July 24, 1966.

Brown, Carol. "A History and Analysis of Radical Activism in Sociology, 1967–1969." *Sociological Inquiry* 40 (1970): 27–33.

Brown, Cynthia Stokes. *Refusing Racism*. New York: Teachers College Press, 2002.

Brown, Julia S., and Brian G. Gilmartin. "Sociology Today: Lacunae, Emphases, and Surfeits." *American Sociologist* 4 (1969): 283–91.

Brown, Norman O. *Apocalypse and/or Metamorphosis*. Berkeley: University of California Press, 1991.

———. *Life against Death*. Hanover: Wesleyan University Press, 1985. First published 1959.

———. *Love's Body*. Berkeley: University of California Press, 1990. First published 1966.

———. "A Reply to Herbert Marcuse." *Commentary* 43 (1967): 83–84.

Brown, Susan Love. "Breaking the Habits of the Heart." *Critical Review* 5 (1991): 379–97.

Buck, Paul H. *General Education in a Free Society*. Cambridge, MA: Harvard University Press, 1946.

Bundy, McGeorge. "An Exchange on 'Veritas at Harvard.'" *New York Review of Books* 24 (May 26, 1977).

Burawoy, Michael. "Antinomian Marxist." In Sica and Turner, *Disobedient Generation*, 48–71.

Burawoy, Michael, and Jonathan VanAntwerpen. "Berkeley Sociology: Past, Present and Future." Berkeley Sociology, personal website of Michael Burawoy, November 2001. http://burawoy.berkeley.edu/PS/Berkeley%20Sociology.pdf.

Burghardt, Gordon M. *The Genesis of Animal Play*. Cambridge, MA: MIT Press, 2005.

Burris, Val. "The Academic Caste System: Prestige Hierarchies in PhD Exchange Networks." *American Sociological Review* 69 (1981): 239–64.

Burtt, Shelley. "Communitarian Ethics and Pluralist Politics." *Journal of Politics* 48 (1986): 750–53.

Buxton, William. "Snakes and Ladders: Parsons and Sorokin at Harvard." In *Sorokin and Civilization*, edited by J. B. Ford, M. P. Richard, and P. C. Talbutt, 31–43. New Brunswick, NJ: Transaction, 1996.

Buxton, William J., and Lawrence T. Nichols. "Talcott Parsons and the 'Far East' at Harvard, 1941–48." *American Sociologist* 31, (2000): 5–17.

Calhoun, Craig, ed. *Sociology in America*. Chicago: University of Chicago Press, 2007.

Calí, Grace. *Paul Tillich First-Hand*. Chicago: Exploration, 1996.

"Calling the Roll of Sooner Classes." *Sooner Magazine* 15 (1943): 57.

Camic, Charles. "*Structure after 50 Years: The Anatomy of a Charter.*" *American Journal of Sociology* 95 (1989): 38–107.

———. "Talcott Parsons before *The Structure of Social Action*." In *Talcott Parsons: The Early Essays*, edited by Camic, ix–lxix. Chicago: University of Chicago Press, 1991.

———. "Three Departments in Search of a Discipline: Localism and Interdisciplinary Interaction in American Sociology, 1890–1940." *Social Research* 62 (1995): 1003–33.

———. "The Utilitarians Revisited." *American Journal of Sociology* 85 (1979): 516–50.

———. *Veblen: The Making of an Economist Who Unmade Economics*. Cambridge, MA: Harvard University Press, 2020.

Capozzola, Christopher. "'It Makes You Want to Believe in the Country': Celebrating the Bicentennial in the Age of Limits." In *America in the 70s*, edited by B. Bailey and D. Farber, 29–49. Lawrence: University Press of Kansas, 2004.

Carman, John B., and Kathryn Dodgson. *Community and Colloquy*. Cambridge, MA: Center for the Study of World Religions–Harvard Divinity School, 2006.

Castoriadis, Cornelius. *The Imaginary Institution of Society*. Cambridge: Polity, 1987.

Cavazza, Fabio L., and Stephen R. Graubard, eds. *Il caso italiano*. Milan: Garzanti, 1974.

Champlin, Charles. Review of *Habits of the Heart* by R. N. Bellah et al. *Los Angeles Times*, May 19, 1985.

Chan, Anita, Richard Madsen, and Jonathan Unger. *Chen Village*. Berkeley: University of California Press, 2009.

Chapman, William. "The Battle of Princeton, 1973." *Washington Post*, March 11, 1973.

Cherry, Conrad. "Two American Sacred Ceremonies." *American Quarterly* 21 (1969): 739–54.

Cherry, Frances. "The Nature of *The Nature of Prejudice*." *Journal of the History of the Behavioral Sciences* 36 (2000): 489–98.

Clapp, Rodney. "Habits of the Heart." *Christianity Today* 33 (1989): 20–30.

Clark, Daniel A. "'The Two Joes Meet. Joe College, Joe Veteran': The G. I. Bill, College Education, and Postwar American Culture." *History of Education Quarterly* 38 (1998): 165–89.

Clark, Jim, and Mischa Gabowitsch. "Sociologists and Their Publishers." *Laboratorium* 1 (2009): 151–59.

Clinton, Bill. *My Life*. New York: Alfred A. Knopf, 2004.

———. "A Vision for America: A New Covenant." In *Preface to the Presidency*, edited by S. A. Smith, 212–22. Fayetteville: University of Arkansas Press, 1996.

Cogley, John. "Scholars Agree that U.S. Is in Religious Crisis, but They Dispute Its Nature." *New York Times*, May 16, 1966.

Cohen-Cole, Jamie. *The Open Mind*. Chicago: University of Chicago Press, 2014.

Coleman, John A., SJ, "Remembering Robert N. Bellah." *America Magazine*, August 5, 2013. https://www.americamagazine.org/content/all-things/remembering-robert-n-bellah.

Collins, Richard C. Review of *The Robert Bellah Reader*, edited by R. N. Bellah and S. M. Tipton. *Virginia Quarterly Review* 83 (2007). https://www.vqronline.org/book-notes-9.

Conant, James B. "President's Report." In *Official Register of Harvard University*, 44: 5–23. Cambridge, MA: Harvard University, 1947.

Conaway, J. "Infighting in the Ivory Tower." *Philadelphia Inquirer*, May 5, 1974.

Cossu, Andrea. "Clifford Geertz, Intellectual Autonomy, and Interpretive Social Science." *American Journal of Cultural Sociology*, October 21, 2019. https://doi.org/10.1057/s41290-019-00085-8.

Cot, Annie L. "A 1930s North American Creative Community: The Harvard 'Pareto Circle.'" *History of Political Economy* 43 (2011): 131–59.

Cox, Harvey. *The Future of Faith*. New York: Harper Collins, 2009.

Cracknell, Kenneth. "Introductory Essay." In *Wilfred Cantwell Smith: A Reader*, edited by Cracknell, 1–24. Oxford: Oneworld, 2001.

Crews, Frederick C. "Love in the Western World." *Partisan Review* 34 (1967): 272–87.

Crout, William R. "Paul Tillich: The Harvard Years." *Bulletin of the North American Paul Tillich Society* 33 (2007): 3–16.

Crowther-Heyck, Hunter. "Patrons of the Revolution. Ideals and Institutions in Postwar Behavioral Science." *Isis* 97 (2006): 420–46.

Cuff, Dana. *The Provisional City*. Cambridge, MA: MIT Press, 2000.

Cully, Kendig B. "Robert Bellah and Civil Religion." *New Review of Books and Religion* 1 (1976): 5.

Danbom, David B. Review of *The Good Society* by R. N. Bellah et al. *Journal of American History* 79 (1992): 1259–60.

Darrow, William R. "The Harvard Way in the Study of Religion." *Harvard Theological Review* 81 (1988): 215–34.

Dart, J. "U.S. 'Civil Religion' Puts Faith in Equality, Follows 'Gospel' of the Founding Fathers." *Los Angeles Times*, July 17, 1976.

Davis, Derek H. Review of *The Robert Bellah Reader*, edited by R. N. Bellah and S. M. Tipton. *Journal of Law and Religion* 23 (2007): 347–52.

Davis, Mike. *City of Quartz*. London: Verso, 1990.

Davis, Robert A. "Guidance of Graduate Students." *Journal of Higher Education* 9 (1938): 365–70.

DeParle, Jason. "'Thousand Points' as a Cottage Industry." *New York Times*, May 29, 1991.

Deptula, Nancy M., and Michael M. Hess. *The Edwin O. Reischauer Institute of Japanese Studies*. Cambridge, MA: Harvard University, 1996.

Diamond, Sigmund. *Compromised Campus*. New York: Oxford University Press, 1992.

———. "Veritas at Harvard." *New York Review of Books* 24 (April 28, 1977): 13.

Dickstein, Morris. *Double Agent*. New York: Oxford University Press, 1992.

———. *The Gates of Eden*. Cambridge, MA: Harvard University Press, 1997.

Dinçşahin, Sakir. *State and Intellectuals in Turkey*. Lanham, MD: Lexington Books, 2015.

Disman, Christopher. "The San Francisco Bathhouse Battles of 1984." *Journal of Homosexuality* 44 (2003): 71–129.

Dittes, James E. "Confessing Away the Soul with the Sins, Or, The Risk of Uncle Tomism Among the Humanists: A Reply to Robert N. Bellah." *Bulletin of the Council for the Study of Religion* 2 (1971): 95–98.

Donald, Merlin. *Origins of the Modern Mind*. Cambridge, MA: Harvard University Press, 1991.

Dower, John W. "Sizing Up (and Breaking Down) Japan." In *The Postwar Development of Japanese Studies in the Unites States*, edited by H. Hardacre, 37–84. Leiden: Brill, 1998.

———. *War without Mercy*. New York: Pantheon Books, 1986.

Dozier, Ray. *The Oklahoma Football Encyclopedia*. 2nd ed. New York: Sports Publishing Books, 2013.

Durkheim, Émile. *The Elementary Forms of Religious Life*. New York: Oxford University Press, 2011.

Duster, Troy. *An Oral History with Troy Duster*. Interviews by R. Candida Smith and N. Wilmot. Berkeley: Regional Oral History Office, Bancroft Library, University of California, Berkeley, 2012.

Dworkin, Andrea Sharon. "Bisexual Histories in San Francisco in the 1970s and Early 1980s." *Journal of Bisexuality* 1 (2001): 87–119.

Eden, Philip. "The Cancer of Self-Interest." *Monthly Review* 38 (1986): 37–42.

Eggan, Fred. Review of *Apache Kinship Systems; Wichita Kinship, Past and Present. American Anthropologist* 56 (1954): 124.

Ehrenreich, Barbara. Review of *Habits of the Heart* by R. N. Bellah et al. *Nation*, December 28, 1985.

Eisenstadt, Shmuel N. *Japanese Civilization*. Chicago: University of Chicago Press, 1996.

———. "Mirror-Image Modernities: Contrasting Religious Premises of Japanese and U.S. Modernity." In Madsen et al., *Meaning and Modernity*, 56–77.

———, ed. *The Origins and Diversity of Axial Age Civilizations*. Albany: State University of New York Press, 1986.

Ekbladh, David. *The Great American Mission*. Princeton, NJ: Princeton University Press, 2010.

Ellwood, R. S., Jr. Review of *The New Religious Consciousness*, edited by C. Y. Glock and R. N. Bellah. *Journal of the American Academy of Religion* 46 (1978): 420–21.

Engerman, David C. *Know Your Enemy*. New York: Oxford University Press, 2009.

———. "The Rise and Fall of Wartime Social Sciences: Harvard's Refugee Interview Project, 1950–1954." In *Cold War Social Science*, edited by M. Solovey and H. Cravens, 25–43. Basingstoke, UK: Palgrave, 2012.

———. "Social Science in the Cold War." *Isis* 101 (2010): 393–400.

Erikson, Kay T. "A Return to Zero." *American Scholar* 36 (1966–67): 134–44.

———. "Sociology and the Historical Perspective." *American Sociologist* 5 (1970): 331–38.

Etzioni, Amitai. "Is Bill Clinton a Communitarian?" *National Civic Review* 82 (1993): 221–25.

———. *My Brother's Keeper*. Lanham, MD: Rowman and Littlefield, 2003.

Evans, Paul M. *John Fairbank and the American Understanding of Modern China*. New York: Basil Blackwell, 1988.

Everist, Norma J. Review of *Habits of the Heart* by R. N. Bellah et al. *World and World* 6 (1986): 484–86.

Fan, Shuhua. *The Harvard-Yenching Institute and Cultural Engineering*. Lanham, MD: Lexington Books, 2014.

Feibelman, Julian B. *A Social and Economic Study of the New Orleans Jewish Community*. Philadelphia: University of Pennsylvania, 1941.

Fenn, Richard. "Bellah and the New Orthodoxy." *Sociological Analysis* 37 (1975): 160–66.

Finstuen, Andrew S. *Original Sin and Everyday Protestants*. Chapel Hill: University of North Carolina Press, 2009.

Fiske, Edward B. "Religion: There's Piety in Our Politics." *New York Times*, January 15, 1967.

FitzGerald, Frances. *Cities on a Hill*. New York: Simon and Schuster, 1986.

———. *The Evangelicals*. New York: Simon and Schuster, 2017.

Flacks, Dick. "The Sociology Liberation Movement: Some Legacies and Lessons." *Critical Sociology* 15 (1988): 9–18.

Flores, Ruben. "An Interview with Stephen J. Mennell: Apropos *The Collected Works of Norbert Elias*." *Sociologica* 8 (2014): 1–26.

Footlick, J. K. "Thunderbolts on Olympus." *Newsweek*, March 19, 1973.

Fox, Renée C. *In the Field*. Abingdon, UK: Routledge, 2011.

———. "Talcott Parsons, My Teacher." *American Scholar* 66 (1997): 395–410.

Fox, Richard Wightman. Review of *Habits of the Heart* by R. N. Bellah et al. *American Journal of Sociology* 92 (1986): 183–86.

Freeland, Richard M. *Academia's Golden Age*. New York: Oxford University Press, 1992.

Frohnen, Bruce. "Does Robert Bellah Care about History?" *Intercollegiate Review* 32 (1997): 19–26.

———. *The New Communitarians and the Crisis of Liberalism*. Lawrence: University Press of Kansas, 1996.

Gair, Christopher. *The American Counterculture*. Edinburgh: Edinburgh University Press, 2007.

Galston, William A. "Point of View: Clinton and the Promise of Communitarianism." *Chronicle of Higher Education*, December 2, 1992, A52.

Galston, William A., and Elaine Ciulla Kamarck. *The Politics of Evasion: Democrats and the Presidency*. Progressive Policy Institute, September 1989. https://www.progressivepolicy.org/wp -content/uploads/2013/03/Politics_of_Evasion.pdf.

Gans, Herbert J. "Best-Sellers by Sociologists: An Exploratory Study." *Contemporary Sociology* 26 (1997): 131–35.

———. *Middle American Individualism*. New York: Free Press, 1988.

———. "Sociology in America: The Discipline and the Public." *American Sociological Review* 54 (1989): 1–16.

Geary, Daniel. *Radical Ambition*. Berkeley: University of California Press, 2009.

Geertz, Clifford. *After the Fact*. Cambridge, MA: Harvard University Press, 1995.

———. *The Interpretation of Cultures*. New York: Basic Books, 1973.

———. *Local Knowledge*. New York: Basic Books, 1983.

———. "Religion as a Cultural System." In *Interpretation of Cultures*, 87–125. First published in *Anthropological Approaches to the Study of Religion*, edited by M. P. Banton, 1–46 (London: Tavistock, 1966).

———. "Shifting Aims, Moving Target: On the Anthropology of Religion." *Journal of the Royal Anthropological Institute* 11 (2000): 1–15.

———. "The Work of Robert N. Bellah." *American Sociologist* 42 (2011): 24–27. Drafted 1972.

[Geertz, Clifford, and Robert N. Bellah]. "Program in Social Change." Unsigned statement. *American Sociologist* 42 (2011): 27–29. Drafted 1972.

Geiger, Roger L. *The History of American Higher Education*. Princeton, NJ: Princeton University Press, 2015.

———. *Research and Relevant Knowledge*. New York: Oxford University Press, 1993.

Gilman, Nils. *Mandarins of the Future*. Baltimore: Johns Hopkins University Press, 2003.

Gittinger, Roy. *The University of Oklahoma 1892–1942*. Norman: University of Oklahoma Press, 1942.

Gladden, James W. Review of *Beyond Belief* by R. N. Bellah. *American Sociological Review* 36 (1971): 733–34.

Glazer, Nathan. "What Happened at Berkeley." In *The Berkeley Student Revolt*, edited by S. M. Lipset and S. S. Wolin, 285–303. Garden City, NY: Anchor Books, 1965.

Glock, Charles Y. "Consciousness among Contemporary Youth: An Interpretation." In Glock and Bellah, *New Religious Consciousness*, 353–66.

———. "The Sociology of Religion." In *Sociology Today*, edited by R. K. Merton, L. Broom, and L. S. Cottrell Jr., 153–77. New York: Basic Books. 1959.

Glock, Charles Y., and Robert N. Bellah. *The New Religious Consciousness*. Berkeley: University of California Press, 1976.

Glock, Charles Y., and Rodney Stark. *Religion and Society in Tension*. Chicago: Rand McNally, 1965.

Godfrey, Brian J. *Neighborhoods in Transition*. Berkeley: University of California Press, 1988.

Goldstein, Rebecca. *Incompleteness*. New York: Atlas Books, 2005.

Goodin, Robert E. Review of *Habits of the Heart* by R. N. Bellah et al. *Ethics* 96 (1986): 431–32.

Goodrich, Lawrence J. "Philosophical Tuneup for the US." *Christian Science Monitor*, November 4, 1991.

Gordon, Andrew. *Modern History of Japan*. New York: Oxford University Press, 2003.

Gordon, Tammy S. *The Spirit of 1976*. Amherst: University of Massachusetts Press, 2013.

Gorski, Philip. *American Covenant*. Princeton, NJ: Princeton University Press, 2017.

Gould, Mark. "Axial Age Religious Commitment in Theoretical Perspective." *Sociologica* 7 (2013): 1–18.

Gouldner, Alvin W. *The Coming Crisis of Western Sociology*. New York: Basic Books, 1970.

———. *For Sociology*. New York: Basic Books, 1974.

Graduate Theological Union. *The First Twenty Years*. Berkeley, CA: Graduate Theological Union, 1982.

Grant, William E. "Individualism and the Tensions in American Culture." *American Quarterly* 38 (1986): 311–18.

Greeley, Andrew M. "Habits of the Head." *Society*, May/June 1992, 74–81.

———. Review of *Beyond Belief* by R. N. Bellah. *American Journal of Sociology* 76 (1971): 754–55.

———. Review of *Habits of the Heart* by R. N. Bellah et al. *Sociology and Social Research* 70 (1985): 114.

Greenham, David. *The Resurrection of the Body*. Lanham, MD: Lexington Books, 2006.

Griffiths, Paul. "Impossible Pluralism." In Reno and McClay, *Religion and the Social Sciences*, 44–48.

Grossman, Victor. *Crossing the River*. Amherst: University of Massachusetts Press, 2003.

Guetzkow, Joshua, Michèle Lamont, and Grégoire Mallard. "What is Originality in the Humanities and the Social Sciences?" *American Sociological Review* 69 (2004): 190–212.

Guhin, Jeffrey. Review of *Religion in Human Evolution* by R. N. Bellah. *Sociology of Religion* 74 (2013): 416–17.

———. "Robert Bellah's Catholic Imagination." In *The Anthem Companion to Robert N. Bellah*, edited by M. Bortolini, 127–45. London: Anthem, 2019.

Guseman, Patricia K. Review of *Habits of the Heart* by R. N. Bellah et al. *Rural Sociology* 51 (1986): 133–34.

Guttman, Amy. "Communitarian Critics of Liberalism." *Philosophy and Public Affairs* 14 (1985): 308–22.

Habermas, Jürgen. *Between Naturalism and Religion*. Cambridge: Polity Press, 2008.

Hadden, Jeffrey K. "Editor's Introduction." *Journal for the Scientific Study of Religion* 14 (1975): 385–90.

Halberstam, David. *The Best and the Brightest*. New York: Random House, 1972.

Handler, Richard. "An Interview with Clifford Geertz." *Current Anthropology* 32 (1991): 603–13.

Hanford, A. C. "The College." In *Official Register of Harvard University*, 45: 97–98. Cambridge, MA: Harvard University, 1948.

Hann, Christopher. "Humans and their Hierarchies: Cosmological and Sociological." *Archives européennes de sociologie* 53 (2012): 315–22.

Hanson, Maynard J. "William Judson Holloway, 1929–1931." In *Oklahoma's Governors, 1929–1955: Depression to Prosperity*, edited by L. H. Fischer, 31–53. Oklahoma City: Oklahoma Historical Society, 1983.

Harding, Vincent. "Toward a Darkly Radiant Vision of America's Truth: A Letter of Concern, an Invitation to Re-creation." In *Community in America*, edited by C. H. Reynolds and R. V. Norman, 67–83. Berkeley: University of California Press, 1988.

Harp, Anne B. *The Sooner Story*. Norman: University of Oklahoma Press, 2015.

Harral, Stewart. "Portrait of a Sooner Who Heads the State Press." *Sooner Magazine* 9 (1937): 281.

Harris, Charles H., and Louis R. Sadler. *The Great Call-Up*. Norman: University of Oklahoma Press, 2015.

Harris, John F. *The Survivor*. New York: Random House, 2005.

Hart, D. G. *The University Gets Religion*. Baltimore: Johns Hopkins University Press, 1999.

Hartman, Andrew. *A War for the Soul of America*. Chicago: University of Chicago Press, 2010.

Hartzell, Karl D., and Harrison Sasscer. *The Study of Religion on Campus*. Washington, DC: Association of American Colleges, 1967.

"The Harvard Tercentenary Celebrations." *Nature* 138 (1936): 667–70.

Hauerwas, Stanley. "A Communitarian Lament." *First Things*, January 1992, 45–46.

Hauser, Philip M. "Samuel Andrew Stouffer, 1900–1960." *American Statistician* 14 (1960): 36.

Hearn, Charles R. *The American Dream in the Great Depression*. Westport, CT: Greenwood, 1977.

Helquist, Michael. "Beyond the Baths: The Other Sex Businesses." *Journal of Homosexuality* 44 (2003): 177–201. First published 1984.

Herberg, Will. *Protestant, Catholic, Jew*. Garden City, NY: Doubleday, 1955.

Hernandez, Javier C. "Summer Resigns." *Harvard Crimson*, February 22, 2006.

Hershberg, James. *James B. Conant*. Stanford, CA: Stanford University Press, 1995.

Heyck, Hunter. *Age of System*. Baltimore: Johns Hopkins University Press, 2015.

Hill, Samuel S., Jr. Review of *Beyond Belief* by R. N. Bellah. *Journal of the American Academy of Religion* 41 (1973): 447–48, 450.

Hilzenrath, David S. "Raisa's Woman to Women Chat." *Washington Post*, December 11, 1987.

Hoehl, Lockwood. "An Interview with Robert Bellah, 'We're in the Lull between Two Storms,'"
    Witness 62 (1979): 7–9, 13.

Holbrook, Clyde A. *Religion: A Humanistic Field*. Englewood Cliffs, NJ: Prentice-Hall, 1963.

Holland, Darrell. "Cardinal Urges Work for the Common Good." *Plain Dealer*, May 29, 1989.

Homans, George C. *Coming to My Senses*. New Brunswick, NJ: Transaction Books, 1984.

Homans, George C., and Orville T. Bailey. "The Society of Fellows at Harvard University."
    American Scientist 37 (1949): 91–106.

Hopkins, George O. "Harry B. Rutledge: Oklahoma's N. E. A. Secretary." *Sooner Magazine* 5
    (1935): 146–50.

Horn, Heather. "Where Does Religion Come From?" *Atlantic*, August 17, 2011.

Horowitz, Daniel. *The Anxieties of Affluence*. Amherst: University of Massachusetts Press,
    2004.

———. *Jimmy Carter and the Energy Crisis of the 1970s*. Boston: Bedford/St. Martin's, 2005.

Horwitt, Sanford D. "Democratic Vistas." *Washington Post*, September 8, 1991.

Hunter, James Davidson. Review of *Habits of the Heart* by R. N. Bellah et al. *Journal for the
    Scientific Study of Religion* 25 (1986): 373–74.

Ingham, John. Review of *Habits of the Heart* by R. N. Bellah et al. *Canadian Journal of History* 21
    (1986): 292–94.

Institute for Advanced Study. *A Community of Scholars. The Institute for Advanced Study Faculty
    and Members 1930–1980*. Princeton, NJ: Institute for Advanced Study, 1980.

"In the Mail. . . ." *Sooner Magazine* 11 (1938): 2.

Isaac, Jeffrey. "Epistemic Design: Theory and Data in Harvard's Department of Social Relations."
    In *Cold War Social Science*, edited by M. Solovey and H. Cravens, 79–95. Basingstoke, UK:
    Palgrave, 2012.

———. "Theorist at Work: Talcott Parsons and the Carnegie Project on Theory, 1949–1951."
    Journal of the History of Ideas 71 (2010): 287–311.

———. "Tool Shock: Technique and Epistemology in the Postwar Social Sciences." *History of
    Political Economy* 42, Suppl. 1 (2010): 133–64.

———. *Working Knowledge*. Cambridge, MA: Harvard University Press, 2012.

"Ivory Tower Tempest." *Time*, March 19, 1973.

Jameson, Frederic. "On *Habits of the Heart*." In *Community in America*, edited by C. H. Reynolds
    and R. V. Norman, 97–112. Berkeley: University of California Press, 1988.

Jaspers, Karl. *The Origin and Goal of History*. New Haven, CT: Yale University Press, 1953.

Jencks, Christopher, and David Riesman. *The Academic Revolution*. Garden City, NY: Double-
    day, 1968.

Jendrysik, Mark S. *Modern Jeremiahs*. Lanham, MD: Lexington Books, 2008.

Jenkins, Philip. *Decade of Nightmares*. New York: Oxford University Press, 2006.

Joas, Hans. "A Conversation with Robert Bellah." *Hedgehog Review* 14 (2012): 72–78.

———. *Do We Need Religion?* Abingdon, UK: Routledge, 2016.

———. "Habits of the Heart." *The Immanent Frame* (blog), August 11, 2013. https://tif.ssrc.org
    /2013/08/11/habits-of-the-heart/.

———. *The Sacredness of the Person*. Washington, DC: Georgetown University Press, 2013.

Johnsen, Thomas. "Reaffirming Bedrock Civic Values in a Society Devoted to the Individual."
    Christian Science Monitor, June 17, 1985.

Johnson, Benton. Review of *The Broken Covenant* by R. N. Bellah. *Contemporary Sociology* 6 (1977): 82–83.

Johnston, Barry V. *Pitirim A. Sorokin*. Lawrence: University Press of Kansas, 1995.

———. "Sorokin and Parsons at Harvard: Institutional Conflict and the Origin of a Hegemonic Tradition." *Journal of the History of the Behavioral Sciences* 22 (1986): 107–27.

Jones, Don G. Review of *The Broken Covenant* by R. N. Bellah. *Sociological Analysis* 37 (1976): 183–87.

Jones, Landon Y., Jr. "Bad Days on Mount Olympus: The Big Shoot-Out at the Institute for Advanced Study." *Atlantic Monthly* 233 (1974): 37–46, 51–53.

Kagan, Jerome. *The Three Cultures*. Cambridge: Cambridge University Press, 2009.

Karabel, Jerome. *The Chosen*. Boston: Houghton Mifflin, 2005.

Karcher, Barbara C., Jack O. Balswick, and Ira E. Robinson. "Empiricism, Symbolic Realism, and the Mystique of the Extreme." *Sociological Quarterly* 22 (1981): 93–103.

Kathan, Boardman, and Nancy Fuchs-Kreimer. "Civil Religion in America: A Bibliography." *Religious Education* 70 (1975): 541–50.

Kaysen, Carl. *Report of the Director 1966–1976*. Princeton, NJ: Institute for Advanced Study, 1976.

Keen, Sam. "Norman O. Brown's Body: A Conversation between Brown and Warren G. Bennis." *Psychology Today* 4 (August 1970): 43–47.

Keen, Sam, and G. T. Harris. "The Elegance of Math Can't Measure the Rich Record of Human Belief." *Psychology Today* 9 (1976): 9, 60, 63.

Keller, Morton, and Phyllis Keller. *Making Harvard Modern*. New York: Oxford University Press, 2001.

Kelly, William. *A History of Fort Dix, New Jersey*. Fort Dix, NJ: Information Office of the US Army Training Center, 1967.

Kenen, Stephanie H. "Who Counts When You're Counting Homosexuals? Hormones and Homosexuality in Mid-Century America." In *Science and Homosexualities*, edited by V. A. Rosario, 197–218. New York: Routledge, 1997.

Kennedy, David M. *Freedom from Fear*. New York: Oxford University Press, 1999.

Kerr, Clark. *The Gold and the Blue*. Vol. 1, *Academic Triumphs*. Berkeley: University of California Press, 2001.

———. *The Uses of the University*. Cambridge, MA: Harvard University Press, 2001. First published 1966.

Khalil, Osamah F. *America's Dream Palace*. Cambridge, MA: Harvard University Press, 2016.

Killen, Andreas. *1973 Nervous Breakdown*. New York: Bloomsbury, 2006.

Klausner, Samuel Z. "Scientific and Humanistic Study of Religion: A Comment on 'Christianity and Symbolic Realism.'" *Journal for the Scientific Study of Religion* 9 (1970): 100–106.

Knöbl, Wolfgang. "Theories that Won't Pass Away: The Never-ending Story of Modernization Theory." In *Handbook of Historical Sociology*, edited by G. Delanty and E. F. Isin, 96–107. London: Sage, 2003.

Korom, Philipp. "The Prestige Elite in Sociology: Toward a Collective Biography of the Most Cited Scholars (1970–2010)." *Sociological Quarterly* 61 (2020): 128–63.

Koschmann, J. Victor. "Intellectuals and Politics." In *Postwar Japan as History*, edited by A. Gordon, 395–423. Berkeley: University of California Press, 1993.

Kristol, William. "Beyond Individualism?" *Commentary* 80 (1985): 76–79.

Kroeber, Alfred L., and Talcott Parsons. "The Concepts of Culture and of Social System." *American Sociological Review* 23 (1958): 582–83.

Kroeber, Theodora. *Alfred Kroeber*. Berkeley: University of California Press, 1970.

Kruse, Kevin M., and Julian E. Zelizer. *Fault Lines*. New York: W. W. Norton, 2019.

Lant, J. L. *Our Harvard*. New York: Taiplinger, 1982.

Lardner, James. "Amitai Etzioni Prescribes for Society's Ills." *Washington Post*, December 27, 1982.

Lasch, Christopher. "The Communitarian Critique of Liberalism." In *Community in America*, edited by C. H. Reynolds and R. V. Norman, 173–84. Berkeley: University of California Press, Berkeley, 1988.

————. "The Search for Meaning in a Narcissistic Age." *In These Times*, June 26–July 9, 1985, 18–19.

Latham, Michael E. *Modernization as Ideology*. Chapel Hill: University of North Carolina Press, 2000.

Le Beau, Bryan F. *The Atheist*. New York: New York University Press, 2003.

Lerner, Daniel. *The Passing of Traditional Society*. New York: Macmillan, 1958.

Levy, David W. *The University of Oklahoma: A History*. 2 vols. Norman: University of Oklahoma Press, 2015.

Levy, Marion J., Jr. "Contrasting Factors in the Modernization of China and Japan." *Economic Development and Cultural Change* 2 (1954): 161–97.

————. *The Structure of Society*. Princeton, NJ: Princeton University Press, 1952.

Lewenstein, Bruce V. "Was There Really a Popular Science 'Boom'?" *Science, Technology, and Human Values* 12 (1987): 29–41.

Lewis, Anthony. "The System: We Have Really Seen the Future and It WORKS! It WORKS! It WORKS!" *New York Times*, July 4, 1976.

Lewis, Lionel S. "On Subjective and Objective Rankings in Sociology Departments." *American Sociologist* 3 (1968): 129–31.

Lieberson, Stanley. "Einstein, Renoir, and Greeley: Some Thoughts about Evidence in Sociology." *American Sociological Review* 57 (1992): 1–15.

Lindsay, D. Michael. "Good Habits of Mind." *Commonweal*, April 3, 2007.

Lipset, David. *Gregory Bateson*. Englewood Cliffs, NJ: Prentice-Hall, 1980.

Lipset, Seymour M. *The First New Nation*. New York: W. W. Norton, 1963.

————. "Political Controversies at Harvard, 1636 to 1974." In *Education and Politics at Harvard*, edited by S. M. Lipset and D. Riesman, 3–278. New York: McGraw-Hill, 1975.

Lipset, Seymour M., and Paul Seabury. "The Lesson of Berkeley." In *The Berkeley Student Revolt*, edited by S. M. Lipset and S. S. Wolin, 340–49. Garden City, NY: Anchor Books, 1965.

Lipsitz, Lewis. "If, as Verba Says, the State Functions as a Religion, What Are We to Do Then to Save Our Souls?" *American Political Science Review* 62 (1968): 527–35.

Lockman, Zachary. *Contending Visions of the Middle East*. Cambridge: Cambridge University Press, 2010.

————. *Field Notes*. Stanford, CA: Stanford University Press, 2016.

Lockwood, Joan. "Bellah and His Critics: An Ambiguity in Bellah's Concept of Civil Religion." *Anglican Theological Review* 57 (1975): 416–23.

Lowell, A. Lawrence. "Dormitories and College Life." *Harvard Graduates' Magazine*, June 1904.

Luhmann, Niklas. *Introduction to Systems Theory*. Cambridge: Polity, 2013.

Lukes, Steven. "The Rhetoric of Thick Consensus." *Contemporary Sociology* 21 (1992): 425–26.

"Luther Hutton Bellah." *Sooner Magazine* 3 (1931): 301–2

Lynd, Alice, and Staughton Lynd. *Stepping Stones*. Plymouth, UK: Lexington Books, 2006.

Lynn, Robert Wood. "Civil Catechetics in Mid-Victorian America." *Religious Education* 68 (1972): 5–27.

Macey, David. *The Lives of Michel Foucault*. London: Random House UK, 1993.

MacIntyre, Alasdair. *After Virtue*. Notre Dame, IN: Notre Dame University Press, 2007. First published 1981.

Madsen, Richard. *Morality and Power in a Chinese Village*. Berkeley: University of California Press, 1984.

———. "Robert Bellah: In Memoriam." *Hedgehog Review* 15 (2013): 96.

———. "Weber for the 21st Century." *The Immanent Frame* (blog), November 9, 2011. http://tif .ssrc.org/2011/11/09/weber-for-the-21st-century/.

Madsen, Richard, William M. Sullivan, Ann Swidler, and Steven M. Tipton, eds. *Meaning and Modernity*. Berkeley: University of California Press, 2002.

"Magazine Is Passed Around." *Sooner Magazine* 9 (1937): 195.

Manseau, Peter. "The Big Bang." *Bookforum*, September–November 2011. http://www .bookforum.com/inprint/018_03/8302.

Marangudakis, Manussos. "Multiple Modernities and the Theory of Indeterminacy." *Protosociology* 29 (2012): 7–25.

Marcuse, Herbert. "Love Mystified: A Critique of Norman O. Brown." In *Negations: Essays in Critical Theory*, 171–86. London: MayFly, 2009. First published in *Commentary* 43 (1967).

Martin, David. "Searching for the Agorà." *Times Literary Supplement*, September 20, 1985.

———. "What Should We Now Do Differently?" *The Immanent Frame* (blog), November 16, 2011. http://tif.ssrc.org/2011/11/16/what-should-we-now-do-differently/.

Marty, Martin E. *The New Shape of American Religion*. New York: Harper, 1959.

———. Review of *Habits of the Heart* by R. N. Bellah et al. *Christian Century*, May 15, 1985, 499–501.

———. Review of *The Broken Covenant* by R. N. Bellah. *American Journal of Sociology* 82 (1976): 230–32.

———. "The Sociologists' Religion under Glass." *National Catholic Reporter*, April 9, 1969.

Mathewes, Charles. "The Evolution of Religion." *American Interest*, July/August 2012.

Mathisen, James. "Twenty Years after Bellah: Whatever Happened to American Civil Religion?" *Sociological Analysis* 50 (1989): 129–46.

Mattingly, Paul H. *American Academic Cultures*. Chicago: University of Chicago Press, 2017.

Mattson, Kevin. *What the Heck Are You Up To, Mr. President?* New York: Bloomsbury, 2009.

Maxa, Rudy. "A Sociologist at the White House? Etzioni Is a Man for All Reasons." *Washington Post*, January 27, 1980.

McAdams, Dan. Foreword to *Explorations in Personality* by H. A. Murray, vii–xxxvi. New York: Oxford University Press, 2008.

McDowell, Edwin. "Harper's Wins Rights to Reprint 'The Lover.'" *New York Times*, August 15, 1985.

McKeon, Zahava K. "General Introduction." In *Selected Writings of Richard McKeon*, Vol. 1, *Philosophy, Science, and Culture*, edited by McKeon and W. G. Swenson, 1–21. Chicago: University of Chicago Press, 1998.

McKeon, Richard. "Philosophic Semantics and Philosophic Inquiry." In *Selected Writings of Richard McKeon*, Vol. 1, *Philosophy, Science, and Culture*, edited by Z. K. McKeon and W. G. Swenson, 209–21. Chicago: University of Chicago Press, 1998.

McNall, Scott. "Is Democracy Possible?" *Sociological Forum* 2 (1987): 167–76.

Melzer, Arthur M., et al., eds. *The Public Intellectual*. Lanham, MD: Rowman and Littlefield, 2003.

Mendieta, Eduardo. "Religious Origins." *Contexts* 11 (2012): 72–74.

Merton, Robert K. "Remembering the Young Talcott Parsons." *American Sociologist* 15 (1980): 68–71.

Mettler, Suzanne. *Soldiers to Citizens*. New York: Oxford University Press, 2005.

Mews, Stuart. "Paul Tillich and the Religious Situation of American Intellectuals." *Religion* 2 (1972): 122–40.

Mieczowski, Yanek. *Gerald Ford and the Challenges of the 1970s*. Lexington: University Press of Kentucky, 2005.

Miles, Jack. Review of *Religion in Human Evolution* by R. N. Bellah. *Journal of the American Academy of Religion* 81 (2013): 852–64.

Miller, James. *The Passions of Michel Foucault*. New York: Anchor Books, 1993.

Miller, Stephen. *Excellence and Equity*. Lexington: University Press of Kentucky, 1984.

Mills, C. Wright. *Power, Politics and People*. Edited by I. L. Horowitz. New York: Oxford University Press, 1963.

Mitchell, Douglas. "Creating Community through Communication." *Schools, Studies in Education* 13 (2016): 243–48.

Moberg, David O. Review of *The New Religious Consciousness*, edited by C. Y. Glock and R. N. Bellah. *American Journal of Sociology* 83 (1978): 1074–77.

Moltmann, Jürgen. "Political Theology." *Theology Today* 28 (1971): 6–23.

Moore, Deborah D. *G.I. Jews*. Cambridge, MA: Harvard University Press, 2004.

Moore, Kelly. *Disrupting Science*. Princeton, NJ: Princeton University Press, 2008.

Morrison, Karl F. "The Holy of Holies Was Empty: Robert Bellah's Quest for Wisdom." *Contemporary Sociology* 41 (2012): 721–32.

Moyers, Bill. *A World of Ideas*. New York: Doubleday, 1989.

Mulder, John M. "The Bicentennial Book Band." *Theology Today* 32 (1975): 277–86.

Müller-Doohm, Stephan. *Habermas*. Cambridge: Polity, 2016.

Mullins, Nicholas C. *Theories and Theory Groups in Contemporary American Sociology*. New York: Harper and Row, 1973.

Münch, Richard. "Talcott Parsons and the Theory of Action. I: The Structure of the Kantian Core." *American Journal of Sociology* 86 (1981): 709–39.

Murphey, Murray G. "On the Scientific Study of Religion in the United States, 1870–1980." in *Religion and Twentieth Century American Life*, edited by M. J. Lacey, 136–71. Cambridge: Cambridge University Press, 1989.

Myers, Robert J. "The Good Society Redux." *Society*, May/June 1992, 70–73.

Najita, Tetsuro, and Irwin Scheiner, eds. *Japanese Thought in the Tokugawa Period*. Chicago: University of Chicago Press, 1978.

Nefsky, Marylin F. Review of *Imagining Japan* by R. N. Bellah. *Sociology of Religion* 66 (2005): 85–86.

Nelson, Benjamin. "Is the Sociology of Religion Possible?" *Journal for the Scientific Study of Religion* 9 (1970): 107–11.

Neuhaus, Richard J. "Habits of the (Academic) Heart." *Public Interest* 83 (1986): 99–104.

———. "Review of *Reconstructing Public Philosophy* by W. M. Sullivan. *Journal of Law and Religion* 1 (1983): 435–38.

———. "Robert Bellah and Social Democracy." *First Things* 1 (1990): 61–72.

Nichols, Larry T. "The Establishment of Sociology at Harvard: A Case of Organizational Ambivalence and Scientific Vulnerability." In *Science at Harvard University: Historical Perspectives*, edited by C. A. Elliott and M. Rossiter, 191–222. Bethlehem, PA: Lehigh University Press, 1992.

Nicholson, Ian A. M. *Inventing Personality*. Washington, DC: American Psychological Association, 2003.

Nicolaus, Martin. "Fat-Cat Sociology: Remarks at the American Sociological Association Convention." *American Sociologist* 4 (1969): 154–56.

———. "The Professional Organization of Sociology: A View from Below." In *Radical Sociology*, edited by J. D. Colfax and J. L. Roach, 45–60. New York: Basic Books, 1971. First published 1969.

Novak, Michael. "America as Religion." *Religious Education* 71 (1976): 260–67.

———. "Habits of the Left-Wing Heart." *National Review*, June 28, 1985, 37.

Novick, Peter. *That Noble Dream*. Cambridge: Cambridge University Press, 1988.

Ogles, Richard H., Marion J. Levy Jr., and Talcott Parsons. "Culture and Social Systems: An Exchange." *American Sociological Review* 24 (1959): 246–50.

Oppenheimer, Martin, Martin J. Murray, and Rhonda F. Levine, eds. *Radical Sociologists and the Movement*. Philadelphia: Temple University Press, 1991.

Otten, Michael A. *University Authority and the Student*. Berkeley: University of California Press, 1970.

Owens, B. Robert. "Producing Parsons' Reputation: Early Critiques of Talcott Parsons' Social Theory and the Making of a Caricature." *Journal for the History of Behavioral Sciences* 46 (2010): 165–88.

Packard, George R. *Edwin Reischauer and the American Discovery of Japan*. New York: Columbia University Press, 2010.

Parmar, Inderjeet. *Foundations of the American Century*. New York: Columbia University Press, 2002.

Parsons, Talcott. *Action Theory and the Human Condition*. New York: Free Press, 1978.

———. "Christianity and Modern Industrial Society." In *Sociological Theory, Values, and Sociocultural Change*, edited by E. Tiryakian, 33–70. New York: Free Press, 1963.

———. "Clyde Kluckhohn and the Integration of Social Science." In W. Taylor et al., *Culture and Life*, 30–57.

———. "Durkheim on Religion Revisited: Another Look at 'The Elementary Forms of the Religious Life.'" In *Action Theory*, 213–32.

———. "The Editor's Column." *American Sociologist* 1 (1966): 182–84.

———. "The Editor's Column." *American Sociologist* 2 (1967): 62–64.

———. "Graduate Training in Social Relations at Harvard." *Journal of General Education* 5 (1951): 149–57.

———. Introduction to *American Sociology*, edited by Parsons, ix–xix. New York: Basic Books, 1968.

———. Introduction to *The Study of Sociology* by H. Spencer, v–x. Ann Arbor: University of Michigan Press, 1961.

———. "Law as an Intellectual Stepchild." *Sociological Inquiry* 47 (1977): 11–58.

———. "The Pattern of Religious Organization in America." *Daedalus* 87 (1958): 65–85.

———. "The Present Position and Prospects of Systematic Theory in Sociology." In *Twentieth Century Sociology*, edited by G. Gurvitch and W. E. Moore, 42–69. New York: Philosophical Library, 1945.

———. "Religion in a Modern Pluralistic Society." *Review of Religion Research* 7 (1966): 125–46.

———. *The Social System*. London: Routledge, 2001. First published 1951.

———. "Some Problems Confronting Sociology as a Profession." *American Sociological Review* 24 (1959): 547–58.

Parsons, Talcott, and Gerald M. Platt. *The American University*. New York: Free Press, 1973.

Parsons, Talcott, and Edward A. Shils, eds. *Toward a General Theory of Action*. Cambridge, MA: Harvard University Press, 1951.

Parsons, Talcott, and Neil J. Smelser. *Economy and Society*. Glencoe, IL: Free Press, 1956.

Patterson, James T. *Restless Giant*. New York: Oxford University Press, 2005.

Pattullo, Edward L. "Dean Bundy Deals with McCarthyism." *Harvard Magazine*, September–October 1998.

Paul, Herman. "Sources of the Self: Scholarly Personae as Repertoires of Scholarly Selfhood." *BMGN—The Low Countries Historical Review* 131 (2016): 135–54.

Payne, Richard K. "Bellah's *Religion in Human Evolution*: Four Theoretical Issues." *Religion, Brain, and Behavior* 2 (2012): 249–55.

Peacock, James L. "America as a Cultural System." In *Community in America*, edited by C. H. Reynolds and R. V. Norman, 37–46. Berkeley: University of California Press, 1988.

Pearson, Birger A. "Religious Studies at Berkeley." *Religion* 29 (1999): 303–13.

Pepper, George. "Religion and Evolution." *Sociological Analysis* 31 (1970): 78–91.

Pettigrew, Thomas. "Gordon Willard Allport: A Tribute." *Journal of Social Issues* 55 (1999): 415–28.

Phelan, Gerald J., SJ. "III. Report on the Discussions at the Symposium on 'the Culture of Unbelief.'" *Bollettino del Segretariato per i non-credenti* 4 (1969): 55–61.

Piven, Frances Fox. "Why Exhortation Is Not a Strategy." *Contemporary Sociology* 21 (1992): 427–28.

Potter, Ralph. "Qualms of a Believer." In *Community in America*, edited by C. H. Reynolds and R. V. Norman, 115–26. Berkeley: University of California Press, 1988.

Power, Willow R. "The Harvard Study of Values: Mirror for Postwar Anthropology." *Journal of the History of Behavioral Sciences* 36 (2000): 15–29.

"President of State Editors." *Sooner Magazine* 30 (1931): 363.

Preston, Samuel. "Paradise Lost." *Contemporary Sociology* 21 (1992): 428–30.

Price, David H. *Cold War Anthropology*. Durham, NC: Duke University Press, 2003.

Rabinow, Paul. *The Accompaniment*. Chicago: University of Chicago Press, 2011.

———. *Reflections on Fieldwork in Morocco*. Berkeley: University of California Press, 2007.

Rabinow, Paul, and William M. Sullivan, eds. *Interpretive Social Science*. Berkeley: University of California Press, 1979.

Raeside, J. "A Night at Camp David." Abridged version. In Horowitz, *Jimmy Carter*, 152–57. Full version published in *East Bay Express*, July 27, 1979, 1, 3–4.

Rajagopal, Arvind. "Interview with Robert Bellah." *Perspectives* 35 (2013): 1, 7, 11.

———. "Talcott Parsons' Favorite Student: An Interview with Robert N. Bellah." *Public Books*, January 6, 2014. https://www.publicbooks.org/talcott-parsonss-favorite-student-an-interview-with-robert-n-bellah.

Ram, Uri. *Israeli Sociology*. Basingstoke, UK: Palgrave, 2018.

Reader, Ian. Review of *Imagining Japan* by R. N. Bellah. *Philosophy East and West* 56 (2006): 351–55.

Regis, Ed. *Who Got Einstein's Office?* New York: Basic Books, 1987.

Reischauer, Edwin O. "Serge Elisséeff." *Harvard Journal of Asian Studies* 20 (1957): 1–35.

Reischauer, Edwin O., and John K. Fairbank. "Understanding the Far East through Area Studies." *Far Eastern Survey* 17 (1948): 121–23.

Reno, R. R., and B. McClay, eds. *Religion and the Social Sciences*. Eugene, OR: Wipf and Stock, 2015.

Reynolds, L., Jr. "The Later Years (1880–1953)." In *The Harvard Divinity School*, edited by G. H. Williams, 165–229. Boston: Beacon, 1954.

Rhoades, Lawrence J. *A History of the American Sociological Association, 1905–1980*. Washington, DC: American Sociological Association, 1981.

Richardson, Herbert. "Civil Religion in Theological Perspective." In Richey and Jones, *American Civil Religion*, 161–84.

Richey, Russell E., and Donald Jones, eds. *American Civil Religion*. New York: Harper and Row, 1974.

Rieder, J., and N. Wiley. Review of *The Cultural Contradictions of Capitalism* by Daniel Bell, *Legitimation Crisis* by Jürgen Habermas and Thomas McCarthy, and *The Fiscal Crisis of the State* by James O'Connor. *Contemporary Sociology* 6 (1977): 411–24.

Rieff, Philip. Review of *The Culture of Unbelief*, edited by R. Caporale and A. Grumelli. *Contemporary Sociology* 1 (1972): 505–7.

Riesebrodt, Martin. "Dangerous Evolutions?" *The Immanent Frame* (blog): November 23, 2011. http://tif.ssrc.org/2011/11/23/dangerous-evolutions/.

Riker, William H. "Learning to Love the 'Me Generation.'" *Wall Street Journal*, March 27, 1985.

Riley, John W. "Talcott Parsons: An Anecdotal Profile." *American Sociologist* 15 (1980): 66–68.

Roark, Anne C. "Study Assails Values of the New Right as 'Cancerous.'" *Los Angeles Times*, January 25, 1985.

Robbins, Thomas. "Old Wine in New Bottles." *Journal for the Scientific Study of Religion* 16 (1976): 310–13.

Robbins, Thomas, Dick Anthony, and Thomas E. Curtis. "The Limits of Symbolic Realism: Problems of Empathic Field Observation in a Sectarian Context." *Journal for the Scientific Study of Religion* 12 (1973): 259–71.

———. "Reply to Bellah." *Journal for the Scientific Study of Religion* 13 (1974): 491–95.

"Robert Bellah Talks about Real Happiness." *Door* 105 (1989): 16–17, 36–37.

Roberts, Nicole E. "The Plight of Gay Visibility: Intolerance in San Francisco, 1970–1979." *Journal of Homosexuality* 60 (2013): 105–19.

Robertson, Roland. Review of *The Broken Covenant* by R. N. Bellah. *Sociological Analysis* 37 (1976): 184–87.

Rockefeller Foundation. *The Search for a Value Consensus: Papers Presented at a Rockefeller Foundation Conference (New York, New York, March 28–29, 1978)*. New York: Rockefeller Foundation, 1978.

Roderick, Kevin. *Wilshire Boulevard*. Los Angeles: Angel City, 2005.

Roetz, Heiner. *Confucian Ethics of the Axial Age*. Albany: State University of New York Press, 1993.

Rofes, Eric. *A Walking Tour of South of Market in the 1970s*. Scribd, accessed November 22, 2020. https://www.scribd.com/document/257572676/70s-Walking-Tour.

Rohde, Joy. *Armed with Expertise*. Ithaca, NY: Cornell University Press, 2013.

Roof, Wade Clark. Review of *The New Religious Consciousness*, edited by C. Y. Glock and R. N. Bellah. *Society* 14 (July 1977): 94–95.

Rorabaugh, W. J. *Berkeley at War*. New York: Oxford University Press, 1989.

Rostow, Walt W. "The Take-Off into Self-Sustained Growth." *Economic Journal* 66 (1956): 25–48.

Roszak, Thomas. *The Making of a Counter Culture*. Garden City, NY: Anchor Books, 1969.

———. "Professor Dionysus." *New Politics* 5 (1966): 123–24.

Runciman, W. G. *The Theory of Cultural and Social Selection*. Cambridge: Cambridge University Press, 2009.

Ruppert, R. "Fundamental Question: Is It Spiritual?" *Seattle Times*, April 17, 1976, A6.

Ryan, Alan. "Disunited States." *New Republic*, November 4, 1991, 28–31.

Sackley, Nicole. "Cosmopolitanism and the Uses of Tradition: Robert Redfield and Alternative Visions of Modernization During the Cold War." *Modern Intellectual History* 9 (2012): 565–95.

Salkever, Stephen G. "Aristotle's Social Science." *Political Theory* 9 (1981): 479–508.

———. *Finding the Mean*. Princeton, NJ: Princeton University Press, 1990.

Sandel, Michael. *Liberalism and Its Critics*. New York: New York University Press, 1984.

Sanoff, Alvin P. "Individualism Has Been Allowed to Run Rampant." *US News and World Report*, May 27, 1985.

Santana-Acuña, Alvaro. *Ascent to Glory*. New York: Columbia University Press, 2020.

Savio, Mario. "An End to History." In *The Berkeley Student Revolt*, edited by S. M. Lipset and S. S. Wolin, 216–19. Garden City, NY: Anchor Books, 1965.

Scaff, Lawrence A. *Max Weber in America*. Princeton, NJ: Princeton University Press, 2011.

Schmookler, Andrew B. *The Parable of the Tribes*. Berkeley: University of California Press, 1984.

Schneider, David. *American Kinship: A Cultural Account*. Chicago: University of Chicago Press, 1968.

———. *Schneider on Schneider*. Durham, NC: Duke University Press, 1995.

Schnur, Susan. "A Good Society Needs Better Habits." *USA Today*, September 26, 1991.

Schrecker, Elizabeth W. *No Ivory Tower*. New York: Oxford University Press, 1986.

Scialabba, George. "Of Politics and Platitudes." *Los Angeles Times*, October 20, 1991.

Secretariatus pro non credentibus. *On Dialogue with Non-believers*. Washington DC: United States Catholic Conference, 1968.

Segal, Robert A. *Religion and the Social Sciences*. Atlanta, GA: Scholars Press, 1989.

Selznick, Philip. "The Idea of a Communitarian Morality." *California Law Review* 75 (1987): 445–64.

——. "Reply to Glazer." In *The Berkeley Student Revolt*, edited by S. M. Lipset and S. S. Wolin, 303–12. Garden City, NY: Anchor Books, 1965.

Shah, Emant. *The Production of Modernization*. Philadelphia: Temple University Press, 2011.

Shapley, Deborah. "Institute for Advanced Study: Einstein Is a Hard Act to Follow." *Science* 179 (1973): 1209–11.

Shenker, Israel. "At Institute for Advanced Study, Opposing Sides Dig In for Fight." *New York Times*, March 4, 1973.

——. "Dispute Splits Advanced Study Institute." *New York Times*, March 2, 1973.

——. "Institute for Advanced Learning Meets to Resolve Governance." *New York Times*, March 25, 1973.

Shepherd, William C. "Religion and the Social Sciences: Conflict or Reconciliation?" *Journal for the Scientific Study of Religion*, 11 (1972): 230–39.

Shields, Jon A. "Framing the Christian Right: How Progressives and Post-War Liberals Constructed the Religious Right." *Journal of Church and State* 53 (2011): 635–55.

Shils, Edward A. *A Fragment of a Sociological Autobiography*. London: Routledge, 2006.

Shilts, Randy. *The Mayor of Castro Street*. New York: St. Martin's, 1982.

Shin, Jean. "Robert Bellah Honored for a Career of Scholarship." *Footnotes* 35 (2007): 3.

Shulman, Bruce J. *The Seventies*. New York: Free Press, 2001.

Sica, Alan, and Stephen P. Turner, eds. *The Disobedient Generation*. Chicago: University of Chicago Press, 2005.

Sides, Josh. *Erotic City*. New York: Oxford University Press, 2009.

Silk, Mark. "Notes on the Judeo-Christian Tradition in America." *American Quarterly* 36 (1984): 65–85.

Simons, William M. Review of *Habits of the Heart* by R. N. Bellah et al. *Annals of the American Academy of Political and Social Science* 483 (1986): 187.

Simpson, Ida Harper, and Richard L. Simpson. "The Transformation of the American Sociological Association." In *What's Wrong with Sociology?*, edited by S. Cole, 271–91. New Brunswick, NJ: Transaction, 2001.

Smelser, Neil J. "The Marshall Lectures and Economy and Society." *Sociological Inquiry* 61 (1991): 60–67.

——. *Neil Smelser: Distinguished Sociologist, University Professor and Servant to the Public*. Interviews conducted by Jess McIntosh and Lisa Rubens, 2011–2012, Regional Oral History Office, The Bancroft Library. Berkeley: University of California, Berkeley, 2013. https://digitalassets.lib.berkeley.edu/roho/ucb/text/smelser_neil.pdf.

——. "On Collaborating with Talcott Parsons: Some Intellectual and Personal Notes." *Sociological Inquiry* 51 (1981): 143–53.

——. *Reflections on the University of California*. Berkeley: University of California Press, 2010.

——. "Sociological and Interdisciplinary Adventures: A Personal Odyssey." *American Sociologist* 31 (2000): 5–33.

————. *Theory of Collective Behavior*. New York: Free Press, 1962.

Smilde, David. Review of *Religion in Human Evolution* by R. N. Bellah. *American Journal of Sociology* 119 (2013): 549–51.

Smith, Dennis. *Barrington Moore*. London: Macmillan, 1983.

Smith, Dusky Lee. "The Sunshine Boys: Toward a Sociology of Happiness." In *Radical Sociology*, edited by J. D. Colfax and J. L. Roach, 28–44. New York: Basic Books, 1971. First published 1964.

Smith, Jonathan Z. "A Damned Good Read." *The Immanent Frame* (blog), December 21, 2011. https://tif.ssrc.org/2011/12/21/a-damned-good-read/.

————. *To Take Place*. Chicago: University of Chicago Press, 1987.

Smith, Marian W. Review of *Apache Kinship Systems* by R. N. Bellah. *Man* 54 (1954): 14.

Smith, M. Brewster. Review of *Habits of the Heart* by R. N. Bellah et al. *Contemporary Psychology* 21 (1986): 173–74.

Smith, Wilfred C. "Comparative Religion: Whither—and Why?" In *The History of Religions*, edited by M. Eliade and J. Kitagawa, 31–58. Chicago: University of Chicago Press, 1959.

————. "Excerpt from 'Memorandum on the Center for the Study of World Religions,' September 1966." In Carman and Dodgson, *Community and Colloquy*, 41.

————. *Islam in Modern History*. Princeton, NJ: Princeton University Press, 1957.

————. "The Place of Oriental Studies in a Western University." *Diogenes* 16 (1956): 104–11.

Solovey, Mark. *Shaky Foundations*. New Brunswick, NJ: Rutgers University Press, 2010.

Sparrow, John C. *History of Personnel Demobilization in the United States Army*. Washington, DC: Department of the Army, 1952.

Spohn, William C., SJ. "Virtue and American Culture." *Theological Studies* 48 (1987): 123–35.

Stark, Werner. "Humanistic and Scientific Knowledge of Religion: Their Social Context and Contrast." *Journal of the American Academy of Religion* 38 (1970): 168–73.

Starr, Kevin. *The Dream Endures*. New York: Oxford University Press, 1997.

————. *Embattled Dreams*. New York: Oxford University Press, 2002.

————. *Endangered Dreams*. New York: Oxford University Press, 1996.

————. *Material Dreams*. New York: Oxford University Press, 1990.

Stauffer, Robert E. "Bellah's Civil Religion." *Journal for the Scientific Study of Religion* 14 (1975): 390–95.

Stausberg, Michael. "Bellah's *Religion in Human Evolution*: A Post-Review." *Numen* 61 (2014): 281–99.

Stein, Judith. *Pivotal Decade*. New Haven, CT: Yale University Press, 2010.

Steiner, Bruce E. Review of *The Broken Covenant* by R. N. Bellah. *Journal of American History* 62 (1976): 964–65.

Steinfels, Peter. "Up from Individualism." *New York Times Book Review*, April 14, 1985, § 7, 1.

Stevens, Wallace. *Letters of Wallace Stevens*. Edited by H. Stevens. New York: Alfred A. Knopf, 1966.

————. *Opus Posthumous*. Edited by M. J. Bates. New York, Alfred A. Knopf, 1957.

Stewart, Jim. *Folsom Street Blues*. San Francisco: Palm Drive, 2011.

Stiehm, Jamie. "Community and Communitarians: Only Academic?" *Nation*, July 18, 1994.

Stone, Brad Lowell. "Statist Communitarianism and Civil Society." *Intercollegiate Review* 32 (1997): 9–18.

Story, Ronald. *Harvard and the Boston Upper Class*. Middletown, CT: Wesleyan University Press, 1980.

Stouffer, Samuel A., ed. *The Behavioral Sciences at Harvard*. Cambridge, MA: Harvard University Press, 1954.

Suleski, Ronald S., ed. *The Fairbank Center for East Asian Research at Harvard University*. Cambridge, MA: Harvard University Press, 2005.

Sullivan, William M. "After Foundationalism: The Return to Practical Philosophy." In *Antifoundationalism and Practical Reasoning*, edited by E. Simpson, 21–44. Edmonton, AB: Academic Printing and Publishing, 1987.

———. *Reconstructing Public Philosophy*. Berkeley: University of California Press, 1982.

———. *Work and Integrity*. New York: HarperBusiness, 1995.

Sullivan, William M., and Robert N. Bellah. "American Values, Citizenship and the Political Economy: Prospect for the '80s." In *Critical Choices for the '80s*, 12th Report of the National Advisory Council on Economic Opportunity, 29–47. Washington, DC: Government Printing Office, 1980.

Sunstein, Cass R. "Beyond the Republican Revival." *Yale Law Journal* 97 (1988): 1539–90.

Sutton, Francis X. "The Ford Foundation: The Early Years." *Daedalus* 116 (1987): 41–91.

———. "The Ford Foundation's Transatlantic Role and Purposes, 1951–81." *Review (Fernand Braudel Center)* 24 (2001): 77–104.

Swartz, Mimi. "The Mythic Rise of Bill Don Moyers." *Texas Magazine*, November 1, 1989.

Sweet, Leonard I. Review of *American Civil Religion*, edited by R. E. Richey and D. G. Jones. *Church History* 44 (1975): 546–47.

Swidler, Ann. "Culture in Action: Symbols and Strategies." *American Sociological Review* 51 (1986): 273–86.

———. *Organization without Authority*. Cambridge, MA: Harvard University Press, 1979.

———. *Talk of Love*. Chicago: University of Chicago Press, 2001.

Swyngedouw, Jan. "Ikado Fujio: A Japanese Cosmopolitan." *Japanese Journal of Religious Studies* 7 (1980): 208–26.

———. "In Memoriam Yanagawa Keiichi, 1926–1990." *Japanese Journal of Religious Studies* 17 (1990): 347–48.

Synnott, Marcia Graham. *The Half-Opened Door*. New Brunswick, NJ: Transaction, 2010.

Szanton, David, ed. *The Politics of Knowledge: Area Studies and the Disciplines*. Berkeley: University of California Press, 2003.

Tanenbaum, Marc H. "Civil Religion: Unifying Force or Idolatry?" *Religious Education* 70 (1975): 469–73.

Tatlow, Didi Kirsten. "Mao's Spell and the Need to Break It." *New York Times*, December 28, 2011.

Taubman, William. *Gorbachev*. New York: Simon and Schuster, 2017.

Taylor, Charles. "Foucault on Freedom and Truth." *Studies in Humanities and Social Sciences* 2 (1996): 152–83.

———. *Modern Social Imaginaries*. Durham, NC: Duke University Press, 2003.

Taylor, Walter W., John L. Fischer, and Evon Z. Vogt. *Culture and Life*. Carbondale: Southern Illinois University Press, 1973.

Tesler, Michael, and David O. Sears. *Obama's Race*. Chicago: University of Chicago Press, 2010.

of the group in the phrasing of their research questions and the usage of similar conceptual and methodological tools. Together with the four volumes of Jeffrey Alexander's *Theoretical Logic in Sociology*, they all came out of the University of California Press between 1982 and 1984—a fact that filled Bellah with fatherly pride.[6]

Thanks to their solo work, Tipton and Madsen had gotten tenure at Emory University in Atlanta and the University of California, San Diego, while Sullivan had moved back to his alma mater, Philadelphia's La Salle University, as an associate professor of philosophy. Still at Stanford as an assistant professor, Ann Swidler was awarded a Guggenheim Fellowship for the academic year 1982–1983 that she used to finalize both *Habits of the Heart* and the original analytical approach to the study of culture she had been developing for a while. Her essay, titled "Culture in Action," was finally published in 1986. In it, Ann attacked the idea of values as a causal element, and used instead a "tool-kit" metaphor that was quite different from Bob's hermeneutic approach. She saw culture as a repertoire of sorts from which actors draw symbols and practices to construct middle- and long-term "strategies of action." The scope and intensity of the causal impact of culture depends on actors living through "settled" or "unsettled" times—the hypothesis being that the more fluid and dynamic the situation, the more culture becomes refined and explicit, often in the form of an ideology, and thus influences the daily lives of social actors and their "styles" of action.[7]

The first half of the 1980s had been such a period of unsettling transformation, one in which the American people had learned new ways "of organizing individual and collective action, practicing unfamiliar habits" until they had become routine. The United States had changed, albeit not as much as its president had promised in 1980. The ambitious tax-cut plan presented in February 1981 as the centerpiece of the neoconservative revolution had been criticized and obstructed in Congress by liberals and fiscal conservatives alike. It was only after he survived an assassination attempt in March that Reagan had been able to force through the Democrat-controlled House a lesser version of his original bill, in which smaller tax cuts were not matched, as requested by Budget Director David Stockman and other die-hard neocons, by proper spending reductions. Reagan's subsequent attack on social security had been resisted by Democrats, and the intransigent pursuit of supply side economics, combined with an exceptional growth in military spending, entirely financed by federal deficit, had worsened the economic recession. Only in 1983, and mainly thanks to the policies of the Federal Reserve's Paul Volker, a Carter études en sciences sociales in Paris—he and Jenny married in 1981 at the Women's Faculty Club of the University of California. As an undergraduate student, Hally performed at the Jacob's Pillow Festival in July 1981 and got her BFA in 1982, two years earlier than expected. Fulfilling one of her mother's aspirations, she pursued a career as a ballerina and worked with various companies in Los Angeles, New York, and San Francisco, where she became a member of the corps de ballet of the Opera in 1985. At that point, Jenny and Christian had grudgingly decided to move to the "uncivilized and uncultured" metropolis where Bob and Melanie had spent their youth—and where Christian could attend the Graduate School of Management of the University of California, Los Angeles. Having passed the California bar exam, Jenny found employment at Gibson, Dunn, and Crutcher, a legal firm founded in 1890 whose Parisian office would soon allow her and Christian to return to the place where they had first met.[4]

I

The years between 1978 and 1985 were also a time of consolidation and growth for the junior members of the Habits group. The steady progress of their collective project confirmed Sharpe in his conviction that the humanities could give an original contribution to the understanding of contemporary American society, and even suggest solutions to major social and cultural problems. The Ford Foundation thus launched Humanistic Perspectives on Major Contemporary Issues, a new program to sponsor research on social justice and common values through a small number of individual awards. Prominent scholars and literati were asked to nominate young scholars, who would then undergo a rigorous review process. Since the adoption of a comparative-historical method and the willingness to write for an educated lay audience were highly appreciated by the Foundation, and given the involvement of Bellah, Swidler, Tipton, and Sullivan in various review committees, the Habits group easily became the midwife, as well as the first grantee, of the new award.[5]

While fully committed to the collective project, Bill and Steve had also completed their monographs, *Reconstructing Public Philosophy* and *Getting Saved from the Sixties*, while Dick had finished two: *Chen Village* with Anita Chan and Jonathan Unger, and his own *Morality and Power in a Chinese Village*, which won the 1984 C. Wright Mills Award of the Society for the Study of Social Problems. Though conceived at different times and quite dissimilar in object, structure, and style, the four books were clearly influenced by the work

Thomas, Michael C., and Charles C. Flippen. "American Civil Religion: An Empirical Study." *Social Forces* 51 (1972): 218–25.

Tillich, Hannah. *From Time to Time*. New York: Stein and Day, 1973.

Tillich, Paul. *The Courage to Be*. New Haven, CT: Yale University Press, 1953.

Tipton, Steven M. *Getting Saved from the Sixties*. Berkeley: University of California Press, 1982.

———. "Moral Languages and the Good Society." *Soundings* 69 (1986): 165–80.

Tiryakian, Edward A. Review of *Habits of the Heart* by R. N. Bellah et al. *Sociological Analysis* 47 (1986): 172–73.

Toby, Jackson. "Samuel A. Stouffer: Social Research as a Calling." In *Sociological Traditions from Generation to Generation*, edited by R. K. Merton and M. White Riley, 131–51. New York: Ablex, 1980.

Torpey, John, and John D. Boy. "Inventing the Axial Age: The Origins and Uses of a Historical Concept." *Theory and Society* 42 (2013): 241–59.

Touraine, Alain. "What Is Daniel Bell Afraid Of?" *American Journal of Sociology* 83 (1977): 469–73.

Triplet, Rodney G. "Harvard Psychology, the Psychological Clinic, and Harry A. Murray." In *Science at Harvard University: Historical Perspectives*, edited by C. A. Elliott and M. Rossiter, 223–50. Bethlehem, PA: Lehigh University Press, 1992.

Trotter, Jake. *I Love Oklahoma/I Hate Texas*. Chicago: Triumph Books, 2012.

Troy, Gil. *Morning in America*. Princeton, NJ: Princeton University Press, 2005.

Turner, Stephen P. *American Sociology*. Basingstoke, UK: Palgrave, 2014.

———, ed. *The Cambridge Companion to Weber*. Cambridge: Cambridge University Press, 2000.

Turner, Victor. "Symbolic Studies." *Annual Review of Anthropology* 4 (1975): 145–61.

Tyler, Ralph W. "Study Center for Behavioral Scientists." *Science* 123 (1956): 405–8.

University of California. "Professor Robert N. Bellah 1971 Recipient of Harbison Gifted Teaching Award, Grant." *University Bulletin* 20 (December 1971): 55.

Urban, George. "A Conversation with Daniel Bell: On Religion and Ideology." *Encounter* 60 (1983): 10–24.

US Department of Commerce. *Fifteenth Census of the United States: 1930. Population. Reports by States Showing the Composition and Characteristics of the Population for Counties, Cities, and Townships or Other Minor Civil Divisions*, vol. 3, pt. 2. Washington, DC: Government Printing Office, 1932.

VanAntwerpen, Jonathan. "Resisting Sociology's Seductive Name: Frederick J. Teggart and Sociology at Berkeley." In *Diverse Histories of American Sociology*, edited by A. J. Blasi, 141–77. Leiden: Brill, 2005.

Velasco, Antonio de. *Centrist Rhetoric*. Lanham, MD: Lexington Books, 2010.

Veterans Administration Guidance Center. Pamphlet. Circa 1946.

Vidich, Arthur. *With a Critical Eye*. Knoxville, TN: Newfound, 2009.

Vidovic Ferderbar, Dragica. Review of *Imagining Japan* by R. N. Bellah. *Asian Studies Review* 29 (2005): 428–29.

Voegelin, Eric. *The Collected Works of Eric Voegelin*. Vol. 5, *Modernity without Restraint*. Columbia: University of Missouri Press, 2000.

———. *Order and History*. Columbia: University of Missouri Press, 2001.

Vogt, Evon Z., and Ethel Albert, eds. *People of Rimrock*. Cambridge, MA: Harvard University Press, 1966.

Vree, Dale. "Diagnosing America's Troubled Ethos and Culture." *New Oxford Review*, July–August 1985.

Wade, Simeon. *Foucault in California*. Berkeley, CA: Heyday Books, 2019.

Wallace, Anthony F. C. "Revitalization Movements." *American Anthropologist* 58 (1956): 264–81.

Wallach, John R. "Contemporary Aristotelianism." *Political Theory* 20 (1992): 613–41.

Wallerstein, Immanuel. "The Unintended Consequences of Cold War Area Studies." In *The Cold War and the University*, by N. Chomsky, I. Katznelson, R. C. Lewontin, D. Montgomery, L. Nader, R. Ohmann, R. Siever, Wallerstein, and H. Zinn, 195–228. New York: New Press, 1997.

Wallis, Roy. Review of *The New Religious Consciousness*, edited by C. Y. Glock and R. N. Bellah. *Contemporary Sociology* 6 (1977): 472–74.

Warner, Lloyd. *American Life*. Chicago: University of Chicago Press, 1953.

Warsford, Victor L. Review of *Habits of the Heart* by R. N. Bellah et al. *Journal of Thought* 21 (1986): 106–17.

The War-Time Program at Harvard. Pamphlet. Harvard University, 1943.

Webb, Jim. *Born Fighting*. New York: Broadway Books, 2004.

Webster, David. *Fire and the Full Moon*. Vancouver: UCB Press, 2009.

Wecter, Dixon. *The Age of the Great Depression, 1929–1941*. New York: Macmillan, 1948.

Weinstein, Michael A. "Disconnected Moralizing." *Journal of Politics* 48 (1986): 746–48.

West, Cornel. "The Struggle for America's Soul." *New York Times Book Review*, September 15, 1991.

What about Harvard? Vol. 42 of the *Official Register of Harvard University*. Cambridge, MA: Harvard University, 1945.

White, Lonnie J. *Panthers to Arrowheads*. Austin, TX: Presidial, 1984.

White, Morton. Letter to the editor. *Atlantic Monthly* 233 (1974): 38–39.

———. *A Philosopher's Story*. University Park: Pennsylvania State University Press, 1999.

———. *Religion, Politics, and Higher Education*. Cambridge, MA: Harvard University Press, 1959.

White, Thomas Joseph. "Sociology as Theology." In Reno and McClay, *Religion and the Social Sciences*, 34–39.

Williams, Daniel K. *God's Own Party*. New York: Oxford University Press, 2010.

Williams, Robin M. Jr. *American Society*. New York: Alfred A. Knopf, 1951.

———. "Talcott Parsons: The Stereotypes and the Realities." *American Sociologist* 15 (1980): 64–66.

Wilson, Logan. *The Academic Man*. New York: Oxford University Press, 1942.

Wimberley, Ronald C., Donald A. Clelland, Thomas C. Hood, and C. M. Lipsey. "The Civil Religious Dimension: Is It There?" *Social Forces* 54 (1976): 890–900.

Winnicott, Donald W. *Playing and Reality*. London: Routledge, 2005. First published 1971.

Winters, Yvor, ed. *Poets of the Pacific. Second Series*. Stanford, CA: Stanford University Press, 1949.

Wolfe, Alan. "Is Sociology Dangerous?" *Tikkun* 1 (1986): 96–101.

———. "Origins of Belief: Robert N. Bellah Explores the Emergence of Religion in Antiquity." *New York Times*, October 2, 2011.

Wolin, Sheldon S., and John H. Schaar, eds. *The Berkeley Rebellion and Beyond*. New York: Vintage Books, 1970.

Wollenberg, Charles M. *Berkeley*. Berkeley: University of California Press, 2008.

Wood, Richard L. "American Habits: Robert Bellah and Cultural Reformation." *Christian Century*, September 4, 2007, 33–37.

———. "A Short Essay in Memory of Robert N. Bellah (1927–2013)." *Sociologica* 6 (2013): 76–80.

Woodard, William P. "Hideo Kishimoto, 1903–1964. In Memoriam." *Contemporary Japanese Religions* 5 (1964): 102–6.

Woodward, Kenneth L. "The American Self." *Newsweek*, April 29, 1985.

———. "Incomplete Candor." *Newsweek*, July 25, 1977.

———. "Looking Past Number One." *Newsweek*, September 30, 1991.

Wuthnow, Robert. *The Consciousness Reformation*. Berkeley: University of California Press, 1976.

Wycliff, Don. "A Critic of Academia Wins Applause on Campus." *New York Times*, September 12, 1990.

Yanagawa, Keiichi. "From a Science of 'Behavior' to a Science of 'Understanding.'" *Japanese Journal of Religious Studies* 9 (1982): 285–94.

Yates, Wilson. Review of *Religious Aesthetics* by F. B. Brown and *Beauty and Holiness* by J. A. Martin Jr. *Theology Today* 48 (1991): 212–18.

Zhang, Zhouxiang. "Traditions Deepen Our Grasp." *China Daily*, December 16, 2011.

INDEX

for the Bellahs, 192; funeral service for, 198; Hally and, 167, 172; lawsuit and compensation for the accident that killed, 242; photos of, 84, 109; Tammy's death, reaction to, 166

Bellah, Hallie Virginia, 10–11, 16, 49

Bellah, Lillian (née Neely), 4–5, 8–11, 16, 22, 26, 30, 33, 52, 236, 365n17, 365n19

Bellah, Luther Hutton, III: birth of, 4; name changed from, 10; photo (baby) of, 5; in "SnapShots," 7. *See also* Bellah, Robert Neelly

Bellah, Luther Hutton, Jr.: and Mex, 3–4; as newspaperman, 4, 6–8, 24; photo of, 2; as a soldier at the southern border, 2–3; as a soldier in World War One, 3; as a teenager, 1; at the University of Oklahoma, 3–4; as William A. Lee, 9

Bellah, Luther Hutton, Sr., 1

Bellah, Melanie Claire (née Hyman): as an editor of *Blue and White*, 14; as an undergraduate at Stanford, 32–33; birth of, 32; Communist Party, expulsion from, 35–36; death of, 333; extramarital affairs, 195–96, 332; genealogy of, 32; health problems, 293, 332–33; in Japan, 82; legal career of, 120, 149, 153, 155–56, 167, 172, 241–42; marriage, status of, 46, 48–49, 108, 194–96, 202–3, 213–14, 216, 236, 293–94, 333; meeting and marriage to Robert, 32–33; as a mother, 50, 57–58, 66, 77, 81–82, 87, 108, 149–50, 158, 165–67, 191–94; Parsons and, 46–47; photos of, 14, 34, 84, 214, 297; Tammy, book about, 241–42, 293; Tillich and, 333

Bellah, Robert Neelly: in the army, 22–26; birth of, 4; childhood of, 10–15; Communist Party, expulsion from, 35–36; death of, 357–58; as editor of *Blue and White*, 13–14; father, unfinished relationship with, 52, 91, 112–13, 215; as a father, 57–58, 81, 150, 158, 164–67, 191–94; first solo trip across the country, 16–17; joyful seriousness of, 359–61; marriage of, 31–33,

46; name changed to, 10; National Humanities Medal, recipient of, 295–97; "nothing is ever lost" principle/mantra, 316, 338, 344–46, 352, 356; "The One Male," 204, 215; photos of, 5, 12, 14, 34, 72, 84, 159, 214, 247, 279, 285, 297, 348, 360; sexuality of, 198–99, 202–5, 207, 213–19, 235–36, 238–39; son, desire for having a, 374n33; as a teacher, 139–42, 147–48, 265–66, 292; as undergraduate at Harvard, 17, 20–22, 26–31, 36

—works by: *Apache Kinship Systems,* 49, 330; "Baigan and Sorai: Continuities and Discontinuities in Eighteenth-Century Japanese Thought," 186; "Between Religion and Social Science," 126, 144, 184; *Beyond Belief* (see *Beyond Belief: Essays on Religion in a Post-Traditional World* (Bellah)); *Broken Covenant* (see *Broken Covenant, The: American Civil Religion in Time of Trial* (Bellah)); "Brown in Perspective," 139, 301; "Civil Religion in America," 96, 98, 113, 138, 170–71, 183, 188, 259, 283, 298, 319; "Confronting Modernity: Maruyama Masao, Jürgen Habermas, and Charles Taylor," 352–53; *Émile Durkheim on Morality and Society,* 142–43; "The Five Religions of Modern Italy," 158, 319; "Flaws in the Protestant Code," 291, 319; "Glock paper," 65, 83, 95, 98–99, 322; "God, Nation, and Self in America," 312–13; *The Good Society* (with Madsen, Sullivan, Swidler, and Tipton) (see *Good Society, The* (Bellah, Madsen, Sullivan, Swidler, and Tipton)); *Habits of the Heart* (with Madsen, Sullivan, Swidler, and Tipton) (see *Habits of the Heart: Individualism and Commitment in American Life* (Bellah, Madsen, Sullivan, Swidler, and Tipton)); "The Heritage of the Axial Age: Resource or Burden," 324, 328; "The House Divided," 288–89, 415n12; "Human Conditions for a Good

A NOTE ON THE TYPE

This book has been composed in Arno, an Old-style serif typeface in the
classic Venetian tradition, designed by Robert Slimbach at Adobe.